HISTORICAL DICTIONARY

The historical dictionaries present essential information on a broad range of subjects, including American and world history, art, business, cities, countries, cultures, customs, film, global conflicts, international relations, literature, music, philosophy, religion, sports, and theater. Written by experts, all contain highly informative introductory essays of the topic and detailed chronologies that, in some cases, cover vast historical time periods but still manage to heavily feature more recent events.

Brief A–Z entries describe the main people, events, politics, social issues, institutions, and policies that make the topic unique, and entries are cross-referenced for ease of browsing. Extensive bibliographies are divided into several general subject areas, providing excellent access points for students, researchers, and anyone wanting to know more. Additionally, maps, photographs, and appendixes of supplemental information aid high school and college students doing term papers or introductory research projects. In short, the historical dictionaries are the perfect starting point for anyone looking to research in these fields.

HISTORICAL DICTIONARIES OF RELIGIONS, PHILOSOPHIES, AND MOVEMENTS

Jon Woronoff, Series Editor

Jesus, by Daniel J. Harrington, S.J., 2010

Metaphysics, by Gary Rosenkrantz and Joshua Hoffman, 2011

Shinto, Second Edition, by Stuart D. B. Picken, 2011

The Friends (Quakers), Second Edition, by Margery Post Abbott, Mary Ellen Chijioke, Pink Dandelion, and John William Oliver Jr., 2011

Lutheranism, Second Edition, by Günther Gassmann with Duane H. Larson, and Mark W. Oldenburg, 2011

Hinduism, New Edition, by Jeffery D. Long, 2011

Calvinism, by Stuart D. B. Picken, 2012

Hobbes's Philosophy, by Juhana Lemetti, 2012

Historical Dictionary of the Chinese Communist Party, by Lawrence R. Sullivan, 2012

New Religious Movements, Second Edition, by George D. Chryssides, 2012

Catholicism, Second Edition, by William J. Collinge, 2012

Radical Christianity, William H. Brackney, 2012

Organized Labor, Third Edition, by James C. Docherty and Sjaak van der Velden, 2012

Historical Dictionary of Organized Labor

Third Edition

James C. Docherty
Sjaak van der Velden

The Scarecrow Press, Inc.
Lanham • Toronto • Plymouth, UK
2012

Published by Scarecrow Press, Inc.
A wholly owned subsidiary of The Rowman & Littlefield Publishing Group, Inc.
4501 Forbes Boulevard, Suite 200, Lanham, Maryland 20706
www.rowman.com

10 Thornbury Road, Plymouth PL6 7PP, United Kingdom

Copyright © 2012 by James C. Docherty and Sjaak van der Velden

British Library Cataloguing in Publication Information Available

Library of Congress Cataloging-in-Publication Data

Docherty, J. C.
  Historical dictionary of organized labor / James C. Docherty, Sjaak van der Velden.
— 3rd ed.
    p. cm. — (Historical dictionaries of religions, philosophies, and movements)
  Includes bibliographical references.
  ISBN 978-0-8108-6196-1 (cloth : alk. paper) — ISBN 978-0-8108-7988-1 (ebook)
  1. Labor movement—History—Encyclopedias. 2. Labor unions—History—
Encyclopedias. I. Velden, Jacobus Hermanus Antonius van der, 1954- II. Title.
  HD4839.D58 2012
  331.8803—dc23

                                                                              2012003173

♾™ The paper used in this publication meets the minimum requirements of American National Standard for Information Sciences—Permanence of Paper for Printed Library Materials, ANSI/NISO Z39.48-1992.

Printed in the United States of America

Contents

Editor's Foreword

Organized labor has been around for a long time, indeed, for centuries, and it has gone through good times and bad times. Now it is passing through a bit of both. In the regions where unions struck root first and were long strongest, namely Western Europe and North America, the situation is preoccupying, to say the least. This is shown by falling memberships and also definite setbacks in legislation, rights, and earnings. On the other hand, unions are making very definite progress in places where they had previously had the most difficulty, namely Eastern Europe and the Third World. There are more members than ever, not just marginally but substantially so, and this is already a fairly long-term trend. Not everywhere, but in enough places to make a difference, the legislation is stronger, labor rights are more extensive, and even earnings are usually up, although starting from a rather low base.

So the overall situation projects a very mixed picture, and only by viewing it from all angles can one even begin to grasp where organized labor stands today. Such an understanding is obviously the goal of the *Historical Dictionary of Organized Labor,* now appearing in its third edition. A good place to start is the chronology, which traces this very long evolution marking the high points and the low points globally or in specific countries. This is fleshed out in the Introduction, which traces the major trends. But the bulk of the information appears in the dictionary section, with numerous entries on significant persons and events as well as literally dozens of specific countries and noteworthy trade unions. The labor movement has its own terminology, which it is essential to know, and the most important terms have their own entries while a broader range appears in the glossary. It is also full of acronyms, many so well known by insiders that they use them regularly rather than the actual names, and readers who are less familiar would be wise to check in the list. Those who want more specific figures should once again turn to the many, essentially updated appendixes. And anyone seeking further information will be helped considerably by the bibliography.

The first two editions of this volume were written by James C. Docherty, who also wrote the *Historical Dictionary of Australia* (1992, 1999) and the *Historical Dictionary of Socialism* (1996, 2004). An Australian, he got to know the unions the best way, by being a union member for several decades, and he also learned about them through a long career with, among others, the Australian Bureau of Statistics, the federal Department of Industrial Relations, the federal Department of Immigration, and the National Centre for Australian Studies at Monash University. This third edition, strongly rooted in the previous two, was written by Sjaak van der Velden. He is Dutch and studied history at Leiden University, where he wrote a thesis on strikes in the Netherlands. But, like Jim Docherty, he also learned about unions by being an active member. Then, in 2007, he built an international HUB on labor conflicts for the International Institute of Social History, and presently hosts the repository on labor conflicts there. Most recently, he co-organized the International Conference on Strikes and Social Conflicts in Lisbon. He, too, has written extensively, including numerous articles and 10 books. This cumulative work is precious since it provides both a long and broad view of the labor movement by persons who know it from inside.

Jon Woronoff
Series Editor

Organized Labor: World Membership, 1870–2010

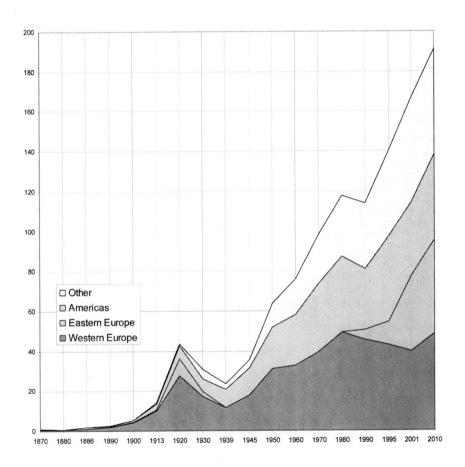

	Western Europe	Eastern Europe	Americas	Other
1870	0	0	0	0
1880	1	0	0	0
1886	1	0	1	0
1890	2	0	0	0
1900	4	0	1	0
1913	10	1	3	1
1920	28	9	6	1
1930	17	3	6	5
1939	11	0	9	3
1945	18	0	14	4
1950	31	0	21	12
1960	33	0	25	18
1970	40	0	34	25
1980	49	0	38	30
1990	46	5	30	33
1995	43	12	43	43
2001	40	38	37	52
2010	49	47	43	53

U.S. 2010 Union Membership by Division

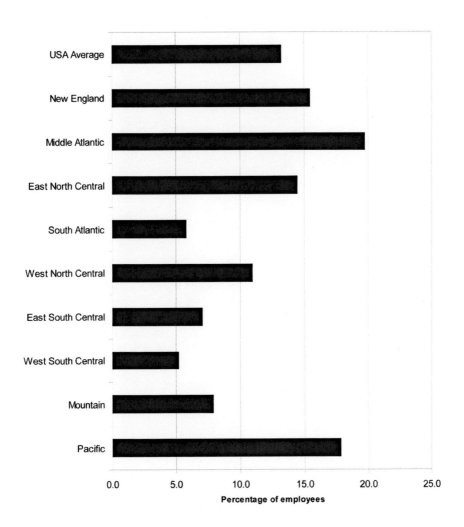

Census Division	2010
Pacific	17.9
Mountain	7.9
West South Central	5.2
East South Central	7.0
West North Central	10.9
South Atlantic	5.8
East North Central	14.5
Middle Atlantic	19.8
New England	15.5
U.S. Average	13.2

Preface

In the decade and half since this dictionary was first published, its subject has undergone many changes, but its aims have remained the same. It continues to be an introduction and invitation to the historical study of organized labor. It is about what organized labor has done or tried to do rather than what it ought to have been. It is about a mass movement with powerful enemies as its activities challenge the political–economic order. They have always resisted its presence, even if they have used different means. In Western nations, organized labor receives generally negative media coverage. It is routinely portrayed as a threat to the operation of a free-market economy by those who effectively own and control that economy. The crude violence toward organized labor of the past may have largely gone in Western nations, but continues to be standard practice in the developing countries. Yet others have criticized organized labor for not being part of the vanguard of radical economic and social change. This work takes no position on what organized labor should or should not be, but views it in its own terms, setting out its characteristics and trends. It also makes a plea for organized labor to be treated less as a marginal topic in the general and economic histories of most countries.

The *Dictionary* is not a one-volume encyclopedia, but a work of first resort for the subject. It is designed as a research tool and to complement the *Historical Dictionary of Socialism* (2006) by Peter Lamb, also published by Scarecrow Press. It provides 495 entries covering most countries, international as well as national labor organizations, major labor unions, leaders, and other aspects of organized labor such as changes in the composition of its membership. References to ideas and political parties have been kept to a minimum because they are addressed in *Historical Dictionary of Socialism*. There are appendixes containing a glossary of terms, lists of leaders of international labor organizations, and union membership statistics. Much of this information is difficult to obtain and no other work brings it together as it has been in this *Dictionary*.

The entries are biased toward institutions because they have usually been the stage of organized labor for most of its history. They are also a useful way of capturing the unsuccessful as well as the successful part of the historical process. The entries are selective and make no claim to cover everything or even to be necessarily representative. They are primarily concerned with the 20th century and the present and reflect our judgments about what is important in a work of this kind.

Our first aim in this dictionary is to make the subject as accessible as possible. Many of the works on organized labor assume a familiarity with the subject that not all their readers may have. Those unfamiliar with the topic should consider reading first the introduction and then the entries on the **United Kingdom, France, Germany, Italy,** the **United States,** and **Japan.** The appendixes and the bibliography, which also contains a guide to relevant Internet websites, are designed to complement the entries and to act as signposts for finding out more about subjects that have neglected in the body of the Dictionary.

Our second aim is to show the variety of labor studies. Economists, political scientists, sociologists, and lawyers have long been well represented in this field, often long before historians showed any interest. These disciplines are valuable as they ask new questions about organized labor or offer improved frameworks for analysis. Similarly, labor relations has much to offer by its synthetic approach even though its concerns are typically with the present rather than the past.

Our third aim is to encourage a greater international outlook on the topic than is apparent in most works on organized labor. In an era of globalization, the need for this may seem self-evident, but studies of organized labor are still prone to stress the special features of the country being studied rather than show how they fit into and shape global trends.

The limitations of space in a work covering such a large subject like this one mean that many important matters often must be treated with brutal brevity, which increases the chances of errors and misleading statements. Where these occur, they are our responsibility alone and we would appreciate being told of them. That disclaimer aside, it is our pleasure to thank those who have helped make this work happen. These are Agustin Santella (Argentina), Linda Briskin (Canada), Heiner Dribbusch (Germany), Deborah Hirtes, Dave Lyddon (United Kingdom), Howard Scott (United States), Kurt Vandaele (Belgium), and Wessel Visser (South Africa).

To facilitate the rapid and efficient location of information and to make this book as useful a reference tool as possible, extensive cross-references have been provided. Within individual entries and other parts of the text, terms that have their own dictionary entries are in **boldface type** the first time they appear. Related terms that do not appear in the text are indicated in the *See also. See* refers to other entries that deal with the topic.

Sjaak van der Velden
James C. Docherty

Acronyms and Abbreviations

AATUF	All-African Trade Union Federation (1961–1973)
ACFTU	All-China Federation of Trade Unions (1950)
ACTU	Australian Council of Trade Unions (1927)
ACWA	Amalgamated Clothing Workers of America (1914)
AEU	Amalgamated Engineering Union (United Kingdom: 1920); Australian Education Union
AFL	American Federation of Labor (1886–1955)
AFL-CIO	American Federation of Labor–Congress of Industrial Organizations (1955)
AFRO	African Regional Organisation of the International Confederation of Free Trade Unions (1960)
AFSCME	American Federation of State, County, and Municipal Employees (1932)
AFT	American Federation of Teachers (1916)
ALP	Australian Labor Party (1891)
ALU	American Labor Union (1898–1905)
AMWU	Amalgamated Metal Workers' Union (Australia: 1973)
APLN	Asia-Pacific Labour Network (1995)
APRO	Asian and Pacific Regional Organisation of the International Confederation of Free Trade Unions (1984)
ASCJ	Amalgamated Society of Carpenters and Joiners (United Kingdom: 1860–1971; Australia: 1860–1992)
ASE	Amalgamated Society of Engineers (United Kingdom: 1851–1920)
ATLU	Antigua Trades and Labour Union (1939)
ATUC	African Trade Union Confederation (1962–1973)
AWU	Australian Workers' Union (1894)
BWI	Building and Wood Workers' International (2005)
CCOO	*Confederación Sindical de Comisiones Obreras* (Union Confederation of Workers' Commissions) (Spain: 1960s)
CEC	*Confédération Européenne des Cadres* (European Confederation of Managers) (1989)

CEF	*Confédération Internationale des Fonctionnaires* (International Confederation of Public Servants) (1955)
CELU	Confederation of Ethiopian Labour Unions (1963)
CEOSL	*Confederación Ecuatoriana de Organizaciones Sindicales Libres* (Ecuadorian Confederation of Free Trade Unions) (1962)
CESI	*Confédération Européenne des Syndicats Indépendants* (Confederation of Independent European Trade Unions) (1990)
CETU	Confederation of Ethiopian Labor Unions (1963)
CFDT	*Confédération Française Démocratique* (French Democratic Confederation of Labor) (1964)
CGIL	*Confederazione Generale Italiana del Lavoro* (General Confederation of Italian Labor) (1944)
CGL	*Confederazione Generale di Lavoro* (General Confederation of Labor) (Italy: 1906–1924)
CGS	*Confederación General de Sindicatos* (General Confederation of Trade Unions) (El Salvador: 1958)
CGSL	*Confédération Gabonaise des Syndicats Libres* (Confederation of Free Trade Unions of Gabon) (1992)
CGT	*Confédération Générale du Travail* (General Confederation of Labor) (France: 1895); *Confederación General de Trabajo* (General Confederation of Labor) (Mexico: 1921); *Central Geral dos Trabalhadores* (General Confederation of Labor) (Brazil: 1986); *Confederación General del Trabajo* (General Confederation of Labor) (Argentina: 1930)
CGT-FO	*Confédération Générale du Travail-Force Ouvrière* (General Confederation of Labor-Workers' Strength) (France: 1948)
CI	Communications International (1997–2000)
CIF	*Confédération Internationale des Fonctionnaires* (International Confederation of Public Servants) (1955)
CIO	Congress of Industrial Organizations (United States: 1933–1955)
CIT	*Confederación Interamericana de Trabajadores* (Interamerican Confederation of Workers) 1948–1951)
CITUB	Confederation of Independent Trade Unions of Bulgaria (1944)
CNETU	Council of Non-European Trade Unions (South Africa: 1942–1955)
CNSLR	*Confederatia Nationala a Sindicatelator Libere din Romànìa* (National Free Trade Union Confederation of Romania) (1990)

CNT	*Confederación Nacional de Trabajadores Libres* (National Confederation of Free Workers) (Dominican Republic: 1962)
CNTD	*Confederacion Nacional de Trabajadores Dominicanos* (National Confederation of Domican Workers) (1971)
COB	*Central Obrera Boliviana* (Bolivian Workers' Confederation) (1952)
COHSE	Confederation of Health Service Employees (United Kingdom: 1946–1993)
COSATU	Congress of South African Unions (1985)
CPUSTAL	*Congreso Permanente de Unidad Sindical de Los Trabajadores de America Latina* (Permanent Congress of Trade Union Unity of Latin American Workers) (1964)
CROM	*Confederación Regional Obrera Mexicana* (Regional Confederation of Mexican Wage Earners) (1918)
CSA	*Confederación Sindical de Trabajadores y Trabajadoras de Las Americas* (Trade Union Confederation of the Americas) (2008)
CSEU	Confederation of Shipbuilding and Engineering Unions (United Kingdom: 1891)
ČS-KOS	*Česka a Slovenská Konfederace Odborových* (Czech and Slovak Confederation of Trade Unions) (1989)
CSTC	*Confédération Syndicale des Travailleurs du Cameroun* (Union Confederation of Cameroon Workers) (1992)
CTAL	*Confederación de Trabajadores de America Latina* (Confederation of Latin American Workers) (1938–1962)
CTC	*Confederacion de Trabajadores de Colombia* (Confederation of Colombian Workers: 1938–1992); *Confederación de Trabajadores de Cuba* (Confederation of Workers of Cuba: 1959)
CTM	*Confederación de Trabajadores de Mexico* (Confederation of Mexican Workers) (1936)
CTV	*Confederación des Trabajadores de Venezuela* (Confederation of Workers of Venezuela) (1936)
CTW	Change to Win (United States: 2005)
CUT	*Central Unica de Trabajadores* (United Workers' Center) (Chile: 1953–1973); *Central Unitaria de Trabajadores* (Chile: 1988); *Central Unica dos Trabalhadores* (Brazil: 1983)
CWU	Communications Workers' Union of America (1945)
DAF	*Deutsche Arbeitsfront* (German Labor Front) (1933–1945)
DBB	*Beamtenbund und Tarifunion* (Public Sector Association and Wage Union) (1918)

DGB	*Deutscher Gewerkschaftbund* (German Trade Union Federation) (1947)
DISK	Confederation of Progressive Trade Unions (Turkey: 1967)
DMV	*Deutscher Metallarbeiter-Verband* (German Metal Workers' Union) (1891–1933)
EI	Education International (1993)
EPZ	Export Processing Zones (*maquiladores, maquilas*) (1965)
ETUC	European Trade Union Confederation (1973)
ETUF	Egyptian Trade Union Federation (1956)
EU	European Union (1993)
FDGB	*Freier Deutscher Gewerkschaftsbund* (Free Confederation of Trade unions) (1945–1990)
FICSA	Federation of International Civil Servants' Associations (1952)
FIET	*Fédération Internationale des Employés, Techniciens et Cadres* (International Federation of Commercial, Clerical, Professional, and Technical Employees) (1921)
FIMEE	Federation of Industrial Manufacturing and Engineering Employees (Australia: 1911)
FIOM	*Federazione Italiana Operai Metallurgici* (Italian Union of Metal Workers) (1901–1924; 1944–1972)
FNV	*Federatie Nederlandse Vakbeweging* (Netherlands Trade Union Confederation) (1980)
FOA	*Federación Obrera Argentina* (Argentinian Workers' Federation) (1901–1902)
FOTLU	Federation of Organized Trades and Labor Unions of the United States of America and Canada (1881)
FPKg	Federation of Trade Unions of Kyrgyzstan
FTU-B	Federation of Trade Unions-Burma (1991)
FUT	*Frente Unitario de Trabajadores* (United Workers' Front) (Ecuador: 1971)
GFJTU	General Federation of Jordanian Trade Unions (1954)
GFTU	General Federation of Trade Unions (United Kingdom: 1899)
GFWTU	General Federation of Workers' Trade Unions (Yemen: 1990)
GLU	Gambia Labour Union (1928)
GMWU	General and Municipal Workers' Union (United Kingdom: 1924)
GSEE	General Confederation of Greek Labor (1918)
GTUC	Ghana Trades Union Congress (c.1956)

GUF	Global Union Federations (called International Trade Secretariats to January 23, 2002)
GWU	Gambia Workers' Union (1958)
HKCTU	Confederation of Trade Unions of Hong Kong (c. 1997)
HKFTU	Hong Kong Federation of Trade Unions (1948)
HKTUC	Hong Kong and Kowloon Trade Union Council (1949)
IALHI	International Association of Labour History Institutions (1970)
IBT	International Brotherhood of Teamsters, Chauffeurs, Warehousemen, and Helpers of America (1903)
ICATU	International Confederation of Arab Trade Unions (1956)
ICEM	International Federation of Chemical, Energy, Mine, and General Workers (1964)
ICFTU	International Confederation of Free Trade Unions (1949–2006)
ICTUR	International Centre for Trade Union Rights (1987)
IFBWW	International Federation of Building and Woodworkers (1934)
IFCTU	International Federation of Christian Trade Unions (1920)
IFFTU	International Federation of Free Teachers' Unions (1928)
IFJ	International Federation of Journalists (1952)
IFPAW	International Federation of Plantation, Agricultural, and Allied Workers (1960)
IFTU	International Federation of Trade Unions (1901–1945)
IFWPAU	International Federation of Workers in Public Administration and Utilities (1907–1935)
IG Metall	*Industriegewerkschaft Metall* (Metal Workers' Industrial Union) (Germany: 1950)
IGF	International Graphical Federation (1949)
IIRA	International Industrial Relations Association (1966)
ILGWU	International Ladies' Garment Workers' Union (United States: 1900–1995)
ILO	International Labour Organization (1919)
IMF	International Metalworkers' Federation (1904–1995)
ISAMMETU	International Secretariat for Arts, Mass Media, and Entertainment Trade Unions (1965–1995)
ITF	International Transport Workers' Federation (1898)
ITGLWF	International Textile, Garment, and Leather Workers' Federation (1970)
ITH	*Internationale Tagung der Historiker der Arbeiterbewegung* (International Conference of Labour Historians) (1964)

ITS	International trade secretariats (called *global union federations* after January 23, 2002)
ITU	International Typographical Union (United States: 1869)
ITUC	International Trade Union Confederation (2006)
IUF	International Union of Food, Agricultural, Hotel, Restaurant, Catering, Tobacco, and Allied Workers' Associations (1994)
IUFAWA	International Union of Food and Allied Workers' Associations (1920)
IWW	Industrial Workers of the World (United States: 1905)
KOR	*Komitet Obrony Robotnikow* (Workers' Defense Committee) (Poland: 1976)
LIGA	Democratic League of Independent Trade Unions (Hungary: 1989)
LO	*Landsorganisationen i Sverge* (Labor Union Federation of Sweden) (1898); *Landsorganisasjonen i Norge* (Labor Union Federation of Norway) (1899); *Landsorganisationen i Denmark* (Federation of Danish Trade Unions) (1898)
MEI	Media and Entertainment International (1995–2000)
MIF	Miners' International Federation (1890–1995)
MSzOSz	*Magyar Szakszervezetek Országos Szövetsége Tagszervezeteinek Címlistája* (National Confederation of Hungarian Trade Unions) (1990)
MWF	Mineworkers' Federation of Great Britain (1890–1945)
NACTU	National Council of Trade Unions (South Africa: 1986)
NALC	Negro American Labor Council (1960)
NALGO	National and Local Government Officers' Association (United Kingdom: 1946–1993)
NEA	National Education Association (United States: 1857)
NLRB	National Labor Relations Board (United States: 1934)
NLU	National Labor Union (United States: 1866–1876)
NSZZ	*Solidarnosc Niezalezny Samorzadny Zwaiazek Zawodowy* (Independent, Self-Governing Trade Union Solidarity) (Poland: 1980)
NUPE	National Union of Public Employees (United Kingdom: 1928–1993)
OATUU	Organization of African Trade Union Unity (1973); Organization of American Trade Union Unity (1973)
OBU	One Big Union
OECD	Organization for Economic Cooperation and Development
ÖGB	*Österreichischer Gewerkschaftsbund* (Austrian Federation of Labor Unions) (1945)

OPZZ	*Ogolnópolskie Porozumienie Zwiazków Zawodowych* (All-Poland Alliance of Labor Unions) (1984)
ORIT	*Organización Regional Interamericana de Trabajadores* (Inter-American Regional Organization of Workers) (1951–2008)
ÖTV	*Gewerkschaft Öffentliche Dienste, Transport und Verkehr* (Public Service, Transportation, and Traffic Labor Union) (Germany: 1896–1933; 1949–2001)
PAC	Political Action Committees (United States: 1940)
PAFL	Pan-American Federation of Labor (1918–1940)
PSI	Public Services International (1935)
PTTI	Postal, Telegraph, and Telephone International (1920–1997)
PTUC	Pacific Trade Union Community (1980–1995)
SACTU	South African Congress of Trade Unions (1955)
SAF	*Svenska Arbetsgivaresöforreningen* (Swedish Employers' Confederation) (1902)
SAK	*Suomen Ammattiliittojen Keskusjärjestö* (Central Organization of Finnish Trade Unions) (1930)
SATUC	South Africa Trade Union Council (1954)
SEIU	Service Employees International Union (United States: 1921)
SGB	*Schweizerischer Gewerkschaftsbund* (Swiss Labor Union Confederation) (1880)
SSF	*Syndicats sans Frontières* (Trade Unions without Borders) (Switzerland: c. 1997)
SZOT	*Magyar Szakszervezetek Országos Tanácsá* (Central Council of Hungarian Trade Unions) (1948–1989)
TGWU	Transport and General Workers' Union (United Kingdom: 1922–2007)
TUAC	Trade Union Advisory Committee to the Organization for Economic Cooperation and Development (1948)
TUC	Trades Union Congress (United Kingdom: 1868); (Ghana: 1953)
TUCA	Trade Union Confederation of the Americas (2008)
TUCAMW	Trade Union Confederation of Arab Maghreb Workers (1991)
Türk-Is	Confederation of Turkish Trade unions (1952)
UADW	Universal Alliance of Diamond Workers (1905–2000)
UATUC	Union of Autonomous Trade Unions of Croatia (1990)
UAW	United Auto Workers (official title: United Automobile, Aerospace, and Agricultural Implement Workers of America, International Union) (1935)

UDT	*Union Djiboutienne du travail* (Djibouti Labor Union) (1992)
UFCW	United Food and Commercial Workers' International Union (United States: 1979)
UGT	*Unión General de Trabajadores* (General Union of Workers) (Spain: 1888); *União Geral de Trabalhadores* (General Workers' Union) (Portugal: 1978)
UGTA	*Union Générale des Travailleurs Algériens* (General Workers' Union of Algeria) (1956)
UGTT	*Union Générale Tunisienne de Travail* (General Tunisian Union of Labor) (1946)
UGTU	*Union Syndicale des Travailleurs de Centralafrique* (Labor Union of Central African Workers) (c. 1978)
UMWA	United Mine Workers of America (1890)
UNI	Union Network International (2000–2009); UNI Global Union (2009)
UNISON	UNISON—The Public Service Union (United Kingdom: 1993)
UNT	*Unión Nacional de Trabajadores* (National Union of Workers) (Mexico 1997)
UNTC-CS	*União Nacional dos Trabalhadores de Cabo Verde-Central Sindical* (National Union of United Workers of Cape Verde-Central Union) (c. 1990)
UNTM	*Union Nationale des Travailleurs du Mali* (National Union of Workers of Mali) (c. 1960)
UST	*Union des Syndicats du Tchad* (Federation of Chad Labor Unions)
USTC	*Union Syndicale des Travailleurs de Centrafrique* (Labor Union of Central African Workers) (1980)
USWA	United Steelworkers of America (1942–2008)
UTC	*Union de Trabajadores de Colombia* (Union of Workers of Colombia) (1946–1992)
Ver.Di	*Vereinte Dienstleistungsgewerkschaft* (United Services Labor Union) (Germany: 2001)
VGCL	Vietnam General Confederation of Labor (1946)
WCL	World Confederation of Labor (1968–2006)
WCOTP	World Confederation of Organizations of the Teaching Profession (1952–1993)
WFTU	World Federation of Trade Unions (1945)
WLU	Western Labor Union (United States: 1898)
WRA	Workplace Relations Act (Australia: 1996)
WU	Workers' Union (United Kingdom: 1898–1929)

Chronology

1152 B.C. Egypt: The pharaoh's tomb makers refuse to work over the failure of the pharaoh's officials to supply them with grain.

A.D. 301 Roman Empire: Emperor Diocletian issues an Edict of Maximum Prices, which also sets maximum wage rates.

544 Byzantine Empire: Emperor Justinian forbids laborers, sailors, and others to demand or accept wage increases on penalty of having to pay the treasury three times the amount demanded.

1345 Florence: Cinto Brandini is hanged for attempting to form an organization among woolcombers.

1347–1353 The "Black Death"—bubonic plague—kills between a quarter and one third of the population of Western Europe. The shortage of labor fuels demands for higher pay.

1351 England: The Statute of Labourers prohibits laborers from demanding wage increases and employers from granting them.

1383 England: Early use of the term *journeyman* to describe a group of London saddlers who had combined to raise their pay.

1387 England: A group of London journeymen cordwainers (shoemakers) attempt to form a union.

1393 France: Strike by vineyard workers in Burgundy.

1411 England: Colchester municipal authorities outlaw payment in kind for weavers.

1448 England: Maximum wage law.

1490 Genoa: Shipbuilding employees organize to resist wage reductions; they did so again in 1526.

1504 Venice: Labor dispute in printing.

1524 **England:** Municipal authorities in Coventry fix maximum wage rates in the textile industry, specify payment in money, and forbid payment in kind.

1539 **France:** Strike by printing employees in Lyon over long hours. They form a union and attack strikebreakers.

1548 **England:** Parliament passes the Bill of Conspiracies of Victuallers and Craftsmen, which introduces the concept of combinations as conspiracies into English law.

1560 **England:** Some London saddlers combine to raise their pay.

1562 **England:** The Statute of Artificers gives justices of the peace the power to set the wages of artisans and laborers, sets down the hours of labor, and provides penalties for breach of contract by employers and employees. It also requires a seven-year apprenticeship as a qualification to be a journeyman.

1675 **Genoa:** Uprising by 10,000 silk workers over the introduction of French ribbon-looms, which enable a single worker to weave 10 to 12 ribbons at a time.

1696 **England:** Organized journeymen felt makers in London try to resist a wage cut.

1701 **England:** Payment in kind outlawed in the textile and iron industries.

1706 **England:** Journeymen weavers in the west accused of trying to force their employers to only employ members of their union.

1718 **England:** The free emigration of skilled artisans and skilled operatives prohibited by law; similar legislation was again passed in 1750 and 1765.

1721 **England:** London journeymen tailors accused by their employers of forming a "combination" of 7,000 to raise their wages and reduce their work day by one hour.

1726 **England:** Parliament passes an Act to Prevent Unlawful Combinations of Workmen Employed in the Woollen Manufactures.

1731 **England:** First recorded use of the "round robin" in the British navy as a method of voicing grievances.

1765 **England:** First sign of organization among coal miners at Newcastle in northeast England.

1768 **England:** Parliament passes the Tailors' Act, which imposes jail terms of two months on any London journeyman who demands pay above the legal maximum and on any master who pays a higher amount.

1769–1773 England: Unrest among London's silk workers over mechanized looms and French competition. Workers' clubs evolve into unions, which threaten industrial sabotage to gain standardized wages. They gain the Spitalfields Act in 1773, which provides a procedure for the setting of wages and piece-rates.

1772 England: London journeymen tailors petition parliament for higher pay because of rising living costs.

1773 Scotland: Trial of 12 leaders of weavers from Paisley, near Glasgow. Thousands had taken part in the strike and used force to prevent the use of strikebreakers. The leaders threaten to take their followers to North America if their demands are not met. Seven are found guilty. **England:** London cabinetmakers and tradesmen in the royal dockyards go on strike for higher pay.

1773–1776 England: A government register of emigrants to North America shows that of the 6,190 emigrants whose occupations were known, 49 percent were artisans, mechanics, or craftsmen.

1780s United States: Formation of trade societies by journeymen in Philadelphia to meet annually with masters to settle the price of their labor.

1786 United States: First strike of employees in a single trade (Philadelphia printers).

1790 France: Journeymen carpenters in Paris form a union. Following complaints by employers, it was suppressed by the law *Le Chapelier* (1791), which was also applied to employers' organizations and made strikes illegal.

1791 United States: First recorded strike in the building trades by Philadelphia carpenters.

1792 England: Seamens' strike in the northeast.

1794 England: Rises in the cost of living because of the war with Napoleon lead to some successful strikes for higher pay by London journeymen tradesmen between 1794 and 1813. **United States:** Formation of the Federal Society of Journeymen Cordwainers (shoemakers) in Philadelphia; the society lasts until 1806.

1796 England: Debate in the House of Commons concerning a proposal to permit justices of the peace to fix a minimum wage.

1797 England: Henry Maudslay invents a metal cutting lathe with a slide rest; perfected in 1800, the lathe plays a major role in shaping the working conditions of metal workers.

1798 Canada: First union formed.

1799   England: Parliament passes the first Combination Act. This act, and the second act of 1800, outlawed labor disputes but did not prohibit employees from improving wages and conditions. **Scotland:** Abolition of serfdom for coal miners.

1800   England: Parliament passes the second Combination Act. The act includes provision for arbitration in labor disputes.

1810   France: The Penal Code prohibits strikes and efforts to strive for wage rises in combination. Countries occupied by France got the same legislation.

1812   Canada: In Saint John, New Brunswick, building unions attempt to exclude American immigrants to maintain the shortage of skilled labor. **England:** Frame breaking made an offense punishable by death in a move aimed at the Luddites, who continue to attack woolen machinery for the next two years.

1813   England: Repeal of the wage clause of the Statute of Artificers of 1562.

1814   England: Repeal of the apprenticeship clause of the Statute of Artificers of 1562. One of the petitions to parliament opposing its repeal was signed by 30,517 journeymen.

1817   England: Suppression of the "Blanketeers" march planned from Manchester to London.

1818   United Kingdom: Robert Owen requests the Congress of Aix-la-Chapelle to urge governments to legally limit ordinary working hours of employees in manufacturing.

1819   England: "Peterloo" Massacre at Manchester.

1824   England: Repeal of the Combination Acts of 1799 and 1800.

1825   England: Outlawing of picketing by the Combination of Workmen Act. Repeal of a law that had prohibited the emigration of artisans to continental Europe. **United States:** Boston construction workers strike unsuccessfully to reduce their work day to 10 hours; they strike again, unsuccessfully, in 1830.

1826   England: Formation of Journeymen Steam Engine Makers' Society in Manchester; known as "Old Mechanics," it was the forerunner of the Amalgamated Society of Engineers (1851).

1827   England: Carpenters and joiners form a general union. **United States:** Journeymen in Philadelphia form the Mechanics' Union of Trade Associations, the first citywide federation of local unions in the United States.

1829   Australia: Formation of a labor union by shipwrights in Sydney, New South Wales.

1833   England: The Factory Act outlaws the employment of children under 9 and sets a maximum of nine hours work per day for employees aged between 9 and 13 years. The act appoints inspectors to enforce its provisions and was the ancestor of modern factory laws. The National Regeneration Society in Lancashire advocated general strikes for the eight-hour work day. **United States:** Formation of the General Trades Union in New York; it was a confederation of tradesmen that was copied by more than 12 other American cities; it lasted until 1837.

1834   England: Six agricultural laborers (the "Tolpuddle Martyrs") sentenced to transportation to Australia for forming a union (March 18). **France:** Revolt by silk workers in Lyon, after the government attempted to suppress labor unions (April 9–13).

1839   England: The Chartist Convention votes in favor of a national strike to achieve its objectives (July 28).

1841   France: First factory legislation; it regulates child labor.

1842   United Kingdom: Formation of Miners' Association of Great Britain and Ireland; it claimed 70,000 members, or a third of the coal mining industry. **United States:** A Massachusetts judge rules that it was not illegal for a union to strike for higher pay, in *Commonwealth v. Hunt.*

1843   France: First collective agreement; it sets wage rates for printers.

1844   England: Four-month coal miners' strike in Durham and Northumberland; the strike was unsuccessful. **Ireland:** Formation of Dublin Regular Trades' Association; it perished in the 1847 depression.

1845   Prussia: Labor unions prohibited. **United Kingdom:** The National Association of United Trades for the Protection and Employment of Labour advocates Boards of Trade, that is, bodies to conciliate and arbitrate in labor disputes.

1846   Chile: Artisans form a mutual aid society.

1847   United Kingdom: William Dixon and W. P. Roberts, two of the leaders of the Miners' Association, become the first union officials to stand for election to parliament. The Miners' Association collapsed the next year.

1848   England: Marx and Engels publish the *Manifesto of the Communist Party.* **France:** Government forcibly closes down the national workshops that had been set up to provide employment; several thousand are killed and thousands of others arrested during the "June Days." **Germany:** Formation of the first national German labor union, the National Printers' Association (*Nationaler Buchdrucker-Verein*).

1849 United States: Organization of the first labor union in the anthracite coalfields of Pennsylvania by an English immigrant, John Bates.

1850 United States: Police kill two picketers in New York, the first labor fatalities in a United States strike.

1851 United Kingdom: Formation of the Amalgamated Society of Engineers in England.

1852 United Kingdom: William Newton, a leader of the Amalgamated Society of Engineers, stands for election to the British House of Commons. **United States:** Formation of the National Typographical Union, the first national labor union in the United States.

1857 Argentina: Mutual aid society among the printers; the society was made into a union in 1877. **United States:** Formation of the National Education Association.

1858 Scotland: Formation of the Glasgow Trades' Council.

1859 United Kingdom: Molestation of Workmen Act makes "peaceful" picketing lawful. A strike by London building employees leads to the formation of the London Trades Council in 1860.

1860 United Kingdom: Formation of the Amalgamated Society of Carpenters and Joiners.

1861 Germany: The legal ban on labor unions is lifted in Saxony, followed by Weimar (1863), and the North German Confederation (1869), but there is no legal right to form unions.

1862 United Kingdom: A delegation of French workers, allowed to visit the London Exhibition, demand freedom of association and the right to strike on their return.

1863 England: Foundation of the Co-operative Wholesale Society at Manchester.

1864 France: Lifting of the legal ban on strikes. **United Kingdom:** Formation of the International Workingmen's Association, or the First International, in London (September 28).

1866 Netherlands: Formation of unions by printers and diamond cutters. **United States:** Formation of the National Labor Union in Baltimore (August); 77 labor union delegates claimed to represent 60,000 members; the union lasts until 1872.

1867   United Kingdom: Second Reform Act gives the vote to the better-off urban working class. A Conciliation Act also becomes law.

1868   United Kingdom: Formation of the Trades Union Congress at Manchester (June 2–6).

1869   United States: Formation of the National Colored Labor Union (December) by black intellectuals and labor leaders; it tried to affiliate with the National Labor Union but was refused.

1870   Austro-Hungarian Empire: Legalizing of labor unions in what is now Austria.

1871   Canada: Formation of first local trade assemblies (councils). **Spain:** Formation of a printers' union in Madrid. **United Kingdom:** Labor unions legalized (June 29), but objections by organized labor led to an improved law in 1876.

1872   United Kingdom: Joseph Arch founds the Agricultural Labourers' Union.

1874   France: A factory law introduces a system of inspectors and outlaws child labor and women working underground. **United Kingdom:** Election of Alexander Macdonald and Thomas Burt, two coal mining labor leaders, to the House of Commons.

1877   United States: Nationwide railroad strikes (July 16 to August 5) marked by rioting and use of the U.S. Army and state guards.

1878   New Zealand: Legalizing of labor unions. **United States:** Formation of the International Labor Union.

1879   France: Formation of first national labor union by hatters. **Australia:** First Intercolonial Trade Union Congress held in Sydney; subsequent congresses were held in 1884, 1886, 1888, 1889, 1891, and 1898.

1880   Switzerland: Formation of the *Schweizerischer Gewerkschaftsbund* (Swiss Labor Union Federation) by socialist labor unions.

1881   Canada: The Knights of Labor forms its first assembly. **South Africa:** The Amalgamated Society of Carpenters and Joiners forms a branch at Cape Town. **Spain:** After the legalization of labor unions, the *Federación de Trabajadores de la Región Española* (Federation of the Workers of the Spanish Region) is formed. **United States:** Formation of the Federation of

Organized Trades and Labor Unions of the United States and Canada, the forerunner of the American Federation of Labor, in Pittsburgh.

1883 **Bulgaria:** Formation of a printers' union. **United States:** First attempt to form an industrial union in the railroad industry, the Brotherhood of Railroad Trainmen.

1884 **France:** Legalizing of labor unions (March 21).

1886 **Canada:** Formation of the Canadian Trades and Labour Congress. **France:** Formation of the first national trade union center, *Fédération Nationale des Syndicats Ouvriers* (National Federation of Workers' Unions). **Scandinavia:** Beginning of regular conferences between labor leaders of Sweden, Denmark, and Norway. **United States:** Labor riots in Chicago (May 4); founding of the American Federation of Labor (December 8).

1887 **France:** First Catholic labor union formed among white-collar workers. **United States:** Burlington railroad strike (February 27, 1888, to January 5, 1889).

1888 **Spain:** Formation of the *Unión General de Trabajadores* (General Union of Workers). **Denmark:** Blacksmiths and Ironworkers' Union formed. **United Kingdom:** International labor union conference held in London; it claimed to represent 850,000 British union members and 250,000 union members in Europe. The conference was a failure. Strike by women match workers in London for higher pay and improved health and safety.

1889 **France:** Formation of Second International in Paris. **Germany:** Strikes for higher wages and regulation of women's and children's work. **United Kingdom:** London longshoremen's strike (August–September).

1890 **International:** In many countries May Day is celebrated in commemoration of the 1886 Chicago riots and to demand the eight-hour work day. **Australia:** 50,000 workers take part in the Maritime Strike (August–December) over freedom of contract; the strike, which extended to New Zealand, failed. **Switzerland:** The Canton of Geneva legally recognizes agreements between employers and unions; it was one of the first laws of its kind. **Austro-Hungarian Empire:** Formation of the Austrian Union of Metalworkers and Miners formed.

1891 **Australia:** Labor unions form the Labor Party in New South Wales and South Australia. **France:** First collective agreement in the mining industry. **Germany:** Defeat of a strike by 20,000 German coal miners in the Ruhr; formation of the *Deutscher Metallarbeiter-Verband* (German Metalworkers'

Union), Germany's first industrial union. **Norway:** Formation of Iron and Metal Workers' Union.

1892   France: Voluntary conciliation and arbitration law. **France:** Foundation of the National Federation of Labor (*Bourses du Travail*). **Germany:** Labor unions hold their first national congress. It resolves to encourage the formation of national unions and agrees to work for the formation of industry-based unions. **United States:** Major labor dispute at the Homestead Steel plant near Pittsburgh (June–November).

1893   Belgium: General strike (April). **United States:** First successful biracial strike, in New Orleans.

1894   Australia: Formation of the Australian Workers' Union. **Ireland:** Formation of the Irish Trades Union Congress. **New Zealand:** Becomes the first country in the world to introduce compulsory conciliation and arbitration for labor disputes. **United Kingdom:** Beatrice and Sidney Webb publish *The History of Trade Unionism,* the first scholarly investigation of labor unions. **United States:** Pullman railroad strike.

1895   China: Formation of the first unions in the Canton region. **France:** *Confédération Générale du Travail* (General Confederation of Labor) founded in France; it absorbed the National Federation of Labor (*Bourses du Travail*) in 1902.

1896   Uruguay: Formation of the first union federation.

1897   Austro-Hungarian Empire: Formation of the Czechoslovak Trade Union Federation. **Japan:** Steelworkers form a union. **United Kingdom:** Workmen's Compensation Act; the law applies only to blue-collar employees. Formation of the Scottish Trades Union Congress.

1898   France: Failure of first general railroad strike. **Korea:** Longshoremen form a union. **United Kingdom:** Workers' Union formed.

1899   Australia: First Labor Party government in the world in Queensland; it lasts one week. **Austro-Hungarian Empire:** The Hungarian Trade Union Council (formed 1891) is set up on a permanent basis. **Egypt:** Formation of the first labor union among cigarette workers. **France:** Formation of the first company union.

1900   International: The first international May Day to demand the eight-hour work day (May). **Japan:** Formation of unions by employees in metalworking, printing, railroads, teaching, and firefighting; they are suppressed by legislation later in 1900.

1901 Albania: First strikes among shoemakers and waterfront workers. **Argentina:** Formation of the first union federation; it soon split into anarchist, syndicalist, and socialist factions, foreshadowing similar splits in Chile, Brazil, Uruguay, and Paraguay. **Denmark:** International labor union conference in Copenhagen (August 21); the conference set up the International Secretariat of the National Trade Union Federations, which was officially renamed the *International Federation of Trade Unions* in 1919. **Italy:** Italian Metal Workers' Union (*Federazione Italiana Operai Metallurgici*) formed. **United Kingdom:** The House of Lords upholds an appeal by the Taff Vale Railway Company against the Amalgamated Society of Railway Servants, which cost the society £23,000 in damages (July).

1902 Belgium: General strike. **Philippines:** Creation of a national federation by craft labor unions. **United States:** A major strike by anthracite coal miners results in the appointment of a presidential arbitration commission by President Theodore Roosevelt.

1903 Brazil: Strike by textile workers in Rio de Janeiro. **Canada:** Formation of the National Trades and Labour Congress by organizations excluded by the Trades and Labour Congress (that is, by the Knights of Labor and unions not part of American unions). **Netherlands:** Major strikes by railroad and longshoremen. **Switzerland:** White-collar unions form their own federation.

1904 Australia: First national Labor government, with Protectionist support (April 27 to August 12). **Bulgaria:** Creation of socialist and Marxist labor union federations; the two bodies merged in 1920.

1905 Dutch East Indies (modern Indonesia): Formation of first labor union by Dutch and indigenous railway employees. **Nigeria:** Formation of first substantive labor union of indigenous employees in Africa (civil servants in Lagos). **Russian Empire:** Meeting of All-Russian Conference of Trade Unions and attempts to overthrow czarism. **United States:** Creation of the Industrial Workers of the World in Chicago.

1906 Bolivia: Formation of the first labor union. **France:** The *Confédération Générale du Travail* adopts the radical Charter of Amiens, which advocates the general strike to eliminate capitalism and affirms the independence of trade unions from political parties. **Germany:** The Mannheim Agreement declares the equality of unions and the Social Democratic Party in providing leadership for the working-class movement. **Italy:** Foundation of the *Confederazione Generale di Lavoro* (General Confederation of Labor). **Russian Empire:** Unions made legal (March), but a government crackdown follows after 1907. **United Kingdom:** The Trades Disputes Act protects unions from prosecution by employers over breach of contract under common law.

1907 Argentina: General strike in Buenos Aires by 93,000 employees. **Canada:** The Industrial Disputes Investigation Act enables the federal government to appoint a tripartite board to try to resolve labor disputes on application by the employers or the unions. **Switzerland:** Catholic unions form their own federation.

1909 Hong Kong: Formation of first labor union. **Spain:** Over 175 shot in riots led by revolutionary syndicalists in Catalonia over the calling up of reservists for the war in Morocco during "Tragic Week" (July); attacks on churches and convents. Government executes anarchist leader, Francisco Ferrer. **Sweden:** General strike by 300,000 employees. **United Kingdom:** House of Lords upholds the Osbourne Judgement declaring political levies by labor unions illegal (December 2).

1910 France: First old age pension law. **Spain:** Formation of the *Confederación Nacional del Trabajo* (National Confederation of Workers) by anarchists.

1911 International: Seamen's strike in Belgium, the Netherlands, and the United Kingdom (June). **United Kingdom:** First national railway strike; it lasts for two days.

1912 Italy: Syndicalists form their own labor federation. **Japan:** Bunji Suzuki forms a labor union. **United States:** The Lloyd-LaFollette Act and other legislation forbid American federal employees from going on strike.

1913 France: Clerical workers form the first national Catholic union. **United Kingdom:** Syndicalists from 12 countries attempt to form a Syndicalist International in London.

1914 International: In most countries affected by the outbreak of the First World War the union movement halts strikes.

1916 United States: American Federation of Teachers formed (April).

1917 Russia: Bolshevik Revolution (November).

1918 Germany: November Pact (Stinnes-Legien Agreement) made between major employers and organized labor. **Greece:** Formation of the General Confederation of Greek Labor. **India:** B. P. Wadia forms the Madras Union. **United States:** Formation of Pan-American Federation of Labor in Texas (November 13).

1919   Argentina: The army suppresses a general strike with much bloodshed. **British Guiana:** Formation of the British Guiana Labour Union. **Canada:** Six-week general strike in Winnipeg; sympathetic strikes also occur in other Canadian cities, notably in Vancouver. **France:** Formation of the *Confédération Française des Travailleurs Chrétiens* (French Confederation of Christian Workers) representing 100,000 Catholic workers in 321 unions (November); formation of the International Labour Organisation (ILO) from the Versailles Peace Treaty. Formation of the International Organisation of Employers in 1920 also results from the creation of the ILO. **Soviet Union:** Formation of the Third International (communist); known as the *Comintern,* it was disbanded in 1943. **United Kingdom:** Seven-day national railroad strike; it resulted in the employees gaining the eight-hour work day in 1920. **United States:** Defeat of general steelworkers' strike.

1920   France: The split in the Socialist Party results in the formation of the Communist Party. Railroad and general strike fails. **India:** Formation of All-India Trades Union Congress representing 64 unions with about 150,000 members. **United Kingdom:** formation of the Amalgamated Engineering Union.

1921   Canada: Formation of the Catholic Confederation of Labour in Quebec.

1921–1922 France: The *Confédération Générale du Travail* splits. The communists and syndicalists form the *Confédération Générale du Travail Unitaire,* which joins the Red International of Labor Unions in 1923.

1922   Hong Kong: Successful general strike by seamen against an attempt to suppress their union. **South Africa:** Army kills 230 white strikers during Rand revolt. **United Kingdom:** Formation of Transport and General Workers' Union.

1924   Italy: Abolition of nonfascist labor unions (January 24). **United Kingdom:** Formation of the General and Municipal Workers' Union.

1925   China: Formation of the All China General Labor Federation.

1926   France: Syndicalists form their own labor federation. **Portugal:** The government dissolves the *Confederaçao Geral de Trabalho* (the peak labor organization formed in 1913). **United Kingdom:** General (May 4–12) and coal mining (May–November) strikes.

1927   Australia: Formation of the Australian Council of Trade Unions. **Canada:** Formation of the All-Canadian Congress of Labour. **China:** Chiang

Kai-shek purges the communists from organized labor in Shanghai and kills about 5,000 (April).

1928   Colombia: Army kills several hundred strikers during a dispute with the U.S.-owned United Fruit Company.

1930   Argentina: Formation of the *Confederación General del Trabajo* (General Confederation of Labor). **Colombia:** Labor unions made legal. **United Kingdom:** British government begins to encourage the development of labor unions in its colonies in Africa, Asia, and the Caribbean (September).

1931   Dutch East Indies (Indonesia): Confederation of native employees joins the International Federation of Trade Unions.

1932   United States: Anti-Injunction (Norris-LaGuardia) Act provides freedom of association to organized labor.

1933   Germany: Labor unions suppressed (May 2); imprisonment of labor leaders in Dachau concentration camp. **United States:** Section 7(a) of the National Industrial Recovery Act gives unions the undisputed legal right to recruit employees and collectively bargain for employees.

1934   France: First successful general strike over the need to resist fascism.

1935   Norway: Conclusion of basic agreement between organized labor and employers. **United States:** National Labor Relations Act (Wagner Act) protects the right of labor unions to organize and engage in collective bargaining.

1936   France: Syndicalists, communists, and other labor organizations hold a unity congress (March). The election of the Popular Front leads to new laws on a 40-hour work week, paid holidays, collective bargaining, and compulsory conciliation and arbitration (this last law was suspended in 1939). The Matignon Agreement provides for the unions' right to organize, an end to antiunion practices, collective bargaining, pay increases of 7 to 12 percent, and the election of shop stewards (June 7). **New Zealand:** Amendments to the Industrial Conciliation and Arbitration Act makes union membership compulsory for any employee subject to a registered award of industrial agreement; this provision remained part of New Zealand law until 1991.

1937   British East Africa: Banning of the Labour Trade Union of East Africa. **France:** A decree legalizes labor unions in the French colonies of West and Equatorial Africa (March 11). **French-speaking Africa:** White-collar workers form the first labor unions in Tunisia, in Bamako (Mali), and in Dakar (Senegal). **New Zealand:** Formation of the Federation of Labour. **Switzerland:** An accord between employers and unions in the engineering industry eventually became the model for a national social partnership in Swiss industrial relations.

1938 Caribbean: The West Indies Royal Commission (Lord Moyne) recommends the encouragement of organized labor. **Sweden:** Saltsjobaden Agreement between unions and employers. **United States:** Formation of the Congress of Industrial Organizations (CIO); John L. Lewis becomes president.

1939 Canada: Expulsion of the Canadian branches of the CIO international unions from the Trades and Labour Congress. **Cuba:** Formation of the *Confederación de Trabajadores de Cuba* (Confederation of the Workers of Cuba). **France:** The *Confédération Générale du Travail* expels communist affiliates over their support of the Soviet pact with Nazi Germany. **United States:** The Hatch Act prohibits federal employees from active participation in federal election campaigns and from providing organizational support for candidates.

1940 Canada: The expelled CIO unions and the All-Canadian Congress of Labour merge to form the Canadian Congress of Labour. **France:** Dissolution of all three national labor organizations (November 9). **Japan:** Suppression of all independent labor unions and employers' organizations (June). **United Kingdom:** The Colonial Development and Welfare Act 1940 links the payment of assistance funds to fostering labor unions in British colonies.

1942 Egypt: Legalizing of labor unions.

1943 Canada: The Order-in-Council P.C. 1003 creates a legal framework for collective bargaining and mechanisms for resolving disputes.

1944 France: The provisional government restores free labor unions (July).

1945 Austria: Formation of the *Österreichischer Gewerkschaftsbund* (Austrian Federation of Trade Unions) (April 13). **Germany:** Resurgence of labor unions at the factory level in West Germany (March–August). By August 1945, nearly one million union members had been officially recognized in unions in the British zone. **Netherlands:** Formation of a permanent union–employer policy body, the Foundation of Labor (May). **United Kingdom:** Representatives from 53 countries attend the World Trades Union Conference in London (February 6–17). The conference led to the creation of the World Federation of Trade Unions in Paris on September 25. The International Federation of Trade Unions ceased to exist after December 31.

1946 Belgian Congo: Labor unions formed by Africans legalized; European labor unions had been permitted in the Congo since 1921. A multiracial labor federation was formed in 1951 but split along racial lines. **Canada:** Rand Formula introduced into industrial relations. **United Kingdom:** Major dispute in the transportation industry over the closed shop.

1947   France: General strike. **United States:** Taft-Hartley Act outlaws political levies by labor unions and the closed shop (June 23). The act provides for the immediate dismissal of striking American federal government employees and prohibits their reemployment by the government for three years.

1948   International: International Labour Organisation Convention No. 87 (Freedom of Association and Protection of the Right to Organize). The Universal Declaration of Human Rights proclaims the right of individuals to form and join trade unions to protect their interests (Article 23, Part 4). **France:** Strike by coal miners accompanied by much violence; 30,000 troops sent in by the government. **Japan:** Public sector employees forbidden to strike. **Peru:** Formation of the *Confederación Interamericana de Trabajadores* (Interamerican Confederation of Workers) (January 10) in Lima. **West Germany:** The number of union members reaches five million.

1949   International: International Labour Organisation Convention No. 98 (Right to Organize and Collective Bargaining). **Australia:** Communist-led coal miners' strike. The federal Labor government sends in troops to mine the coal (June 26 to August 15). **United Kingdom:** Formation of the International Confederation of Free Trade Unions (December), which claims 54 million members. **United States:** Introduction of the General Schedule, in its present form, for white-collar employees of the American federal government; its origins go back to pay reforms of 1923, which were based on pay legislation of the 1850s. CIO expels communists.

1950   International: The International Confederation of Free Trade Unions establishes the European Regional Organization (November). **Germany:** Formation of *IG Metall* (Metal Workers' Industrial Union). **Kenya:** Army crushes a general strike in Nairobi.

1951   Guatemala: Castillo Armas, with U.S. support, overthrows President Jacobo Arbenz, executes labor organizers, and suppresses the country's 533 unions. **Mexico:** Formation of the *Organización Regional Interamericana de Trabajadores* (Inter-American Regional Organization of Workers) in Mexico City (January).

1955   United States: The American Federation of Labor (AFL) and the CIO agree to merge, with George Meany as president, to form the American Federation of Labor–Congress of Industrial Organizations (AFL-CIO).

1956   Canada: The Trades and Labour Congress and the Canadian Congress of Labour merge to form the Canadian Labour Congress. **Japan:** First *Shunto* or Spring Offensive.

1959   United States: Wisconsin legislature passes the first public-sector bargaining law, which gives state employees the right to join unions.

1960   International: The International Confederation of Free Trade Unions establishes the African Regional Organization to represent organized labor in Africa (November). **Canada:** Merger of the Canadian and Catholic Confederation of Labour to form the Confederation of National Trade Unions. **United States:** *Labor History* journal begins publication in New York.

1963   International: International Confederation of Free Trade Unions holds its first World Youth Rally in Vienna, Austria (July 9–19).

1964   United Kingdom: House of Lords upholds the original decision in the *Rookes v. Barnard* case. This loophole in the Trades Disputes Act (1906) made union officials liable for damages for threatening to strike in breach of contracts of employment; it was closed by the Trades Disputes Act (1965).

1966   International: International Industrial Relations Association is formed.

1967   United States: The Taylor Act in New York State imposes penalties on public-sector employees who went on strike; the penalties were increased in 1969, 1974, and 1978 and have been enforced.

1968   International: The International Federation of Christian Trade Unions renames itself the *World Confederation of Labor*. **France:** During the "French revolution of '68," 10 million workers go on strike (May). **United Kingdom:** Report of the Royal Commission on Trade Unions (Donovan Commission).

1969   Germany: The *September Streiks* signal the end of the postwar period of very low strike incidence. **United States:** The AFL-CIO disaffiliates from the International Confederation of Free Trade Unions (February) and sets up the Asian-American Free Labor Institute with U.S. State Department support.

1970   European Economic Community: Creation of the Standing Committee of Employment, the first formal European-level committee of its kind to include representatives from organized labor (December). **United States:** The Pay Comparability Act applies the principle of pay comparability with the private sector to American federal government employees in its present form. A successful national strike by postal workers leads to the Postal Reorganization Act 1970, which separates pay determination in the postal service from the rest of federal employment, outlaws strikes, gives the unions the right to engage in collective bargaining, and provides for compulsory arbitration in case of disputes. President Richard Nixon attempts to delay the statutory federal pay adjustment deadline during his freeze on pay and prices; the National Treasury Employees Union (founded in 1938) takes its case to the Supreme Court and wins what has been claimed to be the largest backpay award in history: $600 million.

1972   United Kingdom: Miners massively go out on strike for the first time since 1926.

1973   International: Formation of the European Trade Union Confederation; it claimed 37 million members. **South Africa:** Strikes by black workers in Durban lead to the arrest of the leaders and the suppression of black unionism.

1974   India: Strike by railway workers. **United Kingdom:** Labour Party and the Trades Union Congress agree to a Social Contract.

1976   Poland: Formation of an Organizing Committee for Free Trades Unions in Silesia and an independent labor union committee following a strike wave. **West Germany:** Extension of the Co-determination Law to companies with 2,000 or more employees.

1977   Soviet Union: Vladimir Klebanov and five others announce the formation of an Association of Free Trade Unions of Workers in Moscow (November). **Spain:** Organized labor gains minimum legal freedom; full legal freedom was not granted until 1985.

1979   International: First United Nations resolution calling on member countries to release any person detained "because of their trade union activities." **Romania:** A dissident, Paul Goma, announced the formation of the Romanian Workers' Free Union. **South Africa:** The government appoints the Wiehahn Commission to investigate trade unionism; the commission successfully recommended that black labor unions be legally recognized. **United States:** The AFL-CIO and President Jimmy Carter reach a national accord under which the unions agree to restrain wage claims in return for a package of economic and social measures (September).

1980   Brazil: Five-week strike by metalworkers. **Poland:** Formation of Solidarity (September 22). **Sweden:** National lockout by employers (May). **Turkey:** A military coup results in restrictions on labor unions.

1981   International: Reaffiliation of the AFL-CIO with the International Confederation of Free Trade Unions (November). **Chile:** Formation of a centrist labor union. **United States:** A strike by the Professional Air Traffic Controllers' Organization (August 3) leads to the firing of strikers and their replacement by military controllers and civilian controllers who returned to work.

1982   Germany: Cuts to social services inspire 500,000 to join in union protests. **Turkey:** Trial of 52 labor leaders (February–March). **United States:** Federal government takes away air traffic controllers' union's right to bargain collectively (February) after its defeat in the 1981 strike.

1983   Australia: The Australian Council of Trade Unions and the Australian Labor Party negotiate an accord covering economic policy to be followed if the Labor Party won the federal election (February). The accord operates between March 1983 and March 1996.

1984   International: The International Confederation of Free Trade Unions conducts the first survey of violations of trade union rights in the world. **Germany:** Introduction of 38-hour work week in the steel industry. **New Zealand:** Abolition of access to compulsory arbitration in interest disputes except in "essential" industries. **Spain:** The government and the *Unión General de Trabajadores* (General Union of Workers) agree to a social and economic pact to control wage claims as an antiinflationary measure. The pact breaks down after 1986. **United Kingdom:** The Employment Act requires secret ballots for labor union officials and for strikes.

1985   United States: Hormel strike, Austin, Minnesota.

1986   Germany: *Neue Heimat* affair; the mismanagement of the cooperative housing project damaged the prestige of labor unions. **United Kingdom:** Defeat of London printing unions over the introduction of new technology at Rupert Murdoch's Wapping plant.

1987   Germany: *IG Metall* gains the 37-hour work week for members from April 1, 1988; other unions also gained reductions in their working time. **Ireland:** Government, unions, and employers agree to the Programme for National Recovery (April). **Taiwan:** Formation of a Labor Party (November) after the lifting of martial law.

1988   International: The International Trade Secretariats sign the first framework agreement with a multinational corporation, Danone.

1989   Japan: Merger of two major labor federations, *Rengo* and *Sohyo,* to form *JTUC-Rengo* (November 21), with 7.6 million members.

1990   Italy: Strikes in a wide range of essential services legally prohibited (June). **United States:** The Federal Employees Pay Comparability Act signed into law by President George Bush (November 5).

1991   Albania: Formation of the first independent labor unions and national labor federation (February). **Cuba:** Formation of the Independent Cuban General Workers' Union (October 4); it continues to be denied official recognition by the government. **Morocco:** Creation of the Trade Union Confederation of Arab Maghreb Workers. **New Zealand:** The Employment Contracts Act abolishes the arbitration system and the system of compulsory union membership, which had operated since 1936.

1992   International: Signing of European Union Treaty in Maastricht (February 7); it includes a social policy agreement that gave European-wide labor and employer federations an enhanced formal role in the social policy of the European Union. **China:** Suppression of the China Free Trade Union Preparatory Committee (formed at the end of 1991). **Georgia:** Formation of Georgian Trade Union Amalgamation (December 18).

1993   International: Formation of Education International. **European Community:** Formal recognition of the European Trade Union Confederation, EUROCADRES, and the *Confédération Européene des Cadres* as "social partners" for European-wide dialogue on social policy matters. **India:** National strike by millions of employees against the national government's economic reforms (September 9). **Indonesia:** Government bans the first congress of the independent Indonesia Prosperity Labor Union (August). The union, formed in November 1990, claimed 50,000 members but had twice been refused official registration by the Department of Manpower. **Poland:** Strikes by Solidarity over low pay and staff cuts (May). **United Kingdom:** The Trade Union Reform and Employment Rights Act becomes law (July 1). Creation of the International Centre for Trade Union Rights in London.

1994   International: The International Labour Organisation adopts a Convention and Recommendation designed to protect the conditions of part-time workers. The International Confederation of Free Trade Unions launches a campaign against child labor (June). **European Community:** European Commission's White Paper on Social Policy recognizes employers' organizations, unions, and voluntary associations as partners in the development of social policy (August). **Indonesia:** Muchtac Pakpahan, the leader of the independent Indonesia Prosperity Labor Union, is sentenced to three years in jail for allegedly inciting riots in Medan in April (November 7); his sentence is extended to four years in January 1995. **Vietnam:** A new labor law requires every foreign joint enterprise to establish a labor union within six months (June).

1995   International: The International Confederation of Free Trade Unions announces that 528 union activists were murdered during 1994 (June).

Merger of the Miners' International Federation and the International Federation of Chemical, Energy, and General Workers' Unions to form the International Federation of Chemical, Energy, Mine, and General Workers' Unions (November). The International Confederation of Free Trade Unions forms the Asia-Pacific Labour Network. **United States:** The United Steelworkers, the United Auto Workers, and the International Association of Machinists agree to a merger (July). Lane Kirkland steps down as president of the AFL-CIO (August) and is replaced by John J. Sweeney (October).

1996   International: International unions inaugurate the first International Commemoration Day for Dead and Injured Workers to focus attention on occupational health and safety (April 28). Campaign by the International Federation of Commercial, Technical, and Clerical Employees for union recognition by the U.S. firm Toys "R" Us in 60 countries. **South Korea:** Labor law changes ending job security guarantees (December) produce a wave of strikes in 1997.

1997   Canada: Strike by public high school teachers (October 27–November 10) and by postal workers (November). **China:** At least three labor protests in Sichuan province over job losses in state-owned industries; two labor activists in Shenzhen are sentenced to three and a half years in jail for setting up an independent trade union in May 1994 (June). **India:** Murder of Bombay union leader Datta Samant (January 16). **Israel:** National labor strikes over privatization (November). **United States:** End of the longest strike ever, at Las Vegas; the strike began in 1991 over the rehiring of 550 employees.

1998   France: Introduction of a 35-hour working week for enterprises that employed 20 or more employees. **Greece:** Public sector strikes over labor market reform (July 23). **Peru:** National strike (October 30). **Russia:** Blockades and strikes by coal miners over unpaid wages (May). General strikes in main cities over unpaid wages and low pay (October 7). **South Korea:** Unions agree to economic reform laws in return for concessions (increasing unemployment payments, allowing unions to engage in politics, and allowing public sector teachers to form unions) (February 14); auto workers' strike over mass layoffs and privatization (July 14–15). **Ukraine:** Strike by coal miners over unpaid wages (May 4).

1999   International: International Labour Organisation adopts the Worst Forms of Child Labour Convention (No. 182). **Germany:** Creation of the Alliance for Jobs, Training, and Competitiveness, a national forum of labor unions, employers, and government.

2000   International: Creation of Union Network International (January 1). International Confederation of Free Trade Unions' Annual Survey of

Violations of Human Rights shows that 209 union activists were killed in 2000 compared with 140 in 1999. **France:** Organized labor gains a 35-hour working week law. **Russia:** Three labor union federations with a total of 30 million members affiliate to the International Confederation of Free Trade Unions (November).

2001   Germany: Creation of *Ver.di,* the world's biggest labor union (March 21). **United States:** President George W. Bush signs Executive Orders that direct employers to notify union members that they could opt out of dues collected from members that were used for political activity and forbade "project labor agreements" whereby only unionized companies can bid for government contracts. The Bush administration also indicates that it would overturn workplace safety rule laws on ergonomics (March).

2002 France: Dilution of 35-hour week labor law (December). **Germany:** *IG Metall* conducts a successful series of strikes that gain an immediate 4-percent pay rise and a further 3.1-percent rise from June 1, 2003. **India:** Unions lead 10 million to protest government plans to privatize state-run companies (April 16). **Italy:** General strikes over planned labor reforms to remove reinstatement of employees for wrongful dismissal (April 16). Labor protests over the giant auto company, Fiat (established in 1899), laying off 20,000 employees (November 26). **Portugal:** General strike over government spending cuts required to meet the financial requirements of membership of the European Union (mid-November). **South Africa:** Two-day general strike over the government's privatization policy (October). **United Kingdom:** Formation of Amicus from merger of the Amalgamated Engineering and Electrical Union and the Manufacturing, Science and Finance Union (January). **United States:** Lockout of longshoremen shuts down all ports on the West Coast over introduction of new technology and job security (September 29–October 9). **Venezuela:** Strike by oil workers protesting over president Hugo Chávez remaining in office leads to general strike (December 2–February 3, 2003).

2003 International: International Confederation of Trade Unions calls for the World Confederation of Labor to join with it in building a unified global trade union movement to meet the challenges of globalization (May). A United Nations convention protecting the rights of migrant workers comes into force (July 1); among other things, it guarantees migrant workers the right to trade union representation. **Austria:** General strike over government cuts to state pensions (June). **France:** Rolling transport strikes over government plans to reform the state pension scheme (May and June). **Germany:** Strikes in the chemical and metals manufacturing industries in the east in support of the 35-hour week (June). **Nigeria:** Violence during a general strike over oil price rises (July).

2004   Cambodia: Two leading labor union leaders, Chea Vichae and Ros Sovannareth, are murdered (January, May). **Netherlands:** strikes and mass demonstrations stop government plans to change pension scheme (October). **United States:** A 20-week strike by 70,000 Southern California grocery workers to protect health benefits and stop imposition of a vicious two-tier wage system ends (February).

2005   Australia: Organized labor holds national protest rallies over federal radical labor relations reforms designed to reduce the power of unions, but the reforms become federal law (November). **Norway:** A report by the research institute Fafo shows that the trade union movement is not doing enough to embrace ethnic minorities (October). **United Kingdom:** Unite the Union is formed from the amalgamation of Amicus and the Transport and General Workers' Union (27 April). Women now make up the majority of British union members, the first time this has happened in the world.

2006   International: The International Confederation of Free Trade Unions and the World Confederation of Labor amalgamate to form the International Trade Union Confederation (1 November). **France:** One million people take part in demonstrations and strikes against government attempts to reform youth labor laws (March). **United States:** Solidarity partnership between AFL-CIO and National Education Association (June). Seven major national unions representing six million workers disaffiliate from the AFL-CIO and form a new coalition called Change to Win, devoted to organizing labor (September).

2007   India: Hindustan Unilever locks out striking workers as part of a series of union-busting activities by the company (July). **Mauritania:** The Islamic Republic of Mauritania was the last country on the globe that not only forbade slavery but also made slavery punishable. **United States:** Hollywood writers began a successful strike for better monetary compensation (November).

2008   United States: After the 2007 merger between Amicus with the Transport and General Workers Union to form Unite the Union, the new organization merged with the United Steelworkers to Workers Uniting.

2009   Canada: In Toronto, 24,000 municipal workers belonging to two separate unions (CUPE Local 416, representing the outside workers, and CUPE Local 79, representing the inside workers) struck 35 days following six months negotiating with the municipality over contract renewal (June). **Egypt:** A wave of strikes taking place during the year across almost all sectors demonstrated mounting discontent at the 28-year rule of President Hosni Mubarak and poverty. **Germany:** The first nationwide strike of cleaners was won after 10 days (November). **Russia:** Two unidentified persons attack Evgeniy Ivanov, chair of the grass-roots organization at "General Motors Avto," in the entrance to his apartment house. They hit him several times in the face, stating "greetings from the union" (February).

2010   China: A series of high-profile strikes in foreign-owned auto parts plants spread throughout the coastal regions. This wave was remarkable: it caused concessions granted to workers, it initially received publicity in the Chinese media, and it helped push prospects for showcase union reform onto the agenda (May–July). **Egypt:** Strikes and demonstrations lead to the fall of President Mubarak. One of the first measures of the new military regime is a ban on strikes. **Netherlands:** Cleaners won a nine-week strike for an improved collective agreement of 150,000 workers. In December the union is rewarded with the UNI GLOBAL UNION's world cup. **Nigeria:** After nationwide strikes, the president announces a bill that will double minimum wages (November).

2011 Australia: The Australian Council of Trade Unions considers launching a landmark case before the Fair Work tribunal to give casual employees the opportunity to be classed as permanent and receive greater benefits (December). **Burma:** The president signs a new law allowing unions and strikes (October). **Greece:** The European Trade Union Federation issues its Athens Manifesto concerning the economic and social effects of the Western government cutbacks in response to the debt crisis (May). Tens of thousands take part in seven general strikes during 2011 to protest government austerity policies. **Iran:** Pressure from the International Trade Union Confederation and the International Transport Workers' Federation results in the release of Ebrahim Madadi, a leader of the Tehran bus drivers' union, the Vahed Syndicate; he had been imprisoned since 2008 charged with endangering national security (30 November). **Liberia:** Organized labor recognizes that unity is needed to stand up to multinational companies and decides on a merger (April). **South Africa:** Widespread strikes in metal and other industries over pay claims (August). **Turkey:** The International Trade Union Confederation supports protests by the Education International over the sentencing of 25 Turkish trade unionists to six years in prison for alleged terrorism (2 December). **United Kingdom:** The Trades Union Congress holds a Day of Action over planned pension cuts by the national government; nearly a million employees strike in support (30 November). **United States:** Large-scale strikes and protests in Wisconsin and Ohio over a new anti–collective bargaining bill (February). The executive of the AFL-CIO issues its "America Wants to Work: A Call to Action" statement (3 August).

Introduction

Organized labor is about the collective efforts of employees to improve their economic, social, and political position. It can be studied from many different points of view—historical, economic, sociological, or legal—but is fundamentally about the struggle for **human rights** and social justice. As a rule, organized labor has tried to make the world a fairer place. Even though it has only ever covered a minority of employees in most countries, its effects on their political, economic, and social systems have been generally positive. History shows that when organized labor is repressed, the whole society suffers and is made less just.

This dictionary could be seen as a study in failure and success. Since 1980, organized labor in most Western countries has faced falling **membership**, defeats by employers, and a general loss of direction and power. Eastern Europe since the falling apart of the **Soviet Union** and many developing countries in more recent years have witnessed a growth of membership. The result of this has been a growth of global membership from 118 million in 1980 to 175 million in 2010.

Against this very mixed contemporary background, it is timely to take stock of the history of organized labor, to see where it came from and where it has been. This introduction presents a general view of the development and growth of organized labor as a historical movement in a global perspective, explores some of the characteristics of organized labor, and analyzes the main trends since 1980.

Labor in History

The Beginnings of Organized Labor in an Unfree World

Labor unions are usually defined as voluntary organizations of employees created to defend or improve the pay and conditions of their members through bargaining with their employers. As institutions, labor unions have existed only in the last 200 years—that is, with the advent of the Industrial Revolution—but in fact organized labor has existed throughout history. It is simply that in a documentary record dominated by the powerful, labor, unless it caused trouble, was hardly mentioned.

Bargaining between rulers and the ruled has always occurred to some degree. Often this bargaining took the form of petitions by labor to their rulers complaining about some matter in the hope of redress. In 1152 B.C., the Egyptian pharaoh's tomb makers struck work over the failure of their rulers to supply them with grain; it was history's first recorded labor dispute. The Old Testament records that during the Israelites' Egyptian bondage, their foremen complained to the pharaoh about the lack of straw they needed to make their quota of bricks. The Old Testament also records the pharaoh's haughty dismissal of their complaints (Exodus 5:6–23).

Rulers from ancient times saw any unauthorized gatherings or organizations as a threat to social order. This can be shown by two examples from the Roman Empire. In about A.D. 54, there was a disturbance among the silversmiths of Ephesus over the threat to the trade in cult objects for the worship of Diana caused by the preaching of St. Paul. A local official pointed out that the gathering was illegal and could lead to the use of force by the Romans (Acts, 19:23–40). A second example occurred in about A.D. 110 when Pliny the Younger, the governor of the troubled province of Bithynia, requested permission from the emperor Trajan to allow a fire brigade of 150 members to be organized. Trajan denied the request on the grounds that the brigade might become a focus for political opposition, as had happened elsewhere in Asia Minor.

With much of the labor performed by tied labor forces or slaves, there was little scope for the formation of a large body of free individuals who earned their living by their labor in the societies of classical Greece and Rome. Indeed, the concept of "labor" as a general function in these societies scarcely existed. Both the Greek and Latin words for *work* (ἔργον and *labor*) were associated with unremitting toil, compulsion, and slavery. The purpose of the government was to maintain the social and economic order. The Roman emperor Diocletian's well-known edict of maximum prices of A.D. 301 laid down maximum **wages** as well.

Despite government policy, some groups did engage in rudimentary forms of collective bargaining. Evidence for this comes from the early Byzantine Empire. In A.D. 544, one of the "new" laws of the emperor Justinian I forbade sailors and laborers from demanding or accepting pay increases on penalty of having to pay the treasury three times the amount at issue.

Although distant in time, these precedents showed the attitudes of the rulers toward their subjects that were held until fairly recently in recorded history. In the absence of political bargaining, most groups often had to resort to rebellion to make their presence felt. Usually they had no agenda for social reform, although the Mazdakite movement in sixth century A.D. Persia, with its curiously modern call for redistribution of wealth, was an exception.

During the Middle Ages in Western Europe, religion could also be an outlet for those seeking social change, as shown by the activities of revolutionary millenarians. It is interesting to note it was the radical wing of organized labor that was to continue the millenarian tradition through its imagery of a bright and shining tomorrow (*see* ICONOGRAPHY). Organized labor emerged very slowly from the economic and urban population growth of Western Europe from about A.D. 1200. The money economy of capitalism began to assume greater importance, as signaled by the revival of regular gold coin production at Florence and Genoa in 1252. Although the broad pattern of economic and social development across Western Europe differed widely, some common elements were present. Of particular significance was the rise of a wage-earning group in the population, whose existence is documented in Portugal as early as 1253. Wage earners, especially skilled members, were the founders of the first labor unions.

The Birth of Organized Labor in England

Among the Western nations, England can claim special importance because it was there that many of the institutions and much of the lexicon of organized labor had their origins. From about A.D. 1100, guilds or societies of masters and journeymen were the main agents of economic regulation. They could fix the price of their products, had responsibility for maintaining their quality, and controlled entry into their trade through an **apprenticeship** system. The guilds could also set the wages of journeymen. The word *wages* was known to be in use in England by about 1330.

Journeymen were men who, having served an apprenticeship and become qualified in their trade, were employed by a master. Once qualified, they could find themselves in an awkward position in the medieval labor force. They were conscious of being in a socially superior position compared with peasants, but could suffer from changes in price levels through being tied to the money economy of the towns. At the same time, opportunities for advancement to a master could be limited or nonexistent.

These conditions gave rise to persistent attempts by journeymen in many trades and others to organize themselves for higher pay, a process that was assisted by the Black Death (1347–1353), which may have killed off as many as a third of the population in England, mainly the working poor. In 1381, the Corporation of the City of London forbade congregations or alliances among the trades. In 1383, some journeymen saddlers of London were accused of having formed "covins" (a term of conspiratorial suggestion first recorded in 1330) to raise their pay.

With the decline of the guilds after 1500, the English parliament started to make laws covering a wider range of economic regulation. In 1548 parliament passed a general law prohibiting combinations among artisans and laborers. This law, the Bill of Conspiracies of Victuallers and Craftsmen, was significant for introducing the concept of combinations as conspiracies into English law. Other laws passed in the 1550s were designed to preserve the economic order; they applied to the textile industry (one of the first industries to employ large concentrations of employees) and restricted how many looms a person could own and outlawed gig-mills. In 1562, the Statute of Artificers gave justices of the peace the power to set the wages of artisans and laborers and provided penalties for breach of contract by employers and employees. The statute also laid down that a seven-year apprenticeship was required for a man to become a journeyman.

England's economic growth, and particularly its rate of technological change from 1700, made the intent of the 16th-century labor laws increasingly difficult to apply to an increasingly dynamic economy with its fluctuating levels of real wages. It was also an economy with a growing labor force employed in manufacturing. In 1980, P. H. Lindert used samples from burial registers to gauge occupation change in England before 1800. His revised estimates, although tentative, suggest that the importance of commercial and industrial occupations in the pre-1800 economy had been underestimated by Gregory King, who used hearth tax returns and other sources. Lindert estimated that between 1700 and 1803, the number of males employed in manufacturing doubled from 155,000 to 324,000, a modest rate by later standards but impressive for the time. These developments also provided unintended fertile soil for the germination of labor unions. Despite the antiunion laws, journeymen and others continued to form secret labor unions and, from at least 1717, to conduct strikes. The term *strike* acquired its modern meaning as early as 1763. By 1769, settling **labor disputes** had become an important part of the duties of justices of the peace.

In his 1980 study, C. R. Dobson documented 383 labor disputes in Britain between 1717 and 1800 that covered more than 30 trades; of these, most occurred among wool combers, weavers, and wool spinners (64); seamen and ships' carpenters (37); tailors and staymakers (27); bricklayers, carpenters, and building laborers (19); and coal miners (18). Disputes over wages and working hours accounted for 71 percent of disputes, 9 percent were over the employment of apprentices or other persons, and 6 percent were over innovation and machinery.

The evidence assembled by Dobson is important for showing that even before the start of the Industrial Revolution, labor disputes and labor organizations were established, if unwelcome, features of British society. Similar features are also found in the Low Countries where an extensive woolen industry existed. Dobson also showed that the groups who took part in disputes were similar to those who were to play a prominent role in later periods—weavers, coal miners, and building workers—and that the issues that concerned them most were wages and working hours. In this period, labor unions had no legal standing but were clearly a presence even if shadowy as organizations.

It was no accident that 56 percent of all the disputes between 1717 and 1800 were over wages. Real wages fluctuated considerably from year to year in the 18th century, making it all too easy for the living standards of groups of employees to fall behind the cost of living. Falls in the standard of living were most conducive to increased activity by organized labor, especially during the 1790s when England's wars with France caused real wages to fall by 42 percent and led to some successful strikes for higher pay by London journeymen. Parliament responded to the labor unrest by the Combination Acts of 1799 and 1800, which, it has been argued, were largely wartime security measures aimed primarily at labor disputes rather than labor unions as such.

The next 25 years were difficult for organized labor. The Industrial Revolution gathered pace, and with it came a host of technological changes that benefited some groups in the labor force and destroyed the livelihood of others. The legal suppression of strikes encouraged illegal outlets, such as the organized destruction of machines in the woolen industry by the Luddites between 1811 and 1813. Parliament and organized labor differed fundamentally on economic policy. Organized labor wished to preserve the preindustrial economic order with its extensive regulations. Parliament was determined to move toward a free-enterprise economy with minimal government regulation. The triumph of the new economic order based on manufacturing was symbolized by the repeal of the wages clause of the Statute of Artificers (1562) in 1813 and the apprenticeship clause in 1814. There was opposition to both actions. One petition presented to parliament opposing the repeal of the apprenticeship clauses was signed by 30,517 journeymen (13,000 in London and 17,517 outside it), an action that gave some indication of the extent of organized labor at the time.

Organized labor and social protest were closely allied. Much of the social protest of the period was economic in origin and intent. Two well-known examples were the planned march to London by some Manchester weavers (the "Blanketeers") of 1817, who were dispersed by the government after the arrest of their leaders, and the "Peterloo" Massacre at Manchester when a militia charge killed 11 people in a crowd that had gathered for a political demonstration for parliamentary reform in 1819.

Although the Combination Acts were repealed in 1824, they were replaced by new legislation in 1825 that effectively prohibited strikes. Despite this, labor unions continued to survive. Francis Place estimated that in this period there were about 100,000 journeymen in London, all potential candidates for union membership. The word *union* itself seems to have come into use at this time in its modern sense in the shipping and shipbuilding industries. By 1834, the term *employee* had also come into use.

During the first half of the 19th century, two elites were evident among the artisans who composed organized labor in England: an older elite of carpenters, tailors, potters, and curriers and a new elite in ironworking, engineering, and the new manufacturing industries. Other occupations, most notably those of handloom weavers, were destroyed by mechanization of their trade. New unions began to emerge: journeymen steam engine makers (1826), carpenters (1827), a national union of coal miners in 1842 that claimed 70,000 members for a time, carpenters and joiners (1860), and, most famous of all, the **Amalgamated Society of Engineers** (1851).

According to the first directory of British labor unions published in 1861, there were 290 trades with unions in London alone, nearly all of them in manufacturing or construction. How many members of labor unions there were in England before 1860 is not known with precision, but the available evidence suggests it was small and the numbers varied widely depending on the state of the economy. The Grand National Consolidated Trades Union in 1834 is thought to have had only about 16,000 members. Even well-known unions had relatively small memberships. Both the Amalgamated Society of Engineers and the Friendly Society of Operative Stonemasons had only 5,000 members each in 1850–1851. These and other figures suggest that total union membership for Britain in the early 1850s was about 50,000 and fell to about 40,000 in 1860.

There was significant growth in the membership of skilled unions in the 1860s. The Amalgamated Engineers grew from 21,000 members in 1860 to 35,000 by 1870, the Ironfounders from 8,000 to 9,000, and the newly formed **Amalgamated Society of Carpenters and Joiners** from 618 to 10,200. At the 1869 meeting of the **Trades Union Congress (TUC)** there were 40 unions represented claiming a total membership of 250,000.

The Example of England

Outside of Britain before 1835, labor unions seem to have existed only in **France**, the **United States**, **Canada**, and the colony of New South Wales in **Australia**. After the French Revolution in 1789, journeymen carpenters in Paris formed a union that aroused complaints by employers; the union was suppressed by the law *Le Chapelier* (1791), which was also applied to employers' organizations. Strikes were forbidden by the Penal Code of 1810. In North America, the idea of labor unions was imported from England by journeymen immigrants. A British register of American emigrants maintained between 1773 and 1776 showed that of the 6,190 emigrants whose occupations were known, 49 percent were artisans, mechanics, or craftsmen. The first American union was the Federal Society of Journeymen Cordwainers (or shoemakers) in Philadelphia; formed in 1794, the society lasted until 1806. In Canada, unions in the building industry made their presence felt at Saint John, New Brunswick, as early as 1812 when they tried to exclude American immigrants to maintain the shortage of skilled labor. In Australia, at least two unions were formed by 1835: one among Sydney shipwrights (1829) and the other among cabinetmakers (1833).

In this period, governments often made little distinction between social unrest and calls for greater democracy and labor unions. The spirit of the age was shown by a revolt by silk workers in Lyon, France, in 1834 after the government attempted to suppress labor unions. Yet despite the harshness of its laws, the environment in England was, in practice, much freer than elsewhere in Europe. For example, in 1825 the British government repealed a law that had prohibited the emigration of artisans to continental Europe, legislation that had been in English statutes since 1718. If they could survive the severe economic fluctuations of the period and the social consequences of technological change brought by industrialization, labor unions could succeed.

European visitors to England in the 1860s were impressed by its labor unions. In 1862, a deputation of French labor leaders was allowed by Napoleon III to visit the London Exhibition. They returned with a high opinion of English working conditions and unions and asked to be granted freedom of association and the right to strike, freedoms that were not really available under English law.

In 1869, the Comte de Paris (Louis Philippe d'Orleans) published a sympathetic study, *The Trade Unions of England,* which was translated into English; it had previously been reprinted six times in French and a German translation was prepared as well. In 1868, Max Hirsch, a German mechanical engineer, toured England and was much influenced by what he saw of the skilled unions, particularly their attempts to settle disputes amicably, and by their independence from political parties. On his return he organized a new group of liberal unions known as **Hirsch-Duncker Trade Associations,** which were based on these ideas. Similarly, the constitution of the TUC provided the model for the American Federation of Organized Trades and Labor Unions of the United States and Canada, the forerunner of the American Federation of Labor. In Australia, New Zealand, and Canada, British immigration reinforced Britain as the model for organized labor throughout most of the 19th century.

It was no accident that England, as the first industrial nation in the world, should have been the birthplace of organized labor. In European, if not

American, terms it was a land of liberty, as underscored by the Second Reform Act of 1867, which gave the vote to the better-off urban working class, that is, to most of the union members of the time. This early accommodation of labor by the political system, expressed through its alliance with the Liberal Party, marked England off from the rest of Europe and held back the formation of a purely labor party. In other parts of Europe, the political wing of labor was often stronger than its industrial wing.

There were other important differences between the history of British organized labor and that of many other parts of the world. First, British society was divided primarily by social class rather than religion, race, or ethnicity, a fact that eased recruiting. Second, as the center of a global empire up to 1939, British unions were freed from the need to participate in any struggle for national independence. Third, they operated in an advanced and relatively wealthy society, even though the distribution of that wealth was highly uneven.

The Role of the State

The spread of the Industrial Revolution, population growth, and rising literacy during the 19th century gave rise to the well-studied phenomenon of the "rise of the working class." Crude repression, the traditional method used by governments to maintain control, continued in many countries such as **Russia**, but from about the 1860s onward the need for skilled workers gradually made this option less acceptable. What was needed was a way of encouraging working-class demands and protests into acceptable constitutional channels. By a process of trial and error, organized labor gradually became accepted by a number of governments as one way of achieving this goal. In various ways, often unintentional, the form of organized labor was influenced by the state. This can be shown by the responses of governments to the growth of organized labor in a number of countries.

In Britain, the supportive response of the British government to the moderate trade unionism of the 1860s and 1870s (as indicated also by the Trade Union Act of 1871) contrasted with its hostility to the radicalism of Chartism in the 1840s. It was this moderation that earned the labor unions the scorn of Karl Marx and Friedrich Engels. The growth of unions, especially moderate ones, seems to have been implicitly encouraged by governments in a number of European countries with the object of reducing support for socialism. In France, the government legalized labor unions in 1884 and provided financial assistance to the *Bourses du Travail* (the coordinating centers for local unions), provided they remained out of the control of extremists. This was in the starkest contrast to the state's violent suppression of the unemployed during the "June Days" in 1848 and the bloodshed of the Paris Commune in 1871. In **Germany**, the labor unions operated in a legal twilight but operated nevertheless if they avoided politics; as well, Bismarck attempted to undercut the threat of socialism not just by banning the Social Democratic Party (1878) but also by a number of social reforms such as sickness insurance (1883). In this sense, organized labor, far from operating in a political void, was the target of manipulation by the political culture.

Even benign actions by the state affected organized labor. For example, the introduction of compulsory conciliation and arbitration procedures in Australia and **New Zealand** assisted the growth of unions by easing the process of gaining recognition from employers for bargaining but also encouraged an unduly large number of unions.

The spread of the Industrial Revolution from about 1870 and the economic and social changes it brought challenged the social order. Industrial and urban growth fed the growth of organized labor and raised awkward questions about the distribution of wealth, political reform, and, ultimately, what form future society should take. Radical political creeds arose to offer answers— **anarchism**, **socialism**, **syndicalism**, and Marxist-Leninism—creeds that continued to stimulate and divide organized labor throughout most of the 20th century and made them a continuous object of attention by the state.

During World War I, governments needed the active cooperation of organized labor to maintain the high level of armaments production to fight the war. In the United Kingdom, France, Germany, and the United States, organized labor enjoyed a degree of acceptance by the state that it had not previously enjoyed. In the United Kingdom, France, and the United States, organized labor was courted by the highest levels of government and coopted into the war effort. The economic difficulties of the 1920s and 1930s brought new pressures to bear on the relations between the state and organized labor that were resolved by widely differing methods. In France (1936), formal accommodations between government, employers, and unions were agreed to, which had long-lasting results for organized labor. In **Norway** (1935), **Switzerland** (1937), and **Sweden** (1938), employers and organized labor came to agreements that had the support of their governments. Fascism was the other response to the economic problems of the interwar years. With its emphasis on centralized control justified on the grounds of maintaining national unity, fascism was hostile to any independent source of political power. As such, organized labor was a leading victim of fascist repression. German labor leaders were among the first inmates of Dachau concentration camp. In **Italy** (1924), Germany (1933), and **Japan** (1940), organized labor was incorporated into the **corporatist** apparatus of totalitarian government, examples that were copied by **Brazil** (1931), **Greece** (1931), **Portugal** (1933), and **Yugoslavia**

(1935). That said, fascist policies had an enduring effect on organized labor. In Italy, the fascist legacy to organized labor consisted of the legal recognition of unions, a unitary labor organization, compulsory financial contributions, and legally binding collective agreements. In Germany, the forcible organization of labor into national industry groups was a powerful precedent for the simplified labor union structure of the post-1945 era.

During the Cold War, democratic governments intervened in the affairs of organized labor, overtly and covertly, throughout the world to resist **communist** influence in countries like Italy. Of lasting significance in this period was the creation of the **International Confederation of Free Trade Unions** in London in November 1949 as a counter-organization to the communist **World Federation of Trade Unions**. In these ways organized labor has been shaped by the actions of governments (*see* GOVERNMENT CONTROL OF ORGANIZED LABOR).

The Growth of Organized Labor

The growth of organized labor is one of the unsung success stories of modern world history. In 1870, there were about 790,000 labor union members in the world; in 1900, there were about 5 million; in 1970, there were 98 million; and, in 2011 there were 175 million. As these figures exclude communist and other authoritarian countries where unions are not allowed to bargain freely, they are all the more impressive. Few other world movements have grown so much without the use of force or direction from above.

Of the 790,000 union members in the world in about 1870, most lived in Britain (289,000) or the United States (300,000). France had about 120,000 members and Germany and the Austro-Hungarian Empire together had about 81,000. Labor unions also existed in Australia and Canada, but their membership was tiny, probably no more than 10,000 in total. Union growth after 1870 was neither steady nor sure. The original base of recruitment, the skilled trades, was expanded to include employees in mass employment such as the railroads, laborers, and the less skilled and finally, from 1890 onward, groups like **women** and **white-collar** employees. Even so, the rise in world union members was heavily dependent on the condition of the trade cycle and on events peculiar to countries with large memberships. For instance, in the United States, union membership reached its pre-1900 peak in the mid-1880s with about one million members—or 53 percent of the world total—but then fell to 869,000 by 1900. This collapse was brought about by internal conflict over what form organized labor should take, in particular, the fight between the **American Federation of Labor** and the **Knights of Labor**. In contrast, union membership in Britain advanced from 581,000 in the mid-1880s to 2 million by 1900.

The 20th century opened with a blossoming of organized labor. Between 1900 and 1905, labor unions appeared in Japan (although they were quickly suppressed) and among indigenous workers in Africa (Lagos, **Nigeria**), the **Philippines**, and in the Dutch East Indies (**Indonesia**). Union membership grew also in Southern and Eastern Europe until, by 1913, there were 14 million union members in the world, a remarkable development compared with 50 years before even if organized labor remained a largely European movement. Of the 14 million union members in 1913, 76 percent were in Europe; of the remaining 3 million, most were in North America or Australia. This meant that unionism was essentially European in structure and outlook. Although the **International Federation of Trade Unions** tried to build up a truly international membership, in practice it remained a largely European organization during its life from 1901 to 1945.

Less obvious, but more serious, was the relatively small proportion of employees enrolled by organized labor in most countries. In 1913, only Australia (31 percent) had more than 20 percent of its employees in labor unions. Within Europe, the highest levels of union enrollment of employees were in Germany (18 percent), Netherlands (17 percent), and Britain (16 percent). With 9 percent of its employees in labor unions in 1913, the United States was comparable with Sweden and Norway (each with 8 percent). Not only did organized labor embrace a small minority of employees, its membership was heavily concentrated in mining, manufacturing, construction, and transportation. Furthermore, the vast majority of union members were men in blue-collar occupations.

Between 1913 and 1920, there was an explosion in world union membership based on high inflation largely caused by military expenditure, falling real wages, and the recruitment of large numbers of white-collar workers such as teachers. It was a period of wartime dislocation and political revolution. By 1920, organized labor could claim 44 million members worldwide, three times what it had been in 1913. Of the gain of 30 million, 18 million occurred in Western Europe, 8 million in Eastern Europe, and less than 4 million in the Americas. For the first time, too, organized labor emerged in India and Japan.

The year 1920 was a high point in the strength of organized labor, with about half of the employees in Germany, Austria, and Britain belonging to unions, a reflection of their governments' need to enlist the support of organized labor to fight World War I. Considered by region, 63 percent of union members were in Western Europe, 19 percent in Eastern Europe, and 15 percent in the Americas.

Organized labor's new importance was officially recognized by the formation of the **International Labour Organisation** in 1919. After 1920, the fortunes of organized labor fell considerably. By 1930, it could claim only 31 million members worldwide, a net loss of 13 million members. The economic crisis of the 1920s and the revived hostility of the employers cost labor dearly. Those countries where organized labor had grown the most in the period from 1913 to 1920 were those that suffered the largest losses after 1920: Germany (3.6 million), Italy (3.4 million), the United Kingdom (3.5 million), and the United States (1.6 million). In all, European unions lost 16 million members in the 1920s and North America lost 1.6 million. These losses were only partly offset by membership gains in Latin America, Asia, and Australasia of 3.6 million.

With the rise of fascism and the onset of the Depression, the growth of organized labor ceased. In Italy, the unions' declining labor membership enabled their suppression by Mussolini in 1924. In 1933, the free unions of Germany with their 5.6 million members were snuffed out and many of their leaders arrested and imprisoned. In both Italy and Germany, the fascist government suppressed labor movements that were already in decline. The remaining independent labor unions of Japan were suppressed in 1940. Ironically, it was the 1930s that saw a rebirth of American labor unions, whose membership during the decade rose from 3.2 to 7.9 million, even though this growth only restored the proportion of employees in unions to about where it had been in 1920. The other main areas of labor union membership growth were in Britain and Scandinavia.

After World War II, organized labor became embroiled in Cold War politics. In 1945, the former international body of organized labor, the International Federation of Trade Unions, dissolved itself and was replaced by the World Federation of Trade Unions, which was the first truly global organization of labor unions. It lasted in this form until 1949, when the noncommunist countries withdrew and set up their own international body, the International Confederation of Free Trade Unions, whose membership rose from 48 million at its formation to 175 million by 2010. Meanwhile, the World Federation of Trade Unions continued as an organization.

What happened to these international labor bodies was probably unavoidable given the international climate of the times, but what was more significant and encouraging was the strong revival of organized labor in Germany, Italy, and Japan. By 1950, these three countries had a total labor union membership of 16 million or a quarter of the world's membership. The United States also continued to have a growing labor union membership: from 7.9 million in 1940 to 13.4 million in 1950.

The 30 years from 1950 to 1980 marked another high point in the history of organized labor, with world membership growing from 64 to 118 million. The industries where organized labor was traditionally strong, such as manufacturing and other areas of mass employment, grew to meet the demands of postwar economies. Labor also enjoyed a far more sympathetic political environment, particularly in Western European democracies where **social-democratic, socialist, and labor parties** governed or were major political players.

Yet even in the time of its greatest strength, the structural problems that have always bedeviled organized labor remained. Since the 1960s, much of the growth in the labor force has been in the service sector—that is, those industries other than agriculture, mining, and manufacturing—industries with many women and white-collar workers, groups that organized labor either neglected or found difficult to recruit.

Two broad observations may be made about the course of the history of organized labor between 1870 and 1980. First, union membership has grown mightily, if unevenly, from lowly beginnings in hostile political and legal environments to a position of strength where governments had to take account of its views. This growth was achieved by democratic means. Unlike communism, organized labor has come from below rather than being imposed from above by a self-proclaimed representative of the employees. Second, through its political struggles, organized labor has helped change society for the better by fighting for improved working conditions and greater sharing of the gains of economic growth. These successes need to be remembered in any assessment of the history of organized labor. It is also vital to appreciate the many internal difficulties faced by organized labor, which are the subject of the next section.

The Character of Organized Labor

The Divisions of Organized Labor

So far, it has been convenient to view organized labor as a single entity to show how it developed and spread as a world movement. But organized labor has never been a single entity, and its divisions are as important as its similarities both within and between countries. Organized labor has always reflected faithfully its country of origin in all important respects.

The most widespread division in the history of organized labor has been that between the skilled and the less skilled (*see* CRAFT UNIONS). As has already been mentioned, the strongest labor unions developed among groups of skilled men, and it was these groups that were largely responsible for its survival before the 1880s. Skilled men, of course, had many advantages over the less skilled; they could command higher pay, were harder to replace, and so had more bargaining power with an employer. Furthermore, they had already made a substantial investment of time and effort in their employment through the apprenticeship system. As a result, it was all too easy for the skilled to look down on or fear the less skilled, rather than make common cause with them. At the same time, the less skilled presented a potential threat to skilled men, especially when technological change reduced the skills needed for a job and opened the way for the less skilled to be trained to replace them.

This problem has been a critical issue for organized labor throughout much of its history. It came to the forefront spectacularly with the Knights of Labor in the United States in the 1880s; the Knights were the first labor organization in the world to recruit the unskilled as well as the skilled. The problem gave rise to debate about how organized labor should be organized, by industry or by occupation. An industry-based union implied that all within that industry could be eligible to be recruited into a union, whereas unions based on craft or skilled occupations implied that many employees within the industry would be left out (*see* INDUSTRIAL UNIONS). As labor unions emerged among the traditionally less skilled, new problems arose. For example, the American Federation of Labor, the body that only accepted affiliates organized along craft lines, also included unions of unskilled employees even in the late 19th century. With union growth came the problem of which unions had the right to recruit which employees. With no clear answer in many cases, there was often much conflict between unions about who had recruitment rights. As a result, national labor federations often had to adjudicate in interunion disputes.

The second divide in organized labor was between **blue-collar** and white-collar workers and the distinctions of social "class" this implied. In late 19th-century Germany, it was called the *Kragenlinie* or "collar line." Although white-collar unionism began to emerge in a number of countries in the 1900s, it was generally moderate in character and aloof from manual union organizations and their concerns until after 1945 (*see* WHITE-COLLAR UNIONISM).

As well as these sources of division, organized labor has been and is divided by religion. Before World War II, organized labor in Western Europe (apart from Britain) was divided by religion, specifically into Catholic and non-Catholic movements, with the non-Catholic unions largely being socialist in outlook. Since 1945, with the exception of Germany and Austria, this division has persisted in continental Europe despite efforts to unify the movements in France, Belgium, and Switzerland (*see* CATHOLICISM).

Politics has been a fourth source of division in organized labor. Before 1920, the dominant form of political division was between socialists (of varying degrees) and nonsocialists. After 1920, communism became an important and sometimes dominant element in labor union politics. More generally, the persistent political division in labor unions was between right wing and left wing. **Race and ethnicity** has been, and is, a fifth source of division in organized labor. In some countries, notably South Africa, it assumed huge proportions up to the 1990s.

Ways and Means: Achieving Objectives

Since the late 19th century, organized labor, despite its divisions, has sought to change the rules by which work is governed. The means for achieving this goal has been through **collective bargaining**, preferably to have as an outcome a signed, legally enforceable agreement that sets out wages and conditions of employment. Although labor disputes attract publicity and may be dramatically or even violently conducted, in democratic societies the process of collective bargaining is more usually slow, detailed, and dull. When organized labor is unable to secure a collective agreement, it may resort to a withdrawal of labor (the strike), but this is a relatively rare event outside of certain industries such as mining, transportation, and metals manufacturing.

Where collective bargaining is not permitted or fails, organized labor may turn to politics for assistance to achieve its objectives. It may seek to lobby parties—for example, the use of **political action committees** in the United States—or, if this fails to deliver satisfactory outcomes, to form its own political parties, as happened in Australia, Britain, and Scandinavia (*see* AUSTRALIAN LABOR PARTY; BRITISH LABOUR PARTY). Since the 1950s, international labor organizations have become adept in forming specific organizations to lobby larger political organizations to seek a voice for labor or to press particular claims (*see*, for example, ASIA-PACIFIC LABOUR NETWORK).

For most of its history, organized labor has not tried to change the essential features of capitalism, but it has tried to mitigate its worst effects. By slowly chipping away at the economic system through improved labor laws and collective agreements, organized labor has brought about incremental, but important economic and social changes that have provided benefits that extend well beyond its immediate membership. Indeed, organized labor is one of the principal forces for economic fairness in most democratic societies.

An Assessment of Organized Labor

Given the divisions within organized labor and the other formidable obstacles it has had to face, it is surprising that it has survived and grown at all.

The key to its success may be found in its continual concern with the practical and attainable rather than the theoretical or ideal. Although the history of organized labor is punctuated by widespread and often short-lived social eruptions, to survive as organizations, labor unions have to become recognized, to make rules and agreements governing how work is to be performed and paid, and to seek change in an incremental rather than revolutionary fashion. This is the discipline of reality, of having to deal with the world as it is rather than how it ought to be, as advocated by political or social theorists. This is not to say that organized labor has not been often profoundly influenced by ideas, but it typically assesses those ideas in terms of their practicality.

Whether they admit it or not, labor unions are political beings. By definition, they represent a potential challenge to the existing distribution of power, goods, and services in society, which accounts for their repression by government throughout much of history. They might be won over by government, but that implicit challenge is always present. Their participation in the political process can take many forms such as lobbying governments or simply providing career stepping stones for upwardly mobile middle-class aspirants, as has happened through labor parties in countries such as Britain and Australia or in a number of African nations since the 1960s.

Unions are also primarily reactive in character. Typically, they work to preserve and protect the pay and conditions of members. Strikes are generally a last resort of unions and occur when other measures have failed. Periods of inflation are especially productive of labor disputes because they upset the distribution of real wages across and within the employed labor force. This was particularly evident in most countries between about 1910 and 1920, and in the 1970s. Similarly, in periods of rising prosperity, unions seek to gain what they see as their share through strikes for improved pay and conditions.

Union membership size, although important, is no guide in itself to bargaining strength with employers. Some numerically large unions representing relatively poorly paid employees may have little bargaining power, while others, particularly those in key industries such as transportation and communications, may have a lot. Even so, few unions are powerful enough in their own right to be able to bargain effectively on a large scale (e.g., with governments). Organized labor learned long ago to cooperate through national bodies (*see* TRADES UNION CONGRESS).

None of this is to say that labor unions are ideal organizations. Like any institution, they can become corrupt if their leaders pursue their own or some other body's interests to the neglect of their members. Where this has occurred, such as in the celebrated case of the **Teamsters** in the United States in the 1950s and 1960s, it receives widespread attention but, by and large, these are exceptions. Despite all the dire predictions to the contrary, unions continue to go about their work and have remained democratic institutions. This is not to say that all members participate in their activities all of the time; usually union activities are confined to the committed few, but unions do offer the possibility for all to participate if they choose to do so. As Germany and Austria since 1945 show, organized labor can also be a powerful force for promoting and sustaining democracy.

Organized Labor Since 1980

Global Economic Change and the "Crisis of Labor"

Since 1980, organized labor in most of the Western world has been on the defensive. The topic that has received the most publicity and pessimistic academic study has been the "crisis of labor," that is, the decline of union membership and power in Western countries, particularly in the United States and the United Kingdom. The recession of 1981–1982 greatly reduced employment in industries in which organized labor had traditionally been strong, such as **coal mining**, steel, and manufacturing as a whole. General economic problems enabled organized labor to be blamed by conservative governments and their economic advisers in the United States and the United Kingdom as barriers to economic efficiency. There is a fundamental cultural clash between the advocates of free-market forces as an economic policy with its emphasis on deregulation, and organized labor, which is passionately in favor of regulation and government intervention to counteract market failures.

Many economic trends adverse to organized labor since 1980 have been evident. They include a fall in the proportion of well-paid, full-time jobs with benefits; the end of reliable career ladders or long-term employment outside of government service; the increasing use of contractors and the decline of the employer–employee legal relationship; competition from Third World countries (especially from their **export processing zones**) to employees in Western economies and the broader phenomenon of **globalization**; and major shifts in employment away from manufacturing toward the service sector and away from blue-collar workers to white-collar and managerial jobs. The period has also seen a growth of inequality and a decline in the quality of working life, characterized by longer working hours and greater insecurity of employment. Technological change in the form of the better use of computers in the workplace has brought rising productivity but also a spread of the likelihood of unemployment to white-collar employees.

The result of all these trends has been a significant fall in the number of union members in Western countries. Between 1980 and 2010, their numbers in Western Europe fell from 49.3 to 48.3 million and in North America from 23.5 to 10.3 million, trends that seem to support a widespread view among commentators that organized labor was a movement with a past but no future. It was largely overlooked that in the same period, its membership in Africa, Asia, and Latin America grew, pushing its global membership up by 48 percent from 118 to 175 million.

Ironically, at a time when organized labor in Western countries was falling, there was a considerable improvement in the quality of statistical information about its membership in the form of household surveys, mainly in North America, Australia, and the United Kingdom, although sometimes too for Western Europe. Since the 1980s, these surveys have shown that organized labor occupies the relatively privileged parts of the labor force. Their members tend to have higher incomes, higher levels of benefits, and better working conditions, and are more likely to work for government or larger enterprises than nonunion members.

Although the general economic trends in the developed countries of the past 30 years have been unfavorable to organized labor, they are not the sole reason for the declining density of union membership among employees. All too often, the leadership of organized labor has made the defense of the labor union as an organization their first priority. Amalgamations of unions protect the edifice of organizations by making them more efficient, but may be detrimental to the interests of the members at the grassroots. Similarly, unduly close relationships between the leadership of organized labor and government of the day can too easily lead to the neglect of the interests of members. A return to the core business and attitude of the unions may possibly be the way to overcome the "crisis of labor." In the final analysis, the only resource organized labor can trade is the wages and working conditions of its members.

Developing Countries: Some Cause for Optimism

Organized labor has always faced huge, if not impossible, obstacles in developing countries, as the Third World is now called, and the economic difficulties of the 1980s provided a convenient excuse for the repression of unions as impediments to economic growth. In 1984, the International Confederation of Free Trade Unions began to conduct annual surveys of violations of trade union rights in the world. These reports make for harrowing reading; they document the murder, torture, and imprisonment of union leaders and the denial of official recognition of labor unions that are not controlled by the government.

Needless to say, those countries with the worst record of human rights also have appalling records of the violation of trade union rights. Despite all this, organized labor has grown in many developing countries over the past 30 years. In Africa, organized labor grew from 1.1 to 14.2 million members between 1980 and 2011; in Asia, membership growth was from 23.4 to 30.1 million. In Latin America, membership growth was from 14.6 to 24.1 million. There are indications that governments may come to realize that political freedom is an indispensable condition to sustained economic growth.

Eastern Europe: The Unexpected Revival

Eastern Europe has been the unexpected chapter in the history of international organized labor since 1980. In 1920, there were about 8.5 million union members in Eastern Europe or about 19 percent of the world's total. There were only 2.5 million by 1930, and thereafter independent organized labor effectively disappeared in a welter of repression first by fascism and then by communism.

The formation of "Solidarity" in September 1980 was a milestone in the emergence of independent organized labor, not just in **Poland** but for what it foreshadowed for Eastern Europe as a whole. The 1990s saw the demise of communism and the emergence of organized labor in the Baltic States and in Russia itself, developments barely imaginable in 1980. In 2011, there were 46.9 million union members in Eastern Europe or about 23 percent of the world's total, that is, comparable with its share in 1920. In November 2000, the International Confederation of Free Trade Unions made the historic decision to admit three Russian labor federations as affiliates with their combined membership of 30 million. It was the first time that any Russian labor unions had been admitted to membership of a democratic, international labor organization.

In summary, then, despite a sea change of adverse economic trends and well-publicized declines of organized labor members in Western economies, the world membership of organized labor has increased from 118 to 175 million—a rise of 48 percent—between 1980 and 2010. A loss of nearly 10 million members in Western Europe between 1980 and 2001 was repaired in 2010 when the total loss for the entire period was back at only 0.7 million. This small loss was more than offset by gains of 44 million in Eastern Europe, 13 million in Africa, 7 million in Asia, and 9 million in Latin America. Of course, this membership growth will take time to translate into the kind of power and favorable institutional arrangements enjoyed by unions in Western Europe and quite possibly may never eventuate at all. Nevertheless, this unpublicized growth testifies to the dynamism of organized labor in a global economy that has undergone huge changes since 1980.

CONCLUSION

By any measure, organized labor has had an extraordinary history in the 20th century. Certainly, the facts of its growth are undeniable. In 1900, there were just 5 million union members, but 5 million by 2010.

Labor unions came into existence because they were wanted. As economies industrialized, so the stress on society grew. The upsetting of power relationships and the redistribution of wealth that came in the wake of industrialization brought friction. Everything that has happened to organized labor since 1980—membership decline, defeats in major strikes, a feeling that it is no longer needed, the threat of technological change, the transferring of jobs to low-wage countries—has all happened before in some form. One thing that seems constant in the history of organized labor is the temptation for employers and conservative governments to take advantage of its weaknesses to attack unions, a policy that can sometimes revive them.

Organized labor is essentially about economic democracy, and how governments treat labor unions is usually a fair indication of the real level of democracy in their society. True, organized labor can cause disruption through strikes, but the economic cost pales before the cost of industrial accidents, high labor turnover, and the lower productivity of sullen employees. Properly consulted, unions can be a force for higher productivity and economic achievement through reducing labor turnover and making for more contented employees. Industrial society has many built-in conflicts that create the demand for unions. Organized labor can be, and has been, frequently suppressed, but unless the mainsprings of its grievances can be satisfied, it will not go away.

There is nothing new in the unions' quest for a more just world or in the generally hostile global politico-economic environment they face. Such difficulties have always confronted organized labor in some form or another. But, despite confident predictions to the contrary, organized labor has not disappeared; indeed, its membership has continued to grow, as discussed, in the Third World and Eastern Europe. For as Britain's greatest labor union leader, **Ernest Bevin**, said in 1923, "We live not for today, but for the future."

A

ACCORD. *See* UNION–GOVERNMENT AGREEMENTS.

ACTIVITIES. *See* COLLECTIVE BARGAINING; OCCUPATIONAL HEALTH AND SAFETY; POLITICAL ACTION COMMITTEES; POLITICS; SOCIAL-DEMOCRATIC, SOCIALIST, AND LABOR PARTIES.

AFGHANISTAN. There is no early history of organized labor in Afghanistan. A small independent union movement existed between 1967 and 1978, but in general the country has lacked all of the prerequisites for its development, being economically backward, politically repressive or unstable, and with a society based largely on ethnic and tribal loyalties. This was further complicated by Soviet invasion, arrival of the Taliban, and intervention of the **United States**. Afghanistan has never been represented in the **International Confederation of Free Trade Unions**. In 2010, the **New Unionism Network** mentioned a number of small, independent unions with more than 450,000 members.

AFRICAN REGIONAL ORGANIZATION (AFRO). AFRO is an international regional labor organization established by the **International Confederation of Free Trade Unions (ICFTU)** to represent its affiliated members in Africa. The idea for AFRO originated from a recommendation of the fifth congress of the ICFTU, which was held in Tunis, **Tunisia**, in 1957, but AFRO was not formally established until 1993. In December 1997, AFRO held a pan-African conference on **child labor**. In 2010, the **International Trade Union Confederation** had 92 country affiliates in Africa with a combined membership of 13.6 million. *See also* TRADE UNION CONFEDERATION OF ARAB MAGHREB WORKERS.

AGE. From early on the bulk of labor union members have been middle-aged men who first served a period of **apprenticeship** or some kind of skilled training preparatory to joining a union in their early twenties. **Coal mining** was an important exception to this generalization because miners could start

21

to earn adult wages in their teens and teenagers were a feature of coal mining union membership up to the 1950s. The availability of official surveys of union membership since the 1970s has enabled the age structure of organized labor to be known in detail and how it has changed over time. Three common patterns are evident from these surveys. First, as expected, the surveys show that the proportion of union members is always higher in the older ages than the younger ones, regardless of the year selected. This happens mostly because younger workers are more likely to change jobs and be less settled in their employment than older, more experienced employees. Second, the proportion of employees under 25 joining labor unions has fallen by about half since the 1980s. For example, in **Canada**, the proportion of 17- to 24-year-olds who were members of labor unions fell from 26 to 14 percent between 1981 and 2004. Third, as a result of young employees not joining unions, there has been an aging of the remaining members. For instance, in **Australia**, the median age of male union members grew from 38 to 44 years between 1983 and 2010 and for female union members from 32 to 48 years. A comparable rise in the ages of labor union membership has also occurred in the **United States**. Although statistics on the age structure of union members in most other Western economies are not readily available, it is generally thought that it is aging.

AGRICULTURE. Despite its historical importance as an employer of labor in most countries, labor unions have been a relatively minor feature of labor relations in agriculture in 20th-century history. This is because few labor union members are employed in agriculture in industrialized economies. For example, the percentage of employees in agriculture and related industries who were members of labor unions in the United States in 2010 was only 1.6 percent compared with 12 percent for all industry sectors. In contrast, labor unions among plantation workers in Central and South America have been an important part of national labor movements. Agricultural labor in these countries has been traditionally characterized by low pay and poor working conditions, and is subject to frequent violence by employers and military governments. *See also* INTERNATIONAL FEDERATION OF PLANTATION, AGRICULTURAL, AND ALLIED WORKERS.

ALBANIA. Albania was ruled by the Ottomans until 1912 and was economically backward. Organized labor in Albania emerged only from 1901 when shoemakers at Shkodra and longshoremen at Durrës conducted localized strikes. In 1920, Albania finally became independent and the first national labor union was formed among teachers in 1924. In the 1930s, Korça became the center of organized labor in Albania. Further development of organized labor was stifled by Italian and German occupation (1939–1944) and by the establishment of a severe Stalinist regime under Enver Hoxha. Although the constitution of 1946 encouraged the formation of labor unions, this trend was reversed in 1950 when the constitution made the unions subordinate to the ruling Communist Party.

The totalitarian regime began to crumble in 1985. In 1990, the ruling communist oligarchy agreed to the creation of other parties. In December 1990, there was a round of strikes and in January 1991 strikes were legalized. In February 1991 the first independent labor unions were formed as well as a national labor federation. In October 1991, the legal status of unions and their contracts with employers were upheld by legislation. The right to strike was restricted by labor laws in 1991, and the government arrested strikers in 1993. However, the economic backwardness of Albania continued. A mission to Albania by the **International Confederation of Free Trade Unions** estimated unemployment at about 25 percent. There was a **general strike** on 16 September 1996 over price rises and demands for pay increases linked to inflation. Two Albanian unions are affiliated to the **International Trade Union Confederation (ITUC)**. The 2010 ITUC report mentioned that trade union rights are recognized by law but that members and organizers are too frequently harassed. In addition, all public sector employees are denied the right to strike.

ALGERIA. Algeria was a colony of **France** from 1830 to 3 July 1962. The first labor unions were formed by French settlers and their example provided the model for the emergence of organized labor among native Algerians from the 1940s. The *Union Générale des Travailleurs Algériens* (UGTA), or General Union of Algerian Workers, was formed in 1956 and affiliated with the **International Confederation of Free Trade Unions (ICFTU)** in the same year. It remained an affiliate until 1963 when it withdrew; in this affiliation period the UGTA claimed a **membership** of 8.9 million. In 1959, Aissar Idir, the first general secretary of the UGTA, died in a French military prison following his detention and torture. From 1963 to 1988, the UGTA was under the control of the *Front de Libération Nationale* (National Liberation Front), the political party that ruled Algeria. But the UGTA then restored internal democracy and asserted its autonomy by breaking all links with political parties. The ICFTU sent several missions to Algeria between 1989 and 1995. In 1996, the UGTA was readmitted to the ICFTU as a national, genuinely independent, and democratic organization with 1,350,000 members. The independent stance of the UGTA, particularly its calls for social justice, has made it the object of attacks by Islamic fundamentalists and the government. Between 1992 and 1994, 300 members of the UGTA were killed by Islamic fundamentalists. On 28 January 1997, Abdelhak Benhamouda, aged 51, the staunchly democratic leader of the UGTA, was assassinated outside the organization's headquarters. In 2009, the UGTA declared a membership of 1.5 million. A legal right to strike does exist. In many instances government and police have nevertheless made it almost impossible to go on strike. The 2010 **International Trade Union Confederation** survey noted that protest actions were banned and repressed and that the right to strike was limited by the government.

ALLIANCE FOR LABOR ACTION. The Alliance for Labor Action was the name of a campaign initiated by **Walter Reuther**, the president of the **United Auto Workers**, in alliance with the **Teamsters** to recruit new union members among **white-collar** employees and in service industries in 1969. The Alliance was formed outside of the **American Federation of Labor–Congress of Industrial Organizations** (AFL-CIO), from which the United Auto Workers had disaffiliated (July 1968) and from which the Teamsters had been expelled (1957). Later the chemical and distributive unions joined. Based in Atlanta, Georgia, the Alliance's campaign had poor results, partly because of hostility from the AFL-CIO, which regarded the Alliance as a rival organization. After Reuther's death in an airplane crash in 1970, the Alliance lost momentum and was disbanded in December 1971.

AMALGAMATED ENGINEERING UNION (AEU). The AEU was formed in the **United Kingdom** from the **amalgamation** of the **Amalgamated Society of Engineers (ASE)** and several other smaller unions on 1 July 1920. For most of its history, the ASE had only admitted skilled engineering employees, that is, workers who had completed an **apprenticeship**, but in 1926 it began to admit lesser skilled workers, mainly because of the effects of technological change and also to counter competition from unions such as the **Workers' Union**. By 1939, it had 390,900 members compared with 168,000 in 1933. World War II boosted the demand for engineering workers. In 1942, **women** were admitted to the ranks of the AEU for the first time; by 1943 they made up 139,000 of its 825,000 members. In 1943, too, the AEU became Great Britain's second largest union, a position it retained for most of the postwar period.

The AEU continued to grow with the economy and also through amalgamation with other unions, notably with the 72,900 strong Amalgamated Union of Foundry Workers (formed in 1946) in January 1968. Between 1962 and 1979, the membership of the AEU rose from 982,200 to a peak of 1,483,400. In 1971, the Technical, Administrative, and Supervisory Section (TASS) joined the AEU, which renamed itself the Amalgamated Union of Engineering Workers; in 1988 the TASS left to join the Association of Scientific, Technical, and Managerial Staffs to form the Manufacturing, Science and Finance Union and the AEU reverted to its former title. During 1991, the AEU and the other members of the **Confederation of Shipbuilding and Engineering Unions** won a campaign that reduced the working week from 39 to 37.5 hours for many of its members. On 1 May 1992, the AEU merged with the Electrical, Telecommunications, and Plumbing Union to become the Amalgamated Engineering and Electrical Union. Between 1986 and 1994, the membership of the AEU fell from 858,000 to 781,000. In 2001, the AEU had a membership of 728,200 before it merged with the Manufacturing, Science, and Finance Union to form **Amicus** in January 2002. *See also IG METALL.*

AMALGAMATED METAL WORKERS' UNION (AMWU). The AMWU has been one of the strongest labor unions in **Australia**. It began as the New South Wales branch of the English-based **Amalgamated Society of Engineers** in 1852 with 27 members. From 1920 to 1973, it was called the Amalgamated Engineering Union and the AMWU from 1973 to 1990. Its members were skilled metal workers, and it was one of the few unions to offer members sickness, accident, unemployment, and strike payments. From 1915, it began to admit lesser skilled metal workers into its ranks. Between 1920 and 1969, its membership rose from 16,000 to 149,300. In 1968, it formally severed its links with its British parent union. After 1945, the AMWU was one of the leading unions in gaining higher pay and better conditions for its members through **labor disputes**. From 1972, it grew by **amalgamation** with other unions, namely the Association of Drafting, Supervisory, and Technical Employees (1990) and the Vehicle Builders Employees' Federation (originally formed in 1912) in 1993. In February 1995, it merged with the Printing and Kindred Industries Union (formed in 1916) and was renamed the Australian Manufacturing Workers' Union, which claimed a membership of over 130,000 in 2009.

AMALGAMATED SOCIETY OF CARPENTERS AND JOINERS (ASCJ). A British and international union, the ASCJ was formed in London in June 1860 with 618 members following a strike in 1859–1860 to win the nine-hour working day. The employers responded with a lockout and a demand that the strikers sign an undertaking that they would not join a labor union. The strong financial support given by the other unions, particularly the **Amalgamated Society of Engineers**, caused the employers to withdraw their demand. Membership of the ASCJ rose to 10,178 by 1870 and to 17,764 by 1880, making it one of the most powerful craft unions.

The ASCJ was also an international union; it established branches in **Ireland** (1866), the **United States** (1867), Scotland (1871), **Canada** (1872), **New Zealand** (1875), **Australia** (Sydney, 1875; Adelaide, 1878; and Melbourne, 1879), and **South Africa** (1881). In Australia, the New South Wales branch of the ASCJ claimed 33,000 members in 1890. In the United States, the ASCJ provided a model for the formation of the Brotherhood of Carpenters and Joiners in Chicago in 1881 by Peter J. McGuire. The Brotherhood proved to be far more successful than the ASCJ in recruiting members. In 1923, the Canadian branches of the ASCJ were closed and merged with the American Brotherhood. In 1911, the English ASCJ merged with the Associated Carpenters and Joiners' Society of Scotland (founded in 1861). Further amalgamations followed that transformed the original **craft union** into an **industrial union** that eventually gave rise to the Union of Construction and Allied Technical Trades in 1971. In Australia, the ASCJ retained its separate identity until 1992. *See also* UNITED KINGDOM.

AMALGAMATED SOCIETY OF ENGINEERS (ASE). Since 1851, engineering unions have played a central role in the history of organized labor in the **United Kingdom**. The first continuous labor organization in the engineering industry was the Journeymen Steam Engine, Machine Makers, and Millwrights' Friendly Society formed in Manchester in 1826 and known as "Old Mechanics." The ASE was largely formed from the merger of "Old Mechanics" and the Smiths' Benevolent Sick and Burial Society in 1851. Membership began at 5,000 and reached 11,000 by the end of 1851. The formation of the **Amalgamated Society of Engineers (ASE)** in 1851 was hailed by **Beatrice and Sidney James Webb** as a pivotal event in the history of organized labor as marking the first of "model" unions with well-developed organizations, high contribution fees, and sickness, **unemployment**, superannuation, and funeral benefits. The ASE was the target of a nationwide lockout by employers in 1852. Defeated, some members left Britain to form a branch of the ASE in New South Wales, **Australia**, in 1852. In 1851 the ASE founded its first branch in **Ireland**; it also set up branches in **Canada** (1853), the **United States** (1861), **New Zealand** (1864), and **South Africa** (1891). With the creation of these branches, the ASE became an international as well as a British union, an example later followed by the **Amalgamated Society of Carpenters and Joiners**.

In 1897–1898, the ASE suffered an important defeat by a lockout organized by the engineering employers, an event that led it to become a prime mover in the formation of the **General Federation of Trade Unions** in 1899. During the lockout, over £28,000 was given by European unions (half came from German unions) and overseas branches of the ASE. Faced with intense competition from American unions, the ASE closed down its American branches in 1920, whereas in Australia, the ASE went on to become one of the major unions as the **Amalgamated Metal Workers' Union**. In 1913, the ASE had 17,000 members (or about 10 percent of its total membership) in nine countries outside of Great Britain. In Britain, the membership of the ASE grew from 100,000 in 1910 to 174,300 in 1914. As a result of the demand for munitions during World War I, membership reached 298,800 in 1918. In 1916, George Nicoll Barnes (1859–1940), a former secretary of the ASE, joined Lloyd George's wartime government as minister for **pensions**. From 1905, the ASE supported the creation of a single union for the engineering industry and in 1918 persuaded 17 unions in the industry to conduct ballots for **amalgamation**; nine of these bodies agreed to amalgamate to form the **Amalgamated Engineering Union**. In 1920 just before the amalgamation, the ASE had 423,000 members. *See also DEUTSCHER METALLARBEITER-VERBAND; FEDERAZIONE ITALIANA OPERAI METALLURGICI.*

AMALGAMATION. Amalgamation—that is, the merging of a labor body with one or more other labor bodies—has been an important feature of the history of organized labor in most countries. In the **United Kingdom** and in countries where organized labor had British roots (**United States, Canada, South Africa, Australia,** and **New Zealand**), there were by the late 19th century relatively large numbers of unions organized by occupation or **craft**. As these unions tried to recruit new members, they soon came into conflict with other unions, and one of the functions of national labor federations such as the **Trades Union Congress** and the **American Federation of Labor** was often to adjudicate in jurisdictional (or demarcation) disputes between unions. One solution to this problem was amalgamation, which had the added advantage of better-funded union administrations. A number of large unions have grown by amalgamation, notably the British **Transport and General Workers' Union** and the Australian Federated Miscellaneous Workers' Union.

Amalgamation has accounted for much of the general fall in the number of unions in English-speaking countries. In Australia, the number of unions officially recorded fell from 573 in 1911 to 132 in 1996, after which date more recent data is not available. In the United Kingdom, the peak number of unions was reached in 1920 when there were 1,384 unions. By 2001, there were 226 unions; in 2010, only 177 remained. In New Zealand, the number of unions was greatest in 1937 at 499, but by 1973 this figure had dropped to 309 and between 1985 and 2010 from 259 to 157. Because of its longer tradition of **industrial unions**, the decline in the number of unions in **Germany** has been comparatively low. In the United States, the number of unions affiliated with the **American Federation of Labor–Congress of**

Industrial Organizations was only 55 in 2010, compared with 139 in 1955. Between 1956 and 1994, there were 133 union amalgamations, of which 40 occurred between 1986 and 1994. Since the recession of the early 1980s, there has been continual economic pressure on unions generally to maintain their strength through amalgamation. Although amalgamations may benefit labor unions as organizations, it can be detrimental to their relations with their members at the grassroots level.

AMERICAN FEDERATION OF LABOR (AFL). The AFL was the leading federation of American organized labor from the early 1890s. It grew out of the Federation of Organized Trades and Labor Unions of the **United States** and **Canada**, which was formed in Pittsburgh in 1881. Based on the British **Trades Union Congress**, it represented 50,000 members and gave autonomy to affiliated unions. It faced strong competition for members from the **Knights of Labor**. Interunion fighting prompted **Samuel Gompers** to lead a campaign by craft unions that resulted in the setting up of the AFL in Columbus, Ohio, on 8 December 1886. The AFL was based on craft unions, not on unions organized by industries. This led to jurisdictional or demarcation disputes between member unions over which organizations had the right to recruit certain members, particularly in coal mining, which the **United Mine Workers of America** declared as its preserve in the "Scranton Declaration" in 1901.

During World War I, the AFL became the recognized spokesman of American organized labor, and it had the support of the National War Labor Board. By 1920 the AFL represented four million employees, but this gain rapidly fell away in the face of a sustained offensive by employers for the "open shop." The Depression reduced the AFL to only 2.1 million members by 1933. The membership was disproportionately concentrated in coal mining, railroads, and construction. Gompers, the AFL president since its formation (with one short break in 1894), died in 1924 and was succeeded by **William Green**, who was president until his death.

Reflecting its **craft union** roots, the AFL was always a conservative organization, and dissatisfaction with its neglect of mass production workers enabled **John L. Lewis**, the president of the United Mine Workers' Union, to set up a rival to the AFL based on **industrial unions**, the Committee of Industrial Organizations, in 1935, which officially became the **Congress of Industrial Organizations (CIO)** in 1938. In 1937, the AFL had 3.4 million members compared with 3.7 in the CIO, and in 1938 all CIO member bodies of the AFL were expelled in the United States and in Canada. Competition for members with the CIO, compounded by its less conservative policies, ensured that rivalry continued with the AFL into the late 1940s. In 1952,

George Meany was elected president of the AFL, and a formal merger with the CIO occurred in December 1955.

AMERICAN FEDERATION OF LABOR–CONGRESS OF INDUS-TRIAL ORGANIZATIONS (AFL-CIO). The AFL-CIO was formed by the merger of the two rival national labor federations in the **United States** in December 1955. The **Taft-Hartley Act** of 1947 and the worsening political climate for organized labor encouraged the two bodies to consider joining forces. The deaths of the presidents of both bodies in 1952 (**William Green** of the American Federation of Labor and **Philip Murray** of the Congress of Industrial Organizations), who were bitter rivals, also made the **amalgamation** of the two organizations far easier. **George Meany**, who replaced Green as AFL president, worked hard to achieve unity, as did his counterpart in the CIO, **Walter Reuther**. Meany became president of the AFL-CIO, a post he held until 1979. In 1957, the AFL-CIO expelled the **Teamsters** and the Laundry Workers and the Bakers' Union for corruption.

Although officially nonpolitical, the AFL-CIO has always been closely associated with the Democratic Party. In its international dealing in labor affairs, the AFL-CIO has followed conservative policies, as shown by its withdrawal from the **International Confederation of Free Trade Unions** between 1969 and 1981. Since the early 1980s, the AFL-CIO has petitioned the United States government to exclude **China**, **Malaysia**, and **Thailand** from the generalized system of preferences for their abuses of **human rights** and labor union freedom. In 1979, **Joseph Lane Kirkland** succeeded Meany as AFL-CIO president and held the post until 1995. He was succeeded by **John J. Sweeney**.

In 1973, the AFL-CIO had 114 affiliated unions with a total membership of 13.4 million. Between 1991 and 2001, the number of its affiliated unions fell from 89 to 66 and the total membership they represented fell from 13.9 to 13 million. In 2002, the AFL-CIO stated as its mission: "to bring social and economic justice to our nation by enabling working people to have a voice on the job, in government, in a changing global economy and in their communities." Despite these words, the decline of membership continued. A group of dissatisfied unions, including the Teamsters, split and formed **Change to Win**. As a result the AFL-CIO only counted 9 million members in 2010. Adding the membership of **Working America**, the total number was 12.2 million out of a total union membership for the United States of 14.7 million.

AMERICAN FEDERATION OF STATE, COUNTY, AND MUNICI-PAL EMPLOYEES (AFSCME). The AFSCME was founded in 1932 by a small group of **white-collar**, professional state employees in Madison,

Wisconsin, as the Wisconsin State Administrative, Clerical, Fiscal and Technical Employees Association. In 1935, with help from the **American Federation of Labor** (AFL), the Association successfully resisted through lobbying and demonstrations draft state legislation aimed at dismantling the state's civil service system and was granted an AFL charter. By the end of 1936, AFSCME had emerged as a national labor union with 10,000 members that was recognized by the AFL. Before the 1970s, the AFSCME grew steadily rather than quickly, from 73,000 in 1946 to 237,000 in 1965. In 1958, the AFSCME forced New York City Mayor Robert Wagner to grant **collective bargaining** rights to unions representing city employees.

In 1961, President John F. Kennedy issued Executive Order 10988, which legitimized collective bargaining for federal employees and helped create a favorable atmosphere for similar demands from all public employees. These developments worked to the advantage of the AFSCME, which used them to get collective bargaining frameworks established in a number of states. Its membership rose from 647,000 in 1975 to a million by 1985 and to 1.6 million (including retirees) by 2010. The AFSCME has a history of using the political process and lobbying to achieve its goals. A survey of AFSCME members in March 2001 found that 53 percent were **women**, 29 percent had household incomes of $60,000 or more, and 31 percent had college or postgraduate education.

AMERICAN FEDERATION OF TEACHERS (AFT). Although formed in April 1916, the origins of the AFT can be traced to the Chicago Federation of Teachers, which was formed in 1897. Faced with a hostile environment, particularly the lack of a framework for **collective bargaining** until the 1960s, membership growth was slow and uncertain, falling from 9,300 to 3,700 between 1920 and 1924. Opportunities for growth in the 1930s were hampered by an internal struggle with **communism**. During World War II, the AFT was able to negotiate contracts with educational authorities in Montana and Washington states and conducted its first strike in St. Paul, Minnesota, in 1946. Between 1939 and 1955, the membership of the AFT grew from 32,100 to 46,000. In 1957, the AFT lost nearly 7,000 members when local unions that refused to admit African-Americans were expelled. An early affiliate of the **American Federation of Labor–Congress of Industrial Organizations (AFL-CIO)**, the AFT achieved a major success in the early 1960s when its New York locals gained collective bargaining rights and, in 1963, the AFT dropped its no-strike policy. Against a background of discontent over the failure of teachers' salaries to keep up with the private sector, the membership of the AFT climbed from 97,000 to 396,000 between 1965 and 1975 and to 499,00 by 1987.

The AFT faced a formidable competitor in its efforts from the **National Education Association (NEA)**, which had opposed collective bargaining for teachers before 1963. Efforts to merge the two unions nationally failed because of the affiliation of the AFT with the AFL-CIO. Finally, in 2001, the AFT and the NEA signed the NEAFT Partnership, a pledge by both organizations to "work together on behalf of our members and on behalf of all those whom our members serve." The Partnership recognized the independence of both unions and their commitment "to nurturing and improving public education above all. We are determined to fight for family needs, which must be met in order to make our public schools the equalizer they have been and should be for society. This encompasses quality of life issues, such as health care for all Americans, safe neighborhoods and a caring government." In 2010, the AFT claimed a membership of 900,000.

AMERICAN LABOR UNION (ALU). The ALU was a short-lived radical organization formed by the Western Federation of Miners in 1898 as the Western Labor Union to supplement the eastern-dominated **American Federation of Labor (AFL)**. A **socialist** organization, the ALU attempted to recruit employees ignored by the AFL, that is, the lesser skilled, **women**, and immigrants. The Western Labor Union was fiercely opposed by the AFL and changed its name to the ALU in 1902 to compete directly with the AFL, as advocated by Eugene V. Debs. The ALU also advocated **industrial unions** instead of **craft unions**, which were the basis of the AFL. Despite its wider recruiting ambitions (it claimed 100,000 members), the core of the ALU was the Western Federation of Miners. The ALU was one of the parent organizations of the **Industrial Workers of the World**, which continued its main aims after 1905, after which time the ALU ceased to exist. *See also* UNITED STATES.

AMICUS. Amicus, from the Latin meaning "friend" or "ally," was formed in the **United Kingdom** from the merger of the **Amalgamated Engineering and Electrical Union** and the Manufacturing, Science and Finance Union in January 2002. With 1.1 million members, it became the second largest British labor union, after **UNISON**. In 2007, Amicus merged with the Transport and General Workers Union to form **Unite the Union**.

ANARCHISM. The term *anarchism* was derived from an ancient Greek word meaning "without government." As a political philosophy, it owed much to Pierre-Joseph Proudhon (1809–1865), who regarded the state as a negative element in society that should be abolished. Mikail Alexandrovich Bakunin (1814–1876), a Russian political thinker, propagandist, and activist, absorbed Proudhon's ideas and was one of the leading anarchists of the 19th century. In the International Working Men's Association (generally known as the first international), Bakunin was an opponent of Karl Marx's ideas about the socialist state. Anarchism, as envisaged by Bakunin, sought the overthrow of the state and its replacement by democratically run cooperative groups covering the whole economy. It attracted support from certain intellectuals and in rural areas where the local political and economic system was repressive and ignored demands for reform. It drew much support from **Spain** and **Italy**, where it formed a strand of political thinking with **syndicalism**, called **anarcho-syndicalism**. Anarcho-syndicalists envisage the overthrow of capitalism by a **general strike** guided by the union. Because of their association with political violence, anarchists were excluded from mainstream socialism from 1896. **Immigration** spread anarchist ideas to Latin America; in 1919, the anarchists attempted to form a federation covering the whole of Latin America.

In Spain, the anarchists formed their own federation, the *Confederación Nacional del Trabajo* (National Confederation of Labor), in 1910 and anarchists remained important until their destruction during the Spanish Civil War (1936–1939). From 1940 to about 1990, anarchism failed to attract a significant following, but in the 1990s began to grow again. Much of the violence that occurred in the protests about **globalization** from the late 1990s was committed by self-styled anarchists who had no knowledge of the theoretical background of 19th century anarchism. *See also* ARGENTINA; CHILE; COMMUNISM; SYNDICALISM.

ANARCHO-SYNDICALISM. *See* ANARCHISM; SYNDICALISM.

ANGOLA. Free labor unions and strikes were forbidden when Angola was a colony of **Portugal** up to 1974, although organizations among European employees existed from 1897. In the 1960s, the *Liga Geral dos Trabalhadores de Angola* (General Union of Angolan Workers) was an affiliate of the **International Confederation of Free Trade Unions (ICFTU)**, but only as an organization in exile. Angola was admitted to full affiliation with the ICFTU in 2002 and claimed 51,000 members in the *Central Geral de Sindicatos Independentes e Livres de Angola* (General Centre of Independent and Free Unions of Angola). In February 2006 the Strike Act had been revised under which the right to strike has been strictly regulated. A tripartite system of collective bargaining is recognized, but union rights are not consistently enforced. In 2007, the survey of **violations of trade union rights** reported that the situation in the country still made it difficult for the unions to enforce their rights; this complaint was repeated in subsequent years.

ANTIGUA AND BARBUDA. Antigua and Barbuda was a colony of the **United Kingdom** to 1981. The legal right to register a labor union was granted in 1939. The Antigua Trades and Labour Union (ATLU), a labor union closely related to the labor party, was the first Antiguan labor organization to take advantage of this law; it registered in 1939 and claimed 7,000 members by 1975. After a split from the ATLU in 1967 the Antigua Workers' Union was formed. The ATLU was an affiliate of the **International Confederation of Free Trade Unions** (ICFTU) by 1975. In 2007, there still were 7,000 union members in Antigua and Barbuda or 75 percent of the employees.

APPRENTICESHIP. Apprenticeship is a system of vocational training for teenagers characterized by on-the-job instruction and technical training. In England, apprenticeship was first regulated in the 14th century, and a seven-year apprenticeship was set down in law in 1562; this was repealed in 1814, despite protests from organized labor. Apprenticeship has historically been favored by organized labor as a way of maintaining skill standards for craft occupations and as a means of controlling the supply of labor, both unqualified as well as skilled. Apprenticeship has largely been a feature of specialist craft occupations, particularly in **manufacturing**, but has also been extended to service occupations such as hairdressing. In the 20th century, technological change and rising education levels have diminished the importance of apprenticeship. As a method of trade training, apprenticeship has the disadvantage of being less available to students who leave school during low points in the trade cycle because that is usually the time when employers cut down on the number of new apprentices to lower their wages cost. *See also* YOUTH.

ARBITRATION. *See* CONCILIATION AND ARBITRATION.

ARGENTINA. Argentina has one of the oldest labor movements in Latin America; in 1857, printers formed a mutual **benefit** society, which they made into a union in 1877. The first union federation was formed in 1891 but did not last long. Ten years later, the next federation was formed, the *Federación Obrera Argentina* (FOA), or Federation of Workers of Argentina, which was renamed *Federación Obrera Regional Argentina* one year later. The FOA soon split into **anarchist, syndicalist,** and **socialist** factions. All workers organizations recognize the FOA as their origin.

Like North America and Australasia, the population of Argentina was built on **immigration**; in the case of Argentina, the bulk of the immigrants up to the 1930s came from **Italy** and **Spain**. Most immigrants settled in the eastern part of the country. They played an important role in the formation of the labor movement, but the *criollos* had their part too.

Despite its early beginning, union membership was low in the 19th century. In 1908, a government survey estimated that there were only 23,400 union members in Buenos Aires, and even by 1920, national membership had only reached 68,000. Despite these low membership figures, Argentina experienced a **general strike** in 1902, and also in 1904 and 1905. In the 1907 general strike, 93,000 took part. By 1930, when the *Confederación General del Trabajo* (CGT), or General Confederation of Labor, was formed by socialist and syndicalist unions, the number of union members had grown to 280,000. Other rival labor federations were formed by anarchists and **communists**. In 1935 the CGT split into a syndicalist wing (*Unión Sindical Argentina*) and a socialist-communist CGT. From 1943 the CGT became an active participant in **politics** through Colonel Juan Perón. In the turmoil that followed Perón's removal in 1955, the CGT was suppressed by the military government and forced underground, but reemerged in 1961.

Thereafter, political rather than industrial concerns dominated Argentinean labor as governments both military and democratic attempted to deal with the country's severe economic problems; these policies produced factional divisions within the CGT. The union was suppressed after the 1976 military coup d'état but managed to continue its existence. The legal status of the CGT was restored in 1986 following intervention by the **International Labour Organization**. In 1988, Law 23551 established a framework for the administration of labor unions, **collective bargaining**, and **labor disputes**. In 2001, there were claimed to be 4.4 million union members in Argentina compared with 2.5 million in 1990. In 2001–2002, the country's economic crises threatened to undermine political stability and the relatively favorable status of organized labor. Despite the severity of the crisis in 2002, the survey of **violations of trade union rights** reported that labor unions had managed to survive surprisingly well. According to the 2009 report, unionists suffered from intimidation, dismissals, and attacks. Membership even grew between 2002 and 2009 causing a stable percentage of employees organized in unions. *See also* TOSCO, AGUSTIN GRINGO; VANDOR, AUGUSTO.

ARMENIA. The first trade unions were formed in 1905–1907. Part of the former Soviet Union from 1920 to September 1991, there was no history of organized labor in Armenia. The Council of Trade Unions of Armenia was established in 1921 but subordinate to the Communist Party; it was not independent. After the fall of **communism** 24 unions signed the Declaration on the foundation of the Confederation of Trade Unions of Armenia (CTUA). In 2007, the CTUA had 29,665 members but it has not been affiliated to the **International Trade Union Confederation**. In 2010, membership had fallen to 24,133. The economy remains undeveloped and the population poor.

ASIA AND PACIFIC REGIONAL ORGANISATION (APRO). APRO is an international regional labor organization formed by the **International Confederation of Free Trade Unions (ICFTU)** in 1984. It began in Karachi, Pakistan, in May 1951, as the Asian Regional Organisation. It was later moved to **India** and then to **Singapore**, where it remains. In 2007, APRO had affiliates in 28 countries and represented 30 million members. In 2007, following the merger of the ICFTU and the **World Confederation of Labor**, the organization adopted the name **Regional Organisation for the Asia and the Pacific**.

ASIA-PACIFIC LABOUR NETWORK (APLN). APLN was formed by the **International Confederation of Free Trade Unions** in 1995 to lobby for social dialogue with the governments of the Asia-Pacific Economic Cooperation Forum (APEC; formed in 1989 to promote free trade and investments) on economic and social issues such as debt, corruption, structural imbalances, and **child labor**. To date, its overtures have been rejected. APLN and APEC have 21 country members.

AUSTRALIA. The first labor unions in Australia arose among shipwrights in 1829, but it was not until after the gold rushes in the 1850s that organized labor became more important. Before the 1880s, most unions were formed by employees in a limited range of occupations, but in the 1880s there was an upsurge of "new" unionism, which embraced a wider range of occupations. By 1890, there were about 200,000 union members covering about 23 percent of all employees, giving Australia, briefly, the highest level in the world. Between 1878 and 1900, the six colonies that made up Australia—there was no national government until 1901—passed laws that recognized labor unions. In 1879 the labor unions held their first intercolonial congress in Sydney; subsequent congresses were held in 1884, 1886, 1888, 1889, 1891, and 1898. Between August and December 1890, 50,000 workers in Australia and **New Zealand** took part in the great Maritime Strike over freedom of contract; the strikers suffered defeat. Between July and September 1894, the unions suffered a second major setback as a result of the wool shearers' strike in Queensland. The depression of the early 1890s, which was aggravated by a severe drought, retarded economic growth and caused union membership to fall to 97,000 (or about 9 percent of employees) in 1901.

The unions also used **politics** to improve their position. Following the introduction of public payment of a salary to members of parliament in New South Wales in 1889, the Sydney Trades and Labour Council resolved to support labor candidates, a decision that resulted in the election of 35 labor members to Parliament at the 1891 election, an event that marked the birth of what later was called the **Australian Labor Party**. Greatly assisted by the introduction of compulsory **conciliation and arbitration** as a means of settling labor disputes—a system that eased the process for unions to **collectively bargain** with employers by granting them legal recognition—union **membership** rose to 498,000 or 34 percent of employees in 1913, the highest level in any country at the time. As in other countries, **white-collar** unions began to organize during the 1900s, but most union members continued to be predominantly male **blue-collar** employees. With the establishment of the Federated Miscellaneous Workers' Union in 1915 (a union that recruited employees not recruited by other unions), the structure of organized labor remained relatively unchanged until the late 1980s. Australian labor unions have been a mixture of large and small organizations since the 1890s. Between 1913 and 1995 the proportion of unions with less than 1,000 members fell from 80 to 49 percent and the number of unions fell from 432 to 142.

After 1913, union membership rose and fell according to the state of the economy and the distribution of employment by industry. Unionism was strongest among blue-collar workers and skilled tradesmen. It was weakest among casual employees and white-collar workers. As a proportion of employees, unions reached their height in Australia in 1953, when 63 percent of employees were members.

Since the early 1980s, the structure and size of union membership in Australia has changed considerably, affected by the economy and politics. Between 1983 and 1996, the federal Labor government and the **Australian Council of Trade Unions** (ACTU) worked closely to achieve economic growth and other objectives through a series of **accords**. The pay rises this process delivered to all employees reduced the necessity to join unions, and between 1982 and 1996 the number of union members fell from 2,567,600 to 2,194,300, and the proportion of employees who were union members fell from 49 to 31 percent. With the election of the conservative Liberal-National government in March 1996, the special relationship between organized labor and the federal government ended abruptly. In 1996, the government passed the Workplace Relations Act (WRA), which curbed labor unions and restricted the right to strike. In 2002, only 23 percent of all employees were union members; in the private sector, only 18 percent of all employees were union members. The WRA was amended by the Workplace Relations Amendment (Work Choices) Act 2005 that came into force in March 2006 and went even further in imposing limitations on workers' rights. This legislation was used against workers and trade unionists and as a result workers were dismissed, prosecuted, and fined. In 2009 the **International Trade Union Confederation** (ITUC) concluded that the new legislation was still in effect although the new Labor government's Fair Work Act provides stronger rights for workers and unions. A year later the ITUC was a little more optimistic about union rights. Between 1995 and 2010, the decline in the proportion of employees who were labor union members in Australia (33 to 18 percent) was greater than in the **United States** (15 to 12 percent). The total number of members in 2010 was 1.4 million.

AUSTRALIAN COUNCIL OF TRADE UNIONS (ACTU). The ACTU is the national body representing labor unions in **Australia**. The idea of a single body representing Australian labor unions was first suggested by William Gutherie Spence (1846–1926) at the 1884 Intercolonial Trade Union Congress, but it failed to attract support although subsequent congresses considered ways of federating the various peak labor bodies in the various colonies. The creation of a national government in 1901 and a federal system of **conciliation and arbitration** in 1905 created a new incentive to form a national body. But despite further national congresses in 1902, 1907, 1913, and 1916, it was not until the national conference of 1921 that the first steps were taken to form a peak national labor body, and even then two further conferences were needed (in 1922 and 1925) before the ACTU was formed in Melbourne, Victoria, in 1927. The ACTU was invited to join the **International Federation of Trade Unions** in 1936 but did not accept. Until the late 1950s, the powers of the ACTU were limited, with real power continuing to reside with the state trades and labor councils.

It was not until 1943 that the ACTU created its first salaried position, and it was only in 1949 that it had its first full-time president, Albert E. Monk, who held the post until 1969. In 1953, the ACTU joined the **International Confederation of Free Trade Unions** and remains by far its largest member in Oceania. The growing importance of national wage cases and the convenience for national governments of dealing with a single labor body further strengthened the ACTU. In 1968, the then largest labor union, the **Australian Workers' Union**, affiliated with the ACTU. In 1980, the Australian Council of Salaried and Professional Associations joined the ACTU, as did the other major **white-collar** body, the Council of Australian Government Employees, in 1981. By 1981, all significant unions and union groupings had become affiliated with the ACTU and it represented about 2.5 million employees.

The ACTU was at its greatest influence when the **Australian Labor Party** (ALP) ran the national government from March 1983 to March 1996. At the March 1983 national election, the ALP won office and the former ACTU president from 1970 to 1980, Bob Hawke, became prime minister. Although the ACTU remains based in Melbourne, most large labor unions have their headquarters in Sydney. Between 1986 and 1993 the number of unions affiliated with the ACTU fell from 162 to 94, largely in response to a campaign led by the ACTU for the **amalgamation** of unions. In 2009, the ACTU had 26 affiliated unions and represented 1.9 million members.

The ACTU has had an affirmative action policy for many years and elected its first female president, Jennie George, in 1996. After George stepped down, she was replaced by Sharan Burrow in May 2000 who remained president until 2010. In 2002, half of the ACTU executive's members were **women**. In recent years, the ACTU has conducted "living wage" campaigns for lower-paid employees and against long **working hours**. It has also played a significant role in promoting democracy and trade unionism in the Pacific and southeast Asia. The objective of the ACTU for 2010 was to remind the government that Australian workers cannot live with second-rate safety standards because reducing death, injury, and illness at work is a top priority for working people and unions. *See also* PACIFIC TRADE UNION COMMUNITY; UNION–GOVERNMENT AGREEMENTS.

AUSTRALIAN LABOR PARTY (ALP). The ALP is one of the oldest and most successful continuous political parties based on organized labor in the world. It had its beginnings in a decision of the Sydney Trades and Labor Council in January 1890 to support candidates in the 1891 election following the introduction of state payment of the salaries of members of parliament in 1889. Support for a direct role in **politics** by organized labor was boosted by its defeat in the Maritime Strike of 1890. Labor unions have continued to provide the basis of the ALP ever since. It represented the culmination of efforts to elect working-class representatives to Parliament, which began in the late 1870s. It drew part of its inspiration from the British Liberal Party, the main political outlet for the organized English working class in the 19th century. By the mid-1900s, the ALP had been set up in all Australian states. Its features of a platform of policies and disciplined voting by its elected members began a new era in Australian politics. Usually represented by its opponents as a "left-wing" party, the ALP has always been a moderate social democratic party, although it did contain some radical groups. There have been two major splits in the ALP. The first was in 1916–1917 over military conscription, and the second occurred in 1955 over attitudes to communism.

The ALP formed national governments in 1908–1909, 1910–1913, 1914–1915, 1929–1932, 1941–1949, 1972–1974, and 1983–1996, but its longest terms of government success have been in the states. Notable ALP prime ministers have been William Morris Hughes (1915–1916), James H. Scullin (1929–1932), John Curtin (1941–1945), Ben Chifley (1945–1949), Gough Whitlam (1972–1974), and Bob Hawke (1983–1991); before becoming prime minister, Hawke was president of the **Australian Council of Trade Unions** (ACTU) from 1970 to 1980. In September 2002, the federal parliamentary

ALP leader, Simon Crean a former ACTU president, succeeded in reducing bloc voting by organized labor at ALP state conferences from 60 to 50 percent. The ALP was returned as the federal government in the elections of November 2007 led by Kevin Rudd. He was deposed by his deputy, Julia Gillard, in August 2010, and in the elections shortly afterward the ALP lost ground and was returned a minority government dependent upon the support of three independents.

AUSTRALIAN WORKERS' UNION (AWU). From the 1900s to 1969, the AWU was the largest labor union in **Australia**. It began as a sheep shearers' union in Ballarat, Victoria, in 1886. In 1894, the AWU was founded in Sydney, New South Wales, from the **amalgamation** of shearers' and laborers' unions, with a claimed membership of 30,000. The membership of the AWU was open to all employees. The AWU expanded by amalgamation with other unions, first with the rural laborers' union in 1894 and then with unions of semiskilled workers in rural, general laboring, and mining occupations between 1912 and 1917. By 1914, the AWU had 70,000 members.

The AWU has been a powerful but conservative force in Australian organized labor and in the **Australian Labor Party**. In the 1950s the AWU had about 200,000 members. Structural changes in industries and occupations, as well as internal disputes, have reduced the AWU membership since 1970 from 160,000 to 115,500 by 1990. In November 1993, the AWU amalgamated with the Federation of Industrial Manufacturing and Engineering Employees (FIMEE), formerly the Federated Ironworkers' Association (formed in 1911) and was officially renamed the AWU-FIME Amalgamated Union. Two years later the name was changed back to The Australian Workers' Union. It had a membership of about 170,000 in 1999 and 135,000 ten years later.

AUSTRIA. Labor unions were legally tolerated within the present borders of Austria in 1870; the unions claimed 46,600 members by 1892 and 119,000 by 1900. Union growth was hampered not just by political and religious divisions in Austrian society but also by the large proportion of the labor force employed in **agriculture**. In 1920, 41 percent of the labor force was employed in agriculture, a proportion that had only dropped to 32 percent by 1934. Even so, as in other Western European countries, union **membership** grew substantially after 1913 from 263,000 to a million by 1920, when it reached 51 percent of employees, a level comparable with **Germany**. To a large extent, the union growth that occurred just after World War I was the result of legislative change. The newly created Austrian Republic, following the German example, sought to tie organized labor into the new political order by laws in 1919–1920, which set up chambers of labor (modeled on the chambers of commerce) within the works' council law of 1919; these laws set up an ordered industrial relations system with compulsory union membership. By 1930, union membership had declined to 38 percent of employees in response to the economic dislocation of the 1920s and the Depression. Unions were also caught up in the turmoil of Austrian **politics**. After a short civil war in 1934, the **socialist** unions along with the Social Democratic Party were repressed and placed under the control of a labor federation run by the Catholic unions. After the annexation of Austria by Germany in 1938, all Austrian organized labor was incorporated into the ***Deutsche Arbeitsfront***.

The end of World War II saw the immediate rebirth of free organized labor in Austria. Wartime imprisonment of all labor leaders by the Nazis encouraged the Catholics, socialists, and communists to bury their differences and form the *Österreichischer Gewerkschaftsbund* (Austrian Federation of Labor Unions) in April 1945. **Blue-collar** and **white-collar** workers are traditionally organized in separate unions. Composed of 15 unions, the *Österreichischer Gewerkschaftsbund* has worked with government to promote balanced economic growth and a stable democratic government. The laws of 1919–1920, which set up works' councils, were the basis of the "social partnership" that became characteristic of the corporatist approach to organized labor followed by Austria throughout the post-1945 period. During this period, industrial peace was prevalent. In 2001, there were 1.4 million union members in Austria compared with 1.6 million union members in 1994; over this period, union membership among Austrian employees fell from 49 to 43 percent. In 2010, the number of union members had fallen to 1.2 million.

AZERBAIJAN. Azerbaijan has been independent of the former Soviet Union since August 1991. Organized labor in Azerbaijan has progressed despite the government's use of Soviet-era laws. In 1993, an independent journalists' union was formed after two journalists were beaten up on government orders. Azerbaijan became an affiliate of the **International Confederation of Free Trade Unions** in 2000. In 2001, there were 735,000 union members in Azerbaijan, organized in the Azerbaijan Trade Union Confederation. In 2007, the **International Trade Union Confederation**'s survey of **violations of trade union rights** reported that there was little respect for collective bargaining in Azerbaijan even though it had been legal to form labor unions since 1994. Unions reported that many employers did not recognize unions and one of these employers even dismissed 700 union members. He did so despite the new 2006 law that stipulated that a written consent by the union is requested if an employer wants to dismiss his personnel.

B

BAHAMAS. A colony of the **United Kingdom** to 1973, labor unions emerged in the Bahamas after 1943 when unions were, in effect, legalized; the law was broadened in 1958. The first union was the Bahamas Federation of Labor (est. 1942), but this union ceased to exist in 1969. By 1969, the Bahamas had become an affiliate of the **International Confederation of Free Trade Unions** (ICFTU). In 2001, there were 2,500 union members in the Bahamas, mainly organized in the Commonwealth of the Bahamas Trade Union Congress and the National Congress of Trade Unions.

The Industrial Relations Act strongly limits the right to strike. In 2010 the government was reported to still have wide powers to interfere in union activities while employers in the hotel sector in 2008 laid off employees on a massive scale.

BAHRAIN. Until 1971 Bahrain was a British protectorate in which the ruling elite has been since the 18th century the al-Khalifa family. Independent labor unions are not allowed in Bahrain. In 1983, the government introduced a joint work council system that included elected workers' representatives, who in turn elect 11 members to the General Committee of Bahrain Workers. About 60 percent of the labor force are expatriate even though official policy is to replace them with Bahraini workers. These migrant workers are hardly protected by law against maltreatment. Although they share the same rights to form work councils as the locals they prefer not to do so because they are not protected against dismissal. The 2010 survey of the **International Trade Union Confederation** mentioned that many construction workers were threatened with arrests and dismissals because they sought better working conditions.

BALTIC STATES. *See* ESTONIA; LATVIA; LITHUANIA.

BANGLADESH. Bangladesh was called *East Pakistan* until December 1971 when it forcibly seceded from West Pakistan. Organized labor in Bangladesh dates from the 1920s, mainly in cotton manufacturing. After the creation of **Pakistan** in 1947, Indian labor unions set up a labor union federation in East Pakistan to mirror the All-India Trade Union Congress, but under Indian tutelage. Despite ratification of **International Labour Organization** conventions 87 and 98 relating to the right to **collective bargaining** and the right to **strike**, respectively, organized labor in East Pakistan was effectively muzzled. The creation of Bangladesh did not lift the restrictions on organized labor, and labor relations remained turbulent, reflecting the poverty of Bangladesh and its political instability. By 1975, organized labor in Bangladesh was divided among three national labor federations; two were affiliated with the communist-led **World Federation of Trade Unions** and the third, the Bangladesh Jatio Sramik League, was an affiliate of the **International Confederation of Free Trade Unions (ICFTU)**. By 1989, there were four national labor organizations affiliated with the ICFTU. In 2001, these affiliates had a combined **membership** of 888,700. In 2010, the six affiliates of the **International Trade Union Confederation (ITUC)** had a total membership of 876,000. Only 5 percent of all employees were union members compared with 38 percent in the formal sector.

The ICFTU and the **global union federations** have urged the labor federations of Bangladesh to work closely together. In 2007, the ITUC's survey of **violations of trade union rights** reported that there was a growth in legal restrictions on organized labor and that a climate of political violence toward labor unions continued. This climate resulted in firing, arrests, torture, and even the death of a worker. The 2009 survey mentioned increased restrictions on workers rights and intensified exploitation during 2008. Although the state of emergency was lifted at the end of 2008, repressions and labor conflicts continued throughout 2009.

BARBADOS. Barbados was a colony of the **United Kingdom** to November 1966. The framework for labor relations in Barbados was created in 1939 with the implementation of the Trade Disputes (Arbitration and Enquiry) Act. This act followed riots two years earlier. These riots were also followed by the formation of an organization. This Barbados Workers' Union was registered in 1941 and claimed 25,000 members by 2007. Barbados has been an affiliate of the **International Confederation of Free Trade Unions** since 1951.

Under the labor law, employers are not obliged to recognize unions but many do so. The right to strike is not granted to essential workers. In the 2010 **International Trade Union Confederation** survey a few examples were mentioned of employers using strategies to curtail unions.

BASQUE COUNTRY. Although part of **Spain**, the Basque Country has been a recognized affiliate of the **International Confederation of Free**

Trade Unions since 1951 through the *Solidaridad de Trabajadores Vascos* (Solidarity of Basque Workers), which was formed before the Spanish Civil War (1936–1939), declared illegal after the War, and forced to be an exiled organization until the end of the dictatorship of General Francisco Franco in 1975 and the legalizing of labor unions in Spain in 1977. In 2001, the Basque Country remained affiliated with the ICFTU through the *Euskal Sindikatua*. In 2010, it claimed a **membership** of 115,000.

According to the survey of **violations of trade union rights** in January 2006, furniture deliverers for the multinational IKEA dismissed striking workers in the Vizcaya region, which is a violation of the right to **strike**.

"BATTLE OF THE OVERPASS." The "battle of the overpass" was the name given to a violent incident on 26 May 1937, on an overpass to the Ford Motor Company between **Congress of Industrial Organizations** organizers and Ford's private police force. The organizers, who included **Walter Reuther** and Richard Frankensteen, had planned to hand out leaflets at Ford. Ford refused to recognize unions and ordered the organizers to leave. In the fight that followed, Reuther and Frankensteen were beaten up by Ford's police in front of the press. The incident was the subject of some famous photographs in the *Detroit News* and typified the violence of U.S. labor relations in the 1930s. *See also* UNITED AUTO WORKERS (UAW).

BEAMTENBUND UND TARIFUNION **(DBB).** Founded in 1918, the predecessor of the DBB was dissolved by the Nazis in 1933. It reemerged after the war and now the DBB (Civil Service Association and wage union) has over 1.23 million members in the public service sector and the privatized services. It is the second largest union in **Germany**.

BECK, DAVID (1894–1993). Beck was one of the main figures in the **Teamsters** from the mid-1930s to the mid-1950s. Born in Stockton, California, he joined the Teamsters in 1914 and, after service in World War I, was elected to his first position within the union in 1923. He became a full-time organizer for the union in 1927 for the Northwest. In 1940, he became an international vice president. In 1949, he was the fraternal delegate of the **American Federation of Labor** to the British **Trades Union Congress**. In 1952, Beck was elected international president of the Teamsters. He supported Dwight D. Eisenhower's campaigns in the 1950s and became a vice president of the **American Federation of Labor–Congress of Industrial Organizations** (AFL-CIO) between 1953 and 1957. In 1957, he was accused of corruption and embezzlement of union funds by Senator McClellan and expelled from the AFL-CIO. Beck served a 30-month jail term between 1962 and 1965 for federal income tax evasion. He later became a millionaire from real estate dealings in Seattle, Washington.

BELARUS. Independent of the former Soviet Union since August 1991, Belarus has remained the closest of the former Soviet territories to its authoritarian past. An independent trade union movement was begun by miners and workers in the capital, Minsk. In November 1993, the Belarus Free Trade Union and the Belarussian Independent Trade Union formed a **strike** committee and together with political opponents of the government called a strike for 15 February 1994. The government declared the strike illegal and imprisoned and harassed the organizers. Under the 1996 constitution, the president of Belarus has, in effect, a monopoly of political power and rules by decree. In January 1999, all previously registered labor unions had to reregister or be banned. The Labor Union law of January 2000 violates trade union rights, according to the assessment of the **International Confederation of Free Trade Unions** in 2002. In 2007, the **International Trade Union Confederation**'s survey of **violations of trade union rights** reported that the government's violations of trade union rights caused the **European Union** trade preferences to be withdrawn. The 2010 survey stated that antiunion legislation and practice remained firmly in place. They even deteriorated in general, but an unprecedented court ruling reinstating a dismissed trade union activist may give some hope for the future.

BELGIUM. It is common knowledge that the first Belgian unions were organized by spinners and weavers in the cotton industry in 1857, but according to new insights the first union was probably founded in 1842 by Brussels typographers. From the start organized labor was weak and divided by religion and ethnicity. Nevertheless, this did not mean the absence of working-class discontent; this forced the middle classes in 1886 to acknowledge the "social question." In April 1893, about 200,000 employees took part in a national **strike**. Catholic and **socialist** labor unions emerged in the 1880s, but even their combined efforts at recruitment yielded poor results. By 1900, there were only 42,000 union members, accounting for 3 percent of all employees. Only 10 percent of employees were unionized by 1913, but, in common with other Western European countries, union growth was substantial to 1920, when there were 850,000 union members, accounting for 37 percent of employees. Since 1960, the Catholic labor federation (*Confédération des Syndicats Chrétiens/Algemeen Christelijk Vakverbond,* formed in 1912) and the socialist labor federation (*Fédération Générale du Travail de Belgique/ Algemeen Belgisch Vakverbond*), formed from a labor body set up in 1898, have developed a closer working relationship to strengthen their bargaining position with employers. Apart from these, a much smaller liberal union (*Centrale Générale des Syndicats Libéraux de Belgique/Algemene Centrale der Liberale Vakbonden van België*) has existed since 1930. In 1990, about 54 percent of Belgian employees were members of labor unions. In 2002, Belgium had 1.85 million labor union members, covering 40 percent of Belgian employees. This relatively high proportion of union membership is a result of the Ghent-system of unemployment insurance, whereby unions play an important role in the payment of **unemployment benefits**.

The right to form unions and to strike is strongly enshrined in law. Since the mid-1980s a growing number of employers have tried to gain the legal prohibition of strikes, particularly since 2009. In 2010, the three national trade union centers lodged a complaint before the European Union for violation of the right to strike against the State for allowing employers to counter collective action by a preventive strategy. *See also* CATHOLICISM.

BELIZE. Known until 1973 as British Honduras, Belize was a colony of the **United Kingdom** to September 1981. The British authorities legalized trade unionism in the 1930s. The National Trade Union Congress of Belize has been an affiliate of the **International Confederation of Free Trade Unions** since 1992, when it claimed 2,400 members.

Although a legal right to form unions exists, especially on the banana plantations and other export processing zones, this right does not exist in practice as employers are more persuasive in court. The 2010 Annual Survey of **violations of trade union rights** states that the government blocks union negotiations.

BENEFITS. Although the benefits of being a member of a labor union are generally considered in terms of higher pay—the **union wage differential**—it has long been common for labor unions to negotiate other nonwage benefits as part of **collective bargaining**. Depending on the economic health of the industry concerned, these benefits might include plans that provide above-average retirement, health care, and insurance benefits. National government surveys in both **Australia** and the **United States** since the mid-1990s have shown consistently that union members generally enjoy access to and participation in a significantly higher level of nonwage benefits than nonunion members. For example, in August 2005, only 10 percent of Australian union members did not have leave entitlements in their main job compared with 32 percent of nonunion employees. In March 2006, the U.S. survey found that, in keeping with previous surveys, union members had higher levels of access to the most important nonwage benefits of employment; for instance, not only did 84 percent of union members have access to retirement benefits compared with 57 percent of nonunion members, but the access to the best retirement benefits, defined benefits, differed greatly. Only 15 percent of nonunion employees had access to a defined-benefit retirement plan compared with 70 percent for union members. Developing countries often have a bigger proportion of workers in the informal economy in which benefits are difficult to achieve.

BENIN. Benin was a colony of **France** before August 1960, when it was called *Dahomey*. A national labor organization existed in Benin in the 1950s, when it joined the *Union Générale des Travailleurs de l'Afrique Noire* (General Union of Workers of Black Africa) in 1957. After independence, organized labor in Benin became intertwined with **politics**. In 1969, the Benin labor body the *Confédération nationale des Syndicats libres* (National Confederation of Free Trade Unions) was admitted to membership of the **International Confederation of Free Trade Unions** (ICFTU). The ICFTU was concerned about the efforts of the Benin military government to form a single national labor organization under its control. In 1973, the *Confédération nationale des Syndicats libres* merged with the *Union Génerale des Syndicats du Dahomey* (General Union of the Trade Unions of Dahomey), which had been formed in 1964. Through this body, Benin remained a member of the ICFTU and its successor the **International Trade Union Confederation** (ITUC), but continued being a hostage to political instability and poverty. Unions are only allowed to be formed after government approval. Strikes are legally allowed but also strongly regulated. In 2009, the ITUC complained that striking workers met with intimidation; several union leaders received dead threats. In 2010, the authorities still acted with hostility toward the unions.

BERMUDA. In Bermuda, a British dependent territory, the foundations of a labor relations system were laid by the Trade Union and Trade Disputes Act (1946). After the introduction of this law, the Bermuda Industrial Union was formed in 1946, drawing most of its **membership** from black residents; by 1975, it claimed 6,000 members. Bermuda has been a member of the **International Confederation of Free Trade Unions** and its successor, the **International Trade Union Confederation**, since 1969 and had 9,000 members in 2011.

BEVIN, ERNEST (1881–1951). Bevin was the greatest leader to emerge from organized labor in the **United Kingdom** in the 20th century. Born into poverty in Somerset, he held a number of lowly jobs until finding work as a van driver in 1901. His formal education was very limited. Like other labor leaders of his generation, he was a Methodist. He gained some further education from the Quaker Adult School and joined the Socialist Party in Bristol, where he became a speaker and an organizer. In 1908, he became active in the Right to Work movement for the unemployed. During the **strike** by dockers (longshoremen) at Avonmouth, he organized the dock carters as part of the Dock, Wharf, Riverside, and General Workers' Union so they could not be used as strikebreakers. In 1911, he became a full-time official of the Dockers' Union. An outstanding negotiator, Bevin became one of the Union's three national organizers in 1913. He realized that strong, centralized authority was as vital for unions as rank-and-file support.

In 1915–1916, Bevin was sent as the fraternal delegate of the **Trades Union Congress (TUC)** to the **American Federation of Labor**, a trip that gave him an international outlook on the world of organized labor. In 1920, his brilliant advocacy for the dock workers before the Industrial Court won him national recognition, as did his leadership of the Council of Action's campaign to boycott the supply of military equipment to **Poland** for use against the Russian revolutionaries. In 1921, Bevin was the pivotal figure in the **amalgamation** of 14 unions to create a new mass union, the **Transport and General Workers' Union (TGWU)**, which by the late 1930s had grown to be the largest union in Britain and, for a brief time, the largest in the world.

In 1925, Bevin became a member of the general council of the TUC, a position he held until 1940; in 1937, he was chairman of the TUC. During the 1930s, Bevin successfully fought **communist** influence within the TGWU. In 1937–1938, he conducted a tour of the British Commonwealth and was able to bring about improved labor relations. In 1940, he was made minister for labor, a position responsible for organizing Britain's labor force during World War II. Bevin's last official position was foreign secretary from 1945 to just before his death. *See also* DEAKIN, ARTHUR.

BLACK LABOR MARKET. The *black labor market* refers to employment in jobs for which the income is not declared for taxation and social security. It is a subset of the term *black economy,* which came into use in the late 1970s. This form of labor engagement often removes workers from occupational health and safety protection and is a traditional source of low pay. In 2000, it was estimated that 48 percent of nonagricultural employment in North Africa was in the black or informal sector. Including agricultural employment, the percentage rises. In a country like **India,** it rises beyond 90 percent. The percentages for developed countries probably are around 15. Labor unions oppose the black labor market as its lower labor costs threaten the pay and conditions of their members. *See also* BONDED LABOR.

BLUE-COLLAR/WHITE-COLLAR. *Blue-collar* and *white-collar* are terms to describe manual occupations (meaning literally to work with the hands) and nonmanual occupations (meaning to work with the brain rather than the hands), respectively. Although of U.S. coinage, both terms have entered general English usage, although the color blue—whether of caps or coats—was associated with servants and other menial occupations in England from the 17th century. The term *white-collar,* referring to a clerical occupation, was used in the United States from about 1920; *blue-collar* was coined in about 1950 and was in general English usage by the 1960s.

One of the outstanding features of the labor force in advanced capitalist economies in the 20th century has been the shift away from blue-collar to white-collar occupations. The trend in the British labor force seems to have been typical for other countries. Between 1911 and 1951, the proportion of blue-collar jobs in the labor force fell from 75 to 64 percent and has continued to decline ever since. By 2000, only about one third of the labor force in Western economies worked in blue-collar jobs.

Historically, these terms have strong connotations of social class. A manual occupation was the membership badge of the working class and a white-collar occupation indicated middle-class membership. These social distinctions were reinforced by labor laws and from about 1910 were reflected in the occupational classifications of population censuses, which presented a carefully graded hierarchy of occupations from managers at the top to laborers at the bottom. The *Code de Travail* (Code of Labor) in **France**, which was published between 1910 and 1936, distinguished between the superior intellectual qualities of white-collar work and those required for blue-collar jobs. Labor laws passed in **Greece** (1920), **Italy** (1926), and France (1924, 1935) defined the division between blue- and white-collar jobs and provided for different systems of payment. Blue-collar workers received wages; white-collar workers were paid salaries. White-collar workers were paid more but less frequently and received preferential treatment in the case of their employers' bankruptcy. Although the legal distinction between blue-collar and white-collar employees has tended to lessen since the 1950s, it remained a feature of labor law in most Western European countries in the late 1990s.

Organized labor worldwide reflected the social division between blue-collar and white-collar workers. In 1900, less than 10 percent of union members worked in white-collar jobs, but after 1910 the proportion of white-collar members began to slowly rise. Even so, the **iconography** of organized labor tended to pay homage only to blue-collar work ("real" work) as opposed to the work performed at a desk by a white-collar employee. Heavy manual work was more amenable to being presented as heroic rather than working in safety and comfort at a desk. Generally not welcome in organized labor,

BÖCKLER, HANS • 49

white-collar unions and their federations tended to remain outside its ranks until the 1960s.

Since the 1970s, technological change has blurred the social distinction between blue- and white-collar jobs. A white-collar job no longer carries the social status it did 50 years ago. Over the same period, the proportion of blue-collar jobs in the labor force has declined and the proportion of white-collar jobs has risen as a result of changes in types of work and through social mobility. In 2000, the British Department of Trade and Industry recognized these changes when it ceased to publish statistics on union **membership** divided by blue- and white-collar jobs following the introduction of a new classification of occupations. In 2001, 48 percent of union members in the **United States** were employed in white-collar jobs, and 45 percent were in **Australia**. In both countries, employees in blue-collar jobs were still more likely to be union members than were white-collar employees. For organized labor, these trends have meant that a substantial part of its membership in Western economies works in white-collar jobs even though it has become harder to compare these changes with the past because of changes to the classification of official occupational statistics since 2000. *See also* WHITE-COLLAR UNIONISM.

BÖCKLER, HANS (1875–1951). Böckler was one of the leading architects of the revived post-1945 labor movement in **Germany**. The son of a coachman, he qualified as a gold and silver smith and joined the *Deutscher Metallarbeiter-Verband* (German Engineering Union) and the Social Democratic Party in 1894. After being wounded in 1916, he left the army to become an official of the Engineering Union. In 1927, he became the Düsseldorf area chairman of the General German Trade Union Federation and was elected to the Reichstag in 1928. In 1944, Böckler managed to avoid capture by the Nazis for his part in the July plot to kill Adolf Hitler.

After the Nazis' defeat, the Allies adopted different policies on the revival of the labor unions. The British policy, following the Potsdam Agreement, which encouraged organized labor, was to allow the revival to come gradually from the local level first and to be carefully supervised, whereas leaders like Böckler preferred to organize centralized democratic unions following in many respects the organizational framework of the former Nazi *Deutsche Arbeitsfront*. Böckler and other leaders were advised on the future structure of organized labor by a delegation from the British **Trades Union Congress** in 1945. The individual independent labor unions that had been approved set up a first so-called *Deutscher Gewerkschaftbund* (Confederation of German Trade Unions) in the British zone on 22–25 April 1947, with Böckler as its head. Realizing the need for the labor movement to be better informed, Böckler was the prime mover in 1946 in creating the Institute for Economic

Science to give organized labor expert advice for its policies and positions. Also in 1946, Böckler, in an address to the first labor conference in the British zone, made clear his support for the unions to be represented on the managing and supervisory boards of companies, thereby laying the foundation for the introduction of *Mitbestimmung* (codetermination). In October 1949, the federations of German labor unions in the British, American, and French zones of occupation were merged into the present *Deutscher Gewerkschaftbund,* and Böckler was elected chairman by 397 out of 474 votes, a position he held until his death.

BOLIVIA. Organized labor in Bolivia has a violent history. The first trade union in Bolivia was formed in 1906, but organized labor was torn by political ideologies—**socialism, anarchism**, and, later, **communism**—as well as facing opposition from the government, and handicapped by the poverty of Bolivia's people. The first national Bolivian national congress was held in 1927. The Bolivian miners' unions federated in June 1944. Following the successful revolution of the National Revolutionary Movement, organized labor formed the *Central Obrera Boliviana* (COB), or Bolivian Workers' Confederation, in 1952. Until 1963, the COB worked with the leftist government and gained significant advantages, notably concession of its demand for "workers' control" of mines. A military coup in November 1964 ended the alliance between the government and the COB. Thereafter, Bolivia's labor unions were the focus of government repression. A **general strike** led by the COB in May 1965 resulted in hundreds of deaths. In 1974, the COB and organized labor generally were banned by the government. There were widespread violations of human rights in Bolivia in the 1970s, which were exposed after a secret mission to the country by the British National Union of Miners in April 1977. The left-wing COB was not an affiliate of the **International Confederation of Free Trade Unions** (ICFTU), preferring affiliation with the communist **World Federation of Trade Unions**. Bolivia's membership of the ICFTU in the 1950s and 1970s was through one of its smaller unions. Civilian government was restored in Bolivia in 1982. In 1993, the government introduced free-market reforms, which resulted in a wave of **strikes** during 1995. In 2001, Bolivia and **Uruguay** were the only South American countries not to be members of the ICFTU. In 2009, the **International Trade Union Confederation** reported that the general climate for organized labor in Bolivia continued to be repressive, despite hopes for a restoration of trade-union rights and a new Constitution improving trade union rights. In 2011 strikes were still strictly regulated but they continued to take place.

BONDED LABOR. Bonded labor is a form of **forced labor** in which a worker is bonded to an employer, often to repay a debt lent to the worker at an inflated interest rate. Bonded or indentured labor was a feature of the labor force of colonial North America. It was common in Asia, particularly in **India**. Since 1945, bonded labor has been illegal in India but is widespread in practice; it has been estimated that there were 10 million bonded laborers in India in 1999. The **International Confederation of Free Trade Unions** has been associated with Anti-Slavery International since 1997. In 2009, the United Nations estimated that there were 27 million workers of both sexes and all ages enslaved. *See also* SLAVERY.

BOSNIA and HERZEGOVINA. One of the six republics that made up the former **Yugoslavia**, Bosnia and Herzegovina has been a separate nation since 1991. The country's war-torn history in the 1990s has precluded the emergence of organized labor. In 2007, the **International Trade Union Confederation** noted that although **collective bargaining** existed all over the country, the right to establish unions in fact needed prior authorization. Since 2002, the government has been refusing to register the Confederation of Trade Unions of Bosnia and Herzegovina. Dismissals and threatening of unionists by private sector employers also frequently take place. In spite of government hostility, there were 223,000 union members in 2010.

BOTSWANA. There were some labor unions in Botswana, a colony of the **United Kingdom** up to September 1966, before independence, but their **membership** was slight; even by 1974, Botswana's unions had a total of only 1,400 members. By 1986, the membership of the Botswana Federation of Trade Unions—as indicated by its returns to the **International Confederation of Free Trade Unions**—had risen to 14,000 and to 18,000 by the 1990s. Unlike most other postindependence African countries, Botswana has remained a stable democracy, a condition that has maintained organized labor and reflected its relatively prosperous economy.

The 2004 Trade Disputes Act effectively prohibits most strikes. Even though the right to strike legally exists, the procedures are so complex that unions always lose their case. In addition, many employers use dismissals and other unfair tactics to discourage collective bargaining. In 2009 and again in 2010, the survey of **violations of trade union rights** concluded that it is impossible to strike legally.

BRAZIL. The first labor unions were formed in Brazil in the 1900s but, as in other countries separated from **Portugal** or **Spain**, organized labor developed along the political and religious divisions of the mother country, as shown by the formation of **Catholic, socialist, anarchist,** and **communist** unions. Although Brazil claimed 270,000 union members by 1930, these divisions and the economic world crisis allowed the government of Getúlio Vargas to force all unions to become officially registered in 1931, a move that Vargas used to outlaw the communist and anarchist unions. Vargas, who ran the government until 1945, used the example of fascist **Italy** to build a corporatist state in which unions were controlled by government nominees or supporters and received their finances from compulsory contributions by all employees regardless of whether they were union members. Since 1945, as in other Latin American countries, the labor unions have played a central role in the campaign against authoritarian government and in favor of democracy, although their efforts have been hampered by internal political divisions. The 1950s and 1960s were marked by a high level of labor disputes and the growth of communist support. In 1964, an antiunion military junta seized government. This government declared most **strikes** illegal and banned free unions.

Massive strikes all over the country were pivotal to the redemocratization process during the late 1970s. During the process the *Central Unica dos Trabalhadores* (CUT), or Single Workers' Center, was founded in August 1983. After the reintroduction of civilian government in 1985 the *Central Geral dos Trabalhadores* (CGT), or General Confederation of Labor, was formed in August 1986. An unconditional right to strike was established in 1988 for all employees except the police and the military. In 2000, three Brazilian labor federations were members of the **International Confederation of Free Trade Unions**: the CGT with 2.2 million members, the CUT with 4.6 million members, and the *Força Sindical* (Union Strength; formed in 1991) with 2.1 million members. In 2001, there were 8.9 million labor union members in Brazil covering 21 percent of employees. On 27 October 2002, Luiz Inacio "Lula" Da Silva (1945–), a former leader of the metal workers' union in the 1970s, was elected president, the first occupant of the position with a background in organized labor. His election raised hopes for improvement in the treatment of organized labor in Brazil, but rural violence and land disputes still exist. Lula stayed in office until 1 January 2011 when he was succeeded by a partisan.

The 2009 survey of **violations of trade union rights** paints a grim picture of the blatant violation of union rights by a number of employers with four union leaders murdered in Brazil in that year. *See also* DA SILVA, LUIZ INACIO.

BRENNER, OTTO (1907–1972). One of the main post-1945 labor leaders in **Germany**, Brenner was born in Hanover and began his working life as a general laborer but eventually worked his way up to electrical engineer. He joined the *Deutscher Metallarbeiter-Verband* (German Metal Workers' Union) in 1922. He was a co-founder of the *Sozialdemokratische Arbeiterpartei* (Social Democratic Workers' Party) in 1931. Arrested by the Gestapo in 1933, he was jailed for two years and was under police surveillance until 1945. With Hans Brümmer, he was joint leader of *IG Metall* from 1952 to 1956 and then led the union alone until his death. Under Brenner's leadership, *IG Metall* was at the front of the movement in West Germany for **shorter working hours**. In 1958, Brenner warned of the dangers of unemployment caused by technological change. In 1969, he was elected president of the European Confederation of Free Trade Unions, the forerunner of the **European Trade Union Confederation**.

BRITAIN. *See* UNITED KINGDOM.

BRITISH GENERAL STRIKE. The British General Strike, which took place between 4 and 12 May 1926, was the largest single confrontation between the government and organized labor that has ever occurred in the **United Kingdom**. The immediate background to the **strike** was the government's decision in 1925 to return Britain to the gold standard, a move that increased the price of British exports and encouraged employers to instigate pay cuts to maintain their position in world trade. At the center of the strike were grievances by the coal miners over wage cuts and their efforts to gain the support of other unions. Although employees gave a high level of support to the strike—a record 162 million working days were lost through labor disputes in 1926—the Stanley Baldwin government was well prepared and used special constables, university students, and other volunteers to take the place of strikers. The coal miners remained on strike until August, when they admitted defeat and returned to work on the employers' terms. As a result of the strike, the **Trades Union Congress** (TUC) issued an invitation for talks on the reform of British industrial relations in 1927. Although the offer was ignored by the employers' association, the offer was taken up by Sir Alfred Mond, the chairman of Imperial Chemical Industries, who met with Ben Turner of the TUC in a series of talks that ran into 1928; these talks led to the Mond-Turner Report, which suggested that organized labor should have a role in making national economic and industrial relations policies. The idea was rejected by the **employers' organizations** and the talks were abortive. The government enacted the Trade Disputes Act in 1927, which outlawed the secondary boycott and strike, the mechanisms on which the strike had been based. This law, although not used, was repealed by Clement Attlee's Labour government in 1946. *See also* GENERAL STRIKES; LABOR DISPUTES.

BRITISH LABOUR PARTY. Formed in 1900 as the Labour Representation Committee, the British Labour Party has been one of the leading continuous political parties in the world based on organized labor. Labour officials first began contesting British parliamentary elections in 1847, but none were successful until 1874 when Alexander Macdonald (1821–1881) and Thomas Burt (1837–1922), two coal miners' leaders, were elected to the House of Commons. In 1867, the franchise was widened to include relatively well-off urban working-class males. Because of its ability to work with the Liberal Party for labor objectives, the **Trades Union Congress** was slow to see the need for organized labor to support its own political party. In 1892, Keir Hardie (1856–1915) succeeded in having a resolution for separate labor representation carried at the TUC, but no action followed. It was the **Taff Vale Case** that galvanized organized labor into supporting a separate labor party; in 1906, the Labour Representation Committee was renamed the *Labour Party.* Membership was at first open only to unions, but in 1918 individuals were allowed to join. During World War I, a number of Labour members were participants in the government.

In 1918, the Labour Party adopted a socialization objective that called for government control of most of the economy, and in 1922 became the official opposition party for the first time. In 1923–1924, the Labour Party formed a minority government under Ramsay MacDonald. In the 1930s the Labour Party fared badly in elections and directed its policies toward producing detailed reformist programs. During World War II, members of the Labour Party, such as **Ernest Bevin**, participated in Winston Churchill's government. In 1945, Labour, under Clement Attlee (who had been leader of the party since 1935), won government for the first time and proceeded to implement wide-ranging reforms. Labour was defeated in 1951 and did not win government again until 1964. Thereafter, the Labour Party's electoral record in national British politics was mixed: Labour lost power in 1970, regained it in 1974, lost again in 1979 after the **"winter of discontent"** when militant labor struck massively. After 1979 Labour spent 18 years in the political wilderness during which time it tried to regain public support by setting the unions at a distance. The changes resulted in a landslide victory in 1997 for New Labour under Tony Blair. It won a second victory in June 2001 and a third in May 2005. However, despite these wins, relations between the Blair government and organized labor have been cool. The government has shown no obvious bias in favor of organized labor and has been accused by organized labor's left of being too close to big business. Certainly the election of the Labour Government in 1997 has done little to arrest the slow decline in the **membership** of organized labor. Although the number of employed British union members averaged about 7.3 million between 1995 and 2008, the proportion of employees who were union members fell from 29 to 25 percent. There were continued falls in 2009 and 2010 as a result of the global financial crisis and the failure of unions to recruit additional men in full-time employment. In 2010, there were 6.9 million union members accounting for 24 percent of employees. *See also* UNITED KINGDOM.

BRUNEI. Brunei is a sultanate that became independent from British rule in 1984. The sultan rules by decree. As a consequence of large oil and gas reserves, the indigenous population of Brunei enjoys a high standard of living. However, 40 percent of the workforce are foreigners. Only 5 percent of the employees in the oil sector are organized in unions. **Strikes** are legal but seem not to occur. The 2009 Annual Survey of **violations of trade union rights** mentions virtually no union activity.

BUILDING AND WOOD WORKERS' INTERNATIONAL (BWI). At its World Congress in Buenos Aires, on 9 December 2005, the **International Federation of Building and Wood Workers** and the World Federation of Building and Wood Workers created a new **global union federation**, the BWI. The BWI is a global union federation, grouping free and democratic unions with members in the building, building materials, wood, forestry, and allied sectors.

The BWI groups together 318 labor unions representing around 12 million members in 130 countries. Its headquarters is in Geneva, **Switzerland**. Regional Offices and Project Offices are located in **Panama** and **Malaysia, South Africa, India, Burkina Faso, Bosnia and Herzegovina, Lebanon, Kenya, South Korea, Russia, Argentina, Peru**, and **Brazil**.

BULGARIA. The first labor union in what is now Bulgaria, but was then part of the Ottoman Empire to 1908, was formed in 1883 by printers. Other unions were formed after that date, and a Socialist Party was set up in 1893. In 1904, two labor federations were formed. Despite its small membership (there were 2,700 members in 1904 and about 29,000 union members in 1911), organized labor conducted 537 **strikes** up to 1910, of which 161 won gains for the strikers. During World War I, Bulgarian organized labor developed a revolutionary character; in 1920, when the two labor federations merged, union **membership** reached 36,000 and attained its pre-1945 peak of 49,800 in 1923. Bulgaria was an affiliate of the **International Federation of Trade Unions** from 1904 to 1913 and from 1921 to 1933. A military coup in June 1923 brought a fascist-style government to power, which banned many labor unions. Although there was some revival of organized labor after 1927, union membership had fallen to 18,900 by 1933. After the withdrawal of the

Nazis in 1944, the Confederation of Independent Trade Unions of Bulgaria (CITUB) was formed; it became a pillar of the **communist** regime and was given a range of responsibilities concerning labor administration. Bulgaria was a model of communist orthodoxy until the late 1980s.

In February 1989, some members of the intelligentsia formed an independent labor union, *Prodrepka* (Support). In spite of the imprisonment of some of its leaders, it claimed 100,000 members by December 1989 and played a central part in the popular uprisings that broke the communist political monopoly. The challenge posed by *Prodrepka* for the leadership of organized labor prompted the CITUB to reform itself and call a **general strike** in December 1990, a move that helped to cause the fall of the government. As in **Poland**, disputes over the ownership of union assets have been a major issue since the end of communism. In December 1991, the democratically elected government seized the assets of the Communist Party, including those of the CITUB. In June 1992, the CITUB and *Prodrepka* agreed that union property should be returned to organized labor and divided between them. In 1993, *Prodrepka* was a member of the **International Confederation of Free Trade Unions** with 321,200 members. By 2001, these two affiliates had a combined membership of 555,350. In 2007, the **International Trade Union Confederation (ITUC)** reported frequent harassment of union officials and members who were relocated, downgraded, or even dismissed. After international action, the Parliament removed on 12 October 2006 the ban on strikes in the energy, communication, and healthcare sectors, and provided for the mediation and conciliation procedures. In 2010 the prohibition of strikes in public administration still remained in force. The ITUC also reported ongoing frequent harassment of trade union activists.

BURKINA FASO. Called *Upper Volta* until 1984, Burkina Faso was a colony of **France** up to 1960. As in other French colonies, organized labor followed the example of French settlers and reflected divisions within French organized labor. In 1947, the first national union federation was formed as a branch of the French *Confédération Générale du Travail* (CGT), or General Confederation of Labor. In the 1960s, the *Organisation Voltaique des Syndicats Libres* (Organization of Free Trade Unions of Volta) was established and was admitted to membership of the **International Confederation of Free Trade Unions (ICFTU)**; it claimed 6,000 members by 1966. Organized labor remained fragmented and weakened by too many unions. Nevertheless, in January 1966, the unions successfully conducted a **general strike** to bring down the government. Burkina Faso has continued to be a member of the ICFTU. Following the suspicious death of the journalist Norbert Zongo in 1998, a Workers' Front was formed to defend organized labor and basic

human rights generally; the Workers' Front was the target of government repression in 2000. In 2001, the ICFTU reported that there were still many restrictions on organized labor, particularly over the government's ability to use public sector employees to break **strikes**. There were 59,500 union members in Burkina Faso in 2001. In 2002, the ICFTU reported that a climate of government intimidation toward organized labor prevailed in Burkina Faso. The same was true in 2006, when the six national trade unions who organized a national strike in May reported threats and intimidation against their members. In 2008 the right to strike was broadened, but at the same time this right was violated as a response to numerous protests. In 2010, excessive restrictions to the right to strike still remained.

BURMA. Burma was part of British India from 1886 to 1937 and has been independent of the **United Kingdom** since 1947. Organized labor in Burma emerged among Indian and Chinese imported workers in the 1920s. In 1926, the British administration legalized labor unions, and this principle was incorporated into the 1948 constitution. By 1961, there were 173 registered unions with a total **membership** of 64,000, but thereafter Burma's history was dominated by political instability, military repression, and rebellious ethnic groups. In 1964, the Socialist Program Party government abolished independent organized labor and, in 1968, set up its own system of grassroots committees to control labor. Following thousands of deaths in student riots in 1988, the military took power, renamed the country *Myanmar,* and suppressed all vestiges of organized labor.

In 1991, the Federation of Trade Unions–Burma (FTU-B) was formed in secret in **Thailand** and is forced to operate along the borders of Burma because of the severity of military repression. By 1997, the FTU-B claimed to have an underground national network of sympathizers within Burma. Virtually all factories in Burma are owned by the military government. **Forced labor** is a general feature of the labor force, despite Burma's ratification of **International Labour Organization** Convention No. 87— Forced or Compulsory Labor (1930). The **International Confederation of Free Trade Unions (ICFTU)** has consistently drawn attention to the government of Burma as one of the worst **human rights** offenders in Asia; dozens of trade union activists are in jail. Burma has never been a member of the ICFTU.

The 2010 survey of the **International Trade Union Confederation** mentioned the inhuman attitude of the military government when it refused to allow international help in response to Cyclone Nargis, which killed over 140,000 persons. Trade unions were still repressed, but in 2011 the regime announced freedom to organize and to strike.

BURUNDI. Since independence from Belgium in 1962, the country suffered from military coups and ethnic rivalries that cost the lives of hundreds of thousands people. The right to form unions and the right to **strike** are severely limited. According to the survey of **violations of trade union rights**, 2008 was a bad year for trade union rights and the survey for the following years showed no improvement.

C

CAMBODIA. After the Japanese occupation, France tried to regain control over the country, which had been a French protectorate since 1863. In 1953, Cambodia became independent but became involved in the **Vietnam** War. In 1975, the Khmer Rouge took power and renamed the country *Kampuchea.* The Khmer Rouge used terror to try to rebuild the economy on an agricultural basis, and millions starved. After years of internal war, a constitutional monarchy was installed in 1993.

Three years later, the Free Trade Union of the Kingdom of Cambodia was founded. The right to form unions is restricted, as is the right to strike. There is a whole battery of antiunion practices. In 2011, 300 striking garment workers were victimized.

CAMEROON. Cameroon was under French administration for the United Nations to 1960. Accordingly, its labor unions developed along French lines with the usual French ideological divisions. Cameroon has been represented in the **International Confederation of Free Trade Unions (ICFTU)** since 1953. By 1975, there were about 40,000 union members. The first union federation was formed in 1948, and in 1971 Cameroon's four union federations agreed to merge. Labor unions were regulated by law in 1974. The 1992 labor code required government approval for workers to form a trade union. Between December 1993 and January 1994 there was a **strike** caused by large pay cuts in the public sector; the strike was defeated by violence and intimidation. A delegation to Cameroon by the ICFTU and its **African Regional Organization** was able to get an assurance from the government that it would not interfere in the internal affairs of the country's labor federation, the *Confédération Syndicale des Travailleurs du Cameroun* (Union Confederation of Cameroon Workers). The 1992 Labor Code permits labor unions to be formed, but the ICFTU has complained about government interference in the internal affairs of unions. When the cumbersome procedures for calling strikes are not met, heavy sanctions follow. In contrast to other Third World countries, the ICFTU found that the country's **export processing zones** generally conformed with internationally recognized labor standards.

In 2008, a transport strike gave way to riots to which the security forces responded with brutal force. The repression of union activities continued in 2010. In 2010, there were 200,000 labor union members in Cameroon.

CANADA. Evidence of organization among skilled mechanics in Canada exists from the 1790s, and seven such bodies were known to have existed by 1829. They made their presence felt at Saint John, New Brunswick, as early as 1812 when they tried to exclude American immigrants to maintain the shortage of skilled labor in the building industry. Up to the early 1870s, the **United Kingdom**, through **immigration**, was the dominant influence on the shaping of Canadian organized labor as shown by the establishment of Canadian branches of British unions such as the **Amalgamated Society of Engineers** in 1853 and the **Amalgamated Society of Carpenters and Joiners** in 1872. However, in the 1860s, international craft unions came into the Canadian colonies, including the Iron Molders International Union.

With the growth of the United States economy after the Civil War and its greater interrelationship with the Canadian economy after the early 1870s, the United States increasingly came to dominate the politics and structure of organized labor in Canada. The **Knights of Labor** set up their first assembly in Canada in 1881, the same year that saw the formation of the Federation of Organized Trades and Labor Unions of the United States and Canada in Pittsburgh. Its successor, the **American Federation of Labor (AFL)**, soon established a presence in Canada. Conflict arose with the Knights of Labor, and in 1902 the Canadian Trade and Labour Congress (formed in 1886) expelled the Knights and all other unions that were part of an American (or "international") union. The excluded unions formed their own federation, the National Trades and Labour Congress, in Canada in 1903, which was renamed the Canadian Federation of Labour in 1908. In 1906, the **Industrial Workers of the World** created its first organization in Canada; as in the United States, it largely recruited the lesser-skilled employees. **Catholic** unions in Quebec created a provincial federation in 1921. In common with other countries, Canada experienced a wave of **labor disputes** after World War I, notably the **general strike** in Winnipeg in 1919. The **One Big Union** movement also found support at the same time. Despite the growth of organized labor, the proportion of employees enrolled in unions remained low. In 1920, for example, only 15 percent of Canadian employees were union members compared with 17 percent in the **United States**, 42 percent in **Australia**, and 26 percent in **New Zealand**. Unions accounted for 33 percent of Canadian employees by 1950 and this level remained relatively unchanged thereafter; moreover, unlike other countries, Canada did not suffer a sharp decline in union **membership** during the 1980s.

For most of the 20th century, about half of Canada's union members have been members of American unions, a feature that ensured that the political divisions and events of the United States, such as the formation of the **Congress of Industrial Organizations (CIO)**, were also part of the history of Canadian organized labor. This particular chapter was closed in 1956 when the Trades and Labour Congress (the Canadian equivalent of the AFL) and the Canadian Congress of Labour (the Canadian equivalent of the CIO) merged to form the Canadian Labour Congress, which remains the largest labor federation in the country, with 1.5 million members in 2001. Since 1974, a number of Canadian unions have split from the American unions to be fully independent in **collective bargaining**. In 2009, there were 4.2 million union members in Canada, compared with 3.9 million in 1995. Canada has always been a member of the **International Confederation of Free Trade Unions (ICFTU)**, and, despite the country's excellent **human rights** record, the ICFTU has been critical of restrictions on trade union rights and the right to strike imposed by some provincial governments, particularly in the **public sector** (especially at the federal level) or "essential services." In its 2009 survey, the **International Trade Union Confederation** expressed concern about an antiunion trend in legislation and practices based on a hostile political climate.

CAPE VERDE. Cape Verde became independent from **Portugal** in July 1975, and the first labor union was formed in Cape Verde in 1976. Cape Verde was not represented in the **International Confederation of Free Trade Unions (ICFTU)** until 1990, when its affiliate, the *União Nacional dos Trabalhadores de Cabo Verde-Central Sindical* (UNTC-CS), or National Union of Workers of Cape Verde-Central Union, claimed 15,000 members. In December 1991, the government closed part of the social center building of the UNTC-CS and handed the keys to a rival labor organization. The dispute continued for three years and led to calls for intervention by the ICFTU. In 2010, there were 35,000 union members in Cape Verde. There is a legal right to strike, but the government has on occasion ordered strikers back to work.

CARIBBEAN CONGRESS OF LABOUR. This regional international labor organization was formed in 1960 to lobby Caribbean governments on labor issues and to provide training and research. Between 1990 and 2010, the number of employees it represented rose from 122,600 to 500,000 in 17 countries. Most of its country members are also members of the **International Trade Union Confederation**.

CATHOLICISM. Catholics and Catholicism have played a major role in shaping the history of organized labor. Because the growth of **socialism** in

Western Europe was often associated with anticlericalism, it led to a Catholic reaction. At Ghent, an Anti-Socialist League was set up in 1878. In **France**, the first Catholic labor union was formed among **white-collar** workers in 1887. The 1891 papal encyclical *Rerum Novarum* ("Of New Things") rejected socialism but recognized and supported the need for social justice and cooperation between employers and employees within industrial society, thereby encouraging Catholics to participate in labor unions under the guidance of spiritual leaders. Because of the papal promotion of cooperation, Catholicism is often associated with corporatism.

In **Germany**, the first Catholic unions were formed in 1894, and by 1919 had a combined **membership** of one million. In France, the first national Catholic union was formed among clerical workers in 1913. In **Switzerland**, Catholic unions formed their own federation in 1907. A French Catholic labor federation, *Confédération Française des Travailleurs Chrétiens* (French Confederation of Christian Workers), was formed in 1919; it claimed to represent 100,000 employees. An international body, the International Federation of Christian Trade Unions (the forerunner to the **World Confederation of Labour [WCL]**), was formed at The Hague in 1920, the culmination of efforts begun in 1908. Although Catholic labor organizations were important, they did not represent the full extent of Catholic activity in organized labor, for Catholics were also active in the non-Catholic organizations, which generally retained their numerical superiority over the purely Catholic ones.

The emergence of **communism** from the early 1920s presented Catholicism with its greatest ideological challenge of the century, as it had many of the features often associated with a religion. Communism was officially condemned by the Vatican in the encyclical *Domini Redemptoris* ("Redemption of the Lord") in 1937. From that time onward, Catholics were important as a group in fighting communist infiltration of organized labor in the 1940s and 1950s. Catholic unions remain a feature of organized labor in Western Europe, but in Germany and **Austria** their support is limited because the pre-World War II divisions within organized unions were seen as contributing to the success of fascism. Catholicism has been the driving force behind the WCL.

CENTRAL AFRICAN REPUBLIC. The Central African Republic became independent of **France** in 1960, at which time organized labor in the country had about 2,000 members. The government of Jean-Bédel Bokassa brought the unions under the control of one organization in 1964. The Central African Republic has been represented in the **International Confederation of Free Trade Unions** since 1980 by the *Union Syndicale des Travailleurs de Centrafrique* (USTC), or Labor Union of Central African Workers. **Strikes** in the Central African Republic, such as those conducted by public sector employees in April 1994 over unpaid salaries, have been met by government military forces. Despite the establishment of a democratic government in 1993, relations between the government and organized labor remain difficult. In 1999, the general secretary of the USTC, Sunny-Colé, was arrested and beaten up by the presidential security unit and only released after international pressure. In 2007, the **International Trade Union Confederation (ITUC)** reported about police intimidation and the prevention by employers of union meetings at the workplace. The ITUC considered the 2009 Labor Code to be inadequate and complained in 2010 that unions were not respected. In 2010, there were 11,000 union members in the Central African Republic.

CHAD. Independent of **France** since August 1960, organized labor in Chad began as branches of French unions; they claimed 1,500 members by 1960. In 1962, the government required official approval before a trade union could be formed and banned any political activity by unions. The unions were brought under **government control** by one union body in 1965. In 1975, **strikes** were banned after a military coup, and in 1976 **public sector** employees were forbidden to form trade unions. Despite the hostile legal and political environment, Chad has been represented in the **International Confederation of Free Trade Unions** since 1987 by the *Union des Syndicats du Tchad* (UST), or Federation of Chad Labor Unions. Strikes in the public sector over the government's failure to pay salaries in 1994 and 1995 were met with violence by the government; at least five union leaders were murdered in 1994. In July 1994, the government and the UST agreed to a social pact that resulted in an agreement to pay the salaries due; the International Monetary Fund warned the government that the pact was a serious violation of its aid package and could result in its cancellation. In 1996, the ban on strikes ended. In 2007, the **International Trade Union Confederation** reported that the government appeared to be engaged in an attempt to curtail the UST. In the same year, the legislation was amended to make organizing strikes more difficult. In 2010, basic trade union rights were still frustrated by government intervention. There were 42,000 union members in Chad in 2010.

CHANGE TO WIN. The Change to Win Federation is a coalition of five labor unions in the **United States** formed in 2005 as an alternative to the **American Federation of Labor–Congress of Industrial Organizations** (AFL-CIO). The coalition is associated with strong advocacy of the **organizing** model. Worried about the continued decline in the share of employees who were union members, five unions came together in 2003 to push reform in the AFL-CIO. Their main concern was an effort to start organizing unorganized workers. Two years later the informal partnership, joined by the

Teamsters and the **United Food and Commercial Workers**, formed Change to Win, which introduced a program for reform of the AFL-CIO.

The CTW's members were largely service-sector unions that represented large numbers of **women, immigrants**, and people of color, as opposed to the manufacturing unions. On the eve of the 2005 AFL-CIO convention, the two largest Change to Win affiliates, **Service Employees International Union** and the Teamsters, announced that they were leaving the AFL-CIO. Others followed. In 2005, Change to Win held its founding convention and announced the formation of a federation dedicated primarily to organizing. In 2009, reunification talks between the AFL-CIO and CTW failed. At that time the CTW had 5.5 million members.

CHILD LABOR. The elimination of child labor was a general objective of organized labor in the 19th century, not just on the grounds of the protection of children but also to reduce their competition with adults. As children were cheaper to employ than adults, they tended to reduce the wages of adults. Early 19th-century British social reformers like Robert Owen (1771–1858) opposed the employment of children. Union pressure for legislation to regulate factory employment and exclude child labor effectively began in 1833 in England, but progress was slow and grudging. In the **United States, Samuel Gompers**, although generally suspicious of government labor laws, supported them if they were aimed at eliminating child labor. The National Child Labor Committee (formed in 1904) induced most states to pass child labor legislation, but Supreme Court opposition delayed the passing of a national law to directly prohibit child labor until 1949. The **International Labour Organization (ILO)** has sought to reduce the incidence of child labor but with limited success outside of Western economies. The first ILO Convention concerning child labor was adopted in 1919: The Minimum Age (Industry) Convention, 1919 (No. 5). It was followed by the Minimum Age for Employment Convention 1973 (No. 138).

The **International Confederation of Free Trade Unions** and its successor, **International Trade Union Confederation**, have been campaigning against child labor since 1986. Child labor remains widespread in developing countries, with many poor families seeing child labor as essential for their economic survival. On 8 January 1995, the Indian National Trade Union Congress and the Centre of Indian Trade Unions signed a pact with the ILO to work toward the elimination of child labor. In 1999, the ILO adopted the Worst Forms of Child Labour Convention (No. 182), which was based on the ICFTU's Child Labor Charter released in 1998. *See also* BONDED LABOR; MINIMUM AGE; SLAVERY.

CHILE. The first labor organizations in Chile were founded as mutual aid associations by artisans in 1847. The growth of unions was slowed by hostile governments, which violently suppressed **strikes** in 1890 and 1907; the 1907 strike was led by nitrate employees, of whom over 2,000 were killed by the army. The first national labor federation in Chile was set up in 1909. **Anarchism** attracted a wide following, and an anarchist labor federation existed between 1931 and 1936. The number of union members was claimed to be 150,000 by 1923 and 204,000 in 1927. A new labor federation was created in 1936, but during 1946–1947 it split into **communist** and **socialist** factions. A reformed national labor federation, the *Central Unica de Trabajadores* (CUT), or Central Workers Union, was established in 1953; left-wing in character but independent of any political party, it became affiliated with the **International Confederation of Free Trade Unions (ICFTU)**. During the 1960s, there was a general rise in labor unrest, a reflection of the deep divisions in Chilean society. In 1970, Salvador Allende, the leader of the Popular Unity Coalition, was elected president with the CUT as his major ally. In September 1973, the Allende administration was overthrown in a military coup that had the backing of the administration of Richard Nixon in the **United States**. Not only were strikes, unions, and **collective bargaining** suppressed, but 13,000 people were arrested and at least 2,200 were executed by the Pinochet administration.

Labor unrest during the 1980s gave rise to a new, broad-based labor federation, the *Central Unitaria de Trabajadores* (CUT), or Unified Workers' Center, in August 1988, which actively worked for the restoration of democratic government (achieved in 1990) and labor law reform. In 1992, there were about 720,000 union members in Chile (about 24 percent of employees) of whom 425,000 were affiliated with the Unified Workers' Center. Between 1983 and 1993, the number of unions in Chile rose from 4,401 to 11,389. In 1994, the Unified Workers' Center was admitted to membership of the ICFTU. In 2001, it was estimated that about 12 percent of Chilean employees were union members. On 11 September 2001, the senate of Chile adopted a labor union rights law; the ICFTU has complained that the law does not go far enough, but noted that for the first time in the history of Chile, 10 military officers were found guilty of the murder of a labor union official, Tucapel Jiménez, under the dictatorship of General Augusto Pinochet.

Since 2007, monitoring by the **International Trade Union Confederation** has indicated greater respect by the government for organized labor and progress in the application of labor standards.

CHINA. The first Chinese labor unions were formed in the Canton region from 1895; they were followed by a union of seamen formed in the British colony of **Hong Kong SAR** in 1909, who successfully defended their union by a **strike** in 1922 against an attempt to suppress it. In the same year, the first national congress of Chinese labor was held, which led to the formation of the All China General Labor Federation in 1925. Organized labor drew much of its support from the industrial city of Shanghai. In 1927, Chiang Kai-shek of the nationalist Kuomintang movement purged the **communists** from organized labor in Shanghai, which resulted in the killing of about 5,000 people. In 1930, there were said to be 2.8 million labor union members in China, but free labor bodies were never able to get established primarily because neither the communists nor the Kuomintang supported an independent labor movement.

In 1950, the communist government, which had taken power on the Chinese mainland under the leadership of Mao Zedong a year earlier, adopted a labor union law that recognized only the All-China Federation of Trade Unions (ACFTU) under the control of the Communist Party. During the Cultural Revolution, even the state-sponsored ACFTU was forbidden, but it was restored in 1978. The 1992 Trade Union Law (amended in 2001) has not led to the recognition of any independent labor organizations. The ACFTU is the largest trade union in the world with 239 million members (2010).

In 1989, there was an attempt to form independent labor unions, but these bodies and the Free Trade Union Preparatory Committee (formed at the end of 1991) were suppressed by the government in 1992. China has never been a member of the **International Confederation of Free Trade Unions** (ICFTU) or its successor, the **International Trade Union Confederation**. On 1 January 1995, a labor law came into effect that set down minimum general conditions of employment for the first time. The absence of an officially recognized labor movement has not meant the absence of **labor disputes** in China, which are known to have occurred on a large scale (there were 520,000 labor disputes in 2008), particularly following the **privatization** of many state-owned enterprises in the 1990s. In 2002, the ICFTU was particularly critical of abuses of trade union rights in China and noted a wave of **strikes** during March to May 2002, particularly in the northeastern provinces. In 2009, this criticism remained valid. There still is no right to strike or form independent unions. In 2009 and 2010, strike waves swept the country and especially the Guandong region. The sometimes victorious 2010 wave was seen by some observers as the beginning of the end of China as a low-wage country. *See also* TAIWAN.

CITRINE, WALTER McLENNAN (1887–1983). Born to a Liverpool seaman and nurse, Citrine began his career as an electrician and became active in the Independent Labour Party and the electrician's union of Liverpool.

Citrine became assistant general secretary of the **Trade Union Congress (TUC)** in 1924 and general secretary in 1926. He held the post for 20 years. Citrine also served as president of the **International Federation of Trade Unions** (1928–1945) and chairman of the **World Federation of Trade Unions** (1945–1946). As TUC general secretary, Citrine proved to be an efficient administrator and a highly skilled organizer. The 1926 **General Strike** definitively convinced Citrine to abandon the conflict model; the unions should try to remove reasons of conflict and develop into reliable negotiators. Identified with the conservative wing of English labour, Citrine nevertheless opposed plans by the Labour Government in 1931 to cut **unemployment benefits**. He published a number of books, including *The Trade Union Movement of Great Britain* (1926) and his autobiography *Men and Work* (1964). Citrine upset many in the Labour movement when he accepted a knighthood in 1935 and a peerage in 1946. Until his retirement in 1957, he was chairman of the British Electricity Authority. *See also* UNITED KINGDOM.

COAL MINING. With engineering, coal mining was one of the main pillars of organized labor in most Western countries. Between the early 1900s and the late 1930s coal miners' unions were the largest single labor unions in both the **United Kingdom** and the **United States**. Within both countries, labor unions among coal miners emerged on a regional basis after 1840, but their attempts to form effective national bodies floundered until the 1890s. The similarity in the two countries was explained not just by the geographical separation between coalfields but also by the presence of British immigrants among the union leaders in the early history of coal mining in the United States. The first labor union in the anthracite coalfields of Pennsylvania was organized by an English immigrant, John Bates, in 1849. Later, Daniel Weaver and Thomas Lloyd, both immigrant miners from Staffordshire, formed the American Miners' Association in 1861.

Between 1854 and 1902, nearly 191,000 miners of all kinds emigrated from Britain; of the 184,000 whose destinations are known, 109,200 went to the United States, 11,000 to **Canada**, and 24,900 to **Australia** and **New Zealand**. The bulk of this migration occurred between 1854 and 1871, when 70,400 British miners emigrated. In 1890, 58 percent of coal miners in Pennsylvania were foreign-born; in Australia, 76 percent of coal miners in the largest coalfield, at Newcastle, New South Wales, were foreign-born in 1891.

Because coal was the main source of energy in the Western world up to the 1950s, coal miners' unions were able to command considerable influence within organized labor, but since that time, technological changes have reduced the number of miners needed and other sources of energy have lessened the reliance on coal. Between 1910 and 1940, the amount of energy supplied to the U.S. economy from coal fell from 85 to 50 percent. Coal mining had also been a major source of **labor disputes** in Australia, Britain, and the United States before 1950. Today **China** is the world's largest coal producer with five million people active in the sector. *See also* IMMIGRATION; MINEWORKERS' FEDERATION OF GREAT BRITAIN (MWF): UNITED MINE WORKERS OF AMERICA [UMWA]; Table 16, Appendix D.

CODETERMINATION. *See MITBESTIMMUNG.*

COGHLAN, TIMOTHY AUGUSTINE (1855–1926). An Australian statistician and historian, Coghlan was born in Sydney to Irish parents. Coghlan became the colonial statistician of New South Wales in 1886, a post he held until 1905 when he became agent-general in London. As a statistician, he achieved acclaim both in Australia and internationally; in 1893, he was made a Fellow of the Royal Statistical Society in London. Coghlan not only reorganized the statistical collections of New South Wales, he systematically extended the collections and communicated their results in appealing publications with text and tables, notably in the yearbook *The Wealth and Progress of New South Wales,* which was first published in 1887. He was particularly interested in the emergence of the labor movement and the growth of labor unions as well as movements in wages and prices. Because of his accuracy and his inside knowledge of political affairs, his publications remain an important source for the study of labor in **Australia**. His great work, *Labour and Industry in Australia,* was published in four volumes in 1918 by Oxford University Press, and continues to be an indispensable source for economic, political, and labor history in the last half of the 19th century. *See also* LABOR HISTORY; LABOR STATISTICS.

COLLECTIVE BARGAINING. Collective bargaining is the decision-making process whereby employers and unions negotiate the wages and conditions of employment. This process may also include governments. The form of collective bargaining varies. Unions and employers may bargain directly with each other or through a third party, such as an independent negotiator or a tribunal established by the government. Bargaining structures can vary also. Bargaining can take place with just a single enterprise or across a whole industry or a whole country. The types of collective bargaining that are used reflect the particular histories and cultures of the countries concerned. For example, collective bargaining in the private sector in the **United States** and the **United Kingdom** is generally done without any government participation whereas, in **Australia** government industrial tribunals continue to play an active part in the bargaining process. In **Brazil**, collective bargaining is only open to unions registered by the government. *See also* UNION–GOVERNMENT AGREEMENTS.

COLOMBIA. Associations of employees were formed in Colombia from the 1850s, but the first unions did not appear until around 1909. A **strike** by banana laborers at the U.S.-owned United Fruit Company in December 1928 resulted in the deaths of several hundred strikers. Unions and **collective bargaining** were fostered by a law of 1931. A union federation was formed in 1935 but soon split between **socialists** and **communists**. It was reunited as the *Confederacion de Trabajadores de Colombia* (CTC), or Confederation of Colombian Workers, in 1938. Colombia had two union federations affiliated with the **International Confederation of Free Trade Unions (ICFTU)** by 1951, the CTC and the Catholic *Union de Trabajadores de Colombia* (UTC), or Union of Workers of Colombia, formed in 1946, but they were rivals and it was not until 1958 that the two bodies, with the support of the ICFTU, agreed to work together. In 1986, the center-left *Central Unitaria de Trabajadores* (Central Union of Workers) was founded. The CTC and the UTC merged in 1992 with a few other unions into the *Confederacion General de Trabajadores Democraticos*.

Although collective bargaining and trade unions were legalized in 1975, organized labor in Colombia has had a difficult history marked by political instability and repression, a reflection of the country's narrow economic base and poor economic performance. In its annual surveys of **violations of trade union rights**, the ICFTU has consistently made special mention of the savagery of labor relations and **human rights** abuses in Colombia, specifically the killing of labor union activists. Between 1987 and 2000, between 2,500 and 3,200 union activists were killed in Colombia; in 2002, 184 were killed, compared with 185 in 2001. In 2006, this number had fallen to 78, but this was hardly proof of better relations. The 2009 survey confirmed this by mentioning the assassination of 49 unionists and a 25 percent rise in antiunion violence. According to the **International Trade Union Confederation** this sad position of Colombia as the country with the most assassinations per year is still true. Besides, national and international companies used harassment, persecution, and repressive actions against unions.

COMMONS, JOHN ROGERS (1862–1945). Born in Ohio, Commons became a political reformer on the side of labor and one of the foremost political economists in the **United States**. Based in Wisconsin, he played a significant role in drafting progressive labor laws between 1905 and 1911 and served on the state's Industrial Commission between 1911 and 1913. Outside of Wisconsin, he helped to found the American Association for Labor Legislation in 1906, served on the Commission on Industrial Relations between 1913 and 1915 and was president of the National Consumers' League from 1923 to 1935. Among his many achievements was his founding of the Wisconsin school of **labor history**, one of the first systematic, scholarly endeavors of its kind anywhere. His publications included *A Documentary History of American Industrial Society* (1910–1911, 10 vols.) and *History of Labor in the United States* (1918–1935, 4 vols.).

COMMONWEALTH TRADE UNION COUNCIL. This international body, based in London, was formed in 1979 to promote the interests of employees in the 50 countries that make up the Commonwealth, that is, the former British Empire. In 2004, the council was transformed into the **Commonwealth Trade Union Group**. In 2009, there were some 30 million employees in the Groups' member countries. The group acts in unison with the **International Trade Union Confederation**.

COMMONWEALTH TRADE UNION GROUP. *See* COMMONWEALTH TRADE UNION COUNCIL.

COMMUNICATION WORKERS OF AMERICA (CWU). The CWU is the largest telecommunications union in the world. It grew out of the organization of telephone workers in the 1890s by the International Brotherhood of Electrical Workers and the Commercial Telegraphers' Union. The modern union began as the National Federation of Telephone Workers, which was formed at Chicago in June 1939 with 45,000 members. By 1945, the Federation had grown to 170,000 members. Following a failed strike against the American Telephone and Telegraph Company, the Federation renamed itself the Communication Workers' Association in 1947 and was reorganized along more central lines. In 1949, it joined the **Congress of Industrial Organizations** to avoid further jurisdictional or demarcation disputes with other unions in the telecommunications industry and became affiliated with the **American Federation of Labor–Congress of Industrial Organizations** in 1955. **Membership** of the CWA rose from 180,000 in 1950 to 260,000 in 1960 and to 573,000 by 1983. In 2009, its membership was over 700,000 in the **United States** and **Canada**. *See also* POSTAL, TELEGRAPH, AND TELEPHONE INTERNATIONAL.

COMMUNICATIONS INTERNATIONAL (CI). The CI was named the **Postal, Telegraph, and Telephone International** until August 1997. The change in name was made in response to mergers and other changes in the organization of global telecommunications. On 1 January 2000 the CI merged with the **International Graphical Federation**, the **Media Entertainment International**, and the *Fédération internationale des employés, techniciens et cadres* (International Federation of Commercial, Clerical, Professional, and Technical Employees) to form the **Union Network International Global Union**.

COMMUNISM. In reaction to the support for their national governments during World War I by social-democratic parties many radical social-democrats split off. The establishment of the Bolshevik regime under Vladimir I. Lenin following the Russian revolution in 1917 and the formation of communist parties from the split off radical social-democrats in other parts of the world after 1918 began a new era in the history of organized labor. Underlying these changes was an upsurge of working-class discontent based on sharp inflation during and after World War I and the economic slump of the early 1920s. Following Lenin, communist theory and practice regarded labor unions as the primary vehicle of working-class organizations and, as such, ideal for infiltration and mobilization on behalf of revolution; this was the purpose of the Communist International (Comintern), which was established in March 1919. Noncommunist bodies that proved resistant to infiltration, notably the **International Federation of Trade Unions**, were made the targets of propaganda wars of ridicule and scorn.

As organizations, labor unions were often poorly equipped to deal with communist infiltration because of the low proportion of members who usually attended union meetings. As well, many communists gained election to union posts because of their dedication and hard work. The communist presence was notable in the leadership of certain industries such as **coal mining**, engineering, transportation, and the waterfront; during the Depression of the early 1930s, communists were often the leaders of moves to mobilize the unemployed into movements. With Hitler's attack on the Soviet Union in June 1941, the communist parties in the West were instructed to cooperate with their governments. In 1943, the Comintern was officially disbanded.

The end of World War II and the start of the Cold War saw a renewal of the Russian-led campaign to infiltrate organized labor, a campaign that brought about a split of the **World Federation of Trade Unions** and the creation of the **International Confederation of Free Trade Unions** in 1949. The improvement in the world economy after the early 1950s and determined campaigns to remove communists from key union positions largely eliminated communism as a major force within organized labor in the West. Nevertheless, individual communist leaders continued to be important in organized labor until the 1980s. With the collapse of the Soviet Union in 1991, the threat of communism largely disappeared, and the former labor union federations in Russia and Eastern Europe converted themselves into organizations that professed to be democratic to compete with the emergence of new labor union organizations that had no history of being run by communist governments. In Western Europe, few communist-oriented labor federations remain, the only notable exception being the *Confédération Générale du Travail* (General Confederation of Labor), in **France**. *See also* CATHOLICISM; SOCIALISM.

CONCILIATION AND ARBITRATION. Conciliation and arbitration are two methods that can be used for settling **labor disputes**. Following legislation in 1562 to fix maximum levels of wages, local courts in England acted as industrial tribunals and as wages boards. By 1769, conciliation in labor disputes had become an important part of the work of English magistrates. The Combination Act of 1800 included an arbitration clause. During the 19th century, conciliation and arbitration gradually became features of the method of resolving labor disputes in England.

Conciliation refers to the voluntary use of a mediator who tries to reach a settlement that both employer and employees would accept. Failing that, resort could be made to arbitration, where a settlement would be proposed by a board or an individual. The first conciliation legislation was passed in **Britain** in 1867, but the system had mixed success. In the wave of labor disputes in the late 19th and early 20th centuries, governments considered making conciliation and arbitration compulsory; that is, the parties in dispute would be legally compelled to accept the settlement of a board or tribunal. In the **United Kingdom**, labor unions generally opposed compulsory conciliation and arbitration. Nevertheless, compulsory arbitration as a means of settling disputes was used in **Germany** (1923–1928), **France** (1915–1919, 1936–1939, and 1940–1951), Kansas (1920–1925), **Norway** (1945–1952), and **Turkey** (1947–1963, 1980–1982).

Compulsory conciliation and arbitration achieved its most lasting success in **Australia** and **New Zealand**. In 1894, New Zealand introduced compulsory arbitration into its legal system, and it remained there until removed by far-reaching reforms in 1991. In Australia, industrial tribunals were established under federal and state laws between 1896 and 1912. In the early 1900s, there was considerable interest in these labor experiments from the United Kingdom, France, and the **United States**. In 1907, the British government sent Ernest Aves (1857–1917) on a fact-finding mission to Australia and New Zealand to investigate compulsory conciliation and arbitration; he reported that these systems seem to work well in their particular environments but concluded that the different legal and economic environment of the United Kingdom made their adoption inappropriate. Since the mid-1980s, both federal and state governments in Australia have encouraged greater reliance on **collective bargaining**, although the essentials of the conciliation and arbitration system remain intact.

CONFEDERACIÓN DE TRABAJADORES DE AMERICA LATINA **(CTAL).** The CTAL, or Confederation of Latin American Workers, was formed in 1938 by Vincente Lombardo Toledano, a Mexican Marxist. A left-wing international federation, it had close links with the **Congress of Industrial Organizations**. During World War II, the CTAL actively promoted organized labor in Latin America and supported the work of the **International Labour Organization**. In 1945, the CTAL joined the **World Federation of Trade Unions (WFTU)** and became its regional affiliate for Latin America. The CTAL remained with the WFTU after the withdrawal of its noncommunist members in 1948. In 1963, the CTAL was officially disbanded and replaced by the *Congreso Permanente de Unidad Sindical de los Trabajadores de America Latina y el Caribe* (Permanent Congress of Trade Union Unity of Latin American Workers).

CONFEDERACIÓN INTERAMERICANA DE TRABAJADORES **(CIT).** The CIT, or Inter-American Confederation of Workers, was the successor body to the Pan-American Federation of Labor. Formed on 10 January 1948 in Lima, **Peru**, the other founding member countries of the CIT were **Bolivia, Brazil, Chile, Colombia, Costa Rica, Cuba, El Salvador**, Dutch Guiana (**Surinam**), **Mexico, Panama, Puerto Rico**, and the **United States**. The **American Federation of Labor (AFL)**, represented by **George Meany** and others, was the prime mover in the creation of the CIT, which also had the support of the U.S. Department of State in its efforts to insulate Latin America from European fascism. The CIT soon became a victim of regional and international politics. In 1949, it was expelled from Peru by the government crackdown on organized labor and was then caught up in the politics of the Cold War. In 1951, the CIT reorganized itself into the *Organización Regional Interamericana de Trabajadores* the regional branch of the **International Confederation of Free Trade Unions**. After the ICFTU merged into the **International Trade Union Confederation** in 2008, ORIT was dissolved and renamed **Trade Union Confederation of the Americas.**

CONFEDERACIÓN SINDICAL DE TRABAJADORES Y TRABAJADORAS DE LAS AMERICAS **(CSA).** The CSA, or the Trade Union Confederation of the Americas (TUCA), is the largest regional workers' organization in the Americas. Founded in 2008 in Panama City, it represents more than 50 million workers belonging to 65 national trade union organizations distributed in 29 countries. TUCA/CSA is the regional organization of the **International Trade Union Confederation**.

CONFÉDÉRATION EUROPÉENNE DES CADRES **(CEC).** The CEC (European Confederation of Managers), also known as *EUROCADRES,* was formed in 1989 to represent the interests of managers, executives, and professional staff. Since December 1993, it has been formally recognized by the **European Union** as a "social partner" for European-level dialogue on social policy matters. In 2009, the CEC represented 1.5 million employed managers in Europe, compared with 800,000 in 1993. The CEC supports professional equality between men and **women** and programs to improve their access to jobs involving supervision, responsibility, and autonomy; the specific presence of a representation of executives and managerial staff in all the information, consultation, and participation bodies in the company; and adaptations to supplementary **pensions** in Europe to promote the free movement of labor.

CONFÉDÉRATION EUROPÉENNE DES SYNDICATS INDÉPENDANTS **(CESI).** The CESI, or European Confederation of Independent Trade Unions, was created in 1990 to represent the interests of a range of independent labor organizations. Its country membership in 1993 consisted of **Belgium, Germany, Iceland, Italy,** the **Netherlands, Portugal, Spain,** and the **United Kingdom** as well as **Sweden, Norway** (to July 1994), the **Czech Republic** and **Slovakia,** and the **Public Services International**. Since 1994, the CESI had admitted affiliates from **Bulgaria, Hungary, Poland,** and **Romania**. In 2005, the CESI was granted "social partner" status for European-level dialogue on social policy matters by the European Commission. In 2008, the European Federation of Public Service Employees affiliated. Two years later the CESI represented eight million members, compared with five million in 1993. *See also CONFÉDÉRATION EUROPÉENNE DES CADRES;* EUROPEAN TRADE UNION CONFEDERATION.

CONFÉDÉRATION GÉNÉRALE DU TRAVAIL **(CGT).** The CGT, or General Confederation of Labor, has been the oldest continuous important labor organization in **France** since its formation at Limoges in 1895; it absorbed the National Federation of *Bourses du Travail* in 1902. In 1906, the CGT adopted the radical Charter of Amiens, which called for wage increases and **shorter working hours** by dispossessing the "capitalist class" and supported the **general strike** as a means of achieving that end; the charter also made the CGT independent of any political party or philosophy. Between 1914 and 1920 the number of union members represented by the CGT grew from 400,000 to 2.5 million, but, as before 1914, the CGT was riven by tensions between its right and left wings. In 1921–1922, the CGT split when the **communists** and **syndicalists** formed their own federation, the *Confédération Générale du Travail Unitaire,* which joined the Red International of Labor Unions in 1923. In 1936, the CGT and the *Confédération Générale du Travail Unitaire* held a unity congress that resulted in the latter's readmission to the CGT. Membership of the CGT soared to between four and five million by 1936. Nevertheless, tensions between the communists and noncommunists remained.

In 1948 many of the noncommunists in the CGT left to form their own body, the *Confédération Générale du Travail-Force Ouvrière,* leaving the CGT effectively under the control of the French Communist Party (formed in 1920). The CGT has been the most important Western European affiliate of the communist **World Federation of Trade Unions** since 1949, but its power has been declining since the 1970s. Between the early 1970s and 1988, the membership of the CGT fell from 2.3 million to 800,000 and to 650,000 by 1999. In the 1990s, the CGT started cutting most of the links with the Communist Party, after which membership increased again to 710,000 at present. In 2001, the CGT was the only major national labor federation in Western Europe that was not an affiliate of the **International Confederation of Free Trade Unions,** but it became a member of the **International Trade Union Confederation** in 2006.

CONFÉDÉRATION INTERNATIONALE DES FONCTIONNAIRES **(CIF).** The CIF (International Confederation of Public Servants) is a Paris-based labor organization that was formed in 1955. In 2001, it had 11 members in eight countries and was associated with the *Confédération Européenne des Syndicats Indépendants.*

CONFEDERATION OF HEALTH SERVICE EMPLOYEES (COHSE). The COHSE was a British health workers' union formed in 1946 from the merger of the Mental Hospital and Institutional Workers' Union (founded in 1910) and the Hospital and Welfare Services Union (founded in 1918). Between 1948 and 1982, its membership grew from 25,000 to 230,000. In 1993, it merged with two other labor unions to create **UNISON.**

CONFEDERATION OF SHIPBUILDING AND ENGINEERING UNIONS (CSEU). The CSEU began in 1891 as the Federation of Engineering and Shipbuilding Trades. It provided a forum for **collective bargaining** for British **white-** and **blue-collar** unions in shipbuilding and engineering. In its present form, it was constituted in 1936, but until World War II it was not a fully representative body. Wartime cooperation with the Foundry Union and the **Amalgamated Engineering Union** on the national negotiating body, the National Engineering Joint Trades Movement (formed in 1941) helped to allay suspicions and, in 1944, the Foundry Union joined the CSEU, followed by the Amalgamated Society of Engineers in 1946. In 1989, the CSEU had 22 affiliated organizations representing two million members. In 2001, the CSEU represented about 1.2 million union members. In 2010 and 2011, the CSEU complained about job losses in the engineering industry and restrictions imposed by British labor laws on organized labor.

CONGO (REPUBLIC). The administration of French Equatorial Africa allowed Africans to form unions in 1944 and legalized these in 1952. The present territory of Congo was granted independence by **France** in 1960. In August 1963, the unions successfully resisted the attempts of the Fulbert Youlou government to impose a one-party state. The unions formed the *Confédération Syndicale Congoliase* (Congolese Trade Union Confederation) in 1964. A comprehensive labor law was introduced in 1975 to regulate the unions; union **membership** was then about 22,000. By 1995, Congo was represented in the **International Confederation of Free Trade Unions** by two affiliates with a combined membership of 80,800.

Despite civil war in the early 21st century, there were 112,000 union members in the Congo by 2010. This is surprising as employers regard organized labor with contempt and the legal framework for trade union rights remained weak.

CONGO (DEMOCRATIC REPUBLIC). A colony of **Belgium** until 1960, labor unions existed only among Europeans before 1945. Called Zaire from 1971 to 1997, organized labor claimed 325,000 members by 1965, according to the returns by its four affiliates of the **International Confederation of Free Trade Unions** (ICFTU), of whom 300,000 were members of the *Confédération des Syndicats libres du Congo* (Confederation of Free Trade Unions of the Congo), formed in 1961. Thereafter, the fortunes of organized labor in the Democratic Republic of Congo have reflected its unstable and violent political history. There was no representation from the Congo in the ICFTU between 1965 and 1995. In 2002, the ICFTU reported that although trade union rights existed on paper, they were ignored in practice against a background of fragile peace following the civil war and economic collapse. In 2006, two union activists were kidnapped and tortured because they were critical of the conditions at the company where they worked. In 2009, employers still showed hostility toward the unions. Despite massacres and forced migration, organized labor claimed 492,000 union members in the Democratic Republic in 2010.

CONGRESO PERMANENTE DE UNIDAD SINDICAL DE LOS TRA-BAJADORES DE AMERICA LATINA **(CPUSTAL).** The CPUSTAL or Permanent Congress of Trade Union Unity of Latin American Workers was an international labor federation formed in 1964 with 18 countries from Latin America and the Caribbean. It succeeded the *Confederación de Traba-jadores de America Latina*. Closely associated with the **World Federation of Trade Unions**, it had 25 member countries in 1990 and claimed 20 million members. The CPUSTAL faced much opposition from right-wing governments and was defunct by 2001. *See also ORGANIZACIÓN REGIONAL INTERAMERICANA DE TRABAJADORES.*

CONGRESS OF INDUSTRIAL ORGANIZATIONS (CIO). The CIO was a national labor federation in the **United States** from 1935 to 1955. Unlike its competitor, the **American Federation of Labor** (AFL), the CIO practiced **industrial unionism** and sought to organize the unskilled. Although there had been earlier attempts to recruit the unskilled into the ranks of organized labor, notably by the **Knights of Labor** and the **Industrial Workers of the World**, the results of their efforts had been short-lived. The AFL only supported unions based on "craft" or occupation and ignored the unskilled and those employed in the mass production industries that emerged after 1900. During the 1920s, the **membership** of American unions declined in the face of company unionism, well-organized campaigns for the open shop, and an unsympathetic political and legal environment. In 1929, a group of **socialists** and progressive labor unionists led by A. J. Muste set up the Conference for Progressive Labor Action to win the AFL over to industrial unionism and recruitment of the unskilled, but their efforts failed.

The possibility for success came in 1933 in the form of Section 7(a) of the National Industrial Recovery Act, which provided for the right of employees to form unions for **collective bargaining** free from employer interference. Despite the known existence of a high level of support for unionism in mass production industries, the leadership of the AFL successfully resisted all efforts to charter new industrial unions at its 1934 convention. **John L. Lewis**, the president of the **United Mine Workers of America**, itself an industrial union, assumed the leadership of the dissidents to the AFL policy and, along with **Sidney Hillman** of the Amalgamated Clothing Workers, **David Dubinsky** of the **International Ladies' Garment Workers' Union**, and five other labor leaders, formed the Committee for Industrial Organization in November 1935. In August 1936, the 10 unions that had affiliated with the CIO were suspended by the AFL following successful organizing drives by the CIO in the steel, automobile, radio, and rubber industries.

The CIO unions went on to win three major industrial victories for union recognition. The first was achieved by a large-scale sit-down **strike** at the Goodyear Tire and Rubber Company, which won union recognition for the CIO's United Rubber Workers in 1936. In March 1937, the CIO won an unexpected major victory by negotiating union recognition for the Steel Workers Organizing Committee from U.S. Steel. The committee negotiated a 10 percent pay raise, an 8-hour day, and a 40-hour week. The third victory for union recognition was won by the **United Auto Workers** (UAW) against the General Motors Corporation, also in 1937. In 1938, the CIO was expelled from the AFL. The last major victory by the CIO was the gaining of recognition by the UAW from the Ford Motor Company after a 10-day strike in 1941. By 1939, the CIO claimed that its affiliated unions had a combined membership of 1.8 million compared with 3.9 million for the AFL. World War II more than doubled the membership of the CIO to 3.9 million, making it equal to that of the AFL.

However, the CIO never again regained the recruiting initiative it had seized in the late 1930s because the AFL began to recognize industrial unionism within its own ranks, as shown by the conversion of large affiliates like the **Teamsters** into industrial unions and by the defection of John L. Lewis and his United Mine Workers of America from the CIO in 1940. The Cold War also harmed the CIO, which had always been a more militant body than the AFL. On 5 November 1955, the two organizations agreed to merge as the **American Federation of Labor–Congress of Industrial Organizations (AFL-CIO)**. At the time of its merger, the CIO had an affiliated membership of 4.6 million.

COOK ISLANDS. A dependency of **New Zealand**, the Cook Islands have been an affiliate of the **International Confederation of Free Trade Unions/ International Trade Union Confederation** since about 1993 through their Cook Islands Public Service Association, Inc., which had a **membership** of 1,200 in 2010.

COSTA RICA. The first union in Costa Rica was created in 1905. In 1943, non-Catholic and **Catholic** union federations were formed. Despite its democratic government, union growth has been limited by the narrow basis of the economy and by unemployment as well as by political and religious divisions. Also employer opposition prevented workers from joining unions. In the early 1980s, multinational banana companies together with the U.S. embassy, the Costa Rican government, and the Roman Catholic hierarchy created an alternative to independent labor unions. These *solidarista* associations try to replace trade unions and workers' rights under the pretext of peaceful labor relations. They act in the tradition of *el solidarismo*, which dates back to the 1940s.

In 1997, Del Monte allowed his banana workers the right to organize after international pressure. By 1976, the three national labor federations had only about 30,000 members. Between 1958 and 1991, the **membership** of the Catholic federation increased from 12,000 to 56,700. Costa Rica has been represented in the **International Confederation of Free Trade Unions** since 1951 and claimed 45,000 members in 2001. Since 2007, the **International Trade Union Confederation** has reported increases in antiunion violations; its two affiliates claimed 138,000 members in 2010.

***CÔTE D'IVOIRE* (IVORY COAST).** As a colony of **France** until 1960, organized labor in the *Côte d'Ivoire* before the 1950s consisted of overseas branches of French unions. The indigenous unions that emerged after 1950 became associated with the independence movement, but after independence came under pressure to become part of a one-party political system. The *Côte d'Ivoire* has been affiliated with the **International Confederation of Free Trade Unions** by the *Union Générale des Travailleurs de Côte d'Ivoire* (General Union of the Workers of the Ivory Coast) since 1992. Under its law, the president of the *Côte d'Ivoire* can end a strike by compulsory **arbitration**. A strike by 700 workers at a government-owned enterprise over management's refusal to allow democratic trade union elections between May 1993 and April 1995 resulted in the deaths of 14 strikers and strikers' evictions from company-owned housing. Between 1991 and 2001, the number of union members in the *Côte d'Ivoire* declined from 400,000 to 120,000, and the economy suffered from a civil war in 2003. In 2009, the **International Trade Union Confederation** complained about continuous intimidation and repression of strikers. Its two affiliates claimed a total of 328,000 members in 2010. In the northern regions, both government and rebels repressed strikes.

COUNCIL OF NORDIC TRADE UNIONS. An international labor organization representing **Denmark, Finland, Greenland, Iceland, Norway,** and **Sweden,** this Council has existed since 1972 in its present form, but its origins date to 1886. The purpose of the Council is to provide a forum for topics of mutual interest and to exchange information. In 2009, the Council represented 9 million members, compared with 7.2 million in 1990.

CRAFT UNIONS. Historically, craft labor unions have been based on craftsmen, that is, those skilled **blue-collar** occupations requiring the completion of an **apprenticeship** to attain a formal qualification of competency. Because of their relatively high pay and strategic position in the workplace to disrupt production, craft unions have often been able to exercise economic power disproportionately greater than their numbers and were at the forefront of the leadership of organized labor in the **United Kingdom** and the **United States** in the 19th century. Up to the 1960s, craft unions had especially been a feature of **printing** and metals **manufacturing**. Generally, **membership** of craft unions was closed to employees who had not completed a relevant apprenticeship, and craft unions attempted to regulate their working environment closely by upholding unwritten work rules, such as reserving particular jobs for skilled workers. Notable examples of craft unions have included the **Amalgamated Society of Engineers**, and craft unions have often been leaders in the establishment of national union federations such as the British **Trades Union Congress** and the **American Federation of Labor**. Technological change since the 1960s has effectively brought about the end of craft unions, which usually **amalgamated** with other unions. *See also* INDUSTRIAL UNIONS.

CROATIA. Organized labor emerged in Croatia in 1904, and in 1907, Croatia became a member of the **International Federation of Trade Unions**. By 1913, membership of the country's unions had grown to 7,000. From October 1918 to its dissolution in June 1991, Croatia's labor movement was intertwined with the violent history and ethnic politics of the republic of **Yugoslavia**. However, the situation changed with independence. The largest labor organization in Croatia, the Union of Autonomous Trade Unions of Croatia (UATUC), was formed in 1990 by dissident unions and former communist unions. The UATUC applied to join the **International Confederation of Free Trade Unions** (ICFTU) in 1992 and was admitted in January 1997. In 2001, the ICFTU reported that although the legal framework for organized labor had improved, the right to **strike** was still limited despite criticism by the **European Union**. In 2009, the government used EU regulations as a pretext to reduce the rights of public workers and trade unions. The Labour Code in force in 2010 allows for more flexibility and liberalization. Private employers still resist union organizing by dismissing activists. In 2010, there were 278,000 union members in Croatia compared with 650,000 in 1997.

CUBA. The first Cuban labor union was formed among tobacco employees in 1868, and over the next 15 years a number of **craft unions** were set up. A congress of Cuban employees was held in 1892 and passed resolutions calling for independence from **Spain** and the eight-hour day. **Anarchism**, as in other Latin American countries, was an important force within organized labor; an anarchist labor federation was created in 1925. In 1933, there was a **general strike** that succeeded in gaining some progressive legislation, but a second general strike in 1935 was repressed and organized labor crushed.

It revived in 1938, and in January 1939 the *Confederación de Trabajadores de Cuba* (CTC), or Confederation of Workers of Cuba, was formed. Cuba was represented in the **Confederation of Free Trade Unions** from 1951 to 1959. Fidel Castro's triumph over Fulgencio Batista was greatly assisted by a general strike in 1959. With Castro's victory, strikes were forbidden and organized labor was gradually deprived of its independence; Cuba then had 1.2 million union members. The CTC was renamed *Central de Trabajadores de Cuba* under Castro and became affiliated to the **World Federation of Trade Unions**. In October 1991, an Independent Cuban General Workers' Union was created, but it has always been denied recognition by the government and even by 2010 this had not changed. Independent union members continued to be persecuted and exiled. The right to strike is still not recognized in law.

CURAÇAO. The biggest of the islands that made up the Netherlands Antilles, Curaçao saw early efforts by Roman-Catholics to organize workers during the years between the two World Wars. Only after World War II did modern unions emerge. Curaçao has been a member of the **International Confederation of Free Trade Unions** since at least 1957. Union **membership** in Curaçao fell from 9,000 in 1957 to 6,000 in 1988 and to 5,100 in 2001. It was 5,800 in 2009 when the island became a country within the Kingdom of the **Netherlands**.

CYPRUS. Organized labor in Cyprus emerged in 1910, four years before the island was annexed by the **United Kingdom**. British colonial authorities repressed the early unions. The first trade union law was enacted in 1932, but comprehensive labor laws were only introduced during World War II. The first labor federation was established in 1941. Organized labor was part of the struggle for independence, which was gained in 1960. From 1963, divisions between Greeks and Turks on Cyprus became evident and were formalized after the division of the island with the Turkish invasion in 1974. Cyprus has been represented in the **International Confederation of Free Trade Unions** since 1951. In 2010, its two affiliates with the **International Trade Union Confederation** claimed a combined membership of 74,000.

CZECH REPUBLIC. The Czech Republic was created in 1993 from the division of **Czechoslovakia**. It has been represented since the division in the **International Confederation of Free Trade Unions** by the Czech-Moravian Confederation (formerly known as the Chamber) of Trade Unions, which claimed a **membership** of 1.3 million in 2001. In January 2001, a new labor code was introduced that strengthened the legal position of organized labor but excluded the **public sector** from **collective bargaining**. In 2007, the **International Trade Union Confederation** reported difficulties with organizing but also some progress. The economic crisis has, however, been used to set union rights a few years back and made workers vulnerable to antiunion harassment. In 2010, trade union activities became difficult as a result of the economic crisis and union membership had fallen to 445,000.

CZECHOSLOVAKIA. Before 1918, Czechoslovakia was part of the Austro-Hungarian Empire. The first labor union was set up by journeymen drapers at Liberec in 1870 and had 3,500 members after a year. Unions became part of the political struggle for independence as well as pursuing industrial objectives. A labor federation was formed in 1897, and some members attended as observers at the conferences of the **International Federation of Trade Unions** in 1901 and 1902. Reflecting the diversity of the society, unions were divided along national, political, and religious lines. In 1905, the unions made their presence felt through protests for the eight-hour day as well as for the universal franchise. By 1913, there were 318,000 union members; some were in German unions and others were members of **Catholic** or Protestant unions. In 1919, the Czech and German labor federations became affiliates of the IFTU and remained affiliated until 1938. By 1920, there were 1.7 million union members in the Czechoslovak Republic. Unlike most of its neighbors, Czechoslovakia had a large industrial base; in 1921, 37 percent of the labor force was employed in **manufacturing**. Union **membership** peaked at 1,738,300 in 1928, when there were 583 unions. Under the Nazi occupation (1938–1945), free unions were suppressed and compliant ones created.

As a result of their leadership of the partisans during World War II, the **communists** gained much popular support. In 1945, the communists formed their own labor federation, the Central Council of Trade Unions. Noncommunist unions reestablished themselves, but their independence was short-lived and, from 1948, the communist federation was the sole national labor center. During the "Prague Spring" in 1968, the unions actively supported Alexander Dubček's program of reforms. The 12 industrial unions were divided into 58 new unions with a high degree of independence. After the Soviet invasion and the fall of Dubček in April 1969, these initiatives were suppressed.

After the collapse of the communist regime in November 1989 in the so-called Velvet Revolution, organized labor carried out its own internal reforms, which produced a united federation of Czech and Slovak unions, *Ceska a Slovenská Konfederace odborových* (ČS-KOS), with a membership of six million. Following the peaceful division of the country into the **Czech Republic** and **Slovakia** in 1993, the ČS-KOS was also divided along Czech and Slovak lines. At the time of the division, there were 2.6 million members in the Czech Republic and 1.2 million in Slovakia.

D

DA SILVA, LUIZ INACIO [Lula] (1945–). Da Silva was born on 27 October 1945 in the hinterland of Pernambuco State, **Brazil**. Later on, he added "Lula" to his name of birth. Lula means squid, but is also the nickname of people called "Luiz." When Luiz was seven years old his family moved to São Paulo State. After basic education Lula started working at a local cleaner. Later he got a placement in a training course and graduated as a metalworker. After the 1964 military coup, Lula worked in Villares Industries in São Bernando do Campo, in the industrial heartland of São Paulo State. His brother Frei Chico brought him into contact with the labor movement.

Lula made a rapid career in the unions and in 1975 he was with an overwhelming majority elected president of the Metalworkers Union of São Bernardo do Campo and Diadema, a 100,000-strong union. Lula re-directed the Brazilian labor movement, leading to the first strikes in 10 years. The massive strikes and mass meetings were met with police intimidation. State repression caused Lula to consider creating a political workers' party. In 1980, Lula, together with union members and others, founded the *Partido dos Trabalhadores* (PT, Workers Party). In the same year, a metalworkers strike provoked government intervention and the imprisonment of Lula and other union leaders for 31 days. In 1983, he took part in the establishment of the *Central Única dos Trabalhadores* (United Workers' Federation).

The PT nominated Lula for the presidential elections of 1989, but he lost by a slim margin. In 1994 and 1998, Lula ran again for president in vain. After the PT allied with other political parties under a platform of social inclusion Lula was elected president of the republic in 2002, the first left-wing head of state since the military coup of 1964. Promising to promote economic growth and the diminishing of social differences he was re-elected in 2006. In 2010, Lula was legally not allowed to run again, but a fellow party member, Dilma Vana Rousseff, won the elections.

DEAKIN, ARTHUR (1890–1955). One of the leading British labor leaders in the 1940s, Deakin was born in Sutton Coldfield, Warwickshire, and moved to Wales in the early 1900s where he worked in a steel plant. During this period, he became a Primitive Methodist and a teetotaler. In 1910, he moved to north Wales where he was a member of several unions including the **Amalgamated Society of Engineers** but transferred to the Dock, Wharf, Riverside, and General Workers' Union and became a full-time organizer for the Union in 1919. When the Union became part of the **Transport and General Workers' Union** (TGWU) in 1922, Deakin became, in effect, its manager for north Wales. After holding various local government positions, he became national secretary of the General Workers' part of the TGWU and moved to London, where his abilities were recognized by the general secretary, **Ernest Bevin**, who made Deakin his protégé. When Bevin joined Winston Churchill's War Cabinet in 1940, Deakin became the acting general secretary of the TGWU; he became permanent in the position with Bevin's retirement in 1946. In the same year, he also became president of the **World Federation of Trade Unions** and, like his patron, Bevin, strongly opposed the communists, who were against the Marshall Plan for aiding postwar Europe. Indeed, Deakin played a central role in the foundation of the **International Confederation of Free Trade Unions** in 1949. Deakin continued to play an important part in fighting **communism** within the **Trades Union Congress**, of which he was president in 1951–1952.

DENMARK. Organized labor developed relatively strongly in Denmark from the mid-1850s after the abolition of the guilds. By 1890, there were 218 unions with about 31,000 union members; in 1900, there were 96,000 union members or about 14 percent of employees, a level comparable with the **United Kingdom** (13 percent). This strength owed much to an agreement reached between the Federation of Danish Trade Unions (the *Landsorganisationen i Denmark* [LO], formed in 1898) and the government in 1899 over the right to organize; the unions were also given the task of running the unemployment insurance program. This agreement enabled Danish unions to enjoy a privileged position within European countries of the time and continued to sustain them thereafter. Unlike many other European countries Danish unions are not divided along political or religious lines, but rather along educational lines. The LO organizes skilled and unskilled workers; another union organizes teachers, nurses, and bank workers; and a third represents employees with a higher education.

In the post-1945 period, Denmark continued to have a high level of union **membership**; it rose from 52 percent of employees in 1950 to 80 percent in 1980 and even by 1991 remained at 81 percent. In 2010, there were 1.7 million union members compared with two million in 2001. About 80 percent of Danish employees are union members.

DEUTSCHE ARBEITSFRONT **(DAF).** The DAF (German Labor Front) was set up by the Nazis to control the German labor movement between

1933 and 1945. After November 1933, the DAF also included all employers. The DAF covered the whole labor force and by 1939 had control of about 20 million people. During World War II, it was used to maintain production of war materials and to settle **labor disputes**. The members of the DAF were organized among 18 *Reichbetriebsgruppen* or industrial groups. Although not a free labor organization, the structure of the DAF foreshadowed the 16 industrial groups (*Industriegewerkschaften*) in West Germany, which were created between 1948 and 1950. *See also* BÖCKLER, HANS; *DEUTSCHER GEWERKSCHAFTSBUND*.

DEUTSCHER GEWERKSCHAFTSBUND **(DGB).** The DGB (Confederation of German Trade Unions) is the leading labor union federation of **Germany**. The first German union confederation, the *Allgemeiner Deutscher Gewerkschaftsbund* (General German Trade Union Federation), was formed in 1868 and claimed to represent 142,000 employees, but was able to achieve little as a result of Otto von Bismarck's repressive Anti-Socialist Laws, which were in force from 1878 to 1890. In 1890, a new labor federation, the *Generalkommission der Gewerkschaften* (General Council of Trade Unions), was formed with **Carl Legien** as its president.

In 1919, this body was reorganized as the *Allgemeiner Deutscher Gewerkschaftsbund* (General German Trade Union Federation), a title it retained until its suppression by the Nazis in 1933. After Germany's defeat in 1945, unions were at first only allowed to organize within state boundaries but, with the lifting of this restriction, a first confederation under the label of the *Deutscher Gewerkschaftsbund* (DGB) was set up in the British zone under the leadership of **Hans Böckler** in April 1947. This DGB was in some ways but not formally the predecessor of the later DGB. There was a broad consensus among postwar trade unionists that the new German trade union movement should cover all currents within the labor movements and overcome the prewar split in socialist, Christian, and liberal trade unions. In 1949, the American and French authorities had given their agreement to extend the confederation to all their zones in West Germany and to their sectors in Berlin. The official foundation of the DGB as the trade Confederation of German Trade Unions in the new Federal Republic of Germany (*Bundesrepublik Deutschland*) took place in October 1949 in Munich. The DGB was granted only weak powers by the affiliated unions, which kept full control of their own finances and remained solely responsible for collective bargaining. By 1950, the DGB had a total **membership** of nearly 5.5 million, of whom 83 percent were **blue-collar** employees and 15 percent were **women**. Until 2001, one union, *IG Metall*, accounted for about a quarter of its total membership. Although a nonpartisan confederation and not formally affiliated with the German Social

Democratic Party (*Sozialdemokratische Partei Deutschlands*), the DGB has been closely associated with it in practice. Following the formal reunification of Germany in October 1990, the membership of the unions affiliated with the DGB rose from 7.8 to 9.8 million members between 1989 and 1994. Its membership in 1994 consisted of 62 percent blue-collar workers and 31 percent women. Since 1994, the DGB has experienced a decline in the membership of its affiliates to 7.8 million in 2000 and 6.3 million in 2009, prompting greater moves toward **amalgamation**. In 2009, the DGB consisted of eight industry unions (compared with 16 in 1994), but its power over its larger affiliates was very limited. The eight industrial groups covered by its affiliated unions were construction, **agriculture**, and environment; mining, chemicals, and energy; rail transport; **education** and science; metal manufacturing, woodworking, textiles, and garments; food beverages and catering; **police**; and the many industry groups covered by *Ver.di* (commerce, banking, and insurance; media and the arts; public and private services and transportation [public and private]; and postal and communication workers).

***DEUTSCHER METALLARBEITER-VERBAND* (DMV).** The DMV (German Metal Workers' Union) was the first **industrial union** to be formed in **Germany**. The first German metal workers' unions were formed in 1868–1869, but **membership** growth was slow before 1891, when representatives of a number of separate metal unions formed a single industrial union, the *Deutscher Metallarbeiter Verband* (DMV) with 23,200 members. Because it recruited unskilled as well as skilled workers, the DMV was regarded with suspicion by the older **craft unions**. For instance, the Berlin metal workers did not join the DMV until 1897 and then only on the condition that they retain their independence. For an industrial union, the growth of the DMV was slow—50,000 in 1896, 100,000 in 1901, and 554,900 by 1913—largely because the DMV was denied recognition by employers in the new large-scale heavy industry plants. Granted recognition during World War I in 1916, the membership of the DMV rose to 786,000 by 1918 and to 1.6 million in 1919, a level it held until 1923, making it briefly the largest single union in the world. The DMV proved incapable of retaining these gains after 1924 because of the economic crisis and also internal weaknesses. In particular, it failed to recruit the young; between 1919 and 1931, the percentage of members under 20 fell from 23 to 12 percent. By 1928 membership had fallen to 944,000. The DMV was to the left of most of the German labor movement. It was dissolved by the Nazis on 2 May 1933, and many of its leaders were imprisoned. *See also* BRENNER, OTTO.

DJIBOUTI. A colony of **France** to June 1977, labor unions were scarce. Apart from local branches of French unions, only two unions existed by

1975. The French Overseas Labor Code of 1952 remained in force in 1994, despite the government's promise to update the country's labor laws. In July 1993, the secondary school teachers formed a union that received legal recognition; it called a **strike** in January 1994 over the nonpayment of salaries, prompting a round of government repression and intimidation. Djibouti has been represented internationally in organized labor since 1994 by the *Union Djiboutienne du travail* (UDT), or Djibouti Labor Union, which claimed 13,000 members in 2010.

In 2002, the **International Confederation of Free Trade Unions** reported that there was considerable government interference with organized labor. Since 2002, it has remained very difficult to exercise trade union rights in Djibouti with strikes being violently repressed and the UDT having to cancel meetings of its congress.

DOMINICA. Independent of the **United Kingdom** since November 1978, organized labor in Dominica had emerged by the late 1940s, and Dominica was an affiliate of the **International Confederation of Free Trade Unions** by 1951. By 1995, it reported a union **membership** of 1,900. The government since the 1990s has severely curtailed the right to strike. In 2010, there were about 1,700 union members in Dominica, covering less than 10 percent of the workforce.

DOMINICAN REPUBLIC. Organized labor emerged during the U.S. occupation between 1916 and 1924. A union federation was formed in 1930. The dictator General Rafael Trujillo tried to suppress the federation, but it survived despite much loss of life. In 1946, Trujillo set up a union federation controlled by the government. Following a mission to the Dominican Republic in 1957, the **International Confederation of Free Trade Unions (ICFTU)** boycotted the oppressive Trujillo government; Trujillo was assassinated in 1961. In 1962, organized labor split along political lines, with the moderate bodies setting up the *Confederación Nacional de Trabajadores Libres* (National Confederation of Free Workers). It was affiliated with the ICFTU by 1965 and became the *Confederacion Nacional de Trabajadores Dominicanos* (CNTD), or National Confederation of Dominican Workers, in 1971. The militant union bodies opted to resist the government. Civil war in 1965–1966 resulted in U.S. occupation. The political environment for organized labor only began to improve after the 1978 elections. After pressure by the CNTD, a labor code introduced in 1992 provided legal protection for labor unions and required that a union had to have a **membership** of more than half of the employees at an enterprise for it to be recognized as the representative for **collective bargaining**. Economic reforms from the 1980s led to the establishment of **export processing zones**, in which unions were, in effect, not permitted, and working conditions and pay were substandard. Although workers could form labor unions in 2009, they are effectively excluded from export processing zones and sugar plantations. Antiunion strategies, such as lay-offs, further undermine workers' rights.

DONOVAN COMMISSION. The *Donovan Commission* was the popular term for the British Royal Commission on Trade Unions and Employers' Associations, which reported to the government in 1968. Named after its chairman, Lord Donovan, it made a comprehensive investigation of industrial relations and institutions. The commission found that **Great Britain** had two systems of labor relations, a formal and an informal system. The formal system, based on law and official institutions, was less important than the informal system, based on the behavior of unions, shop stewards, and employers. It argued that **collective bargaining** should be extended with the agreement of employers and unions and that legislative reform of the formal system was not a practical option. Despite the commission's findings, which were the product of careful research, including some pioneering survey investigations, British conservative governments since 1980 have placed primary reliance on the law as a means of controlling and reducing the power of organized labor. The lasting legacy of the Donovan Commission was the inauguration of official workplace surveys. *See also* EMPLOYMENT ACTS; *ROOKES V. BARNARD.*

DUBINSKY, DAVID (1892–1982). A leading U.S. labor leader, Dubinsky was born in Russian **Poland**, and began his working life as a baker. He took part in a successful **strike** in 1907, after which he spent 18 months in jail. Exiled to Siberia, he escaped on the way and went underground until he gained an amnesty in 1910. In 1911, he emigrated to the **United States** and joined the **International Ladies' Garment Workers' Union** in New York. From 1918, he occupied various senior offices in Local 10 of the union and became secretary-treasurer in 1929 and president in 1932, a position he held until 1966. Thereafter, Dubinsky emerged as one of the main labor leaders in the United States. He was a labor adviser to the National Recovery Administration from 1933 to 1935 and an executive council member of the **American Federation of Labor (AFL)** in 1935 but resigned after the suspension of the **Congress of Industrial Organizations (CIO)** in 1937. Nevertheless, Dubinksy opposed the CIO as an independent body. In 1940, he reaffiliated his union with the AFL, and in 1945 was again on its executive council. He also took an active part in labor **politics** and was a founder of the American Labor Party in 1936. Dubinsky was a participant in the formation of the **International Confederation of Free Trade Unions** in 1949.

E

ECUADOR. Organized labor emerged in Ecuador in its main port of Guayaquil in 1920, mainly as a result of the rise in the cost of living caused by the inflation of World War I. Although union protests over the cost of living were suppressed, the unions formed a federation to campaign for rights; its efforts led to the labor law of 1928. A national **Catholic** federation was formed in 1938 and in June 1944 the **industrial unions** set up their own labor federation. A third national federation was formed in 1962 and was affiliated with the **International Confederation of Free Trade Unions**; by 1975, this organization was renamed as the *Confederación Ecuatoriana de Organizaciones Sindicales Libres* (CEOSL), or Ecuadorian Confederation of Free Trade Unions. In 1964, the military government denied the unions the right to **strike**, but they and students successfully forced the government to resign. Despite their differences, the three labor federations have tended to cooperate in the *Frente Unitario de Trabajadores* (FUT), or United Workers' Front. FUT tried to achieve common goals such as a larger social security system and the nationalization of the petroleum industry. Internal division aside, slow economic growth as well as political hostility have made it difficult for organized labor to accomplish significant gains since the 1970s. A fresh challenge came in the 1990s with government efforts to reform the economy along free market principles. In 1991, the labor law was amended to discourage the formation of unions in small enterprises that are an important part of the economy of Ecuador. There was a strike wave over government policies, particularly over petrol price rises and redundancies. In 1994, there was a nine-week strike by teachers that was only brought to an end by the government threat to declare a state of emergency and subject teachers to military discipline. Hyperinflation in 2000 and a fall in gross domestic product of 7.5 percent led to widespread labor protests in January 2001, which were met by government repression and the unlawful detention of the leaders of organized labor, including José Chávez, the president of the CEOSL. During demonstrations by teachers in June 2001, four people were shot dead. Since then, intimidation and violence toward organized labor has been routine and there is no right to strike in practice. Violations are widespread in both the public and private sectors. Employers try to promote *Solidarismo* movements.

EDUCATION. Education was seen as a prerequisite for self-confident union members in the labor movement in the late 19th century and it was one reason why early unions were strongly opposed to **child labor**.

Labor unions in education have historically concerned school teachers. In the **United Kingdom**, the National Union of Elementary Teachers was formed in 1870; it renamed itself the National Union of Teachers in 1888 and conducted its first **strike** in 1914 against the Education Authority in Herefordshire. In 1919, the union agreed to admit uncertified teachers as members, gained a national pay scale, and adopted an equal pay for **equal work** policy. In **Australia**, the first teachers' union was formed in Victoria in 1878. Other teachers' bodies were formed in Queensland in 1889 and New South Wales in 1895. The New South Wales Teachers' Association was formed in 1918 and formally registered as a labor union in 1919. The first teachers' strike occurred in western Australia in July 1920 when they joined the majority of the **public sector** in a three-week strike for increased pay to compensate for inflation; the strike was largely successful. The first teachers' strike in Victoria occurred in 1965 and in New South Wales in 1968. In the **United States**, the Chicago Federation of Teachers was formed in 1897 and affiliated with the **American Federation of Labor** in 1902. In 1916, the **American Federation of Teachers (AFT)** was created and grew to 9,300 members by 1920. Thereafter, it had a difficult history marked by a fall of **membership** in the 1920s (down to 3,700) and an internal struggle with **communists** in the 1930s. Even by 1940 only about 3 percent of teachers were members of the federation. Despite a national no-strike policy up to 1963, teachers did strike at the state level in 1946 largely because of the failure of teachers' salaries to keep pace with comparable occupations in the private sector. The AFT faced strong competition from the **National Education Association (NEA)** from 1960; since 1987, the NEA has been the largest labor union in the United States and in 2010 was the largest union in the world. *See also* WHITE-COLLAR UNIONISM.

EDUCATION INTERNATIONAL (EI). The EI was formed in 1993 from the merger of the **International Federation of Free Teachers' Unions** (formed in 1928) and the World Confederation of Organizations of the Teaching Profession (formed in 1952). It is based in Brussels and has 402 affiliated unions in 173 countries representing almost 30 million members, mostly **women**. Its president is Susan Hopgood of the Australian Education Union. EI promotes the development of democratic organizations for teachers and other education workers. EI tries to foster good relations between education workers in all countries.

EGYPT. The first Egyptian labor union was formed among cigarette workers in 1899, and by 1911 there were 11 unions claiming a total of 7,000 members. As often happened in other colonial societies, labor unions became part of the movement for independence. They participated in the revolution of 1919, which led to the formation of a monarchical government in 1922. In the early 1920s, the unions were led by the Egyptian Socialist Party (formed in 1921), but an attempted **general strike** in 1923 was suppressed. During the 1930s, Egyptian organized labor became intertwined with **politics**. Unions were legalized in 1942. After the overthrow of the monarchy in 1952 under Colonel Gamal Abdel Nasser, organized labor and the political system became increasingly integrated. In 1962, the president of the Egyptian Trade Union Federation (formed in 1956) was made minister of labor, a trend later followed by **Guinea** and **Tanzania**. Strikes do occur in Egypt, but they are regarded as a form of public disorder and are illegal. The government response to strikes is to use the **police** to repress them violently. However, in 2006 there were more than 220 strikes, which made this year the strongest wave of labour protest since 1945. In 2008, a demonstration in Mahalla was savagely repressed, leaving six people dead. The year 2008 saw the emergence of an independent union within a department of the ministry of finance, a unique event. Because there is no independent organized labor in Egypt, it has never been a member of the **International Confederation of Free Trade Unions** or the **International Trade Union Confederation**. In 2010, a strike movement was the beginning of popular protest that turned to be an introduction to the resignation of President Mubarak in 2011. The military council that took power soon issued a ban on strikes.

EL SALVADOR. Organized labor formed its first national federation in 1922; a reformed federation was set up in 1924 and drew support from plantation workers. A revolt in 1932 against the dismissal of the elected government by the military dictatorship of Maximiliano H. Martinez was savagely repressed with the slaughter of up to 20,000 peasants, an event that cowed organized labor until the mid-1950s. In 1957, the *Organización Regional Interamericana de Trabajadores* (ORIT), or Inter-American Regional Organization of Workers, held a congress that resulted in the foundation of the *Confederación General de Sindicatos* (General Confederation of Labor Unions) in 1958 and its swift affiliation to the **International Confederation of Free Trade Unions**. Although some liberalization was extended to organized labor by the government from 1962, mainly in response to fears caused by the communist revolution in **Cuba**, progress was limited by the inequitable distribution of land ownership, unemployment, and vigilante violence, as well by the dependence of the economy on a few staples such as coffee for its growth. The country was torn apart by civil war from 1980 to 1992, during which perhaps 10,000 trade unionists lost their lives. Since 1992, organized labor has continued to face hostility from the government and legislative restrictions; for example, El Salvador only ratified International Labor Convention No. 87 (Freedom of Association and Protection of the Right to Organize) in 2006, but it has so far not come into force. In 2009, the new left-wing administration legally registered trade unions. Private companies continued to intimidate workers and deny their right to organize.

EMPLOYERS' ORGANIZATIONS. Employers' organizations, like labor unions, have existed at least since Adam Smith's well-known discussion of their secret activities in *The Wealth of Nations* (Book I, Chapter VIII) in 1776. As shapers of national labor policy or participants in **collective bargaining**, formal employers' organizations in most countries emerged after 1880 partly in response to strikes and the rise of organized labor. The general pattern was usually for employers in an industry to organize first and create a national body later. In the **United Kingdom**, the ship owners formed a national federation in 1890, as did the engineering employers in 1896; the engineering federation organized two lockouts in 1896 and 1922 and defeated the unions both times. In 1919, the British Employers' Confederation was formed. In 1965, the Confederation of British Industry was created from a merger of the British Employers' Confederation, the Federation of British Industries, and the National Association of British Manufactures. The Chambers of Commerce remained separate from these bodies.

In the **United States**, the shoemakers' employers organized an association as early as 1789. In 1899, the National Metal Trades Association was formed. The National Association of Manufacturers was set up in 1895, and in 1903 it adopted an "open shop" policy to fight unions. The Chamber of Commerce of the United States was founded in 1912. In **France**, the *Le Chapelier* law of 1791 banned organizations by employees and employers but was largely enforced only against labor unions. The legislation that legalized unions in 1884 also legalized employers to form organizations, but those organizations that were created were confined to particular industries. A national employers' organization was only created in 1919 and even then was set up at the behest of the government; it was dissolved in 1940. The present principal employers' organization in France, the *Conseil National du Patronat Français,* was created in 1945. In **Germany**, a national federation of employers in manufacturing (*Vereinigung der Deutschen Arbeiterverbände*) was formed in 1913; it was joined by another national body (*Reichsverband der Deutschen Industrie*) in 1919. The **November Pact (Stinnes-Legien Agreement)** of

1918 encouraged the formation of employers' organizations by making such associations responsible for representing employers in **collective bargaining**. In the 1930s, the Nazis incorporated the employers' organizations into the *Deutsche Arbeitsfront*.

In 1950, the West German employers created the first comprehensive national employers' organization, the *Bundesvereinigung der Deutschen Arbeitgeberverbände* (Confederation of German Employers' Associations) to conduct national collective bargaining. In **Italy**, a national employers' organization was established in 1910; it became known by its shortened title, *Confindustria* (Confederation of Industry), after 1920. In 1923, *Confindustria* successfully opposed a proposal by the fascist government of Benito Mussolini to integrate employers and unions in one body; it retained its autonomy and went on to remain a part of industrial relations in Italy after 1945.

In **Japan**, a national federation of chambers of commerce was formed in 1892. In 1917, the Japan Economic Federation was formed to prevent the legal recognition of labor unions. In 1938, the government set up the Greater Japan Patriotic Industrial Association (known as *Sampō*); all employers' organizations and unions were forced to join this body as part of the war effort in June 1940. *Nikkeiren*, the Japanese Federation of Employers' Associations, was formed in 1948.

In **Australia**, the first employers' organizations designed to deal with unions were formed by coal mine owners in 1872. The first national body was formed by building employers in 1890. In 1903, the various State Chambers of Manufactures formed a national body. Until the 1970s, employers' organizations were largely state-based and relatively ineffective as national organizations. In 1977, the first national umbrella employer organization, the Confederation of Australian Industry, was formed as a counterpart to the **Australian Council of Trade Unions**; in 1992, this body merged with the Australian Chamber of Commerce to form the Australian Chamber of Commerce and Industry. The Business Council of Australia, a group of large employers, was created in 1983 to shape industrial policy. In **New Zealand**, the New Zealand Federation of Employers' Associations was formed in 1902. In 1992, the New Zealand Employers' Federation had 10,000 individual employer members and 51 affiliated business organizations as members. The New Zealand Business Roundtable, an employer body made up of large firms, was created in the mid-1970s to discuss and prepare general economic policies.

The International Organization of Employers, formed in 1920, is the only international body of its kind; it provides the employers' representatives to the **International Labour Organization** of 150 national organizations from 143 countries.

EMPLOYMENT ACTS. Between 1980 and 1993, Conservative governments in the **United Kingdom** introduced a number of laws to limit the power of labor unions, following the **"winter of discontent."** The Employment Act of 1980 limited **picketing** to employees who were directly engaged in a **strike**, expanded the exemptions from the closed shop, introduced public funding for secret ballots for the election of full-time union officials, and required secret ballots before unions engaged in strikes. The idea of strike ballots was first suggested in the Conservative Party's policy paper, *Fair Deal at Work,* which was published in 1968 and was also recommended for certain kinds of strikes in a **British Labour Party** policy document, *In Place of Strife,* published in 1969. The Employment Act of 1982 outlawed the pre-entry closed shop and demanded that post-entry closed shops must be supported by 85 percent of employees in a ballot. The secret ballot provisions of the 1980 act were boycotted by the **Trades Union Congress** and had little effect.

In 1984, the government published a Green Paper (a statement of government proposals) on proposed changes to the industrial law, which reintroduced the debate about public funding for secret ballots for the election of full-time union officials and before industrial disputes. This was followed by a White Paper (a statement of government intentions) and the Trade Union Act of 1984, which required secret ballots for the election of full-time officials and for the holding of strikes not more than four weeks before they were due to start; the strike provision came into force on 26 September 1984. The Employment Act of 1988 enabled a union member to apply to the court for legal action against the union if it engaged in industrial action without the support of a ballot. The Employment Act of 1990 provided for a right of complaint to an industrial tribunal for any employee refused employment because he or she did or did not belong to a union, made unions potentially liable for common law actions if any of their officials (including shop stewards) initiated industrial action without written repudiation, and gave employers greater power to dismiss employees who engaged in unofficial industrial action. This act has been interpreted as a return to the **Taff Vale Case**.

The Trade Union Reform and Employment Rights Act 1993 became law on 1 July and built on the trends evident in British labor law since 1980. Among other things, the law created a new legal right that enabled any individual, employer, or union member whose supply of goods and services was affected by a dispute that did not meet these conditions to initiate civil law proceedings against the union. The legislation also required unions about to engage in a labor dispute to conduct first an independently scrutinized postal ballot among members and to provide the employer with at least seven days' written notice.

The election of the British Labour Party in May 1997 did not result in the repeal of these employment acts, and although the level of labor disputes in the United Kingdom was low in the 1990s, this decline seems to have been caused by economic circumstances rather than the legislative environment. *See also* DONOVAN COMMISSION.

EQUAL PAY FOR EQUAL WORK. Equal pay for equal work originally refers to **women** receiving the same pay as men provided they perform work of equal value. In the **United States**, equal pay for women was raised as early as 1837. In the **United Kingdom**, the **Trades Union Congress** passed resolutions in support of equal pay for women in the 1890s. Union support for equal pay, although based on **human rights** concerns, was also influenced by the desire to prevent women from being used to undercut union wage rates. The entry of large numbers of women into jobs traditionally done by men, such as in transportation or metal working, was generally only tolerated in wartime, but they were expected to leave these jobs at war's end. In the United Kingdom, women were only admitted to the **Amalgamated Engineering Union** in 1942. In **Australia**, industrial tribunals set women's pay rates at 55 percent that of men's in the 1920s and 1930s and raised them to 75 percent in 1950.

In 1951, the **International Labour Organization** adopted the Equal Remuneration Convention (No. 100), which called for equal pay for men and women for work of equal value. In 1958, the Australian state of New South Wales introduced "equal pay for equal work" legislation, which was followed by the other states by 1968. In 1969 and 1972, the Australian federal industrial tribunal handed down decisions in favor of equal pay for equal work for employees covered by federal awards. In 1970, the United Kingdom government introduced the Equal Pay Act. Despite these changes, women's pay in the private sector still lags behind men's.

Since modern globalization, a pay gap also exists between the established and migrants. Permanent staff accuses migrants of bringing down wages while temporary workers are angry about being underpaid for doing the same job as colleagues. The unions' response to this is to demand equal pay for equal work.

EQUATORIAL GUINEA. Independent of **Spain** since October 1968, organized labor in Equatorial Guinea never had the opportunity to develop, either under Spanish rule or since independence. In 1976, the London-based Anti-Slavery Society published a report on **forced labor** and **slavery** in Equatorial Guinea. In 1990, the independent Equatorial Guinea Trade Union was formed, but failed to gain legal recognition or any reform of the country's denial of trade union rights. The Independent Services Trade Union in the

public sector has also been unable to secure legal recognition since 1995. Despite the government's ratification of the eight core labor standards of the **International Labour Organization** in 2001, it has since then suppressed all attempts to create independent labor unions, according to the **International Trade Union Confederation (ITUC)**. In 2008, a strike at a Chinese company was brutally repressed: two workers were killed, about 100 were arrested, and 400 were repatriated. There were no **strikes** in 2009 and Equatorial Guinea was not represented in the ITUC .

ERITREA. Eritrea was formed as an independent nation in 1993 after a 30 years' war against **Ethiopia**. By 1995, the National Confederation of Eritrean Workers (founded in 1979) had been admitted to affiliation to the **International Confederation of Free Trade Unions**; it was closely monitored by the government, however. As a result of tensions with bordering countries, the Eritrean people have suffered from increasing repression and violations of union rights.

ESTONIA. Organized labor was only able to emerge in Estonia after it gained independence from **Russia** in 1921; previously it had been part of the Russian Empire. By 1923, there were 30,000 union members and a national labor federation had been formed by 1927 and joined the **International Federation of Trade Unions (IFTU)**. The number of union members reached 50,000 by 1932, and the national labor federation retained its membership of the IFTU until 1939. In 1940, an independent labor movement ceased to exist in Estonia, when, like the other **Baltic states**, it was annexed by the Soviet Union. From 1957 to 1994, the Estonian Seamen's Union was accorded membership in exile by the **International Confederation of Free Trade Unions (ICFTU)**.

In the late 1980s, the Soviet Union began to fragment, allowing organized labor to reemerge. In 1989, the communist labor federation of Estonia joined the independence movement. In March 1990, Estonia and the other Baltic states declared their independence from the Soviet Union. Nevertheless, the political climate remained dangerous, as was shown by the murder of two visiting Swedish union officials who made contact with the independent labor movement. Violations of union rights have since then been frequent. In 1994, Estonia became the first Baltic state to be represented in the ICFTU by the Association of Estonian Trade Unions; it claimed 65,000 members in 2001.

In 2000 the trade union law was adopted that guaranteed the right to organize. However, the recession of 2008 hit the economy hard and led to antiunion behavior in the private sector. The ban on strikes for public servants was prolonged for over 15 years.

ETHIOPIA. Although a member of the **International Labour Organization** from 1923, Ethiopia did not legally recognize labor unions until 1962 and unions had to form and operate secretly. The first union was formed among the railroad workers in 1947. In 1954, the unions formed the first national labor federation, which was reformed into the Confederation of Ethiopian Labour Unions (CELU) in 1963. Assisted by both the **International Confederation of Free Trade Unions (ICFTU)**, which it joined, and the **American Federation of Labor–Congress of Industrial Organizations**, the **membership** of the CELU grew from 28,000 in 1964 to 85,000 in 1974, but organized labor fell foul of the military council (the Dergue) that replaced Emperor Haile Selassie. The Dergue regime formed its own labor federation. Strikes were forbidden and the CELU was caught up in a policy of government hostility and prolonged civil war, economic destruction, and famine. In 1986, the CELU changed its name to the Confederation of Ethiopian Trade Unions (CETU) and in 1994, the CETU reaffiliated with the ICFTU. It ceased its membership by 1997 as it was brought increasingly under **government control**. In 2010, the **International Trade Union Confederation** reported that the government still closely monitored organized labor.

EUROPEAN TRADE UNION CONFEDERATION (ETUC). The ETUC is the major international labor organization of Western Europe. Although the **International Federation of Trade Unions** was mainly a European body for most of its life between 1901 and 1945, the first moves to form a regional labor federation of European bodies were made in November 1950 when the **International Confederation of Free Trade Unions (ICFTU)** established the European Regional Organization. The creation of the European Coal and Steel Community prompted a number of national labor federations as well as the **International Metalworkers' Federation** and the **Miners' International Federation** to form the Committee of Twenty-One to represent the interests of organized labor. Following the creation of the European Economic Community by the Treaty of Rome in 1958, the ICFTU formed the European Trade Union Secretariat, which incorporated the Committee of Twenty-One.

Further changes in the structure of Western European organized labor were also prompted by wider changes in the supranational European political framework. In 1968, the ICFTU members of the Free Trade Area set up the Trade Union Committee for the European Free Trade Area. In 1969, the European Trade Union Secretariat reshaped itself as the European Confederation of Free Trade Unions. In February 1973, these two bodies agreed to merge as the **European Trade Union Confederation (ETUC)**. Up to 1991, the membership of the ETUC was largely confined to noncommunist labor bodies in Western Europe, but since that time, the ETUC has admitted affiliates from Eastern European countries.

The ETUC has always operated as a lobbying body for organized labor, but at its 1991 congress it resolved to take an active role in **collective bargaining** for the whole of Europe. Its role assumed added significance after the signing of the **European Union** Treaty (7 February 1992); appended to the treaty was a social policy agreement that gave European-wide labor and **employers' organizations** an enhanced formal role in preparing and implementing the social policy of the European Union. In December 1993, the ETUC was one of three European-wide labor bodies that were granted formal "social partner" status by the European Commission for European-wide dialogue on social policy matters.

Although both the Commission and the ETUC wanted to advance this dialogue to collective bargaining, this course has been opposed by the Union of Industrial and Employers' Confederations of Europe even though the ETUC had reached an agreement with the European Center of Public Enterprises for such a move in September 1990. In 1994, the ETUC claimed 46 million members (compared with 37 million in 1973) in 21 countries. In 2009, the ETUC had 82 national labor federations as affiliates from a total of 36 European countries representing a total of 60 million members. *See also CONFÉDÉRATION EUROPÉENNE DES CADRES.*

EUROPEAN UNION (EU). The EU has its origins in the European Economic Community in 1957; its present title dates from 1 November 1993. The rise of the EU has been paralleled by changes in the **European Trade Union Confederation (ETUC)**, the primary lobby group for European organized labor. The EU's concern with economic and social issues, particularly since the 1970s, has made it an increasingly important vehicle through which European labor can try to achieve its objectives. The European Union Treaty, signed at Maastricht on 7 February 1992, appended a social policy agreement that gave European-wide organized labor and **employers' organizations** an enhanced formal role in the social policy of the European Union. In 1993, the European Commission formally recognized the ETUC and the *Confédération Européenne des Cadres* as "social partners" for European-wide dialogue on social policy matters. In August 1994, the European Commission's White Paper on Social Policy recognized employers' organizations, labor unions, and voluntary associations as partners in the development of social policy. In 1996, the European Commission directive on European Works' Councils came into force; it meant that any company with more than 1,000 employees, of whom at least 150 worked in a minimum of two EU member countries, had to set up a work's council or at least a formal procedure for informing and consulting staff about matters affecting their working lives. In 1999, a European Commission directive setting a limit on **working hours** became operational in the **United Kingdom**.

In 2000, the EU adopted the Lisbon Agenda intended to make Europe the most competitive economy in the world. To obtain this, labor was supposed to accept liberalization. In reaction in 2003 and 2006 longshoremen successfully struck Europe-wide to oppose liberalization of port labor as stipulated in an EU directive. In February 2002, the EU, after much lobbying by the **International Confederation of Free Trade Unions**, incorporated trade union rights in its regulations on tariff preferences for 2002–2004.

EXPORT PROCESSING ZONE (EPZ). Also known as Free Trade Zones or *maquiladores* or *maquilas* (assembly plants), the term *EPZ* refers to areas designated by governments in Third World countries since the 1960s where foreign companies can produce goods and services with minimal taxation and without the legal restraints of the labor regulations that might apply elsewhere in the country. In practice, export processing zones are generally zones of exploitation for their employees, characterized by low wages and poor working conditions. EPZs were first set up in northern **Mexico** on the U.S. border in 1965. The first EPZ in Africa was established in **Mauritius** in 1970 and Asian countries followed, beginning with the **Philippines**. Labor unions are either prohibited or actively discouraged by violence. In 2002, the **International Confederation of Free Trade Unions** estimated that about 80 percent of employees in EPZs were **women** and that they earned about half of what their male counterparts were paid. There were about 3,500 EPZs in the world in 2006 employing 66 million workers, of which 40 million were Chinese.

FALKLAND ISLANDS. A British dependency, which was successfully retaken by the **United Kingdom** after the Argentine invasion in June 1982, the Falkland Islands has only one labor union, the General Employees Union; formed in 1943, it has been an affiliate of the **International Confederation of Free Trade Unions** since 1949. Between 1975 and 1990, the membership of the General Employees Union fell from 450 to 150. There were no affiliates from the Falkland Islands in the **International Trade Union Confederation** in 2010.

FÉDÉRATION INTERNATIONALE DES EMPLOYÉS, TECHNICIENS ET CADRES **(FIET).** The FIET, or the International Federation of Commercial, Clerical, Professional, and Technical Employees, was an **international trade secretariat** formed in 1921 from a failed earlier international clerical body that had operated from Hamburg, **Germany**, between 1909 and 1914. The FIET was primarily a European body until 1949, after which time it expanded into other continents. The main industries represented by the FIET were in the **service sector**: banking, insurance, commerce, retailing, and social services. Between 1976 and 1994, the affiliated membership of the FIET rose from 6.2 to 11 million. It is based in Geneva. In January 2000, the FIET merged with **Communications International**, the **International Graphical Federation**, and the **Media Entertainment International** to form the **Union Network International**. *See also* WHITE-COLLAR UNIONISM.

FEDERATION OF INTERNATIONAL CIVIL SERVANTS' ASSOCIATIONS (FICSA). Founded in 1952, the FICSA represents the staff employed by the United Nations and its specialized agencies, including the **International Labour Organization**. Based in Geneva and New York, the FICSA had 29 affiliated associations or unions in 2009. *See also* WHITE-COLLAR UNIONISM.

FEDERAZIONE ITALIANA OPERAI METALLURGICI **(FIOM).** The FIOM (Italian Union of Metal Workers) was formed in 1901 and operated until 1924, when it was suppressed by the fascist government along with the other free unions in **Italy**. Its membership growth was slow, a reflection of the slow industrialization of the Italian economy. In 1906, it signed the first collective agreement in Italy, which gave the union the closed shop and the right of employees to elect members to grievance committees. From 10,000 members in 1913, it had only reached 40,000 by 1918, but by 1920 it had grown to 152,000, a rise that reflected the demands of World War I. By 1923 its membership had fallen to 20,000. It was revived in 1944. A union known for its militancy in the 1960s, its **membership** grew from 167,000 in 1968 to 278,700 in 1972, when it merged with two other metal unions to form an **industrial union** for the metal industry.

FIJI. Labor unions were first formed in Fiji in 1939 but had an unstable history, largely in response to the ethnic tensions between Indians and native Fijians, with unions tending to be either ethnically Indian or native Fijian. In 1957, the Fiji Industrial Workers' Congress, which had been formed in 1952, was admitted to membership of the **International Confederation of Free Trade Unions (ICFTU)**, thereby becoming the third part of Oceania to be a member after **New Zealand** and **Australia**. In 1966, the Fiji Industrial Workers' Congress was reformed as the Fiji Trade Union Congress; by 1975, it had 23,000 members. In 1970, Fiji became an independent democratic nation from **Britain**, but by the late 1980s economic difficulties fed racial tensions between native Fijians and the economically better-off Indian Fijians, who made up about half the population. Two military coups in support of the rights of native Fijians in 1987 resulted in restrictions on labor unions and the reintroduction of the Tripartite Forum, made up of unions, employers, and government representatives. Fiji's poor economic performance undercut efforts to attain political stability. There was another coup in May 2000 by elements of the military, although civilian rule was restored with military support in July 2000. At that date an estimated 55 percent of the employees were unionized. In 2002, the ICFTU reported that although **collective bargaining** and the right to **strike** are legally recognized, there was a general failure by the government to enforce these rights. It remained relatively easy for employers to dismiss trade union activists, particularly after the military takeover in December 2006. At first, the provisional government was inclined to respect trade union rights, but over time it has come to view organized labor as one of its opponents.

FIMMEN, EDO (EDUARD CARL) (1881–1942). President of the International Transport Workers' Federation, Fimmen was born in Nieuwer Amstel (now part of Amsterdam) in the **Netherlands** to German-born parents. He was fluent in French, German, and English. By the early 1900s, Fimmen was a committed protestant Christian, antimilitarist, and socialist, and had adopted the pseudonym *Edo*. He campaigned against prostitution and in favor of **equal pay** for **women**. He was employed as clerk and, following a **general strike** in 1903, he helped found the General Dutch Federation of Trade and Office Clerks in October 1905. In January 1906, this federation affiliated with the new Netherlands Federation of Labor Unions and Fimmen became its secretary in 1907, holding the position until February 1916 and then serving the federation in other roles until 1919.

As early as 1910, Fimmen began to be active in international labor unions when he became a secretary of the German-based International Shop Assistants Secretariat. World War I interrupted his activities, but in April 1919 he became secretary of the **International Transport Workers Federation (ITF)**. He used this position to organize opposition to the Allied intervention against the Soviet Union, to support left-wing politics, oppose fascism, and to help union leaders he knew personally who suffered in fascist countries. The priority he gave politics, particularly his support for cooperation with communists as opposed to purely labor union activities, drew criticism from some within the federation. The ITF itself was weakened by the loss of member organizations in fascist Italy, Spain, and Germany; in 1931, it had a **membership** of 2.3 million, compared with 3 million in 1920. He organized a conference of the exiled union leaders in April 1935. Illness and the outbreak of World War II in 1939 forced Fimmen to leave Europe for Mexico, where he died. He is remembered as an outstanding leader of the ITF, which honored him in 1942 and 1952. A statue for Fimmen was erected in Rotterdam in 1997 to celebrate the centennial of the ITF. Fimmen wrote a number of publications, including two in English, *The International Federation of Trade Unions* (1922) and *Labour's Alternative: The United States of Europe or Europe Limited* (1924).

FINLAND. Organized labor in Finland emerged on a significant scale in the 1900s. In 1907, at the initiative of the Social Democratic Party, 18 unions held a congress that claimed a total **membership** of 25,000 out of 175,000 nonagricultural employees. Strongly influenced by **communism**, this body was banned by the government in 1930, and the Social Democratic Party reorganized a noncommunist body, the *Suomen Ammattiliittojen Keskusjärjestö* (SAK), or Central Organization of Finnish Trade Unions. In 1922, a separate **white-collar** federation was formed to restore real pay levels, which had been sharply eroded by the inflation that followed World War I; the white-collar federation, unlike the other labor federation, was politically independent. After a steady growth, organized labor collapsed at the end of the 1920s.

Political oppression and the legal ban of organized labor in 1929 and 1930 caused union coverage of Finnish employees to collapse to 5 percent in 1930, compared with 25 percent in 1920, but it recovered strongly after 1944 with the improvement of the political climate for labor. Between 1965 and 1970, union **membership** in Finland rose from 642,900 to 945,300, raising its coverage of employees from 42 to 57 percent, an increase brought about by diminished internal conflict within organized labor, the introduction in 1960 of the **Ghent system** of unemployment insurance, and the establishment of a centralized **collective bargaining** system. The SAK remained the dominant labor federation in the post-1945 period; in 2010, it had 800,000 members compared with the Confederation of Unions for Professional and Managerial Staff (382,000) and the Finnish Confederation of Professionals (418,000). Despite economic difficulties, Finnish organized labor continues to cover the majority of employees and its officials are well represented in Parliament.

FLAGS OF CONVENIENCE (FOC). An international system of merchant ship registration whereby a ship owner in a country with a Western economy registers ships in a Third World country to avoid paying high taxes and wages and providing good working conditions; the system began in the 1920s when U.S. ship owners began registering ships in **Panama**. Since the 1970s, the share of global merchant shipping sailing under flags of convenience has risen from 20 to over 50 percent. The **International Transport Workers' Federation (ITF)** has denounced the FOC system since 1948. Often poorly maintained, FOC ships are more prone to accidents that cause environmental damage. In 2000, twice as many FOC ships were shipwrecked as other ships. The ITF has estimated that about 2,000 merchant sailors a year die in accidents at sea, mainly in FOC ships. In 2002, the top FOC countries were Panama, **Liberia**, **Malta**, **Bahamas**, and **Cyprus**. The top ship ownership countries of FOCs were **Greece**, **Japan**, the **United States**, **Norway**, and **Hong Kong SAR**. In 2009, the ITF covered about a quarter of FOC vessels with global agreements, ensuring basic pay and conditions to over 123,000 seafarers.

FORCED LABOR. Throughout recorded history, the performance of the work needed by society has been linked with coercion. Labor in classical Greek and Roman society depended heavily on agricultural laborers tied to the land and **slavery**. With the rise of market economies in Western Europe after 1300, the first free labor forces in the modern sense of the term began to emerge slowly on a significant scale. Although most working people had effectively little economic freedom, the Industrial Revolution brought a far greater range of choices of employment and the crude notion of a forced labor force receded, although pockets of feudal arrangements remained even in the **United Kingdom**; for example, Scottish coal miners were not fully emancipated from lifetime bondage until 1799. Slavery was abolished in the British Empire in 1807, in the **United States** in 1865, and was the target of an international conference in 1890. Serfdom in **Russia** was abolished in 1861. Forced labor in a legal sense in **Britain** became confined to convicts, who were exported to North America from 1655 to 1776 and **Australia** until 1868. Within British prisons, labor was regarded by the authorities as therapeutic and useful for offsetting administrative costs. Before World War II, forced labor in some form and to varying degrees was a feature of the African colonies of **Belgium** and **France**.

Organized labor has generally been hostile to prison labor because it could be used to undercut the price of goods produced by union members. In 1934, the U.S. Supreme Court denied the state of Alabama an injunction to stop the sale of goods made by prisoners. Nazi **Germany** and **Japan** both made extensive use of forced labor by civilians as well as by prisoners of war. Forced labor has also been a feature of communist regimes, notably in the former Soviet Union. The **International Labour Organization** passed a Convention against Forced Labor (No. 29) in 1930. The **International Confederation of Free Trade Unions** and its successor, the **International Trade Union Confederation**, have repeatedly denounced the use of forced labor in a number of countries, most notably **Burma**. In 2010, 12.3 million people are supposed to be in forced labor.

FRANCE. Early forms of labor organization existed in France long before the effects of the Industrial Revolution became evident during the 19th century. For example, there is a record of a **strike** by vineyard workers in Burgundy as early as 1393 and by printers at Lyons in the 16th century. As in **Britain**, journeymen were the leaders in forming labor unions. Following the revolution in 1789, journeymen carpenters in Paris took advantage of its promise of political freedom by forming a union in 1790, but the employers objected and it was suppressed by the law *Le Chapelier* (1791), which was also applied to **employers' organizations** and made strikes illegal. Despite the legal prohibition on strikes, there was a revolt by silk workers in Lyons after the government attempted to suppress labor unions in April 1834. Some progress toward peaceful labor relations occurred in the early 1840s, as evidenced by the making of a collective agreement in the printing industry in 1843, but otherwise the government was quick to use force against the working class, as shown by the "June Days" in 1848, when it shut down employment workshops for the unemployed, a move that resulted in some thousands of deaths and the arrest of thousands of others.

In 1862, a deputation of French labor leaders was allowed by Napoleon III to visit the London Exposition. They returned with a high opinion of English working conditions and unions and asked to be granted freedom of association and the right to strike. Strikes were legalized in 1864, but, although legalizing unions was considered in 1868, nothing was done. In 1869, the Comte de Paris published a sympathetic study, *The Trade Unions of England,* which was reprinted six times, but the official attitude toward unions was colored by the bloodshed of the Paris Commune (1871).

By the 1880s, the government realized that there were advantages to encouraging labor unions as a means of tempering revolutionary tendencies by the working class. In 1884, it legalized strikes and labor unions and provided financial assistance to the *Bourses du Travail* (the coordinating centers for local unions), provided they remained out of the control of political extremists. The first national trade union center (the *Fédération Nationale des Syndicats Ouvriers* [National Federation of Workers' Union]) was opened in 1886. A **Catholic** labor union was formed among **white-collar** workers in 1887, the first sign of an important division within French organized labor; the Catholic unions went on to form their own national labor federation in 1919. **Collective bargaining** began in the **coal mining** industry in northern France, but remained limited in scope because of the importance of small enterprises in the economy. In 1895, a new national labor federation, the *Confédération Générale du Travail* (CGT), or General Federation of Labor, was formed; it absorbed the National Federation of *Bourses du Travail* (founded in 1892) in 1902. **Syndicalism**, a doctrine that had its origins in the revolutionary tradition of France, became an important influence on organized labor, particularly with its emphasis on the use of **general strikes**.

Yet French organized labor never attained the strength of its counterparts in other major European countries. In 1920, a high-water mark for organized labor in Europe, only 12 percent of French employees were members of unions, compared with 53 percent in **Germany**, 39 percent in **Italy**, and 48 percent in the **United Kingdom**. Subsequently, French labor was weakened by divisions caused by **communists**. Despite the **Matignon Agreement** in 1936, which provided for the unions' right to organize, an end to antiunion practices, collective bargaining, pay increases, and the election of shop stewards, French organized labor remained relatively weak even though an impression of strength might have been created by dramatic events such as the national disturbances of May 1968. Although the reasons for the weakness of French organized labor since 1945 are complicated, they stem in large part from its deep political and religious divisions. Aside from the Catholic labor federation, the *Confédération Française des Travailleurs Chrétiens* (French Confederation of Christian Workers, formed in 1919), the most important division occurred in April 1948 when the noncommunist unions of the CGT withdrew and formed their own federation, the *Confédération Générale du Travail-Force Ouvrière* (CGT-FO), or General Confederation of Labor-Workers' Strength. A third national labor federation, the *Confédéra-*

tion Française Démocratique (CFDT) or French Democratic Confederation of Labor, was formed in 1964.

From a high point of 38 percent of employees in unions in 1950, there was a steady decline thereafter to 21 percent in 1960 and 17 percent in 1980. Between 1989 and 2001, union coverage of French employees fell from 11 to 9 percent, the lowest level for any large Western industrialized country. Also, unlike most other Western industrialized countries, France still has no single, dominant national labor federation. In 2001, organized labor was divided between three national federations: the CGT (650,000 members), the CGT-FO (300,000 members), and the CFDT (765,000 members). Yet despite its very low level of union membership, France has experienced a high level of **labor disputes** in recent years compared with Germany and the United Kingdom, particularly surrounding the introduction of the 35-hour week in February 2000. In May and June 2003, the unions conducted rolling strikes in protest over government plans to reform the government **pension** scheme. This conflict was still not solved in 2010 and the **International Trade Union Confederation** noted obstacles to trade union activities.

Activists sometimes face discrimination such as disciplinary sanctions or suspension of their careers. In addition, the **International Labour Organization** received a complaint concerning the creation of police files about trade union participation. These files are considered a threat to union activity.

FREEDOM OF ASSOCIATION. The **International Labour Organization** (ILO) first considered drafting a Convention on Freedom of Association to protect labor unions in 1925, a concern prompted by the incorporation of unions under **government control** in fascist **Italy**. Among the ILO member countries of the time, there were two main kinds of laws relating to unions. Under the first kind of law, unions were unlawful unless their formation and operation were authorized by the government. Under the second kind of law, unions were legally recognized and operated without government control. Examples of countries following this second kind of law were the **United Kingdom** (1871), **New Zealand** (1878), and **France** (1884). However, the 1925 proposal failed, mainly because the representatives of organized labor within the **International Federation of Free Trade Unions** were unable to agree on a course of action, with some fearing that such a convention could limit the freedoms the unions already had. The present ILO Convention (87) on Freedom of Association and Protection of the Right to Organize was not passed until 1948. It was augmented by Convention No. 98 (Right to Organize and Collective Bargaining) in 1949. The ILO established the Freedom of Association Committee to monitor the operation of these conventions in 1951.

FRENCH POLYNESIA. Acquired piecemeal by **France** by 1889, organized unions in this group of south Pacific islands were mainly overseas branches of French unions. In 1990, a Polynesian union based on Tahiti, *A Tia I Mua,* was admitted to **membership** of the **International Confederation of Free Trade Unions** as the affiliate for French Polynesia with 5,000 members, although the largest labor union in French Polynesia is the Confederation of Workers' Union of Polynesia. Unions organized a **general strike** in June 2010 against the government to create a national unemployment insurance in response to job losses following the economic crisis. After two weeks, the dispute was settled and the **International Labour Organizations** asked to look into the feasibility of an unemployment fund.

FRIENDLY SOCIETY. A friendly society (or mutual society, benevolent society, or fraternal organization) is a mutual association for insurance, **pensions**, savings, or banking. People joined together for a common financial or social purpose. Before the existence of modern insurance and the welfare state, these kinds of societies provided financial and social services to individuals. Friendly societies therefore were important in many people's lives. Many of these societies still exist. Early unions often served the same purpose and sometimes even grew out of a friendly society. The historical relationship between unions and European medieval guilds that also were a kind of friendly societies is, however, disputed. *See also* NORWAY; RAILROADS.

FULL-TIME/PART-TIME EMPLOYMENT. Before the 1960s, most employees in Western countries were employed full time; that is, they worked about 40 or 44 hours a week. Part-time employment emerged in the early 1930s as a temporary expedient to cope with the Depression. With the entry of more **women** into the labor force, particularly married women, there was a growth in demand for fewer working hours. Official labor force household surveys in many countries collect statistics on full-time and part-time employment—with full-time employment defined as 35 hours or more a week—and these have shown a general rise in part-time employment since the 1970s. In 1994, the **International Labour Organization** adopted a convention to protect the conditions of part-time workers.

Organized labor has generally found it harder to recruit part-time workers as members, as was shown by results from labor force surveys in 2010. In the **United States**, 13 percent of full-time employees were union members, but only 6 percent of part-time employees. In the **United Kingdom**, 28 percent of full-time employees were union members compared with 21 percent of part-time employees. *See also* WORKING HOURS.

G

GABON. Gabon has been independent of **France** since 1960, and indigenous organized labor developed along the French model. One of its labor federations was an affiliate of the **International Confederation of Free Trade Unions (ICFTU)** by 1965, with 6,100 members. In 1964, Gabon became a one-party state and formed a single labor federation under party control from the country's 70 unions in 1969; the 1978, labor law reaffirmed this system. The government-aligned union center COSYGA (formerly known as Gabonese Trade Union Confederation) evolved into a more independent organization after 1991. In the same year the *Confédération Gabonaise des Syndicats Libres* (CGSL), or Confederation of Free Trade Unions of Gabon, was formed. By 1992, this independent union had become affiliated to the ICFTU and gained government recognition as Gabon's second labor federation. The CGSL conducted an unsuccessful **general strike** in February 1992 over inflation and falling living standards. The political environment for organized labor in Gabon is difficult. Although the right to strike exists in theory, in practice it does not and trade unionists are regularly harassed, dismissed, or beaten up. In 2010, the president restricted the right to strike. The two labor federations are represented in the **International Trade Union Confederation** and have a combined **membership** of 42,000.

GAMBIA. Gambia has been independent of the **United Kingdom** since 1965, and organized labor in Gambia began effectively in October 1928 when the Gambia Labour Union (GLU) was formed by Edward Francis Small (1890–1957) and the first **strike** was conducted. In 1935, the GLU was officially registered under the 1932 Trade Union Act. By 1953, the GLU was affiliated with the **International Confederation of Free Trade Unions**. By 1965, the Gambia Workers' Union, founded in 1958, had replaced the GLU as Gambia's ICFTU affiliate; its **membership** was small, being only 3,000 by 1988. Gambia is remarkable for being one of the few African countries not named in the survey of **violations of trade union rights** since 2002.

GENERAL AND MUNICIPAL WORKERS' UNION (GMWU). The GMWU was one of the largest labor unions in the **United Kingdom** from its formation on 1 July 1924 following the **amalgamation** of three unions: the National Union of General Workers, which was founded by Will Thorne (1857–1946) in 1889 as the National Union of Gasworkers and General Labourers of Great Britain and Ireland (it had 202,000 members in 1924); the National Amalgamated Union of Labour, which had about 53,000 members in 1924; and the Municipal Employees' Association, which was founded in 1894 and had about 40,000 members in 1924. Known officially as the *National Union of General and Municipal Workers,* the GMWU drew the bulk of its **membership** from lesser skilled employees, particularly those in the gas industry and local government. There was much overlap between the kinds of employees it recruited and those of similar general unions, particularly the **Transport and General Workers' Union**.

At its creation, the GMWU had 298,200 members. This number fell during the Depression to 207,700 in 1932, but by 1940 the GMWU had 493,740 members and 715,460 by 1950. Between 1945 and 1992, the GMWU was Britain's third largest union in most years. Membership rose to 786,140 by 1962 and to a peak of 964,800 in 1979. An important feature of this growth was the share of **women** members. Between 1924 and 1940, the proportion of women members in the GMWU rose from 9 to 18 percent and to 20 percent by 1950. By 1976, 34 percent of the total membership were women, a proportion that had increased to 36 percent in 1994. In 1972, the GMWU set up a new section to recruit **white-collar** employees.

Between 1963 and 1979, the GMWU absorbed five small unions. In 1982, it combined with the Amalgamated Society of Boilermakers, Shipwrights, Blacksmiths, and Structural Workers (itself a production of amalgamation with other unions, the oldest of which was formed in 1834) to create the General Municipal, Boilermakers' and Allied Trade Union. In 1989, this union amalgamated with the Association of Professional Executive, Clerical, and Computer Staff (originally formed as the National Union of Clerks in 1890) to form a union known simply as the **GMB**.

GENERAL FEDERATION OF TRADE UNIONS (GFTU). The GFTU was formed in Manchester, England, in January 1899 by a number of relatively large unions, including the **Amalgamated Society of Engineers** with 85,000 members, the Gas and General Labourers' Union (with 48,000 members), the National Amalgamated Union of Labour with 22,000 members, and the National Union of Boot and Shoe Operatives (with 22,000 members). A moderate body, the purpose of the GFTU was to provide mutual support and to resolve **labor disputes**. At its formation, its constituents had about 310,400 members or about a quarter that of the **Trades Union Congress** (TUC), which regarded the GFTU as a competitor. Although the GFTU aspired to be a large organization, it found it difficult to move beyond representing **craft unions**, a feature that won it respect and support from **Samuel Gompers**. The number of members it represented rose from 884,000 in 1912 to over a million by 1920, but the withdrawal of the ASE in 1915 and other unions severely weakened the GFTU. The general secretary of the GFTU from 1907 to 1938 was William A. Appleton (1859–1940). As well as its useful role in labor dispute settlements and labor **politics**, the GFTU was **Britain**'s representative in the **International Federation of Trade Unions** until it was supplanted by the TUC between 1918 and 1922. In 2001, the GFTU had 34 affiliates, mainly smaller, skilled unions, and represented 252,000 members, compared with 277,900 in 1988. **Membership** was even lower in 2010 when numbers stopped at 215,000.

GENERAL STRIKES. General strikes, in the sense of a widespread **labor dispute** that affects a city, region, or country, feature prominently in the history of organized labor; there is no hard-and-fast definition because these labor disputes can assume a variety of forms. The followers of **anarchism** and **syndicalism** in the late 19th century and early 20th centuries saw the general strike as a means of overthrowing the existing social order and replacing it with a fairer one. They saw their view confirmed by the general strikes that took place in **Russia** during the 1905 revolution. The strike wave of the late 19th century was often an expression of working-class discontent, with many participants not being members of labor unions, as occurred in **Belgium** in 1893. A general strike could also be international in its effects; the Maritime Strike that was called by unions in eastern Australia in 1890 was also supported by unions in **New Zealand**. After 1900, general strikes were usually called by labor unions.

General strikes have also occurred in cities (for instance, Philadelphia in 1910; Brisbane, Australia, in 1912; Seattle in 1919; and Winnipeg, Canada, in 1919) and countries (such as Sweden in 1909 and Argentina in 1909 and 1919). The 1920s were a high point of the use of the general strike: **Portugal** (1919, 1920, and 1921), **France** (1920), **Norway** (1921), **Hong Kong SAR** (1922), **Egypt** (1923), **South Africa** (1922), and the **United Kingdom** (1926). Usually these general strikes were suppressed (for example, in **Cuba** in 1935 or in **Kenya** in 1950) by military force or led to punitive legal actions by the government (for instance in **South Korea** in 1946–1947). On occasions the general strike has achieved some improvements (for instance in Cuba after the general strike in 1933). Although general strikes have continued to occur in Western Europe since 1945—for instance in France (1947, 1968) and Denmark (1973)—their incidence has declined. Yet they remain an option for labor in an intolerable political environment, as happened in

Bulgaria in 1990 and **Bangladesh** in 1994. In the 1990s, general strikes, such as in Greece in 1998, have often centered on labor market reforms or **privatization**. Others, such as in **Venezuela** between December 2002 and January 2003, have had purely political objectives. Since 2008, the general strike has reemerged in Western Europe, particularly in **Greece**, **Portugal**, France, and **Spain**, to resist cuts in government expenditure caused by the financial crisis. *See also* BRITISH GENERAL STRIKE; "WINTER OF DISCONTENT."

GEORGIA. Part of the Russian Empire to November 1917, Georgia briefly enjoyed independence to 1921, when it was forced to join the Soviet Union. Always strongly nationalistic, Georgia's people began in 1988 to demand independence. In June 1990, Georgia's labor unions seceded from the Soviet trade unions and declared their political independence. Over the next three years, the Georgian labor unions fought against attempts by the communist government of Zviad Gamsakhurdia to take control of organized labor for his own ends. Finally, on 18 December 1992, Georgia's labor unions formed the Georgian Trade Union Amalgamation, consisting of 26 of the country's 30 unions. The Georgian economy in the first half of the 1990s was weakened by the victory of the separatist movement in Abkhazia (which resulted in an influx of 200,000 refugees), high inflation, and the general disruption caused by the transition to a free-market economy. In 2001, Georgia was admitted to affiliation with the **International Confederation of Free Trade Unions**. In 2007, the **International Trade Union Confederation** reported that the new Labour Code had diminished trade unions' bargaining rights since July 2006. The code also made it very easy to dismiss workers, for which the World Bank praised the code.

In 2008, a military conflict with Russia resulted in the loss of many lives, including trade union members. Fear of losing jobs caused 20,000 union members to leave their union. In 2010, conditions were still bad for **organized labor**.

GERMANY. In terms of historical importance and influence in Europe, organized labor in Germany has been second only to the **United Kingdom**. This importance derived not just from the numerical size of Germany's labor unions during the first two decades of the 20th century, but also from the pivotal role German labor leaders played in promoting international labor unionism. Organized labor came relatively late to Germany. The first national German labor union, the National Printers' Association (*Nationaler Buchdrucker-Verein*), was not established until 1848. Despite the spread of industrialization after 1850, political repression retarded the growth of unions. In 1861, the legal ban on labor unions was lifted in Saxony, followed by Weimar (1863) and the North German Confederation (1869), but there was no legal right to form unions. In 1863, Ferdinand Lasalle (1825–1864) founded the German Workingmen's Association, which had as one of its aims the legalizing of labor unions. Yet by 1869 there were only 77,000 union members, of whom 30,000 were enrolled in liberal or "yellow" **Hirsch-Duncker Trade Associations**. Further progress of organized labor was retarded by Otto von Bismarck's Anti-Socialist Laws of 1878, which were not repealed until 1890.

In 1892, German labor unions held their first national congress at which they agreed to encourage the formation of national and **industrial unions**. In 1894, the **Catholics** began organizing their own unions, a step that marked the beginning of the third division of pre-1933 German organized labor, along with the conservatives (the Hirsh-Duncker Trade Associations) and the **socialists** (the Free Trade Unions). By 1913, the Free Trade Unions had 2.5 million members, the Catholic unions 218,200, and the Hirsh-Duncker Trade Associations 106,600. At that time, Germany had the second highest total number of union members in the world after the United Kingdom. **White-collar** unions were formed after 1900, and their **membership** grew from 567,700 in 1906 to 941,300 by 1913. **Collective bargaining** also emerged during the 1900s; by 1913, two million employees were covered by agreements negotiated by collective bargaining.

World War I boosted membership to 10.5 million in 1920, but the hyperinflation of the war and the economic disruption that followed it made this level unsustainable. Nonetheless, the labor unions were largely responsible for the defeat of the right-wing Kapp *putsch* in Berlin in 1920. In 1923, the government created an **arbitration** service to deal with **labor disputes** and even made the service compulsory if the parties could not agree. The legitimacy of organized labor was not accepted by many large employers in the late 1920s. Between October and December 1928, 220,000 engineering employees were locked out by their employers in the Ruhr; and although the dispute was settled by mediators, the employers were harshly critical of their efforts. The economic downturn turned into full depression by 1931, and its resultant very high unemployment (44 percent by 1932) destroyed the power of organized labor and made its suppression by Adolf Hitler a relatively easy matter. On 2 May 1933, Germany's unions were suppressed and many of their leaders were sent to the Dachau concentration camp. The former unions were coordinated into the German Labor Front (***Deutsche Arbeitsfront***).

In reviewing the relative political weakness of German organized labor before 1933, it is important to realize that for all the industrial growth after 1850, a large part of the German economy remained in **agriculture**; even in 1933, the proportion of the labor force employed in agriculture was 29 percent.

The revival of organized labor in western Germany began when the advancing Allied armies were petitioned for permission to form labor unions in March and April 1945. By August 1945, nearly one million union members had been officially recognized in unions in the British zone, where official policy was favorable to their growth as a means of promoting democracy. In this they were very successful, for Germany's labor unions went on to play a fundamental role in promoting and sustaining democracy in West Germany. The situation was completely different in the eastern part of Germany, somewhat confusingly named the German Democratic Republic (*Deutsche Demokratische Republik* [DDR]). In the DDR there was only one trade union, the Free Confederation of Trade unions (*Freier Deutscher Gewerkschaftsbund* [FDGB]). The FDGB was formed in 1945 to overcome the prewar diffusion, but soon became an undercover organization of the communist party. As a part of the specific role attributed to unions in the GDR, the FDGB even had 61 seats in the East German Parliament. The union was not a free union and was not given the right of free collective bargaining.

Determined to avoid the mistakes of the past, West German unions were to be organized along industry lines, sectarian divisions were to be avoided, and unions were to have a say in the decision-making process of large enterprises, a policy that made it possible for Germany to put pressure on the **South African** government to permit black labor unions. Despite the impressive gains made by organized labor since 1950, only 33 percent of employees were union members by the late 1980s, which was below the levels of neighboring **Austria**, **Belgium**, and **Denmark**.

Although the formal reunification of Germany in October 1990 opened up new recruiting opportunities for organized labor, it also presented many problems because of the economic backwardness of the former East Germany where the FDGB was dissolved. At first there were impressive gains in membership, but these had been largely lost by 1999 as a result of the recession of the early 1990s, the lackluster performance of the German economy, persistently high unemployment, and the high cost of the economic integration of the former East Germany. In 2003, only 22.6 percent of German employees were union members, but organized labor continues to carry much political weight in Germany.

Nevertheless, there is still room for improvement in conditions for German organized labor. For example, in 2007, the Swedish retailer Hennes and Mauritz was accused of bullying union activists. More generally, civil servants are denied the right to strike in spite of the ongoing efforts of the **International Labour Organization** since 1959 to move the government to grant this right. *See also* BÖCKLER, HANS; BRENNER, OTTO; *DEUTSCHE ARBEITSFRONT; DEUTSCHER METALLARBEITER-*

VERBAND; DEUTSCHER GEWERKSCHAFTSBUND; HIRSH-DUNCKER TRADE ASSOCIATIONS; *IG METALL;* LEGIEN, KARL; *MITBESTIM-MUNG;* UNION-GOVERNMENT AGREEMENTS.

GHANA. Ghana has been independent of the **United Kingdom** since March 1957; organized labor began in the 1920s and gained legal regulation in 1941. In 1945, the Gold Coast Trades Union Congress was formed and was an affiliate of the **International Confederation of Free Trade Unions (ICFTU)** by 1953 with 74,000 members; later it was renamed the Trades Union Congress of Ghana (GTUC). As in other African colonies and territories, organized labor was aligned with movements for independence. By 1965, the GTUC had ceased to be a member of the ICFTU and did not rejoin until 1992; in 1993, it claimed 556,500 members. Since 1965, under successive military dictatorships that governed the country until 1992, **strikes** were effectively illegal in Ghana, but despite the country's postindependence political and economic difficulties, the environment for organized labor has remained positive. In 2010 legal restrictions on striking and forming labor unions continued.

GLOBAL UNION FEDERATIONS (GUF). Before 23 January 2002, GUFs were known as **International Trade Secretariats** (ITSs). In 2009, there were 11 GUFs, compared with 16 ITSs in 1995. They were **Educational International; Building and Wood Workers' International; International Arts and Entertainment Alliance; International Federation of Chemical, Energy, Mine, and General Workers' Unions; International Federation of Journalists; International Metalworkers' Federation; International Textile, Garment, and Leather Workers' Federation; International Transport Workers' Federation; International Union of Food, Agricultural, Hotel, Restaurant, Catering, Tobacco, and Allied Workers' Associations; Public Services International;** and **Union Network International**. The GUFs maintain a common global unions website. *See also* GLOBALIZATION.

GLOBALIZATION. The term *globalization* came into general use in the late 1990s to describe the process of acceleration in the interdependence of the international economy since about 1980, particularly with reference to trade, technological transfers, and information. Supporters of globalization hail its general economic benefits, such as increasing the volume of world trade, reducing poverty, and keeping prices down. Opponents of globalization complain about its potential threat to the sovereignty of nations, and international and regional organized labor has been long concerned about job losses from advanced industrial economies to the developing countries.

In November and December 1999, organized labor took part in the protests about globalization at the World Trade Organization meeting in Seattle, but because it conducted its protest peacefully, it received little publicity in the mass media compared with the violence used by **anarchist** and other anti-capitalist groups. Led by the **International Confederation of Free Trade Unions (ICFTU)**, organized labor called for the inclusion of social justice issues in the debate about globalization and for the inclusion of **International Labour Organization (ILO)** standards in tariff agreements. Symbolic of the need by international organized labor to address globalization directly was the renaming of the **International Trade Secretariats** as **global union federations** in January 2002.

In March 2002, the ICFTU presented a submission to the first meeting of the ILO World Commission on Globalization in which it acknowledged that globalization had "created unprecedented wealth and resources" but at the price of "a still-widening gap in incomes both inside and between countries and enduring unacceptable levels of absolute poverty." It cited an associated growth in human rights abuses with globalization, such as forced labor, child labor, and the exploitation of women workers in export processing zones throughout the Third World. The ICFTU was especially critical of the lack of social responsibility shown by the World Trade Organization, the International Monetary Fund, and the World Bank in addressing the need for ILO international standard-setting for labor as well as the need by multinational corporations to exercise due social responsibility and accountability.

The ICFTU and the GUFs continue to lobby the United Nations, the World Bank, the International Monetary Fund, and regional economic groups on behalf of the rights of workers. On 28 May 2003, the ICFTU's general secretary, **Guy Ryder**, called for the religious international labor body, the **World Confederation of Labour**, to join with the ICFTU in building a unified global trade union movement capable of better meeting the challenges of globalization. This call resulted in the formation of the **International Trade Union Confederation** on 1 November 2006. The financial and economic crisis that shook the world since 2008 made observers from organized labor less enthusiastic about globalization.

GMB. The main British general union, the GMB was formed in 1989, largely from the General, Municipal, Boilermakers and Allied Trade Union whose initials were used to form the title. Almost anyone can become a member regardless of where they are employed. It is affiliated to the **Trades Union Congress** and the **British Labour Party**. In 2009, the GMB had 601,000 members, compared with 683,900 in 2001 and 790,000 in 1994.

GOMPERS, SAMUEL (1850–1924). Gompers was the outstanding national labor leader in the **United States** from the late 1880s until his death. He was also an important figure in international labor. Born in London, he and his family arrived in New York in 1863, where he began work as a cigar maker and attended night classes to improve his education. He joined the Cigarmakers Local 15 in 1864 and made the union the basis of his career. Gompers was one of the principal founders of the Federation of Organized Trades and Labor Unions of the United States and Canada in 1881 and of its successor, the **American Federation of Labor (AFL)**, in 1886; he became the first president of the AFL, a position he held, with the exception of 1894, until his death. Although originally attracted to **socialist** ideas in the early 1870s, Gompers turned to unionism as the means to improve the position of labor. He was an admirer of English unionism and used it as a model for reorganizing the Cigarmakers' Union, particularly its emphasis on high membership fees and unemployment, sickness, and death benefits. He based the Federation of Organized Trades on the British **Trades Union Congress**. He and the socialists became enemies.

By the late 1870s, Gompers had developed the set of beliefs—later known as the doctrine of **voluntarism**—that he applied throughout his labor career. He believed that unionism, organized along occupational rather than industrial lines and using **strikes**, was the correct path to improving the position of employees. He distrusted the state as a means of achieving this end and opposed not only unions supporting political parties but also laws designed to set maximum hours and **minimum wages** and establish health and unemployment insurance. At the same time, he supported the restriction of **child labor**. Voluntarism, as espoused by Gompers, made the United States a notable exception to the views held by organized labor in other countries and led to friction with the **International Federation of Trade Unions**. With the collapse of the **Knights of Labor** from the late 1880s, Gompers and the AFL became the undisputed national center of American organized labor, but it was a narrow movement based on better-off employees that largely ignored the unskilled and immigrants. Gompers's ideas prevailed until the Depression and the rise of the **Congress of Industrial Organizations** in the 1930s. Gompers also played a significant role in setting up the **International Labour Organization.**

GOVERNMENT CONTROL OF ORGANIZED LABOR. Since 1920, governments that have been unwilling to tolerate an independent organized labor movement have generally suppressed them first and then set up their own labor organizations as agents of control. In communist countries, governments have suppressed independent organized labor on the grounds that, as **communism** represented the working class, an independent labor movement was not needed. By 1922, organized labor in **Russia** had been brought under the complete control of the Communist Party. In 1924, nonfascist labor unions were suppressed in **Italy**, an example followed by **Greece** (1931), **Brazil** (1931), **Germany** (1933), **Portugal** (1933), **Yugoslavia** (1935), and **Spain** (1940). In the 1960s, it was common for newly independent countries in Africa and Asia to bring organized labor under government control through the creation of single national labor organizations, even though organized labor typically played an active role in independence movements. Government control of unions was an issue during the revolts of 2010 and 2011 in Arab countries. *See also DEUTSCHE ARBEITSFRONT;* EGYPT; POLITICS; UNION–GOVERNMENT AGREEMENTS.

GOVERNMENT EMPLOYMENT. *See* PUBLIC SECTOR.

GREAT BRITAIN. *See* UNITED KINGDOM.

GREECE. The development of organized labor in Greece was hampered by the country's lack of economic growth and dependence on **agriculture**; in 1920, half the Greek labor force was employed in agriculture. The first union was formed by carpenters at the Syros shipyard in 1879, but it was not until 1918 that the General Confederation of Greek Labor (GSEE) was founded. Throughout the 1920s, conflict between **socialists** and **communists** weakened organized labor. Beginning in 1914, legislation was passed to regulate unions, and from 1931 to 1936, the state brought organized labor under its control, using the example of fascist **Italy**. This was obvious in 1946 when the government nominated the executive of the General Confederation of Greek Labor. Between 1967 and 1974, Greece was run by a military government, which seized control by a coup.

In 1968, sections of organized labor formed a group to work for the restoration of democracy. With the collapse of the military government, this group continued its activities but redirected its focus at improving democracy within organized labor, particularly with respect to the GSEE. Following organized labor's complaints to the **International Labour Organization** over government interference in the confederation, a new leadership took over and conducted a **strike** against proposed antistrike legislation in 1990, in which more than a million participated. Even so, the General Confederation of Greek Labor has been continuously represented in the **International Confederation of Free Trade Unions** since 1951. In the 1990s, Greek unions have engaged in **labor disputes** over the **privatization** of government businesses and moves to reform the labor market. In 1998, there was a **general strike** by **public sector** employees over labor market reforms and general strikes have continued to be a feature of Greek politics. In 2005, there were about 6400,000 union members in Greece, covering about 23 percent of employees. The **International Trade Union Confederation** has been concerned about violations of trade union rights in Greece and attacks on union activists. In its surveys of **violations of trade union rights** for 2009 and 2010, it had drawn attention to the attack with sulphuric acid on Constantina Kuneva, secretary of the All Attica Union of Cleaners and Domestic Workers, after enduring pressure, intimidation, and death threats. It considered the investigation into this barbaric act to have been slow and inefficient.

GREEN, WILLIAM (1872–1952). Green succeeded **Samuel Gompers** as president of the **American Federation of Labor (AFL)** in 1924 and held the post until his death. Born in Cochocton, Ohio, into a **coal-mining** family of English-Welsh immigrants, Green became a coal miner, like his father, at 16. He became active in coal mining unionism in 1891 and served as president of the Ohio District of the **United Mine Workers' of America (UMWA)** in 1906. He served two terms in the Ohio Senate for the Democratic Party, where he achieved the passage of a workman's compensation law in 1911. In 1912, he was made the international secretary-treasurer of the UMWA, a post he held to 1922. From 1914, he served in executive positions in the AFL and attended the Paris Peace Conference in 1919 that led to the creation of the **International Labour Organization (ILO)**. Upon Gompers's death on 3 December 1924, Green became president of the AFL with the support of the president of the UMWA, **John L. Lewis**.

As AFL president, Green maintained the policy of backing **craft unions** as the preferred model for organized labor and ignored the need for recruiting union members among lesser skilled workers and **women**. As a result, the employers' organizations were able to continue their offensive against organized labor, assisted by a weakening economy in the late 1920s, culminating in the Depression, with little resistance. By 1930, only 9 percent of U.S. employees were union members, the same level as in 1913, and nearly half of what it had been in 1920. In contrast, Green's career prospered from 1933 under the presidency of Franklin D. Roosevelt. Green served on the National Labor Board in 1934 and on the governing board of the ILO from 1935 to 1937.

The creation of the **Congress of Industrial Organizations (CIO)** by John L. Lewis in 1935 led to Green's resignation from the UMWA in 1938, following the AFL's expulsion of the unions that supported the CIO. Although the two national labor federations supported the Allied effort during World War II, they remained rivals. After World War II, the AFL began to recognize industrial unions. Green died on 21 November 1952, 12 days after the death of his CIO counterpart, **Philip Murray**. The deaths of these rivals greatly assisted the merger of the AFL and the CIO in December 1955. *See also* MEANY, GEORGE.

GRENADA. Grenada has been independent from the **United Kingdom** since February 1974, and organized labor has followed a British pattern of development. **Collective bargaining** was first regulated by the Labour Ordinance of 1940, which was extended to labor unions in 1951. The unions formed the Grenada Trades Union Council in 1955. Grenada has been represented in the **International Confederation of Free Trade Unions** and its successor, the **International Trade Union Confederation**, since 1951 and had about 8,000 members by 2009.

GUATEMALA. Organized labor in Guatemala began in the early 1900s. Efforts were made to form union federations in 1912 and 1928, but under the military dictatorship of General Jorge Ubico, all activities by organized labor were suppressed from 1931 to 1944. Yet by 1951 a legal framework had been created in Guatemala that enabled **collective bargaining** to occur. In 1957, Guatemala was admitted to membership of the **International Confederation of Free Trade Unions (ICFTU)** and has retained its representation since. Despite interference in its external affairs by the **United States**, widespread violence against labor unions, and 30 years of murderous civil war from the mid-1960s to the mid-1990s, organized labor declared a **membership** of 150,000 to the ICFTU by 1989. Guatemala has figured largely in the annual survey of **violations of trade union rights** for the murder of labor union leaders (2,000 unionists are said to have been murdered during the late 1980s), a legal system that discriminates against employees generally, and violence toward efforts to form labor unions in the country's **export processing zones**. In 2009, the right to **strike** remained difficult to exercise in practice because of threats, attacks, kidnapping, and raids. Some U.S. employers, such as Coca-Cola, have a long history of antiunion practices. *See also* INTERNATIONAL UNION OF FOOD, AGRICULTURAL, HOTEL, RESTAURANT, CATERING, TOBACCO, AND ALLIED WORKERS' ASSOCIATION; VIOLATIONS OF TRADE UNION RIGHTS.

GUINEA. Independent from **France** since October 1958, organized labor in Guinea was largely confined to French employees until the 1950s. There were only 2,600 union members in Guinea by 1953, but this had grown to 39,000 by 1955 after a successful **general strike**. After independence organized labor came under the control of the government. Guinea was not represented in the **International Confederation of Free Trade Unions** until 1997. In 2007, there was a general climate of government intimidation and violence toward organized labor in Guinea. In 2008, striking miners were dismissed and striking policemen beaten up by the army, leaving three dead. In 2009, the ban on trade union activities was lifted, but this did not prevent troops from killing many demonstrators later that year.

GUINEA-BISSAU. Guinea-Bissau has been independent from **Portugal** only since September 1973; organized labor had to operate in secret before then because of Portuguese rule. A General Union of Guinea-Bissau Workers existed by the 1960s and was an affiliate in exile of the **International Confederation of Free Trade Unions (ICFTU)** from 1965 to 1975. Guinea-Bissau was admitted to membership of the ICFTU in December 1997. Conditions for organized labor continued to be difficult. The national union center was subject to intimidation before a three-day strike. In 2009, it was still virtually impossible to exercise trade union rights. Even so, Guinea-Bissau had 50,000 labor union members in 2010.

GUYANA. Independent from the **United Kingdom** since May 1966, the first labor union in Guyana was the Guiana Labour Union in 1919, followed by the Manpower Citizens' Association in 1936, which recruited Indian employees of the sugar plantations. In 1940, the unions formed the Guyana Trades Union Congress. In 1942, the colonial administration introduced three ordinances that provided a legal framework for **collective bargaining** and union registration. By 1953, there were 30 unions in Guyana and the country had two unions affiliated with the **International Confederation of Free Trade Unions (ICFTU)**, with a combined **membership** of 8,600. Thereafter, political and ethnic tensions polarized organized labor. Guyana did not rejoin the ICFTU until 1965, when the Guyana Trades Union Congress claimed to represent 45,000 members. In 2001, the Guyana Trades Union Congress claimed to represent only 15,000 members. In 2002, the ICFTU reported that that there was political and ethnic discrimination toward organized labor in Guyana and restrictive **strike** legislation remained in place. In 2010, Guyana was not represented in the **International Trade Union Confederation**.

HAITI. The country was ruled by the Duvalier family from 1957 to 1986. It became the poorest country in the Western hemisphere during this period. There have been political turmoil and military intervention since. Political killings are still endemic.

"Papa Doc" Duvalier eliminated the existing union movement when he came to power. After 1986, unionists were still under attack, although on a less massive scale. The 2009 survey of the **International Trade Union Confederation** mentioned that no steps had been taken to harmonize legislation with **International Labour Organization** standards, despite the promise by the new government to do so. The rights to organize and to strike were still severely limited. The new regime of Michel Martelly raises hope that the situation will improve.

HILLMAN, SIDNEY (1887–1946). An important U.S. labor leader, Hillman was born in **Lithuania**. He studied to be a rabbi until 1902, when he moved to **Russia**; there he studied economics. For his part in labor agitation, he spent eight months in jail. On his release, he emigrated to the **United States** in 1907, where he settled in Chicago. Hillman worked as a clerk for two years, then became a garment cutter and a member of the United Garment Workers' Union of America (formed in 1891). Between September 1910 and January 1911, Hillman was the leader of a **strike** against Hart, Schaffner, and Marx in Chicago. The success of this strike fed discontent with the conservative leadership of the union, and in 1914 Hillman led a breakaway group of members who formed the Amalgamated Clothing Workers of America (ACWA). Hillman became its first president. The second result of the 1910–1911 strike was the setting up of **arbitration** machinery that was extended to other parts of the clothing industry. Hillman was a dedicated supporter of **industrial unionism** and led the ACWA through an industry-wide lockout between December 1920 and June 1921 and the exclusion of racketeers during the 1920s. He served on the federal Labor Advisory Board (1933) and on the National Industrial Recovery Board (1935). In 1935, he became one of the leaders of the **Congress of Industrial Organizations**. A political moderate, Hillman supported the American Labor Party and the Democratic Party.

HIRSCH-DUNCKER TRADE ASSOCIATIONS. Hirsch-Duncker trade associations were a group of labor unions that operated in **Germany** from 1869 to 1933. They were begun by Max Hirsch (1832–1905), a mechanical engineer, and Franz Duncker, a newspaper publisher. Hirsch made a tour of England in 1868 and came back with the idea that German unions should imitate those of England as he perceived them—that is, independent from political parties, in favor of the amicable settlement of labor disputes, and avoiding the use of **strikes**. In 1869, he and Duncker organized a national federation of unions with 30,000 members among eight trade associations. Although the Hirsch-Duncker associations were exempt from the Anti-Socialist Law of 1878 because of their lack of political affiliation. Their growth was slow; it was not until 1902 that their combined **membership** reached 102,600. Despite claims of political and religious neutrality, the associations were linked with left-wing liberalism, a political area to which other groups could make better claim. After reaching a peak membership of 226,000 in 1920, the associations' membership declined to 149,800 by 1931. They were dissolved by the Nazis in 1933 and were not reestablished after 1945.

HOFFA, JAMES P. (1941–). The only son of **James Riddle Hoffa**, James P. Hoffa was born in Detroit, Michigan, and completed his education at the University of Michigan as a lawyer in 1966. He joined the **Teamsters** in 1959 and worked as a laborer in Detroit and Alaska in the 1960s. Between 1968 and 1983, he was a Teamster attorney representing members in workers' compensation cases, social security, and personal legal matters; he also represented Teamster joint councils and local unions. He was administrative assistant to the president of Michigan joint council 43 between 1993 and 1998. In 1999, Hoffa was easily elected general president of the Teamsters on a platform of reform; he was reelected in 2001 and 2006. Under his leadership, the Teamsters conducted an independent, internal investigation of the history and current status of the influence of organized crime in the Teamsters and released it to the public in March 2002. The teamsters' **membership** grew for the first time in decades under Hoffa.

HOFFA, JAMES RIDDLE (1913–c. 1975). Hoffa was one of the most controversial labor leaders in recent U.S. history. Born in Brazil, Indiana, Hoffa worked in various service sector jobs before he became involved with organized labor in 1931. He became a member of the **Teamsters** in 1934. He advanced steadily in the Teamsters, was made a vice president in 1952, and was president from 1957 to 1971. In the course of his union career, Hoffa developed links with the Mafia. In 1964, he was convicted of jury tampering, fraud, and conspiracy over the disposition of union benefit funds and began a 13-year jail sentence in 1967, which was commuted by President Richard Nixon in 1971. As president, Hoffa's contribution to the Teamsters as a union was to enlarge its **membership** in the transportation and storage industry (under Hoffa, the Teamsters' membership grew from 1,417,400 to 1,789,100), to introduce the first nationwide contract in the industry (1964), and to expand the union's health and medical program. Hoffa disappeared in 1975 and has been presumed to have been murdered by the Mafia. His career was the subject of the 1993 film *Hoffa*, starring Jack Nicholson and Danny DeVito. *See also* HOFFA, JAMES P.

HONDURAS. The first labor union in Honduras was formed in 1917 among tradesmen, but organized labor could make little progress because of government opposition; under the dictatorship of General Tuburcio C. Andino organized labor was suppressed from 1932 to 1949. Between 1950 and 1963, a more favorable political environment enabled the formation of unions. A successful **strike** by 10,000 banana plantation workers against the U.S.-owned United Fruit Company led to union recognition and the country's first collective agreement in 1954 and general government recognition of labor unions and the right to strike. From 1959 Honduras was represented with the **International Confederation of Free Trade Unions (ICFTU)**. In 1963, the military took power and suppressed organized labor; they held power more or less continuously until 1982. By the 1990s, the main concern of the ICFTU with regard to Honduras had turned to harsh working conditions and physical abuse of women workers in the country's **export processing zones**, particularly by Korean-owned firms. Only an estimated 14 percent of employees are unionized. The right to strike and form unions remained tenuous in Honduras in 2008 when a number of companies did everything in their power to destroy organized labor. Companies in the banana business harassed trade unions and three members of a bank workers union were arrested. A *coup d'état* in 2009 destroyed all remaining union rights and the elected administration that followed did nothing to restore them. The two Honduras affiliates of the **International Trade Union Confederation** in 2010 claimed a total **membership** of 305,000.

HONG KONG SAR (CHINA). Hong Kong was a dependent territory of the **United Kingdom** until June 1997, after which Hong Kong became a Special Administrative Region (SAR) of **China**. The first labor union in Hong Kong was formed in 1900, and its waterfront unions conducted a major **strike** in 1922. The first labor federation was formed in 1923. Although strikes and trade unions were illegal before the ordinance of 1948, the colonial administration appointed an official in 1938 to arbitrate in labor disputes and to regulate unions. The Hong Kong Federation of Trade Unions (HKFTU) was formed in 1948, and the Hong Kong and Kowloon Trade Union Council (HKTUC) was established in the following year. Hong Kong has been represented in the **International Confederation of Free Trade Unions (ICFTU)** since 1951. Despite being a British colony, the legal status of labor unions in Hong Kong lagged behind that of other British colonies by the 1970s, a state of affairs that drew criticism from the ICFTU and the British **Trades Union Congress** in the 1970s.

The transfer to Chinese rule in 1997 caused the decline of the HKTUC, which was oriented toward Taiwan and the emergence of the independent Confederation of Trade Unions of Hong Kong, which identifies with opposition politics. Since 1997, the ICFTU has been critical of the Hong Kong authorities' failure to create an institutional framework that provided for labor union rights and **collective bargaining**. In 2010, the **International Trade Union Confederation** concluded that workers and unions continued to have little room for promoting their interests or defending their rights. Despite this, there were many successful strikes in 2009.

HUMAN RIGHTS. Organized labor has always supported human rights issues, even if that support has been tinged with economic considerations. The exclusion of children from factory employment, for example, could be justified on the grounds of the protection of their welfare, but the employment of children also posed a threat to adult wages. Similarly, the attempts of the **American Federation of Labor–Congress of Industrial Organizations** to deny tariff preferences to certain countries such as **Indonesia** for abuses of trade union rights could also be interpreted as reducing competition from countries with low wage economies. More clearly, the support for human rights by organized labor was evident in the case of the apartheid system in **South Africa**, where German and Swedish unions were able to exert pressure on the boards of their companies operating in South Africa to adopt progressive codes of conduct that excluded racist practices.

In 1985, the **International Confederation of Free Trade Unions** began to publish annual surveys of **violations of trade union rights** in the world, which document the murder, torture, and imprisonment of union leaders and denial of official recognition of labor unions that are not controlled by the government. Its successor, the **International Trade Union Confederation**, has continued to conduct this survey. Those countries with the worst record of human rights violations also have the worst record of violation of trade union rights. The Middle East usually attracts significant attention in this regard, but of late attention has been given to Asia and Africa. *See also* CHILD LABOR; FORCED LABOR; INTERNATIONAL LABOUR ORGANIZATION; SLAVERY.

HUNGARY. Organized labor within the modern borders of Hungary emerged during the 1860s and grew in parallel with the Social Democratic Party, which set up a council of labor unions in 1891; this was reorganized on a permanent basis in 1899. In 1898, there were 126 unions with a combined **membership** of 23,000. In 1907, the unions claimed a combined membership of 130,000, but the hostile political climate reduced this to 112,000 by 1912. Hungary was an affiliate of the **International Federation of Trade Unions** from 1905 to 1939. In 1919, Hungary's political framework was shattered by the attempted creation of a communist republic, which was replaced by a provisional government of labor and **socialists** and then by a right-wing counterrevolutionary government led by Admiral Miklós Horthy, who suppressed organized labor. His regime lasted until 1944. The imposition of **communist** rule meant that it was impossible for an independent labor movement to operate until 1986. In 1956, independent workers' councils managed to stage a **general strike** against the Soviet regime. The movement was suppressed, however.

In 1989 Hungary became independent from the **Soviet Union** and the state-led union centre *Magyar Szakszervezetek Országos Tanácsá* (SZOT), or Central Council of Hungarian Trade Unions, was dissolved. The country became a market economy at high speed. By 1995, two national labor federations existed: the *Magyar Szakszervezetek Országos Szövetsége Tagszervezeteinek Címlistája* (MszOSz), or National Confederation of Hungarian Trade Unions, formed in 1990 from the former SZOT with 895,000 members, and the Democratic League of Independent Trade Unions (LIGA), formed in 1989 with 98,000 members. The LIGA, MszOSz, and the Autonomous Trade Union Federation were members of the **International Confederation of Free Trade Unions** in 2001. Together, their membership was 766,000 or about 29 percent of all employees. A national survey by the MszOSz in 2001 found widespread violations of **freedom of association**, discrimination against organized labor, and breaches of labor law. Amendments to the labor code in September 2002 have improved the legal environment for organized labor in Hungary, but discrimination against unions continues. According to the **International Trade Union Confederation**, union organizing in multinationals is difficult and trade union rights in the public sector are limited. The three Hungarian affiliates of the ITUC claimed a combined membership of 630,000 in 2010.

I

ICELAND. In 1944, Iceland became fully independent from **Denmark**. In 1916, seven unions created the Icelandic Federation of Labor with 650 members. The first attempt at forming a labor federation had been made in 1907, but it collapsed in 1910. By 1923, union **membership** had reached 4,000. Between 1925 and 1927, three regional labor federations were created. Despite legal restrictions, many **labor disputes** have occurred in Iceland. State and local government employees organized their own labor federation in 1942. Union membership grew from 4,500 in 1927 to 30,000 in 1960 and 82,900 in 2001. By 2010, the Icelandic affiliates of the **International Trade Union Confederation** declared a total membership of 130,000 covering most employees. *See also* COUNCIL OF NORDIC TRADE UNIONS.

ICONOGRAPHY. Throughout its history, organized labor has made extensive use of public symbols to express and create unity and to win support. Painted silken banners depicting the activities and aspirations of union members seem to have been derived from coats of arms in **Britain** and began to be used from about 1807. About three quarters of the union banners used by organized labor in Britain from 1837 until the 1970s were made by a firm founded by George Tutill (1817–1887); Tutill's banners were also exported throughout the British Empire. Banners were carried on May Day or **Labor Day** and to encourage solidarity during **labor disputes**. Common themes in the iconography of organized labor were the appeal to unity (e.g., in slogans like "the unity of labor is the hope of the world") and secular millenarianism (the promise of a better future often symbolized by a rising sun) and how it might be achieved through **socialism** or **communism**. Traditionally, the iconography of organized labor has depicted **blue-collar** employment.

Union labels have also been used to promote goods produced by union members; they were first used in the **United States** by the Cigar Makers' International Union in 1874. In 1884, the **Knights of Labor** and other unions used union labels as part of their boycott campaign. Organized labor has also used badges and medals to promote **membership**; the **general strike** in Brisbane, Australia, in 1912 was prompted by managements' objections to government street car employees wearing membership badges. Other outlets for the use of union iconography were the labor press from the 1880s and, from the 1930s, film. In 1954, the **International Confederation of Free Trade Unions** began to create a catalog of films made by organized labor and held screenings at their own film festivals held every two years. Since the late 1990s, the World Wide Web has been an important medium through which unions can spread their ideas and messages about actions undertaken. *See also* INDUSTRIAL ARCHAEOLOGY.

IG METALL. IG Metall was the largest labor union in **Germany** and the largest union in any democratic country in the world between 1950 and 2001. Since 1965, it has had over two million members or a third of Germany's total trade union **membership**. Based on engineering employees, the sheer size of *IG Metall* has made it a major force in post-1945 German labor history. *IG Metall* was formed at a congress in Hamburg, 18–22 September 1950, with a membership of 1.3 million. Its leader between 1954 and 1972 was **Otto Brenner**. *IG Metall* played a prominent part in **labor disputes** and in gaining pay increases and **shorter working hours** for its members. In 1977, the first debates were held within *IG Metall* for gaining a 35-hour work week.

In 1984, *IG Metall* conducted a **strike** that reduced the working hours of its members to 38.5 hours, and in February 1988 signed an agreement that gave many of its members a work week of 36.5 hours. Following the reunification of Germany in 1989, *IG Metall* actively recruited in the former East Germany to raise its membership to 3.6 million by 1992. On 21 April 1994, *IG Metall* negotiated an agreement with the employers' metal trades federation for a 35-hour week to begin on 1 May 1994. In 1994, *IG Metall* had three million members, but by 1997 membership had fallen to 2.6 million, of whom 18 percent were **women**. This decline was a reflection of the slow growth of the German economy and the cost of the integration of the former East Germany.

In the mid-1990s, *IG Metall* moved to the forefront of German labor unions in its adoption of policies aimed at combating discrimination on the grounds of **race and ethnicity**. In 1994, about 10 percent of the membership of *IG Metall* were non-German, of whom about half were from Turkey or of Turkish descent. By 2000, membership had increased slightly to 2.7 million but in 2010 it had fallen to 2.4 million. In 2008, *IG Metall* launched a campaign using the threat of warning strikes to gain an 8 percent pay rise, but, faced with the global financial crisis, it accepted a 4.2 percent rise. *See also DEUTSCHER METALLARBEITER VERBAND.*

IMMIGRATION. Immigration from Western Europe has played an important role in spreading organized labor to other countries. In the **United Kingdom**, some sections of organized labor actively encouraged emigration as a way of reducing unemployment. Several English unions, notably the **Amalgamated Society of Engineers** and the **Amalgamated Society of Carpenters and Joiners**, were able to establish branches in North America, **South Africa**, and Australasia through immigration. As a major source of skilled employees, British immigrants were particularly important in the founding of labor unions in **Canada**, the **United States**, **Australia**, and **New Zealand** before 1900. Similarly, organized labor in Latin America was much influenced by Spanish and Italian immigrants. In the United States, immigrants were disproportionately represented in organized labor because they were the backbone of the industrialized labor force in the large cities.

Up to 1890, the industrialized labor force of the United States was dominated by British, Irish, and German immigrants, but thereafter immigrants from **Russia**, Eastern Europe, **Italy**, and Scandinavia assumed greater importance. By 1910, 20 percent of the labor force of the United States was foreign-born. Not only that, 72 percent of immigrants were urban dwellers, compared with 36 percent for the native-born. The occupations that loomed large in the history of organized labor were immigrant-dominated; in 1910, 48 percent of coal miners were foreign-born, as were 45 percent of woolen textile workers, and 37 percent of cotton textile workers. The harsh lot of many immigrant employees—low pay, long hours, and poor and unsafe working conditions—generated justifiable discontent and created a large social divide in American society, whose established unions (because they tended to represent the better-off native-born) proved ill-equipped to heal. Nevertheless, union activity was one source of upward social mobility for the foreign-born. Gary M. Fink estimated in 1984 that of the 80 top labor leaders in the United States in 1900, 40 percent were foreign-born, and that even by 1946 this proportion had only fallen to 20 percent. In Australia, immigration has been a feature of organized labor for over a century, and between 1976 and 1999 a steady 24 percent of union members were born overseas.

In Western Europe, immigration from Eastern Europe, Northern Africa and Turkey, the Caribbean, and sub-Saharan Africa since the 1970s has fed the **black labor market** and heightened issues of **race and ethnicity**. Although the leadership of European organized labor officially opposes racism, there are doubts about the degree to which the rank-and-file share their views.

On 1 July 2003, the United Nations Convention on Migrant Workers came into force. Among other things, it required countries that ratified the convention to guarantee migrant workers the right to labor union representation. The **International Trade Union Confederation** has expressed concern that none of the countries receiving large numbers of migrants—that is, in North America, Western Europe, Australasia, and the Middle East—have ratified the convention. In Asia and the Middle East, immigrants generally have the worst conditions of employment, pay, and official protection. *See also* COAL MINING.

INDIA. A British colony until 1947 this "sovereign socialist secular democratic republic" has been governed by the Indian National Congress for most of the period since. Roughly two thirds of the labor force work in **agriculture**.

Before 1918, there was very little organized labor in India. Those unions that had been formed were confined to skilled and better-off employees. The industrialization brought by World War I created a more favorable climate for the creation of unions. In 1918, B. P. Wadia created the Madras Union, which was based on textile employees. Stimulated by low wages, wartime inflation, and the rise of the independence movement, the next two years brought an increase in unions and union **membership**. In 1920, the All-India Trades Union Congress was formed, representing 64 unions with about 150,000 members. In the interwar years, India's unions and labor federations became divided between moderates and **communists**. As in other countries, industrial and political aims (that is, support for independence) became mixed. In 1947, the government sponsored a new noncommunist labor federation, the Indian National Trade Union Congress, thereby setting a precedent for the various labor federations to be associated with a particular political party.

Between 1950 and 1970, the number of union members rose from 2.3 million to 4.9 million. Although Indian unions operate in a relatively benign legal environment compared with most other Asian countries, their power to influence governments has been limited. For example, a **general strike** by millions of employees against the national government's economic reforms on 9 September 1993 had no effect on government policy. There were 11.8 million union members in 2001 in India, compared with 10.3 million in 1995. On 6 April 2002, unions led 10 million workers in protests over government plans to **privatize** state-run companies. In 2009, the **International Trade Union Confederation (ITUC)** was again critical of government restrictions of the right to strike, particularly in the state of Tamil Nardu and in **export processing zones** generally. To remove a union, Unilever closed down a factory in 2008. In 2009, a protesting worker, Ajit Kumar Yadav, was killed during a demonstration of over 100,000 workers from 70 auto companies. In 2010, the three Indian affiliates of the ITUC had a total membership of 15.2 million, of whom 8 percent were self-employed women. *See also* CHILD LABOR; LOKHANDE, NARAYAN MEGHAJI.

INDONESIA. Indonesia was ruled by the **Netherlands** as the Dutch East Indies from the 17th century to 1949. It had no organized labor until 1905, when Dutch and indigenous railway employees formed a union. A labor federation, the *Persatuan Pergerakan Kaum Buruh* (United Workers' Movement) was founded in 1919, but it only lasted until 1921. **Communism** and nationalism were features of organized labor from the 1920s to the 1960s. By 1930, there were 32,000 union members in Indonesia, and in 1931 a revived labor federation of indigenous employees was admitted to the **International Federation of Trade Unions**.

In 1933, the Dutch government announced the lowering of military wages to which the indigenous crew of the *Zeven Provinciën* (Seven Provinces) started a mutiny assisted by a few European marines. Prime minister Colijn ordered a bombing, leaving 23 personnel dead. Under Japanese occupation during World War II, all unions were suppressed. Since independence, labor unions have been bound up with the government. Some sections of organized labor participated in the communist insurgency in the 1950s and early 1960s, but these were suppressed in an extensive crackdown that followed the attempted coup of 1965. The Suharto regime that took power following the coup stressed national unity and consensus. Strikes and free unions were therefore curbed. Since 1973 labor unions have been incorporated into the apparatus of government, although remaining nominally independent under the All-Indonesian Labor Federation. Although three Indonesian labor federations have been members of the **International Confederation of Free Trade Unions** since 1969, in the early 1990s their **membership**, and those of a fourth body, was suspended because of their lack of independence from **government control**.

An independent union, *Setia Kawan* (Prosperity Labor Union), was formed in November 1990; it claimed 50,000 members in 1993 but has twice been denied registration as a legal body, and its leadership has been harassed by the military. In August 1993, the government banned the union's first congress. There is also another independent labor body, the Center for Indonesian Working-Class Struggle. Muchtar Pakpahan (1958–), a lawyer and the leader of the Prosperity Labor Union, was arrested on 13 August 1994 over riots in Medan, Sumatra, that occurred in April 1994 because of demands for raising the **minimum wage**, **freedom of association**, the investigation of the death of Rusli (a striker), and compensation for dismissed rubber factory workers.

On 7 November 1994, Pakpahan was sentenced to three years in jail, a decision that brought protests from labor leaders in **Australia** and the **United States**. On 16 January 1995, Pakpahan's sentence was increased to four years by the North Sumatra High Court. After the collapse of the Suharto government in May 1998, the government of Bacharuddin Jusuf Habibie released Pakpahan and other labor organizers. It also agreed to ratify **International Labour Organization (ILO)** Convention 87 on freedom of association and the right to organize labor unions. Although Convention 87 and the other seven core standards of the ILO were ratified by 2001, trade union rights in practice have proved difficult to exercise in Indonesia, with violence and intimidation of organized labor continuing to be commonplace. In 2001, four Indonesian unions were affiliated with the **International Trade Union Confederation (ITUC)** with a total **membership** of 432,600. In 2003, the right to strike and **collective bargaining** were curtailed by legislation, and police violence against union activists continued. In 2008, the government ignored the violations of law by employers and declared strikes illegal. In 2009, the government continued to undermine workers' rights. Despite this hostile environment, the two Indonesian affiliates of the ITUC claimed a combined membership of one million in 2010. *See also* SASTRADIREDJA, SUPARNA.

INDUSTRIAL ARCHAEOLOGY. Industrial archaeology is a branch of archaeology devoted principally to the physical remains and technology of the Industrial Revolution. It emerged in the 1960s and is also associated with efforts to recreate the living conditions in industrial centers through open-air museums such as those of Beamish in northeast England, at Dudley in the English Midlands, the Hagen Westphalian Open-Air Museum in **Germany,** or the Ignacy Lukasiewicz Open Air Museum of the Oil Industry in **Poland**. *See also* ICONOGRAPHY.

INDUSTRIAL DEMOCRACY. *Industrial democracy* is a term with a wide spectrum of meanings but indicating some degree of control by employees in the decisions and processes that affect their working lives. At its most extreme, it can mean that the employees should be the managers of their employment. This has been a particularly popular view in the left wing of organized labor and expressed in the term *workers' control.* In its milder forms, especially in the 1970s, it has been used to justify greater consultation with employees as a means for raising labor productivity. *See also MITBESTIMMUNG*; SYNDICALISM.

INDUSTRIAL PSYCHOLOGY. Industrial psychology is primarily concerned with human relations at work. There have been a number of schools of thought within the field reflecting the kinds of employment dominant in the economy. One of the earliest was "scientific management," which was founded by an engineer, Frederick Winslow Taylor (1856–1915), who had been employed by the Midvale Steel Company in the 1880s. Taylor developed his ideas at a time when technological changes in the steel industry enabled managements to break the power of skilled employees and replace them with lesser skilled workers. Employees were assumed to be relatively unintelligent and motivated largely to earn more by agreeing to close supervision in the performance of monotonous work of low skill content. Scientific management was suitable for industries engaged in high-volume production in which the tasks could be broken down into a series of repetitive steps such as assembly lines.

The "human relations" school was founded by an Australian-born psychologist, (George) Elton Mayo (1880–1949), who conducted a series of experiments for the management of the Western Electric Company in Chicago between 1924 and 1927. One of Mayo's findings was the important role played by informal groups in the performance of factory work and their significance for work habits and attitudes.

In 1943, A. H. Maslow published a psychological theory of motivation, which proposed that employees' satisfaction depended on a hierarchy of needs: physiological needs, safety, love or social needs, self-esteem, and self-fulfillment. In the 1950s and 1960s, F. Herzberg built on Maslow's work to stress the need for the work itself to have or produce a sense of achievement, advancement, and responsibility as factors that motivated employees to perform more productively. In the 1970s, *industrial democracy* (a term with a variety of meanings) was given more attention in the management literature as a means of promoting higher productivity and lower absenteeism. In practical terms, it has encouraged greater consultation by management of its employees. As a general rule, the results of the research carried out by industrial psychologists have been of far greater interest and use to management than they have to organized labor. This is because the research has often been commissioned by employers and because the research itself often ignored unions and why they might be supported by employees. *See also* EMPLOYERS' ORGANIZATIONS.

INDUSTRIAL SOCIOLOGY. Industrial sociology is a branch of sociology concerned with work, its organization, and its effects. Although there were earlier investigations, industrial sociology had its origins in the work of British pioneers such as Henry Mayhew in the 1850s and 1860s and Charles Booth in the 1890s. These investigators collected data on employment, living conditions, income, and costs among the working class in London. In the **United States**, important studies were carried out of particular groups such as coal miners (for example, by Peter Roberts in 1904) and clothing employees. In the 1930s, studies by industrial sociologists in many countries documented the debilitating effects of long-term unemployment; for example, E. W. Bakke published *Citizens without Work* in 1940. Others published their findings as official government reports. Common themes in industrial sociology in the period from 1945 to 1980 were how the working class was responding to greater affluence, the monotony of mass production, and family relationships.

Labor unions as such were not studied much before the pioneering works of **Beatrice and Sidney Webb** in the 1890s. In 1952, an American investigator, Joseph Goldstein, published *The Government of British Trade Unions,* which examined the workings of the **Transport and General Workers' Union** and estimated that branch attendance at union meetings never exceeded 15 percent of the **membership**. Subsequent studies have confirmed Goldstein's findings of low membership participation in the affairs of most large unions. In 1974, Harry Braverman wrote *Labor and Monopoly Capital: The Degradation of Work in the Twentieth Century,* in which he developed a critical analysis of scientific management. His general thesis is the deskilling of labor by which management gains complete control of the labour process.

Since 1980, industrial sociologists have often been concerned with the social effect of economic change; the effects of steel plant closures on communities, for instance, have been studied in many countries. *See also* LABOR HISTORY.

INDUSTRIAL UNIONS. In theory, industrial unions are labor unions that only recruit their members from a particular industry regardless of whether the employees in the industry have completed an **apprenticeship**, in contrast to **craft unions**. The issue of how organized labor should be organized— whether by particular trade or by industry—was often raised in the late 19th century, but assumed greater importance in the early 20th century with the growth of unions. In 1905, the **Industrial Workers of the World** agreed that it should consist of five main industry groups: mining, manufacturing, building, transportation, and public service distribution. Concerned about their autonomy, craft and other smaller labor unions resisted the advocates of industrial unions. In turn, the advocates of industrial unions, particularly drawing on **syndicalism**, regarded craft unions as organizations that maintained divisions among the working class and rendered organized labor vulnerable to attack. The debate assumed urgency in **Germany** after World War II when leaders like **Hans Böckler** succeeded in reestablishing organized labor along the lines of industrial unions. This was possible because of the smashing of the previous mix of craft and industrial unions in Germany by the Nazis, but elsewhere the goal of purely industrial unions has proved elusive for organized labor in democratic societies. The main difficulty with industrial unions has been defining an "industry" for practical purposes. In 2010, organized labor is still characterized, despite numerous **amalgamations** over the past 50 years, by a mixture of types of unions, some organized around an industry (e.g., **education**), a particular occupation (e.g., the U.S. Brotherhood of Railroad Signalmen), or a conglomerate of occupations (e.g., **Amicus**).

INDUSTRIAL WORKERS OF THE WORLD (IWW). The IWW, popularly known as the "Wobblies," was the American expression of **syndicalism**, which was influential in international organized labor from the early 1900s until about 1920. Although the works of European theorists such as Karl Marx and Georges-Eugène Sorel were known, the IWW owed its origins to the violent labor environment of the mining industry in the western **United States**. The prime mover in the formation of the IWW was the radical Western Federation of Miners, a body that originated in the Butte Miners' Union, established in 1878. After defeats in disputes in 1903 and 1904, particularly at Cripple Creek, Colorado, the Western Federation of Miners called a convention in 1904 in Chicago to form a single organization for the working class, which led to the creation of the IWW in 1905. The convention adopted a radical platform that declared that the employers and workers had nothing in common and agreed to build an organization that admitted all employees regardless of sex, **race**, or nationality, an idea dormant in American organized labor since the demise of the **Knights of Labor** in the late 1880s. It also agreed that the IWW should be made up of five main industry groups: mining, **manufacturing**, building, transportation, and public service distribution, an idea that later became very influential in international organized labor.

By 1906, the IWW claimed 14,000 members but was able to mobilize far greater support among poorly paid and exploited workers. It campaigned for free speech in the late 1900s, which provoked vigilante violence, and conducted America's first sit-down **strike** at the General Electric plant at Schenectady, New York, in 1906. The IWW proved adept at mobilizing working class discontent, for example among the largely immigrant textile employees at Lawrence, Massachusetts, in 1912, but not at creating lasting organizations. With the entry of the United States into World War I in 1917, the IWW came under direct attack from the federal government, which raided IWW offices and arrested the bulk of the leadership. Of the 105 leaders arrested, 91 were convicted, including William Haywood (1869–1928). At its height, between 1919 and 1924, the **membership** of the IWW ranged between 58,000 and 100,000.

Although the IWW continued to live on after 1924, it was no longer a significant force. In its heyday, it led the mobilizing of unskilled workers in **agriculture** and lumber and, more important, drew public attention to their deplorable working conditions. The IWW also provided members for the American Communist Party. Although primarily an American organization, the IWW was an important force in **Canada** and was a focus for left-wing activity in **Argentina**, **Australia**, **Mexico**, **New Zealand**, and **South Africa**; its most lasting legacy was its advocacy of the **One Big Union**. The IWW continues as an international organization and maintains a website.

INDUSTRIEGEWERKSCHAFT METALL. *See IG METALL.*

INTERNATIONAL ASSOCIATION OF LABOUR HISTORY INSTI-TUTIONS (IALHI). The IALHI was formed in Stockholm in 1970, mainly by the Swedish Archives of Labor, the *Deutscher Gewerkschaftsbund*, the German Friedrich Ebert Foundation, the Dutch International Institute of Social History, the British Labour Party, the Swiss Archives of Society, and the **Trades Union Congress**. It brings together archives, libraries, document centers, museums, and research institutions specializing in the history and theory of the labor movement from all over the world. It fosters lending of materials wherever possible among members, encourages the interchange of publications and duplicates and sponsors publications such as bibliographies, lists of holdings, and surveys. *See also* LABOR HISTORY.

INTERNATIONAL BROTHERHOOD OF TEAMSTERS, CHAUF-FEURS, WAREHOUSEMEN, AND HELPERS OF AMERICA. *See* TEAMSTERS.

INTERNATIONAL CENTRE FOR TRADE UNION RIGHTS (ICTUR). ICTUR was established in London in 1987 as an organizing and campaigning body with the fundamental purpose of defending and improving the rights of trade unions and trade unionists that are threatened throughout the world. In 1993, ICTUR was recognized as an important international organization and granted accredited status with both the United Nations and the **International Labour Organization**. The ICTUR is an independent forum for discussion and debate. It operates on a very small budget and relies heavily on the good-will of its networks of contributors and supporters worldwide. Since 1993, it has published *International Union Rights*.

INTERNATIONAL CONFEDERATION OF ARAB TRADE UNIONS (ICATU). The ICATU was formed in Damascus, Syria, in March 1956, by national labor bodies in **Egypt**, **Jordan**, **Lebanon**, **Libya**, and **Syria**. The aims of the ICATU included the improvement of living standards of Arab employees but also support for national struggles for independence against colonial rule. The ICATU promoted training and study courses for union officials from 1969. Two forces weakened the potential effectiveness of the ICATU: the repression of organized labor by Arab governments and the left-wing character of the ICATU. The ICATU split in 1978 and its headquarters were transferred from Egypt to Syria in protest against President Sadat's visit to **Israel**. In 1992, the ICATU had 16 member nations and had close links to the **World Federation of Trade Unions**. During the 2004 congress, it was clear that differences exist between democratic forces and party-dominated unions. In 2010, the General Secretariat expressed its solidarity with the Egyptian people in seeking the overthrow of the Mubarak regime.

INTERNATIONAL CONFEDERATION OF FREE TRADE UNIONS (ICFTU). The ICFTU was the largest international body representing organized labor in noncommunist countries between its formation in December 1949 and 2006. After the replacement of the **International Federation of Trade Unions** (IFTU) by the **World Federation of Trade Unions** in 1945, there was growing concern over infiltration of the new body by **communist** organizations controlled by the **Soviet Union**. This concern was strongest in the **United States**, the **United Kingdom**, and the **Netherlands**, which set up the ICFTU in 1949. At its foundation, the ICFTU had members in 51 countries, which represented 48 million union members, of whom 43 percent were in Western Europe and 31 percent in North America. Despite its strong support for independent labor unions from its formation, many of the ICFTU's members in Latin America, Africa, and Asia were guilty of violations of this principle. In 1985, the ICFTU began to publish annual surveys of **violations of trade union rights** in the world. The ICFTU checked applicant organizations carefully to ensure that they were independent and not mouthpieces of their governments.

By the 1960s, the ICFTU had broadened its perspective to include progressive social goals. In 1969, the politically conservative **American Federation of Labor–Congress of Industrial Organizations** (AFL-CIO) withdrew from the ICFTU and did not rejoin until 1981. The absence of the AFL-CIO reduced the budget of the ICFTU by one quarter.

The ICFTU had four regional organizations: the **European Trade Union Confederation**; the *Organización Regional Interamericana de Trabajadores* (Inter-American Regional Organization of Workers), formed in 1951; the **Asian and Pacific Regional Organisation**, formed in 1984 from the Asia Regional Organization, formed in 1951; and the **African Regional Organization**, formed in 1960.

After 1989, some labor federations from former East European communist countries were admitted to membership of the ICFTU. By 1995, organized labor in Eastern Europe accounted for only 9 percent of the 125 million members in the ICFTU. However, in November 2000, the ICFTU took the historic decision to admit the **Russian** labor federations as affiliates, a move that boosted the union **membership** represented by the ICFTU by 30 million and the proportion of its members living in Eastern Europe to 24 percent. As well as country members, **global union federations** have been associated with the ICFTU, although retaining their autonomy. In 2001, the ICFTU had a membership of 156 million or about 93 percent of all global labor union members. On 1 November 2006 the ICFTU merged with the **World Confederation of Labour**. The two formed the **International Trade Union Confederation**.

INTERNATIONAL CONFERENCE OF LABOUR AND SOCIAL HISTORY (ITH). The ITH is an international network of associations, research institutes, and historians of labor and social movements. It has more than 100 members from 5 continents. It was founded in 1964 in Vienna (Austria) as *Internationale Tagung der Historiker der Arbeiterbewegung,* or the International Conference of Labour Historians. It originally served as a platform of dialogue between the Western and Eastern scientific communities of labor historians.

Since the fall of the Berlin Wall, ITH redefined its mission as a forum of international scholarly exchange in the field of labor and social history. The Conference has reoriented toward a global South–North orientation; it emphasizes a global approach to labor and social history and focuses on transnational topics. ITH sets a high value on communicating scholarly research to an interested public outside the scientific community. Its main activity is the organization of the annual Linz Conferences and the publication of conference papers. *See also* LABOR HISTORY.

INTERNATIONAL FEDERATION OF BUILDING AND WOODWORKERS (IFBWW). The IFBWW **global union federation** was formed on 1 April 1934 through the merger of the Woodworkers' International (formed in 1904) and the Building Workers' International (formed in 1903). Later in 1934, two other **international trade secretariats**, the Painters' International (formed in 1911) and the Stoneworkers' International (formed in 1904), joined the IFBWW, which has been based in Geneva since 1970. The affiliated **membership** of the IFBWW was 2.2 million in 1975 and 3.5 million in 1992. In 2005, the IFBWW claimed 10 million members and 287 affiliated labor unions in 124 countries. At its Congress in Buenos Aires on 9 December 2005, the IFBWW and the World Federation of Building and Wood Workers created a new joint global union federation, the **Building and Wood Workers' International**.

INTERNATIONAL FEDERATION OF CHEMICAL, ENERGY, MINE, AND GENERAL WORKERS' UNIONS (ICEM). The ICEM **global union federation** was created in 1964 from the merger of the International Federation of General Factory Workers (formed in 1907) and the International Federation of Industrial Organizations and General Workers' Unions (formed in 1947). The IFCEGW faced competition from the International Federation of Petroleum and Chemical Workers (formed in 1954) until its denouncement by Victor George Reuther as a "front" for the U.S. Central Intelligence Agency, an action that led to the folding of the federation in 1976. Between 1976 and 1992, the affiliated **membership** of the IFCEGW rose from 4 to 6.3 million members. In 1995, it merged with the **Miners' International Federation**. In 2009, ICEM claimed a membership of over 20 million and 467 affiliated labor unions in 132 countries. The ICEM seeks to obtain global agreements with multinational corporations on workers' rights, pay, and working conditions. Its activities include representing workers' interests within the United Nations, its agencies, and other intergovernmental bodies.

INTERNATIONAL FEDERATION OF CHRISTIAN TRADE UNION. *See* WORLD CONFEDERATION OF LABOR.

INTERNATIONAL FEDERATION OF FREE TEACHERS' UNIONS (IFFTU). The IFFTU **international trade secretariat** was originally formed as an entirely European body in 1928 but was reorganized as a global labor body in 1951 in Paris. Its **membership** increased from 2.3 million in 1976 to 19 million in 1993. It was based in Brussels. In 1993, it was reorganized as **Educational International** following its merger with the **World Confederation of Organizations of the Teaching Profession**.

INTERNATIONAL FEDERATION OF JOURNALISTS (IFJ). The first efforts to form an international labor organization among journalists date from 1926. The IFJ was formed in 1952 by noncommunists who split from the **communist**-dominated International Organization of Journalists. Up to the late 1980s, the IFJ was neither an **international trade secretariat** nor a formal associate of the **International Confederation of Free Trade Unions**, but it was both by 1993. Membership of the IFJ was 81,900 in 1976 and 350,000 in 1994. It is based in Brussels. In 2010, the IFJ claimed a **membership** of 600,000 in more than 100 countries. The IFJ has a particular concern with **human rights** and the freedom of the press. Reporting world events is a dangerous occupation; in 2009, IFJ documented the deaths of 139 journalists among its affiliates. *See also* WHITE-COLLAR UNIONISM.

INTERNATIONAL FEDERATION OF PLANTATION, AGRICULTURAL, AND ALLIED WORKERS (IFPAW). The IFPAW **international trade secretariat** was created in 1960 by the merger of the International Landworkers' Federation, which was formed by some European agricultural labor unions in 1921, and the Plantation Workers' International, which was organized by the **International Confederation of Free Trade Unions** in 1957 to represent Third World plantation employees; the International Federation of Tobacco Workers joined this body in 1958. Between 1976 and 1992 the affiliated **membership** of the IFPAW was stationary at three million. In 1988, the IFPAW signed an agreement with the French food multinational, Danone, on **collective bargaining**, one of the first of its kind. In 1994, the IFPAW merged with the **International Union of Food and Allied Workers' Associations**. *See also* AGRICULTURE.

INTERNATIONAL FEDERATION OF TRADE UNIONS (IFTU). The IFTU was the first continuous general international organization of labor unions. Officially called the *International Secretariat of the National Trade Unions Federations* until 1919, the IFTU was formed in Copenhagen on 21 August 1901, by labor representatives from **Belgium, Denmark, Finland, France, Germany, Norway, Sweden,** and **United Kingdom**. The original impetus for the formation of the IFTU came from J. Jensen, the leader of the Danish labor unions, who had attended a conference held by the **General Federation of Trade Unions** in London in 1900. Its largest affiliates between 1901 and 1913 were the United Kingdom and Germany. The **American Federation of Labor** (AFL) joined the IFTU in 1911 but left officially in 1919; it did not reaffiliate until 1937. Before 1913, the IFTU devoted itself to collecting money to help unions and strikers engaged in **labor disputes**, and to exchanging information. World War I split the IFTU along national lines, and it was not reestablished until 1919. Up to 1919, the IFTU was led by **Carl Legien**.

After 1919, the IFTU participated in European **politics**, a policy that led to the withdrawal of the AFL. The IFTU invited the **Russian** trade unions to its conferences, but these moves were met with hostility from the communist government, which regarded the IFTU as a competitor for the leadership of organized labor. The Russians established Profitern, the labor arm of the Comintern, as a rival to the IFTU. The IFTU continued to aid labor unions in affiliated countries and carried out fact-finding missions of workers' conditions in **Austria** and Belgium (1920) and the Saar and Upper Silesia (1921). Throughout its life, the IFTU was essentially a moderate, European-based organization and the voice of organized labor in the **International Labour Organization**. In 1927, the IFTU established an International Committee of Trade Union Women, which lasted until 1937; it considered issues such as **equal pay for equal work**, domestic service, working from home, and the **women**'s peace campaign.

In the 1930s the IFTU tried to widen its **membership; India** joined in 1934, **Mexico** in 1936, **New Zealand** in 1938, and **China** in 1939. The **Aus-**

tralian Council of Trade Unions was invited to join in 1936 but did not accept. At its conferences in 1931 and 1932, the IFTU adopted the 40-hour work week and a comprehensive social program as objectives. Despite its best efforts, the IFTU was weakened by the suppression of organized labor by fascism and undermined by **communism** and lack of support from the AFL for most of its life. The IFTU gave way to the **World Federation of Trade Unions** and ceased to exist on 31 December 1945. *See also* INTERNATIONAL CONFEDERATION OF FREE TRADE UNIONS; SOCIAL-DEMOCRATIC, SOCIALIST, AND LABOR PARTIES.

INTERNATIONAL GRAPHICAL FEDERATION (IGF). The IGF was founded in Stockholm in 1949 through the **amalgamation** of three international printing and graphical trades bodies—the International Typographical Secretariat (formed in 1889), the International Federation of Lithographers (formed in 1896), and the International Federation of Bookbinders and Kindred Trades (formed in 1907)—and eight British graphical trades labor unions. Based in Brussels, the IGF is mainly a European body. Its affiliated **membership** increased from 806,300 in 1976 to 1.2 million in 1994. In January 2000, the IGF merged with **Communication International**; **Media Entertainment International**; and the *Fédération internationale des employés, techniciens et cadres* **(FIET)**, or the International Federation of Commercial, Clerical, Professional, and Technical Employees to form the **Union Network International**. *See also* PRINTING.

INTERNATIONAL INDUSTRIAL RELATIONS ASSOCIATION (IIRA). The IIRA was formed in 1966 to encourage the study of industrial relations on a purely academic level. The general purpose of the Association is to promote the study of industrial relations throughout the world in the relevant academic disciplines. The Association has 47 institutional members and over 1,000 individual members worldwide, including prominent industrial relations scholars and practitioners. Subjects such as **globalization**, changes in information technology, gender, HIV/AIDS at the workplace, occupational safety and health, labor law, human resource management, labor standards, social dialogue and many other topics are largely discussed during its congresses. The IIRA is located in the office of the **International Labour Organization** (ILO) in Geneva, Switzerland.

INTERNATIONAL LABOUR ORGANIZATION (ILO). Created in 1919 as part of the peace process to end World War I, the ILO is a permanent world organization composed of representatives of governments, **employers' organizations**, and organized labor. The ILO's function is the protection and improvement of working people through the setting of legal minimum standards and technical assistance. The first steps toward the creation of such a body were taken in **Switzerland** in the late 1880s. The Belgian government supported the Swiss initiatives, and the International Congress of Civil Reforms in Brussels in 1897 called for the setting up of an international body to protect labor. The Swiss-based International Association for Labor Legislation was formed in 1900 and held a number of international conferences, which stimulated government interest in forming a permanent body to protect employment conditions. An important precedent for the creation of the ILO occurred in 1904 when **France** and **Italy** signed a treaty regulating the employment conditions of their nationals working in each other's country.

World War I disrupted these efforts, but the need for the active support of labor to fight the war gave organized labor an enhanced standing with the British, French, and German governments. In 1916, a congress held by organized labor in the **United Kingdom** was attended by representatives from France, Italy, and **Belgium**; it prepared specific proposals to be incorporated into the treaty expected to end the war and suggested an international commission to implement them. In Germany, **Carl Legien**, concerned that the **International Federation of Trade Unions (IFTU)** might be broken up, convened a counter-conference at Berne in 1917. Organized labor in France and **Germany** strongly supported the idea of an international body to safeguard the interests of labor. During the preparations for the Versailles Treaty, a Labor Commission was formed of 15 members drawn from the **United States**, France, the United Kingdom, Italy, **Japan**, Belgium, **Cuba**, **Czechoslovakia**, and **Poland**; the Commission was chaired by **Samuel Gompers**.

Overcoming many political and ideological differences, the commission succeeded in having these principles incorporated in the treaty: respect for labor, the right of association, adequate wages, an 8-hour work day or 48-hour week, abolition of **child labor, equal pay for equal work**, migrant workers to be given the same treatment as nationals, and an inspectorate system for protecting labor. Although the final outcome of the peace process was a disappointment for organized labor in Europe, the compromises reflected the political reality of the time. Under the ILO constitution, the governing body was to have 12 representatives from governments, 6 from employers, and 6 from employees; however, in practice, employee representation was dominated by the IFTU. The ILO became an affiliated agency of the League of Nations.

The ILO was able to achieve relatively little in its first 20 years. The fascist suppression of free unions in Italy raised the issue of **freedom of association** in a very stark way, but the ILO was unable as an organization to agree on a course of action. Its representation was also inadequate; the United States did not join until 1935. Its recommendations for reducing the mass unemployment of the early 1930s through increased government spending were ignored by member governments. Despite its difficulties, the ILO succeeded in starting the first continuous collections of international **labor statistics**.

In 1946, the ILO became the first specialized agency to be associated with the United Nations. In the late 1940s, the ILO adopted two fundamental propositions regarding organized labor: Convention 87 (Freedom of Association and Protection of the Right to Organise, 1948) and Convention 98 (Right to Organise and to Bargain Collectively). In 1951, the governing body of the ILO set up a standing Freedom of Association Committee to oversee the operation of these and other conventions relating to organized labor. Although there is no specific ILO convention setting down the right to **strike**, Article 3 of Convention 87 stating that unions had the right to "draw up their constitutions and rules, to elect their representatives in full freedom, to organize their administration and activities and to formulate their programmes" has been interpreted as including a right to strike. The extent of ratification by member governments of the ILO of these and similar conventions varies, as does the degree of respect for them among those governments that have. The United States withdrew from the ILO between 1977 and 1980 because of disagreements with its policies.

Organized labor is represented in the ILO by the **International Trade Union Confederation**, which uses the **international standard-setting** of the ILO, specifically seven core labor standards, in its assessment of **violations of trade unions rights**: forced or compulsory labor (Convention No. 29, 1930), freedom of association and protection of the right to organize (Convention No. 87, 1948), right to organize and **collective bargaining** (Convention No. 98, 1949), equal remuneration for work of equal value (Convention No. 100, 1951), discrimination in employment and occupation (Convention No. 111, 1958), minimum age for employment (Convention No. 138, 1973), and worst forms of child labor (Convention No. 182, 1999). *See also* LABOR DISPUTES; OCCUPATIONAL HEALTH AND SAFETY; THOMAS, ALBERT.

INTERNATIONAL LADIES' GARMENT WORKERS' UNION (IL-GWU). The ILGWU has played a significant role in the history of organized labor in the **United States**. Formed in New York City in March 1900, the ILGWU received a charter from the **American Federation of Labor** (AFL) three months later. Its **membership** grew from 2,200 in 1904 to 58,400 in 1912, much of which consisted of Jewish and East European immigrants. Successful **strikes** in New York City in 1909 and 1910 secured the union's future. The 1910 cloak makers' strike gained a 54-hour work week over six days, the closed shop, **arbitration** for the settlement of disputes, and the abolition of home-based work and subcontracting, which were important means of keeping wages in the trade low. Other important initiatives of the ILGWU in this period were union health centers (1913) and the preparation of an employer-funded unemployment plan (1919). By 1920, the ILGWU had grown to 195,400, but this success was undermined by **communists**, who dominated the leadership until 1928.

The newly elected leadership of Benjamin Schlesinger and **David Dubinsky** took over a union with debts of $800,000 and a financial membership of only 40,000. Assisted by the **National Industrial Recovery Act**, the ILGWU was rebuilt; by 1935, its membership had grown to 168,000 and most of the debts had been repaid. Under Dubinsky's leadership, the ILGWU was at the center of the struggle within organized labor to promote **industrial unionism** and in the formation of the **Congress of Industrial Organizations**. It left the AFL in 1938 but rejoined in 1940. In 1973, the union had a membership of 427,600, of whom about 80 percent were **women**. Diversity of **race and ethnicity** remained characteristic of its membership. In 1992, the ILGWU had 143,000 members. In 1995, the ILGWU merged with the Amalgamated Clothing and Textile Workers' Union to form the Union of Needletrades, Industrial, and Textile Employees.

INTERNATIONAL METALWORKERS' FEDERATION (IMF). The IMF was the largest of the **international trade secretariats** until 1995. It began as the International Metallurgists' Bureau of Information in 1893 and took its final name in 1904. In 1921, the IMF accepted a new constitution, which included a call for international cooperation to improve wages and conditions and for workers to take over the means of production. By 1930, the IMF had a **membership** of 1.9 million, but by 1938 the Depression and fascism had reduced its membership to only 190,000. By 1947, its membership had grown to 2.7 million. The IMF played a major role in defeating the attempt of the **communist**-led **World Council of Trade Unions** to absorb the various International Trade Secretariats in 1948–1949 and in the formation of the **International Confederation of Free Trade Unions** (ICFTU) in 1949. In 1994, the IMF claimed 16 million members among its 165 affiliated unions. In 1995, the IMF merged with the International Federation of Chemical, Energy, and General Workers' Unions to form the **International Federation of Chemical, Energy, Mine, and General Workers' Unions** (ICEM).

INTERNATIONAL ORGANIZATION OF EMPLOYERS. *See* EMPLOYERS' ORGANIZATIONS.

INTERNATIONAL SECRETARIAT FOR ARTS, MASS MEDIA, AND ENTERTAINMENT TRADE UNIONS. *See* MEDIA ENTERTAINMENT INTERNATIONAL.

INTERNATIONAL STANDARD-SETTING. *International standard-setting* refers to the work of the **International Labour Organization (ILO)** in devising suitable standards for the protection and improvement of working conditions, especially in relation to **working hours**, the protection of **women** and children, adequate wages, social security, **freedom of association**, and vocational and technical **education**. The framing of such standards is difficult because the standard of living in the member countries of the ILO differs so greatly, as do their politics and economies. At the same time, there is an obvious need for such standards.

INTERNATIONAL TEXTILE, GARMENT, AND LEATHER WORKERS' FEDERATION (ITGLWF). The ITGLWF is a **global union federation** formed in 1970, although international bodies among European textile labor unions dated from 1894, and among shoemakers and leather employees from 1907. In 1960, the Textile Workers' Asian Regional Organization was created with 1.5 million members. Other similar regional bodies were formed, and these were the basis of the ITGLWF. Based in Brussels, the **membership** of the ITGLWF was 5.2 million in 1976, 7 million in 1994, and 10 million in 2010.

INTERNATIONAL TRADE SECRETARIATS (ITS). ITSs have been an important feature of the European labor movement throughout the 20th century and of the international labor movement since 1945. The secretariats represented individual occupations or particular industries. They emerged as formal organizations among hatters (Paris, 1889), cigar makers (Antwerp, 1889), shoemakers (Paris, 1889), miners (Manchester, 1890), glass workers (Fourmies, **France**, 1892), typographers (Berne, 1892), tailors (Zurich, 1893), metal workers (Winterthur, **Switzerland**, 1893), textile workers (Manchester, 1894), furriers (Berlin, 1894), lithographers (London, 1896), brewery workers (Berlin, 1896), transportation workers (London, 1897, this secretariat absorbed the railroad workers who had formed a secretariat in Zurich in 1893), foundry workers (1898), stone workers and stone cutters (1902, 1904), building workers (Berlin, 1903), carpenters (Hamburg, 1903), wood workers (Amsterdam, 1904), pottery and china workers (1905, 1906), diamond workers (Antwerp, 1905), bookbinders (Nuremberg, 1907), hairdressers (Stuttgart, 1907), municipal and public services (Mainz, 1906), factory and unskilled workers (this secretariat lasted from 1908 to 1914), postal workers (Marseilles, 1910), hotel and restaurant workers (Amsterdam, 1911), and painters (Hamburg, 1911).

By 1913, the trade secretariats claimed a total **membership** of 5.6 million, of which the largest were those of the miners (1.2 million), metal workers (1 million), transportation workers (860,000), and textile workers (533,000). By

1939, important new secretariats had emerged among teachers (1928) and government employees (1935).

After 1945, international labor organizations along occupational lines were important among civil servants, journalists, transportation workers, metal workers, miners, teachers, postal workers, textile workers, and plantation and agricultural employees. Despite attempted **communist** infiltration in 1948–1949, the international trade secretariats preserved their independence. Since 1949, they were associated with the **International Confederation of Free Trade Unions**. One way in which the ITSs tried to improve the conditions of their members is through agreements negotiated with multinational corporations to provide a framework for **collective bargaining**; the first of these was negotiated with the French corporation, Danone, in 1988. In January 2002, the ITSs were renamed **global union federations**.

INTERNATIONAL TRADE UNION CONFEDERATION (ITUC). The ITUC results from the 1 November 2006 merger between the **International Confederation of Free Trade Unions** with the **World Confederation of Labour**.

The ITUC represents 175 million workers in 155 countries and territories and has 311 national affiliates. It continues the work of both predecessors including the survey of **violations of trade union rights**. The ITUC follows the historic role of trade unionism: to better the conditions of work and life of working women and men and their families, and to strive for **human rights**, social justice, gender equality, peace, freedom and democracy. *See also* AP-PENDIX C.

INTERNATIONAL TRANSPORT WORKERS' FEDERATION (ITF). The ITF is a **global union federation** that grew out of the International Federation of Ship Dock and River Workers, which was formed by Tom Mann (1856–1941) and some European labor leaders in London in 1896. It became the ITF in 1898. World War I disrupted the ITF, and it was reestablished in 1919 through the efforts of Dutch, Swedish, and British labor unions. In 1920, the ITF had three million members, all of them in Europe; by 1931, **membership** had fallen to 2.3 million. The ITF provided valuable services to the Allied war effort during World War II. As of 1948, the ITF began to seek affiliates from outside Europe. Since 1949, the ITF has been working closely with the **International Confederation of Free Trade Unions** and its successor to draw attention to the hazards of the use of **flags of convenience** in world merchant shipping. By 1976, half of the 4.1 million members of the ITF were in developing countries. In 2010, the ITF claimed 779 unions representing over 4,600,000 transport workers in 155 countries. Because it has many waterfront union affiliates, the ITF can exert considerable power if it chooses. For example, in 2006, the ITF successfully resisted a second attempt by the **European Union** to open up port services to labor market competition after 6,000 dockers from 16 European countries were joined by longshoremen from **Australia** and the **United States**.

INTERNATIONAL UNION OF FOOD, AGRICULTURAL, HOTEL, RESTAURANT, CATERING, TOBACCO, AND ALLIED WORKERS' ASSOCIATIONS (IUF). The IUF is a **global union federation** that was formed in 1994 from the merger of the **International Union of Food and Allied Workers' Associations** and the **International Federation of Plantation, Agricultural, and Allied Workers**. In 1997, the IUF negotiated an agreement to provide a framework for **collective bargaining** with a number of multinational corporations. In 2010, the IUF had over 12 million members in 336 labor unions in 120 countries.

INTERNATIONAL UNION OF FOOD AND ALLIED WORKERS' ASSOCIATIONS (IUFAWA). The IUFAWA was an **international trade secretariat** established in 1920 from the **amalgamation** of the international federation of brewery employees (formed in 1896) and baking and meat employees. Until 1945 the IUFAWA was a European body, but afterward it expanded into North America (1950), Latin America (1953), Africa (1959), and East Asia (1961). In 1980, the IUF, with the support of international organized labor, campaigned against Coca-Cola over the exploitation of plantation workers in **Guatemala**. **Membership** of the Geneva-based IUFAWA was 2.1 million in 1978 and 2.3 million in 1992. In 1994, the IUFAWA merged with the **International Federation of Plantation, Agricultural, and Allied Workers** to form the **International Union of Food, Agricultural, Hotel, Restaurant, Catering, Tobacco, and Allied Workers' Association**.

INTERNATIONAL UNIONS. International labor unions are those that have branches in more than one country. The term is commonly applied to American unions with branches in **Canada**, but could also be applied to **Ireland**. Other international unions have been the **Amalgamated Society of Carpenters and Joiners** and the **Amalgamated Society of Engineers**. *See also* IMMIGRATION.

IRAN. Organized labor began in Iran when printers formed a union in the early 20th century. A national labor federation was formed in 1920 and fought for the eight-hour working day; it claimed 8,000 members by 1922. The first labor legislation was introduced in 1923. Under the right-wing regime of Reza Khan, organized labor was forced to operate and grow in secrecy. In 1944, the Unified Trade Union of Iranian Workers was formed, with a **membership** of about 150,000, and became an affiliate of the **World Federation of Trade Unions**. It had about 180,000 members by 1945. Organized labor played an active role in the oil nationalization campaign between 1946 and 1953, and there were large-scale **strikes**. By 1951, the Iranian Trades Union Congress had affiliated with the **International Confederation of Free Trade Unions** and remained an affiliate until 1959, representing 65,000 union members. The overthrow of the Mohammed Mossadeq government and its replacement by the son of Reza Khan, Mohammad Reza Shah Pahlavi, with secret British and U.S. support, resulted in renewed repression and the outlawing of labor unions that were not controlled by the government. After the fundamentalist Islamic Revolution in 1978 and 1979, organized labor has remained ruthlessly repressed. Many thousands of activists were arrested and imprisoned. Strikes are illegal, but nevertheless occur: 181 strikes took place from March 1998 to March 1999. Strikers and activists are often sentenced to sadistic penalties, including execution. The **International Trade Union Confederation** documented the flogging of four labor activists in 2009, two of them women: Sousan Razani and Shiva Keriabadi who were sentenced to 70 and 15 lashes respectively.

IRAQ. There was no independent organized labor in Iraq in the 20th century after the violent suppression of the first trade unions in the 1920s. There was only one legal labor organization after 1945, the General Federation of Trade Unions, which was controlled by the ruling Ba'ath Party until the overthrow of Saddam Hussein in April 2003. Laws from the old regime, including the union restrictions, have not been replaced so far. The 2009 report by the **International Trade Union Confederation** reported the assassination of a trade unionist. Others have been tortured or fallen victim to the bands sowing terror across the country after the fall of Saddam Hussein. In 2009, a strike wave occurred but the Iraqi government continued repressing and punishing union activity in 2010 also.

IRELAND. The existence of unions by the 18th century in Ireland is known from a law of 1729, which outlawed combinations among journeymen, with a penalty of three months' hard labor. Similar laws were passed in 1743 and 1757. Despite the intimidating legal climate, unions were formed. In May 1788, journeymen cabinetmakers in Belfast formed a union; their minute book survives, making it one of the oldest documents of its kind. As a part of the **United Kingdom** until 1922, Irish organized labor was much influenced by the English model, but it also took some important initiatives of its own. In

1844, the Regular Trades' Association was formed in Dublin; it perished in the 1847 depression, but it was one of the first city labor councils in Britain. British unions were active in Ireland from 1851, beginning with the **Amalgamated Society of Engineers**. By 1900 about three quarters of the 67,000 union members in Ireland belonged to British unions; in 1940, this proportion had fallen to 30 percent and was stable at about 14 percent between 1955 and 1985.

In 1894, the Irish Trade Union Congress was formed, with 50,000 members among its affiliates. Originally intended to act as an auxiliary to the British **Trades Union Congress**, it went its own path from 1901; in 1945, it was challenged by the formation of a new peak labor body, the nationalist Congress of Irish Unions, but in 1959 these two bodies merged to become the Irish Congress of Trade Unions. Union **membership** in Ireland rose from 189,000 in 1922 to 285,000 in 1950 and to 490,000 in 1980. Despite some losses in the 1980s, union membership reached 677,600 by 1995 and 758,800 by 2001, or 59 percent of employees. Irish immigrants have played a significant role in the history of organized labor in the **United States**, **Australia**, and **New Zealand**. In 2010, the Congress of Irish Unions claimed 833,000 members.

ISRAEL. Organized labor in what is now Israel began in 1920 with the formation of leagues by both Arab and Jewish workers. The creation of the *Histadrut* (General Federation of Labor in Israel) in December 1920, representing 4,400 workers, was a pivotal event in the history of organized labor in Israel. Unlike the labor federations in most other countries, the socialist *Histadrut* was a state in miniature with wide political and economic goals within its promotion of Zionism and consumer cooperation. In 1933, there were 35,400 union members within the present borders of Israel. In the next year, some members of the *Histadrut* formed the National Labor Federation, which rejected the idea of class struggle and supported separate bodies for employees and employers. Nevertheless, the *Histadrut* continued to be the dominant labor organization after the declaration of the state of Israel in 1948; in 1945, it claimed 150,000 members and 300,000 by 1995. *Histradut* has been more than a labor union but is also the owner of many enterprises. In 2001, the *Histadrut* had about 450,000 union members and about the same number who were self-employed or housewives. Individuals join the *Histadrut* directly and are then placed in the union that covers their occupation. The *Histadrut* has close ties with the Labor Party, which was formed in 1968 and has been represented in the **International Confederation of Free Trade Unions** and its successor since 1957.

After the 1967 Arab–Israeli war, Israel occupied the West Bank and Gaza, suppressing the independent **Palestinian** union movement. In the late 1990s,

Israel granted both territories limited autonomy in accordance with the Oslo Accords. In 2009, the **International Trade Union Confederation** reported that although the rights of Israeli employees were fairly well respected, there was legal discrimination against Palestinian workers and no protection for migrant workers who come mainly from Asia. Also, the right to strike was undermined by court rulings and employer behavior. In 2010, Histadrut claimed 450,000 members. *See also* PALESTINE.

ITALY. Although organized labor in its modern form developed during the last half of the 19th century, there is evidence of earlier organizations in cities such as Florence from the 14th century. In 1675, an estimated 10,000 silk workers in Genoa rioted over the introduction of French ribbon looms, which enabled a single worker to weave 10 to 12 ribbons at a time; the workers burnt the new looms. Medieval guilds lasted longer in Italy than in other parts of Western Europe and were only abolished piecemeal on a regional basis between 1770 and 1821. At the same time, as in other parts of Western Europe, artisan journeymen were the vanguard of organized labor. In 1853, they held a regional conference of friendly societies, bodies that were forerunners of labor unions. Although the first labor union was formed in the **printing** industry in Turin, and a national printers' body was created in 1872, there was little in the way of unions elsewhere until after 1880.

Nevertheless, the absence of formal unions did not indicate the absence of **labor disputes**; 634 occurred between 1860 and 1878, mainly in the north and mostly over wages. The example of the French *Bourse du Travail* (labor union center), particularly that founded at Marseilles in 1888, was influential in Italy and led to the formation of chambers of labor (*Camera del Lavoro*) beginning in Milan in 1891. By 1893, the chambers had about 41,000 members. Government policy toward organized labor turned hostile in the 1890s, and it tried to suppress the unions between 1894 and 1899.

After a last attempt at official suppression in Genoa in 1900, labor unions began to emerge and create new national organizations, exemplified by the formation of the *Confederazione Generale di Lavoro* (CGL), or General Confederation of Labor, in 1906. Although there was impressive national growth in Italian union **membership** after 1900, the labor movement was divided on political and religious lines. Revolutionary **syndicalism** attracted much support from rural workers employed on large estates and claimed 200,000 members in 1908. The syndicalists formed their own labor federation in 1912 and were opposed by the **socialist** unions. As well, the **Catholic** unions, which were first formed in 1894 and claimed 107,600 members by 1910, made up a separate strand of organized labor. In 1920, they formed their own federation, the *Confederazione Italiana dei Lavoratori* (Italian Confederation of Workers), with 1.2 million members of whom 79 percent were employed in **agriculture** or textiles **manufacturing**. The socialist federation, the CGL, had 2.2 million members, of whom about 34 percent worked as farm laborers and most of the others in manufacturing.

Politically, Italy was still immature in 1920; there was little opportunity for labor leaders to gain the experience of government they needed. There was much labor unrest in 1919 and 1920, but the Socialist Party failed to translate this into practical political gains and continued to preach revolution; it was further weakened by a split caused by the **communists** in 1921. Divided, organized labor lost support and declined. Between 1920 and 1924, the membership of the CGL collapsed from 2.2 million to 201,000. On 24 January 1924, Benito Mussolini's fascist government abolished the nonfascist labor unions of Italy. The CGL voted itself out of existence in 1927. The fascist government introduced a number of important principles into Italy's system of industrial relations that were to have lasting consequences. It brought in a centralized system of **collective bargaining** under which unions that were part of the Confederation of Fascist Corporations were legally recognized as partners, as well as a compulsory system of pay deductions for union dues. Italy's corporatism was imitated by **Germany, Greece, Spain, Portugal**, and **Brazil**.

On 3 June 1944, all three sections of organized labor—socialist, communist, Christian Democrat (Catholic)—agreed to the "Pact of Rome," which provided for the setting up of a new united labor confederation, the *Confederazione Generale Italiana del Lavoro* (CGIL), or General Confederation of Italian Labor, which was made up of equal representation from these three groups. This unity did not last; following a wave of **strikes** and unrest led by the communists of the CGIL, the Christian Democratic unions formed their own federation in 1948, as did the republican and democratic socialists in 1949. The Christian Democratic federation, the *Libera Confederazione Generale Italiana dei Lavarotori,* or Free General Italian Confederation of Workers, received support for its establishment not only from the Catholic church but also from the **American Federation of Labor–Congress of Industrial Organizations** (AFL-CIO) and the U.S. Central Intelligence Agency as a counter to the communist-dominated CGIL. In 1972, the three labor federations formed an alliance, which collapsed in 1984 and was only partly restored. Rank-and-file dissatisfaction with the three federations in 1987–1988 led to the formation of grassroots committees known as *comitati di base* or "cobas," which sought the repeal of a law of 1970 giving the federations legal rights in **collective bargaining**. In June 1990, the government prohibited strikes in a wide range of essential services. In 1994, Italy's 10 "autonomous" labor unions (which operated mostly in the **public sector**) formed a federation, the *Intesa Sindicati Autonomi* (Pact of Autonomous Unions), which claimed to represent six million employees. In 2001, there were about four million union members in Italy, covering about 27 percent of employees. Italian labor union membership figures have been remarkable since the 1960s for their high proportion of **retired employees**. In 2010, the three Italian affiliates of the **International Trade Union Confederation** declared a combined membership of 12.2 million, but many of these were retired employees. *See also FEDERAZIONE ITALIANA OPERAI METAL-LURGICI.*

IVORY COAST. *See CÔTE D'IVOIRE.*

J

JAMAICA. Jamaica was a colony of the **United Kingdom** until August 1962; the first labor union in Jamaica was formed by longshoremen in 1918 and labor unions were legalized in 1919. Reflecting Jamaican society generally, organized labor in Jamaica has been divided by racial and class conflicts. Important milestone events in the history of organized labor in Jamaica since 1930 have been the formation of the Bustamente Industrial Trade Union in 1938, the Trades Union Congress of Jamaica in 1948, and the National Workers' Union of Jamaica in 1952. Jamaica was represented in the **International Confederation of Free Trade Unions** since 1953, but no Jamaican union is affiliated to the **International Trade Union Confederation** in 2010. The Jamaican Confederation of Trade Unions has about 140,000 union members.

In 2002, the ICFTU complained that no labor unions had been formed in the country's **export processing zones**, that the right to strike was denied to employees in the **public sector**, and that **collective bargaining** remained restrictive in Jamaica. These issues have continued. The surveys of **violations of trade union rights** for 2009 and 2010 complained that employers still tried to deny the right to organize and strike and about the undue intervention by the Ministry of Labour in terminating strikes.

JAPAN. The first recorded labor disputes in Japan date from 1870 and the first union was formed among steelworkers in 1897. Other unions were formed among employees in **printing, railroads,** teaching, and firefighting; their total **membership** reached 8,000 in 1900, but they were suppressed by law. Japanese government opposition to unions continued until 1945, and unions were denied legal recognition. Nevertheless, a Japanese labor movement did emerge from 1912 when Bunji Suzuki formed a labor union called the *Yuai-kai* (Workers' Fraternal Society); government hostility forced it to pretend it was a cultural and moral body in its early years. In 1917, some employers formed the Japan Economic Federation to prevent the legal recognition of labor unions. By 1920, there had been significant growth in organized labor in Japan, with total membership reaching 103,000. In 1921, the *Yuai-kai* established Japan's first labor federation, the *Nihon Rodo Sodomei*. In the 1920s and 1930s, Japanese organized labor was split between social democrats, **socialists**, and **communists**. In 1940, when all independent unions and **employers' organizations** were compulsorily merged into a body run by the government, there were only 9,500 union members compared with 408,700 in 1935.

As in **Germany**, the end of World War II brought an explosive growth in organized labor; in December 1945, Japanese employees were legally allowed to form unions, to engage in **collective bargaining**, and to strike. The release of communists and other radicals from jail enabled them to rejoin the unions and fight the hardship and poverty of the immediate postwar period through **strikes**. In 1948, the right to strike was withdrawn from **public sector** employees. Between 1945 and 1950, the number of labor union members increased from 380,700 to 5.8 million and the number of unions rose from 509 to 29,144. A Japanese delegation attended the founding congress of the **International Confederation of Free Trade Unions (ICFTU)** in London in November and December 1949, and Japan was a full member of the ICFTU by 1951.

Three labor federations were formed in 1946 and multifederations based on political as well as industrial differences remained a feature of Japanese organized labor thereafter. The largest federations were the *Domei* (that is, the Japanese Confederation of Labor, which evolved out of *Sodomei,* the Japanese Federation of Trade Unions, originally formed in 1946 to cover private sector employees) and the socialist, mainly public sector *Sohyo,* General Council of Trade Unions of Japan. *Sohyo* was formed in 1950 when the noncommunists split from the communist-dominated *Sanbetsu-Kaigi* (or Congress of Industrial Unions of Japan, originally formed in 1946). In 1987, *Domei* and some other federations as well as unaffiliated unions formed a new private sector federation, now referred to as "old" **Rengo** (Japanese Trade Union Federation). In 1989, this body merged with *Sohyo* to create "new" *Rengo,* which claimed 7.7 million members by 1992 or about two thirds of total labor union membership. New *Rengo* has also engaged directly in **politics** by supporting opposition candidates in elections.

From 1946 to 1960, the level of **labor disputes** in Japan was relatively high; an annual average of 458 working days per thousand employees were lost through labor disputes between 1946 and 1950, 468 between 1951 and 1955, and 437 between 1956 and 1960. In 1956, the *Shunto,* or Spring Offensive, was begun by *Sohyo* and became an annual coordinated drive to gain wage increases. Since the mid-1970s, the level of labor disputes in Japan has decreased.

As a proportion of employees, union membership has declined steadily since its peak of 56 percent in 1950 to 19 percent in 2005. This decline has largely occurred in the private sector, with union coverage of government employees remaining high. Japan continues to be a nation with a large number of labor unions; there were 61,178 unions in 2005, compared with 70,839 in 1995 and 41,561 in 1960. Since 1945, organized labor in Japan has become important in world terms; with 10.1 million members in 2009, Japan accounted for almost 6 percent of the membership of the **International Trade Union Confederation (ITUC)**. In 2009, the ITUC complained about the strong legal restrictions on government employees' union rights, including the ban on public sector strikes. Foreign workers often end up in sweat shops with hardly any rights. *See also* CHINA; SOUTH KOREA.

JOB SHARING. Job sharing generally refers to the splitting of a full-time job into two part-time positions in Western countries. Although first proposed in the 1970s, job sharing is largely a development of the 1980s and has been especially beneficial to **women** employees with young children. Although it came to be accepted by most unions when it was done on a voluntary basis, it was often treated with suspicion at first as a possible threat to the conditions of full-time employees.

JORDAN. Although the first labor union among Arab workers in Jordan was formed in Haifa in 1920, organized labor effectively dates from 1954 with the formation of the General Federation of Jordanian Trade Unions (GFJTU), but has since had a difficult history caused by government restrictions. In 1965 and 1969, Jordan was represented in the **International Confederation of Free Trade Unions**, but not again until 1995, when it was represented by GFJTU, which claimed 200,000 members. In 2009, the **International Trade Union Confederation** reported that all unions must belong to the GFJTU. Organized labor faces many restrictions in practice and Jordan's one million foreign employees are still denied the right to join unions. The right to **strike** is heavily curtailed. Throughout 2009 strikes and demonstrations by migrant workers were brutally broken up by the police.

JORDAN, BILL [WILLIAM BRIAN] (1936–). General secretary of the **International Confederation of Free Trade Unions (ICFTU)** from 1995 to 2001, Jordan was born and educated in Birmingham, England. He began work as a machine tool fitter at the age of 15. In 1966, he became a shop steward convenor with the **Amalgamated Engineering Union** and rose to become the president of the Amalgamated Engineering and Electrical Union in 1986, a post he held until becoming general secretary of the ICFTU. He was a member of the general council of the **Trades Union Congress** from 1986 to 1995 and over the same period served on the executive of the **International Metalworkers' Federation** and was president of the European

Metalworkers' Federation. During his period as general secretary of the ICFTU, there was a sustained offensive against **child labor** and a major increase in the **membership** of the ICFTU (from 126 to 156 million), mainly brought about by the accession of the labor federations of **Russia** in 2000. In 2000, he was made a Baron (life peer) in recognition of his contribution to British and international organized labor.

K

KAZAKHSTAN. Independent of the former Soviet Union since December 1991, the emergence of independent organized labor in Kazakhstan was hampered by a 1990 Soviet labor law that required **collective bargaining** to be carried out between management and a "conference" representing employees. However, the law did not define how or by whom the "conference" was to be convened. This omission has enabled the former government-controlled unions to be parties to collective agreements and freeze out independent unions. Despite considerable government opposition, including violence, the coal miners formed an independent labor union in 1992 and conducted a **strike** in May 1994. In July 1995, a mission from the **International Confederation of Free Trade Unions (ICFTU)** and the **Miners' International Federation** visited Kazakhstan but was unable to secure a fair settlement for the coal miners because the judicial system was biased in favor of the former government-run unions. In 2002, the ICFTU reported that antiunion practices by employers were widespread. In 2010, Kazakhstan was not represented in the **International Trade Union Confederation**.

KENYA. A colony of the **United Kingdom** until December 1963, labor unions among African workers emerged in the late 1940s and were largely preoccupied with the independence movement. After independence, the government was hostile to the existence of an independent labor movement. For example, on 1 May 1994, the government arrested Joseph Mugalla, the general secretary of the Central Organisation of Trade Unions, over threats to call a **general strike** in support of wage claims. Kenya was represented in the **International Confederation of Free Trade Unions (ICFTU)** from 1953 to 1959 and again since 1991 by the Central Organisation of Trade Unions (established 1965). In 2001, the ICFTU reported that unions in Kenya were restricted in practice in their right to organize, particularly in the country's **export processing zones**. There were about 233,500 union members in Kenya in 2001. In 2007, the **International Trade Union Confederation** complained that workers are prevented from unionizing or going on legal strikes. In 2009, legal amendments favored trade union activities, but **collective bargaining** remained difficult.

KIRIBATI. Independent of the **United Kingdom** since July 1979, the Kiribati Trades Union Congress (established 1982) has been represented in the **International Confederation of Free Trade Unions** since 1993, when it claimed a **membership** of 2,600. No strikes have been recorded since 1980 because heavy penalties exist.

KIRKLAND, JOSEPH LANE (1922–1999). Kirkland was president of the **American Federation of Labor–Congress of Industrial Organizations (AFL-CIO)** from 1979 to 1995. Born in Camden, South Carolina, he was employed as a merchant marine pilot between 1941 and 1946 and as a nautical scientist in the Hydrographic Office of the U.S. Navy Department between 1947 and 1948. In 1945 and 1946, he was a member of the International Organization of Masters, Mates, and Pilots (formed in 1887). He graduated with a science degree from Georgetown University in 1948. In the same year, he joined the **American Federation of Labor** as a researcher and was assistant director of its social security department between 1953 and 1958. His writing ability was recognized in the AFL-CIO, and in 1961 he was made executive assistant to its president, **George Meany**.

In 1969, Kirkland was elected secretary-treasurer of the AFL-CIO. In the 1960s, he coordinated the AFL-CIO's civil rights campaign and fought racial discrimination in unions. He lobbied for a fair employment clause in the Civil Rights Act (1964), played an active role in the war on poverty, and helped to raise over $2 million for the A. Philip Randolph Institute's antighetto programs. In 1979, he negotiated a national accord with the Jimmy Carter administration in which the AFL-CIO promised to restrain wage claims to help control inflation in return for greater measures to protect the poor, limits on corporate profits, and an undertaking not to use unemployment as a means of lowering inflation. As AFL-CIO president, Kirkland followed a more moderate path than Meany. Under him, the AFL-CIO rejoined the **International Confederation of Free Trade Unions** in 1981. In 1986, Kirkland was elected president of the Trade Union Advisory Committee to the Organization of Economic and Community Development (founded in 1948). In 1995, Kirkland was succeeded by **John J. Sweeney** as AFL-CIO president.

KNIGHTS OF LABOR. The Knights were the first mass labor organization in the **United States** to recruit unskilled workers as well as African-Americans and **women**, and the organization has been described as a form of **syndicalism**. Originally formed in 1869 as a secret society by some garment cutters in Philadelphia, the Knights rejected the wage system and supported cooperation and education as a means of improving the position of workers. Between 1878, when it became a national body, and 1881, the **membership**

of the Knights rose from 9,000 to 19,000 and was open to all who earned their living through manual labor either as employees or as small farmers. Between 1881 and 1893, the Knights were led by Terrence V. Powderly (1849–1924). The Knights supported the abolition of **child labor**, government inspection of mines and factories, and the nationalization of banks and **railroads**. The Knights was a centralized organization, and membership grew from 49,500 in 1883 to a peak of 703,000 in 1886, of which about 10 percent were African-Americans and 10 percent were women. Most of this growth occurred as a result of successful **strikes** against railroad companies in 1884.

After 1886, the membership of the Knights declined rapidly following their defeat in a strike against Jay Gould's Southwestern Railroad (1886), factional fighting within the Knights, and a prolonged struggle with the **craft unions** represented by the **American Federation of Labor**. One of the major problems faced by the Knights was the gulf between the expectations of the rank-and-file and the moderation of the senior leadership, a gulf exposed by the leadership's refusal to endorse the nationwide eight-hour campaign in 1886. The Knights were also active outside the United States, forming off-shoots in **Canada** (1881), the **United Kingdom** (where they claimed 10,000 members by 1889), **Belgium**, **Ireland**, **Australia** (1890), and **New Zealand**. Within the United States, the membership of the Knights ebbed rapidly from 511,400 in 1887 to 220,600 by 1889. Although a spent force after 1890, the Knights claimed 20,200 members in 1900 and continued to publish a journal until 1917. Some of their ideas were carried on by the **Industrial Workers of the World** (IWW) after 1905.

KOREA. *See* NORTH KOREA; SOUTH KOREA.

KOSOVO. Kosovo has been independent from **Serbia** since 2008. The essential rights of organized labor are guaranteed by the United Nations, but are frequently violated by employers. Laws to help organized labor were expected to be enacted in 2010 but failed to materialize.

KUWAIT. Kuwait has been ruled by monarchs for over 200 years without interference from political parties. Based on oil, the economy has attracted so many foreign workers that they constitute 80 percent of the workforce. Although it is possible to form labor unions in Kuwait, it is very difficult. In 1968, the Kuwait Trade Union Federation was founded; it is the sole legal trade union. In 1994, the law required that at least 100 workers were required to form a labor union, of whom at least 15 had to be Kuwaiti nationals.

Expatriate workers have to live in Kuwait for at least five years before they can join a labor union, but they cannot hold office or vote in union ballots or at union meetings. Expatriate domestic servants are often mistreated and can be prosecuted if they leave their employers. In 2009, the **International Trade Union Confederation** drew attention to the restrictions on trade union rights. Hundreds of migrant workers were arrested and deported when they struck against bad working conditions and low wages. The Labour Code that was passed at the end of 2009 did nothing to improve conditions for immigrant employees or organized labor in general.

KYRGYZSTAN. Independent since August 1991 from the former Soviet Union, of which it had been formally a part since 1924, there is no early history of organized labor in Kyrgyzstan. The 1992 Labor Law recognized the right of workers to form unions but the right to **strike** was not specifically protected and strikes were made illegal. The law recognized the right to **collective bargaining** but generally was more in favor of attracting foreign investors than protecting workers' rights. In 2007, the **International Trade Union Confederation (ITUC)** noted that trade unions successfully prevented attempts to remove some union rights but in 2008 a district court suspended the president of the Federation of Trade Unions of Kyrgyzstan (FPKg). As a result the FPKg lost its ITUC status and had not regained it by 2010.

L

LABOR DAY. Labor Day, a public holiday celebrated in the **United States** and **Canada** on the first Monday of September, was begun by the **Knights of Labor** as a march in New York City in 1882; other marches were held in 1883 and 1884 to celebrate labor. Oregon was the first U.S. state to legislate Labor Day as a public holiday in 1887. The U.S. Congress declared it a public holiday in 1894. Labor Day public holidays are also a feature of **Australia** and **New Zealand**, though largely devoid of their original significance.

LABOR DISPUTES. Labor disputes, whether in the form of **strikes** or lockouts, are the most consistently visible sign of the presence of conflicts between employers and labor. There have been labor disputes since the earliest times—the first recorded labor dispute occurred in **Egypt** in 1152 B.C. among the pharaoh's tomb-makers—and they predate unions as formal, continuous organizations. In 18th-century England, 383 labor disputes were recorded between 1717 and 1800, and these led to the first sustained efforts to create legal mechanisms for their resolution. As the Industrial Revolution developed, labor disputes and other kinds of collective action such as rallies and demonstrations began to replace older forms of social protest such as food riots and tax revolts.

From about 1830, the first systematic efforts were made to collect information on disputes both by officials and by individuals. In **France**, official monitoring began in 1830 even though strikes were treated as a crime before 1864. Elsewhere in Europe, monitoring of disputes in some form had begun in the **United Kingdom** (1870) and **Italy** (1871), activities that often grew into official national statistical collections by the 1890s. In the **United States**, in 1888, the Massachusetts Bureau of Statistics published a time series for its labor disputes from 1825 to 1886 and continued to publish statistics into the 20th century, as did New York State, even though a national series of U.S. dispute statistics was begun in 1881. Other countries followed: **Denmark** (1897), **Canada** (1901), **Netherlands** and **Germany** (1901), **Sweden** and **Norway** (1903), **New Zealand** and **South Africa** (1906), **Finland** (1907), **Australia** (1913), and **Japan** (1914). In 1927, the **International Labour**

Organization began publishing dispute statistics for all the countries that collected them.

This monitoring was in response to a general rise in the level of disputes in Western Europe and North America from the late 1860s to the outbreak of World War I in 1914 and from 1917 to about 1930. **General strikes** occurred in some countries such as in **Belgium** (1893), Netherlands (1903), Sweden (1909), Britain (1926), and France (1968). The year 1920 was one of the high points of disputes based on rising inflation and falling real wages in the aftermath of World War I. The causes of these waves of disputes included political as well as economic objectives. Many employees who were not formally union members took part in labor disputes.

Governments before 1914 were more concerned with disputes as a threat to political stability than as a cost to the economy. Labor disputes are unlike most other social phenomena in that they can change greatly from one year to the next and often occur in waves. There have been three major international waves of labor disputes: 1869 to 1875, 1910 to 1920, and 1968 to 1974. The relationship between labor disputes and the trade cycle is complicated, but there is a clear association between the frequency of disputes and the state of the trade cycle. In good economic times, there are usually more disputes than when the cycle is depressed.

On occasion, particularly intense labor disputes have politicized some of their participants. For instance, two of the thousands of strikers who were victimized after the great railroad strike of 1917 in New South Wales, Australia, were drawn into politics: Joseph Benedict Chifley (1885–1951), who was Australia's prime minister from 1945 to 1949, and John Joseph Cahill (1891–1959), who was premier of New South Wales from 1952 to 1959.

In 1984, two Danish economists, Martin Paldam and Peder J. Pedersen, examined data for 18 Organisation for Economic Co-operation and Development (OECD) countries between 1919 and 1979 and found a positive link between nominal wage rises and the number of labor disputes. They found that changes in real wages were only negatively related to changes in labor disputes in the United States and that in other countries the relationship was either positive or insignificant. They also suggested that there was a cultural-linguistic divide in the labor dispute record of these countries between 1919 and 1979. They distinguished high-conflict countries as belonging to the Anglo-Saxon group (United Kingdom, **Ireland**, United States, Canada, Australia, and New Zealand) or the Latin group (France and Italy), low-conflict countries as belonging to the German-Nordic group (**Austria**, **Denmark**, Germany, Netherlands, Norway, Sweden, and **Switzerland**), and a fourth group that did not fit easily into any category (Belgium, Finland, and Japan). They could not discern any long-term pattern in the labor dispute levels of the Anglo-Saxon or Latin groups, but in the German-Nordic group there was a strong falling trend of disputes since the peak level of the early 1920s.

Labor disputes are unevenly distributed in the economy. Certain industries, particularly **coal mining**, engineering, and transportation, have frequently accounted for a major part of the disputes in many countries. From the 1970s a "tertiarisation of industrial conflict" has been noted following the tertiarisation of the economy. Since 1980, the number of disputes has fallen to very low levels in most countries, a trend that has been attributed to the decline in the strength of organized labor and profound economic shifts.

The study of labor disputes has been approached from two main directions: the sociohistorical approach, which examined their statistical characteristics within and between countries over time, and the "rational expectations" approach, which treats labor disputes as one possible result of rational decision-making by bargainers with incomplete information. This latter approach has been popular among labor economists since about 1970, although it was first suggested by the economist John R. Hicks in 1932. Although the two approaches proceed from widely different attitudes and assumptions, it is clear that there is no agreed single model that can be applied to labor disputes for all periods.

For all the drama that can accompany large labor disputes, they account for only a tiny proportion of the work days lost in most Western economies compared with other sources of loss such as illness and industrial accidents. The lost production caused by disputes is usually quickly made up. Nevertheless, governments remain sensitive to the level of disputes as an indicator of political stability and the countries' reliability as international traders. Consequently, the legal right to strike is circumscribed in various ways even in many Western countries. Legal notice of a strike is required in some countries. In Japan, most of the **public sector** is denied the right to strike, as are federal government employees (since 1912) and most state employees in the United States, with the exception of those in Hawaii and Pennsylvania. Finally, the international statistics on disputes for any period must be treated with considerable caution, as many countries understate their true level of disputes and use incomparable definitions. Data compiled by the British Department of Industry indicated that within the countries of the OECD, the average number of working days lost per thousand employees in 1996 to 2000 was 59, compared with an average of 66 between 1991 and 1995. Since 2006, strikes in many countries affected by the global financial crisis have risen sharply. *See also* BRITISH GENERAL STRIKE; CONCILIATION AND ARBITRATION; GENERAL STRIKES; LABOR STATISTICS; STRIKES; "WINTER OF DISCONTENT."

LABOR HISTORY. Credit for the first truly scholarly investigation of organized labor must go to **Beatrice** (1858–1943) and **Sidney James Webb** (1859–1947), who published their *The History of Trade Unionism* in 1894.

In the **United States**, John R. Commons (1862–1945) founded the Wisconsin school of labor history, one of the first systematic, scholarly endeavors of its kind anywhere, and published the 10-volume *A Documentary History of American Industrial Society* in 1910–1911 and a four-volume *History of Labor in the United States* between 1918 and 1935. In **Australia**, T. A. Coghlan (1855–1926) published a four-volume general account, *Labour and Industry in Australia from the First Settlement in 1788 to the Establishment of the Commonwealth in 1901,* in 1918. In 1921, J. T. Sutcliffe published *A History of Trade Unionism in Australia.*

However, this impetus was not sustained, and the scholarly examination of the history of organized labor tended to languish in the 1930s and 1940s and did not revive until the 1960s, when it benefited from an upsurge of interest in social and economic history, stimulated by works such as E. P. Thompson's *The Making of the English Working Class* (1963). Academic journals devoted to labor history began in the United States (1960), Australia (1962), and Canada (1976). Academics lost interest in the 1980s, but following the recent global revival of labor unrest, academia has shown renewed interest.

LABOR-MANAGEMENT REPORTING AND DISCLOSURE ACT. *See* LANDRUM-GRIFFIN ACT.

LABOR PARTIES. *See* SOCIAL-DEMOCRATIC, SOCIALIST, AND LABOR PARTIES.

LABOR STATISTICS. Most of the earliest labor statistics were collected through the census of population and housing: the **United Kingdom** census included a question on occupation from 1811 and the **United States** census included a question on industry from 1820. From the 1860s, there was growing demand for better statistical information about labor. Several American states, notably Massachusetts (1869), Pennsylvania (1870), and Ohio (1877), established statistical bureaus that collected data on wages, prices, and **labor disputes**.

The demand for better statistics did not just come from governments and employers; organized labor was well aware of the importance of accurate statistics. The International Working Men's Association (the first International) as early as 1866 invited all workers of Europe and America "to collaborate in gathering the elements of the statistics of the working class." Aim III of the **Knights of Labor** was the establishment of a Bureau of Labor Statistics "so that we may arrive at correct knowledge of the educational, moral and financial condition of the laboring masses." The U.S. Bureau of Labor was created in 1884 and made an independent organization in 1888. From about 1890, many countries began to publish official statistics on topics, such as labor disputes, trade union **membership**, wages, prices, employment, and unemployment. In 1893, the British government began to issue a national statistical publication with commentary, the *Labour Gazette*, which continues to the present as the *Employment Gazette*. In **Australia**, the federal government began publishing a compendium of national labor statistics, the *Labour Report*, in 1912 and continued it until 1972. The U.S. Bureau of Labor Statistics began to publish the *Monthly Labor Review* in 1915, a publication that continues to the present.

In 1940, the United States began to collect labor force statistics from a regular household survey, an example followed by **Canada** (1954), Australia (1960), and many other countries since. One important byproduct of these surveys has been their ability to match labor union membership with a range of socioeconomic and demographic characteristics. Such information began to be available for the United States in 1973 (although the present survey began in 1983), from 1983 for Australia (with a pilot survey being held in 1976), in 1984 for Canada, in 1987 for **Sweden**, and in 1989 for the United Kingdom.

The main agency for the collection of international labor statistics is the **International Labour Organization**, which has been publishing its *Year Book of Labour Statistics* since 1927. ILO Convention 160 (Labor Statistics, 1985) called on member countries to regularly compile and publish statistics on employment, unemployment, earnings, working hours, consumer prices, household expenditure, occupational injury and diseases, and labor disputes. This convention was a revision of Convention 63 (Statistics of Wages and Hours of Work, 1938). The Organisation for Economic Co-operation and Development to which 30 countries are members also collects and publishes labor statistics.

LABOR UNIONS AS EMPLOYERS. Because of their role as representatives of employees and their traditionally small size as organizations, it has tended to be forgotten that labor unions as organizations are also employers, and the topic has not been researched. However, the increased **amalgamation** of labor unions since the 1980s has meant that labor unions have become larger organizations and therefore more likely to be employers in their own right. Information on unions as employers is scanty, but in the **United States**, official survey figures show that there was an average of 138,400 people employed by its labor unions between 2001 and 2005, that is, 1 employee for every 114 union members. In **Australia**, wage and salary data for 2004–2005 implied that there were about 6,500 persons employed by labor unions or 1 employee for every 300 union members. In the **Netherlands**, the mergers and financial problems of labor unions even resulted in a number of strikes by union employees against the unions they worked for.

LANDRUM-GRIFFIN ACT. This act, known officially as the *Labor-Management Reporting and Disclosure Act,* was a major piece of U.S. federal labor law that was passed in September 1959. It was aimed at reducing corruption within unions as exemplified by the **Teamsters**. It set down minimum standards to ensure democratic elections, but it also extended the ban of the **Taft-Hartley Act** on secondary boycotts and allowed the states to assume jurisdiction in relatively minor **labor disputes**.

LAOS. The Lao People's Democratic Republic has been ruled by the Communist Party since 1975. The Party also controls the Federation of Lao Trade Unions. No unions are allowed outside the Federation and strikes are forbidden in law. The **International Trade Union Confederation** survey of **violations of trade union rights** documents the arrest in 2009 of nine rural workers during a demonstration.

LATVIA. Organized labor was only able to emerge in Latvia after it gained independence from **Russia** in 1920; previously, it had been part of the Russian Empire. In 1921, the labor federation of Latvia joined the **International Federation of Trade Unions** and remained a member until 1933. In 1923, Latvia claimed a trade union **membership** of 23,660. In 1940, an independent labor movement ceased to exist in the Baltic States after their annexation by the Soviet Union.

In the late 1980s, the Soviet Union began to fragment, allowing organized labor to reemerge. During March 1990, Latvia and the other **Baltic states** declared their independence from the Soviet Union. Labor unions were legalized in Latvia in December 1990, although there was conflict over the ownership of the property of the former communist labor federation. The right to **strike** was recognized in 1998, although with limitations. In 1997, the Free Trade Union Confederation of Latvia was admitted to membership of the **International Confederation of Free Trade Unions (ICFTU)** and claimed a membership of 207,400 in 2001. During 2001, the government made efforts to bring Latvia's laws in line with the conventions of the **International Labour Organization** and the **European Union**. In 2002, the ICFTU conceded that progress had been made with Latvia's legal environment for organized labor, but that government did not regard labor unions as partners in social dialogue and that there was much opposition to unions in the private sector. The 2009 survey of **violations of trade union rights** by the **International Trade Union Confederation** observed that there was a trend of employer hostility toward organized labor and **collective bargaining**.

LAVAL CASE. Swedish unions took action in 2004 against the Latvian Laval company over the working conditions of Latvian construction workers in the town of Vaxholm who were paid according to the standards of **Latvia**. Laval refused to sign a collective agreement, and the unions responded with a blockade of the work place. The Labour Court of **Sweden** referred the case to the European Court of Justice, which ruled in 2007 that the right of businesses to supply cross-border services is more fundamental than the right to **strike**. The **European Trade Union Confederation** fears that as a consequence, equality for migrant workers according to the conditions of the host country is under attack and social dumping will follow.

LAW. *See* EMPLOYMENT ACTS; LANDRUM-GRIFFIN ACT; NATIONAL INDUSTRIAL RECOVERY ACT; RIGHT-TO-WORK LAWS; *ROOKES V. BARNARD;* TAFT-HARTLEY ACT; WAGNER ACT.

LEBANON. An independent nation since 1943; it had been previously administered by **France** under a mandate from the League of Nations. Labor unions in Lebanon were first formed in the 1940s. Reflecting its society, organized labor was fragmented along religious, ethnic, and political lines. Lebanon has been represented in the **International Confederation of Free Trade Unions** since 1951, but by a number of affiliates since 1965; in 1996, Lebanon had 13 affiliates, the most of any country at the time. The biggest affiliate is the General Confederation of Lebanese Workers with more than half of organized labor. Between 1975 and 1990, Lebanon suffered from civil war, which claimed 150,000 lives and inflicted massive economic damage. In 2009, the **International Trade Union Confederation** expressed its concern that **Palestinian** workers, who are regarded to be stateless, are not allowed to form unions. The right to **strike** is limited, as is the right to organize demonstrations. A **general strike** in May 2008 met with army intervention.

LEGIEN, CARL (1861–1920). Carl Legien was one of the leading labor leaders in **Germany** before 1914. Born in Marienburg, he was raised in an orphanage after the death of his parents. Apprenticed as a turner in 1875, he settled in Hamburg after military service. He joined the turner's union in 1886 and became its chairman. In 1890, he was elected chairman of the *Generalkommission der Gewerkschaften*, the National Federation of Trade

Unions, a position he held until his death. He used his position to build a strong national union organization and to maintain the independence of the union movement from the control of the Social Democratic Party. He was a strong opponent of the **general strike** as advocated by **syndicalism**. He was president and secretary of the **International Federation of Trade Unions** from 1901 to 1919. Ironically, for someone who opposed general strikes, it was Legien who issued the call for the general strike in Berlin that defeated the proto-fascist Kapp Putsch in 1920.

LESOTHO. Lesotho has been independent from the **United Kingdom** since October 1966 but economically dependent on **South Africa** since then; organized labor had emerged sufficiently by the 1960s to form the Basutoland Federation of Labour, which was admitted to the **International Confederation of Free Trade Unions (ICFTU)** in 1979, declaring a **membership** of 12,000. Changing its name to the Lesotho Federation of Trade Unions by 1983, the federation remained in the ICFTU to 1993, against a backdrop of political instability and military rule between 1986 and 1995. The ICFTU has been critical of the environment for organized labor in the 1990s. In 2007, the **International Trade Union Confederation** reported that, because of complicated legal procedures, there have not been any legal **strikes** for many years, although strikes do occur. Labor unions in the private sector could not be formed without permission and had to be registered by the registrar of trade unions. Harassment of union activists remained commonplace.

LEWIS, JOHN LLEWELLYN (1880–1969). John L. Lewis was the most important miners' leader in the **United States** in the 20th century. He was born in Lucas, Iowa, and began working as a coal miner at 16. In 1909, he gained his first office with the **United Mine Workers of America**, progressing to vice president in 1917 and president in 1920, a position he held until 1960. Lewis was a controversial figure who devoted much of his energies in the 1920s to fighting and expelling rivals from within the union, the **membership** of which fell from 500,000 to 75,000 between 1920 and 1933. Lewis realized the need for legal support in rebuilding the union and was a prime mover behind Section 7(a) of the **National Industrial Recovery Act** of 1933, which gave employees the right to collectively organize and bargain without employer interference. A supporter of **industrial unions**, Lewis saw the potential for organizing the semiskilled and led the campaign to form the **Congress of Industrial Organizations**. He served as its president from 1938 to 1940, resigning in opposition to the policies of President Franklin D. Roosevelt. In 1946 and 1948, Lewis led a series of **strikes** that resulted in the coal mine owners paying a bounty on each ton of coal mined, which was used to finance health, welfare, and retirement benefits for miners. Lewis's last major achievement was the first federal Mine Safety Act (1952). *See also* COAL MINING.

LIBERIA. Despite its name and origins as a haven for freed U.S. slaves since 1847, Liberia has not enjoyed a history of liberty. There was no legal framework for organized labor or **collective bargaining** until 1963. A national labor union federation was formed in 1960; modeled on the U.S. **Congress of Industrial Organizations**, it gained affiliation with the **International Confederation of Free Trade Unions** by 1965, but by 1989 had been replaced as Liberia's affiliate by the Liberian Federation of Labor Unions. In 2007, Liberia was mentioned in the survey of **violations of trade union rights** because the government tried to interfere in internal trade union affairs. In 2008, a historic collective agreement was signed by the Firestone rubber plantation. The same year saw the removal of a 1980 decree that had banned **strikes** but in 2009 a legal framework for trade union activities was still lacking.

LIBYA. Libya has been independent from **Italy** since December 1951. Organized labor in Libya only dates from after 1945; under Benito Mussolini's rule, labor unions were outlawed. The Libyan General Workers' Union was formed in 1952 and was an affiliate of the **International Confederation of Free Trade Unions (ICFTU)** from 1953 to 1959, when it amalgamated with another labor federation to form the Libyan National Confederation of Trade Unions. However, after the coup by Colonel Mummar al-Qaddafi in September 1969, organized labor in Libya ceased to function and its affiliation with the ICFTU also ended; at that time Libya had about 35,000 union members. In 2010, the **International Trade Union Confederation (ITUC)** reported that Libyan workers were still denied any right to organize independent labor unions and **collective bargaining** was heavily curtailed. The report was also critical of the government's disregard of the rights of migrant workers and the virtual prohibition of strikes. The General Trade Union Federation of Workers claimed to be more independent than during the past, but the ITUC concluded that it is still under strict **government control**. The uprisings in **Tunisia** and **Egypt** that started in 2010 were followed by a popular revolt in Lybia resulting in the death of Qaddafi.

LIECHTENSTEIN. Liechtenstein is a constitutional monarchy with a high standard of living, thanks to its financial services as the main economic sector. There is freedom of unions and strikes. The single union, *Kiechtensteiner Arbeitnehmer Verband* (Liechtenstein Employees' Association), has 1,200 members and covers about 13 percent of employees.

LITHUANIA. Organized labor was only able to emerge in Lithuania after it gained independence from **Russia** in 1918; previously it had been part of the Russian Empire since 1795. A labor federation existed in Lithuania by 1926 and was a member of the **International Federation of Trade Unions** until 1927, but after a military government took power, the number of union members fell from 18,500 in 1927 to 1,200 by 1932. In 1940, an independent labor movement ceased to exist in Lithuania and the other **Baltic states** after their annexation by the Soviet Union.

In the late 1980s, the Soviet Union began to fragment, allowing organized labor to reemerge. The first independent labor union in the post-1940 period in the Baltic states was formed in Lithuania in 1988. During March 1990, all three Baltic states declared their independence from the Soviet Union. In Lithuania, an independent workers' union, the Lithuanian Workers' Union, was formed in 1989 and claimed 150,000 members by 1992. In 1991, the Lithuanian government nationalized the property of the **communist** labor federation and introduced the Collective Agreements Law, which hindered the formation of new labor unions. Lithuania was represented in the **International Confederation of Free Trade Unions** by 1997. In 2001, its two labor federation members claimed a combined **membership** of 91,600. In 2007, the **International Trade Union Confederation** was critical of restrictions on the right to join unions and of the excessive ban on **strikes**. Besides, the national confederation, the *LPSS solidarmus* suffered government interference in its activities. Legislation in 2008 relaxed restrictions, but antiunion behavior continued. At least three trade unionists were dismissed in 2010.

LOBBYING. *See* POLITICS.

LOKHANDE, NARAYAN MEGHAJI (1848–1897). Generally regarded as the father of organized labor in **India**, Lokhande started his career with the railroads and the postal department. Afterward, he joined the Mandavi Textile Mills as storekeeper in 1870. This mill-life experience exposed him to the miserable living conditions of the mill hands and it prompted him to organize them. Before the Factory Act of 1881, no legislation existed to protect employees, who toiled in appalling conditions that could be endured for only a few years. Many were women and children, causing growing concern about the exploitative nature of factory work. Despite the employers' resistance, the government enacted the Factory Act of 1881. The enforcement of the law was minimal, so Lokhande saw the need to establish a union in 1884, the Bombay Mill Hands Association—the first labor organization in India. That year also witnessed the appointment of a Factory Commission because the concerns of adult mill workers had so far been ignored. The Association and Lokhande placed many formal grievances before the government. They also gathered thousands of signatures of mill workers, submitted memoranda, and gave valuable evidence before the Commission. He also established a hospital for the poor so they would have access to medical facilities. In 1896, he was involved in relief work when Bombay and its suburbs were in the grip of the plague. This tireless work itself led to his death from the plague. Despite all his achievements, Lokhande was a forgotten figure until 2005 when he was commemorated on a postage stamp.

LUXEMBOURG. Luxembourg has been a sovereign nation since 1867, when organized labor also began to develop. Like its neighbor, **Belgium**, its organized labor has been divided by religion. The *Confédération Générale du Travail* (General Confederation of Labor), the main labor federation, was formed in 1919. A **Catholic** labor federation was formed in 1920. Union **membership** was 18,000 in 1930. Unions were suppressed by the Nazis, and, although an attempt was made to build a unified labor movement after 1944, it had failed by 1948 through the defection of **communists** and Catholics. Luxembourg has always been a member of the **International Confederation of Free Trade Unions**. Between 1970 and 1990 the number of union members in Luxembourg rose from 52,000 to 75,000, divided among labor federations that cater to **white-** and **blue-collar** unions, Catholic unions, private sector white-collar unions, and **craft unions**. In 2010, the two Luxembourg affiliates of the **International Trade Union Confederation** had a total membership of 104,500.

MACEDONIA (FORMER YUGOSLAV REPUBLIC). Macedonia was part of **Yugoslavia** until 1991. Unlike **Yugoslavia (Federal Republic)**, there was no significant continuous history of organized labor in Macedonia—although some unions are known to have been formed in 1905—which remains the poorest of the republics that made up the former Yugoslavia.

In 2010, the **International Trade Union Confederation (ITUC)** was concerned about serious limitations on the right to **strike** in Macedonia and changes to labor laws wanted by international financial institutions that disadvantaged organized labor. There were 5,300 union members in Macedonia.

MADAGASCAR. Independent from **France** since June 1960, Madagascar had labor unions by 1937. Madagascar was represented in the **International Confederation of Free Trade Unions** by 1953 and has retained its affiliation ever since, despite political uncertainty. In 1995, there were about 30,000 union members in Madagascar. In 2007, the **International Trade Union Confederation (ITUC)** reported government hostility to labor unions in "essential services" and particularly in **export processing zones**. The right to **strike** is recognized but not easy to use because of complicated procedures. Despite this, and a political crisis in which dozens of civilians were killed, the four Madagascan affiliates of the ITUC claimed a total of nearly 78,000 members in 2010.

MALAWI. A former colony of the **United Kingdom** and independent since July 1964, Malawi was previously called *Nyasaland.* It was unusual among colonies in having an ordinance regulating labor unions in 1932 before there was any real presence of organized labor. The Nyasaland Trades Union Congress was formed in 1956 and was admitted to the **International Confederation of Free Trade Unions (ICFTU)** in 1957; it was reformed as the Trades Union Congress of Malawi in 1964 and has remained an affiliate of the ICFTU ever since. After independence, organized labor fared poorly. Hastings Banda, who led the independence movement and was the first prime minister, declared himself president for life in 1971 and ran a one-party government to 1994 that committed abuses of trade union and **human rights**. By

1995, Malawi had about 45,000 labor union members. In 2007, the **International Trade Union Confederation** reported that, although labor unions and collective bargaining were legally recognized in Malawi, they were severely regulated and **strikes** were easily declared illegal. In 2010, 50 workers were dismissed for striking and the ITUC confirmed that employers and government still resisted unions.

MALAYSIA. The first labor unions in the Malayan Peninsula were created by the Chinese in the **Singapore** area, starting with a union of engineering mechanics in 1875. Other unions were formed later by Indian employees. In 1939, there were 43 unions. By 1947, there were about 200,000 members of labor unions, of which about half belonged to unions controlled by **communists**. The Malaysian Trades Union Congress (originally called the *Malayan Trade Union Council*) was formed in 1950. The development of Malaysian labor unions was retarded by the economic dominance of **agriculture** until the late 1980s and by the period of the Emergency (1948–1960), which forced governments to devote their efforts to fighting the communist insurgency. Since becoming independent from the **United Kingdom** in 1957, Malaysian governments have tolerated rather than encouraged labor unions. In 1967, the Industrial Relations Act gave the government the power to use compulsory arbitration to settle **labor disputes** if **conciliation** failed. To encourage foreign investment in 1981, labor unions were excluded from **export processing zones**, which mainly produced electronic goods. Under pressure from the **American Federation of Labor–Congress of Industrial Organizations**, this policy was relaxed in September 1988 to permit in-house unions in these zones. Malaysia has been represented continuously in the **International Confederation of Free Trade Union** and its successor since 1951. They have been critical of the Malaysian government and policies of hindering **collective bargaining** and the free operation of labor unions. In 2010, there were 400,000 union members in Malaysia, compared with 350,000 in 1992. In 2009, the **International Trade Union Confederation (ITUC)** complained that the Trade Union Act (2008) obstructed the creation of independent and strong unions; the ITUC documented many examples of employers' destroying labor unions and abuse of migrant employees.

MALDIVES. Independent from the **United Kingdom** since 1965, the Maldives became a presidential republic three years later but only became a multiparty state in 2005. The 2008 constitution guarantees freedom of association and the right to **strike**. The Tourism Employees Association of Maldives, which was formed in 2008, seems to have been the first labor union ever formed on the Maldives. In 2009, all the leaders of a strike at the Bandos Island Resort lost their jobs.

MALI. Mali has been independent of **France** since September 1960; organized labor in Mali originally consisted of the overseas branches of French labor unions. After independence, organized labor was placed under **government control** through the *Union Nationale des Travailleurs du Mali* (UNTM), or National Union of Workers of Mali. In 1993, this organization was admitted to membership of the **International Confederation of Free Trade Unions**, when it claimed 130,000 members. The growing independent attitude of the UNTM provoked the government to fund a breakaway union centre. The **International Trade Union Confederation** surveys of **violations of trade union rights** since 2007 have documented the arrests of union leaders and dismissals of activists such as the 100 strikers from the Morilla gold mines in 2010.

MALTA. Fully independent from the **United Kingdom** since 1964, the first Maltese labor union was formed among waterfront fitters under English influence in 1884, but it was not until 1945 that a legal framework for labor unions and **collective bargaining** was established. Malta has been represented continuously in the **International Confederation of Free Trade Union** and its successor, the **International Trade Union Confederation**, since 1951 by the General Workers' Union (formed 1943); it claimed 36,000 members in 2001. Since 1959, a rival union center exists, claiming 31,000 members in 2001. In 2002, the government introduced a law that would allow for compulsory arbitration in **labor disputes**. In 2008, there were 84,000 union members in Malta of which only 60,000 remained in 2011.

MANUAL/NONMANUAL. *See* BLUE-COLLAR/WHITE COLLAR.

MANUFACTURING. Manufacturing, also known as the *secondary sector,* covers all those economic activities that result in the production of tangible goods. It was the first economic sector in which organized labor arose from about 1350, in Western Europe. Modern organized labor emerged in the 18th century in the **United Kingdom**. **Printing** was the earliest part of manufacturing to produce organized labor. With the advent of the Industrial Revolution from 1850, engineering and metal working, together with **coal mining**, became important parts of the backbone of organized labor. In the United Kingdom, this was most evident in the **Amalgamated Society of Engineers**, formed in 1851. Between 1892 and 1970, about 40 percent of all British union members were employed in some area of manufacturing, of whom about half were employed in metal working and engineering. Since the 1970s, the strength of manufacturing unions within organized labor in industrial countries has declined along with employment in the industry. In the United Kingdom, for example, only 20 percent of employees in manufacturing in

2010 were union members compared with 33 percent in 1995. Over the same period, the percentage of employees in manufacturing in the **United States** fell from 18 to 11 percent. Even in upcoming **China** the number of employees in manufacturing fell from 86.2 million in 1990 to 83.1 million in 2002.

MATERNAL PROTECTION. The provision of legal safeguards for employed mothers was recognized by the **International Labour Organization** by Convention No. 3 (Maternal Protection) in 1919, which was revised in 1952 as Convention No. 103. Paid leave for maternity (that is, during and after pregnancy), however, generally only became a feature of **women**'s employment in the 1980s.

MATIGNON AGREEMENT. The Matignon Agreement was a landmark agreement in the history of labor relations in **France**. It was reached between the Socialist government of Léon Blum, the *Confédération Générale du Travail* (CGT), or General Confederation of Labor, and **employers' organizations** on 7 June 1936. The agreement provided for the unions' right to organize, an end to antiunion practices, **collective bargaining**, pay increases of 7 to 12 percent, and the election of shop stewards. One problem with the agreement was that by extending bargaining rights to all representative unions rather than to a single bargaining body, it tended to inhibit the development of strong collective bargaining units representing employees.

MAURITANIA. Independent from **France** since November 1960, organized labor in Mauritania has been under **government control** since 1971, and the government reserved the right to recognize or dissolve labor unions. Foreign workers do not have the right to form labor unions. On 16 October 2000, a march organized by the Free Confederation of Mauritanian Workers was declared illegal by the government and 40 participants were arrested. In December 2001, Mauritania was admitted to membership of the **International Confederation of Free Trade Unions (ICFTU)**. The ICFTU was critical of the Mauritanian government's failure to make good on its promises to reform its labor laws, made to the **International Labour Organization** since 1993. It remained critical of the Labor Code of 2004. In addition, successive military governments have harassed organized labor and the **International Trade Union Confederation** was unable to report any improvements in 2010.

MAURITIUS. Independent from the **United Kingdom** since March 1968, organized labor in Mauritius developed in the 1940s—as evidenced by the formation of the Mauritius Trades Union Congress in 1946—and came to reflect the country's ethnic and political divisions. Mauritius has been represented in the **International Confederation of Free Trade Unions** since

1951; between 1951 and 1995, its reported **membership** rose from 10,000 to 67,000 and the Mauritius Labour Congress, which was formed in 1963, was the country's representative at the ICFTU since 1965. Mauritius established the first **export processing zone** in Africa in 1970. In 2001, the ICFTU was critical of the low level of union membership in the export processing zones of Mauritius, even though such membership is legal; in 2002, it noted that some improvements had been made. The 2009 and 2010 surveys of the **violations of trade union rights** conducted by the **International Trade Union Confederation** reported harassment of union activists and that workers in the export processing zones have virtually no trade union rights.

MBOYA, THOMAS JOSEPH ODHIAMBO (1930–1969). Tom Mboya was the son of relatively poor members of the Luo tribe (the second largest tribe at that time) in **Kenya**, then a British colony. Despite the poor environment he grew up in, Mboya was educated at school and completed secondary school. But when he ran out of money he was unable to complete the examinations. Mboya later was able to attend the sanitary inspectors' school in Nairobi because he was given a stipend. Working as an inspector in Nairobi, he became secretary of the African Employees Union. In 1952, he founded the Kenya Local Government Workers Union. When the Mau Mau rebellion against the European land ownership started in 1951, the colonial British government responded with the declaration of a state of emergency. In 1952, Jomo Kenyatta, the leader of the Mau Mau, and over 500 others were detained. Most of them belonged to the Kikuyu tribe, the largest of the country. Tom Mboya accepted the post of treasurer in the Kenya African Union (KAU), thus controlling most of the opposition to British rule. The British banned the KAU in 1953, leaving the newly created Kenya Federation of Labour in control of the "official" opposition. With the support of the British Labour Party, Mboya went to the **United Kingdom** to study industrial management. By the time he returned, the Mau Mau rebellion had ended in a bloodbath leaving 10,000 Mau Mau and only just over 100 Europeans dead. The existing union movement was mostly involved in the struggle for independence, in which Mboya played a big role. When he attended a convention of African nationalists at Accra, Ghana, he regarded it as "the proudest day of my life." After achieving independence and the declaration of a republic in 1963, Jomo Kenyatta became Kenya's first president. Ethnic rivalries between the Luo and the Kikuyu developed rapidly. Mboya was considered a potential successor to Kenyatta, but a Kikuyu murdered him in 1969.

MEANY, GEORGE (1894–1980). Meany was president of the **American Federation of Labor (AFL)** from 1952 to 1955 and of the **American Federation of Labor–Congress of Industrial Organizations (AFL-CIO)** from

1955 until 1979. Born in New York City, Meany completed an **apprenticeship** as a plumber in 1915 and based his union career on the United Association of Plumbers and Steam Fitters of the United States and Canada. In 1939, he was elected secretary-treasurer of the AFL, but it was not until the late 1940s that he could exercise any real power. He was the first director of the AFL's League for Political Education (1948) and served on the executive board of the **International Confederation of Free Trade Unions (ICFTU)** during 1951. A skilled negotiator, he played a major role in the merger of the AFL with the **Congress of Industrial Organizations** to form the AFL-CIO in 1955. A Catholic, Meany waged a determined campaign against **communism** and labor rivals such as **Walter Reuther**; he was also opposed to racial or religious discrimination in organized labor. A right-wing Democrat, Meany refused to give the AFL-CIO's endorsement to the left-wing George S. McGovern, the Democratic nominee for president in 1972. Under his leadership, the AFL-CIO left the ICFTU in 1969 over its stance on **politics** and did not rejoin until 1981. Meany was succeeded as AFL-CIO president by a more moderate figure, **Joseph Lane Kirkland**.

MEDIA ENTERTAINMENT INTERNATIONAL (MEI). Originally called the *International Secretariat of Entertainment Trade Unions,* the MEI was an **international trade secretariat** set up in 1965 in Brussels at a conference of the **International Confederation of Free Trade Unions**. In 1984, it became an autonomous part of the *Fédération internationale des employés, techniciens et cadres* **(FIET)**, or the International Federation of Commercial, Clerical, Professional, and Technical Employees. The secretariat was not a success; between 1973 and 1992 its **membership** fell from 470,000 to 100,000. In 1993, it merged with the International Federation of Trade Unions of Audio-Visual Workers (founded in 1974) to form the International Secretariat for Arts, Mass Media, and Entertainment Trade Unions (ISAMMETU). In December 1995, the ISAMMETU renamed itself the *MEI* and in January 2000 it merged with **Communication International**, the **International Graphical Federation**, and the FIET to form the **Union Network International**.

MEMBERSHIP OF ORGANIZED LABOR. The membership of organized labor tends to be drawn from the better-off sections of the labor force or from industries characterized by large employers. The first labor unions were made up of skilled artisans, such as in **printing**, and later by skilled metal workers in **manufacturing**. Unions among large-scale industries such as **coal mining**, textiles, and **railroads** tended to be formed after about 1860. Unions among the lesser skilled employees mostly only began late in the 19th century. The industrial composition of union membership changed considerably in the 20th century in response to shifts in employment. In 1900, about half of all union members in the **United States** were employed either in mining or in manufacturing, but since 1950 their share of union membership has declined. In 2010, only 10 percent of union members were employed in mining or manufacturing in the United States compared with 17 percent in 2001.

Other industries (excluding **agriculture**) have accounted for a growing share of union members, again in response to employment shifts within the labor force. These industries cover a great range of economic activities, from construction to education and from government employment to personal services. Transport and communications accounted for 22 percent of union members in **Australia** and the United States in 1900, but only for 11 percent in the **United Kingdom**. By 2001, the share of union members employed in transport and communications was about 10 to 11 percent in all three countries.

Household surveys of the labor force since 1980 have shown that the proportion of employees in these industries (sometimes called the tertiary or **service sector**) varies greatly. For example, in 2001, the proportion of employees in wholesale and retail trade who were union members was 4.7 percent in the United States, 15.2 in Australia, and 12 percent in the United Kingdom. In contrast, the proportion of employees in government employment in 2001 was consistently high in all three countries: 37 percent in the United States, 59 percent in the United Kingdom, and 48 percent in Australia.

Until the 1960s, **women** made up only about 20 percent of union members but have more than doubled their share in Australia, the United Kingdom, and the United States. Since 2005, there have been more women labor union members than men in the United Kingdom. An exception to this trend was **Germany**, where the proportion of women members only grew from 18 to 32 percent between 1960 and 1997. Statistics on the ages of union members have only become available with household labor force surveys since the 1970s. These surveys show that younger employees, particularly teenagers, are less likely to be union members than middle-aged employees. In 2010, only 12 percent of employees aged 20 to 24 were union members in the United Kingdom, compared with 23 percent of those aged 30 to 34 years. In the United States, only 4 percent of employees aged 16 to 24 were union members compared with 13 percent of employees aged 25 and over in 2010. *See also* FULL-TIME/PART-TIME EMPLOYMENT; WHITE-COLLAR UNIONISM; Appendix D.

MEXICO. As in Western Europe, the first organizations among workers in Mexico were mutual-aid societies, which were formed in the main urban areas between 1835 and 1864. Although de facto unions emerged after 1876, it was not until 1906 that organized labor made its presence felt through **strikes** by miners (Cananea) and textile workers (Rio Blanco); these were violently suppressed by the Porfirista dictatorship. The Constitution of 1917 recognized labor unions and the right to strike and was a tangible victory from the revolution of 1910. In May 1918, the *Confederación Regional Obrera Mexicana* (CROM), or Regional Confederation of Mexican Wage Earners, was established with 75 organizations that claimed a million members. Militant at first, the CROM became more allied with the government, a trend that promoted the creation by **anarchists** of a radical alternative labor federation, the *Confederación General de Trabajo,* or General Confederation of Labor, in 1921. By 1923, union **membership** in Mexico had fallen to about 800,000 but then rose to 2.1 million by 1927.

The Depression beginning in 1929 reduced union membership to 500,000 by 1932, but by 1934 organized labor claimed 2.6 million members. In 1936, a third labor federation, the *Confederación de Trabajadores de Mexico* (CTM), or Confederation of Mexican Workers, was formed. Because the CTM had the affiliation of oil workers, miners and metal workers, railroad employees, and peasants, it became the dominant federation and developed close links with the ruling political party. Since 1936, other labor federations were founded, usually to the left of the CTM. In 1997, the *Unión Nacional de Trabajadores,* or National Union of Workers, was created by dissident organizations located in the telecommunications sector and especially among health workers in the public sector.

Mexico joined the **International Federation of Trade Unions** in 1936 and has been an active participant in pan-American labor bodies such as the **Pan-American Federation of Labor** and the *Organización Regional Interamericana de Trabajadores.* In 1966, the *Congreso del Trabajo,* or Congress of Labor, was set up to provide a single voice for organized labor. Mexico has been represented in the **International Confederation of Free Trade Unions (ICFTU)** and its successor since 1951. In 1965, the Mexican government established the first **export processing zone** near the U.S. border to assemble goods for foreign-owned companies at low wages. In 2001, Mexico's affiliate in the ICFTU, the CTM, claimed a membership of 1.5 million. In 2007, the **International Trade Union Confederation (ITUC)** noted that, although the general legal environment for organized labor was acceptable, in practice there were **violations of trade union rights** in the **public sector** and the export processing zones. The ITUC documented 2 deaths and 41 injuries during a demonstration by miners in 2009 over the illegal dismissal of a union leader. Six labor activists were killed in 2009. The ITUC was unable to report any improvements in conditions for organized labor in Mexico in 2010.

MINERS' INTERNATIONAL FEDERATION (MIF). The MIF was set up in **Belgium** in 1890 by representatives of miners' unions from **Austria**, Belgium, **France**, **Germany**, and the **United Kingdom**. Between 1913 and 1931 its claimed **membership** rose from 1.2 to nearly 1.5 million. In the late 1950s, the MIF began to prepare standards for miners; it released a miner's charter in 1957 and a charter for young miners in 1958. In 1976, the MIF had 887,500 members, of whom 628,700 were in Europe, 203,800 in Asia, and 8,800 in the **United States**. In 1994, the MIF had 58 affiliated unions that represented 4.2 million members. In 1995, the MIF merged with the **International Federation of Chemical, Energy, Mine, and General Workers**. *See also* COAL MINING.

MINEWORKERS' FEDERATION OF GREAT BRITAIN (MWF). From the early 1890s to the late 1930s, the Mineworkers' Federation (its official title from 1932) was the largest labor union in the **United Kingdom** and the largest single labor union in the world until 1919. The federation grew out of discussions among delegates representing regional groups of employees in **coal mining** who met to coordinate wage claims against the mine owners. The Yorkshire Miners' Association (formed in 1858) took the initiative to form the federation in 1889. In 1890, the MWF showed its strength by leading a campaign that resulted in a 5-percent wage rise. In 1892, the federation claimed 150,000 members among its affiliates, compared with only 36,000 in 1889. Thereafter, the federation's membership grew rapidly as large affiliates joined: the Scottish Miners' Federation joined in 1894, the South Wales Miners' federation in 1898, and, finally, the Durham Miners' Federation in 1908. Originally formed in 1869, the Durham Miners' Federation had 121,800 members when it affiliated with the MWF. Between 1900 and 1910, the membership of the federation rose from 363,000 to 597,000, but it continued to be an umbrella organization covering a multitude of labor unions, often with a regional rather than a national outlook. In 1944, when the federation had 603,000 members, it was made up of no less than 22 largely autonomous districts. Wartime centralization of coal mining organization and bargaining hastened the conversion of the federation into the National Union of Mineworkers in January 1945. *See also* UNITED MINE WORKERS OF AMERICA.

MINIMUM AGE. The legal specifying of a minimum age of employment in an industry has been one way of controlling the exploitation of children and teenagers in the labor force. The first effective factory legislation in England in 1833 outlawed the employment of children under nine years of age. In 1919, the **International Labour Organization (ILO)** approved Convention

No. 5, which set 14 as the minimum age for entry into industrial employment. This convention was revised in 1937 to raise the minimum age to 15 for most forms of employment. Since 1970, the ILO has introduced two additional conventions to address the minimum age and **child labor**: minimum age for employment (Convention No. 138, 1973) and worst forms of child labor (Convention No. 182, 1999).

MINIMUM WAGE. The term *minimum wage* refers to the principle that an employee in a country or an industry should be paid a minimum amount. The idea of a minimum (or living) wage was an important aspiration in the history of organized labor, naturally so in the 19th century when wages were often barely adequate to live on, particularly in certain industries such as clothing **manufacturing**. The first modern minimum wage law was passed in the **United Kingdom** in 1773; this was the Spitalfields Act, which gave English silk weavers a minimum wage that lasted as a principle until about 1820, but other textile employees were not successful. In 1779, English stocking handloom workers rioted after a proposed minimum wage law for the industry was rejected by Parliament. In 1811, petitions for a minimum wage from weavers in England and Scotland with a total of 77,000 signatures were also rejected by Parliament. In 1796, the English Parliament debated a minimum wage law that had been proposed by Samuel Whitebread, but the measure failed to attract support.

Pressure for minimum wages caused governments to act in various ways to provide a minimum wage. Some countries (the **United States** in 1938 and **France** in 1950) have provided a minimum wage through national legislation. Others, such as **Australia** and **New Zealand**, have used **conciliation and arbitration** to set minimum wages in particular industries. There was no legal minimum wage legislation in the United Kingdom before 1999; this followed commitments the **British Labour Party** had adopted in the early 1990s but was only able to implement after its victory in the 1997 elections.

The effects of minimum wage laws have been criticized by some economists since the 1970s as hurting rather than helping low-skilled employees. They have argued that such laws raise the cost of their labor above the market rate and thereby increase their unemployment. The economic effect of a minimum wage depends on the level at which it is set and whether employers have a monopoly on the labor they wish to hire. Too high a minimum wage rate could add to unemployment but, in cases in which employers enjoy monopoly conditions, a minimum wage can help low-skilled workers because the additional labor cost could be paid out of profits. *See also* WAGES.

MITBESTIMMUNG. Mitbestimmung is a German term meaning "the right to have a voice in the economic decision-making of firms"; it is usually translated as *codetermination*. *Mitbestimmung* was expressed through direct labor representation at the various levels of decision making within a firm. The idea of codetermination came from the desire of organized labor to replace the authoritarian order of pre-1918 **Germany** with one that embodied both political and economic democracy. This goal was given practical expression in the Works' Councils Law of February 1920, which provided for elected employee–employer councils in enterprises employing more than 20 employees and for the election of a works' steward in enterprises with fewer than 20 employees; the idea for these councils grew out of the government's attempts during World War I to enlist the support of organized labor for the war effort in return for recognition. The principles of codetermination remained popular in German organized labor throughout the 1920s. In 1928, the *Allgemeiner Deutscher Gewerkschaftsbund,* or German General Trade Union Federation, formally adopted *Wirtschaftsdemokratie,* or economic democracy, a philosophy designed to counter **communism**. In contrast, what little support there was for codetermination among large employers in the early 1920s rapidly declined as the decade progressed.

With the revival of free German labor unions in 1945, codetermination was widely adopted and was first applied at the Klöckner steel works in early 1946. Codetermination was encouraged in the British occupational zone (but not in the American zone) as a means of promoting and sustaining democracy in the economy.

An extended form of codetermination, *Montan-Mitbestimmung,* was applied to companies that derived more than half their income from steel, iron, or coal in 1951. Under legislation passed in 1952 and 1972, all enterprises with five or more employees were able to have works' councils. In 1976, the principle of codetermination was extended to the supervisory boards of enterprises with 2,000 or more employees. Although in theory works' councils are distinct from labor unions, in practice those elected to the councils from the unions are usually shop stewards. Although only 39 percent of German firms had works' councils in 1992, the proportion varied according to the size of the firm, with 13 percent among those with 5 to 20 employees, 34 percent among those with 21 to 50 employees, 53 percent among those with 51 to 159 employees, 97 percent among those with 151 to 300 employees, and 88 percent among those with more than 300 employees. *See also* AUSTRIA; BÖCKLER, HANS; EUROPEAN UNION; SLOVENIA.

MOLDOVA. Moldova has been independent from the former **Soviet Union** since August 1991; organized labor in Moldova has faced considerable economic, political, and social obstacles to its development. Moldova is the poorest country in Europe. Although parliamentary elections have been held in Moldova since February 1994, its labor laws reflect the repressive

Soviet era. The Council of the General Federation of Trade Unions of the Republic of Moldova has faced official discrimination and the right to **strike** is restricted. High unemployment also restricts the potential of the unions to organize and bargain collectively. Moldova was represented in the **International Confederation of Free Trade Unions** by 2006 and its affiliate reported 450,000 members to the **International Trade Union Confederation (ITUC)** in 2010, compared with 326,000 in 2006. The ITUC considered that the national labor legislation in Moldova still fell short of the standards of the **International Labour Organization** in 2010.

MONGOLIA. In 1917, the first two trade unions were established, mainly by Russians. After the murder of trade unionists by a White Russian baron in 1920, it took only one year before the unions were reestablished. In August 1927, 4,056 union members formed the First Congress of Mongolian Trade Unions, establishing the Confederation of Mongolian Trade Unions in the form it maintained until the late 1980s. A **communist** state from 1924 until March 1990, independent organized labor in Mongolia has, of necessity, a brief history. Nevertheless, the Confederation of Mongolian Trade Unions had been reformed by November 1994 and left the **World Federation of Trade Unions**. It was admitted to membership of the **International Confederation of Free Trade Unions** in the same year; it claimed a **membership** of 450,000 to the **International Trade Union Confederation** in 2010.

MONTENEGRO. This former part of the Federal Republic **Yugoslavia** emerged as an independent state in June 2006. It joined the **International Labour Organization** and its confederation of independent labor unions with 61,000 members affiliated with the **International Confederation of Free Trade Unions** soon afterward. Since 2007, the **International Trade Union Confederation** has drawn attention to employer hostility toward organized labor and inadequate labor legislation to protect unions and their right to **strike**.

MONTSERRAT. A dependent territory of the **United Kingdom**, the Montserrat Trades and Labour Council was formed in 1948 and was an affiliate of the **International Confederation of Free Trade Unions** from 1957 to the 1980s, when it was replaced by the Montserrat Allied Workers' Union (formed in 1973); in 2001, it reported a **membership** of 193. It is also part of the **Commonwealth Trade Union Group**.

MOROCCO. Morocco has been independent of **France** since March 1956; organized labor in Morocco dates from 1936 when the colonial administration allowed European workers to form labor unions. However, Moroccan workers were denied the legal right to form labor unions until 1951, although the colonial administration tolerated Moroccan **membership** of unions in 1946. As in other African countries, organized labor in Morocco was associated with the independence movement and Moroccan workers preferred to form their own unions rather than join European ones. The *Union Marocaine du Travail,* or Moroccan Union of Workers, formed in March 1955, was admitted to the **International Confederation of Free Trade Unions (ICFTU)** in 1957 but had ceased its membership by 1965; it did not reaffiliate until 1993, when it claimed a membership of 410,600. As late as the 1990s, union leaders who had been missing since the 1960s were found to be in jail or dead. Since 1994, the right to **strike** has been restricted in Morocco, and by 2002 the ICFTU reported that organized labor had little real legal protection for its activities and spoke of **police** violence against labor demonstrations. In 2008, the **International Trade Union Confederation (ITUC)** noted the greater tolerance of the authorities toward workers' protests. Organized labor in Morocco was, however, still harassed during 2010. Despite this, the three Moroccan affiliates of the ITUC claimed a combined membership of 1.1 million in 2010.

MOZAMBIQUE. Mozambique has been independent of **Portugal** since June 1975; organized labor in Mozambique effectively dates from 1965, when limited rights of **collective bargaining** were granted to bank and **railroad** employees, even though some European workers there had formed organizations as early as 1898. From 1975 to the early 1990s, the government did not permit an independent labor movement. Mozambique has only been represented in the **International Confederation of Free Trade Unions (ICFTU)** and its successor since 1995; it claimed to represent a **membership** of 119,900 in 2001. Since 2002, the ICFTU noted that there was discrimination against employees who went on strike in the **export processing zones**. The **International Trade Union Confederation** considered that the 2007 Labor Code was inadequate to protect organized labor. In 2010, there were 97,000 union members in Mozambique.

MURRAY, PHILIP (1886–1952). Murray was the first president of the **United Steelworkers of America**. He was born in Blantyre, Scotland, and began work as a coal miner at the age of 10. His father was a local coal mining union official. In 1902, he emigrated with his family to the **United States**, where he began working as a coal miner in western Pennsylvania. In 1904, he was elected to his first position within the **United Mine Workers of America (UMWA)**, and in 1912 was elected to its executive board.

Thereafter Murray sat on a number of important labor bodies, including the National Bituminous Coal Production Committee (1917–1918) and the Labor Industrial Advisory Board of the National Recovery Administration (1933).

In 1936, as a vice president of the UMWA, he was put in charge of the campaign to unionize the steel industry by the UMWA's president, **John L. Lewis**. His efforts eventually led to the formation of the United Steelworkers of America, which Murray led from 1942 to his death. In 1940, he took over the presidency of the **Congress of Industrial Organizations** after Lewis's resignation. Lewis had Murray expelled from the UMWA for a combination of personal and political differences; Lewis was a Republican and Murray was a Democrat. After World War II, Murray led major **strikes** in the steel industry (1946, 1949, and 1952) for better pay and conditions. Murray was also active in community affairs; for example, he was a member of the National Association for the Advancement of Colored People. *See also* COAL MINING; GREEN, WILLIAM.

MYANMAR. *See* BURMA.

N

NAMIBIA. Namibia has been independent of **South African** control since 1989; organized labor in Namibia originally consisted of branches of South African unions, both for European and African workers. In 1962, the Union of South West Africa in Exile was formed and was associated with the movement for independence. The first legal **strike** in Namibia took place in November 1992 in the diamond industry following the introduction of new labor legislation. In December 1995, the government prohibited **public sector** employees from participation in **politics**. In 1995, the government established **export processing zones** in which strikes were prohibited for five years. In December 2001, the National Union of Namibian Workers, which had been formed in 1971, was admitted to membership of the **International Confederation of Free Trade Unions** and claimed a **membership** of 65,000. In 2007, the right to organize was withdrawn from prison staff, which violated **International Labour Organization** principles. Managers in the mining industry continued dismissing strikers while excessive restrictions still applied to the right to strike in 2010.

NATIONAL AND LOCAL GOVERNMENT OFFICERS' ASSOCIATION (NALGO). NALGO was one of the largest unions in the **United Kingdom** from 1946 to 1993. It was founded in 1905 as a provincial federation catering to local government officers and was called the *National Association of Local Government Officers (NALGO)*. Between 1905 and 1946, its **membership** grew from 5,000 to 140,000. In 1946, NALGO broadened its recruitment of members to include those in other parts of the **public sector** such as the National Health Service, gas, and electricity. Its title was officially changed to *National and Local Government Officers' Association* in 1952 to reflect these changes in membership, but the acronym NALGO was retained. In 1964, when it became affiliated with the **Trades Union Congress**, its membership had reached 338,300. Like most other **white-collar unions**, NALGO was opposed to **strikes** and connections with the political and industrial aspects of organized labor for most of its life. It was not until 1970 that NALGO authorized its first strike. By 1981, NALGO's membership had reached 706,150; its membership rose to 760,000 by 1991. In 1993, NALGO merged with the **National Union of Public Employees** to create **UNISON**. *See also* WHITE-COLLAR UNIONISM.

NATIONAL EDUCATION ASSOCIATION (NEA). Since about 1987, the NEA has been the largest labor union in the **United States**. Formed in 1857 in Philadelphia, it operated as a professional association of school administrators until 1905, when it admitted teachers as members. Despite a conservative reputation that lasted until the 1960s, the NEA has displayed its progressive side on a number of occasions. In 1866, it formally admitted **women** to full **membership**. In 1914, the NEA passed a resolution supporting **equal pay for equal work**, and in 1972 the NEA representative assembly voted to formally support the passage of the Equal Rights Amendment.

Before 1963, the NEA opposed unionism and **collective bargaining** for teachers but changed this policy, and since 1963 it has been a participant in collective bargaining, as evidenced by its victories in ballots for exclusive bargaining rights against its industrial rival, the **American Federation of Teachers (AFT)**, an affiliate of the **American Federation of Labor– Congress of Industrial Organizations (AFL-CIO)**. The affiliation of the AFT with the AFL-CIO has long been an obstacle to efforts to amalgamate the two unions. In 1992, the NEA gained a major civil rights victory, lobbying successfully to pass the Civil Rights Act, which protects individuals against on-the-job harassment and discrimination and allows victims of employment discrimination to collect compensatory damages.

In 2001, the two organizations agreed to form a cooperative partnership to work together on issues of mutual interest while preserving their independence. Between 1995 and 2006, membership of the NEA rose from 2.2 to 3.2 million members, making it the largest white-collar union in the world and the world's second largest labor union after *Ver.di*. By 2010, the NEA had overtaken *Ver.di* as the world's largest labor union. *See also* EDUCATION; WHITE-COLLAR UNIONISM.

NATIONAL INDUSTRIAL RECOVERY ACT. The National Industrial Recovery Act of 1933 was the cornerstone of modern **collective bargaining** in the **United States**. Under Section 7(a), a provision fought for by the miners' leader, **John Llewellyn Lewis**, employees were given the right to organize labor unions to collectively bargain with employers without harassment, provisions that had been included previously in the federal Railway Labor Act (1926). The National Industrial Recovery Act was declared unconstitutional by the Supreme Court in *Schecter Poultry Corporation v. U.S.* in 1935 and was replaced by the **Wagner Act**. Nevertheless, the shift in the legal environment toward a more favorable view of labor unions indicated by these laws was the basis of a massive recruitment drive by organized labor in the mid-1930s. *See also* AMERICAN FEDERATION OF LABOR; CONGRESS OF INDUSTRIAL ORGANIZATIONS; UNITED STEELWORKERS OF AMERICA.

NATIONAL LABOR RELATIONS ACT. *See* WAGNER ACT.

NATIONAL LABOR UNION (NLU). The NLU was a body created by U.S. organized labor in Baltimore, Maryland, in August 1866 to bring about progressive political reforms. Its agenda included the eight-hour work day, the reduction of monopolies, and producer and consumer cooperatives. The delegates at the inaugural congress represented about 60,000 employees. The main achievement of the NLU was gaining the eight-hour work day law for laborers, workmen, and mechanics working for the federal government. In 1869, it sent a delegate to the first conference of the International Working-men's Association (First international) in Basel, Switzerland. In 1870, the NLU formed a political wing, which created the Labor Reform Party in 1872. The emphasis on **politics** cost the NLU the support of **craft unions** and by 1876 it was defunct. *See also* WORKING HOURS.

NATIONAL LABOUR FEDERATION. The National Labour Federation was formed in Newcastle-upon-Tyne, England, in 1886, with the goal of organizing men and **women** of all trades in contrast to both **craft unions** and **industrial unions**. Any labor union could also join. Its founders were some members of the **Amalgamated Society of Engineers** and Edward R. Pease (1857–1955), a **socialist** and founder member of the Fabian Society. The federation claimed 60,000 members in 1890, mostly in semiskilled jobs in engineering, chemicals, shipbuilding, and construction. By 1892, the federation's **membership** had fallen to 6,000, and it was dissolved in 1894, largely as a result of the depression of the early 1890s and defeats in **strikes**. *See also* KNIGHTS OF LABOR.

NATIONAL UNION OF PUBLIC EMPLOYEES (NUPE). The NUPE grew out of the London County Council Employees' Protection Society (formed in 1888), which became the basis of the Municipal Employees Association in 1894. As a result of a split in 1907, a new body was created, the National Union of Corporation Workers, with a **membership** of 8,000. In 1928, this body changed its name to the NUPE and set about recruiting all employees working for local governments in the **United Kingdom**, a policy that led to conflict with the **General and Municipal Workers' Union** and the **Transport and General Workers' Union**, which managed to exclude the NUPE from affiliation with the **Trades Union Congress** until the 1970s. The membership of the NUPE grew from 10,000 in 1948 to 215,000 in 1962 as a result of recruiting the lower grades of the local government and the National Health Service. Between 1934 and 1962, the NUPE was led by its general secretary, Bryn Roberts, a strong supporter of **industrial unionism**. In 1982, the NUPE had 710,450 members, of whom 65 percent were **women**; membership declined to 658,000 in 1986 and to 551,000 in 1992, of whom 70 percent were women. In 1993, the NUPE amalgamated with the **National and Local Government Officers' Association** to create **UNISON**. *See also* PRIVATIZATION; PUBLIC SECTOR.

NEPAL. Organized labor in Nepal effectively dates from 1947 when the jute and sugar workers went on strike. No union organization was legally permitted until 1964, when the Nepal Labour Organization was formed; by 1975 it had been admitted to membership of the **International Confederation of Free Trade Unions (ICFTU)** and claimed a **membership** of 50,000, but it was not an affiliate in the 1980s. In 1992, the government enacted a labor union law that prohibited antiunion discrimination, but the law has not been followed in practice and the right to **strike** is restrictive. In 1993, the Nepal Trade Union Congress joined the ICFTU and claimed a membership of 140,000. In 2001–2002, the ICFTU reported that the government did not really recognize labor unions as valid representatives of workers, and **police** violence against unions continued. It noted that 200 labor union members had been murdered by Maoist guerrillas during 2002, along with hundreds of other Nepalese. When unions supported the struggle for the restoration of **human rights** and labor rights in 2006, they were the target of police repression: two trade unionists were killed by the police in 2008. Despite its many problems, there were 350,000 labor union members in Nepal in 2010.

NETHERLANDS. Organized labor in the Netherlands began in 1866 when printers formed a national union. A nonreligious labor federation was established in 1871 and a Protestant labor federation in 1877. Organized labor was divided by **politics** as well as religion. In 1893, a social democratic labor union center, the National Labor Secretariat, was created, which claimed to represent 16,000 members. The secretariat stood under the influence of revolutionary **socialists**, which caused its alienation from mainstream labor supporters. Union growth was slow; by the early 1900s there were only about 19,000 union members. Nevertheless, there were major successful **labor disputes** organized by longshoremen and railroad employees in 1903. The **general strike** these strikes developed into was, however, lost. This failure led to the formation of a new national labor federation in 1906. In 1909, a combined **Catholic** and Protestant labor federation was created, but the Catholics withdrew on orders from their bishop. Despite the small size of the country Dutch union leaders played a significant role in international organized labor, notably the histories of the **International Confederation of Free Trade Unions** and the **International Transport Workers' Federation**.

As in other countries, there was considerable growth in union **membership** in the Netherlands between 1913 and 1920, rising from 234,000 to 684,000. This growth took place along deep religious and political divisions, not just because these divisions were present in Dutch society but also because many unions were created by **socialists** or clergy in the absence of large-scale concentrations of manufacturing employment. In 1920, 23 percent of Dutch union members belonged to Catholic unions, 12 percent to Protestant unions, 37 percent to socialist unions, 7 percent to left-wing unions, and 21 percent to some other category. Although these proportions changed over time, the fundamental divisions remained part of the Dutch labor movement despite the formation of a small nondenominational association of labor federations in 1929. During the Nazi occupation, organized labor was banned.

In 1943, secret meetings between the leaders of the employers and the unions led to a new understanding about the conduct of industrial relations after the war. This agreement produced a permanent employer-union body, the Foundation of Labor, in May 1945, which received recognition by government as the leading policymaker in socioeconomic matters. During a short period after the war, a left-wing union emerged and organized large groups of workers. Because the **communist** party took over leadership, most members returned to the revived prewar unions. By 1950, there were nearly 1.2 million union members covering 42 percent of all employees, but since that time the proportion of employees enrolled by unions has steadily declined. In 1976, the social democratic and Catholic unions merged into a new national labor federation, the *Federatie Nederlandse Vakbeweging,* or Netherlands Federation of Labor Unions; the merger was completed in 1981. The Dutch labor movement was significantly reduced by the recession of the early 1980s, which cut the proportion of employees in unions from 32 percent in 1980, to 28 percent in 1995, to 25 percent in 2001 and to 21 percent in 2008. In 2010, the two Dutch affiliates of the **International Trade Union Confederation** claimed a combined membership of 1.7 million. *See also* FIMMEN, EDO; OLDENBROEK, JACOBUS HENDRIK.

NEW CALEDONIA. New Caledonia is still a territory of **France**. Nine labor unions existed in New Caledonia by 1975. New Caledonia has only been an affiliate of the **International Confederation of Free Trade Unions** since

1993, when it claimed to represent 3,600 members. New Caledonia was not represented in the **International Trade Union Confederation** in 2010.

NEW UNIONISM NETWORK. The New Unionism Network is an international group of people who since 2007 have tried to build and revitalize the union movement. It is a network rather than an organization, with no links to any other group. Membership is open to anybody who supports the principles: **organizing**, workplace democracy, internationalism, and creativity.

NEW ZEALAND. New Zealand has an importance in the history of organized labor belied by its small size and location in the southwest Pacific Ocean. It was first settled by Maoris in the mid-14th century and by Europeans from 1840. Exploiting shortages of skilled labor, the first unions emerged in the building trades from 1842. Sustained British **immigration** brought union members as well as the example of labor unions. Printers (1862) and tailors (1865) formed unions, and the British international unions, the **Amalgamated Society of Engineers** (1864) and the **Amalgamated Society of Carpenters and Joiners** (1875), set up New Zealand branches. The first urban trades council was formed in Auckland in 1876, an example followed by other cities and towns in the early 1880s. In 1879, following the successful election of S. P. Andrews, a plasterer, to Parliament, a Working Men's Political Association was formed that was concerned with land tax, tariff protection for local industries, and the prohibition of Chinese immigration.

The most powerful influences on organized labor in New Zealand were **Australia** and the **United Kingdom**. In 1878, New Zealand followed the British example and legalized labor unions. In January 1885, the first New Zealand Trades Union Congress was held in Dunedin following the example set by Australian labor unions from 1879. As in other countries, there was a surge of union growth between 1886 and 1890. In 1886, for example, the Amalgamated Shearers' Union of Australia set up a New Zealand branch and made a special effort to recruit Maoris; in the same year, Christopher Leek founded a mass **railroad** union and called it after the union he had belonged to in England, the Amalgamated Society of Railway Servants. Between 1885 and mid-1890, the number of union members rose from 3,000 to 63,000.

The participation of New Zealand labor in the great Australian Maritime Strike of 1890 (August–November) and the economic depression that set in after it largely destroyed the unions' growth of the late 1880s. It was at this time that New Zealand embarked on a series of social experiments, which attracted international attention in the early 1900s. In 1894, New Zealand became the first country in the world to introduce a compulsory **conciliation and arbitration** system for **labor disputes**. Amending legislation was passed in 1898 that, although it encouraged union formation and growth through official registration, denied unions the right to **strike** once an award of the arbitration court was in force. The New Zealand experiment attracted interest and visits from **France** (F. Challye in 1903), the United Kingdom (**Beatrice and Sidney Webb** in 1898, Ramsay Macdonald in 1906, and Ernest Aves in 1907), and the **United States** (Henry Demarest Lloyd in 1900, V. S. Clark in 1906, and Colonel H. Weinstock in 1909).

The use of compulsion in conciliation and arbitration in labor disputes was adopted by Australia but remained unusual in the rest of the world. The constraints of the arbitration system led to labor disputes particularly as radical unions found they could legally strike if they were not registered organizations under the conciliation and arbitration legislation. There was a disastrous waterfront strike in 1913 that, despite Australian support, depleted the finances of the unions for four years. Radical ideas, particularly for the **One Big Union**, came through the **Industrial Workers of the World**, which formed a branch in New Zealand in 1912. A gold miners' strike at Waihi and Reefton in 1912 was marked by **police** and employer violence, which led to the death of a picketer.

In 1913 the United Federation of Labour was formed and became the leader of organized labor. In July 1916, the New Zealand Labour Party was formed and claimed 10,000 members. Yet compared with Australia, organized labor was weak; in 1920, only 26 percent of employees were union members compared with 42 percent in Australia. In 1928, a coalition government abolished compulsory arbitration to enable wage reductions. In 1935, the Labour Party won a landslide victory and enacted legislation that established a strong regulatory role for government in economic and social management. In 1936, the Industrial Conciliation and Arbitration Act was amended to make union **membership** compulsory for any employee subject to a registered award of industrial agreement, a change that naturally led to a substantial growth in union membership. In 1937, the New Zealand Federation of Labour was formed and joined the **International Federation of Trade Unions** in 1938 and the **International Confederation of Free Trade Unions** in 1951. Another feature of the period was the growth of **industrial unionism** in engineering and printing. With the exception of the 1951 waterfront strike, developments among organized labor were not especially noteworthy again until the late 1960s, when the **white-collar unions** formed a federation; it amalgamated with the New Zealand Federation of Labour in October 1987 to form the New Zealand Council of Trade Unions.

In the mid-1980s, in response to New Zealand's severe economic difficulties, a series of radical reforms were introduced that again made New Zealand a social laboratory, this time for economic deregulation and the free exercise of market forces. In 1984, the government made the first move to abolish compulsory arbitration in interest disputes (a distinction between rights and interest disputes was first introduced into New Zealand legislation in 1973) except in "essential" industries. Yet much of the system first created in 1894 remained in place up to 1991, when the Employment Contracts Act was enacted. The act abolished the arbitration system and its awards and changed the basis of the industrial relations system to the law of contract. It also ended the system of compulsory union membership, which had been introduced into bargaining arrangements in 1936.

Largely because of the economic problems faced by the New Zealand economy, but also because of the removal of the protection of compulsory membership, organized labor has fared poorly since 1991. In 1985, there were 683,000 union members in New Zealand covering 44 percent of employees but, by December 1994, there were only 375,900, covering 23 percent of full-time employees. The reelection of the Labour Party in November 1999 led to the replacement of the Employment Contracts Act by the Employment Relations Act, which made the legal environment fairer for organized labor. In 2000, there were 318,500 union members, covering about 17.5 percent of employees. In 2010, the New Zealand Council of Trade Unions declared a membership of 200,000 to the **International Trade Union Confederation**.

NICARAGUA. Although organized labor had emerged in Nicaragua by 1924, any progress was stifled by the dictatorship of the Somoza family, which was in power from 1936 to 1979. Organized labor reemerged briefly between 1945 and 1949 and again from 1956, with political struggle against the government taking priority. By 1965, Nicaragua had been admitted to membership of the **International Confederation of Free Trade Unions (ICFTU)** and has remained represented in the ICFTU despite a brutal civil war between 1981 and 1990. After the transition to democratic government, Nicaragua opened its first **export processing zone** in 1993. In 1996, the government promulgated a new labor code that removed many of the previous restrictions on forming labor unions, but the right to **strike** remains difficult to exercise in practice. In 2002, the ICFTU was particularly critical of working conditions in the 23 export processing zones, describing them as "close to **slavery**." Official intimidation of organized labor remains common in Nicaragua. The **International Trade Union Confederation** reported continued antiunion policies by Coca-Cola and the brutal suppression of a medical workers' strike in 2009. There was no improvement in conditions for organized labor in 2010.

NIGER. Niger has been independent from **France** since August 1960; organized labor developed under French rule after World War II, but after independence was effectively placed under **government control**. Since 1992, Niger has moved toward democratic rule. In 1993, it was admitted to membership of the **International Confederation of Free Trade Unions**; its affiliate, the *Union des Syndicats des Travailleurs du Niger* (Union of Workers' Unions of Niger), claimed to represent 70,000 members in 2001. Since the strikes of 1994, Niger has been relatively peaceful, although international pressure was necessary to release 22 activists from prison. In 2010, Niger was one of the few African countries not to be mentioned in the survey of **violations of trade union rights**.

NIGERIA. Nigeria has been independent from the **United Kingdom** since October 1960. Organized labor in Nigeria began in 1912 with the formation of the Nigerian Civil Servants' Union; other unions were formed by teachers, miners, and railroad workers in the 1930s. In 1938, the British administration passed a trade union ordinance. The first national union federation was formed in 1943, and by 1957 Nigeria was represented by three affiliates in the **International Confederation of Free Trade Unions (ICFTU)**. At independence in 1960, Nigeria had 631 labor unions representing 520,164 members. Organized labor in Nigeria was large but politically divided and therefore vulnerable to government efforts to place it under control, a process assisted by civil war between 1966 and 1970. Nigeria ceased to be represented in the ICFTU between 1975 and 1990 and was not readmitted until 2000, largely because promises made to an ICFTU delegation in 1993 that organized labor should be free of **government control** were not kept. In 1978, the Nigeria Labour Congress was formed under state sponsorship but it gained considerable autonomy. This independence has been under severe threat from time to time from the military rulers. In 1992, the government established **export processing zones** where organized labor was, in practice, excluded. In 2002, the ICFTU remained critical of the restrictions on the right to organize unions and the right to strike in Nigeria. On 1 February 2002, there was a national **strike** by **police** over wages arrears, which resulted in the dismissal of 153 policemen and the laying of charges against 2,000 others. In 2006, oil workers were attacked by rebel groups, a union member was abducted while in the presence of state officials, and government officials tried to interfere in union affairs. The **International Trade Union Confederation**'s survey of **violations of trade union rights** in 2009 documented the assassination of one union leader and the dismissal of hundreds of activists and called 2010 a violent year for Nigerian organized labor.

NIGHT WORK. Night work is an integral feature of industrial economies, particularly in certain industries such as transportation, storage, and communication, and in some parts of **manufacturing**, such as baking. The problem of night work was recognized in an English law of 1802 designed to protect the health and morals of pauper children taken on as **apprentices**; it forbade any apprentice to work between 9 PM and 6 AM from 1 June 1803. Night work has long been held to be harmful to young employees and **women**, hence the efforts made by the **International Labour Organization** to limit night work to adult males by Conventions No. 4 and No. 6 in 1919. These conventions were revised in 1948 to remove exceptions in the earlier conventions. *See also* WORKING HOURS.

NIHON RODOKUMIAI SORENGOKAI. See RENGO.

NORRIS–LAGUARDIA ACT. The Anti-Injunction (Norris–LaGuardia) Act was a fundamental piece of U.S. federal labor law, which was passed in 1932 and designed to give organized labor full freedom of association. It outlawed yellow dog contracts and prohibited federal courts from issuing injunctions (court orders restraining union activity on the grounds of the prevention of injury to property or other rights) during **labor disputes** except under particular circumstances. The effect of the Norris–LaGuardia Act was weakened by a series of Supreme Court decisions in the 1970s concerning the issuing of injunctions during disputes where there were contracts or **arbitration** machinery. *See also* NATIONAL INDUSTRIAL RECOVERY ACT.

NORTH KOREA (Democratic People's Republic of Korea). An independent state since 1948, having been a colony of **Japan** from 1910 to 1945, North Korea is run on essentially Stalinist principles. There has been no independent labor movement permitted in North Korea since 1925, when the Japanese administration outlawed trade unions. Since 1948, the government-controlled General Federation of Trade Unions of Korea is the only national labor organization allowed. Wages are set by the government and there is no right to **strike** or to engage in **collective bargaining**. The survey of **violations of trade union rights** in 2010 repeated its previous complaints about the total lack of respect for rights of organized labor in North Korea.

NORWAY. Organized labor in Norway began to emerge from the 1860s. As in other European countries, mutual aid or **friendly societies** preceded the formation of unions. The first union was founded by printers in Oslo in 1872. Labor federations were formed in the cities from 1882. In 1887, a political Labor Party was formed. Two pivotal events in Norwegian labor were the establishment of the *Landsorganisasjonen i Norge* (LO), or the Labor Union Federation of Norway, in 1899, and a parallel national organization by employers in 1900. In 1902, the LO and the employers' organization signed their first agreement. A lockout in 1911 gave rise to a law on **labor disputes** passed in 1915 and revised in 1927, which introduced the concepts of rights and interests in disputes in an attempt to control **strikes**. In 1919, another law brought in the eight-hour work day. There was a failed **general strike** in 1921 and other major labor disputes in 1924 and 1931. In 1935, the Labor Party, which had become Norway's largest political party in 1927, won government. In the more cooperative political climate that followed, the first Basic Agreement (1935) was concluded between the LO and the employers' organization, thereby founding a tradition of **collective bargaining** characterized by a mixture of national and industry bargaining. The proportion of employees who were union members in Norway declined from a peak of 60 percent in 1960 to 55 percent in 2007. In 2010, the three Norwegian affiliates of the **International Trade Union Confederation** declared a combined membership of nearly 1.4 million. *See also* DENMARK; SWEDEN.

NOVEMBER PACT (STINNES–LEGIEN AGREEMENT). The November Pact (also known as the Stinnes–Legien Agreement) was signed in **Germany** between the largest **employers' organizations** and the Free (or Social Democratic) labor unions, the **Hirsch-Duncker Trade Associations**, and the **Catholic** unions in November 1918. Designed to stabilize the revolutionary political climate that prevailed in Germany following its defeat in World War I, the agreement recognized the legitimacy of unions to engage in **collective bargaining**, granted the **eight-hour work** day, and provided for workers' committees in enterprises employing more than 50 employees to ensure that the conditions of employment of collective agreements were carried out. The November Pact led to the formation of the *Zentralarbeitsgemeinschaft* or Central Labor Association, an organization designed to implement the pact, but it was not effective after 1924 because of hostility by employers. *See also* LEGIEN, CARL; *MITBESTIMMUNG*.

OCCUPATIONAL HEALTH AND SAFETY. The term *occupational health and safety* covers all aspects of health at work, from the hazards that can cause injury or death to ways of improving the working environment. Knowledge about the risks of particular occupations and from handling certain materials dates from antiquity; the Roman architectural writer Vitruvius (c. 25 B.C.) was aware that lead smelting and lead pipes were harmful to producers and consumers. Over the past two centuries, occupational health and safety has grown as an area of concern for organized labor, particularly in occupations with a high risk of injury or death, such as **coal mining**. The **International Labour Organization** published its first encyclopedia on occupational health and safety in 1930. Since the 1930s, there has been a growth in joint management–union committees with responsibilities for occupational health and safety. General support for occupational health and safety in the workplace has been a standard feature of organized labor, particularly since the 1960s, and has increased as knowledge about hazards has grown. The leaking of toxic gas from the Union Carbide plant in Bhopal, **India**, on 2–3 December 1984, which led to the deaths of 2,600 people and injuries to 200,000 others, was a landmark in general awareness of occupational health and safety; organized labor at the plant had been demanding improved safety conditions for its workers since 1976. The incident raised the profile of occupational health and safety in the **International Confederation of Free Trade Unions.** On 28 April 1996, international labor unions inaugurated the International Commemoration Day for Dead and Injured Workers to focus attention on occupational health and safety.

OLDENBROEK, JACOBUS HENDRIK (1897–1970). Oldenbroek was born and raised in a cigarmaker's family in Amsterdam. He started his professional career as a clerk and soon moved to the headquarters of the Dutch social-democratic union where he met **Edo Fimmen**. In 1919, he accompanied Fimmen to the secretariat of the **International Federation of Trade Unions** and two years later to the **International Transport Workers' Federation (ITF)**, both located in Amsterdam. Meanwhile Oldenbroek was active in the union of office workers and the Dutch social-democratic party.

In the party, Oldenbroek and Fimmen took a leftist stand but the ITF forced them to express more moderate views.

Despite this difference of opinions, the two Dutchmen were allowed to get important positions within the ITF. From 1937, Oldenbroek was second in charge after Fimmen. One of their most prominent activities was the building of an anti-Nazi network of seamen in Germany. When the ITF's headquarter moved to London in 1939, Fimmen and Oldenbroek moved too. Fimmen's illness and death in 1942 made Oldenbroek the actual leader of the ITF. Oldenbroek remained in close contact with the American secret service in their joint effort to get social and economic information out of Germany and the occupied territories.

After the war Oldenbroek played an important role in the formation of the **International Confederation of Free Trade Unions (ICFTU) in 1949**. His career as secretary general of the ICFTU ended in 1960 when he clashed with **George Meany** of the **American Federation of Labor–Congress of Industrial Organizations** over how to encourage organized labor in Africa. The Americans wanted a top-down approach and threatened to draw back from the ICFTU if Oldenbroek did not resign. *See also* NETHERLANDS.

OMAN. Oman is a sultanate where criticism of the Sultan is illegal. The labor law of 1973 did not provide for the existence of labor unions or **collective bargaining** in Oman. **Strikes** were illegal until the 8 July 2006 decree by the government that guaranteed the right to strike and the 31 October decree that granted the freedom to establish trade unions. About half of the labor force are expatriates. Committees of management and workers in enterprises where 50 or more are employed are provided for in law, but not always implemented. The Labor Welfare Board handles individual workers' grievances. In 1993, Oman joined the **International Labour Organization** but its employees have never been represented in either the **International Confederation of Free Trade Unions** or the **International Trade Union Confederation (ITUC)**. There are almost three times as many migrant workers as Omani workers in the private sector. In its survey of **violations of trade union rights** in 2009, the ITUC considered that migrant employees in Oman suffered conditions little better than forced labor.

ONE BIG UNION (OBU). The one big union refers to the idea of organizing all employees into a single union, in contrast to both **craft unions** and **industrial unions**. It originated in the **United Kingdom** in 1834 when Robert Owen (1771–1858) and John Doherty (c. 1798–1854) organized the Grand United Consolidated Trades Union, which briefly attracted a membership of 16,000. In the **United States**, the International Labor Union made the first determined effort to recruit unskilled as well as skilled labor in the late 1870s, an idea followed by the **Knights of Labor** in the 1880s. In the United Kingdom, the idea of an OBU was revived by the **National Labour Federation** in 1886 and by unions such as the **Workers' Union** in 1898 and through federations of existing unions, such as the **General Federation of Trade Unions** in 1899, organizations both created following the defeat of the **Amalgamated Society of Engineers** in the lockout of 1897. The idea of the OBU was revived by the **Industrial Workers of the World** and was an important topic of debate internationally up to the early 1920s. In a limited way, the OBU has found practical expression in union **amalgamations**.

ORGANIZACIÓN REGIONAL INTERAMERICANA DE TRABAJADORES **(ORIT).** The ORIT, or Inter-American Regional Organization of Workers, was formed out of the *Confederación Interamericana de Trabajadores* or Inter-American Confederation of Workers in Mexico City in January 1951 by the representatives of 21 countries. The **United States** delegation was led by **George Meany** of the **American Federation of Labor**, and the **International Confederation of Free Trade Unions (ICFTU)** was represented by Sir Vincent Tewson, the general secretary of the British **Trades Union Congress**.

Originally based in **Mexico**, the ORIT has been based in Caracas, **Venezuela**, since the late 1990s. It was created within the framework of Cold War politics with the aim of resisting **communist** influence in Latin America. Despite its promotion of strong, democratic labor unions, the ORIT came under suspicion of being too close to the U.S. Department of State. The ORIT also faced competition from rival inter-American labor federations, the Marxist *Confederación de Trabajadores de America Latina* (Confederation of Latin American Workers) up to 1962, a **Catholic** labor federation formed in 1954, and the radical *Congreso Permanente de Unidad Sindical de los Trabajadores de America Latina* (Permanent Unity Congress of Labor Unions of Latin American Workers) from 1964 to the l990s. The ORIT is the undisputed primary body for representing the Americas in the ICFTU. In 2001, the ORIT represented 32.4 million union members within the ICFTU or 21 percent of its total **membership**. After the merger that led to the formation of the **International Trade Union Confederation**, ORIT gave way to the **Trade Union Confederation of the Americas–Confederatión Syndical de los Trabajadores y Trabajadoras de las Americas** in 2008.

ORGANIZATION OF AFRICAN TRADE UNION UNITY (OATUU). The OATUU was formed in 1973 from the merger of the All-African Trade Union Federation (AATUF), the African Trade Union Confederation

(ATUC), and the Pan-African Workers' Congress. The AATUF was formed in Casablanca in May 1961. It was the first international trade union federation designed to represent African countries only and was formed to exclude influence of both the **International Confederation of Free Trade Unions (ICFTU)** and the **World Confederation of Labor (WCL)**, which were regarded as too conservative. Those national organizations that did not accept this view formed the ATUC in January 1962 as a rival organization. The merger of the AATUF and the ATUC to form the OATUU was made at the behest of the Organization of African Unity. The affiliation of African labor organizations with international labor bodies created discord within the OATUU, with both the ICFTU and the WCL claiming affiliates among bodies affiliated with the OATUU. In 1988, the OATUU and the WCL signed a formal statement of cooperation. In 2004, the OATUU claimed to represent 53 countries with a combined **membership** of 30 million; in contrast, the ICFTU claimed only 15 million members in Africa.

ORGANIZING. Organizing is a new model for labor unions to recruit new members. It started as a reaction to the plummeting fall in the coverage of employees by organized labor since the 1980s. This model opposes the service model union in which the organization acts in the interest of the members but without active participation of these members themselves.

Specially appointed organizers try to build up confidence and networks within the workforce. Employees are often visited at home where long hours of talk serve as means to win confidence and collect information. During industrial action, the emphasis is on the responsibility of the employees and the use of creative tactics. Organizing successfully started in the **United States** within the **Service Employees International Union** and from there spread to other unions and countries.

P

PACIFIC TRADE UNION COMMUNITY (PTUC). Originally called the *Pacific Trade Union Forum,* the PTUC was set up in 1980 to improve cooperation between organized labor in **Australia** and **New Zealand** and the South West Pacific countries, as well as to campaign against the testing of nuclear weapons in the region. In 1992, the PTUC had 14 country members representing about 3.2 million union members, with the bulk of this **membership** living in Australia, New Zealand, and **Papua New Guinea**. The **Australian Council of Trade Unions** provided the secretariat for the PTUC. In 1995, the PTUC was superseded by the **Asian and Pacific Regional Organization**.

PAKISTAN. Pakistan has been independent of the **United Kingdom** since 1947 when the British Indian Empire was divided into India and Pakistan. Organized labor inherited the labor law framework of British **India**, which dated from 1926, when unions were legalized, and played an active role in the independence movement. The All-Pakistan Trade Union Federation was formed in 1948 to represent unions in both Pakistan (then West Pakistan) and East Pakistan (**Bangladesh**). Between 1951 and 1968, the number of unions in Pakistan rose from 309 to 1,041 and their reported **membership** rose from 393,100 to 522,900, despite restrictions on organized labor imposed by military governments. In 1971, Bangladesh seceded from Pakistan. Pakistan has been represented in the **International Confederation of Free Trade Unions (ICFTU)** since 1951. In 1980, the government established **export processing zones** from which organized labor is effectively prohibited and there is no right to **strike**. In 2001, the ICFTU reported that although Pakistan had about 1.1 million union members, organized labor faced considerable hostility from the military government of General Pervez Musharraf, characterized by the arrest of union leaders; the torture of Nadeem Dar (president of the Leatherfield Labour Union) by the owner of the Leatherfield company; **police** intimidation; and coercion for employees to sign individual, nonunion employment contracts. Despite the release of a new Industrial Relations Act in 2008, the **International Trade Union Confederation** noted that restrictions on organized labor still remained. Trade union rights are still violated and several trade unionists were detained in 2009.

PALESTINE. As of 2011 the Palestinian Authority that governs Gaza and the West Bank is still waiting for independence from **Israel**. The Palestine General Federation of Trade Unions was formed in 1965 with origins dating back to the 1920s. It claimed a membership of 131,000 in the autonomous West Bank (88,000) and the Gaza Strip (43,000). The federation became an affiliate of the **International Confederation of Free Trade Unions (ICFTU)** in November 2002, with 215,000 members. Since 1989, the ICFTU sought to improve relations between the federation and the *Histadrut* of Israel but this effort lost its purpose in the light of the expected independence of Palestine. The blockade of the Palestinian territories by Israel made union organizing very difficult. In 2009, strikes and peaceful May Day demonstrations were repressed by the Palestinian Authority. In 2010, the exercise of freedom of association and collective bargaining remained difficult, especially in Gaza.

PANAMA. Independent from **Colombia** since 1903, organized labor was introduced by the **American Federation of Labor** in 1917 when it formed a section in the canal zone to cater to U.S. employees, but the American example did not really take hold among Panamanian workers until the 1930s, as shown by the formation of the first labor federation in 1939. Panama has been represented in the **International Confederation of Free Trade Unions (ICFTU)** since 1951, but Panamanian organized labor has been weakened by the usual political and religious divisions of Latin America. In 2001, the ICFTU was critical of the Panamanian government's restrictions on trade union rights for the **public sector** and the layoff by the Chiquita Brands International, Inc., of 400 banana workers in a dispute. In 2009, the **International Trade Union Confederation** reported that conditions for organized labor in Panama had not improved and that barriers to trade union organizations still existed. It documented the killing of a labor leader in 2010.

PAN-AMERICAN FEDERATION OF LABOR (PAFL). The PAFL was the first international labor federation formed in the Americas; it operated between 1918 and 1940. It was formed at Laredo, Texas, on 13 November 1918, primarily through the efforts of Santiago Iglesias, the president of the labor federation of **Puerto Rico**, and John Murray of the International Typographical Union in California, working in conjunction with **Samuel Gompers**. The original members of the PAFL were **Colombia, Costa Rica, El Salvador, Guatemala, Mexico**, the **United States**, and Puerto Rico. Iglesias had been lobbying the **American Federation of Labor** for the creation of a Pan-American labor federation since 1900, but his efforts did not begin to bear fruit until 1915. The value of good relations between organized labor in the United States and Mexico was shown in 1916 when Gompers secured the release of Americans taken prisoner during an illegal military raid in Mexico to capture Pancho Villa. The PAFL worked for peace between the United States and Mexico, concerned itself with the international migration of labor in the Americas, and opposed American intervention in the internal affairs of Central American and Caribbean countries. Although the **Dominican Republic, Nicaragua**, and **Peru** joined the PAFL, its effectiveness was reduced by the deaths of its key personnel: Murray in 1919, Gompers in 1924, and Iglesias in 1939. The last conference of the PAFL was held in New Orleans in 1940. *See also CONFEDERACIÓN INTERAMERICANA DE TRABAJADORES.*

PAPUA NEW GUINEA. Independent of **Australia** since September 1975, organized labor in Papua New Guinea developed under Australian influence, with the first unions being confined to European employees. However, the Australian presence was small until World War II, when the country was invaded by the Japanese and was the scene of fierce fighting. The colonial administration was opposed to the formation of labor unions by indigenous employees and it was not until the late 1950s that they began to be formed. The Papua New Guinea Trades Union Congress was formed in 1970 and was an affiliate of the **International Confederation of Free Trade Unions** since 1975. By 1973, there were 41 registered labor unions with a total **membership** of 35,000. In 2001, Papua New Guinea had about 70,000 union members, compared with 60,000 in 1995. Most of the labor force works in the informal sector, which organized labor finds difficult to recruit. Papua New Guinea was not represented in the **International Trade Union Confederation** in 2010.

PARAGUAY. Unions in Paraguay formed a federation in 1917 but were able to make little progress because of the lack of economic development, war with **Bolivia** from 1932 to 1935, and political oscillations; in 1936, organized labor was favored by the government, but a year later unions were restricted. The government sought to interfere with and manipulate organized labor in the 1940s and 1950s. A strike over the **minimum wage** in 1958 was widely supported, but repressed by the Stroessner dictatorship that ruled the country between 1954 and 1989. Paraguay has been represented in the **International Confederation of Free Trade Unions** from 1957 to 1975 and again since 1993. The 1993 labor code protected union leaders, but not union members or ordinary workers, from dismissal. Although the constitution guarantees unions and **collective bargaining**, these rights are restricted in practice by both the Labor Code and employers' behavior. According to the survey of **violations of trade union rights**, organized labor in the private sector was harassed during 2009, but following union protests, there was some improvement in the antiunion attitude of the government in 2010.

PART-TIME EMPLOYMENT. *See* FULL-TIME/PART-TIME EMPLOY-MENT.

PENSION. Pension is a retirement income arrangement to provide people with an income when they are no longer earning a regular income from employment. Such arrangements are called *retirement plans* in the **United States**, *pension schemes* in **Ireland** and the **United Kingdom**, and *superannuation plans* in **New Zealand** and **Australia**. Old-age pensions are regarded as delayed wages.

Generally retirement **benefits** may consist of three pillars, the first set up by a government institution, the second by employers or **employers' organizations** and trade unions, and the third by insurance companies. Recent years witnessed a shift from the first to the second and even to the third pillar in industrialized countries. Responsibility for a good income arrangement thus has to be borne by the individual rather than by a collective agreement. Pensions in developing countries are almost nonexistent because most people work in the informal sector of the economy where workers remain largely unprotected by social security.

PERMANENT CONGRESS OF TRADE UNION UNITY OF LATIN AMERICAN WORKERS. *See CONGRESO PERMANENTE DE UNIDAD SINDICAL DE LOS TRABAJADORES DE AMERICA LATINA.*

PERU. Organized labor in Peru developed in the late 19th century; the first national labor federation was formed in 1919 and a second, under Marxist leadership, in 1929. There were about 25,000 union members by 1930. Because of its association with left-wing politics and support for land nationalization, organized labor was repressed by the military governments that ruled Peru in the 1930s and 1940s. The *Confederación de Trabajadores del Perú* (Confederation of Workers of Peru) was formed in May 1944 and was an affiliate of the **International Confederation of Free Trade Unions (ICFTU)** by 1951. Organized labor in Peru has been caught up in the country's political divisions and by internal divisions based on religion. In 2000, organized labor played an active part in the campaign to get rid of the corrupt and autocratic president, Alberto Fujimori. By 2001, there were three Peruvian labor federations affiliated with the ICFTU claiming a combined **membership** of 265,000. Despite the return to democratic government after the repressive regime of Fujimori, the **International Trade Union Confederation** remained critical of Peru's record of trade union rights during 2008, noting the use of the police to put down a demonstration against the unfair dismissal of three trade union leaders. Labor laws have not been revised since the restoration of democracy and the government still assists employers to break **strikes**.

PHILIPPINES. Although labor unions were not legalized in the Philippines until 1908, **craft unions** were formed after 1899; these unions set up a national federation of labor, *Union Obrera Democratica Filipina* (Democratic Workers Union of the Philippines), in 1902. Tolerated by the U.S. administration rather than encouraged, union growth was slow; by 1930, there were estimated to be only 67,000 union members. The labor movement was also divided between **communists** and noncommunists; the communists were more successful in enlisting union support for independence. After independence from the **United States** in 1946, Cipriano Cid, an official of the **Congress of Industrial Organizations**, set up the Philippines Association of Free Labor Unions. A **Catholic** labor federation, the Federation of Free Workers, was formed in 1950. In 1953, the Philippines was admitted to membership of the **International Confederation of Free Trade Unions (ICFTU)** and has remained represented there.

In 1954, the Republic Act 875 gave labor unions legal protection and the right to engage in **collective bargaining**. Because of deep internal divisions, hostile management, legal complexities, and lack of public support, organized labor was unable to utilize fully the advantages of this law. In 1950, there were only 150,000 union members out of two million nonagricultural employees. In 1963, organized labor engaged directly in **politics** by creating the Workers' Party, but it fared poorly in the Manila elections of that year. In 1965, a new national labor federation, the Philippines Labor Center, was formed, but it did not result in a unified labor movement. From the early 1970s, industrial and political protests in the Philippines became intertwined.

President Ferdinand Marcos declared a state of emergency in September 1972, which was used to suspend the right to **strike** and to arrest labor leaders. In 1974, a new labor code aimed at reorganizing the unions along industrial lines. In 1975, the Trade Union Congress of the Philippines was established; it claimed a million members and remains the largest labor federation in the country. After the overthrow of Marcos in 1986, a new constitution was adopted in February 1987, which promised full legal protection for labor, organized and unorganized. According to government figures, the membership of labor unions in the Philippines grew from 1.9 to 3.8 million between 1980 and 2000. Like **Japan**, there are thousands of unions in the Philippines.

Despite an improvement in the political and legal climate for organized labor, the ICFTU complained to the Philippine government about restrictions on the right to **collective bargaining** and discrimination against unions in 1991–1992. It has also noted the continuation of violence against labor officials and striking employees, such as in 2006 when at least 33 unionists were killed in "an orgy of extrajudicial violence." In 2009, the **International Trade Union Confederation** drew attention to restrictions on the right to strike or form unions and it documented the murder of four labor activists.

PICKETING. *Picketing* refers to labor union members demonstrating outside a workplace, often with placards, in support of the union's claims against the workplace employer during **labor disputes**. The group carrying out the picketing (the "picket line") will also try to encourage employees not engaged in the dispute to stay away from the workplace. They can do this verbally or, on occasion, by violence. Picketing in this sense had entered English usage by 1867. Picketing was outlawed in the **United Kingdom** in 1825, but "peaceful picketing" was legalized in 1859. Violence during picketing was legally prohibited in 1875. The **Employment Act** of 1980 limited legal picketing to employees engaged in a labor dispute. In the **United States**, mass picketing was outlawed by the **Taft-Hartley Act** in 1947. *See also* "WINTER OF DISCONTENT."

POLAND. Organized labor in what is now Poland emerged during the late 19th century in Galicia, then part of the Austro-Hungarian Empire. Other unions were formed in German-controlled Poland but not in the Russian Partition, where unions were illegal before 1906. Organized labor and the Polish Socialist Party (formed in 1892) were closely linked. A national labor federation was created in 1918. Despite the difficult conditions for organizing and the heavily rural nature of the Polish economy, union growth was impressive. In 1920, there were 947,000 union members, who were mostly organized by industry groups. Political pressure by the Socialist Party gained exclusive rights for unions in **collective bargaining** in the 1920s, but the economic difficulties of the period reduced union **membership** from its peak of one million in 1921 to 539,100 by 1924. In 1926, the government forced employees of government-owned enterprises to belong to a government-sponsored union. Nevertheless, union membership reached 979,000 by 1930 and, despite the Depression, there were still claimed to be 738,900 members in 1933. This growth was to some extent a reflection of the increase in **manufacturing** employment, which nearly doubled from 1.3 to 2.5 million between 1921 and 1931. With the imposition of **communist** rule in 1948, an independent labor movement ceased to exist in Poland, although the trend toward an industrialized economy continued. Between 1950 and 1969, the number employed in manufacturing rose from 2.8 to 4 million.

In the 1970s, the first sustained popular challenge to the communist-dominated labor movement and society in Eastern Europe occurred in Poland. From December 1970 to January 1971, there was a wave of **labor disputes** in the Baltic cities that resulted in 44 deaths. Poland's continued economic problems—particularly its high inflation and large overseas debts—depressed living standards and maintained discontent. In September 1976, the Workers' Defense Committee (*Komitet Obrony Robotnikow*) was set up to help those who had lost their jobs in labor disputes. In May 1976, a committee of free labor unions was formed in the Baltic cities. The visit to Poland of the newly elected first Polish pope, John Paul II, in June 1979 provided a focus for economic grievances as well as nationalist, political, and religious feelings. A round of government-decreed price rises in the 1980s led to rolling **strikes** at the Lenin shipyard in Gdansk (the former German city of Danzig), which was the catalyst for the government conceding on 31 August 1980 the right not only to form independent labor unions but also to strike and broadcast religious programs, as well as the right to more civil liberties. It was from these origins that "Solidarity"—*"Solidarnosc" Niezalezny Samorzadny Zwaiazek Zawodowy,* or Independent, Self-Governing Trade Union Solidarity—was formed on 22 September 1980, with an unemployed former electrician, **Lech Walesa**, as its chairman. By December 1980, 40 independent labor unions had been formed and there was a growing movement to create a rural version of Solidarity. On 1 January 1981, the communist labor federation was disbanded, but these gains proved short-lived. The pace of change raised the threat of Russian intervention, a threat that had hung over Poland since the first Partition in 1772.

The government declared martial law in December 1981. In October 1982, Solidarity was driven underground by labor laws that dissolved all labor unions. It survived, but its membership fell from 10 to 1.3 million by 1995. There was much debate about Solidarity's goals, and a splinter organization, Solidarity 80, was formed.

In 1987, Solidarity was admitted to membership of the **International Confederation of Free Trade Unions (ICFTU)**, the first labor organization to be admitted to the ICFTU from Eastern Europe that was not an organization in exile. In November 1984, the former communist labor federation reformed itself as the *Ogolnópolskie Porozumienie Zwiazków Zawodowych* (OPZZ), or All-Poland Alliance of Labor Unions, a nonauthoritarian body that recognized the independence of labor unions. The OPZZ derived its strength from its control of the assets of Solidarity, which enabled it to offer members benefits such as the use of holiday homes. In 1992, the OPZZ had three million members and another 1.5 million members who were **retired employees**.

Despite these national divisions, organized labor in Poland cooperates closely through joint councils at the enterprise level, which has enabled it to conduct many labor disputes since the end of communist rule in early 1990 and to obtain the election of Walesa as the new republic's first president. Since 1990, Solidarity has struggled with the consequences of Poland's conversion from a state-run to a capitalist economy and from a one-party to a democratic society. Both Solidarity and the OPZZ are highly politicized organizations, and from 1992 both bodies have been represented along with representatives from government and **employers' organizations** on a tripartite commission that monitors the economy. In 2001, Solidarity declared a membership of 1.1 million to the ICFTU, which was about 13 percent of employees.

In 2002, the ICFTU reported that changes to the Labor Code reduced the rights of Polish organized labor. In 2010, the two Polish affiliates of the **International Trade Union Confederation** declared a combined membership of 986,000. In 2010, the ITUC judged that antiunion behavior by employers was increasing.

POLICE UNIONISM. Although the police usually appear as the historical enemies of labor unions, they have formed their own unions and have sometimes engaged in **labor disputes**. The inflation of World War I and the failure of police pay to be increased accordingly was the background to police strikes in a number of countries. In the **United Kingdom**, a Police Union was formed in 1918; it engaged in strikes in 1918 and 1919, incidents that led to the legal suppression of police unionism. Legislation in 1964 and 1972 allowed the formation of Police Federations but forbade their affiliation with the **Trades Union Congress**, a ban that has continued to the present. Police unions were formed in the states of **Australia** between 1915 and 1921 and a police strike was held in Melbourne in 1923. Unlike the United Kingdom, however, police unions have been able to affiliate with the national peak labor organization; the Police Federation of Australia was an affiliate of the **Australian Council of Trade Unions** in 2002.

Police unions were also formed in the **United States** in the 1910s. A police strike took place in Boston (1919). The Boston **strike** was the result of the suspension of some of the police, who had joined a new union sponsored by the **American Federation of Labor**. The governor of Massachusetts, Calvin Coolidge, strongly opposed the strike, thereby gaining a greatly enhanced standing with the public that assisted his election as president. Since the 1920s, other police labor disputes have occurred, such as the dispute in New York City in January 1971. During the 1970s, 245 illegal police strikes occurred in the United States. In February 1979, the International Union of Police Associations (formed in 1954) became the first independent law enforcement union to hold an **American Federation of Labor–Congress of Industrial Organizations** charter, based partly on a successful police strike in Memphis, Tennessee. By 1997, this U.S. union had more than 80,000 members. Police unionism has also emerged in other countries such as the **Netherlands** and **Nigeria**.

POLITICAL ACTION COMMITTEES (PAC). PACs were set up by organized labor in the **United States** in the 1940s to circumvent federal legal restrictions on the amount of money organizations, businesses, or individuals could contribute to election campaigns. Since the 1940s, other organizations have set up their own PACs. The importance of PACs was increased by 1971 federal legislation. In 2008, there were 293 PACs run by organized labor, which contributed a total of $80.2 million to candidates. *See also* POLITICS.

POLITICS. By their very nature, labor unions are political institutions, offering a permanent challenge to the economic, political, and social order. In the last half of the 19th century, organized labor in the **United Kingdom** lobbied the Liberal Party to achieve its objectives, particularly legal protection. As labor unions banded together to form national and industry federations, they either worked with the established political order or, where they could not, formed their own political parties, as in **Australia**, **Austria**, **Finland**, **New Zealand**, **Norway**, **Sweden**, and the United Kingdom. The **United States** and **Canada** were unusual among Western nations in their lack of significant political parties based on organized labor, although the **National Labor Union** was an exception.

Tensions could, and did, arise between organized labor and their political parties. For example, in 1906, organized labor in **France** and **Germany** declared its independence from control by political parties. In Third World countries, organized labor almost always played an active role in independence movements. Since 1945, organized labor has supported the efforts of social democratic parties in the Western nations to create welfare states to enhance **social security** and has been an active participant in **union–government agreements**. In both the United Kingdom and Australia, the respective parliamentary labor parties have sought to reduce the influence of organized labor within their parties in response to the decline of union **membership** during the 1990s. *See also* POLITICAL ACTION COMMITTEES; SOCIAL DEMOCRATIC, SOCIALIST, AND LABOR PARTIES.

PORTUGAL. Unions and left-wing political groups developed in parallel in Portugal after 1870, a response to Portugal's poverty and its political conservatism. A Socialist Party was set up in 1875 and **syndicalism** attracted much support. There was considerable labor unrest from the 1880s to the revolution of 1910, which caused the fall of the monarchy and the creation of a republic. By 1913, there were claimed to be 90,000 union members, and a national labor federation, named the *Confederaçao Geral de Trabalhadores* (General Confederation of Labor) from 1913, was created. The next 15 years were chaotic, with **general strikes** being declared in 1919, 1920, and 1921. **Collective bargaining** was legalized in 1924. In 1926, a fascist, military-backed dictator, Antonio de Oliveira Salazar, took power and dissolved the *Confederaçao Geral de Trabalho.* Using the examples of fascist Italy and the Nazi *Deutsche Arbeitsfront,* Salazar established a corporate network of government-controlled unions that required compulsory **membership** in 1933. A general strike called by the left wing of organized labor in 1934 only led to more repression.

An independent labor movement did not begin to emerge once more until 1970, when the present *Confederaço Geral dos Trabalhadores Portugueses-Intersindical Nacional* (General Confederation of Portuguese Workers-National Labor Unions) was formed illegally. After the Carnation Revolution (*Revolução dos Cravos*) in 1974 forced the dictatorship to vanish, conditions for organized labor began to improve. The right to **strike** was conditionally granted in 1974 and the right was extended in 1977. A rival **socialist** labor federation, the *União Geral de Trabalhadores* (UGT), or General Workers' Union, was formed in 1978 and was admitted to membership of the **International Confederation of Free Trade Unions (ICFTU)** in 1987 with 983,700 members; it has remained Portugal's representative in the ICFTU and its successor. In December 1996, the UGT, the government, and representatives of the **employers' organizations** signed a social pact aimed at creating employment and improving training in return for cooperation on improving economic performance. In 2001, the UGT had 251,000 members. In its 2010 survey of **violations of trade union rights**, the **International Trade Union Confederation** judged that antiunion behavior was common in private companies and noted that the right to collective bargaining was limited to the **public sector**.

POSTAL, TELEGRAPH, AND TELEPHONE INTERNATIONAL (PTTI). The PTTI was founded in Milan, Italy, in 1920, although the first international conference of postal, telegraph, and telephone employees had been held in Paris in 1911. As with other **international trade secretariats**, the PTTI was a European body up to 1950, after which time it began to expand globally. **Membership** of the Geneva-based PTTI was 3.2 million in 1975 and 4 million in 1994. In August 1997, the PTTI renamed itself **Communication International**. *See also* COMMUNICATION WORKERS' UNION OF AMERICA.

PRINTING. Printing has an important place in the history of organized labor up to the 1970s. Printing was an unusual trade in that it demanded not just superior technical skills but also a high level of literacy. It was this combination that often placed printers at the forefront of employees both in terms of power at the workplace and as leaders within organized labor. Printing was also a leading industry in technological change, a fact that created problems as well as opportunities for its employees. **Labor disputes** in printing occurred as early as the 16th century in **Italy, France**, and **Switzerland**.

Printers were among the first to form formal unions in many countries, although they had been informally organized long before; for instance, in 1829, printers conducted one of **Australia**'s first **strikes**. In **Germany**, printers formed the first national labor union, the *Nationaler Buchdrucker-Verein* (National Printers' Association), in 1848. The printing industry was often a pacesetter for other industries. The first collective agreement made in France in 1843 set wage rates for printers. The first international labor organization among printers was formed in 1889.

Philadelphia printers carried out the first strike of employees in a single trade in the **United States** in 1786, and a short-lived union existed among New York printers in the late 1770s. In 1804, the New York printers formed a union that lasted until 1815. Ely Moore, the first president of the National Trades' Union, the first U.S. labor federation in 1834, was a printer. In 1852, the National Typographical Association was formed which, after the affiliation of printing unions in **Canada**, renamed itself the International Typographical Union (ITU) in 1869. As a strong **craft union**, the ITU played an influential role in the creation of the Federation of Organized Trades and Labor Unions of the United States and Canada in 1881 and the **American Federation of Labor** in 1886.

Hierarchical occupational divisions were an important feature of the organization of printing work, with compositors being the highest group; their dominance of the ITU led to the creation of separate unions by other printing employees such as stereotypers and electroplaters, photoengravers, bookbinders, and journalists in the last decades of the 19th century. Ethnicity also played a role in the history of the ITU. In 1873, printers employed by the German-language press formed their own union, the German-American *Typographia*, but in 1894 this body merged with the ITU. In 1906, the ITU conducted a successful campaign in book and job-printing firms for the eight-hour work day, laying the foundation for its adoption elsewhere in the printing industry. In 1911, the ITU and other unions formed a printing industry body, the International Allied Printing Trades Association.

Until the 1960s, the printing industry unions throughout the world enjoyed considerable power but, with the coming of new technology, that power waned as many of the older mechanical skills were replaced by electronic machines and, more recently, by computers. Symptomatic of the decline of their power was the defeat of London printing unions over the introduction of new technology at Rupert Murdoch's Wapping plant in London in 1986. *See also* INTERNATIONAL GRAPHICAL ASSOCIATION.

PRIVATIZATION. *Privatization* refers to the sale or partial sale of a government-owned enterprise or agency either to a private sector company or through the sale of shares offered to the general public. Privatization was adopted by the Conservative governments in the **United Kingdom** starting in 1979 as a means of improving the efficiency and productivity of the economy. It was based on the ideas of two economists, Friedrich von Hayek and Milton Friedman.

The economic effects of privatization have been much debated, but privatized concerns can achieve higher productivity and bigger profits at least in the short term if they are able to significantly reduce the number of employees. Generally, organized labor has opposed privatization because of the job losses and intensified work methods it usually brings. From the early 1980s, many Western countries have used privatization to varying degrees as a means of improving their economic performance (for example, **Australia** and **New Zealand**). Since the economic crisis of 2008, privatization has been increasingly criticized.

Since the late 1980s the former communist countries of Eastern Europe have used privatization as part of the transition from planned to market economies. In Asia, privatization has been used both in noncommunist countries (for example, **Indonesia** and **Thailand**) and communist countries such as **Vietnam** and **China**. Privatization has produced major **labor disputes** in countries as different as China (October 1997), **India** (April 2002), and **South Africa** (October 2002). *See also* PUBLIC SECTOR.

PUBLIC SECTOR. In most Western countries, one of the most significant trends in the structure of union membership over recent decades has been the large increase in the proportion of union members employed by the public sector (that is, by government or government agencies) compared with the private sector. Precise measurement of this trend is difficult because the statistics have not always been collected in a convenient form or because frequent changes of national policy (such as over the nationalization of industries in the **United Kingdom** since 1945) drain the meaning from longer-term comparisons even if the data are available.

Nevertheless, the distribution of labor union **membership** for the United Kingdom (taking the public sector to be a combination of union membership employed by national government, local government and education, gas, electricity, water, postal, and telecommunications) suggests that 10 percent of union members were employed by the public sector by 1920, 20 percent by 1940, and 22 percent by 1960.

In 1960, only 6 percent of union members in the **United States** were public-sector employees. The growth of government employment after 1960 and structural changes in the private sector in the 1970s and 1980s (specifically the decline in large-scale **manufacturing** employment and the growth of the **service sector**) combined to raise the proportion of union members employed by the public sector to a historic high. In the United States, the proportion of union members employed by the public sector rose from 11 percent in 1970 to 32 percent in 1983, and to 49 percent by 2010. In 2010, the level of union membership among employees in the public sector remained far higher than in the private sector: 41 percent in Australia, 57 percent in the United Kingdom, and 36 percent in the United States. *See also* PRIVATIZATION; PUBLIC SERVICES INTERNATIONAL; WHITE-COLLAR UNIONISM; WOMEN.

PUBLIC SERVICES INTERNATIONAL (PSI). The PSI is one of the largest **global union federations** in the world. It was formed in 1935 with the merger of the International Federation of Workers in Public Administration and Utilities (IFWPAU) and the Civil Servants' International. The IFWPAU was founded by representatives of local government unions from **Denmark**, **Germany**, **Hungary**, the **Netherlands**, **Sweden**, and **Switzerland** in 1907 at the suggestion of the Dutch. The Civil Servants' Association was created in 1925 in the Netherlands and represented employees of central governments. The activities of the PSI were severely restricted first by the disaffiliation of the British civil servants in 1927 (which was forced by legislation passed after the **General Strike** in 1926) and then by the suppression of organized labor by the Nazis in Germany in 1933. After World War II the PSI was reestablished in London and its membership broadened to take in countries outside Europe. In 1957, persistent lobbying of the **International Labour Organization (ILO)** by the PSI resulted in the formation of a committee for public services, although it was not until the early 1970s that the **public sector** was given greater attention by the ILO. Between 1976 and 1994, the **membership** of the PSI rose from 4.8 to 16 million. In 2010, the PSI claimed to represent 20 million members in 650 union affiliates in 148 countries. *See also* WHITE-COLLAR UNIONISM.

PUERTO RICO. Puerto Rico is a free state that has been associated with the **United States** since 1952; organized labor in Puerto Rico emerged after 1872 but was outlawed by the Spanish administration in 1888. From 1898 to 1952, Puerto Rico was under U.S. administration and the first unions date from 1898. Links with the **American Federation of Labor** began in 1900. Organized labor effectively opted out of **collective bargaining** and sought a political role. In 1934, there was a large-scale sugar workers' **strike**. In March 1940, a new labor federation was formed. By 1951 Puerto Rico had joined the **International Confederation of Free Trade Unions (ICFTU)** and has remained a member. Between the 1960s and the mid-1970s, the proportion of union membership in Puerto Rico who belonged to U.S. unions fell from about 75 to 43 percent. In 1957, two labor federations merged to form the *Federación del Trabajo de Puerto Rico,* or Federation of the Workers of Puerto Rico, which was the country's ICFTU affiliate and claimed a membership of 53,000. In 2009, there was considerable labor unrest in Puerto Rico. Puerto Rico was not represented in the **International Trade Union Confederation** in 2010 by the *Central Puertorriquena de Trabajadores.*

Q

QATAR. There is no organized labor in Qatar and **collective bargaining** is illegal. About 75 percent of the labor force is expatriate. Joint consultative committees of management and workers' representatives are possible under the law, but they do not discuss wages. In theory, **labor disputes** are possible once they have been reported to a **conciliation** board, but in practice they do not occur. In 2002, the **International Confederation of Free Trade Unions** noted that labor unions continued to be banned. Although the new 2005 Labour Code raised hopes for improvements, the **International Trade Union Confederation (ITUC)** reported in 2009 that no unions were created.

Migrant workers still suffer abuse in Qatar despite some recent labor legislation. More than 100 strikers were deported in 2009. Qatar was not represented in the ITUC in 2010.

R

RACE AND ETHNICITY. Racial divisions have been both a unifier and divider in the history of organized labor. There were many instances of the use of different ethnic groups to break **strikes** in the 19th century. In the **United Kingdom**, Welsh, Irish, and Cornish miners were brought in by employers to break strikes. In the **United States**, immigrants were used as strikebreakers in the steel industry. In the 1870s and 1880s, violent anti-Chinese feelings, particularly in the mining industry, helped to promote labor unions in the western United States and southeastern **Australia**. In the United States, one of the objectives of the **National Labor Union**, a labor organization that operated between 1866 and 1876, was the restriction of Chinese **immigration**. It was the refusal of the NLU to accept racial integration that led to the operation of the Colored National Labor Union between 1869 and 1871. In the United States, and later in **South Africa**, organized labor tended to be the preserve of European men, although cooperation could occur, as was shown by the successful biracial strike of 1893 in New Orleans. The **Knights of Labor** were unusual in the mid-1880s in their practice of racial integration.

Attempts at racial integration in the United States for much of the 20th century floundered on the racism of many labor unions. In 1924, the Central Trades and Labor Council of Greater New York supported the creation of the Trade Union Committee for Organizing Negro Workers, but this body was defunct by 1927. In 1935, the Negro Labor Committee was formed in New York State and organized a march on Washington in 1941, which led to the setting up of the Fair Employment Practices Commission in 1943, which was designed to eliminate discrimination in employment in war industries or government on the grounds of "race, creed, color, or national origin." In 1960, A. Philip Randolph and other black leaders set up the Negro American Labor Council (NALC) to fight racial discrimination in unions affiliated with the **American Federation of Labor–Congress of Industrial Organizations (AFL-CIO)**; the council operated throughout the 1960s and its relations with the AFL-CIO were often difficult. In the late 1960s, more radical black union groups came into being that challenged the leadership of the NALC within organized labor.

At its inaugural conference in November 1949, the **International Confederation of Free Trade Unions (ICFTU)** declared its intention to work together to "eliminate throughout the world every kind of discrimination or domination based upon race, creed, color, or sex." However, in practice it was not until the 1960s that the ICFTU was able to devote serious attention to the racial aspect of this resolution, mainly with respect to South Africa where racial discrimination became a legal system supported by white labor unions. The ICFTU actively participated in the events of 1997, the European Year against Racism. Since the 1980s, organized labor has made more efforts to combat racism in its own ranks and in the labor force generally. In 1981, the British **Trades Union Congress** released a major policy statement, *Black Workers: A TUC Charter for Equal Opportunity.* In 1996, *IG Metall* published a handbook concerning racial discrimination at the workplace.

In the United States, 15 percent of American labor union members were African-Americans in 2002, compared with 14 percent in 1983. The percentage of Hispanics among union members rose from 6 percent in 1983 to nearly 10 percent in 2001. African-Americans were more likely to be union members than white or Hispanic Americans; in 2010, 13 percent of African-American employees were union members, compared with 12 percent of white and 10 percent of Hispanic employees.

In the United Kingdom, official surveys of labor union members have also found significant variations in the proportions of employees by race who were union members; in 2001, 29 percent of white employees were union members, compared with 30 percent for blacks and 25 percent for Asians. In 2010, 27 percent of white employees were union members, compared with 29 percent for blacks and 16 percent for Asians.

RAILROADS. The railroads were among the main battle grounds of organized labor between 1870 and 1920. Railway employment was characterized by long hours, dangerous working conditions, and management devices to control employees such as company towns (for instance, Pullman in Illinois and Crewe in England). Management attitudes and organization were based on the army. Occupations were divided horizontally as well as vertically. Despite these drawbacks, the railroads were attractive because they usually offered relatively secure employment and the prospect of promotion with experience and length of service. Under these conditions, unions were slow to emerge although a **friendly society** was set up by English locomotive engine drivers and firemen as early as 1839 and may have had some features of a labor union; locomotive enginemen are known to have formed unions in 1848 and 1860.

In 1865, an attempt to form a provident society by the guards of the Great Western Railway Company was crushed by the dismissal of its leaders. In

1866, locomotive engine drivers and firemen formed a union that demanded the 10-hour work day. The other unions present within the railroad industry before 1870 were those of tradesmen working in the repair workshops. In 1871, the Amalgamated Society of Railway Servants of England, Ireland, Scotland, and Wales was formed and became the largest railroad union in **Britain**; this union was the subject of the **Taff Vale Case** in 1901, which cast doubt on the legal status of labor unions. It amalgamated with two other unions in 1913 to become a genuine **industrial union** and changed its name to the National Union of Railwaymen.

In the **United States**, the Brotherhood of Locomotive Firemen and Enginemen was formed in New York in 1873 with the original aim of providing sickness and funeral **benefits** for members, but it soon became a labor union. In 1883, the formation of the Brotherhood of Railroad Trainmen represented the first attempt to create an industrial union in the railroad industry.

In **Australia**, a locomotive engine drivers' union was formed in Victoria in 1870, and general railway unions, based on the Amalgamated Society of Railway Servants of England, Ireland, Scotland, and Wales, were formed in the various colonies between 1884 and 1899, and in **New Zealand** in 1886.

The railroad industry was the focus of some major **labor disputes** between management and employees. In the United States, there were three national clashes before 1900: in 1877, the Burlington railroad strike of 1888–1889, and the Pullman strike and boycott of 1894. There was a national railroad strike in **France** in 1898. The first national railroad strike in **Great Britain** was in 1911 and lasted two days; it was followed by another in 1919. One of Australia's largest strikes, from August to September 1917, was centered on the railroads. General strikes by Dutch railroad employees have occurred twice: in 1903 for higher wages and in 1944 against the Nazi occupation of the **Netherlands** by the Germans. Until the 1980s, most railroad companies were state-owned. The hype of **privatization** has since caused a lot of labor unrest.

RAMAPHOSA, MATAMELA CYRIL (1952–). One of the leaders of black organized labor in **South Africa**, Ramaphosa was born in the Soweto area of Johannesburg. He studied law from 1972 and became involved in student politics. These activities resulted in being detained in solitary confinement for 11 months in 1974 under the Terrorism Act. In 1976, he was again detained, this time for six months. After his release, he became a law clerk and studied for a degree. After obtaining his degree in 1981, Ramaphosa joined the National Council of Trade Unions as a legal advisor. In 1982, he was requested to start a union for mineworkers: the National Union of Mineworkers (NUM). Ramaphosa was again arrested, but was undeterred from organizing.

Ramaphosa was elected as the first general secretary of the NUM. Under his leadership, union membership grew from 6,000 in 1982 to 300,000 in 1992, nearly half of the total number of black workers in the South African mining industry. As General secretary, he along with James Motlatsi, president of NUM, and Elijah Barayi, vice president of NUM, also led the mineworkers in one of the biggest strikes ever in South African history. In 1985, the NUM helped to establish the Congress of South African Trade Unions. Ramaphosa resigned in 1991, when he was elected secretary general of the African National Congress (ANC). Ramaphosa played a leading role in the Mass Democratic Movement during the political struggle against apartheid and became head of the ANC team that negotiated the end of apartheid with the government. After the first democratic elections in 1994, Ramaphosa became a member of Parliament and played an important role in the government. After he lost the race to become president of South Africa, he resigned from politics in 1997 and moved to the private sector.

REAGAN, RONALD (1911–2004). Reagan was the first U.S. president to have also been an executive officer in a national labor union; between 1959 and 1960, he was president of the Screen Actors' Guild (formed in 1933). Despite this background, his presidency (1981–1989) was hostile to organized labor, as shown by his crushing of the **strike** by the Professional Air Traffic Controllers' Organization in August 1981 by firing over 11,000 strikers and replacing them with military controllers and civilian controllers who returned to work.

British Prime minister Margaret Thatcher and Reagan are together known for their neoliberal attitude toward labor.

REGIONAL ORGANISATION FOR ASIA AND PACIFIC (ITUC ASIA PACIFIC). After the merger of the **International Confederation of Free Trade Unions** and the **World Confederation of Labor** in November 2006, the **Asia Pacific Regional Organisation** was renamed ITUC Asia-Pacific. It is based in Singapore, has 40 affiliated organizations in 28 countries, and claims a membership of 30 million.

RENGO. *Rengo,* an abbreviation for *Nihon Rodokumiai Sorengokai* (Japanese Trade Union Confederation), is the largest labor union federation in **Japan**. It is the product of a series of **amalgamations** with other labor federations. The largest part of *Rengo* began as *Sodomei* (Japanese Federation of Trade Unions) in 1946, which became *Domei* (Japanese Confederation of Labor) in 1964, by which time it had 2.1 million members. In 1987, *Domei* joined with *Sorengo* (National Federation of Trade Unions of Japan; formed in 1979) and *Shinsanbetsu* (National Federation of Industrial Organizations; formed in 1952) to form *Zenmin Roren* (Japanese Private Sector Trade Union Federation, now referred to as "old *Rengo*"). The second part of *Rengo* was the **public sector** labor federation *Sohyo* (General Council of Trade Unions of Japan), which was formed in 1950 when the noncommunist unions split from the **communist**-dominated *Sanbetsu-Kaigi* (Congress of Industrial Unions of Japan), which had been formed in 1946. Left-leaning and militant, *Sohyo* was largely responsible for beginning the ***Shunto*** or Spring Offensive for wage increases in 1956. In November 1989, *Zenmin Roren* and *Sohyo* merged to form *Rengo*. In 2001, Rengo organized a mass campaign of 10 million workers against the government. In 2010, *Rengo* represented 6.6 million union members.

RETIRED EMPLOYEES. Retired employees who were formerly labor union members are a neglected group in analysis or discussions of organized labor but have assumed greater importance since the 1970s with the layoff of older workers in **manufacturing** and the aging of the labor force in most Western economies. In **Germany**, the **United Kingdom**, and the **United States**, union members often retain their **membership** after retirement. In 1986, it was estimated that retired employees on **pensions** made up less than 10 percent of union members in Germany and the United Kingdom, but about 18 percent in **Norway**.

Italy is one of the few countries in the world where organized labor has set up strong organizations of retired employees as autonomous associations within the main labor federations. Between 1951 and 1973, the number of pensioner union members was stable at about 600,000, but thereafter has grown steadily to 1.7 million by 1980 and to 5.1 million by 1996. Between 1970 and 2001, the proportion of total union members in Italy who were retired employees rose from about 8 to 18 percent.

In 2002, the United Auto Workers' Union had 710,000 active members and over 500,000 retired members in the United States and Canada. In addition to its 1.4 million employed members in 2001, the U.S. Service Employees International Union (SEIU) had 120,000 members who were retired. Retired members of the SEIU assist in the election of politicians favorable to organized labor.

Since the late 1990s, concern over maintaining pensions has been an area of interest for European and U.S. organized labor. By 2002, the European Federation of Retired and Elderly Persons operated under the auspices of the **European Trade Union Confederation**. National statistics on the numbers of retired employees who retain their **membership** of labor unions are generally not available. In **Australia**, the United Kingdom, and the United States, the labor force surveys of households that are used to generate statistics on labor union membership all exclude retired employees.

RÉUNION. A territory of **France**, organized labor on Réunion had emerged by the 1970s and conducted **general strikes** over inflation in May 1973 and February 1974. In 2000, Réunion was admitted to membership of the **International Confederation of Free Trade Unions.** In 2010, the Union Interprofessionnelle de la Réunion had 16,000 members and was affiliated with the **International Trade Union Confederation.**

REUTHER, WALTER PHILIP (1907–1970). Reuther was one of the chief labor leaders in the **United States** in the post-1945 period through his presidency of the **United Auto Workers** (UAW), which he held from 1946 until his death. Born in Wheeling, West Virginia, he completed three years of secondary education before entering a tool and die maker **apprenticeship** with the Wheeling Steel Corporation. Fired for union activities by the corporation, he moved to Detroit in 1926. In 1931, he was fired by Ford, again for union activities. Unemployed, he took a world tour during 1933 to 1935 that included Europe, the **Soviet Union**, **China**, and **Japan**. On his return, he became an organizer and then an official of the UAW in Detroit. He was elected to the executive board of the UAW in 1936 and was one of the leaders of the UAW's campaign of sit-down **strikes** during 1937 against General Motors and Chrysler. The UAW's campaign for recognition against Ford was met with violence in which Reuther and Richard Frankensteen were beaten up by Ford's private **police**, an infamous incident dubbed the **"battle of the overpass."** During World War II, Reuther served on a number of federal government boards.

In 1946, his moderate faction won control of the UAW and Reuther became its president. The UAW's strike campaign for better pay and conditions in the motor industry culminated in a contract with General Motors in 1948, which included pay increases based on the official cost of living index. In the same year, Reuther was wounded by a shotgun in an attempted assassination. He became president of the **Congress of Industrial Organizations (CIO)** in 1952 and supported its merger with the **American Federation of Labor (AFL)** in 1955. He served as a vice president but led the UAW out of the AFL-CIO in 1968 following disagreements with its conservative president, **George Meany.** Before his death in a plane crash, Reuther's last major activity was his leadership of the **Alliance for Labor Action.**

RIGHT-TO-WORK LAWS. Under the federal **Taft-Hartley Act** of 1947, U.S. states were given the right to ban the union (or closed) shop within their borders. Under most union shop agreements, new employees typically had 30 days in which to join the union. Right-to-work laws make it possible for employees in unionized workplaces to remain nonunionists and have the general effect of inhibiting union **membership** growth. Within the **United States**, 22 states have such laws; they include all of the south and most of the midwest.

ROMANIA. Organized labor first emerged in what is now Romania among printers who formed **mutual benefit** societies, at Brasov in 1846. During the 1860s, other employees formed associations, which were much influenced by **socialism**. In 1872, a general union was formed that was open to all employees without regard to occupation, sex, or religion. In 1893, the Romanian Social Democratic Party was formed and a national labor federation was set up in 1906. The unions supported the peasant uprisings in 1907. The labor federation was an affiliate of the **International Federation of Trade Unions** from 1909 to 1918 and from 1923 to 1938.

Between 1914 and 1920, union **membership** rose from 40,000 to 300,000, divided among 350 unions. In 1921, the Communist Party was constituted from the former Socialist Party and competed for the leadership of organized labor. Both parties sponsored their own labor federations. After a short period of cooperation, the Communist Party broke away from the united labor federation and was banned by the government in 1923; in 1929, its labor federation was banned too. There were many **labor disputes** in Romania in the late 1920s and early 1930s, a reflection of not just the deterioration in economic conditions but also the rise in **manufacturing** employment from 318,000 in 1913 to 953,000 in 1930. In 1936, a new labor federation was formed, with 310 individual unions representing 80,000 members, but when the fascist government came to power two years later, unions and **strikes** were outlawed. During World War II, the Romanian government was an ally of the Nazis until its overthrow in 1944. With the establishment of a **communist** republic in 1947, organized labor became part of the machinery of government.

An attempted formation of an independent union was made in 1979, but was harshly suppressed. A second clandestine effort was made in 1988, but was suppressed also. Communist rule in Romania was ended by a violent popular uprising between December 1989 and January 1990. In December 1989, *Fratia* ("Fraternity"), a broadly based independent labor union, was formed. The former communist labor federation was dissolved early in 1990 and replaced by what became the *Confederatia Nationala a Sindicatelator Libere din Românìa* (CNSLR), or National Free Trade Union Confederation of Romania. A third independent labor body, *Alfa-Cartel,* was formed by 1991. In the same year, the government legalized the formation of independent labor unions.

As in **Bulgaria** and **Poland**, there have been conflicts between the independent labor organizations over the control of the assets of the former communist labor federations, but in Romania these have been minimized by a high degree of cooperation. In 1993, the CNSLR and *Fratia* joined forces to become the Romanian member of the **International Confederation of Free Trade Unions (ICFTU)**, with a claimed membership of 3.2 million, which represented 39 percent of employees. In 2001, the two Romanian affiliates of the ICFTU claimed a total membership of 400,000.

The 2003 Trade Union Law gave legal recognition of the right to form unions. The right to strike is also recognized, but there exist some limitations and courts tend to declare strikes illegal. Even in 2010, the enforcement of laws to protect organized labor remained difficult. For example, many foreign employers make employment conditional upon the employee agreeing not to become a union member.

ROOKES V. BARNARD. *Rookes v. Barnard* was an important legal case concerning the operation of labor unions in the **United Kingdom**. In 1955, Douglas Rookes, an employee of the British Overseas Airways Corporation, resigned from his union, the Association of Engineering and Shipbuilding Draftsmen. The union, wanting to maintain a closed shop, instigated his dismissal. Rookes sued the union and was awarded substantial damages; the association appealed to the House of Lords, but it upheld the original decision in 1964. The case, which reflected poorly on the attitude of a union toward an individual, opened up a loophole in the Trades Disputes Act (1906) by making union officials liable for damages for threatening to **strike** in breach of contracts of employment. This loophole was closed by the Trades Disputes Act (1965). The legal issue raised by *Rookes v. Barnard* was one of the forces behind the appointment of the **Donovan Commission**.

ROTH, HERBERT OTTO (1917–1994). A librarian and writer, Roth was born in Vienna, **Austria**, the son of a railway engineer. He wrote the first general account of organized labor in **New Zealand**. He was called "Otti" during his years in Austria, but was later known as "Bert" in New Zealand. Although his parents were Jewish, religion played little part in his upbringing. As a young man he was an instinctive leftist, although his family was not particularly political. With the dominance of fascism in Austria in the 1930s, left-wing politics was increasingly clandestine. The German annexation of Austria in March 1938 threatened **socialists** and Jews alike. Bert Roth fled Austria, his escape route taking him first into **Germany**, then across Lake Constance into **Switzerland** and ultimately to **France**. In 1940, he acquired a permit to emigrate to New Zealand. On arrival he described himself to a reporter as a socialist refugee.

Roth quickly became involved in left-wing politics. He mixed with old socialists and **communists**, and a younger bohemian group. Bert Roth never became formally affiliated with particular socialist factions. He described himself as a "champagne socialist."

Roth's greatest contribution to New Zealand history writing was *Trade Unions in New Zealand Past and Present* (1973), which remains the standard introduction to the history of New Zealand unionism. Most of Roth's writing was based on unpublished material, drawn largely from his own private collection, which is an important resource at the Alexander Turnbull Library in Wellington.

RUSSIAN FEDERATION. Before March 1906, unions were illegal throughout the Russian Empire. Their brief legalization produced a surge of **membership** growth to 123,000 by 1907 in the wake of the 1905 Revolution, but this development was wrecked by a government crackdown. There was some revival by organized labor between 1911 and 1914, but it was able to achieve little beyond conducting protest strikes. The revolutionary period between mid-1917 and 1920 saw an explosion of union membership from 1.5 to 5.2 million. The main division in the Russian labor movement was between those who supported the autonomy of organized labor from the political arm of labor (led by the Mensheviks) and the Bolsheviks, who held that the function of the unions was to help overthrow the government and transfer power to the **socialist** party who was said to act on behalf of the proletariat and was renamed the **Communist** Party after 1918. During 1919 and 1920, the Bolsheviks achieved control of the Russian labor movement. At first, the unions played an important role in the program of economic reconstruction known as the New Economic Plan, but from 1922 under Lenin, Stalin, and their successors, the unions operated as agents of centralized communist rule whose main role was to increase economic output.

In 1978, some dissidents tried to form an independent union for professional employees, but it was suppressed by the Soviet government and its leaders imprisoned. The first sign of a mass independent labor movement came in mid-1989 with a wave of **strikes** in northern Russia, the **Ukraine**, and the Urals, which gave rise to Workers' Committees and the formation of an independent miners' union, which joined an independent Confederation of Labor when it was set up in May 1990. In October 1990, the All-Union Central Council of Trade Unions, the central communist body formed in November 1924, transformed itself into the "General Confederation of Unions of the USSR"; it recognized the rights of the newly independent nations within the former Soviet Union and pledged itself to protect union rights.

After the creation of the Commonwealth of Independent States on 8 December 1991, the General Confederation of Unions again reshaped itself to become the Federation of Independent Trade Unions of Russia, made up of seven of the new states (excluding the Ukraine) in April 1992. The organizational continuity of these moves was important for maintaining control of the assets of the former communist labor organization, a vexed issue in most other East European countries. Aside from the emergence of the independent labor organizations in the former Soviet republics, the main independent Russian labor organization is *Sotsprof,* a federation of social democratic and socialist unions formed in about 1990.

An official crackdown on independent organized labor began in August 1992, when there was a strike by air traffic controllers. In the same year, the Boris Yeltsin government began a program of economic reform marked by **privatization** of state-run enterprises. A **collective bargaining** law was introduced in 1993, but changed little in the way the labor code worked, with its many restrictions on the right to strike and the banning of strikes on **railroads**, public transport, civil aviation, communications, energy, and defense. In 1994, trade union efforts to monitor or influence privatization of enterprises to ensure the protection of workers' rights was met with official violence and intimidation.

From the early 1990s, the **International Confederation of Free Trade Unions (ICFTU)** was able to take a growing role in the well-being of Russian organized labor. Beginning with trade union education, the ICFTU campaigned for the payment of wage arrears due to Russian workers, which culminated in the All-Russian Trade Union Day of Action in April 1998. The ICFTU also secured the participation of the **International Labour Organization (ILO)** in the Russian wages campaign. During the economic turmoil of 1998, the ICFTU organized meetings between the leaders of Russian organized labor and the International Monetary Fund and the World Bank. The ICFTU successfully promoted cooperation between Russia's three labor federations. An ICFTU mission to Russia reported favorably on the country's organized labor.

In November 2000, the ICFTU took the historic decision to admit as affiliates the Federation of Independent Trade Unions of Russia, the All-Russian Confederation of Labor (formed in 1995), and the Confederation of Labor of Russia (also formed in 1995). This was the first time that Russia had ever been represented in an independent international labor organization. In 2001, these three federations had a combined membership of 30.5 million. In 2007, the ICFTU noted that, although Russian workers had the right to form unions, collective bargaining for smaller unions was difficult in practice and that generally the political environment for organized labor had worsened since 2001. The ICFTU also considered that amendments to the labor code that came into force on 1 February 2003 imposed rules on union structures. The right to strike is still limited, despite ILO criticism. In 2010, unionists still faced intimidation, dismissals and arrests while some receive death threats.

RWANDA. Independent from **Belgium** since July 1962, the first labor unions were branches of Belgian unions. Since independence, the history of Rwanda has been one of political turmoil and massive ethnic violence, culminating in a genocidal civil war in 1994. In 1993, the *Centrale Syndicale des Travailleurs du Rwanda* (Central Trade Union of Workers of Rwanda) was admitted to the **International Confederation of Free Trade Unions** with 70,000 members. In 2007, the **International Trade Union Confederation** reported that labor unions in Rwanda operated in a climate of antiunion employers and limitations on the right to strike. By 2009, conditions for organized labor had improved, but were still far from ideal because free **collective bargaining** is not guaranteed and the right to **strike** is hampered by lengthy procedures.

RYDER, GUY (1957–). General secretary of the **International Confederation of Free Trade Unions (ICFTU)** from January 2002 and its successor, the **International Trade Union Confederation**, since November 2006. Ryder was born in Liverpool, England. He worked as an assistant in the international department of the **Trades Union Congress** between 1981 and 1985 before serving as secretary of the industry trade section of the *Fédération internationale des employés, techniciens et cadres* (International Federation of Commercial, Clerical, Professional, and Technical Employees) in Geneva from 1985 to 1988. In 1988, he joined the staff of the ICFTU in Geneva and rose to be the director of its office there. He was also secretary of the Workers' Group of the Governing Body of the **International Labour Organization (ILO)** in 1993 to 1998 and other positions with the ILO before becoming general secretary of the ICFTU. In 2002, he listed his priorities as ICFTU general secretary in an interview as responding better to the challenge of **globalization**, increasing the effectiveness of the ICFTU, creating greater opportunities for **women**, and boosting recruitment to combat the aging of the **membership** of organized labor.

S

SABOTAGE. Derived from the French word *sabot* (wooden shoe), sabotage is a means for workers to stop the smooth running of production. When workers threw their *sabots* into a machine, this was called *sabotage*. Sabotage can take different forms, including the go-slow. Organized labor has been reluctant to use sabotage, with the exception of the **Industrial Workers of the World**.

SAFETY. Derived from the French word *sauf*, "safe" means being free of all kinds of failure, damage, error, accidents, harm, or any other undesirable events or circumstances. Safety also means achieving an acceptable level of risk. This can take the form of being protected from the event or from exposure to something that causes health dangers.

Safety has been an important issue for labor unions since the heyday of the Industrial Revolution. Work often was hazardous and some professions such as in the mines or on the docks were infamous for their dangers. The **International Labour Organization (ILO)** keeps more than 40 conventions and recommendations. The most important are Occupational Safety and Health Convention, 1981 (No. 155); Occupational Health Services Convention, 1985 (No. 161); Promotional Framework for Occupational Safety and Health Convention, 2006 (No. 187); and Occupational Safety and Health Recommendation, 2006 (No. 197).

According to the ILO, every year more than 2 million people die from occupational accidents or work-related diseases. It also estimates that there are 270 million occupational accidents and 160 million cases of occupational diseases each year worldwide, but the emphasis is on developing countries where deaths and injuries take a heavy toll, especially among children, migrants, and women.

Since 1995, the **International Confederation of Free Trade Unions** and its successor organizes The International Commemoration Day for Dead and Injured Workers, in memory of workers who die or are injured at work. The ILO has supported this since 2003. In 2007, chromium miners in **Albania** struck over safety for months after the deaths of two colleagues.

SAINT CHRISTOPHER AND NEVIS. St. Christopher and Nevis has been independent from the **United Kingdom** since September 1983; labor unions on St. Christopher and Nevis have been legally recognized since 1940. The islands have been represented in the **International Confederation of Free Trade Unions** since 1951 by the Saint Christopher and Nevis Trades and Labour Union. In 2001, there were about 400 labor union members on St. Christopher and Nevis. **Strikes** have been unknown since 1988.

SAINT HELENA. St. Helena is a territory of the **United Kingdom**. The St. Helena General Workers' Union has been the sole labor union on the island since its formation in 1958; it had about 700 members in 2001 and was represented in the **International Confederation of Free Trade Unions** from 1965 to 2001. In 2010, there was no affiliation with the **International Trade Union Confederation**.

SAINT LUCIA. St. Lucia has been independent from the **United Kingdom** since February 1979; organized labor developed after the establishment of **collective bargaining** arrangements in 1938. The St. Lucia Workers' Union was formed in 1939 and was followed by the St. Lucia Waterfront Worker's Trade Union in 1945. Both unions have been affiliates of the **International Confederation of Free Trade Unions** from 1953 to 2006; by 2010, they had amalgamated to form the National Workers' Union with about 3,000 members. It was affiliated with the **International Trade Union Confederation**.

SAINT VINCENT AND THE GRENADINES. St. Vincent and the Grenadines has been independent from the **United Kingdom** since October 1979; organized labor on St. Vincent and the Grenadines emerged after World War II. By 1957, the United Workers, Peasants, and Ratepayers' Union had become affiliated with the **International Confederation of Free Trade Unions (ICFTU)** and the islands have continued their affiliation since then. In 2001, their ICFTU affiliate was the Commercial, Technical, and Allied Workers' Union, with 2,000 members. In 2010, Saint Vincent and the Grenadines was not represented in the **International Trade Union Confederation**.

SAMSON, MILIANO [ELMO] (1915–1978). The founder of the Laborers' Union of Hawaii, Elmo was born and raised in poverty. When his parents were evicted from their house during a sugar plantation strike in the 1920s, the family had to sleep in a ditch. This memory together with other reminiscences of his life in poverty motivated Samson to get engaged in union activities. After working on a sugar plantation, he worked at the Pearl Harbor Naval Shipyard. Elmo helped to organize the local of the Laborers' Union, which had a **membership** of a few hundred. He also assisted in the formation of the Hawaii Building Trades Council and the Hawaii State Federation of Labor, **American Federation of Labor–Congress of Industrial Organizations**, of which he became a vice president in 1966, the year it was constituted. At the time of his death, the local had 3,500 members.

SAN MARINO. The oldest republic in the world (dating from 1600), San Marino has been represented in the **International Confederation of Free Trade Unions** from 1959 to 2006 by the *Confederazione Democratica dei Lavoratori Sammarinesi* (Democratic Confederation of San Marino Workers) and in the **International Trade Union Confederation** since 2006; it has 5,900 members.

SAUDI ARABIA. Organized labor first made its presence felt in Saudi Arabia in 1953 when 13,000 Saudi nationals successfully went on **strike** in the oil industry to demand equality of conditions with U.S. workers. The government was subsequently presented with petitions asking for permission to form labor unions. Some temporary concessions were made, but these were withdrawn by 1959. Most employees in Saudi Arabia are migrants. **Collective bargaining** and labor unions are forbidden. In 1994, the government advised the **International Confederation of Free Trade Unions** that trade union rights were considered to violate the principles of Islam. Although in theory workers have access to labor courts, in practice it is virtually impossible for expatriate workers to legally enforce their rights. In April 2002, amendments to the labor law allowed for the establishment of workers' committees made up of Saudis and expatriates in firms employing 100 or more as a way of improving work performance. In 2010, conditions for migrant employees in Saudi Arabia had not improved. Expatriates made up about two thirds of employees who are deported if they protest or strike.

SASSENBACH, JOHANN (1866–1940). Johann Sassenbach was born in Breun (now known as Lindlar, **Germany**). After his training time, he became a *sattler* (saddle maker) like his father. As a journeyman, he hiked through Germany, **Switzerland**, **France**, north **Italy**, and **Austria**. After returning in 1889, he joined the just-established association of the saddle makers and related workers and established a branch of the union in the same year in Cologne. Sassenbach moved to Berlin in 1890. He attended advanced education and language courses and lectures at the university. In 1891, he became chair to the saddle makers' union and editor of the *Sattlerzeitung*. In 1895, he also organized the first **socialist** academic conference.

From 1902 to 1921, Sassenbach was a nonsalaried member of the *Generalkommission der Gewerkschaften* (National Federation of Trade Unions). In 1920, Sassenbach was sent to Rome as social attaché of the German Foreign Office. Since 1922, he was secretary and from 1927 to 1931 secretary-general of the **International Federation of Trade Unions**. He was also an author and publisher and can be regarded as the first trade union librarian. The Nazis seized his extensive library and imprisoned him. Sassenbach died in Frankfurt am Main.

SASTRADIREDJA, SUPARNA (1915–1996). Born in Java, Dutch East Indies (**Indonesia**), Sastradiredja died in Amsterdam (the **Netherlands**). He was one of the founders of the trade union of plantation workers, *Sarekat Buruh Perkebunan Republik Indonesia* (Sarbupri, Estate Workers Union of the Rebublic of Indonesia), in 1947 and its secretary-general until 1965. Sarbupri in its initial stage was more engaged in fighting the Dutch during the struggle for independence than in union organizing. In the 1950s, the union, the largest in Indonesia and closely linked to the **Communist** Party, organized massive strikes. When in 1965 a military coup d'état brought the military to power, thousands of communists and union members were slaughtered. Sastradiredja escaped persecution because he was in **China** at the time. In 1978, he moved to the Netherlands, where he died in exile.

SCHEVENELS, WALTER (1894–1966). Walther Schevenels was a Belgian trade union leader and one of the founders of the Metalworkers' Federation of **Belgium**. In 1929, he was appointed assistant general secretary of the **International Federation of Trade Unions**, in 1930 he became general secretary and held the position until 1945. He then became assistant general secretary of the **World Federation of Trade Unions (WFTU)** in charge of the industrial field. Together with the Western European trade unions, he left the WFTU, and, after the creation of the **International Confederation of Free Trade Unions** in 1949, he became in January 1951 secretary general of the European Regional Organisation. He held this position until his death in 1966.

From 1949, he was also secretary general of the Trade Union Advisory Committee of the European Recovery Programme, from 1955 known as the *Joint Trade Union Advisory Committee to the Organisation for European Economic Co-operation* and from 1961 known as the **Trade Union Advisory Committee** to the Organisation for Economic Co-operation and Development. Among his publications are *Forty-Five Years: International Federation of Trade Unions 1901–1945* (Brussels, 1955) and "European Regional

Organisation (ERO), of the ICFTU" in *The European Trade Union Movement within the ICFTU* (Brussels, 1964).

SENEGAL. Senegal has been independent from **France** since April 1960. Organized labor began in Senegal in 1937 in the form of branches of French labor unions; by 1956, total **membership** had risen to 50,000. The *Confédération Nationale des Travailleurs du Sénégal* (National Confederation of Workers of Senegal) was formed in 1969 and in 1993 was admitted to membership of the **International Confederation of Free Trade Unions (ICFTU)** with a claimed membership of 60,000. Despite challenges, Senegal has managed to retain a pluralist political system since independence. The ICFTU reported that, although the 2001 constitution recognized the right to **collective bargaining**, the right to **strike** was curtailed. Similarly, the labor code recognized the right to form labor unions, but these unions had to be approved by the Ministry of the Interior. In 2001, Senegal was represented by two union federations. The ICFTU reported that the government continued to retain the right to grant or withhold approval to form a labor union and that the constitution adopted in January 2001 undermined the right to strike, but admitted that the right to collective bargaining was recognized.

Conditions for organized labor in Senegal have not improved since 2002. In 2010, Senegal had five affiliates with the **International Trade Union Confederation** with a total membership of 191,000. Strikers were dismissed and beaten in 2010.

SERBIA. A former part of the **Yugoslavia (Federal Republic)**, Serbia has been independent since February 2008. Despite the ratification of several **International Labour Organization** conventions, Serbian organized labor faces harassment from employers. Two women labor activists were attacked in 2009.

SERVICE EMPLOYEES INTERNATIONAL UNION (SEIU). The SEIU is a leading U.S. labor union that recruits nurses, doctors, health technicians, workers in local government, state employees, security officers, janitors, and building service workers. It was formed in 1921 as the Building Service Employees International Union and was chartered by the **American Federation of Labor**. It adopted its present name in 1968. Between 1980 and 2010, the **membership** of the SEIU rose from 625,000 to 1.8 million, one of the few unions to successfully exploit the recruitment opportunities presented by the employment growth of the **service sector** by using the **organizing** model; in addition, the SEIU has 120,000 members who are **retired employees**. In

2001, more than half its members were **women** and 20 percent were African-American. The SEIU claims to represent more immigrant workers than any other union in the **United States**. From the early 1980s to 1995, the president of the SEIU was **John Joseph Sweeney**. The SEIU operates a strong, grass-roots political program and has been affiliated with **Change to Win** since 2005. In 2010, the SEIU was the fourth largest labor union in the world.

SERVICE SECTOR. The service (or tertiary) sector is that part of the economy that provides consumer or producer goods (usually intangible) for immediate consumption, in contrast to the primary sector (**agriculture**, forestry, and fishing) and the secondary sector (**manufacturing**). Since World War II, the service sector has become the largest and fastest-growing sector in industrialized economies, both in terms of employment and value of economic output. In 2010, 88 percent of employees in the **United States**, and 87 percent in **Australia** were employed in the service sector.

Within the service sector, the traditionally strong areas of labor union **membership** have been in the **railroads** (up to the 1920s), construction, and since World War II, **education** and communications. Outside of the **public sector**, the service sector, because of its diversity and part-time employment, has partially been a difficult recruiting area for organized labor. For example, in 2010 only 5 percent of employees in wholesale and retail trade in the United States were union members, compared with 22 percent of employees in transportation and utilities.

SEYCHELLES. The Seychelles has been independent from the **United Kingdom** since June 1976; organized labor in the Seychelles emerged in the 1960s. It has been represented in the **International Confederation of Free Trade Unions** since 1989 by its National Workers' Union, which was formed in 1978 uniting all previously existing unions; it claimed 5,000 members in 2001. The Seychelles was not represented in the **International Trade Union Confederation** in 2010.

SHORTER WORKING HOURS. From as early as the 16th century, unions have attempted to reduce **working hours**, or at least resist them being lengthened. There were two disputes in the **printing** industry in **France** in 1539 and 1572 over long working hours. In both the **United Kingdom** and the **United States**, there were moves by organized labor to gain a maximum working day of 10 hours in the 1830s. In the 1880s, there was an international movement by organized labor to reduce the work day to eight hours. This movement was also the beginning of the yearly 1 May manifestations, but for most employees the eight-hour working day was not achieved until the 20th century. Since 1945, metal workers' unions have generally been the vanguard for the reduction of working hours in the United Kingdom, **Germany**, **Italy**, and **Australia**. Since the 1980s, the target working week for organized labor has been the 35-hour week, but outside of France, which introduced the 35-hour working week in 2000 at the behest of organized labor, shorter working hours remain a desired but not an attained goal in Western Europe. Indeed, in December 2002, the French Parliament agreed to dilute the 35-hour week labor law. Furthermore, statistics collected by the **International Labour Organization** indicate that in 2004, 22 percent of French employees worked over 48 hours a week to make ends meet. In general, a worldwide raise in working hours occurred since the 1980s.

SHUNTO. *Shunto* is a Japanese term meaning "spring offensive" and refers to the national process of bargaining over wages, conditions of employment, and other issues between unions, employers, and the government. The *Shunto* was begun in **Japan** in February 1956 by *Sohyo* (General Council of Trade Unions of Japan) as a way of strengthening the power of the unions and of reducing earning differentials between enterprises and the thousands of unions based on them. For decades, the *Shunto* began with an agreement by the unions about the amount of the pay increase they wanted and a corresponding decision by the **employers' organization** (*Nikkeiren*) about the amount of the unions' demand that they were prepared to accept; the unions then formally presented their demands. The *Shunto* moved on to the private sector beginning with the iron and steel, shipbuilding, electrical equipment, and automobile industries.

Later the *Shunto* proceeded to industries such as textiles, petroleum, and food. Pay increases made in the larger enterprises were then applied to medium and smaller enterprises. The *Shunto* reached its climax in April. The increases gained by the *Shunto* in the private sector were used as the basis for the increase for government employees and employees in national enterprises. The *Shunto* has been responsible for gaining wage increases higher than the consumer price index. In 1975, the *Shunto* delivered a pay increase of 32.9 percent, but since 1976 these increases have been less than 10 percent; in 1995, the *Shunto* pay increase was 2.8 percent, its lowest level. Since 1995, the *Shunto* has declined in importance in response to the depressed state of the Japanese economy. *See also RENGO.*

SIERRA LEONE. Independent from the **United Kingdom** since April 1961, organized labor in Sierra Leone effectively dates from the 1920s, although the first attempts to form unions began in 1884. In 1942, there were 11 registered unions with a total **membership** of 800. In 1955, the unions conducted a

general strike. The Sierra Leone Labour Congress came into being in 1976 from the merger of two labor federations formed in 1942 and 1958. It has been the country's affiliate with the **International Confederation of Free Trade Unions** and the **International Trade Union Confederation** and claimed 25,000 members in 2010. There have been tensions between organized labor and the government, but conditions for organized labor have been relatively free. On 8 May 2000, a demonstration for peace by 2,000 union members resulted in the deaths of 19 and the wounding of 50 people by rebel insurgents; three bystanders were also killed. Sierra Leone is one of the few African countries where violations of trade union rights do not occur.

SINGAPORE. After achieving self-rule from the **United Kingdom** in 1959, Singapore joined the Federation of **Malaysia** in 1963. Labor unions emerged in Singapore from 1946 and soon became part of the struggle against British rule. In the early 1950s, Singapore's high level of **labor disputes** was a reflection of the political militancy of organized labor. In 1955, **strikes** were forbidden in essential services. The National Trades Union Congress was officially registered in 1964 but had its origins in a body formed in the 1950s, the Singapore Trades Union Congress. Between 1946 and 1962, the number of labor union members in Singapore grew from 18,700 to 189,000. In 1953, Singapore was admitted to membership of the **International Confederation of Free Trade Unions**. In 1965, Singapore left the Federation of Malaysia and has been sovereign since that time.

With the defeat of political leftists in the early 1960s, organized labor in Singapore was increasingly brought under **government control**. Unions are free to form in the private sector, but forbidden in the public sector. Despite its lack of freedom, the National Trades Union Congress claimed 225,000 members, which represented about 14 percent of employees in 2001. In 2009, the **International Labour Organization** reported that many of the restrictions on trade union rights were not applied because the Minister of Manpower has the power to make exemptions. Migrant workers still have little opportunity to organize and only two strike days have been officially registered since 1978. *See also* MALAYSIA.

SLAVERY. The most extreme form of **forced labor**, slavery is often assumed to be a feature of the past, an institution that died out in the 19th century, but there is much evidence of a resurgence of slavery since the 1980s. In 1994, the Committee against Modern Slavery was established in Paris and between 1997 and 1998 investigated 135 cases, mainly involving Third-World immigrant workers in Western Europe. Slavery reemerged in southwest Sudan in 1989 as part of the civil war waged by the Islamic fundamentalist regime in northern Sudan. There have also been incidents of trafficking in children as slaves in West and Central Africa from 1995 to 2001. The **International Labour Organization** adopted the Worst Forms of Child Labour Convention (No. 182) in 1999 in an effort to combat the practice. In 2007, the Islamic Republic of **Mauritania** was the last country in the world to forbid slavery and make it a criminal offense. In 2008, Anti-Slavery International, a nongovernmental organization based in London, estimated that there were about 12.3 million people who were slaves—that is, they were forced to work through the threat of violence. *See also* CHILD LABOR; *SYNDICATS SANS FRONTIÈRES.*

SLOVAKIA. Formed from the eastern part of **Czechoslovakia** on 1 January 1993, Slovakia was represented in the **International Confederation of Free Trade Unions** (ICFTU) by the Confederation of Trade Unions of the Slovak Republic from 1993; it claimed 338,000 members in 2010, compared with 702,000 in 2001. The ICFTU reported in 2001 that there had been a significant improvement in trade union rights in Slovakia, specifically removing the requirement that lists of names of striking workers be provided to the employer. A labor code was introduced in April 2002 that provided for **collective bargaining**, but no protection for labor unions that go on strike if a part of a collective bargain has not been honored by the employer.

SLOVENIA. Independent from the former **Yugoslavia** since 1991, Slovenia has enjoyed political stability and has made considerable strides from a state-run to a market economy. A centralized system of **collective bargaining** has been in place since 1989. In 1993, independent labor unions were legalized and a codetermination system based on *Mitbestimmung* in **Germany** was introduced to enable unions to influence **privatization**. In 1994, organized labor was a participant in a **union–government agreement** on incomes policy. By 1994, there were four main labor federations, of which the largest was the reformed ex-communist organization. Never a member of the **International Confederation of Free Trade Unions**, Slovenia had about 300,000 union members in 2003 or about 41 percent of the employees. In 2010, this percentage proved rather stable.

SOCIAL-DEMOCRATIC, SOCIALIST, AND LABOR PARTIES. Social-democratic, socialist, and labor political parties grew out of the conviction that the economic and social condition of working-class people needed improvement. They developed in and outside the union movement out of groups whose origins sometimes dated back to the International Working Men's Association (commonly known as the First International). Usually composed of diverse groups and opinions, these parties developed their own characteristics depending on their country of origin, but they were united by their vision of themselves as the political arm of the working class. Despite the formation of socialist groups in the 1880s, such as the Social Democratic Federation, the Socialist League, and the Fabians, it was the relative success of the political alliance of labor unions with the Liberal Party in the **United Kingdom** that delayed the formation of an independent political party based on unions. It was not until 1893 that the Independent Labour Party was formed; it cooperated with the **Trades Union Congress** to form the Labour Representation Committee in 1900; it was renamed the British **Labour Party** in 1906. In **Norway,** a Labor Party was formed in 1887. In **Australia,** the Labor Party was established separately in the colonies of New South Wales and South Australia in 1891. Labor parties were formed in **South Africa** in 1909 and in **New Zealand** in 1916.

In continental Europe, the generally authoritarian political climate encouraged political parties with labor connections to be far more radical, even revolutionary. They drew the bulk of their political ideas from Marxism. This tendency was reinforced by the relative weakness of labor unions for most of the 19th century. The first European social-democratic party was formed in **Germany** in 1863 by Ferdinand Lassalle (1825–1864) as the German Workingmen's Association, and the second, also in Germany, by Wilhelm Liebknecht (1826–1900) and August Bebel (1840–1913) as the Social Democratic Party of Germany in 1866. In 1875, these two parties fused to form the Social Democratic Party. Socialist parties soon emerged in other Western European countries: **Denmark** (1871), **Czechoslovakia** (1872), **Portugal** (1875), **Spain** (1879), **France** (1880), **Belgium** (1885), **Austria** and **Switzerland** (1888), **Sweden** (1889), **Italy** (1892), **Romania** (1893), the **Netherlands** (1882, which split in 1894), and **Finland** (1899).

Socialist parties were formed in Eastern Europe too: **Armenia** (1890), **Poland** (1892), **Bulgaria** (1893), **Hungary** (1894), **Lithuania** (1896), **Russia** (1898), and **Georgia** (1899); a social democratic party was formed in **Latvia** in 1904, and in the **Ukraine** in 1905. In the **United States,** a socialist labor party was formed in 1876, a Greenback-Labor Party in 1878, and a Socialist Party in 1901. A Socialist Party was formed in **Argentina** in 1892.

The Second International Workingmen's Association, which was set up in 1889, was the international forum for many of these parties. Although there was agreement about the need for change, there was much disagreement about the methods for achieving it. By the late 19th century, there were two main tendencies at work in these parties both within their national borders and internationally: those who wanted change by gradual reform within the political order and those who wanted change by full-scale social revolution. The second strand was incorporated into **communism** from 1917.

Electorally successful labor parties, that is, political parties built solely on organized labor, have been relatively rare since 1900 outside of Australia, the United Kingdom, and Scandinavia. Conflict can and does arise between the political and industrial wings of organized labor. One early instance of this occurred in Germany in 1906; it was resolved by the Mannheim Agreement, which declared the equality between the Social Democratic Party and the unions in providing the leadership for the working class. In France, the trade unions declared their independence from all political parties in the Charter of Amiens, also in 1906.

SOCIALISM. As a political ideology, socialism took shape during the 19th century; as a word, it came from the Latin *socius*, meaning "friend" or "ally." Although the term *socialism* was applied to a wide range of beliefs, a shared concern was the need to assume some kind of collective control over the means of production, distribution, and exchange, and to use this control for the greatest good of the members of society. Despite great interest in socialist ideas in organized labor, there was often little understanding of how to translate socialist theories into practice. In many countries, from about 1910, socialists within labor unions began to divide between reformists and revolutionaries, giving rise to **communism**. **Social-democratic, socialist**, and **labor parties** have been the means for introducing socialist policies into mainstream democratic politics, with organized labor being careful to preserve its independence from political parties. The inflationary effects of World War I caused a heightened sense of economic injustice among the working class and led to the incorporation of explicit socialist objectives into the platforms of the **British Labour Party** (1918) and the **Australian Labor Party** (1919). By and large, social-democratic, socialist, and labor parties saw Parliament and legislation as the way to implement socialism before the 1950s, with organized labor playing a secondary role as a means of bringing about incremental improvements in pay and working conditions. However, there have been some important exceptions to the limited role assigned to organized labor within socialism. In the **United Kingdom**, guild socialists in the 1920s envisaged labor unions as the basis for a future socialist state. In Germany, organized labor gave formal support to the principle of economic democracy, an idea that became *Mitbestimmung* (codetermination) after 1945.

SOCIAL SECURITY. Social security has been defined by the **International Labour Organization (ILO)** as embracing social insurance schemes (for occupational injury, health, **pensions**, and **unemployment**), public health, family allowances, war benefits, and special transfers to government employees. The growth of social security systems in Western economies during the 20th century was sought by organized labor not just to improve the conditions of employees generally but also as a means of reducing the competition for positions in the paid labor force from dependent groups such as children, mothers, and the aged. Of special importance was the introduction of **unemployment benefits** because the unemployed were the pool from which strikebreakers were traditionally drawn by employers. In 1950, the **International Confederation of Free Trade Unions** issued a manifesto in favor of social security and old age and sickness insurance in the context of wider support for political and economic democracy.

In 1952, the ILO adopted Convention Number 102 on Social Security (Minimum Standards), which covered the following forms of **benefits**: medical, sickness, unemployment, old age, occupational injury and disease, family, maternity, and invalidity.

Since the 1980s, there has been growing concern by governments about the adverse economic effects of spending on social security. Regardless of their political complexions, Western European governments have tried to reduce social security benefits based on the assumption that their maintenance in the long term is unsustainable because of the aging of their populations. This assumption has been fostered by the neoliberal belief that the state has to retreat from the economy. Their efforts have produced **strikes** in 2003 in **France** and **Austria** and conflict within the German Social Democratic Party. Nevertheless, social security systems are the main means for the redistribution of income from the better-off to the less well-off in Western societies. In 2006, only 41 countries had signed ILO Convention Number 102 on Social Security.

The term *social security* may also refer to basic security as recognized in articles 25 and 26 of the Universal Declaration of **Human Rights**. This security covers food, housing, clothing, education, money, and medical care. Social protection in developing countries is still not significant, but growth of these economies may mean that this situation will change. *See also* MINIMUM WAGE.

SOLOMON ISLANDS. Independent from the **United Kingdom** since 1978, organized labor emerged in the 1970s in the form of the Solomon Islands Council of Trade Unions despite considerable ethnic tension between the indigenous people and the descendants of immigrant **Indian** plantation workers that have led to military coups and the suspension of democratic government. The Solomon Islands were not represented in the **International Trade Union Confederation** in 2010.

SOMALIA. Somalia was formed from a merger of colonial territories of the **United Kingdom** and **Italy** in July 1960; labor unions in Somalia emerged in the 1940s and formed a labor federation in 1949, which was represented in the **International Confederation of Free Trade Unions (ICFTU)** by 1959. Somalia continued to be represented in the ICFTU until 1969. Plagued by clan rivalries and prolonged civil strife since the late 1970s, organized labor effectively ceased to exist. Somalia has not been represented either in the ICFTU or its successor, the **International Trade Union Confederation**, since 1969 when Siyad Barre seized power. Independent unions were not allowed and organizing strikes was punishable by death. In 1991, when Barre's reign was overthrown by guerrillas, civil institutions collapsed and have not been restored. Somalia remains an impoverished country.

SOUTH AFRICA. The first labor union in South Africa was the **Amalgamated Society of Carpenters and Joiners**, which was established by Europeans in Cape Town in 1881. Workers in the Kimberley set up a union in 1884, the Artisans' and Engine-Drivers' Protection Association. The **Amalgamated Society of Engineers** formed a branch in Johannesburg Town in 1893. The Transvaal Federation of Unions was created in 1911. One remarkable feature of this development was the very low **membership** of organized labor in South Africa compared with similar societies such as **Australia** and **New Zealand**. There were only 3,800 union members in 1900 and only 11,900 by 1914, of whom 2,800 were members of the Amalgamated Society of Engineers. As in other countries, the following six years saw a large increase in union membership, to 135,100 by 1920, but this represented only about 12 percent of nonagricultural employees.

A second feature of European labor organization, though not one confined to South Africa, was its hostility to other racial groups. The South African Industrial Federation, which was formed in 1914, was aimed at protecting the jobs of skilled Europeans against unskilled black workers and maintaining racial divisions. The South African branch of the **Industrial Workers of the World**, founded in 1910, was unique in setting up a multiracial body, but it could not survive in such a racially divided society. The first recorded black union, the Industrial Workers of Africa, was formed in 1917, but the largest body, the Industrial and Commercial Workers' Union, was set up in 1919; it claimed 100,000 members by 1925 but was virtually made defunct by 1930. Gandhi also helped to form unions among Indian workers, but the growth of non-European unionism alarmed the Europeans, who went on **strike** in 1922 in protest against the substitution of white for black workers in certain job categories in the mines and against the reduction of wages. In the ensuing conflict, called the Rand Revolt, approximately 230 strikers were killed by the army and the police. The incident led to the election victory of a pro–white labor government in 1924, which would introduce legislation to reduce economic opportunities for non-Europeans—a policy that greatly harmed non-European unionism. Membership of all South African unions grew from 118,300 in 1930 to 272,500 in 1940 and to 408,600 in 1950. In 1942, some black unions formed the Council of Non-European Trade Unions (CNETNU); it claimed 158,000 members by 1945.

With the victory of the National Party in the 1948 elections, total apartheid became government policy, and this also entailed a hostile attitude toward non-European unions, which led to their politicization. In 1954, the South Africa Trade Union Council was formed with unions from all the country's racial groups. In 1955, the South African Congress of Trade Unions was formed from the merger of some independent black unions and the CNETU, but it was crushed by the government between 1962 and 1965 because of its radicalism. After strikes by black workers in Durban in 1973, the government arrested the leaders and tried to suppress black unionism. The government reaction led to concerted support for black unions by international unionism through bodies such as the **International Metalworkers' Federation** and through pressure from the union representatives on the boards of Swedish and German multinational companies operating in South Africa.

In 1977, the government appointed the Wiehahn Commission to investigate trade unionism; the commission successfully recommended that black labor unions be legally recognized and the system of racial reservation of job occupations be abandoned. The recommendations did not mean complete freedom for black organized labor. Rural and domestic workers and state employees were denied access to **collective bargaining** and unions could not affiliate to a political party or support illegal strikes. Nevertheless, black unionism grew despite continued violence; in April 1987, for instance, seven strikers were killed during a railroad strike. In December 1985, the Congress of South African Unions, a mainly black labor federation, was formed; non-racial by policy, it claimed 1.3 million members by 1991. A radical black labor federation, the National Council of Trade Unions, was formed in 1986 and claimed 327,000 members in 1994, when it became affiliated with the **International Confederation of Free Trade Unions (ICFTU)**, the first South African labor federation to be admitted because of apartheid and the restrictions on trade union rights.

The ICFTU had been lobbying hard against South Africa's policies since 1954 and had been actively supporting black organized labor since 1980. Although the apartheid system ended with multiracial elections in 1994, and the legal rights of organized labor were recognized by the 1995 Labour Relations Act and strengthened in March 2002, the ICFTU complained that they are often ignored in practice. Since 2007, the **International Trade Union Confederation** has complained about police violence against strikers, the

violation of trade union rights of subcontracting employees, and the heavy penalties imposed on strikers. In 2010, South Africa was represented by four labor federations in the ITUC with a combined membership of 2.8 million. *See also* RACE AND ETHNICITY; RAMAPHOSA, MATAMELA CYRIL.

SOUTH KOREA (Republic of Korea). The first **labor disputes** on the Korean peninsula date from the 1890s, and the first labor union was formed by longshoremen in 1898, the Song-Jin Dockers' Union. Korea was a colony of **Japan** from 1910 to 1945. Following the suppression of a revolt for independence in 1919, Japanese policy was one of toleration until 1925. In this period, three labor federations were formed (1920, 1922, and 1924). In 1925, the Japanese repressed organized labor by their Public Peace law; at this time there were about 123,000 union members in Korea. With Japan's defeat in 1945, organized labor revived and set up a large, broad-based, **communist** labor federation. It was challenged by an anticommunist, nationalist labor federation with U.S.-backing, the General Federation of Korean Trade Unions, in March 1946. After it led two **general strikes**, the communist federation was outlawed in 1947.

Although in theory labor was able to organize, **collectively bargain**, and strike under the constitution of 1948, in practice it was controlled by the government. In 1958, an independent labor federation was formed, but after a military coup in 1961, all labor unions were broken up and reorganized by the military into 14 industrial unions based on organized labor in **Germany**. Under the labor laws of 1953 and subsequent years, most public sector employees were denied the right to strike. In 1963, unions were legally forbidden from participation in **politics**.

Following the promise of constitutional reforms in June 1987, there was an outburst of independent activity among employees; it is estimated that 400,000 employees joined these unions by August 1987. An independent labor federation, the National Council of Labor Unions, was set up in January 1990 from a body originally formed in March 1984; it claimed about 200,000 members in 1992. Despite the lack of freedom of organized labor in South Korea since 1953, its labor federation has been a continuous member of the **International Confederation of Free Trade Unions (ICFTU)** since 1949. Since the late 1980s, South Korea has had a high level of labor disputes, a reflection of the abrasive nature of its labor relations. The ICFTU has been highly critical of the violent way in which the government has responded to strikes by organized labor. During 2002, 147 labor members were detained by the government and 55 remained detained at the end of the year. During 2006, some strikers were seriously injured and one steelworker killed as a result of police violence. In 2010, the two South Korean affiliates of the **International**

Trade Union Confederation (ITUC) claimed a total membership of 1.7 million and the ITUC has maintained its complaints about the repression of organized labor. *See also* NORTH KOREA.

SOVIET UNION. *See* RUSSIAN FEDERATION.

SPAIN. Organized labor developed slowly in 19th-century Spain, a reflection of the country's economic and political backwardness. In 1871, printers formed a union in Madrid, but unions were not legalized until 1881, an event that led to the formation of the first labor federation, the *Federación de Trabajadores de la Región Española* (Federation of Workers of the Region of Spain), which claimed to represent 58,000 members. This body was replaced in 1888 by the *Unión General de Trabajadores* (UGT), or General Union of Workers, which has continued to be Spain's largest labor federation; it was dominated by the **socialists**. In 1902, the UGT affiliated with the **International Federation of Trade Unions**.

Anarchism was one of the distinguishing characteristics of Spanish labor. It found particular appeal in rural areas and envisaged the overthrow of the state by a **general strike** and its replacement by democratically run cooperative groups covering the whole economy. In 1910, the anarchists formed their own federation, the *Confederación Nacional del Trabajo* (National Labor Federation), which continues to the present as an insignificant organization. Unions and union growth were relatively weak. Between the early 1900s and 1913 the number of union members rose from 26,000 to 128,000.

Violence was also a feature of Spanish labor. During "Tragic Week" (July 1909), over 175 people were shot in riots led by revolutionary **syndicalists** in Catalonia after the calling up of reservists for the war in **Morocco**. The rioters' attacks on churches and convents led to the execution of anarchist leader Francisco Ferrer despite international protests. After World War I, unions grew significantly; between 1920 and 1930 the number of union members increased from 220,000 to 946,000, and by 1936 the UGT claimed two million members.

The Civil War (1936–1939) and the repression that followed under General Francisco Franco eliminated independent organized labor from political life officially in 1940. The UGT continued as an organization in exile in France. It was a founding organization of the **International Confederation of Free Trade Unions (ICFTU)** and maintained the ICFTU's hostility to Franco's regime; for example, in 1952, the ICFTU protested vehemently over the admission of Spain to the United Nations Educational, Scientific, and Cultural Organization. During the 1960s, the **communists** organized employees at the workplace and even led illegal **strikes**.

With the restoration of democracy following Franco's death in 1975, labor unions were legalized in 1977, although full legalization was not granted until 1985. As well as the UGT, the communists organized their own federation from the workplace groups they formed under Franco, the *Confederación Sindical de Comisiones Obreras* (CCOO), or Union Confederation of Workers' Commissions, and the anarchists reemerged, but with only a shadow of their pre-1936 strength. In 1984, the government and the *Unión General de Trabajadores* agreed to a social and economic pact to control wage claims as an antiinflationary measure. The pact, which was opposed by the CCOO, broke down after 1986. In 1980, Spain had about 1.7 million union members, but this figure had declined to about 1.2 million by 1990. In 2010, the four labor federations in Spain affiliated with the **International Trade Union Confederation (ITUC)** claimed a total **membership** of over 2.3 million. The ITUC has been concerned about threats made to organized labor by some multinational companies to discourage **labor disputes**. The global financial crisis and government cuts in spending led to widespread strikes in 2010. *See also* BASQUE COUNTRY.

SPRING OFFENSIVE. *See SHUNTO.*

SRI LANKA. Sri Lanka, formerly known as *Ceylon,* has been independent from the **United Kingdom** since February 1948. Organized labor developed at the end of the 19th century, beginning with the Ceylon Printers' Union in 1893. In 1926, the unions formed the All-Ceylon Trades Union Congress; by 1930, Ceylon had about 114,000 union members. In 1935, labor unions were legalized by the colonial administration. In 1940, the Ceylon Indian Congress Labour Union was formed for the Indian Tamils; it was reformed as the Ceylon Workers' Congress in 1950. Although organized labor in Sri Lanka claimed a large **membership**, it was characterized by fragmentation based on ethnic, political, language, and religious divisions. At independence, there were 1,592 registered unions; of these, 412 unions that reported their membership totaled 398,400. By 1973, 590 unions reported that their total membership was 1.2 million. Sri Lanka was represented in the **International Confederation of Free Trade Unions (ICFTU)** from 1951. Sri Lanka's political stability has been severely challenged by the Tamil insurgency since 1983, which led to emergency regulations and created the opportunity to restrict organized labor as well. The ICFTU was highly critical of the **violation of trade union rights** in Sri Lanka's **export processing zones** in 2000 and 2001, but noted improvements in 2002. In 2009, employers often still refused to recognize unions and the government criminalized **strikes** and other union activities. In 2010, Sri Lanka had four affiliates with the **International Trade**

Union Confederation with a combined membership of 741,000. *See also* INDIA.

STEELWORKERS. *See* UNITED STEELWORKERS OF AMERICA.

STRIKE. A strike is a **labor dispute** initiated by a group of workers, a labor union, or a group of unions, in contrast to a lockout or a labor dispute initiated by an employer or group of employers. In a strike, workers withdraw their labor from the employer. This meaning of *strike* in contrast to *lockout* has been established in English since about 1850. Before 1850, the word *turnout* was used for a strike. The word *strike* comes from Indo-European *streig,* which means "stand still." It was first used in its modern sense in a hiring bond in 1763 between coal owners and miners at Newcastle in northern England and in connection with London tailors in 1764. Although labor disputes are often called *strikes* by the media, in practice the initiator can be difficult to determine, particularly as strikes are often called by labor unions in response to the actions of employers, such as reductions in wages and entitlements or adverse changes to working hours or conditions at work. Strikes in the sense of a broad offensive by labor unions are comparatively rare events and mainly occur in periods of prosperity combined with price inflation; examples include strikes by metal workers' unions in the early 1970s for higher pay. Strikes can take a variety of forms. Although most strikes typically have the extension or defense of wages and conditions as their objectives, they may have purely political objectives (as in the **Netherlands** in 1941 against the maltreatment of Jews by the Nazis and **Venezuela** in 2002–2003) or may be in support of strikes by other labor unions, the so-called sympathetic strikes. Another variety is the unofficial or wildcat strike, in which a local or regional branch of a labor union engages in a strike without the approval of, or even in opposition to, the head office of the union. *See also* GENERAL STRIKES; LABOR DISPUTES; "WINTER OF DISCONTENT."

SUDAN. Sudan has been independent from the **United Kingdom** and **Egypt** since January 1956; organized labor in the Sudan developed after World War II. In 1959, the 4,000-strong anticommunist Central Sudan Government Workers' Trade Unions' Federation, which formed in 1955, joined the **International Confederation of Free Trade Unions** but was not represented subsequently. In the 1960s, organized labor continued to grow but in a fragmented way. In 1971, the government dissolved Sudan's 562 separate labor unions and independent, organized labor ceased to exist. There was some reemergence of organized labor in the 1970s and 1980s, but in 1989 the military took over government and again dissolved the labor unions. In 1992, the government established its own organization to run labor unions. In 2000, a new labor code was introduced, but the ICFTU considered that it had not led to an improvement in Sudan's labor relations and that independent organized labor had been forced underground. The **International Trade Union Confederation** reported that no improvement in conditions for Sudanese organized labor had occurred in 2009 and it had no affiliates there in 2010. In 2011, the southern part of the country became an independent state.

SURINAM. Surinam has been independent from the **Netherlands** since November 1975; organized labor in Surinam began effectively in the late 1940s, with the first labor federation being formed in 1947. By 1964, there were six national labor federations with a combined **membership** of 30,000. Organized labor was divided along political and religious lines. Surinam has been represented continuously in the **International Confederation of Free Trade Unions** since 1951. Surinam was one of the few Latin American countries not to be reported in the survey of **violations of trade union rights** by the **International Trade Union Confederation** in 2007. In 2010, Surinam was represented by two affiliates with the ITUC with a total membership of 10,000.

SUTCLIFFE, JAMES THOMAS (1873–1938). Statistician, economist, and author, Sutcliffe was born in Yorkshire, England. After migration to Australia, he was appointed to a senior position with the Commonwealth Bureau of Census and Statistics (now the Australian Bureau of Statistics) in August 1915 and was made head of its labor and industrial department where he worked on the production of **labor statistics**. In 1920, he served as secretary to the federal government's basic wage commission. In 1927, he resigned from the federal bureaucracy to become general manager of Amalgamated Textile Pty., Ltd., in Sydney, thereby doubling his annual income.

Sutcliffe is best known for his book, *The History of Trade Unionism in Australia,* which was published in April 1921. He began researching Australian organized labor with fellow Bureau employee Gerald Lightfoot (1877–1966) and together they produced a short unpublished history by 1916. Sutcliffe conducted further research on his own and presented his results to the University of Melbourne, which awarded him the Harbison-Higginbotham Scholarship in 1919. In 1921, he worked for the Victorian branch of the Workers' Educational Association as tutor in industrial history. In the same year, the Association published his history of organized labor in Australia. It was the first book of its kind to be based on original research, and it remained the only account until the emergence of academic interest in organized labor 50 years later; as part of that revival, his book was reprinted in 1967. Sutcliffe's study was essentially one of the growth and structure of the institutions of organized labor, an approach that came to be seen as too narrow in terms of the new social history of the 1970s, but one that still retains its soundness as labor unions continue to pursue **amalgamation**. *See also* LABOR HISTORY.

SWAZILAND. Swaziland has been independent from the **United Kingdom** since September 1968; organized labor has faced a difficult challenge to become established. Beginning as a large number of small bodies, the unions could make little headway in a country ruled by a king and a cabinet. A state of emergency has been in force since 1973 and political parties are banned. The Swaziland Federation of Trade Unions was registered in 1973 and became an affiliate of the **International Confederation of Free Trade Unions (ICFTU)** by 1989 with 26,000 members. In 1980, the government prohibited **strikes** by postal, radio, and **education** workers. In its survey of **violations of trade union rights** for 2002, the ICFTU was particularly critical of the government of Swaziland, noting its fiercely antiunion policies and its trial of six union leaders who tried to present a petition to the government. Conditions for organized labor have not improved since 2002. Indeed, Swaziland has been ratifying international labor conventions but violating them in practice. In 2008, a strike by 16,000 women was brutally repressed. In 2010, the **International Trade Union Confederation** had two affiliates in Swaziland representing 76,000 members.

SWEDEN. The first true labor unions in Sweden were formed in the 1880s by skilled men, much under influence from Denmark, to prevent strike-breaking across the borders. In 1886, the first of what became regular conferences was held between labor leaders of Sweden, **Denmark**, and **Norway**. In 1889, the unions formed the Social Democratic Party. But union **membership** growth was very slow; there were only 9,000 members or about 1 percent of nonagricultural employees by 1890. Thereafter, union membership grew steadily to 64,155 or 5 percent of employees by 1900. In 1898, a labor federation for **blue-collar** employees, the *Landsorganisationen i Sverge* (LO), or the Swedish Confederation of Trade Unions, was formed, but the union movement faced a difficult political environment. In 1889, the government enacted a law that prevented strikes; it remained law until 1938. This law, the so-called Åkarp law (named after the home village of the member of parliament who proposed it) was much more subtle. It was not directed immediately against strikes, even though "strike leaders" could be arrested and sentenced to penal servitude; rather, its main aim was to protect strike-breakers. It was not allowed to prevent someone from working. It was further modified several times before 1938, the first time in 1914; the most important year in strike legislation is no doubt 1928.

Yet the unions, together with the Social Democratic Party and the Liberals, demonstrated their power by conducting a **general strike** in 1902 for universal suffrage, which led employers to execute their plan to form the *Svenska Arbetsgivareföreningen* (SAF), or the Swedish Employers' Confederation. In 1906, the SAF and the LO signed an agreement that, although it recognized the unions' right to represent its members in **collective bargaining**, forced the unions to accept the employers' right to hire and fire employees and to control production. A massive but unsuccessful general strike in 1909 (the number of working days lost per thousand employees was 12,677, making it one of the biggest disputes in Sweden's history) hurt organized labor so that it took many years to recover from the dip in membership. Between 1913 and 1920, the number of union members rose from 134,000 to 403,000 and the proportion of employees in unions rose from 8 to 28 percent. Despite large-scale protests, the government enacted laws in 1928 that regulated collective bargaining contracts and set up a labor court to settle disputes. In 1931, **white-collar** employees in the private sector formed their own labor federation.

In 1932, the political climate for labor changed for the better with the election of the first **social-democratic** government. In 1936, the government passed a second major labor law that provided for the recognition of unions and the opening of negotiations by either employers or unions and outlawed the victimization of union members for taking part in legal union activities. This law was the legal confirmation of an existing practice. National government employees formed a labor federation in 1937 and were granted the right to bargain in that year; the benefit was extended to employees of local government in 1940. Of particular significance was the Saltsjöbaden Agreement in 1938 between the LO and the SAF; it specified dispute settlement procedures, the avoidance of disputes, and by implication the avoidance of government intervention. This agreement is generally credited with securing a high degree of industrial peace until the economic problems of the 1970s. By 1940 there were 971,000 union members, covering 54 percent of employees. Since 1950, Sweden has had one of the highest levels of union membership in the world. In 2007, Swedish unions covered 74 percent of employees compared with 87 percent in 1995. In 2009, the **International Trade Union Confederation (ITUC)** complained about attempts by the government to interfere in the process of free collective bargaining. The right to strike seemed to be limited by the consequences of the service directive of the **European Union** as shown in the **Laval case** when unions were sentenced to pay damages and legal costs. In 2010, the three Swedish affiliates of the ITUC declared a total membership of 3.1 million. *See also* COUNCIL OF NORDIC TRADE UNIONS.

SWEENEY, JOHN JOSEPH (1934–). Sweeney was elected president of the **American Federation of Labor–Congress of Industrial Organizations** (AFL-CIO) in October 1995 to replace **Joseph Lane Kirkland** and was re-elected twice since then. He retired in 2009.

Sweeney was born in the Bronx, New York City. His trade union career began as a research assistant with the **International Ladies' Garment Workers' Union**. In 1960, he joined the **Service Employees International Union (SEIU)** as a contract director for New York City Local 32B. He went on to become union president and to lead two citywide **strikes** of apartment maintenance workers. At the time of his election as president of the AFL-CIO, he was serving his fourth four-year term as president of the SEIU, which grew from 625,000 to 1.1 million members under his leadership. He was first elected as an AFL-CIO vice president in 1980. He is the author of *America Needs a Raise: Fighting for Economic Security and Social Justice* and has supported grassroots organizations and campaigns to achieve the objectives of organized labor.

SWITZERLAND. Organized labor in Switzerland began effectively in the late 1860s through contact with German **socialist** labor bodies. In 1873, an unsuccessful attempt was made to form a national federation but, in 1880, the socialist labor unions created the *Schweizerischer Gewerkschaftsbund* (SGB), or Swiss Trade Union Confederation. In 1890, the Canton of Geneva passed a law that recognized agreements between unions and employers; it seems to have been the first legislation of its kind in Europe to legalize **collective bargaining**. In 1900, when the SGB declared its political neutrality, Switzerland had about 90,000 union members, covering about 10 percent of its nonagricultural employees. Switzerland was affiliated with the **International Federation of Trade Unions** from 1902 to 1945. A **white-collar** labor federation was established in 1903 and a **Catholic** labor federation in 1907. A **general strike** in 1918 was crushed by the army.

By 1920, there were 313,000 union members representing about 26 percent of nonagricultural employees. Swiss organized labor developed and grew in a tolerant political climate and in a relatively prosperous economy. In 1937, a peace **accord** was made in the engineering industry that became the basis for a national social partnership between unions and employers from the 1950s. It provided for bargaining in good faith and avoiding strikes or lockouts during the life of agreements. The consensus approach adopted so successfully in industrial relations reflected a wider respect for Switzerland's diversity of people, language, and religion. Spared the ravages of World War II, the Swiss labor movement continues to be formally divided by religion, unlike those of **Germany** and **Austria**. Switzerland was represented in the **International Confederation of Free Trade Unions** from its inceptions in 1949. In 2006, there were 721,000 union members representing about 19 percent of employees. Since 2000, the right to strike in the **public sector** has been permitted in federal employment but had not been extended to all cantons and communes in 2002. There were several dismissals of activists in 2010. *See also SYNDICATS SANS FRONTIÈRES.*

SYNDICALISM. Syndicalism was a set of practices and ideologies developed by French organized labor in the 1890s and 1900s. It derived from the French *syndical,* meaning simply "trade union," but as an ideology *syndicalism* (or *revolutionary syndicalism*) meant the use of unions to gain political and social change. The class war was central to syndicalist thought, which saw governments and political parties, including **socialist** parties, as instruments of working-class oppression. Syndicalist thought stressed direct action, particularly the **general strike**, as the means to gain its objectives. It owed as much, if not more, to work experience as to ideas.

Syndicalism grew out of conditions peculiar to **France**, namely, its revolutionary tradition (1789, 1830, 1848, and 1871), the self-reliant attitude of its working class, the relatively slow growth of industrialization, and the importance of small enterprises in the economy. The French Charter of Amiens (1906), which was adopted by the national organization of French labor, the *Confédération Générale du Travail* (General Confederation of Labor), called for wage increases and **shorter hours** to be won by the taking over of the capitalist class and the general strike. In the **United States**, the **Knights of Labor** have been described as a U.S. version of syndicalism. In **Italy**, syndicalism began to emerge after 1902 as a reaction to reformism in the Italian Socialist Party and developed into an unstable combination of Marxism and populism. In **Spain**, syndicalism remained important until the late 1930s but was destroyed during the civil war. *See also* INDUSTRIAL WORKERS OF THE WORLD; ONE BIG UNION.

SYNDICAT SANS FRONTIÈRES (SSF). SSF, or Trade Union without Borders, is an affiliate of the *Communauté genevoise d'action syndicale* (Community of Union Action of Geneva), which emerged in 1990 to fight for the interests of technical, administrative, and service employees of the United Nations, embassies, and international organizations situated in Geneva, as well as the rights of migrant workers treated as virtual slaves in Europe. SSF seeks the payment of wages for the workers concerned through the courts. *See also* SLAVERY; SWITZERLAND.

SYRIA. Independent organized labor does not exist in Syria. The sole national labor organization, the General Federation of Labor Unions, is run by the ruling Ba'ath party government, which has a long history of repression. For example, in 1980 some engineers and medical doctors who went on **strike** were arrested; 15 years later, their fate was still unknown. In 2010, the **International Trade Union Confederation** noted that there were no free or independent labor unions or the right to freely engage in **collective bargaining**. Workers face severe punishment if they strike. Following the popular revolts of 2010 in **Tunisia** and **Egypt**, Syria also witnessed an uprising.

T

TAFF VALE CASE. The Taff Vale Case was a pivotal legal case in the history of organized labor in the **United Kingdom**. It arose from **picketing** by the Amalgamated Society of Railway Servants to prevent the use of nonunion labor during a **strike** in August 1900 on the Taff Vale railroad in South Wales. The general manager of the railroad, Ammon Beasley, sued the officials of the society for damages to the property of the railroad. The strike was settled through mediation after 11 days, but the company continued to press its claim through the courts. The company won the first round but lost in the court of appeal, after which it went to the House of Lords, which decided against the society in July 1901 and, in a consequent case, declared that the society would have to pay the company £23,000 plus its legal costs of £19,000 (about $100,000 in total), which were huge sums for the time. The Taff Vale Case was immediately followed by two other antiunion decisions by the House of Lords over picketing and boycotting (*Lyons v. Wilkins* and *Quinn v. Leathem*). The Taff Vale Case had three major results. First, it cast doubt on the legal status of labor union activity not just in Britain but in all countries that used British law, particularly **Canada**, **Australia**, and **New Zealand**. Second, it swung opinion within British organized labor around to the idea that it needed its own political party. The Labour Representation Committee, which had been formed in 1900, was upgraded; in 1903, a compulsory levy was made of unions to pay for Labour members of parliament and the committee itself was renamed the Labour Party in 1906. Third, pressure from organized labor on the Liberal government led to the Trade Disputes Act (1906), which granted the unions immunity from actions such as happened in the Taff Vale Case. *See also* BRITISH LABOUR PARTY; *ROOKES V. BARNARD.*

TAFT-HARTLEY ACT. The Taft-Hartley Act, known formally as the *Labor-Management Relations Act,* was a piece of U.S. federal law passed in 1947 to redress the imbalance in the law alleged to have been caused by the **Wagner Act** of 1935. Conservative politicians and employer groups claimed that the Wagner Act only dealt with coercive actions by employers and ignored such acts by unions. The legislation was passed at a time of increasing **labor disputes** generally and in **coal mining** and steel production in particular. Although the Taft-Hartley Act maintained the fundamental freedoms of unions, it imposed a number of important restrictions on them; it outlawed the union or closed shop and allowed the states to pass their own anti–closed shop or **right-to-work laws**. Unions were also made liable to be sued in the federal courts for breaches of contract and had to give at least 60 days' notice of the ending or amending of an agreement. Finally, unions were forbidden to spend any of their funds on political campaigns. Despite some moves to repeal Taft-Hartley Act, it has remained in force. In October 2002, President George W. Bush used it to end a maritime labor dispute on the West Coast, the first time the law had been used since 1978. *See also* POLITICAL ACTION COMMITTEES; UNITED MINE WORKERS OF AMERICA; UNITED STEELWORKERS OF AMERICA.

TAHITI. *See* FRENCH POLYNESIA.

TAIWAN. Following the imposition of martial law in 1949, **strikes** on Taiwan were outlawed and only unions controlled by the Kuomintang Party encouraged. Between 1955 and 1989 the number of members in government-controlled unions rose from 198,000 to 2.4 million. The continuance of martial law was justified by the government on the grounds that Taiwan was still at war with mainland **China**; it was only lifted in 1987, a step that led to a pent-up wave of **labor disputes**. Strikes were permitted by the Arbitration Dispute Law, which allowed employees to strike after mediation but required them to return to work. Nevertheless, striking union members were jailed for striking in 1988 and 1989. In November 1987, a Labor Party was formed and there was significant growth in the **membership** of independent labor unions. Taiwan has been represented in the **International Confederation of Free Trade Unions (ICFTU)** since 1951 by the Chinese Federation of Labor, which claimed one million members in 2001. Membership plummeted since then to 250,000 in 2009. The ICFTU reported negatively about the legal system for organized labor in Taiwan in 2002, but noted an improved attitude toward labor unions by the government since 2000. In September 2002, 60,000 teachers demonstrated for the right to form unions. The 2010 survey of **violations of trade union rights** conducted by the **International Trade Union Confederation** complained that many categories of employees are not allowed to form unions and that strikes are difficult to conduct legally. *See* CHINA.

TAJIKISTAN. Independent from the former **Soviet Union** since 9 September 1991, there is no history of organized labor in Tajikistan. The labor code is ambiguous about the right to form unions, bargain collectively, and conduct strikes. Although **collective bargaining** is known to occur, civil war and ethnic conflict have exhausted the society. Tajikistan was not a member of the **International Confederation of Free Trade Unions** in 2001. In 2007, the **International Trade Union Confederation (ITUC)** repeated its earlier comments that there were ambiguities in the labor law of Tajikistan, mainly in the freedom given to government to restrict the rights of organized labor. The national trade union federation has been very loyal to the autocratic government. The **International Labour Organization** has repeatedly asked for clarification of the law. Tajikistan was not represented in the ITUC in 2010.

TANZANIA. Tanzania was formed in December 1961 from the British territory of Tanganyika and the islands of Zanzibar and Pemba. Unlike most colonies, labor unions were legalized before there were any actual unions; a Trade Union Ordinance was passed in 1932 covering Tanganyika, but there were no unions formed until 1949. The Tanganyika Federation of Labour was formed in 1955 and was admitted to the **International Confederation of Free Trade Unions (ICFTU)** in 1957; it was abolished by the government in 1964, which sought to dominate organized labor. The one-party political system of Julius Nyerere that ran Tanzania gave way to a pluralistic system after 1992. In 1991, the government formed the Organisation of Tanzania Trade Unions, which was admitted to **membership** of the ICFTU in 1994 with a declared membership of 359,900. In 1995, the unions formed the Tanzania Federation of Free Trade Unions as a successor organization, but it was denied legal recognition and was dissolved by the government on 1 July 2000. In 2007, the **International Trade Union Confederation** reported that there was considerable government interference in the affairs of organized labor. There have been strong restrictions on the right to strike in the private sector, whereas **public sector** workers are entirely refused the right to strike. In the autonomous part of Tanzania named *Zanzibar* all strikes are illegal.

TEAMSTERS. Officially known as the *International Brotherhood of Teamsters, Chauffeurs, Warehousemen, and Helpers of America,* the Teamsters was the largest labor union in the **United States** from the mid-1950s to 1987, when it was overtaken by the **National Educational Association**. The Teamsters began as the Team Drivers' International Union in January 1899 with a **membership** of 1,700 based on drivers of horse teams. In 1902, part of the Chicago membership formed a rival body, the Teamsters' National Union, but in 1903 the two organizations agreed to merge as the International Brotherhood of Teamsters. In its early years, the Teamsters was a sprawling confederation of local unions controlled by powerful bosses rather than a unified national organization. It owed much of its organizational success to Daniel J. Tobin, who was its president from 1907 to 1952. In 1910, Tobin gained jurisdiction over truck drivers from the **American Federation of Labor,** a move that enabled it to grow with the fastest parts of the American economy and placed it in a strong bargaining position in many related industries. Even so, membership growth was slow between 1912 and 1930 (from only 84,000 to 98,800), but after 1935 it grew quickly, reaching 441,600 in 1939 and 644,500 by 1945.

In 1955, the Teamsters had 1,291,100 members, the largest membership of any American labor union. Under presidents **Dave Beck** (1952–1957) and **James R. Hoffa** (1957–1971), the Teamsters continued to expand into employment sectors that were related to transportation, such as cold storage, warehousing, baking, laundry work, and canning, despite the convictions of Beck and then Hoffa for corruption and other offenses. In 1957, the Teamsters were expelled from the **American Federation of Labor–Congress of Industrial Organizations (AFL-CIO)** but were readmitted in November 1987. During the 1980s, the leadership of the Teamsters backed **Ronald Reagan** for president, but the reformed leadership that gained power in the late 1980s backed Bill Clinton's presidential campaign. The Teamsters claimed 1.4 million members in 2009. In 1997, the Teamsters successfully conducted a 16-day strike against United Parcel Services that attracted popular and international support. Since 1999, James R. Hoffa's son, **John P. Hoffa**, has been general president. In 2005, the Teamsters disaffiliated from the AFL-CIO and formed the new **Change to Win** organization.

THAILAND. Unofficial organizations among Thai employees existed from the early 1880s. They conducted a number of **strikes** to gain formal recognition, but this was not granted until 1932 and then only lasted until 1934. Legal recognition of unions was not restored until after the Japanese were expelled in 1944; it was withdrawn in 1948, restored in 1955, and revoked in 1958. Unions were again legally recognized between 1972 and 1976, but the military government that took power in October 1976 once again withdrew recognition. Many union members in Thailand work in state-owned enterprises that have been vulnerable to changes in government policy, particularly **privatization.** Following a campaign by the unions, the right to strike was restored in January 1981 but was withdrawn for those employees working in state-owned enterprises in April 1991 following the military coup on 23 February 1991. In June 1991, the president of the Labor Congress of Thailand (formed in 1978), Thanong Po-arn, disappeared and was presumed murdered. Between 1989 and 1991 the number of union members in Thailand dropped from 309,000 to 160,000. In 1993, there were 800 unions and 26 labor federations in Thailand. It was represented in the **International Confederation of Free Trade Unions** from 1951 to 2006 and in its successor, the **International Trade Union Confederation (ITUC)**, from November 2006. In 2010, it was represented by four affiliates with a combined membership of 250,000. The ITUC has been critical of the lack of **collective bargaining** in Thailand and unchecked employer violence toward organized labor, both in 2010 and in earlier years. Migrant employees, mainly **Burmese**, **Laotian**, and **Cambodian**, have been vulnerable to intimidation by Thai employers.

THOMAS, ALBERT (1878–1932). A French labor scholar, newspaper editor, and politician, Thomas was the first director of the **International Labour Organization (ILO)** between 1920 and 1932. During the early 1900s, he carried out research in **Germany**, **Russia**, and the eastern Mediterranean into **socialism**, **syndicalism**, and consumer cooperatives, which he published in 1903. In 1904, he was made assistant editor of the socialist newspaper *L'Humanité*. In 1910, he was elected to the Chamber of Deputies for the Socialist Party, a position he held until 1921. In 1915, he became undersecretary of state for artillery and munitions and minister for munitions in 1916. In 1917, he was ambassador to Alexander Kerensky's government in Russia. As ILO director, he worked tirelessly for the adoption of its conventions by member countries in a very difficult political climate.

TOGO. Togo has been independent from **France** since April 1960; the first unions in Togo were branches of French unions. All of Togo's unions were brought under **government control** in 1972 and 1973. Togo did not move to a pluralistic political system until the early 1990s. In 1992, two Togo labor federations, with a combined **membership** of 67,300, were admitted to the **International Confederation of Free Trade Unions (ICFTU)**. In 2002, the ICFTU was critical of the weak protection afforded to Togo's unions by its laws, even though the right to join unions and to **strike** was legal. It was also critical of the lack of legal protection given to workers in the country's **export processing zones (EPZs)**. In 2006, a new Labor Code removed a few of the earlier weaknesses, but an antiunion climate still prevails in Togo and especially in the EPZs. The **International Trade Union Confederation (ITUC)** reported that there had been no improvement in the environment for organized labor in Togo since 2007. In 2010, the three affiliates of the ITUC in Togo claimed a total membership of 122,000.

TONGA. Independent from the **United Kingdom** since June 1970, organized labor began effectively in the 1970s with the Tonga Teachers' Association, with 222 members in 1976. Later merging with the Nurses' Association, the union became an affiliate of the **International Confederation of Free Trade Unions** in 1990. In 2010, Tonga had no affiliates with the **International Trade Union Confederation**.

TOSCO, AGUSTIN GRINGO (1930–1975). A leader of organized labor in **Argentina**, Tosco was born in Córdoba Province. Tosco became general secretary of *Luz y Fuerza,* the union of the light and power utilities workers, in 1957. He was an advocate of general assemblies rather than representative committees and of demanding more than just wage rises. He opposed bureaucracy in the *Confederación General del Trabajo* and fought lengthy struggles with other leaders in this regard.

Tosco was actively involved in the uprising in the city of Córdoba in May 1969. This uprising was aimed at ending the dictatorship of Juan Carlos Onganía. The *Cordobazo,* as the uprising is called, hastened the end of the Onganía administration. Tosco was condemned to eight years in jail for his role in the revolt, but released after 16 months. He returned to Córdoba but fell victim to persecution after the victory of Peronism in 1973. The *Luz y Fuerza* union was abolished and Tosco went into hiding. When he fell seriously ill, his fear of persecution prevented him from going to the hospital. He died in 1975, and, despite government threats, thousands attended his funeral.

TRADE UNION ADVISORY COMMITTEE TO THE ORGANIZATION FOR ECONOMIC COOPERATION AND DEVELOPMENT (TUAC). The TUAC was formed in 1948 to represent the interests of organized labor (58 national organizations representing 66 million employees) within the Marshall Plan. Since 1962, it has played the same role within the Organization for Economic Cooperation and Development (OECD). The TUAC has consultative status with the OECD and is able to make its views known on multinational corporations, labor market reform, **privatization**, **globalization**, and unemployment.

TRADE UNION CONFEDERATION OF ARAB MAGHREB WORKERS (TUCAMW). The TUCAMW is an international labor organization formed in 1991 by the labor federations of **Algeria, Libya, Mauritania, Morocco,** and **Tunisia** to lobby for the inclusion of social objectives in the Arab Maghreb Union (formed in 1989) to promote greater cooperation among the governments of North Africa. These labor federations had a combined **membership** of 2.2 million in 2001. In November 2001, the TUCAMW signed a joint declaration with the **International Confederation of Free Trade Unions** to strengthen cooperation between the two organizations. With assistance of the **European Trade Union Confederation** a two-year project on trade union reform was drawn up by TUCAMW in 2008–2009. *See also* AFRICAN REGIONAL ORGANIZATION.

TRADE UNION CONFEDERATION OF THE AMERICAS (TUCA). The Trade Union Confederation of the Americas was formed in 2008 as the regional representative of the **International Trade Union Confederation** (ITUC) to replace the *Organización Regional Interamericana de Trabajadores* (Inter-American Regional Organization of Workers). The TUCA has 65 affiliated or fraternal organizations in 29 countries, representing 50 million workers. *See also ORGANIZACIÓN REGIONAL INTERAMERICANA DE TRABAJADORES (ORIT).*

TRADES UNION CONGRESS (TUC). The TUC has been the largest national labor union organization in the **United Kingdom** since its formation in Manchester on 2–6 June 1868. Its constitution provided the model for the Federation of Organized Trades and Labor Unions of the **United States** and **Canada** in 1881, the organization that was the forerunner to the **American Federation of Labor (AFL)**. In 1894, **Samuel Gompers** initiated an annual exchange of fraternal delegates between the AFL and the TUC. The TUC played only a minor role in international labor unionism before 1913; this role was taken by the **General Federation of Trade Unions**. Between 1868 and 1898, the number of members in unions affiliated with the TUC rose from 118,400 to 1.1 million. By 1914, most British unions were affiliated with the TUC. The TUC is essentially a policy-making body for its affiliates; it has no power to direct them, although it acts as the national voice of organized labor in Britain. From 1871, it operated through its parliamentary committee as a lobby to government in the interests of labor. It also provided a national forum for delegates to debate policy matters at its annual congresses. In 1892, Keir Hardie persuaded the TUC to pass a motion calling on its parliamentary committee to draw up a scheme for a fund to pay for the direct representation of labor members of parliament. Nothing came of the proposal and it was not until a conference of the parliamentary committee (representing less than half of the TUC) in 1900 that Hardie succeeded in setting up the Labour Representation Committee, the body that became the **British Labour Party**.

As organized labor grew, the TUC was drawn into adjudicating disputes between its affiliates over which union had the right to recruit particular employees. In 1924, it drew up formal rules for the transfer of members between unions to avoid jurisdictional or demarcation conflicts. In 1939, these rules were codified into six principles known as the *Bridlington Agreement*. The operation of these procedures has been criticized as favoring larger over smaller unions. Under section 14 of the Trade Union Reform and Employment

Rights Act 1993, the unions' power to exclude or expel employees was curtailed, thus giving individuals greater choice about which union to join and so substantially reducing the power of the TUC in deciding on jurisdictional disputes between affiliates. In 1981, the **membership** of affiliates with the TUC reached its highest point of 12.2 million, but by 1992 this membership had fallen to 7.8 million or the level it had in 1950. Over the same period, the number of affiliated unions fell from 109 to 72.

In 2009, the number of British unions affiliated with the TUC was 58 and they represented 6.5 million members. At its 2009 Liverpool conference, TUC delegates debated resolutions relating to bogus self-employment, racism, sexism and homophobia, and the economic crisis. The government was urged to regulate the economy more closely, increase public spending, accelerate the public works programs, and increase the pay of the lowest-paid employees. *See also* IRELAND.

TRANSPORT AND GENERAL WORKERS' UNION (TGWU). From 1937 to 1993, the TGWU was the largest labor union in the **United Kingdom**. Formed in January 1922 by the **amalgamation** of 14 unions from various industries, it began with 350,000 members. In 1929, it absorbed the declining **Workers' Union**, which gave it a recruiting foothold in industries that were to grow significantly in later years. In 1933, the TGWU had 371,000 members, which made it the second largest union in Britain after the **Mineworkers' Federation of Great Britain**. By 1937, the TGWU had 654,500 members. **Membership** continued to rise from the 1930s: 984,000 by 1945, 1.3 million by 1956, and 2.1 million by 1979. Between 1922 and 1978, the TGWU absorbed 84 smaller unions in a wide range of industries. In 2001, the TGWU was Britain's third largest union (after **UNISON** and **Amicus**), with a membership of 858,800, compared with 914,000 in 1994, or 11 percent of all British labor union members. In 2007, the TGWU amalgamated with Amicus to form **Unite the Union**. *See also* BEVIN, ERNEST.

TRINIDAD AND TOBAGO. Independent from the **United Kingdom** since 1962, organized labor began in 1919. In 1973, there were 83 registered unions with a combined **membership** of 95,000. Trinidad and Tobago has been represented in the **International Confederation of Free Trade Unions (ICFTU)** since 1951. In 2001, there were 45,000 union members in Trinidad and Tobago, or about 12 percent of all employees. Although the law of 1972 permitted all workers to join unions and engage in **collective bargaining**, the ICFTU repeatedly noted the government's unwillingness to lift the limitations on the right to **strike** and collective bargaining in the **public sector**.

The **International Trade Union Confederation** repeated these complaints in 2009 and 2010.

TUNISIA. Tunisia has been independent from **France** since March 1956. The first attempt to form a non-European labor union in Tunisia was made in 1924 but it was suppressed by the French administration. The right to form unions was not allowed until 1932. Farhat Hachet (1914–1952), who was eventually murdered by French agents, played a major role in building organized labor in Tunisia and later in the independence movement. Tunisia has been represented in the **International Confederation of Free Trade Unions (ICFTU)** since 1953 by the *Union Générale Tunisienne du Travail* (UGTT), or Tunisian General Labor Union, which was formed in 1946. It claimed a **membership** of 300,000 in 1996. Despite the **socialist** leanings of postindependent governments in Tunisia, there has been much tension between organized labor and governments since the late 1970s. When the UGTT called a **general strike** in 1978, several dozen people were killed. In 2001, when Tunisia had about 533,000 union members, the ICFTU expressed concern about continued government interference in the affairs of organized labor in Tunisia, the level of antiunion activity in the private sector, and the unfair way in which the former general secretary of the UGTT, Ismail Sahbani, was tried for alleged corruption and forgery; he was released from his five-year jail sentence on 21 February 2002, on account of failing health. In 2008 the police violently repressed demonstrations in the Gafsa mining region. Many UGTT members were sentenced to prison.

The suicide by a young Tunisian man, Mohamed Bouazizi, sparked a popular protest against the government at the end of 2010. This movement—initiated by labor unions and intellectuals—ended with the abdication of President Ben Ali in 2011. The Tunisian revolt started a series of similar movements in the Arab world. In 2010, Tunisia was not represented in the **International Trade Union Confederation**.

TURKEY. The first attempts to form labor unions in what is now Turkey began in 1871. Unions in a number of crafts were formed after the 1908 revolution but, faced with a well-organized right-wing government under Mustafa Kemal Ataturk from 1920 and limited industrial development, a mass movement was unable to emerge. The first Turkish labor law was adopted in 1936 and set down minimum standards for employees at workplaces where 10 or more worked, but banned unions, **strikes**, and **collective bargaining**. Unions were legally permitted from 1947 and compulsory **arbitration** was introduced for **labor disputes**. The Confederation of Turkish Trade unions

(*Türk-Is*) was formed in 1952. In 1961, the new constitution guaranteed the right to form unions and introduced a system of collective bargaining.

A left-wing labor federation, the Confederation of Progressive Trade Unions (DISK), was formed as a breakaway organization from *Türk-Is* in 1967 and had about 800,000 members by 1980. In 1976 the Islam-affiliated Confederation of Turkish Real Trade Unions (*Hak-Is*) was founded, soon to be banned. The deterioration in the economy during the 1970s led to a military coup in September 1980. The military government suppressed the DISK because of its militancy and leadership in labor disputes: 1,477 of its members were charged and 264 sentenced to varying jail terms in 1986. Several thousand others fled Turkey. The sentences were revoked in 1991. The military government also restored compulsory arbitration in labor disputes. In 1982, a new constitution was introduced, which was the basis for revised labor laws that recognized labor unions (provided they restricted their activities to one sector of the economy and avoided any links with political parties) and reintroduced collective bargaining. Turkey has been an affiliate of the **International Confederation of Free Trade Unions (ICFTU)** and its successor, the **International Trade Union Confederation (ITUC)**, since 1965, and in 2010 its affiliates declared a combined **membership** of 1.4 million. The repressive political and legal environment of Turkey has led to many international complaints about its **human rights** record, both from the ICFTU and the ITUC. Since 2007, the ITUC has complained repeatedly about continued abuse of human and trade union rights in Turkey. Despite changes to its laws to qualify for membership of the **European Union,** the ITUC considered that Turkish law still fell well short of what was required by international standards.

TURKMENISTAN. Turkmenistan has been independent from the former **Soviet Union** since October 1991; there is no history of organized labor in Turkmenistan and no independent labor movement has arisen since independence. The Soviet single-union system still survives, claiming 1.3 million members in 2001. It was not affiliated with the **International Trade Union Confederation** in 2010.

U

UGANDA. Uganda has been independent from the **United Kingdom** since October 1962; organized labor in Uganda began effectively in 1948. In 1956, organized labor was sufficiently strong to form the Uganda Trades Union Congress; it claimed 1,500 members by 1957, when it became an affiliate of the **International Confederation of Free Trade Unions (ICFTU)**. This association ceased in 1973 when the government brought organized labor under its control. Thereafter, Uganda entered nearly 20 years of dictatorship, violent political oppression, and warfare that only ended in the late 1980s. By 1989, Uganda had been readmitted to the ICFTU; its affiliate was the National Organization of Trade Unions, which declared a **membership** of 130,000. This organization was originally established by the government, which required that all of Uganda's unions in the private sector affiliate with it. The 2000 Trade Union Act required that the minimum number of workers a labor union can represent at a workplace was 1,000 and the union must represent 51 percent of its employees. There were about 146,000 union members in Uganda in 2010, compared with 80,000 in 2001. The restrictions of the 2000 legislation were removed by the Labour Union Act of 2006, but in practice the law was not enforced. In 2007, the survey of the **violations of trade union rights** conducted by the **International Trade Union Confederation** complained that employers in hotels, textiles, construction, and transportation were reluctant to recognize unions, a stance supported by the government. In 2008, 116 employees of a cobalt company were dismissed for striking. In November 2009, an **International Labour Organization** representative criticized Uganda for failing to protect employees' rights.

UKRAINE. Independent of the former **Soviet Union** since December 1991, organized labor free of **government control** has emerged in the Ukraine but has been faced with concerted government efforts to reassert state control even though the right to form and join labor unions was guaranteed in the constitution. In June 1994, the government passed legislation that impeded the rise of independent unions and to prop up the previously state-run labor organizations. Despite the hostile legal framework, independent labor unions were formed by **railroad** engine drivers in 1992 and by workers in parts of the transportation industry by 1994. In 1994, the president of the pilots' and airline crews' union, Viacheslav Buashov, died in suspicious circumstances after falling from the balcony of his apartment. By 1998, the Federation of Trade Unions of Ukraine had been formed. The October 1999 trade union law led to complaints by Ukrainian organized labor to the **International Labour Organization (ILO)** that were supported by the **International Confederation of Free Trade Unions (ICFTU)** and the **International Federation of Chemical, Energy, Mine, and General Workers' Unions**, but the law remained below ILO standards. By 2006, the three Ukrainian affiliates with the ICFTU claimed a total **membership** of 11.6 million. During 2010, violence and intimidation continued to be facts of life for organized labor. Despite this, the Ukrainian affiliates of the **International Trade Union Confederation** declared a combined membership of 10.2 million.

UNEMPLOYMENT BENEFITS. Unemployment **benefits** are payments to the unemployed. National arrangements vary significantly. Benefits are often based on a compulsory semigovernmental insurance system to which employees pay a regular premium sometimes supplemented by employers (**United States, Japan**). In **Australia, Great Britain**, and **New Zealand**, unemployment benefits are funded through income taxes. In countries like **Sweden**, trade unions distribute a significant proportion of the benefits. This arrangement is known as the *Ghent system* after the city in **Belgium** where it originated. Other countries distribute the money through government agencies like Centrelink in Australia, Plan Jefes in **Argentina**, or Service **Canada**.

The sums paid may cover the basic needs or compensate for the lost time proportionally to the previous earned wage. Benefits are generally given only to those registering as unemployed after a specified period during which they have worked as an employee. Other conditions often are that they seek work and are not currently economically active. In recent years, systems in many countries have changed in character. Payments were cut and emphasis shifted from benefit to stimulation of job seeking. The **International Labour Organization** supports this attitude since the adoption of the Employment Promotion and Protection against Unemployment Recommendation (convention 176) in 1988. It has been critical of the benefit cuts, though.

Many developing countries lack any decent unemployment benefits partly because of unreliable employment statistics. Government unemployment insurances in **India** only cover a small number of employees. The African Union in its Declaration on Employment and Poverty Alleviation of 2004, however, acknowledged that poverty, unemployment, and underemployment compromise basic **human rights** and emphasized the urgency of employment creation.

UNION NETWORK INTERNATIONAL GLOBAL UNION (UNI). The UNI was formed on 1 January 2000 as Uni Network International, in response to the challenge of **globalization** to labor unions. It was founded by **Communications International**, the *Fédération internationale des employés, techniciens et cadres* (International Federation of Commercial, Clerical, Professional, and Technical Employees), the **International Graphical Federation**, and **Media Entertainment International**. Negotiations between these organizations for the formation of the UNI began in 1998. A prime goal of the UNI is to lobby the **International Labour Organization** and international trade unions in discussions on reforming the global economy, specifically improving the distribution of wealth.

The UNI is organized around 14 sectors: cleaning and security; commerce; finance; gaming; graphical and packaging; hair and beauty; information technology and services; media, entertainment, and arts; post and logistics; social insurance; sports; telecom; tourism; and temp and agency workers. Three groups cut across these sectors: **women, youth**, and professional and managerial staff. UNI has its global headquarters at Nyon, near Geneva, Switzerland. In 2009, the UNI claimed a **membership** of over 900 unions with 20 million members. In March 2009, UNI changed its name to *UNI Global Union.*

UNION–GOVERNMENT AGREEMENTS. One of the features of relations between governments and unions since the 1940s has been efforts to enlist the support of unions in assisting economic growth. In the **Netherlands**, unions supported a government-controlled wage freeze from 1945 to 1960. In the **United Kingdom, Sweden**, and the **United States**, governments experimented with freezes on wages in the 1960s and 1970s as a means of controlling inflation; these schemes had mixed results. In 1974, for example, the **British Labour Party** and the **Trades Union Congress** agreed to a Social Contract, which provided for a range of economic and social reforms in return for voluntary wage restraint by the trade unions.

It became evident that such schemes had little chance of success without a high level of cooperation by organized labor, which was difficult to achieve in inflationary periods. The acute economic difficulties of the late 1970s and early 1980s prompted governments in a number of countries to sign formal agreements with peak union organizations to achieve improved productivity, higher growth, and a range of other objectives. In September 1979, the **American Federation of Labor–Congress of Industrial Organizations** and the Jimmy Carter administration reached a national accord under which the unions agreed to restrain wage claims in return for a package of economic and social measures, but the accord lapsed with Carter's defeat by **Ronald Reagan**.

One of the most successful union–government agreements was made in the Netherlands and was named the *Poldermodel:* the unions agreed on a wage freeze from 1982 in exchange for a promised growth of jobs; employers, unions, and the government signed the treaty. The Accord between the **Australian Labor Party (ALP)** and the **Australian Council of Trade Unions (ACTU)** was a formal agreement regarding economic and social policy in February 1983. The Accord set out details of policies to be implemented when the ALP was elected to the federal government. It covered prices, wages, and working conditions, nonwage incomes (for instance, earnings from dividends and interest), taxation, government expenditure, **social security**, and health. The Accord grew out of conferences between the ALP and the ACTU in 1979 over new approaches to economic management. The Accord was renegotiated seven times but ceased with the defeat of the Labor Party in the national elections of March 1996. The Accord has been credited with modest general increases in wages and lower levels of **labor disputes** since 1983.

In **Spain**, a social and economic pact between the government and the noncommunist federation of unions (*Unión General de Trabajadores*) was agreed on in October 1984 but broke down after 1986. An accord between unions, the government, and the employers was signed in **Portugal** in 1990 and was judged to have been a success in helping to modernize the economy and introduce social reforms; a new accord was signed in January 1996.

Ireland has also experimented with union–government agreements. In 1987, the Irish Congress of Trade Unions suggested to the government that there should be a conference to produce a national plan for economic growth, including pay and a range of social issues. Such a plan was produced; it was called the *Programme for National Recovery.* It operated for three years (1988–1990) and was generally judged to have been a considerable success. It was replaced by a second and broader program, the *Programme for Economic and Social Progress,* in April 1991. The third program, the *Programme for Competitiveness and Work,* was negotiated in April 1994 and was intended to run until 1997. Unlike the Australian Accord, these programs have included employers and have been negotiated with conservative governments. In **Germany**, the federal Social-Democratic/Green coalition government set up the Alliance for Jobs, Training, and Competitiveness, a national forum of labor unions, employers, and government in 1999. **Israel** had a union–government agreement in 2007 to end a strike promising a 5 percent wage increase in the next two years and labor peace until 2009.

UNION WAGE DIFFERENTIAL. The union wage differential (also called **union wage premium**) refers to the generally higher earnings of union members compared with employees who are not union members. In the **United**

Kingdom, the differential is called the *union wage premium*. This differential is one way of directly measuring the economic effects of unions. In the **United States**, H. G. Lewis estimated that union members earned on average between 10 to 15 percent more than nonunion members between 1923 and 1929; this figure rose to about 25 percent for the period 1931–1933 and fell to between 10 and 20 percent during 1939–1941. Between 1945 and 1949, union members were estimated to earn only about 5 percent more than nonunion members. This gap widened to between 10 to 15 percent in 1957–1958 and has continued to exist. By 2002, the median earnings of **full-time** male employees who were union members were 16 percent higher than nonunion employees; for female full-time employees, the gap was 24 percent.

In 1998, full-time union members in **Canada** earned 22 percent more than full-time nonunion members. In contrast, in **Australia**, a country with a higher level of unionization than the United States, the union wage differential was much less, though it has widened in recent years. In 2007, Australian union members employed full-time earned 16 percent more than nonunion employees compared with 8 percent in 1990.

The reasons why union members earn more than employees who are not union members include their tendency to work in larger enterprises (which usually pay higher wages than smaller ones) and in **manufacturing** or **public sector** industries. *See also* Table 17, Appendix D.

UNION WAGE PREMIUM. *See* UNION WAGE DIFFERENTIAL.

UNISON. UNISON was formed in the **United Kingdom** on 1 July 1993, from the merger of three **white-collar** unions: the **Confederation of Health Service Employees**, the **National Union of Public Employees**, and the **National and Local Government Officers' Association**. Its full title is *UNISON—The Public Service Union*. Negotiations for the merger began in 1978 but took on greater urgency with declining **membership** in the late 1980s. In 1994, UNISON claimed 1.4 million members, of whom 71 percent were **women**. It is the largest labor union in the **Trade Union Congress** and the largest **public sector** union in Western Europe. In 2009, UNISON claimed 1.3 million members. The membership of UNISON is diverse and includes frontline staff and managers working full or part-time in local authorities, the National Heath Service, **police**, colleges and schools, electricity, gas and water utilities, and public transportation.

UNITE THE UNION. Unite the Union was the largest labor union in the **United Kingdom** in 2010 and the fifth largest in the world. It formed from the amalgamation of **Amicus** (1.2 million members) and the **Transport and**

General Workers' Union (761,000 members) in May 2007. Known at first as *The Amalgamated Union,* it adopted its present name in May 2008. In 2009, it claimed a **membership** of 1.6 million, which was a fall of 16 percent compared with 2008. In 2010, the fall had stopped.

UNITED ARAB EMIRATES. Labor unions, **collective bargaining**, and **strikes** are not permitted in the United Arab Emirates. However, a bill allowing the formation of unions was approved by the Ministry of Justice in 2004. This has not been passed, however. In 2001, 91 percent of the labor force were expatriates and liable for deportation if they formed unions or engaged in collective bargaining. In recent years, the Ministry of Labor and Social Affairs has taken some action with regard to complaints of unpaid wages to expatriate workers. When thousands of foreign workers went on strike in 2008, they were deported. Both the **International Confederation of Free Trade Unions** and the **International Trade Union Confederation** have declared that organized labor has no rights in the United Arab Emirates.

UNITED AUTO WORKERS (UAW). The UAW—the general name for the United Automobile, Aerospace, and Agricultural Implement Workers of America International Union—has been one of the leading unions in the **United States** since the 1930s. The UAW grew out of the Carriage and Wagon Workers' International Union, which was formed in the early 1900s. Because of the metalworking nature of the industry, the union became party to many jurisdictional disputes with other unions, which led to the suspension of its charter by the **American Federation of Labor (AFL)** in 1918. The union was renamed the Automobile, Aircraft, and Vehicle Workers' Union of America; although its **membership** reached 40,000 in 1920, it collapsed during the 1920s.

Its revival in the 1930s occurred through the passage of the **National Industrial Recovery Act** in 1933 and the campaign by the AFL to recruit members in the auto industry. These efforts led to the formation of the National Council of Automobile Workers' Unions in 1934, but this did not satisfy the employees' demands for the AFL to charter an **industrial union** for the industry. The AFL issued a limited charter for the UAW in 1935. As before 1918, the UAW became embroiled in jurisdictional disputes with other unions. In 1936, it joined the Committee for Industrial Organizations, the forerunner of the **Congress of Industrial Organizations**, a move that led to the revocation of its charter by the AFL in 1938. The UAW was boosted by the militancy of the employees in the auto industry, and during 1937 led successful campaigns for recognition by General Motors and Chrysler, campaigns that raised membership to 478,500 by 1939. Recognition by Ford came after violence against union organizers in the **"battle of the overpass"** (1937) and pressure from the federal government in 1941. In 1946, the moderate leader **Walter Reuther** emerged as the winner from a long factional battle within the UAW and dominated the union until his death in 1970. In 1945, the UAW had 891,800 members, making it briefly the largest union in the United States. Thereafter, its membership reflected the fortunes of the automobile industry; membership reached a peak of 1.3 million in 1955, but declined slowly after that time. In 2009, the UAW had about 513,000 employed members and over 575,000 members who were **retired employees** in the United States, **Canada**, and **Puerto Rico**.

UNITED FOOD AND COMMERCIAL WORKERS' INTERNATIONAL UNION (UFCW). The UFCW is the second largest union in the **United States** along with the **American Federation of State, County and Municipal Employees**. The UFCW was created in 1979 from the **amalgamation** of the Retail Clerks National Protective Association (formed in 1890) and the Amalgamated Meat Cutters (formed in 1897), with a combined **membership** of 1.1 million. The UFCW has maintained its membership largely through amalgamation. The UFCW absorbed the Retail, Wholesale Department Store Union (formed in the late 1930s) in 1993, the United Garment Workers of America (formed in 1891) in 1994, the United Textile Workers (formed in the late 1890s) in 1995, the Distillery Workers (formed in the mid-1940s) in 1995, and the International Chemical Workers Union (formed in 1944) in 1996. As a result of these mergers, the UFCW now covers a diverse range of industries and is particularly strong in food processing, which accounts for 70 percent of its members. The remaining 30 percent of members work in health care, insurance, department stores, garment **manufacturing**, distillery and wine making, chemical, and textiles. In 2005, the UFCW together with six others unions disaffiliated from the **American Federation of Labor–Congress of Industrial Organizations** to form **Change to Win**. In 2009, the UFCW had 1.3 million members, of whom 40 percent were young workers, which is remarkable considering the general problems organizing **youth**.

UNITED KINGDOM. Although covert organizations among employees are known to have existed throughout history, it was in 18th-century England that organized labor in the form that it is most familiar today began to emerge. Between 1717 and 1800, 383 **labor disputes** are known to have occurred despite legal prohibitions on unions (called *combinations*) and **strikes**. Most of the strikes and unions were organized by journeymen tailors and weavers. These actions led to the first efforts at large-scale industrial relations legislation (as opposed simply to the repression of unions and strikes). For instance, the Spitalfields Act (1773) provided for the statutory setting of wages and piece-rates; the level of wages could be proposed by a joint board of masters and journeymen.

From the late 18th century onward, organized labor was shaped by two great forces: the Industrial Revolution and the gradual growth of democracy in **Great Britain**. These two forces, particularly the indigenous development of the Industrial Revolution in Britain, meant that its organized labor assumed a different character from that of organized labor in other parts of Western Europe. Because of their outlawing by the Combination Acts of 1799 and 1800, unions often disguised their activities as those of friendly societies. Although these acts were repealed in 1824, they were followed by amending legislation in 1825 that reintroduced the common law of conspiracy for certain union actions such as **picketing**.

Nevertheless, unions survived; indeed, the modern use of the word *union* was current in the ship and shipbuilding trades by the mid-1820s. In 1826, a union formed by Manchester engineers became the ancestor of the **Amalgamated Society of Engineers**. In 1827, carpenters and joiners formed a union. Better communications, especially the introduction of a national postal service and the expansion of the **railroads**, assisted with the creation of national labor bodies. In 1842, the Miners' Association of Great Britain and Ireland was formed; it claimed 70,000 members but had collapsed by 1848. It is estimated that only about 10 percent of employees in skilled trades were members of unions (called *societies*). Significantly, the union men were paid for their work on the basis of custom and the nonunion men were paid by market rates. According to the first directory of British labor unions, there were 290 unions in London in 1861.

Organized labor had also begun to play some role in the political system even though the restrictive franchise and the absence of payment of members of parliament limited its activities to lobbying and supporting occasional union officials as parliamentary candidates. In 1859, the National Association of United Trades for the Protection of Labour secured the Molestation of Workmen Act, which freed "peaceful" picketing from common-law actions. In 1851, the Amalgamated Society of Engineers was formed; it was followed by the formation of the **Amalgamated Society of Carpenters and Joiners** in 1860. Both unions were distinctive in founding branches in other countries. Another important development was the creation of federations of unions (trades councils) in the cities and large towns; the London Trades Council was formed in 1860.

The 1860s were a formative period in shaping British unionism. Its relative success and moderate behavior attracted favorable interest and comment from French and German visitors. In 1867, the Second Reform Act gave the vote to the better-off urban working class, who made up the bulk of union members at the time. In June 1868, the **Trades Union Congress (TUC)** was formed in Manchester; it became the largest and almost exclusive labor federation in Britain, and was used as the model for the **American Federation of Labor** in the **United States** and **Canada** in 1881.

Before 1870, union **membership** was largely confined to skilled urban workers and to industries that relied for their labor on large, long-established working-class communities such as **coal mining** and textiles. In the comparatively prosperous early 1870s, other groups of employees formed unions: railroad employees (1871), gas workers, agricultural laborers, longshoremen, and builders' laborers (1872). The depression of the late 1870s reduced union numbers, but they rose again with the return of better conditions in the 1880s. The number of union members affiliated with the TUC rose from 289,000 in 1870 to 464,000 in 1880 and to 581,000 by 1886. As not all unions were affiliated with the TUC, these figures underestimate the real level of union membership. During the 1890s the number of union members doubled from one to two million. The 1890s also saw the rise of a regional consciousness within Britain, as shown by the formation of the Irish Trades Union Congress in 1894 and the Scottish Trades Union Congress in 1897.

The ability of British organized labor to work within the political system through the Liberal Party reduced the imperative for it to form a separate political party despite pressure from its left wing, led by James Keir Hardie. It took the **Taff Vale Case** in 1901 to transform the Labour Representation Committee into the **British Labour Party** in 1906. Despite the legal uncertainties created by the Taff Vale Case and the Osbourne Judgement in 1906, the number of union members grew from 2 to 4.1 million between 1900 and 1913. As well, the Labour Party increased in support and political experience. During World War I the demands of total war led to governments coopting the support of organized labor, as also occurred in **France**, the United States, and **Germany**. In Britain, members of the Labour Party were included in the cabinet for the first time in 1915. In 1917, Whitley councils, made up of representatives from unions and management, were set up in a number of industries. One unintended consequence of the Whitley councils was the promotion of unionism among employees of the national government. Between 1913 and 1920, the number of union members who were national government employees rose from 20,800 to 136,200.

In 1920, largely as a result of official encouragement of organized labor during World War I, union membership reached 8.3 million, or 48 percent of employees. Other aspects of this growth were an increase in **white-collar** unionists (who made up 15 percent of total union members by 1920) and the growth in the proportion of **women** labor union members (from 11 to 16 percent between 1913 and 1920). These changes reflected the rise in the number of **public sector** union members (whose numbers rose from 394,100 in 1913 to 854,900 in 1920).

The generally depressed economic conditions of the 1920s gave rise to high levels of unemployment, which sapped union strength. There was a lockout by engineering employers in 1922, the first since 1897–1898, which forced a wage cut on the industry. The return to the gold standard increased the price of British exports and encouraged employers to reduce wages to compete, steps that added to labor unrest and erupted in the disastrous **British General Strike** of 1926. Persistent high unemployment for the rest of the 1920s cut union membership to 4.8 million by 1930 and lowered its coverage rate to 26 percent of employees. The main positive developments of the 1920s among the unions were the formation of the **Transport and General Workers' Union** in 1922 and the decision of the Amalgamated Engineering Union to admit lesser-skilled employees as members in 1926. After the severe depression of the early 1930s, union membership began to grow again, to reach 6.6 million by 1940.

During World War II, as in World War I, there was a resurgence of organized labor with the coopting of both the Labour Party and the unions into the government and in the management of the economy. At the end of the war in 1945, union membership had grown to 7.8 million. As in other Western countries, organized labor in Britain had to expend some of its energy on resisting **communist** influence in a number of key unions. The **World Federation of Trade Unions** was set up in London in 1945, but its promise of a united global labor movement was dashed by its infiltration by the **Soviet Union**, a development that led organized labor in Britain, the United States, and other countries to form the **International Confederation of Free Trade Unions** in 1949.

Within Britain, union membership in the 1950s was stable: in 1960, 44 percent of employees were union members (the same level as in 1950) and 74 percent worked in blue-collar jobs. The importance of organized labor in the management of the postwar economy was recognized by governments, but their experiments with wage restraint schemes from 1948 to 1950 and from 1951 to 1964 did not attract general union cooperation. The Wilson (Labour) government, which was elected in 1964, was able to secure the participation of the unions in the Prices and Incomes Board, but its efforts to raise productivity were disappointing.

In the mid-1960s the unions were the subject of close scrutiny by the **Donovan Commission**, which presented its report in 1968. But the voluntary approach advocated by the Donovan Commission was swept aside by official concern over Britain's poor economic performance and by frustration over unofficial labor disputes. Both the Conservatives (1968) and the Labour Party (1969) published policy papers that suggested ballots before unions could conduct strikes.

In 1979, organized labor in Britain claimed its highest ever membership—13.4 million—but this high-water mark was not maintained for long. The **"winter of discontent"** wave of strikes in 1978 and 1979 made organized labor unpopular and enabled the Conservative Party under Margaret Thatcher to easily win the May 1979 national elections and introduce a raft of measures, such as the **Employment Acts** and **privatization**, which brought about a radical change for the worse in the political and legal climate for organized labor. The process of consultation between the national government and the TUC that had begun during World War I and had accelerated during and after World War II was abruptly brought to a halt. The Employment Acts aim at restricting closed shops, picketing, and strikes without a ballot of members. The government also showed a determination to win confrontations with unions, a policy that was made plain by its defeat of the 12-month-long coal miners' strike in 1984–1985.

Since 1980, the British labor movement has been a case study of the "decline of labor," caused by a mixture of economic and political forces. The recession of the early 1980s drastically cut employment in the older parts of manufacturing such as steelmaking and shipbuilding, industries that were strongholds of organized labor. Union membership figures from the Certification Office of Trade Unions and Employers' Associations show a fall of 3.7 million between 1980 and 1991, of which nearly 2.5 million occurred between 1980 and 1985. When considered annually, these falls corresponded closely to falls in **manufacturing** employment. The decline was not offset by the growth in employment in the **services sector** because of the diversity of this employment and its often **part-time** or casual nature, which made union recruitment difficult. Neither did the unions show an understanding of the need for recruiting drives in these new areas of employment.

The regional percentage distribution of union members has been relatively stable since 1984, but there have been substantial general declines in the proportion of employees who were union members between 1995 and 2010. In London, the proportion of employees who were union members fell from 30 to 22 percent. In the North West, the fall was from 39 to 31 percent. Over this period, the national proportion of employees who were union members fell from 32 to 27 percent. At the same time, the level of unionization remained higher in Scotland, Wales, Northern Ireland, and the north of England than in southern England.

The 1980s saw the continued decline in the number of small unions, which were usually absorbed by larger ones. From a peak of 1,384 unions in 1920, the number of unions fell to 453 by 1979, to 254 by 1993, and to 179 by 2010. The most important union **amalgamations** since 1992 were those between the Amalgamated Engineering Union and the Electrical Electronic Telecommunication and Plumbing Union in 1992, and the mergers that created **UNISON** in 1993, **Amicus** in 2002, and **Unite the Union** in 2007.

Ironically, it was under the Thatcher government that the quality of statistics about labor union members improved markedly, with the introduction of an annual labor force survey based on households beginning in 1989.

Although Thatcher was replaced as Conservative leader by John Major in 1990, the antiunion policies she had begun continued. On 1 May 1997, the Labour Party (now called "New Labour") under Tony Blair won a landslide victory at the national elections and maintained his majority with a second large win in June 2001. However, the change of government made little difference to organized labor. The Employment Acts were not repealed and the government, mindful of public resentment over the strikes during the "winter of discontent," was careful to keep its distance from organized labor. In turn, the left wing of organized labor has been critical of the New Labour, accusing it of being too close to big business and ignoring the concerns of Labour voters.

During the term of the Labour government, the long-term decline in labor union membership continued. Between 1997 and 2010, the number of union members fell from 6.9 to 6.5 million and the proportion of employees who were union members fell from 31 to 27 percent. Much of this decline has occurred because of a fall in the number of male union members. Since 2005, the majority of British union members have been women, the first time this has happened anywhere in the world. In 2010, women accounted for 55 percent of the membership of British organized labor.

UNITED MINE WORKERS OF AMERICA (UMWA). From about 1905 to 1939, the UMWA was the largest labor union in the **United States**. As in the **United Kingdom**, the home of many of the first generation of U.S. coal miners, organization among miners began at a regional level. A Miners' Association was formed in St. Clair County, Illinois, in 1861; it became the American Miners' Association in 1863, by which time it had spread to the coalfields of Missouri, Ohio, and Pennsylvania. Its success proved short-lived; although it claimed 20,000 members, it had largely collapsed by 1866. Unionism was revived in the late 1870s by the miners of Hocking Valley, Ohio, who formed a new union in 1882. In 1883, the Amalgamated Association of Miners of the United States was formed based largely on the coalfields of Ohio and Pennsylvania. A new body, the National Federation of Miners and Mine Laborers, was formed in Indianapolis in 1885. In 1886, the

Knights of Labor formed a second national miners' union, the Miner and Mine Laborers' National District Assembly No. 135. To avoid competition between the two bodies, a joint conference agreed to the organization of the National Progressive Union of Miners and Mine Laborers, but the Knights of Labor body continued to operate more or less independently.

Finally, in January 1890, the National Progressive Union of Miners and Mine Laborers was reformed as the United Mine Workers of America and was recognized by the **American Federation of Labor (AFL)**. Major defeats in **strikes** and the economic depression of the 1890s reduced the UMWA to only 10,000 members in the mid-1890s, but an unexpectedly successful **general strike** in the bituminous **coal mining** industry in 1898 (which gained its participants a standard wage and the eight-hour work day) boosted **membership** from 97,000 in 1898 to 250,100 by 1904. The UMWA's leader, John Mitchell, used the victory to organize the miners on the anthracite coalfields of western Pennsylvania. In 1902, the UMWA won a famous victory in its strike on the anthracite coalfields after the personal intervention of President Theodore Roosevelt.

Despite the failure to organize the miners of West Virginia and elsewhere, the membership of the UMWA grew to nearly four million by 1920, when the controversial **John L. Lewis** became its president, an office he held until 1960. Under Lewis, the UMWA became a far more centralized body and played a significant role in labor **politics**, notably through the formation of the **Congress of Industrial Organizations**. When it withdrew from the AFL in 1947, it followed an independent path. Lewis's leadership and the diminished importance of coal as an energy source reduced the membership of the UMWA to 213,100 by 1973, compared with its peak of 500,000 in 1945. In 1989, when the UMWA affiliated with the **American Federation of Labor–Congress of Industrial Organizations**, it claimed a membership of 150,000. In 2010, there were only 55,000 union members employed in mining (compared with 66,000 in 2001) or 8 percent of mining employees. *See also* MINEWORKERS' FEDERATION OF GREAT BRITAIN.

UNITED STATES OF AMERICA. Organized labor in the United States emerged in the late 18th century but was largely confined to Philadelphia and New York. British **immigration** injected journeymen and their working habits and attitudes into the colonial economy. A register of emigrants to North America compiled between 1773 and 1776 showed that, of the 6,190 emigrants whose occupations were known, 49 percent were artisans, mechanics, or craftsmen. During the 1780s, journeymen and their employers in Philadelphia began to meet annually to negotiate their wages. The first **strike** in a single trade (**printing**, 1786) and in the building trade (1791) also occurred in Philadelphia. The first formal labor union likewise was formed in Philadelphia in 1794 by shoemakers. The union lasted until 1806, when it was made defunct by an adverse court decision. What little union growth occurred after 1806 was destroyed by the depression of 1819. Unions began to reappear in 1822. In 1827, the first citywide federation of unions was formed at Philadelphia. This federation, along with other federations, was the basis of the 12 Workingmen's political parties, which operated in the late 1820s and early 1830s. The General Trades Union was formed in New York in 1833. Despite these activities, union **membership** was small; there were only about 44,000 in 1835 and in the financial crash of 1837 organized labor collapsed.

Unions did not experience a significant revival until the 1850s; the first national unions began to emerge in the 1850s (e.g., National Typographical Union and the National Molders' Union). The labor shortages and industrial production related to the Civil War set a favorable context for union growth during the war. By 1864, there were 270 unions with a total membership of about 200,000. The growth of industrialization after the Civil War accentuated the worst features of the capitalist economy that had been previously evident, namely long hours and low wages. Old skills became obsolete and the general trend of economic development reduced opportunities for self-employment and independence. **Agriculture** no longer offered the escape valve it had before the Civil War. In addition, mass immigration kept the wages of the unskilled low in the major cities. In 1869, the **National Labor Union** was formed but was unable to provide leadership for labor either politically or industrially. In any case, organized labor suffered greatly following the financial crisis of 1873, which reduced the number of national unions from 30 to 9 by 1877 and the number of union members from 300,000 to about 50,000. Although organized labor was weak in the late 1870s, there was no shortage of discontent, as proved by the massive violent national railroad strikes in 1877, or of labor activity, as shown by the conversion of the **Knights of Labor** into a national body and the formation in 1878 of the first organization that aspired to organize unskilled workers on a mass basis, the short-lived International Labor Union (ILU).

The 1880s saw the emergence of mass unionism in the United States for the first time; there were over a million union members by 1886, of whom 70 percent were members of the Knights of Labor (which realized the ILU's vision more successfully than the ILU itself), but this success disguised serious weaknesses. What advances labor achieved were through the cooperation of **craft union** members in skilled occupations; without this support, the unskilled union members could achieve little. Moreover, much of the membership was new to unionism and its discontent over wages and hours of work applied to immigrants in the large cities. This, and the association of labor with violent protests, made it possible for organized labor to be portrayed as something foreign and outside of mainstream American society, which still had strong agricultural roots.

In 1881, the Federation of Organized Trades and Labor Unions of the United States of America and Canada (FOTLU) at its founding congress initiated the struggle for the eight-hour day. Five years later the **American Federation of Labor (AFL)** was founded from FOTLU. In 1884, the FOTLU had unanimously set 1 May 1886 as the date by which the eight-hour work day would become standard. On Saturday, 1 May, rallies were held throughout the United States by at least 300,000 workers. On 3 May at Haymarket Square, a rally met with police force, leaving two workers dead. A day later eight policemen were killed by a bomb attack at the same square, which was unjustly credited to anarchists. Five of them were executed but later pardoned.

After the Haymarket affair it took until 1888 before the AFL 888 decided to campaign for the shorter work day again. The date of 1 May 1890 was chosen as the day on which workers would strike for **shorter working hours**. The international **socialist** movement decided to join this fight for a universal eight-hour work day.

The demise of the Knights of Labor in the 1890s and the relative success of the better-paid employees represented by the craft unions of the AFL also reinforced, as well as reflected, the far wider dispersal in earnings between the skilled and unskilled compared with the **United Kingdom**. This dispersal was mainly the result of the fact that skilled labor always seemed to be in shorter supply in the United States than in Europe, creating leverage for skilled workers. The barriers to organized labor achieving the fairly high coverage of nonagricultural employees that prevailed in Western Europe and Australasia by 1913 were formidable. They included enormous racial and ethnic divisions; a generally hostile legal environment; and strong, well-organized employers. The AFL added to these barriers by its unwillingness to build a mass union movement among the unskilled, leaving the task to alternative bodies such as the **Industrial Workers of the World**, which challenged the AFL during the years between 1905 and 1917, and the **Congress of Industrial Organizations (CIO)**, which was formed by unions that seceded from the AFL in the 1930s.

But it was in its attitude to politics that American organized labor showed its greatest distinctiveness from the labor movements of other Western nations. In Western Europe and Australasia, labor unions by 1900 were closely associated with **social-democratic, socialist, and labor political parties**. In the United States, this kind of permanent relationship did not exist (though this is not to say that the AFL did not participate in **politics**). The AFL's leadership regarded these relationships with intense suspicion and developed an ideology of **voluntarism,** which put it at odds with bodies such as the **International Federation of Trade Unions.** That ideology, which emerged from the AFL leaders' encounters with hostile courts and unsuccessful efforts to secure legislative reforms, held that workers needed to look to their unions to win better working conditions and that any state intervention was likely to favor employers' interests. Thus the AFL came to oppose minimum wages and other social legislation. But the AFL's voluntarist vision had limited reach. By 1930, only 9 percent of American employees were union members, the same level that had been reached in 1913.

The election of the Franklin D. Roosevelt administration in 1933 and its prolabor stance, as shown by its **National Labor Relations Act** (1935), enabled the emergence of the CIO and its recruitment of millions of semiskilled employees into the ranks of organized labor. The CIO broke with the AFL's craft-based voluntarism and established unions in auto, steel, and electrical manufacturing. The CIO's growth, along with the advantages of government support and labor shortages created by World War II were the main reasons for raising the proportion of employees in unions to 28 percent by 1950, a good result for American labor, but a low figure by Western European and Australasian standards. The proportion of American employees who were union members peaked at 32 percent in 1953 but declined steadily thereafter. The public reputation of organized labor suffered in the 1950s and 1960s with well-publicized inquiries into corruption within certain unions, notably the **Teamsters.** As in other Western economies, the effect of technological change whittled away at the parts of the labor force where labor was traditionally strong such as **coal mining,** steel, printing, and the **railroads.** At the same time, the labor force saw a general shift toward **white-collar** employment and a rising number of **women** employees. Union recruitment of new members was also hampered by **right-to-work laws** in many states. The United States is one of the very few industrialized countries that has not ratified the **International Labour Organization** Conventions 87 (Freedom of Association and the Right to Organize, 1948) and 98 (Right to Organize and Collective Bargaining, 1949).

Politically, organized labor was just one interest group among many, and, although since 1936 it has been allied with the Democratic Party, this alliance has not protected it from antilabor forces within the party. Among reformers, organized labor also suffered from its conservative posture, particularly its slowness in dealing with racial discrimination. From 1980, organized labor in the United States, as in other countries, entered a prolonged crisis, which was epitomized by severe slumps in steelmaking and automobile manufacturing, industries characterized by outmoded production methods. It also faced a hostile political climate under the Republican presidencies of **Ronald Reagan** (1981–1989) and George H. W. Bush (1989–1993). Between 1983 and 1993, the proportion of employees who were union members fell from 20 to 16 percent. Bill Clinton's election to the presidency in 1993—the first Democrat administration since 1981—brought some benefits to organized labor; for example, an antiunion presidential order concerning federal contractors was rescinded. However, in November 1994 the Democrats lost control of both the House of Representatives and the Senate to the Republicans, which limited Clinton's ability to introduce prounion policies for the rest of his administration. In the same year, Clinton successfully extended the North American Free Trade Agreement to Mexico, a move opposed by organized labor, even though it included a very weak subagreement on workers' rights. Also in 1994, the Commission on the Future of Worker-Management Relations drew attention to the continued prevalence of concerted employer hostility to organized labor, as shown by practices such as "union busting," the illegal firing of union supporters trying to form unions in nonunionized workplaces, and a general lack of acceptance of the legitimacy of unions in democratic society, in contrast to Western Europe.

During the Clinton administration (1993–2000), the number of U.S. union members fell slightly from 16.6 to 16.3 million, despite substantial economic growth between 1994 and 2000. Although the presidency of George W. Bush (2001–2009) was predictably antiunion in its policies, U.S. organized labor continued to suffer from long-term problems, some of which are of its own making. Notable among these is a poor public image and an association with racketeering and violence based on events from the 1930s into the 1970s. Under **John Sweeney**, who was elected president of the **American Federation of Labor–Congress of Industrial Organizations (AFL-CIO)** in 1995 and has stated that the George W. Bush administration is "the most anti-worker government since Herbert Hoover," labor has begun to address this problem by broadening the scope of organized labor to include social issues such as education, health, and **pensions**, and by greater participation in grassroots campaigns. But Sweeney's efforts to revive the labor movement did not reverse union declines, which led four of the AFL-CIO's five largest unions to withdraw from the federation in 2005 to form a revival union center called **Change to Win**.

Both the **International Confederation of Free Trade Unions** and the **International Trade Union Confederation** have long been critical of the United States in their surveys of **violations of trade union rights**. Their complaints include the legal exclusion of more than 30 million employees from **collective bargaining**, the harassment of labor union members, the active discouragement of attempts to form unions in the private sector, and legal restrictions on the right to strike and collective bargaining in the **public sector**. Organized labor actively supported the presidential campaign of Barack Obama in 2009, but his administration has delivered little in return. In 2011, there were large-scale protests in Wisconsin, Ohio, and Indiana against laws limiting union rights.

The membership of labor unions in the United States has always varied greatly between states. In 2010, the three states with the highest union membership levels were New York (24 percent), Alaska (23 percent), and Hawaii (22 percent). The three states with the lowest union membership levels were Arkansas, Georgia (both with 4 percent), and North Carolina (3 percent).

UNITED STEELWORKERS (USW). *See* UNITED STEELWORKERS OF AMERICA (USWA).

UNITED STEELWORKERS OF AMERICA (USWA). Despite promising beginnings, the steel industry of the **United States** was a mainly nonunion industry until 1936. The first union was formed by skilled British puddlers in Pittsburgh in 1857. They were joined by the formation of a union among skilled workers in the furnaces and rolling mills in 1861. A united industry union of skilled workers, the Amalgamated Association of Iron and Steel Workers of the United States, was formed in Pittsburgh in 1876. By 1891, this union claimed 24,000 members, but in 1892 it suffered a crushing defeat in a **strike** to resist wage cuts by the Carnegie Steel Company at Homestead, Pennsylvania. In the following years, the Amalgamated proved incapable of meeting the enormous managerial and technological changes that came into steelmaking in the 1890s and 1900s. In particular, the unions faced a general deskilling of jobs, which greatly reduced their bargaining power. Lesser skilled jobs meant that wages could be kept low and that immigrants could be easily recruited. In 1909, the largest steel company, the United States Steel Company, refused to recognize the association and defeated it in a strike. The company was able to maintain a union-free labor force until 1937. By 1912, the United States steelmaking industry was a byword for high productivity but with low wages and long working hours. Discontent among its employees led to the great strike of 1919, which was organized by the **American Federation of Labor (AFL)** through its Iron and Steel Organizing Committee. Despite 300,000 taking part, the strike ended after three and a half months on 8 January 1920, in the utter defeat of the strikers.

The **National Industrial Recovery Act** of 1933 laid the foundation for a revival of unionism in the steel industry. In 1934, the AFL began a campaign to recruit union members in the steel industry, but these efforts were frustrated by the leadership of the Amalgamated, which wanted its almost defunct union to lead the campaign; it was then swept aside in 1936 by the **Congress of Industrial Organizations (CIO)**, which launched its own campaign to unionize the industry. Led by **Philip Murray** on behalf of **John L. Lewis**, the aim of the campaign was to build an **industrial union** for the steel industry and to increase the bargaining power of the **United Mine Workers of America** in negotiating with steel companies that owned **coal mines**. The CIO recruited 200,000 steelworkers for the Steel Workers' Organizing Committee and in secret discussions Lewis secured not only recognition for the Committee from U.S. Steel in March 1937 but also a 10 percent wage increase, an eight-hour work day, and a 40-hour work week. However, the CIO's campaign against the independent steel producers was defeated by violence and a downturn in the demand for steel. **Police** killed 10 strikers and wounded 80 at the steelworks of the Republic Steel Company in South Chicago in May 1937.

In 1942, the Steel Workers' Organizing Committee was reorganized as the United Steelworkers of America and was forced to use the National War Labor Board to compel the independent steel producers to engage in collective bargaining. Murray led the USWA from its formation to his death in 1952. In 1946, the USWA conducted a month-long strike throughout the industry, which yielded it a large pay increase. Through strikes in 1949 and 1952 and bargaining, the USWA gained the closed or union shop and a pension scheme for members. Defeat in the strike of 1959 against management's attempt to change work rules and a downturn in the national economy caused the USWA's **membership** to fall from 1.2 million in 1956 to 876,000 in 1965. By 1975, membership had recovered to the one million mark, but the worldwide crisis in the steel industry in 1982–1983 caused membership to fall to 572,000 by 1985 and to 459,000 by 1992. In 2005, the USWA and the Paper, Allied-Industrial, Chemical and Energy Workers International Union merged to form the largest industrial union in North America, the United Steel, Paper and Forestry, Rubber, Manufacturing, Energy, Allied Industrial and Service Workers International Union (in short, **United Steelworkers [USW]**). With more than 850,000 workers in over 8,000 bargaining units in the United States, Canada, and the Caribbean, USW was the largest industrial union in North America. In 2008, the USW merged with **Unite the Union** to form **Workers Uniting**.

UNIVERSAL ALLIANCE OF DIAMOND WORKERS (UADW). The UADW **international trade secretariat** was formed in Antwerp in 1905, although international conferences among diamond employees began in 1889. By 1913, the UADW had 22,700 members. Between 1975 and 1992, **membership** of the UADW was stationary at about 10,000. The UADW was 1 of 16 international trade secretariats associated with the **International Confederation of Free Trade Unions** in 1995. In November 2000, the UADW merged with the **International Federation of Chemical, Energy, Mine, and General Workers' Unions**. At the time of its merger, the UADW had about 100,000 members. One of its last acts was to accuse the diamond industry of financing wars in **Angola**, **Democratic Republic of the Congo**, **Liberia**, and **Sierra Leone**.

URUGUAY. Organized labor in Uruguay was imported by European **immigration; strikes** were recorded by 1884 and the first union congress was held in 1896 to campaign for the eight-hour day. By 1930, there were 28,000 union members in Uruguay. Organized labor was politically divided, mainly between **socialists** and **communists**. Uruguay was represented in the **International Confederation of Free Trade Unions (ICFTU)** between 1951 and 1975. In June 1973, organized labor conducted a **general strike** against the military government's economic program that was defeated and ushered in a highly repressive response. The ICFTU representative in 1975 was the *Confederación General de Trabajadores del Uruguay* (General Confederation of Uruguay Workers) with 40,000 members. It had existed in various forms since 1951, but was disaffiliated after it came under strict **government control**. Uruguay's government became one of the world's worst offenders of **human rights** abuses, and the country has not been represented in the ICFTU since the 1970s. In 2001, there were about 120,000 union members in Uruguay. In 2010, Uruguay was not represented in **International Trade Union Confederation**.

UZBEKISTAN. Independent of the former **Soviet Union** since August 1991, independent organized labor has failed to emerge in Uzbekistan because of the country's lack of economic and social development. The Federation of Trade Unions of Uzbekistan, the survivor of the former Soviet trade union, is effectively under **government control**. Uzbekistan has never been represented in either the **International Confederation of Free Trade Unions** or the **International Trade Union Confederation**.

V

VANDOR, AUGUSTO (1923–1969). A leader of organized labor in **Argentina**, Vandor began in working life in the navy from 1940 to 1950. After leaving the navy, he joined the Philips factory in Buenos Aires. There he became the steward of the Philips factory local of the *Unión Obrera Metalúrgica* (UOM), or Metalworkers' Union, and in 1954 led a strike for better pay at the facility. He gained a reputation for strategic thinking that earned him the nickname of *El Lobo* (the Wolf). He became prominent in the UOM, but was arrested following the overthrow of the Perón administration in 1955. Introduced to Perón, who was in exile in Santo Domingo in 1958, Vandor was elected secretary general of the UOM, which was the largest union of the *Confederación General del Trabajo* (CGT), or General Confederation of Labor. He represented labor as the leading CGT political strategist and helped the failed efforts to slip Perón into Argentina in 1964. Vandor, fearing that Perón might never manage to return to Argentina, became increasingly critical of Perón. This put him in conflict with the CGT secretary general, José Alonso. They both were candidates in the Mendoza Province gubernatorial campaign, but a conservative candidate was ultimately elected. The rivalry between the two union leaders grew even further, resulting in the ousting of Alonso in 1966 and a split of mind in the CGT. The Ongania military dictatorship drove the two opposing rivals back to each other, after which they made common cause in the view that it was better to negotiate with the regime than to express outright opposition, moves that led to opposition from Perón and the Graphists' Union to the candidacy of Vandor for CGT secretary general in 1968. Augusto Vandor eventually reconciled himself with Perón, but was assassinated in 1969 at his UOM offices, probably by a far-left Perónist group.

VANUATU. Vanuatu has been independent of the **United Kingdom** and **France** since July 1980 and formerly known as the *New Hebrides*. Organized labor in Vanuatu has developed since the 1970s. In 1988, the Vanuatu Council of Trade Unions with 1,500 members joined the **International Confederation of Free Trade Unions** and remained an affiliate until 2006, but it did not join the **International Trade Union Confederation**.

VATICAN. Independent from **Italy** since February 1929, the Vatican was represented in the **International Confederation of Free Trade Unions** by 1987 by the *Associazione Dipendenti Laici Vaticani* (Association of Vatican Lay Workers), which organized the first strike in 1988. It had about 300 members in 2010.

VENEZUELA. Organized labor developed in secret during the dictatorship of General Juan Vincente Gómez between 1908 and 1935. After Gómez's death in 1935, Venezuela began to move gradually toward democracy, aided by organized labor in alliance with peasants and students. The *Confederación de Trabajadores de Venezuela* (CTV), or Confederation of Workers of Venezuela, was formed in December 1936. Also in 1936, organized labor formed a **socialist** political party, *Acción Democrática* (Democratic Action), to work for democracy and social change. The CTV was weakened by divisions between supporters of Democratic Action and **communists**. In 1941, organized labor was legalized, and in 1945 a military coup brought in a democratic government. Democratic Action won the 1947 elections, but a military counter-coup on 24 November 1948 ousted the government and repressed organized labor. The CTV was formally dissolved by the government on 25 February 1949. Democratic rule was not restored until January 1958 following a **general strike**. The CTV was a member in exile of the **International Confederation of Free Trade Unions (ICFTU)** from 1951 (when it claimed 200,000 members) and was a full member from 1959. In 2001, it claimed 750,700 members. Although both the Employment Law of 1990 and the 1999 constitution promote **freedom of association**, the ICFTU noted continued government interference in the affairs of organized labor in its global reports for successive years, particularly the efforts of the Hugo Chávez government to replace organized labor with government-run puppet organizations. Between 2 December 2002 and 3 February 2003, there was an unsuccessful general strike in Venezuela led by oil workers against the Chávez government. In 2006, the Coca-Cola Company successfully avoided **collective bargaining**, despite a 24-hour strike on 2 October. The **International Trade Union Confederation** has continued to report that Venezuelan organized labor is forced to operate in a hostile and violent political environment. Between 2006 and 2010, the number of labor union members fell from 475,500 to 370,000.

VER.DI. *Ver.di,* the shortened version of *Vereinte Dienstleistungsgewerkschaft* (United Services Labor Union), is one of the largest labor unions in the world with 2.3 million members. It was formed in **Germany** on 21 March 2001 by the **amalgamation** of five labor unions: *Gewerkschaft Öffentliche*

Dienste; Transport und Verkehr (ÖTV), or Public Service, Transportation, and Traffic Labor Union, with 1.5 million members; the *Deutsche Ang-estellten-Gewerkschaft* (German Private Sector White-Collar Labor Union) with 450,000 members; the *Gewerkschaft Handel, Banken und Versicher-ungen* (Commerce, Banking, and Insurance Labor Union) with 440,600 members; the *Deutsche Postgewerkschaft* (German Postal Labor Union) with 446,000 members; and the *Industriegewerkschaft Medien* (Media Industrial Labor Union) with 175,000 members. Negotiations for the creation of *Ver.di* began in November 1998. The purpose of the merger was to arrest the decline in the **membership** of the unions (the four constituent unions had 3.4 million members in 1996) and to enable them to compete with large employers. In his inaugural address in Berlin, the president of *Ver.di,* Frank Bsirske, formerly of the ÖTV, stressed the need to recruit new members among **youth** (those under 30) and in the former East Germany. *Ver.di* organizes employees from more than 1,000 professions. Between 2001 and 2010, the membership of *Ver.di* fell from 3 to 2.1 million but it was still the third largest labor union in the world.

VIETNAM. Organized labor in Vietnam originated in the participation by some Vietnamese intellectuals in labor affairs in **France** during World War I. Using this experience, they set up some unions in Vietnam (then French Indochina), beginning in Hanoi in 1920. Most labor organizing thereafter was carried out by **communists**. In 1929, the communists formed a labor federa-tion as part of the struggle for independence from French rule. By 1930, the federation claimed 6,000 members, but it was crushed in 1930–1931 during a major peasant uprising against the French. Despite a new labor code and more toleration of labor organizations in the Popular Front period (1936–1939), these initiatives proved short-lived in the face of widespread discontent in Vietnam, the fall of the Léon Blum government in France, and the start of World War II. During the war, Vietnam was occupied by the Japanese.

In 1946, the North Vietnamese government set up the Vietnam General Confederation of Labor (VGCL) on the Soviet model. In what was South Vietnam, the French **Catholic** labor federation, the *Confédération Française des Travailleurs Chrétiens,* was instrumental in forming the *Confédération Vietnamienne du Travail* (Vietnamese Confederation of Labor), which was based on unions among rice growers and employees in river transportation and later claimed 500,000 members. Two other labor federations were formed in 1952 and 1953, but they never had more than 70,000 members between them. In 1959, Vietnam was represented in the **International Confedera-tion of Free Trade Unions** by the *Union Ouvrière du Viet-nam* (Union of Vietnamese Workers), but this body had ceased to be affiliated by 1965. After the reunification of Vietnam, which was the outcome of the Vietnam war, the VGCL subsumed the labor organizations of the South.

With the opening of the Vietnamese economy to foreign investment and enterprises in the late 1980s, there was widespread exploitation manifested in long hours, low pay, and physical abuse. The federation, with assistance provided by the Australian chapter of the **International Labour Organization**, persuaded the National Assembly at the end of June 1994 to approve a new labor code. The code obliged every foreign joint venture to establish a trade union within six months of beginning operations, allowed the employees of such enterprises the right to **strike**, set up independent courts of **conciliation and arbitration**, protected these employees from wrongful dismissal, and required retrenched employees to be paid severance pay. The first legal strike under the code occurred in August 1994. In 2009, the **International Trade Union Confederation** reported that, although the Vietnamese government further restricted the right to strike, 762 illegal strikes occurred in 2008. The global economic crisis and the subsequent loss of jobs caused a drop in the number of strikes to 216 in 2009.

VIOLATIONS OF TRADE UNION RIGHTS. An annual survey conducted since 1984 by the **International Confederation of Free Trade Unions** and the **International Trade Union Confederation (ITUC)** since 2006. The survey documents the condition of organized labor according to the relevant conventions of the **International Labour Organization (ILO)**. The survey includes information on labor union members murdered or assassinated, injured, arrested, or dismissed, by continent. The survey is one of the main ways in which the ITUC reports on the effectiveness of the ILO's **international standard-setting** and is a prime source of information on the state of organized labor in the world.

VOLUNTARISM. *Voluntarism* is a term with two different meanings. In the **United States**, it referred to a doctrine subscribed to by the **American Federation of Labor (AFL)** and promoted by **Samuel Gompers** from the late 1890s to the early 1930s that stressed the need for organized labor to rely on its own resources for gaining improvement of pay and conditions and not on **politics** or political parties. Voluntarism saw a separation between the political process and organized labor, though the doctrine did not exclude lobbying political parties for favors. Voluntarism was strengthened within the AFL after its crushing failure to organize the steel industry in 1919. The doctrine suited workers in skilled unions that could provide welfare benefits to members but ignored the lesser skilled employees.

In the **United Kingdom**, the term *voluntarism* usually refers to the abstaining by the state from intervention in labor relations, particularly **labor**

disputes, except to support or extend **collective bargaining**. For example, the Advisory Conciliation and Arbitration Service, the British government agency that was established in 1974 to resolve labor disputes, can only operate if the parties to the dispute agree to its participation. Since 1980, British governments have shown a greater willingness to intervene in labor relations and have passed laws to regulate their internal management and behavior. *See also* EMPLOYMENT ACTS.

WAGES. Wages, together with **working hours**, have traditionally been central topics for organized labor in **collective bargaining** with employers. Although the amount of wages was usually of most concern, the method and timing of payment also figured as issues in the 19th century. Payment in goods instead of money (or "truck") was widespread in the **United Kingdom** in the early 19th century even though it was outlawed as early as 1411. Similarly, the common practice of monthly payment of wages imposed undue hardship on employees and forced them into debt to meet day-to-day living costs.

The ability of organized labor to raise wages largely depends on the condition of the trade cycle. One area of wages where organized labor has been traditionally most active is in maintaining the differentials between wages in occupations by means of margins such as for skill or seniority. With the generally higher level of union strength between 1940 and 1980 in most Western countries, organized labor has sought to use economic growth to extend wage claims to cover holidays, severance, and redundancy. It has also tried to use increased productivity as a means of raising wages. The importance of unions in economic management, particularly to control inflation, was recognized by government through various experiments in prices and income policies in the United Kingdom and the **United States** in the 1970s; they attempted to limit general increases in wages.

Official statistics from the United States have also shown important differences in the wages of employees who are members of unions and those who are not union members, not just that union members in general earned more than nonunion employees. For example, the U.S. Employment Cost Index shows that between 1975 and 1982 the wages of union members rose faster than nonunion employees but between 1982 and 1999, the percentage change in the pay of nonunion employees was higher than that of union members. Between 2001 and 2006, the total rise was higher for union members than nonunion employees. Similarly, a study of **labor statistics** for 2003 supported the historical observation that the presence of labor unions lowered wages dispersion in the workplace. *See also* SHORTER WORKING

HOURS; UNION–GOVERNMENT AGREEMENTS; UNION WAGE DIF-
FERENTIAL.

WAGNER ACT. Officially known as the *National Labor Relations Act,* this U.S. federal law, named for its promoter, Senator Robert F. Wagner, was passed by the Senate 11 days before the **National Industrial Recovery Act** (1933) was declared unconstitutional by the Supreme Court. The Wagner Act reaffirmed the legal right of organized labor to recruit and represent employees in **collective bargaining** without interference from employers. A National Labor Relations Board was created to administer the act. The scope of the act was amended by the **Taft-Hartley Act** in 1947.

WALESA, LECH (1943–). Son of a carpenter who was persecuted by the Nazis and himself an electrician, Walesa would become the image of anti-communist resistance and the president of **Poland**. After finishing vocational school, Walesa worked as a car mechanic and in 1967 began working at the Lenin Shipyard in Gdansk. He soon became a trade-union activist, and was persecuted by the **communist** government. When the government raised food prices in 1970, the workers came out in protest. Walesa was the chairman of the strike committee at the shipyard. The harsh reaction by the communists resulted in over 30 workers killed and radicalization of Lech Walesa. Because he was involved in illegal union activities, he was dismissed in 1976 and on a number of subsequent occasions. Frequent arrests also became a part of his life.

Walesa became a member of the underground free trade unions and, although not on the payroll of the yard, he was one of the strike leaders when in 1980 a strike wave occurred in Poland. These strikes led to an agreement with the government granting the workers of the Lenin Shipyard in Gdansk the right to strike and the right to organize an independent union. As a result, the *Solidarnosc Niezalezny Samorzadny Zwaiazek Zawodowy* (Independent, Self-Governing Trade Union Solidarity) emerged of which he became the chairman. In a response to the threatening growth of the union to 10 million members, martial law was imposed and Solidarity outlawed. Walesa was again arrested, but returned to the shipyard after his release in 1983 and was awarded the Nobel Peace Prize that year also.

In the mid-1980s, the underground Solidarity continued. Intense strikes forced the government into negotiations in 1989. The role of Walesa again was important as the face of Solidarity. Step by step, the administration had to give in and in 1990 he even won the presidential elections of a Poland that had broken away from the Soviet bloc. In a few years, Walesa lost much of his popularity during Poland's transition to a market economy. Since 1995, Walesa's role has only been marginal.

WEBB, SIDNEY [JAMES] (1859–1947) AND BEATRICE (1858–1943). Socialists who were influential by their writings about the theory and practice of trade unionism in the **United Kingdom**. Sidney was born in London and started his career as an office clerk. After developing **socialist** ideas, he joined the Fabian Society and argued for reform instead of class warfare. In 1892, he married Beatrice Potter, one year after she asked his support for her research into the cooperative movement. Beatrice published *The Cooperative Movement in Great Britain* in 1891 in which she advocated the forming of workers' cooperatives. Beatrice's income from an inheritance allowed Sidney to give up his job as a civil servant.

Together they wrote the influential *The History of Trade Unionism*, which was published in 1894 and translated into numerous languages. Their joint efforts resulted also in the foundation of the London School of Economics and Political Science in 1895 where Sydney became a professor in 1912. Beatrice was a member of the Poor Law Commission from 1905 to 1909, where she wrote a minority report that anticipated the welfare state as known after World War II. After they joined the Labour Party in 1914, Sydney became a member of parliament (1922–1929).

The *History of Trade Unionism* was revised in 1920 and exerted a major influence, particularly in encouraging an institutional approach to labor unions. The Webbs are especially known today as advocates of the new unionism that surpassed the old version of the union movement. According to their definition, a trade union "is a continuous association of wage earners for the purpose of maintaining or improving the conditions of their employment." This definition is still often quoted but also criticized for neglecting the role of noncontinuous labor bodies in the history of organized labor.

After their visit to the **Soviet Union** in 1932, they became uncritical supporters of the regime, for which they were widely criticized. This did not prevent both the Webbs from continuing to support the Soviet planned economy until their deaths.

WESTERN LABOR UNION. *See* AMERICAN LABOR UNION.

WESTERN SAMOA. Western Samoa was independent of **New Zealand** since January 1962. An association of school teachers existed by 1973, but no labor unions as such. The Public Service Association was the country's affiliate of the **International Confederation of Free Trade Unions** by 1988, with 2,200 members. It remained an affiliate until 2006 but never joined the **International Trade Union Confederation**.

WHITE-COLLAR UNIONISM. Up to the 1940s, white-collar employees were a minor part of organized labor in most Western countries, with unions of **blue-collar** employees being the dominant force. Blue-collar unions tended to regard white-collar unions poorly because their members did not perform "real" work. Typically, white-collar occupations included teachers, salaried government workers, and clerks in all industries. For most of history, distinctions of social class underlay blue- and white-collar work. Blue-collar workers were, by general definition, the working class, whereas white-collar employees often saw themselves as socially superior. In **Germany**, federal laws from 1911 even recognized a "collar line" that treated white-collar workers better than blue-collar workers. White-collar employees were less likely to join unions, particularly if they enjoyed advantageous conditions from their employers.

Although lacking the stature of blue-collar unions within organized labor, unions of white-collar employees have a long history. In the **United States**, the first white-collar unions emerged in the 1830s among retail clerks who wanted employers to adopt a standard early closing time; in 1864, dry goods employees in New York went on **strike** to prevent the imposition of longer hours. In the **United Kingdom**, the first white-collar unions were formed among teachers in the 1860s as a result of school managers being given the right to appoint and dismiss teachers. Yet it was not until the 1880s that sustained growth in the number of white-collar unions occurred. In the United States, the first national white-collar union, the Retail Clerks' National Protective Association, joined the **American Federation of Labor** in 1888. In the United Kingdom, white-collar unions were formed among national government clerks (1890) and postal workers (1891).

As the economies of Western nations matured, the **service sector** grew, and with it the number of white-collar employees. Between about 1910 and 1930, the proportion of white-collar employees in the labor forces of the United States, Germany, and Britain rose from about 13 to about 20 percent. Within organized labor in Britain, **Denmark**, and Germany, one fifth of labor union members were white-collar employees by 1930.

After 1950, white-collar unions grew with the growth in **public sector** employment, particularly as government was more likely to concede recognition to unions than the private sector. At the same time, blue-collar occupations grew relatively slowly and their share of the labor force declined. During the 1960s, white-collar employees became more willing to join unions, and their labor federations joined with the traditional labor bodies based on blue-collar employees. Since the 1990s, the traditional distinction between blue-collar and white-collar jobs has become increasingly blurred because of occupational change and it is no longer used in most official collections of **labor statistics**. For example, in the United Kingdom the long-standing division of occupations between "manual" and "nonmanual" ceased in 2000. White-collar unions have also become more strike prone than during the past. An example of this new attitude is the strike at Chevron in 2008 by the white-collar Petroleum and Natural Gas Senior Staff Association of Nigeria to force the removal of a senior expatriate executive. *See also* BLUE-COLLAR/WHITE-COLLAR; EDUCATION; FEDERATION OF INTERNATIONAL CIVIL SERVANTS' ASSOCIATIONS; NATIONAL EDUCATION ASSOCIATION; UNISON; WOMEN.

"WINTER OF DISCONTENT." This phrase from the opening of William Shakespeare's *Richard III* has been commonly applied to a wave of **strikes** in the **United Kingdom** during the winter of 1978–1979. The number of working days lost per thousand employees was 1,270 in 1979, compared with 410 in 1978. The strikes occurred mainly in transportation, garbage collection, hospitals, cemeteries, and the **public sector**. The year 1979 reported the most working days lost per thousand employees in **labor disputes** since the **British General Strike** in 1926. Many of the strikes were accompanied by violence during **picketing**.

The "winter of discontent" ended the **union–government agreement** between the British **Labour Party** and the **Trades Union Congress** begun in 1974 that had tried to limit voluntarily union wage claims to 5 percent. The strike wave lost organized labor much public support and was a main reason why the Labour government was defeated in the national elections in May 1979 by the Conservative Party led by Margaret Thatcher. Between 1980 and 1993, the Conservative governments passed a series of **Employment Acts** to reduce the power of organized labor.

WOMEN. One of the biggest changes in the post-1950 structure of union **membership** has been the rising proportion of women. In 1913, women made up only 11 percent of labor union members in the **United Kingdom**, 8 percent in **Germany**, and 4 percent in **Australia** and the **United States**. By 1950, women made up 18 percent of labor union members in Britain and Germany, 19 percent in Australia, and 23 percent in **Japan**.

The entry of women into the labor force gathered pace after 1960 both in numbers and in the proportion of women working, making them more likely to be recruited by the largely male-dominated labor unions. Increasingly, women moved into the expanding **white-collar** occupations and were no longer just to be found in low-paid **manufacturing** occupations such as in the clothing industry. The **International Confederation of Free Trade Unions (ICFTU)** estimated that between 1949 and 1970, the proportion of women among its affiliates rose from 7 to 22 percent and to 36 percent by 1996. The ICFTU set up a Women's Committee in 1956, and a secretariat in 1957. In 1962, it introduced specialized training programs for women in Third World countries. In 1992, the ICFTU launched its Positive Action

Program for Women in Development Cooperation with the objective of setting a minimum target of 30 percent for women's participation in all labor union activities. The growing importance of women in organized labor was shown in December 2002 when the ICFTU admitted its first woman into a leadership position: Mamounta Cissé, an African, who was appointed as the second assistant secretary-general of the ICFTU. In 2004, Sharan Burrow, an Australian, became the first woman president of the ICFTU and the **International Trade Union Confederation** from its inception in 2006.

In 2001, the proportion of women in labor unions was 47 percent in the United Kingdom, 43 percent in Australia, and 42 percent in the United States, double what it had been in 1960. In contrast, the proportion of women in labor unions in Germany and Japan changed little over this period. In 2005, women union members outnumbered men in the United Kingdom for the first time and have continued to do so, accounting for 55 percent of members in 2010. The trend was also evident in other Western countries where comparable statistics are available. In 2010, women made up 48 percent of union members in Australia and 46 percent in the United States. *See also* WHITE-COLLAR UNIONISM; Table 13, Appendix F.

WORKERS' UNION (WU). The WU was one of the largest general unions in the **United Kingdom** in the early 20th century. Formed in May 1898, it set out to recruit all employees whether skilled or unskilled and, through militancy, work toward the creation of a **socialist** society. The WU was formed in the wake of the major defeat suffered by the **Amalgamated Society of Engineers** in London in 1897 by the leading labor left-wing leader Tom Mann (1856–1941). The new union barely survived its first few years: **membership** reached 2,000 by the end of 1898, and 4,170 by 1899, but fell to 1,000 by 1902. With the recovery in the economy after 1906, membership rose to 91,000 in 1913 and to 140,000 by 1914. Much of this growth was achieved through the recruitment of poorly paid employees, particularly in engineering and **agriculture**. By 1918, membership reached a peak of 379,000, a quarter of them **women**. Although the WU affiliated with the **Trades Union Congress** in 1917 (after two failed attempts), it was disliked by a number of other unions such as the Agricultural Labourers' Union and especially by the Amalgamated Engineers as a competitor for members.

In 1916, the WU began negotiations for **amalgamation** with the National Amalgamated Union of Labour and the Municipal Employees' Association, which resulted in the formation of a new, but only partly amalgamated, organization, the National Amalgamated Workers' Union, in January 1919; this body claimed 500,000 members in 1920. Thereafter, membership of the WU plummeted to 140,000 in 1923 through economic depression, high turnover of members, and hostility from other unions. The WU never recovered and in 1929 was absorbed into the **Transport and General Workers' Union (TGWU)**, but the WU gave the TGWU an organizational foothold in a number of industries whose employment growth helped it to become Britain's largest union by the late 1930s.

WORKERS UNITING. In 2008, **Unite the Union**, the largest labour organization in the **United Kingdom** and **Ireland**, and the **United Steelworkers of America** (USWA), North America's largest private sector union, signed an agreement clearing the way for the creation of Workers Uniting, the world's first global trade union. Workers Uniting organizes more than three million active and **retired employees** from the **United States, Canada, Great Britain,** and the Republic of Ireland who work in virtually every sector of the global economy.

WORKING AMERICA. This community affiliate of the **American Federation of Labor–Congress of Industrial Organizations (AFL-CIO)** was founded in 2003. It is an effort to combine the strength of the AFL-CIO with three million employees who are not union members because there is no workplace union for them. Working America also tries to extend union activities outside the workplace to local communities and the unemployed.

WORKING HOURS. Although there are few statistics on working hours before the Industrial Revolution, there is an impression that working hours in practice, although long, were more varied before it than after it. Where regulations existed, they prescribed long hours. For example, the English Statute of Artificers (1562) fixed the working hours for **apprentices** at 12 hours in the summer and from daybreak to nightfall in winter. Where work was monotonous, customs like "Saint Monday" were observed by the 18th century. Figures for the **Amalgamated Society of Engineers** in the **United Kingdom** show that the number of hours its members worked in a week varied from 57 to 63 in 1851 and from 56 to 60 by 1869. In **Germany**, the typical work week in manufacturing was 78 hours in the 1860s, 66 hours in the 1870s, and between 58 and 60 hours between 1911 and 1914. The long, monotonous week brought by the Industrial Revolution made the reduction of work hours an important issue for organized labor in Europe and North America.

The Ten Hours movement began with textile employees in England in the 1830s, and the short-lived radical body, the National Regeneration Society (1833–1834), advocated an eight-hour work day. In **Australia**, James Stephens (1821–1889), an English Chartist, played an important role in winning the eight-hour work day in a number of skilled trades in the colony of Victoria in the mid-1850s. In 1869, the **National Labor Union** succeeded in gaining the eight-hour work day for U.S. federal employees. In 1871–1872, engineering and building employees in northeast England won the nine-hour work day through **labor disputes**.

Most governments before 1900 avoided legislating for maximum work hours. The English Factory Act of 1875 laid down a maximum work week of 56.5 hours for **women** and teenagers, but ignored men and people working in **agriculture**. In the 1880s and early 1890s, there was international agitation for the eight-hour work day by organized labor. British **railroad** employees did not get the eight-hour work day until 1920 and then only after a national **strike** in 1919. Since 1945, metal unions have been at the forefront of reducing work hours in Australia, Germany, and the United Kingdom. For example, the first debates about the 35-hour week in Western Europe were conducted within *IG Metall* in 1977. Despite the efforts of organized labor, declining **membership** of labor unions has coincided with increases in working hours in most industrialized countries since the 1980s. In 2006, the **International Labour Organization** reported that the number of working hours worked per person per year in manufacturing was 2,137 in the **United States**, 2,262 in **Japan**, 1,839 in **France**, 2,496 in **Hong Kong**, 2,163 in **Israel**, and 1,986 in **Norway**. In contrast to most other Western industrialized countries, the French Socialist government of Lionel Jospin reduced the working week from 39 to 35 hours in 1997 at the behest of organized labor. Although the change did not produce the additional jobs or lower the unemployment rate as claimed, it has been considered to have raised productivity. In countries where the working week has increased, such as Australia, it has been judged to have been detrimental to family life. *See also* FULL-TIME/PART-TIME EMPLOYMENT; SHORTER WORKING HOURS.

WORLD CONFEDERATION OF LABOR (WCL). The WCL began as the International Federation of Christian Trade Unions (IFCTU), which was formed in The Hague in 1920 and traced its origins to the Ghent Anti-Socialist League, which had been organized in 1878. The IFCTU represented labor unions that objected to the anticlericalism of the **socialist** and **anarchist** labor unions that dominated European organized labor. The entry of the IFCTU into the **International Confederation of Free Trade Unions** was opposed by socialist labor unions in Western Europe, and the IFCTU turned its attention to the Third World and recruiting affiliates from Muslim and Buddhist countries, with the main criterion for membership being belief in a religion rather than adherence to Christianity. In 1968, the IFCTU changed its name to the *World Confederation of Labor.* In 2001, the WCL claimed 26 million members (compared with 19 million in 1992 and 14.5 million in

1973), mainly in Latin America or countries where **Catholicism** was strong. On 28 May 2003, the **International Confederation of Free Trade Unions** issued a call to the WCL to join with it to better meet the challenge of **globalization**. As a result, both organizations dissolved themselves on 31 October 2006 and formed the **International Trade Union Confederation**.

WORLD CONFEDERATION OF ORGANIZATIONS OF THE TEACHING PROFESSION (WCOTP). The WCOTP was made up of two federations, the International Federation of Teachers' Associations and the International Federation of Secondary Teachers, from its foundation in 1952 until February 1993, when it agreed to merge with the **International Federation of Free Teaching Unions** to form **Education International**. An independent, nonpolitical body, the WCOTP had 13 million members in 191 countries at the announcement of its merger. *See also* EDUCATION.

WORLD FEDERATION OF TRADE UNIONS (WFTU). The WFTU was formed in Paris on 25 September 1945 at an international conference of labor organizations to replace the **International Federation of Trade Unions**. The WFTU was ruptured by the Cold War and **communist** opposition to the Marshall Plan. In December 1949, the noncommunist countries withdrew from the WFTU and set up their own international labor organization, the **International Confederation of Free Trade Unions**. The WFTU continued as a communist-dominated organization, but since the collapse of the Soviet Union in 1989 has lost much of its support. Its membership is largely confined to countries where independent organized labor is not permitted. At the 2005 congress, Mohamad Shaban Assouz from Syria was elected president. In 2009, the WFTU claimed to represent 70 million members, compared with 120 million in 2000 and 214 million in 1991.

YEMEN. Part of the Ottoman Empire until 1918, Yemen had a precarious independence until the late 1940s. Poverty, the lack of democratic tradition, and conflict between royalist and extreme **socialist** ideologies made for political instability and warfare that resulted in the splitting of the country in 1967. North and South Yemen were not reunited until May 1990, and the first general election was not held until April 1993. Despite this unpromising political and economic background, Yemeni civil society gave rise to **human rights** and **women's** groups, cooperatives, and labor unions. In 1990, the General Federation of Workers' Trade Unions of Yemen (GFWTU) was created, uniting Yemeni labor unions just before the country's reunification and claimed a **membership** of 350,000. Since 1990, the GFWTU has been an active player in promoting democracy in Yemen and became an affiliate of the **International Confederation of Free Trade Unions** in 2002, with a declared membership of 300,000. In late 2002, a new labor law came into force that met most of the **International Labour Organization** standards, but with some restrictions such as banning **strikes** at ports, airports, and hospitals. Yemen joined the **International Trade Union Confederation (ITUC)** and its affiliate declared a membership of 350,000 in 2010. The ITUC has complained that labor rights remain restricted, an assessment demonstrated by the dismissal of strikers in 2009.

YOUTH. Youth traditionally became union members in most Western countries through the completion of an **apprenticeship**, a system of trade training and employment. Since the 1960s, apprenticeship has declined and this, along with other changes in the labor market, has made it harder for organized labor to recruit youth. By the 1970s, it was noted that youth often had broken work experience (whether through choice or necessity) and that their relatively high labor mobility contributed to their low **membership** of organized labor. Also, youth are often employed in relatively low-skilled jobs in wholesale and retail trade, an industry where union membership is low and labor turnover high. Youth also suffer from disproportionately high levels of unemployment even in periods of prosperity.

In 1999, the **International Confederation of Free Trade Unions** recognized the need for organized labor to make a greater effort to recruit youth into organized labor, but few of its affiliates have done so. Between 1995 and 2010, the total share of union members aged under 25 fell from 23 to 8 percent in **Australia** and from 6 to 4 percent in the **United States**. *See also* CHILD LABOR.

YUGOSLAVIA. The former federal republic of Yugoslavia was created in 1918 from part of the Austro-Hungarian Empire; it lasted until 1991 when it was torn apart by a murderous civil war. Within the borders of the former republic, organized labor first emerged in the form of mutual aid societies in the 1870s. The first labor unions were formed in 1894 in **Slovenia**, in 1904 in **Croatia** and **Serbia**, and in 1905 in **Bosnia-Herzegovina**, **Macedonia**, and **Montenegro**. In 1904, when it became affiliated with the **International Federation of Trade Unions (IFTU)**, Serbia had about 5,100 union members; Croatia became an affiliate in 1907 and Bosnia in 1910. By 1913, the number of union members in these countries was 10,000 in Serbia, 7,000 in Croatia, and 5,000 in Bosnia.

After the creation of Yugoslavia, a Communist Party and a national labor federation were formed in 1919. By 1920, there were 25,000 union members, but following a number of **strikes**, the Communist Party and the labor federation were banned by the government. A new labor federation was formed by the **communists** and those unions not affiliated with any political party. In 1922, the Social Democrats set up a labor federation called the *United Federation of Workers' Unions of Yugoslavia,* which was an affiliate of the IFTU until 1939. From 1934, the United Federation of Workers' Unions of Yugoslavia became more militant through communist influence; in 1935, the government challenged its power by setting up a labor federation modeled on the fascist example of **Italy** and **Germany**. Before its suppression in 1940, the federation claimed 100,000 members.

After the Nazi withdrawal in December 1944, a new labor federation was established in 1945, which adopted its present title, *Savez Sindikata Jugoslaviji,* in 1948. Reflecting Yugoslavia's independence from Soviet control, it withdrew from the **World Federation of Trade Unions** in 1950, although relations improved after 1969. Organized labor in Yugoslavia was given greater freedom than elsewhere in Eastern Europe between 1948 and 1988 (e.g., in being able to conduct local strikes). In late 1988, the first independent demonstrations occurred among Yugoslav employees. Independent labor unions were formed during 1989 by **railroad** engineers and airline pilots. Of the separate republics created by the breakup of Yugoslavia, only Slovenia has not been admitted to membership of the **International Trade Union Confederation**.

YUGOSLAVIA (FEDERAL REPUBLIC). A remnant nation created from the federal republic of **Yugoslavia** in 1991, Yugoslavia (Federal Republic) has been represented in the **International Confederation of Free Trade Unions (ICFTU)** since 2000 by two labor federations in Serbia and Montenegro with a combined membership of 243,700. The ICFTU has reported that procedure for the registration of unions is difficult, requiring the consent of the employer. It also reported harassment of union officials and members in 2002. On 3 February 2003, the name of the country was officially changed to *State Union of Serbia and Montenegro.* In 2006, the two countries declared independence from one another: **Serbia** and **Montenegro.**

Z

ZAIRE. *See* CONGO (DEMOCRATIC REPUBLIC).

ZAMBIA. Zambia has been independent from the **United Kingdom** since October 1964; organized labor in Zambia dates from the early 1930s when there were tensions between European and African miners. Labor unions were legalized in 1949. The Northern Rhodesia Trades Union Congress was an affiliate of the **International Confederation of Free Trade Unions (ICFTU)** by 1957 and claimed 9,300 members. After independence, the government disapproved of union federations or individual unions joining international labor bodies. The Zambia Congress of Trade Unions (formed in 1965) did not affiliate with the ICFTU until 1990 and claimed 299,000 members by 2001. Zambia's dependence on copper exports made its economy vulnerable to the fall in the world price of copper since 1975 and was the underlying cause of economic malaise and social unrest. Although the laws of Zambia tolerate organized labor, both the ICFTU and the **International Trade Union Confederation (ITUC)** have complained about the government's increasingly antiunion policies since 1999 regarding **strikes** over falling pay and living standards, particularly among government employees, and that there had not been a single legal strike in Zambia since 1994. In 2006, strikes were violently suppressed. Chinese-owned companies have been conspicuous in their hostility to organized labor. In 2010, the Zambia Congress of Trade Unions declared a membership of 350,000 to the ITUC.

ZIMBABWE. Zimbabwe has been independent from the **United Kingdom** since April 1980, although ruled by a minority European government that declared its independence in 1965. The first unions were formed by Europeans in the early 20th century. The first African union, the Industrial and Commercial Workers' Union, was formed in 1927. As in other African countries, organized labor was closely associated with the independence movement. Although some biracial unions developed, notably among miners and steelworkers, most unions were of one race only. The Zimbabwe Congress of Trade Unions affiliated with the **International Confederation of Free Trade Unions** in 1991 and claimed a **membership** of 361,000. Since the late

1990s, organized labor has been caught up in the tyranny and violence of the Robert Mugabe government and economic decline. In its survey of **violations of trade union rights** for 2007, the **International Trade Union Confederation (ITUC)** noted the use of workers' committees (begun in 1985) to undermine labor unions, the exemption of the **export processing zones** from labor regulation, and a general climate of heightened violence, harassment, and intimidation by the government against the leaders of organized labor as well as other opponents of the Mugabe government. In September 2006, security forces quelled a demonstration with mass arrests and beatings of union leaders, actions that were publicly supported by Mugabe. In 2008, trade unionists were arrested and tortured, and women activists were sexually assaulted. In 2009, the ITUC reported that the incidence of the violations of trade union rights was lower than in previous years, a reflection of the power-sharing agreement with the opposition.

Appendix A
International Federation of Trade
Unions: Leaders, 1901–1945

Presidents/Country of Origin	Period of Office
Carl LEGIEN (1861–1920)/Germany*	1901–1919
James Henry THOMAS (1874–1949)/United Kingdom	1920–1924
Albert Arthur William PURCELL (1872–1935)/United Kingdom	1925–1928
Walter McLennan CITRINE (1887–1983)/United Kingdom*	1928–1945
Secretary/Country of Origin	
Carl LEGIEN (1861–1920)/Germany*	1901–1919
Jan OUDEGEEST (1870–1950)/Netherlands (joint secretary)	1919–1927
Edo FIMMEN (1881–1942)/Netherlands (joint secretary)*	1919–1927
General Secretary/Country of Origin	
Johann SASSENBACH (1866–1940)/Germany*	1927–1930 (interim)
Walther SCHEVENELS (1894–1966)/Belgium*	1930–1945

*Entry in Dictionary.

Source: Walther Schevenels, *Forty-Five Years: International Federation of Trade Unions* (Brussels: Board of Trustees of the International Federation of Trade Unions, 1956), *passim.*

Appendix B
International Confederation of Free
Trade Unions (1949–2006) and International
Trade Union Confederation (2006–2011):
General Secretaries, 1949–2011

Name	Period of Office
Jacobus Hendrik OLDENBROEK (1897–1970)*	1949–1960
Omer BECU (1902–1982)	1960–1967
Harm G. BUITER (1922–2011)	1967–1971
Otto KERSTEN (1928–1982)	1972–1982
John VANDERVEKEN (1930–)	1982–1992
Enzo FRISO (1927–)	1992–1994
Bill JORDAN (1936–)*	1995–2001
Guy RYDER (1957–)*	2002–2010
Sharan BURROW (1954–)	2010–

*Entry in Dictionary.

Source: Trade Union World, September 1999, p. 36; December 2001–January 2002, p. 30; www.ituc-csi
.org.

Appendix C
International Trade Union
Confederation: Affiliates, February 2011

Country	Affiliated Organization	Members (thousands)
Region	AFRICA	
Algeria	*Union Générale des Travailleurs Algériens*	1,533.0
Angola	*Central Geral de Sindicatos Independentes e Livres de Angola*	51.0
	União Nacional dos Trabalhadores de Angola	215.5
Benin	*Confédération des Organisations Syndicales Indépendantes du Bénin*	53.5
	Confédération Générale des Travailleurs du Bénin	51.5
	Union Nationale des Syndicats des Travailleurs du Bénin	36.0
	Confédération des Syndicats Autonomes du Bénin	53.0
Botswana	*Botswana Federation of Trade Unions*	56.0
Burkina Faso	*Organisation Nationale des Syndicats Libres*	42.5
	Confédération Syndicale Burkinabé	19.0
	Confédération Nationale des Travailleurs Burkinabé	10.5
	Union Syndicale des Travailleurs du Burkina	8.7
Burundi	*Confédération des Syndicats du Burundi*	12.0
	Confédération Syndicale du Burundi	5.5
Cameroon	*Confédération Syndicale des Travailleurs du Cameroun*	150.0
	Confédération des Syndicats Autonomes du Cameroun	75.0
	Unions des Syndicats Libres du Cameroun	50.0
Cape Verde	*Confederaçao Caboverdiana dos Syndicatos Livres*	19.8
	União Nacional dos Trabalhadores de Cabo Verde—Central Sindical	15.0
Central African Republic	*Confédération Syndicale des Travailleurs de Centrafique*	11.1
	Confédération Nationale des Travailleurs Centrafricains	16.0

313

Country	Affiliated Organization	Members (thousands)
Chad	Confédération Libre des Travailleurs du Tchad	42.0
	Union des Syndicats du Tchad	55.0
Comoros	Confédération des Travailleuses et Travailleurs des Comores	5.0
Congo	Confédération des Syndicats Libres et Autonomes du Congo	19.0
	Confédération Syndicale des Travailleurs du Congo	69.0
	Confédération Syndicale Congolaise	25.0
Côte d'Ivoire	Union Générale des Travailleurs de Côte d'Ivoire	208.1
	Confédération des Syndicats libres de Côte d'Ivoire	120.0
Democratic Republic of the Congo	Confédération Démocratique du Travail	51.0
	Confédération Syndicale du Congo	390.0
	Union Nationale des Travailleurs du Congo	51.0
Djibouti	Union Djiboutienne du Travail	13.0
Eritrea	National Confederation of Eritrean Workers	26.0
Ethiopia	Confederation of Ethiopian Trade Unions	203.6
Gabon	Confédération Gabonaise des Syndicats Libres	19.0
	Confédération Syndicale Gabonaise	22.8
Gambia	Gambia Workers' Confederation	52.0
Ghana	Trades Union Congress Ghana	275.0
	Ghana Federation of Labour	48.2
Guinea	Confédération Nationale des Travailleurs de Guinée	100.5
	Organisation Nationale des Syndicats Libres de Guinée	43.0
	Union Syndicale des Travailleurs de Guinée	41.0
Guinea-Bissau	Union Nationale des Travailleurs de Guinée Bissau	50.0
Kenya	Central Organisation of Trade Unions	234.0
Liberia	Liberia Labour Congress	6.0
Madagascar	Fivondronamben'ny Mpiasa Malagasy. Confédération des Travailleurs Malgaches	15.0
	Firaisan'ny Sendikan'ny Mpiasan'ny Madagasikare	25.4
	Sendika Krisitianina Malgasy—Confédération Chrétienne des Syndicats Malgaches	32.8
	Union des Syndicats Autonomes du Madagascar	4.6
Malawi	Malawi Congress of Trade Unions	200.0
Mali	Union Nationale des Travailleurs du Mali	130.0

Country	Affiliated Organization	Members (thousands)
Mauritania	Confédération Générale des Travailleurs de Mauritanie	25.0
	Confédération Libre des Travailleurs de Mauritanie	56.0
	Confédération Nationale des Travailleurrs de Mauritanie	18.5
	Union des Travailleurs de Mauritanie	28.8
Mauritius	Mauritius Trade Union Congress	15.0
	National Trade Unions Confederation	35.0
	Mauritius Labour Congress	10.0
Morocco	Union Marocaine du Travail	320.0
	Confédération Démocratique du Travail	61.5
	Union Générale des Travailleurs du Maroc	750.6
Mozambique	Organiçaô dos Trabalhadores de Moçambique	97.3
Namibia	National Union of Namibian Workers	80.0
	Trade Union Congress of Namibia	42.1
Niger	Union des Syndicats des Travailleurs du Niger	38.0
	Confédération Démocratique des Travailleurs du Niger	35.0
	Confédération Nigérienne du Travail	75.0
Nigeria	Nigeria Labour Congress	2,000.0
	Trade Union Congress of Nigeria	500.0
Rwanda	Congrès du Travail et de la Fraternité au Rwanda	15.0
	Centrale des Syndicats des Travailleurs du Rwanda	70.0
Sao Tome and Principe	Organiçaô Nacional dos Trabalhadores de São Tomé E Principe—Central Sindical	3.3
	União Geral de Trabalhadores de São Tomé e Principe	7.7
Senegal	Confédération Nationale des Travailleurs du Sénégal	64.0
	Confédération Nationale des Travailleurs du Sénégal—Forces du Changement	13.9
	Confédération des Syndicats Autonomes du Sénégal	40.0
	Union Démocratique des Travailleurs du Sénégal	20.0
	Union Nationale des Syndicats Autonomes du Sénégal	53.0
Sierra Leone	Sierra Leone Labour Congress	25.0
	Central Confederation of Trade Unions	8.3
South Africa	National Council of Trade Unions	310.0

Country	Affiliated Organization	Members (thousands)
	Congress of South African Trade Unions	1,800.0
	Confederation of South African Workers' Unions	290.0
	Federation of Unions of South Africa	360.0
Swaziland	Swaziland Federation of Labour	10.9
	Swaziland Federation of Trade Unions	65.0
Tanzania	Zanzibar Trade Union Congress	15.0
	Trade Unions' Congress of Tanzania	350.0
Togo	Confédération Nationale des Travailleurs du Togo	55.0
	Confédération Syndicale des Travailleurs du Togo	79.2
	Union Nationale des Syndicats Indépendants du Togo	8.1
Tunisia	Union Générale Tunisienne du Travail	517.0
Uganda	National Organisation of Trade Unions	146.0
Zambia	Zambia Congress of Trade Unions	350.0
Zimbabwe	Zimbabwe Congress of Trade Unions	242.0
TOTAL AFRICA		**14,182.8**
Region	ASIA	
Bangladesh	Bangladesh Mukto Sramik Federation	204.0
	Bangladesh Free Trade Union Congress	85.0
	Bangladesh Labour Federation	102.0
	Bangladesh Jatyatabadi Sramik Dal	180.0
	Jatio Sramik League	150.0
	Bangladesh Sanjukta Sramik Federation	155.0
Burma	Federation of Trade Unions—Burma	10.0
Hong Kong, SAR China	Hong Kong and Kowloon Trades Union Council	5.0
	Hong Kong Confederation of Trade Unions	170.0
India	Hind Mazdoor Sabha	5,788.8
	Indian National Trade Union Congress	8,200.0
	Self-Employed Women's Association	1,256.9
Indonesia	Confederation of Indonesian Trade Union	506.2
	Konfederasi Serikat Buruh Sejahtera Indonesia	511.0
Japan	Japanese Trade Union Confederation	6,615.6
Korea, South	Federation of Korean Trade Unions	878.6
	Korean Confederation of Trade Unions	812.5
Malaysia	Malaysian Trades Union Congress	400.0
Mongolia	Confederation of Mongolian Trade Unions	450.0
Nepal	Nepal Trade Union Congress—Independent	350.0
	General Federation of Nepalese Trade Unions	330.6
Pakistan	All-Pakistan Trade Union Congress	110.0
	Pakistan Workers' Federation	880.0

Country	Affiliated Organization	Members (thousands)
Philippines	Trade Union Congress of the Philippines	475.0
	Federation of Free Workers	27.0
Singapore	National Trades Union Congress	228.4
Sri Lanka	Ceylon Workers' Congress	190.0
	National Trade Union Federation	400.0
	National Workers' Congress	82.9
	Sri Lanka Nidahas Sevaka Sangamaya	68.0
Taiwan	Chinese Federation of Labor	250.0
Thailand	Labour Congress of Thailand	25.0
	National Congress Private Industrial of Employees	150.0
	State Enterprises Workers' Relations Confederation	50.0
	Thai Trade Union Congress	25.0
TOTAL ASIA		**30,122.5**

Region	MIDDLE EAST	
Azerbaijan	Azerbaycan Hemkarlar Ittifaqlari Konfederasiyasi	735.0
Bahrain	General Federation of Bahrain Trade Unions	10.0
Israel	General Federation of Labor in Israel (Histadrut)	450.0
Jordan	General Federation of Jordanian Trade Unions	120.0
Kuwait	Kuwait Trade Union Federation	34.3
Palestine	Palestine General Federation of Trade Unions	318.0
Turkey	Kamu Emekçileri Sendikalari Konfederasyonu	200.0
	Türkiye Isçi Sendikalari Konfederasyonu (TÜRK-IS)	820.0
	Devrimci Isçi Sendikalari Konfederasyonu	30.0
	Türkiye Hak Isçi Sendikalari Konfederasyonu (HAK-IS)	330.0
Yemen	General Federation of Workers' Trade Unions of Yemen	350.0
TOTAL MIDDLE EAST		**3,397.3**

Region	OCEANIA	
Australia	Australian Council of Trade Unions	1,716.4
Cook Islands	Cook Islands Workers' Association Inc.	1.2
Fiji	Fiji Trades Union Congress	33.0
French Polynesia	Confédération Syndicale A Tia I Mua	3.7
Kiribati	Kiribati Trades Union Congress	2.6
New Zealand	New Zealand Council of Trade Unions	200.0
Samoa	Samoa Trade Union Congress	1.5
TOTAL OCEANIA		**1,958.4**

Country	Affiliated Organization	Members (thousands)
Region	EUROPEAN UNION	
Austria	Österreichischer Gewerkschaftsbund	1,222.2
Belgium	Fédération Générale du Travail de Belgique	1,434.5
	Centrale générale des Syndicats libéraux de Belgique	265.0
	Confédération des Syndicats Chrétiens	1,587.1
Bulgaria	Confederation of Labor (PODKREPA)	153.4
	Confederation of Independent Trade Unions in Bulgaria	220.0
Cyprus	Democratic Labour Federation of Cyprus	9.5
	Cyprus Workers' Confederation	64.9
Czech Republic	Czech-Moravian Confederation of Trade Unions (CMKOS)	444.6
Denmark	Landsorganisationen i Danmark	1,201.3
	Funktionaerernes og Tjenestemaendenes Faellesrad	358.0
	Akademikernes Centralorganisation	147.1
Estonia	Confederation of Estonian Trade Unions (EAKL)	34.0
Finland	Suomen Ammattiliittojen Keskusjärjestö	758.0
	Confederation of Unions for Professional and Managerial Staff in Finland	382.0
	Finnish Confederation of Professionals	418.0
France	Confédération Générale du Travail—Force Ouvrière	800.0
	Confédération Française des Travailleurs Chrétiens	140.0
	Confédération Générale du Travail	660.0
	Confédération Française Démocratique du Travail	814.4
	Union Interprofessionelle de la Réunion	16.0
Germany	Deutscher Gewerkschaftsbund	6,000.0
Great Britain	Trades Union Congress	6,201.4
Greece	Greek General Confederation of Labour	300.0
Hungary	Democratic League of Independent Trade Unions (LIGA)	110.0
	Magyar Szakszervezetel Orszáagos Szövetsége (MSZOSZ)	400.0
	Autonomous Trade Union Confederation	120.0
	National Federation of Workers' Councils	45.2
Ireland	Irish Congress of Trade Unions	833.5
Italy	Confederazione Italiana Sindacati Lavoratori	4,507.3

Country	Affiliated Organization	Members (thousands)
	Unione Italiana del Lavoro	2,174.2
	Confederazione Generale Italiana del Lavoro	5,542.7
Latvia, Republic of	Free Trade Union Confederation of Latvia (LBAS)	110.6
Lithuania	Lithuanian Trade Union Confederation	60.0
	Lithuanian Trade Union "Solidarumas"	8.0
	Lithuanian Labour Federation	18.5
Luxembourg	Confédération Syndicale Indépendantl du Luxembourg	68.5
	Lëtzebuerger Chrëstleche Gewerkschafts-Bond	36.0
Malta	General Workers' Union	30.0
	Confederation of Malta Trade Unions	30.4
Netherlands	Federatie Nederlandse Vakbeweging	1,376.0
	Christelijk Nationaal Vakverbond	336.7
Poland	Niezalezny Samorzadny Zwiazek Zawodowy— "Solidarnosc"	667.6
	Ogólnopolskie Porozumienie Zwiazków Zawodowych	318.0
Portugal	Uniâo Geral de Trabalhadores	260.0
Romania	Confederatia Nationale a Sindicatelor Libere din România—Fratia	520.0
	Confederatia Sindicatelor Democratice din Romania	101.0
	Blocul National Sindical	150.0
	Confederatia Nationala Sindicala Cartel Alfa	1,000.0
Slovakia	Confederation of Trade Unions of the Slovak Republic (KOZSR)	337.6
Spain	Euskal Sindikatua—Basque Country	115.0
	Unión General de Trabajadores	880.0
	Confederación Sindical de Comisiones Obreras	1,200.0
	Unión Syndical Obrera	110.0
Sweden	Landsorganisationen i Sverige	1,564.8
	Tjänstemännens Centralorganisation	975.0
	Sveriges Akademikers Centralorganisation	579.9
TOTAL EUROPEAN UNION		**48,217.9**
Region	REST OF EUROPE	
Albania	Confederation of the Trade Unions of Albania	105.0
	Union of the Independent Trade Unions of Albania	84.0
Belarus	Belarusian Congress of Democratic Trade Unions	9.0

Country	Affiliated Organization	Members (thousands)
Bosnia-Herzegovina	Konfederacija Sindikata Bosne I Hercegovine	223.0
Croatia	Union of Autonomous Trade Unions of Croatia	164.7
	Independent Trade Unions of Croatia— Nezavisni Hrvatski Sindikati	113.6
Cyprus (Turkish part)	Cyprus Turkish Trade Unions Federation	3.5
Georgia	Georgian Trade Union Confederation	235.8
Iceland	Athydusamband Islands (Icelandic Confederation of Labour)	109.3
	Bandalag Starfsmanna Rikis og Baeja	20.4
Kosovo	Bashkimi I Sindikatave të Pavarura të Kosovëj	70.5
Liechtenstein	Liechtensteinischer Arbeitnehmerinnen-verband	1.2
Macedonia	Union of Independent and Autonomous Trade Unions of Macedonia	5.3
Moldova	Confederatia Nationala e Sindicatelor din Moldova	450.0
Montenegro	Confederation of Trade Unions of Montenegro	61.3
Norway	Landsorganisasjonen i Norge	865.6
	Confederation of Unions for Professionals	288.0
	Confederation of Vocational Unions	209.3
Russian Federation	Condeferation of Labour of Russia	1,250.0
	Federation of Independent Trade Unions of Russia (FNPR)	27,800.0
San Marino	Confederazione Democratica Lavoratori Sammarinesi	5.9
	Confederazione Sammarinese del Lavoro	5.0
Serbia	Confederation of Autonomous Trade Unions of Serbia	465.0
	Ujedinjeni Granski Sindikati Nezavisnost	158.0
Switzerland	Schweizerischer Gewerkschaftsbund / Union Syndicale Suisse	377.3
Ukraine	All-Ukrainian Union of Workers' Solidarity	150.0
	Confederation of Free Trade Unions of Ukraine	268.0
	Federation of Trade Unions of Ukraine	8,680.0
Vatican	Associazione Dipendenti Laici Vaticani	0.3
TOTAL REST OF EUROPE		**42,179.0**

Country	Affiliated Organization	Members (thousands)
Region	NORTH AMERICA	
Canada	Canadian Labour Congress/Congrès du travail du Canada	1,500.0
	Confédération des Syndicats Nationaux	300.0
	Centrale des Syndicats Démocratiques	72.5
	Christian Labour Association of Canada	51.0
United States	American Federation of Labor–Congress of Industrial Organizations (AFL-CIO)	8,400.0
TOTAL NORTH AMERICA		**10,323.5**
Region	LATIN AMERICA AND CARIBBEAN	
Antigua and Barbuda	Antigua & Barbuda Workers' Union	3.0
	Antigua & Barbuda Public Service Association	1.0
Argentina	Confederación General del Trabajo de la República Argentina	4,401.0
	Central de los Trabajadores Argentinos	600.0
Aruba (affiliated to the European Union)	Federación de Trahadornan di Aruba	2.5
Barbados	Barbados Workers' Union	15.0
Bermuda	Bermuda Industrial Union	4.0
	Bermuda Trade Union Congress	5.0
Bonaire (affiliated to the European Union)	Federación Boneriana di Trabao	0.5
Brazil	Confederaçâo Nacional das Profissões Liberais	260.0
	Força Sindical	2,100.0
	Central Única dos Trabalhadores	7,464.8
	União Geral dos Trabalhadores	1,350.2
Chile	Central Unitaria de Trabajadores de Chile	400,0
	Central Autónoma de Trabajadores de Chile	107.0
	Unión Nacional de Trabajadores de Chile	92.0
Colombia	Confederación de Trabajadores de Colombia	250.0
	Central Unitaria de Trabajadores	510.5
	Confederación General del Trabajo	700.0
Costa Rica	Confederación de Trabajadores Rerum Novarum	30.0
	Central del Movimiento de Trabajadores Costarricenses	108.0

Country	Affiliated Organization	Members (thousands)
	Sentral di Sindikatonan di Korsou	4.0
Dominica	Dominica Trade Union	0.8
	Waterfront and Allied Workers' Union	0.9
	Dominica Almagamated Workers' Union	2.5
Dominican Republic	Confederación Nacional de Trabajadores Dominicanos	143.0
	Confederación Nacional de Unidad Syndical	105.0
	Confederación Autónoma Sindical Clasista	172.0
Ecuador	Confederación Sindical de Trabajadoras y Trabajadores del Ecuador	110.0
	Central Ecuatoriana de Organizaciones Clasistas	62.5
El Salvador	Central de Trabajadores Democráticos de El Salvador	50.0
	Central Autónoma de Trabajadores Salvadoreños	30.0
Grenada	Grenada Trades' Union Council	8.0
Guatemala	Confederación de Unidad Sindical de Guatemala	30.0
	Central General de Trabajadores de Guatemala	60.0
	Unión Sindical de Trabajadores de Guatemala	17.5
Haiti	Confédération des Travailleurs Haïtiens	65.0
Honduras	Confederación de Trabajadores de Honduras	55.0
	Central General de Trabajadores	250.0
	Confederación Unitaria de Trabajadores de Honduras	295.0
Mexico	Confederación Revolucionaria de Obreros y Campesinos	1,251.0
	Consejo Nacional de los Trabajadores	6.0
	Unión Nacional de Trabajadores	500.0
	Confederación de Trabajadores de Mexico	1,500.0
Nicaragua	Central de Trabajadores de Nicaragua	25.4
	Frente Nacional de los Trabajadores	139.3
	Confederación de Unificación Syndical	30.0
	Central Sandinista de Trabajadores	40.0
Panama	Confederación de Trabajadores de la República de Panamá	40.0
	Confederación General de Trabajadores de Panamá	53.3
	Convergencia Sindical	33.8
Paraguay	Central Unitaria de Trabajadores Auténtica	40.0
	Central Nacional de Trabajadores	120.8
Peru	Central Autónoma de Trabajadores del Perú	12.7

Country	Affiliated Organization	Members (thousands)
St. Lucia	National Workers' Union	3.0
	St. Lucia Seamen, Waterfront and General Workers' Trade Union	1.0
Surinam	Algemeen Verbond van Vakverenigingen in Suriname "De Moederbond"	5.4
	Organisatie van Samenwerkende Autonome Vakbonden	5.0
Trinidad and Tobago	All Trinidad General Workers' Trade Union	0.5
	National Trade Union Centre of Trinidad and Tobago	45.0
Venezuela	Confederación de Trabajadores de Venezuela	250.0
	Allianza Sindical Independiente	120.0
TOTAL LATIN AMERICA AND CARIBBEAN		**24,118.3**
WORLD TOTAL		**175,393,026**

Note: The membership shown is that declared by affiliates.

Source: International Trade Union Confederation.

Appendix D
Organized Labor: Historical Statistics

THE NEGLECT OF LABOR UNION STATISTICS

The tables in this appendix trace the growth and main features of labor union membership in the world since about 1870, with an emphasis on recent developments. The figures refer to labor unions able to engage in collective bargaining in a reasonably free political and legal environment and exclude countries whose unions were (or are) under the effective control of an authoritarian government such as under fascism or communism.

Although, like any historical statistical series, they present problems, the absence of data on labor unions in the main readily available reference books on historical statistics is a powerful reason for their presentation here. For example, B. R. Mitchell, *International Historical Statistics: Europe, 1750–1988* (New York: Stockton Press, 1992), follows his earlier international statistical works and gives data on the negative side of organized labor, that is labor disputes, but ignores labor union membership despite the time series information available in George S. Bain and Robert Price, *Profiles of Union Growth: A Comparative Statistical Portrait of Eight Countries* (Oxford: Basil Blackwell, 1980). The second volume of the monumental data book by Peter Flora et al., *State, Economy, and Society in Western Europe, 1815–1975* (Chicago: St. James Press, 1987), had been planned to include labor union membership data, but this chapter was never completed.

Despite their social and economic importance, neither the United Nations nor the International Labour Organisation (ILO) accept the responsibility to regularly collect and publish global labor union statistics. This is a staggering omission from the global statistical record given that there were 176 million labor union members in the world in 2010. Membership data are gathered by the International Trade Union Confederation, but their efforts could hardly be described as readily available compared with those of the United Nations or the ILO; nor are they complete for a number of countries (namely, the United States, Canada, Germany, Japan, Malta, and Switzerland) as they record only affiliates. Despite these defects, this is the only single international source available from 1949.

The record of the ILO is particularly strange in this field. Since 1927, it has been publishing world labor dispute statistics—information of often dubious accuracy and comparability between countries—but ignores the union membership data that are available for many member countries. The call made in the previous editions of this work for the ILO to remedy this gaping statistical hole in a comprehensive, ongoing, systematic fashion is repeated here, particularly in regard to the growth of female membership of international organized labor.

The need for an international impetus in this area has also been shown by the way in which certain countries have reduced their official statistical collections of labor union membership figures. Examples include Switzerland (which reduced its coverage greatly after 1987) and Australia (which ceased its annual census of labor unions in 1996 and reduced the amount of data it published on union members after 1999).

Virtually the only positive recent development in this field has been the creation of the Database on the Institutional Characteristics of Trade Unions, Wage Setting, State Intervention, and Social Pacts under the leadership of Jelle Visser at Amsterdam. Covering 34 countries with data mainly dating from 1960, this database can be accessed from the Internet. It is especially useful for monitoring trends in Eastern Europe.

ORGANIZED LABOR STATISTICS AS A SOURCE

There are two main categories of organized labor statistics: dispute statistics and union membership statistics. National collections of labor dispute statistics began earlier than for labor union members, largely because such disputes were seen by governments as a threat to the existing political and economic order. These data were easier to compile than for union membership because they could be obtained from employers, the press, and perhaps the labor unions.

In contrast, labor union membership statistics could only be supplied by the unions themselves, which may be unwilling to do so because of political suspicion, hostility, or lack of perceived gain. For instance, the legal recognition of labor unions in Australia in the late 19th century made provision for the registration of unions, but this did not result in the comprehensive registration of unions as there was little benefit to be gained from doing so. But when the system of compulsory arbitration and conciliation was introduced after 1900, unions had to be registered to participate in the benefits of the system. Similarly, India's voluntary system of union registration has meant that its published membership figures since 1932 have underestimated the true level of union membership.

There are two significant obstacles to preparing historical statistics on the membership of labor unions. One is the nature of the membership data. Labor union membership is often very difficult to measure accurately because of high labor turnover in some occupations, retirees who continue to be union members (this is an important feature of labor union membership in the United Kingdom, Germany, and the United States), and the difficulty of keeping track of members who remain members but have ceased to pay their dues. Also, unions may exaggerate their membership to increase their bargaining power with employers or to gain greater representation at general conferences of unions.

The second challenge posed is linking union membership figures to the labor force of their particular countries. The concept of the *labor force* is fairly recent in statistical history, only being adopted widely since the 1930s. Before that, a variety of concepts and definitions were used, which limits international comparisons over time.

THE LABOR FORCE

Understanding the structure of the labor force is essential to studying organized labor and how it fits into the economy and broader society. The main components of the labor force are set out in the following diagrams. The first diagram shows how the principal groups that make up the labor force can be identified within the total population. For the purposes of studying organized labor, the main groups are employers and employees. It must be stressed that this is a comparatively modern way of looking at the labor force and that the relative importance of the relationships shown has changed over time. For example, the proportions of self-employed and those who worked in family enterprises were far higher before 1900 than after it.

Schema of the Labor Force

Total Population			
Labor Force (Includes Unemployed)			
Employed Labor Force			
Employer	Self-Employed	**Employee**	
		Union Member	Nonunion Member

Within the employed labor force, it is important to grasp the distinction between an individual's industry and occupation to appreciate how the various divisions within the labor force have been a source of conflict within organized labor, particularly the century-old debate over whether unions should be organized by occupation or by industry.

The following diagram sets out some of the features of the relationship between industry and occupation. It is based on how the United States classifies its labor force, but the broad principles are used by many other countries. Again, this is a modern way of examining the labor force, and the diagram makes no attempt to capture the large shifts in the industrial and occupational composition of the labor force that have occurred since 1900. Chief among these shifts have been the decline of the primary industrial sector, and since about 1950 the rise of the tertiary or service sector. As well, the occupational composition of the labor force has been greatly altered by technological change and the general maturing of Western economies. This has been most evident in the growth of white-collar jobs and the stagnation in the number of blue-collar jobs. Further consideration of these trends is outside the purpose of this appendix, but it is sufficient to draw the reader's attention to an analytical framework that can also be used for historical research.

Only a few countries in the world are fortunate enough to possess labor force statistics covering the last 100 years. The main source for this informa-

Schema of the Relationship between Industry and Occupation

INDUSTRIES		
Primary	Secondary	Tertiary
Agriculture and mining	Manufacturing	Service (all other industries)
OCCUPATIONS		
White-collar:	White-collar:	White-collar:
Managerial and professional	Managerial and professional	Managerial and professional
Technical, sales, and administrative support	Technical, sales, and administrative support	Technical, sales, and administrative support
Blue-collar:	Blue-collar:	Blue-collar:
Service occupations	Service occupations	Service occupations
Precision production	Precision production	Precision production
Operators, fabricators, and laborers	Operators, fabricators, and laborers	Operators, fabricators, and laborers
Farming, forestry, and fishing		

tion is the population census, which can be used to generate estimates of the number of employees at work not just for the whole economy but for particular industries and occupations. Union membership is linked to the labor force by *union density*—that is, the number of union members as a percentage of the total number of employees or of a particular subgroup of employees, for example, the percentage of employees in the manufacturing industry who are union members.

In 1940, the United States became the first country in the world to collect labor force statistics from a regular household survey, an example followed by other countries since 1945. As well as collecting standard labor force data, these surveys can also be used to monitor labor union membership. These data began to be available in 1973 for the United States (although the present survey began in 1983), in 1976 for Australia (with follow-up surveys held in 1982, 1986, and thereafter every two years to 1992, and then annually), in 1984 in Canada, in 1987 in Sweden, and annually in the United Kingdom since 1989. The European Commission has also included questions on labor union membership in its Eurobarometer Surveys at various times from 1973.

Comparisons of reported membership by unions and by those estimated from household surveys of trade union membership in Australia, the United Kingdom, and Canada in the 1980s suggest that unions tend to overestimate their memberships. Although subject to sampling error, household surveys are a far more reliable source and provide a wide range of sociodemographic information not available elsewhere, such as age, sex, birthplace, and income. Mention should also be made of the national workplace surveys that are available for the United Kingdom from 1980 and for Australia for 1989–1990 and 1995. Using data collected from employers and unions, these surveys offer important insights into labor relations that are not available from other sources, but they do not provide information on the composition of individual unions. Valuable as these surveys are, they suffer from a general lack of comparability across countries for much of the sociodemographic information they contain; this lack of standardization severely handicaps efforts to compare accurately many variables.

Needless to say, these statistics need to be subjected to the same critical scrutiny as any other historical source. What is presented here is done in the spirit of capturing a general picture of changes in union membership over the past 140 years. For many countries, the information is approximate only. Gaps indicate not just lack of data but also times when free trade unionism has been suppressed. Because data for a number of countries are not always available for the year shown, the data for the closest year have been used.

For further information on the problems of labor unions statistics as a source, the discussions in George S. Bain and Robert Price, *Profiles of Union Growth: A Comparative Statistical Portrait of Eight Countries* (Oxford: Basil

Blackwell, 1980), Jelle Visser, "Trends in Trade Union Membership," *OECD Employment Outlook*, July 1991, pp. 97–134, and Clara Chang and Constance Sorrento, "Union Membership Statistics in 12 Countries," *Monthly Labor Review*, December 1991, pp. 46–53, retain their value.

REGIONAL STATISTICS ON LABOR UNION MEMBERS

Most historical discussions of labor union membership statistics are usually concerned with the national level only, but regional unions' membership statistics are an often overlooked topic and of great interest in themselves where available. The availability of these statistics varies greatly between countries, as the following table shows.

Country	Period Available	Source
Australia	1912 to date	*Official Year Book of the Commonwealth of Australia; Year Book Australia*
India	1932–1933 to date	*Statistical Abstract for British India; Statistical Abstract, India*
Japan	1950 to date	*Year Book of Labour Statistics*
Philippines	1982 to date	*Yearbook of Labor Statistics*
Switzerland	1917–1932	*Statistisches Jahrbuch der Schweiz, 1932 ed., p. 298*
United Kingdom	1984, 1989 to date	*Employment Gazette; Labour Market Trends*
United States	1930 to date	*Directory of National Unions and Employee Associations; Statistical Abstract of the United States*

The smallest geographical unit generally available is by state (Australia, India, and United States) or prefecture (Japan), or region (Philippines and United Kingdom). For Australia, unpublished household survey data for below the state level are available from 1986. It should be noted too that regional statistics are particularly susceptible to boundary changes.

STRUCTURE OF THE APPENDIX

Part A contains tables that set out the growth and some features of organized labor in the world since 1870. Part B presents statistics on the membership of organized labor in selected countries. Part C sets out some linkages between organized labor and the labor force for selected countries. Part D compares selected structural changes in the membership of organized labor in Australia, the United Kingdom, and the United States in 1995 and 2010.

A. Organized Labor: International

1. Organized Labor: Global Growth, c. 1870–2010
2. Organized Labor: Global Changes, c. 1870–2010
3. International Federation of Trade Unions: Membership, 1901–1945
4. International Confederation of Free Trade Unions/International Trade Union Confederation: Membership, 1949–2010
5. International Confederation of Free Trade Unions/International Trade Union Confederation: Membership by Region, 1949–2010
6. Organized Labor: Largest Unions in the World, 1900–2010
7. Organized Labor: Unions with a Million or More Members, 2001 and 2010
8. Organized Labor: Reported Murders of Union Activists, 1999–2009

B. Organized Labor: Selected Countries

9. Organized Labor: Membership in Selected Countries, c. 1870–c.1890
10. Organized Labor: Membership in Selected Countries, c. 1900–1940
11. Organized Labor: Membership in Selected Countries, 1950–1970
12. Organized Labor: Membership in Selected Countries, 1980–2006
13. Organized Labor: Women Membership in Selected Countries, 1900–2010

C. Organized Labor and the Labor Force

14. Organized Labor as a Proportion of Employees: Selected Countries, c. 1900–1950
15. Organized Labor as a Proportion of Employees: Selected Countries, 1960–2006
16. Organized Labor by Selected Industry Groups: Australia, U.K., and U.S., 1900–2010
17. Organized Labor: Median Weekly Earnings, Australia and U.S., 1982/1983–2007

D. Organized Labor: Selected Changes in Membership in Australia, the U.K., and the U.S., 1995 and 2010

18. Organized Labor as a Proportion of Employees by Age: Australia, 1995 and 2010
19. Organized Labor as a Proportion of Employees by Age: U.S., 1995 and 2010
20. Organized Labor: Selected Membership Features, Australia, U.K., and U.S., 1995 and 2010

1. ORGANIZED LABOR: GLOBAL GROWTH, c. 1870–2010

Year	Western Europe	Eastern Europe	Americas	Other	Total
		Membership (thousands)			
1870	486	4	300	0	790
1880	545	0	50	11	606
1886	828	0	1,010	53	1,891
1890	1,917	0	325	263	2,505
1900	4,193	235	869	133	5,430
1913	10,060	685	2,787	589	14,121
1920	27,692	8,501	6,367	1,221	43,781
1930	17,357	2,538	6,199	4,780	30,874
1939	11,493	100	9,111	2,920	23,624
1945	17,913	0	13,632	4,020	35,565
1950	31,213	0	20,523	12,063	63,799
1960	32,794	0	25,364	17,853	76,011
1970	39,625	0	34,005	24,687	98,317
1980	49,314	0	38,103	30,317	117,734
1990	45,553	5,000	30,328	33,207	114,087
1995	42,904	11,839	42,503	42,996	140,241
2001	39,999	37,526	36,890	52,268	166,683
2010	48,568	46,866	44,867	52,701	193,001

2. ORGANIZED LABOR: GLOBAL CHANGES, C. 1870–2010

Period	Western Europe	Eastern Europe	Americas	Other	Total
		Membership Change (thousands)			
1870–1880	59	−4	−250	11	−184
1880–1886	283	0	960	42	1,285
1886–1890	1,089	0	−685	210	614
1890–1900	2,276	235	544	−130	2,925
1900–1913	5,867	450	1,918	456	8,691
1913–1920	17,632	7,816	3,580	632	29,660
1930–1930	−10,335	−5,963	−168	3,559	−12,907
1930–1939	−5,864	−2,438	2,912	−1,860	−7,250
1939–1945	6,420	−100	4,521	1,100	11,941
1945–1950	13,300	0	6,891	8,043	28,234
1950–1960	1,581	0	4,840	5,791	12,212
1960–1970	6,831	0	8,641	6,834	22,306
1970–1980	9,689	0	4,098	5,630	19,417
1980–1990	−3,762	5,000	−7,775	2,890	−3,647
1990–1995	−2,649	6,839	12,176	9,789	26,154
1995–2001	−2,905	25,688	−5,614	9,272	26,442
2001–2010	8,569	9,340	7,977	432	26,318

3. INTERNATIONAL FEDERATION OF TRADE UNIONS: MEMBERSHIP, 1901–1945

Year	Number of Country Affiliates	Membership of Affiliates (Thousands)	Percentage of World Union Members
1901	8	1,168.0	21.5
1905	14	2,949.5	—
1910	18	6,118.7	—
1913	21	7,702.4	54.6
1920	21	22,701.1	51.9
1925	21	13,366.4	—
1930	26	13,578.8	49.1
1935	23	9,078.3	—
1939	26	14,638.0	62.0
1945	21	24,751.8	69.6

4. INTERNATIONAL CONFEDERATION OF FREE TRADE UNIONS/INTERNATIONAL TRADE UNION CONFEDERATION: MEMBERSHIP, 1949–2010

Year	Number of Country Affiliates	Membership of Affiliates (Millions)	Percentage of World Union Members
1949	51	48.0	75.3
1953	63	47.3	—
1955	75	54.3	—
1959	97	56.0	73.7
1965	96	60.3	—
1969	95	63.0	64.1
1975	88	51.8	—
1979	87	67.0	52.7
1983	94	84.9	—
1989	97	80.3	70.4
1995	135	124.9	89.4
2001	148	156.5	92.1
2010	300	175.8	92.0

5. INTERNATIONAL CONFEDERATION OF FREE TRADE UNIONS/INTERNATIONAL TRADE UNION CONFEDERATION: MEMBERSHIP BY REGION, 1949–2010

Year	Western Europe	Eastern Europe	Americas	Other	Total Percentage
1949	43.0	—	42.8	14.2	100.0
1959	46.7	—	32.8	20.5	100.0
1969	39.8	7.3	37.0	15.9	100.0
1979	55.2	—	18.3	26.5	100.0
1989	43.6	—	29.1	27.3	100.0
2001	27.3	23.5	20.7	28.5	100.0
2010	26.1	26.7	19.3	27.9	100.0

6. ORGANIZED LABOR: LARGEST UNIONS IN THE WORLD, 1900–2010

Year	Country	Name	Members (millions)
1900	U.K.	Miners' Federation of Great Britain	0.4
1910	U.K.	Miners' Federation of Great Britain	0.6
1920	Germany	*Deutscher Metallarbeiter-Verband* (German Metal Workers' Union)	1.6
1933	U.K.	Miners' Federation of Great Britain	0.5
1937	U.K.	Transport and General Workers' Union	0.7
1950	Germany	*IG Metall* (Metal Workers' Industrial Union)	1.3
1960	Germany	*IG Metall* (Metal Workers' Industrial Union)	1.7
1970	Germany	*IG Metall* (Metal Workers' Industrial Union)	2.4
1980	Germany	*IG Metall* (Metal Workers' Industrial Union)	2.6
1990	Germany	*IG Metall* (Metal Workers' Industrial Union)	3.6
2001	Germany	*Ver.di* (United Services Union)	3.0
2010	U.S.	National Education Association	3.2

7. ORGANIZED LABOR: UNIONS WITH A MILLION OR MORE MEMBERS, 2001 AND 2010

Labor Union/Country	Members (millions)	
	2001	*2010*
Ver.di (United Services Union)/Germany	3.0	2.1
IG Metall (Metal Workers' Union)/Germany	2.7	2.4
National Education Association/U.S.	2.7	3.2
Service Employees' International Union/U.S.	1.4	1.8
United Food and Commercial Workers' International Union/U.S.	1.4	1.3
Teamsters/U.S.	1.4	1.4
American Federation of State, County and Municipal Employees/U.S.	1.3	1.4
UNISON/U.K.	1.3	1.4
Amicus/U.K.	1.1	—
Unite the Union/U.K. [formed from the merger of Amicus and the Transport and General Workers' Union, 2007]	—	1.6
American Federation of Teachers/U.S.	1.1	0.9

8. ORGANIZED LABOR: REPORTED MURDERS OF UNION ACTIVISTS, 1999–2009

Year	Number Murdered
1999	140
2000	209
2001	223
2002	213
2003	129
2004	145
2005	115
2006	144
2007	n.a.
2008	76
2009	101

Countries in Which Activists Were Murdered—2009

Country	Number Murdered
Total	101
Colombia	48
Guatemala	16
Honduras	12
Mexico	6
Bangladesh	6
Brazil	4
Dominican Republic	3
Philippines	3
India	1
Iraq	1
Nigeria	1

9. ORGANIZED LABOR: MEMBERSHIP IN SELECTED COUNTRIES, C. 1870–C.1890

Country	c. 1870	c. 1880	c. 1886	c. 1890
	Membership (thousands)			
Australia	—	11	50	200
Austria	—	—	—	47
Czech part of Austro-Hungarian Empire	4	—	—	—
Denmark	—	—	—	31
France	120	60a	110	232
Germany	77	21	137	357
Ireland	—	—	—	50
Italy	—	—	—	41
Netherlands	—	—	—	16
New Zealand	—	—	3	63
Norway	—	—	—	20
Spain	—	—	—	5
Sweden	—	—	—	9
U.K.	289	464	581	1,109
U.S.	300	50	1,010	325

10. ORGANIZED LABOR: MEMBERSHIP IN SELECTED COUNTRIES, C. 1900–1940

Country	c. 1900	1913	1920	1930	1940
Western Europe	Membership (thousands)				
Austria	119	263	1,004	817	—
Belgium	42	203	920	671	350
Denmark	96	153	362	339	543
Finland	—	28	59	15	66
France	492	1,027	1,053	900	1,300
Germany	850	2,974	10,517	6,925	—
Greece	—	—	—	83	—
Iceland	—	—	1	4	—
Ireland	67	70	189	102	163
Italy	280	435	3,410	—	—
Luxembourg	—	—	—	18	—
Netherlands	19	234	684	625	798
Norway	20	64	143	140	307
Portugal	—	90	100	—	—
Spain	26	128	220	946	—
Sweden	67	134	403	554	971
Switzerland	90	122	313	320	385
U.K.	2,025	4,135	8,348	4,842	6,558

10. ORGANIZED LABOR: MEMBERSHIP IN SELECTED COUNTRIES, C. 1900–1940—CONTINUED

Country	c. 1900	1913	1920	1930
Eastern Europe	Membership (thousands)			
Bosnia	—	5	—	—
Bulgaria	3	30	36	19
Croatia	—	7	—	—
Czechoslovakia	62	318	1,650	1,213
Estonia	—	—	—	13
Hungary	23	115	343	141
Latvia	—	—	—	26
Lithuania	—	—	—	18
Poland	15	160	947	979
Romania	4	40	300	80
Russia	123	—	5,200	—
Serbia	5	10	—	—
Yugoslavia	—	—	25	49

Note: No data are available for 1940.

10. ORGANIZED LABOR: MEMBERSHIP IN SELECTED COUNTRIES, C. 1900–1940—CONTINUED

Country	c. 1900	1913	1920	1930	1940
Other	Membership (thousands)				
Australia	97	498	685	856	956
Canada		176	374	322	362
Ceylon	—	—	—	114	—
China	—	—	—	2,800	—
Dutch East Indies	—	—	—	32	
Egypt	—	7	40	—	—
India	—	—	150	242	511
Japan	8	—	103	354	9
Korea	—	—	—	123	—
New Zealand	24	72	96	102	248
Palestine	—	—	4	20	—
Philippines	—	—	—	67	—
South Africa	4	12	135	118	273
U.S.	869	2,588	4,775	3,162	7,877

11. ORGANIZED LABOR: MEMBERSHIP IN SELECTED COUNTRIES, 1950–1970

Country	1950	1960	1970
	Membership (thousands)		
Australia	1,605	1,912	2,331
Austria	1,291	1,501	1,520
Belgium	1,173	1,468	1,606
Canada	1,006	1,459	2,173
Denmark	714	987	1,143
Finland	269	468	950
France	4,000	2,592	3,549
Germany	5,513	7,687	8,251
India	2,371	3,077	4,887
Ireland	285	319	381
Italy	4,798	2,887	4,646
Japan	5,774	7,662	11,605
Malta	19	30	34
Netherlands	1,160	1,354	1,585
New Zealand	267	332	379
Norway	488	542	759
Sweden	1,278	1,879	2,546
Switzerland	627	728	843
U.K.	9,243	9,835	11,178
U.S.	13,430	17,049	21,248

12. ORGANIZED LABOR: MEMBERSHIP IN SELECTED COUNTRIES, 1980–2006

Country	1980	1990	2000	2006
Australia	2,555	2,660	1,902	1,786
Austria	1,444	1,375	1,187	1,073
Belgium	1,651	1,646	1,705	1,959
Canada	3,397	4,031	4,058	4,441
Denmark	1,605	1,756	1,824	1,745
Finland	1,332	1,527	1,504	1,520
France	3,282	1,968	1,781	1,778
Germany	8,154	8,014	7,928	6,720
Ireland	545	491	550	593
Italy	7,189	5,872	5,184	5,569
Japan	12,369	12,635	11,539	9,961
Netherlands	1,517	1,348	1,574	1,530
New Zealand	516	437	319	398
Norway	938	1,034	1,129	1,176
Sweden	3,039	3,322	2,989	2,931
Switzerland	853	820	735	721
U.K.	11,652	8,952	7,149	7,086
U.S.	20,095	16,740	16,258	15,359

13. ORGANIZED LABOR: WOMEN MEMBERSHIP IN SELECTED COUNTRIES, 1900–2010

Year	U.K.	Germany	Australia	U.S.	Japan
	Women as a Percentage of Total Members				
1900	8	3	—	—	—
1913	11	8	4	4	—
1920	16	—	11	8	—
1930	16	8	14	—	—
1940	17	—	16	9	—
1950	18	18	19	17	23
1960	20	18	20	18	26
1970	25	16	24	24	—
1980	29	21	32	24	—
1990	38	26	37	37	28
1994	44	32	40	40	—
2001	47	32	43	42	—
2010	54	—	48	46	—

14. ORGANIZED LABOR AS A PROPORTION OF EMPLOYEES: SELECTED COUNTRIES, C. 1900–1950

Country	c. 1900	1913	1920	1930	1950
		Percentage of Employees			
Australia	9	34	46	51	59
Austria	3	5	51	38	62
Belgium	3	10	45	28	49
Canada	—	7	15	14	33
Denmark	14	15	35	32	52
Finland	—	14	25	5	29
France	7	13	12	9	38
Germany	6	18	53	34	35
Ireland	—	—	36	19	46
Italy	6	6	39	—	41
Japan	—	—	—	30	56
Netherlands	2	17	36	24	42
New Zealand	8	19	26	19	44
Norway	3	8	20	36	50
Sweden	5	8	28	24	68
Switzerland	10	13	26	26	39
U.K.	13	16	48	9	44
U.S.	6	9	17	3	28

15. ORGANIZED LABOR AS A PROPORTION OF EMPLOYEES: SELECTED COUNTRIES, 1960–2006

Country	1960	1970	1980	1990	2000	2006
			Percentage of Employees			
Australia	50	44	49	40	25	20
Austria	68	63	57	47	37	32
Belgium	42	42	54	54	49	54
Canada	29	31	34	34	31	30
Denmark	57	60	79	75	74	69
Finland	32	51	69	73	75	72
France	20	22	18	10	8	8
Germany	35	32	35	31	25	21
Ireland	50	59	64	57	41	35
Italy	25	37	50	39	35	33
Japan	33	35	31	26	22	18
Netherlands	40	37	35	24	23	22
New Zealand	44	39	48	49	22	23
Norway	60	57	58	59	54	55
Sweden	72	68	78	82	80	75
Switzerland	36	29	31	24	21	19
U.K.	40	45	51	39	30	29
U.S.	26	27	23	16	13	12

16. ORGANIZED LABOR BY SELECTED INDUSTRY GROUPS: AUSTRALIA, U.K., AND U.S., 1900–2010

Year	Australia	UK	USA
	MINING		
1900	21.7	28.1	15.1
1913	8.1	23.4	15.9
1920	6.1	15.1	8.7
1930	5.0	13.5	6.8
1940	5.2	11.7	8.7
1950	3.0	8.2	3.2
1960	2.0	7.5	0.6
1970	1.5	3.3	1.0
1980	2.7	3.3	1.0
1990	2.2	1.9	0.7
2001	1.2	0.3	0.4
2010	2.3	n.a.	0.4
	MANUFACTURING		
1900	14.2	43.7	34.2
1913	29.2	39.2	29.3
1920	32.5	42.2	37.9
1930	34.7	39.2	23.2
1940	39.5	38.0	38.3
1950	38.4	41.0	42.8
1960	36.1	41.7	51.3
1970	35.4	45.0	41.9
1980	24.7	29.4	29.9
1990	19.6	25.2	25.1
2001	16.3	14.9	16.3
2010	9.1	n.a.	9.6
	TRANSPORT AND COMMUICATIONS		
1900	22.5	10.6	21.8
1913	25.2	8.8	20.5
1920	21.7	16.0	24.9
1930	19.1	19.4	26.0
1940	15.6	17.6	21.8
1950	15.2	16.0	26.6
1960	12.1	14.5	13.2
1970	10.3	12.3	12.0
1980	12.0	6.1	12.3
1990	11.1	7.8	11.6
2001	10.2	9.5	10.7
2010	9.0	n.a.	9.5

16. CONTINUED

Year	Australia	UK	USA
	ALL OTHER INDUSTRIES		
1900	41.6	17.6	28.9
1913	37.5	18.6	34.3
1920	39.7	26.6	28.5
1930	41.2	27.9	44.0
1940	39.7	32.7	31.2
1950	43.4	34.8	27.4
1960	49.8	36.3	34.9
1970	52.8	39.4	30.3
1980	60.6	61.2	56.8
1990	67.1	65.1	62.1
2001	72.3	75.3	72.6
2010	79.5	n.a.	80.5

17. ORGANIZED LABOR: MEDIAN WEEKLY EARNINGS, AUSTRALIA AND U.S., 1982/1983–2007

Year	AUSTRALIA		U.S.	
	Union Members	Percentage Over Nonunion Employees	Union Members	Percentage Over Nonunion Employees
	FULL-TIME EMPLOYEES—MALES			
1982–1983	$295	3.1	$411	14.1
1986	$391	4.9	$482	18.3
1990	$506	4.2	$542	15.7
1995	$637	8.5	$640	20.8
1999	$792	6.3	$711	15.8
2002	$912	7.5	$780	16.4
2007	$1,096	10.2	$913	23.7
	FULL-TIME EMPLOYEES—FEMALES			
1982–1983	$234	1.71	$307	22.5
1986	$319	5.02	$368	25.5
1990	$426	7.51	$448	27.2
1995	$555	9.73	$527	26.8
1999	$686	9.77	$608	26.2
2002	$778	8.87	$667	23.5
2007	$919	11.5	$790	33.4
	FULL-TIME EMPLOYEES—PERSONS			
1982–1983	$276	6.88	$398	27.6
1986	$372	7.80	$444	26.8
1990	$484	8.06	$509	23.4
1995	$601	8.49	$602	25.8
1999	$758	8.31	$672	23.2
2002	$866	10.1	$740	20.7
2007	$1,067	15.9	$863	30.2

18. ORGANIZED LABOR AS A PROPORTION OF EMPLOYEES BY AGE: AUSTRALIA, 1995 AND 2010

Australia	Unions Members as % Employees		
MALES	1995	2010	% Change—1995–2010
15–24	24.4	9.6	−60.8
25–34	35.0	15.2	−56.5
35–44	40.6	18.8	−53.7
45–54	41.8	24.1	−42.2
55–64	40.5	24.6	−39.2
All ages	**35.7**	**17.9**	**−49.8**
FEMALES			
15–24	20.7	8.3	−60.1
25–34	29.5	15.3	−48.1
35–44	32.3	19.3	−40.2
45–54	34.4	25.7	−25.4
55–64	33.7	28.4	−15.7
All ages	**29.1**	**18.7**	**−35.6**
PERSONS			
15–24	22.6	8.9	−60.5
25–34	32.3	14.8	−54.0
35–44	36.8	19.0	−48.2
45–54	38.4	24.9	−35.2
55–64	38.1	26.3	−30.9
All ages	**32.7**	**18.3**	**−44.1**

19. ORGANIZED LABOR AS A PROPORTION OF EMPLOYEES BY AGE: U.S., 1995 AND 2010

U.S.	Union Members as % Employees		
MALES	1995	2010	% Change—1995–2010
	Percentage of Employee Union Members		
16–24	6.7	5.0	−25.4
25–34	13.8	10.6	−23.2
35–44	20.4	13.6	−33.3
45–54	25.5	16.3	−36.1
55–64	23.4	16.1	−31.2
All ages	**17.2**	**12.6**	**−26.7**
FEMALES			
16–24	4.4	3.6	−18.2
25–34	10.1	9.5	−5.9
35–44	14.6	12.0	−17.8
45–54	17.9	13.8	−22.9
55–64	15.5	15.3	−1.3
All ages	**12.3**	**11.1**	**−9.8**
PERSONS			
16–24	5.6	4.3	−23.2
25–34	12.1	10.1	−16.5
35–44	17.6	12.8	−27.3
45–54	21.7	15.0	−30.9
55–64	19.6	15.7	−19.9
All ages	**14.9**	**11.9**	**−20.1**

20. ORGANIZED LABOR: SELECTED MEMBERSHIP FEATURES, AUSTRALIA, U.K., AND U.S., 1995 AND 2010

Country	1995	2010	1995–2010
Number of members (thousands)			*Percentage change*
Australia	2,252	1,788	−20.6
UK	7,125	6,536	−8.3
USA	16,360	14,715	−10.1
% Males			
Australia	59.9%	52.0%	−13.2
UK	55.1%	45.5%	−17.4
USA	60.7%	54.3%	−10.5
% Females			
Australia	40.1%	48.0%	19.8
UK	44.9%	54.5%	21.4
USA	39.3%	45.7%	16.2
% Public sector			
Australia	42.1%	37.1%	−11.7
UK	52.3%	62.2%	19.0
USA	42.3%	49.4%	16.6
% Private sector			
Australia	57.9%	62.9%	8.5
UK	47.7%	37.7%	−20.8
USA	57.6%	50.6%	−12.1
% Full-time			
Australia	82.3%	76.6%	−6.9
UK	84.2%	78.4%	−6.9
USA	90.6%	89.4%	−1.3
% Part-time			
Australia	17.7%	23.4%	32.3
UK	15.8%	21.6%	36.5
USA	9.4%	10.6%	12.8

NOTES AND SOURCES FOR TABLES

1. **Organized Labor: Global Growth, c. 1870–2010**
   SOURCES: Tables 2, 3, 4, 8. The membership of the affiliates of the International Confederation of Free Trade Unions and the International Trade Union Confederation have been used as the basis of the world total of union membership from 1950. It should be noted that these figures are incomplete for the United States, Canada, Germany, Japan, Malta, and Switzerland, as well as for periods, and they require upward adjustment. Other sources include H. A. Marquand et al., *Organized Labour in Four Continents* (London: Longmans, Green, 1939), p. 438 (for Mexico in 1940) and Elias T. Ramos, *Philippines Labor Movement in Transition* (Quezon City: New Day, 1976), pp. 8–9 (for the Philippines in 1940).

2. **Organized Labor: Global Changes, c. 1870–2010**
   SOURCES: As for Table 1.

3. **International Federation of Trade Unions: Membership, 1901–1945**
   SOURCES: W. Schevenels, *Forty-Five Years: International Federation of Trade Unions* (Brussels: Board of Trustees of the International Federation of Trade Unions, 1956), pp. 23, 62, 423–425; Tables 1 and 2.

4. **International Confederation of Free Trade Unions/International Trade Union Confederation: Membership, 1949–2010**
   SOURCES: John P. Windmuller, *The International Trade Union Movement* (Deventer: Kluwer, 1980), p. 62; data after 1979 were supplied by the International Confederation of Free Trade Unions and the International Trade Union Confederation.

5. **International Confederation of Free Trade Unions/International Trade Union Confederation: Membership by Region, 1949–2010**
   SOURCES: As for Table 4.

6. **Organized Labor: Largest Unions in the World, 1900–2010**
   SOURCES: H. A Clegg, *A History of British Trade Unions since 1889*, Vol. II (Oxford: Clarendon Press, 1985), p. 570; *Statistiches Jahrbuch für des Bundesrepublik Deutschland*; John Harper Publishing, *Trade Unions of the World* (London: John Harper Publishing, 2001); Internet websites for the organizations shown in Appendix B.

7. **Organized Labor: Unions with a Million or More Members, 2001 and 2010**
   SOURCES: John Harper Publishing, *Trade Unions of the World* (London: John Harper Publishing, 2001); Internet websites for the organizations shown in Appendix B.

8. **Organized Labor: Reported Murders of Union Activists, 1999–2009**

    SOURCES: *Annual Survey of Violations of Trade Union Rights* prepared by the International Confederation of Free Trade Unions and its successor, the International Trade Union Confederation.

9. **Organized Labor: Membership in Selected Countries, c. 1870–c. 1890**

    SOURCES: **U.K.:** B. C. Roberts, *The Trade Union Congress, 1868–1921* (London: George Allen & Unwin, 1958), p. 379. Data are for 1871, 1881, and 1885. (Note: these data refer only to Trade Unions Congress affiliates and so underestimate total union membership, but this seems to be the only time series available for this period.) **U.S.:** Estimates in Lance E. Davis and others, *American Economic Growth: An Economist's History of the United States* (New York: Harper & Row, 1972), p. 220. Data are for 1870, 1880, and 1886. **France:** Val R. Lorwin, *The French Labor Movement* (Cambridge, Mass.: Harvard University Press, 1954), pp. 12, 18, 23; Edward Shorter and Charles Tilly, *Strikes in France, 1830–1968* (Cambridge: Cambridge University Press, 1974), p. 371. Data are for 1870, 1881, and 1886. **Germany:** Michael Schneider, *A Brief History of the German Trade Unions* (trans. Barrie Selman, Bonn: J. H. W. Dietz Nachf., 1991), p. 383. Data are for 1869, 1880, and 1885. **Austro-Hungarian Empire:** Marcel van der Linden and Jürgen Rojahn (eds.), *The Formation of Labour Movements* (Leiden: E. J. Brill, 1990), Vol. II, p. 334. Data refer to 1871. **Spain:** Dick Geary (ed.), *Labour and Socialist Movements in Europe before 1914* (Oxford: Berg Publishing, 1989), p. 245. Data are for 1881. **Australia:** J. T. Sutcliffe, *A History of Trade Unionism in Australia* (Melbourne: Macmillan, 1967), pp. 66–67. Data are for 1879 and 1885. **New Zealand:** H. Roth, *Trade Unions in New Zealand: Past and Present* (Wellington: A. H. and A. W. Reed, 1973), p. 167. Data are for 1885.

    Notes: (1) The 1880 figure for France refers to Paris only. (2) The Australian figure for 1890 was supplied by Michael Quinlan and Margaret Gardner of Griffith University from their database on Australian labor unions and labor disputes.

10. **Organized Labor: Membership in Selected Countries, c. 1900–1940**

    SOURCES: The primary sources were Arthur M. Ross and Paul T. Hartman, *Changing Patterns of Industrial Conflict* (New York and London: John Wiley & Sons, 1960), pp. 200–201; George S. Bain and Robert Price, *Profiles of Union Growth: A Comparative Statisti-*

cal Portrait of Eight Countries (Oxford: Basil Blackwell, 1980); Jelle Visser, *In Search of Inclusive Unionism,* Special Issue, *Bulletin of Comparative Industrial Relations,* No. 18 (Deventer, Netherlands and Boston: Kluwer Law and Taxation Publishers, 1990), p. 18; Marcel van der Linden and Jürgen Rojahn (eds.), *The Formation of Labour Movements* (Leiden: E.J. Brill, 2 vols., 1990), pp. 141, 143, 300, 334, 357, 385, 411, 517, 666; A. P. Coldrick and Philip Jones (eds.), *The International Directory of the Trade Union Movement* (London and Basingstoke: Macmillan, 1979), *passim*; W. Schevenels, *Forty-Five Years: International Federation of Trade Unions* (Brussels: Board of Trustees of the International Federation of Trade Unions, 1956), p. 63; Commonwealth of Australia, Bureau of Census and Statistics, *Labour Reports* (Melbourne/Canberra: Government Printer, 1922–1932).

Other data were drawn from Val R. Lorwin, *The French Labor Movement* (Cambridge, Mass.: Harvard University Press, 1954), p. 23; Edward Shorter and Charles Tilly, *Strikes in France, 1830–1968* (Cambridge: Cambridge University Press, 1974), pp. 371–372; Michael Schneider, *A Brief History of the German Trade Unions* (trans. Barrie Selman, Bonn: J. H. W. Dietz Nachf., 1991), pp. 383–386; Daniel L. Horowitz, *The Italian Labor Movement* (Cambridge, Mass.: Harvard University Press, 1963), pp. 44 n. 106 (1893 data), 59 n. 21, 75, 111, 125; John W. Boyle, *The Irish Labor Movement in the Nineteenth Century* (Washington, D.C.: Catholic University of America Press, 1988), pp. 125, 127; Charles McCarthy, *Trade Unions in Ireland, 1894–1960* (Dublin: Institute of Public Administration, 1977), pp. 622, 635; Leo Wolman, *The Growth of American Trade Unions, 1880–1923* (New York: National Bureau of Economic Research Inc., 1924), p. 124; Lance E. Davis and others, *American Economic Growth: An Economist's History of the United States* (New York: Harper & Row, 1972), p. 220; H. Roth, *Trade Unions in New Zealand: Past and Present* (Wellington: A. H. and A. W. Reed, 1973), pp. 167–170; New Zealand, *Official Year Books*; John P. Windmuller, *Labor Relations in the Netherlands* (Ithaca, N.Y.: Cornell University Press, 1969), p. 39; Dick Geary (ed.), *Labour and Socialist Movements in Europe before 1914* (Oxford: Berg Publishers Ltd., 1989), pp. 245, 254; Augustus D. Webb, *The New Dictionary of Statistics* (London: George Routledge and Sons Ltd., 1911), pp. 602, 606 (data for Austria for 1892 and 1901, and for Hungary and Switzerland for 1906); Gary K. Busch, *The Political Role of International Trade Unions* (London: Macmillan, 1983), pp. 110, 124; Walter Kendall, *The Labour Movement in Europe* (London: Allen Lane, 1975), Statistical Appendix;

U.S. Bureau of Labor Statistics, *Monthly Labor Review,* December 1991, p. 48; Walter Galenson (ed.), *Labor in Developing Economies* (Berkeley and Los Angeles: University of California Press, 1963), pp. 216, 283; *Longman's Trade Unions of the World* (London: Longmans, 2nd ed., 1987), p. 205 for the Palestine figure for 1920.

Note: Irish data are also included in the U.K. figure up to 1920; the 1920 figure shown refers to 1922. They are included here separately for their intrinsic interest.

11. **Organized Labor: Membership in Selected Countries, 1950–1970**
SOURCES: Same as for Table 10; Except for New Zealand and the United States, the 1960 and 1970 data are from the Database on the Institutional Characteristics of Trade Unions, Wage Setting, State Intervention, and Social Pacts under the leadership of Jelle Visser at Amsterdam. The data refer to net membership only.

12. **Organized Labor: Membership in Selected Countries, 1980–2006**
SOURCES: Same as for Table 11.

13. **Organized Labor: Women Membership in Selected Countries, 1900–2010**
SOURCES: George S. Bain and Robert Price, *Profiles of Union Growth: A Comparative Statistical Portrait of Eight Countries* (Oxford: Basil Blackwell, 1980), pp. 37–38, 102, 115, 123–124; United Kingdom Employment Department, *Employment Gazette*, January 1983, p. 26, January 1992, p. 188, May 1995, p. 192; Michael Schneider, *A Brief History of the German Trade Unions* (Bonn: J. H. W. Dietz Nachf., 1991), pp. 82, 184, 384–385, 387; *Statistiches Jahrbuch 1995 für die Bundesrepublik Deutschland*, p. 741; Australian Bureau of Statistics, *Trade Union Statistics, Australia* (Catalogue No. 6323.0) (1980 data); Australian Bureau of Statistics, *Trade Union Members, Australia* (Catalogue No. 6325.0) (1990 data), *Trade Union Members, Australia* (Product No. 6325.0.40.001), p. 19 (1994 data), *Employee Earnings, Benefits and Trade Union Membership* (Catalogue No. 6310.0); Leo Wolman, *The Growth of American Trade Unions, 1880–1923* (New York: National Bureau of Economic Research, 1924), pp. 98–99; James J. Kenneally, *Women and American Trade Unions* (St. Albans, Vt.: Eden Press Women's Publications Inc., 1978), p. 218; *Statistical Abstract of the United States* (data for 1954–1978); U.S. Bureau of Labor Statistics, *Employment and Earnings,* January 1991, p. 229, January 1996, p. 210; *Japan Statistical Yearbook,* 1961, p. 351; Ministry of Labour, Japan, *Year Book of Labour Statistics,* 1991, p. 320.

For 2010, the sources were the data cubes for Australia and the United Kingdom. These are spreadsheets that contain time series on more detailed information than is published. They can be downloaded from the Australian Bureau of Statistics at http://www.abs.gov.au/AUSSTATS/abs@.nsf/DetailsPage/6310.0Aug%202010?OpenDocument and for the United Kingdom from http://www.bis.gov.uk/policies/employment-matters/research/trade-union-stats.

The U.S. data can be downloaded in spreadsheets from http://www.stats.bls.gov/news.release/union2.t01.htm.

Notes: (1) **Germany:** The 1900 figure refers to 1902–1903; the figure for 1930 refers to 1931; the figure for 2001 refers to 1997, after which no further national data were published. (2) **U.S.:** 1913 figure refers to 1910; 1950 figure refers to 1954; 1980 figure refers to 1978. (3) **Japan:** The 1990 figure refers to 1991 and no further data were published.

14. **Organized Labor as a Proportion of Employees: Selected Countries, c. 1900–1950**
Sources: Same as for Table 9; Australian data for 1890 and 1900 calculated by the author; Peter Flora and others, *State, Economy, and Society in Western Europe, 1815–1975* (Chicago: St. James Press, 1987), Vol. II, pp. 689–753 contains a valuable nonagricultural employees series that was used to calculate union density for some countries.

15. **Organized Labor as a Proportion of Employees: Selected Countries, 1960–2006**
Sources: Same as for Table 14; Jelle Visser, "Trends in Trade Union Membership," *OECD Employment Outlook*, July 1991, p. 140; and "In Search of Inclusive Unionism," *Bulletin of Comparative Labour Relations*, No. 18, 1990, pp. 18, 35. These data have been supplemented by the Database on the Institutional Characteristics of Trade Unions, Wage Setting, State Intervention, and Social Pacts, Amsterdam.

16. **Organized Labor by Selected Industry Groups: Australia, U.K., and U.S., 1900–2010**
Sources: **Australia:** *New South Wales Statistical Register*, 1903, pp. 805–806 (1902 data); *Western Australia Printed Papers, Reports Etc. of the Parliament, 1904*, Vol. I, Report of Proceedings under the Industrial Conciliation and Arbitration Act, 1902, pp. 10–14 (1901 data); Commonwealth Bureau of Census and Statistics, *Labour and Industrial Branch Report* (Melbourne: Government Printer), 1912–1922; Commonwealth Bureau of Census and Statistics/Australian Bureau of Statistics, *Labour Report* (Melbourne/Canberra: Government Printer), 1923–1973; Australian Bureau of Statistics, *Trade Union Members, Australia* (Catalogue No. 6325.0), 1982, 1990; *Employee Earnings, Benefits and Trade Union Membership* (Catalogue No. 6310.0). **Note:** The figure for 1900 refers to New South Wales (1902) and Western

Australia (1901) only and the figure for 1980 refers to 1982–1983. For data from 1990 to 2010, the source was a data cube that can be downloaded from the Australian Bureau of Statistics at http://www.abs.gov.au/AUSSTATS/abs@.nsf/DetailsPage/6310.0Aug%20 2010?OpenDocument

United Kingdom: George S. Bain and Robert Price, *Profiles of Union Growth: A Comparative Statistical Portrait of Eight Countries* (Oxford: Basil Blackwell, 1980), pp. 43–78; Department of Labour, *Employment Gazette*, January 1983, p. 27, April 1992, p. 189; *Labour Market Trends,* April 2002, p.S26, and the data cube for 1995 to 2010 that can be downloaded from http://www.bis.gov.uk/policies/employment-matters/research/trade-union-stats

Note: The data necessary to perform the calculation, the number of employees by industry, was not published after 2004.

U.S.: U.S. Department of Commerce, *Historical Statistics of the United States* (Washington, D.C.: U.S. Government Printing Office, 1975), Part 1, p. 178; George S. Bain and Robert Price, *Profiles of Union Growth: A Comparative Statistical Portrait of Eight Countries* (Oxford: Basil Blackwell, 1980), pp. 94–95; Department of Labor, Bureau of Labor Statistics, *Handbook of Labor Statistics 1975—Reference Edition* (Washington, D.C.: U.S. Government Printing Office, 1975), pp. 383, 385; Department of Labor, Bureau of Labor Statistics, *Employment and Earnings*, January issues from 1985 onward. **Note:** data for 1950 refer to 1953 and the data for 1980 refers to 1983.

Note: The data used to construct this table were drawn from two different types of sources: data provided by unions for the period up to 1970 for Australia and the United States, up to 1980 for New Zealand, and up to 1990 for the United Kingdom; and data from household surveys for the remaining years. Consequently, the comparability within the table might be affected to some degree.

17. **Organized Labor: Median Weekly Earnings, Australia and U.S., 1982/1983–2007**
SOURCES: Australian Bureau of Statistics, *Trade Union Members, Australia* (Catalogue No. 6325.0), 1982–1990. The data for 1982 were unpublished and were taken from Table 6 of microfiche from the survey and refer to March to May 1982. The Australian data are the author's calculations from grouped income data from Australian Bureau of Statistics, *Weekly Earnings of Employees (Distribution) Australia, August 1995* (Product No. 6310.0.40.001) and *Employee Earnings, Benefits and Trade Union Membership* (Catalogue No. 6310.0); U.S. Department of Labor, Bureau of Labor Statistics, *Employment and Earnings* (January issue from 1985 onward).

Note: The data necessary for the calculation for Australia were not published after 2007.

18. **Organized Labor as a Proportion of Employees by Age: Australia, 1995 and 2010**

    SOURCE: Australian Bureau of Statistics data cube available at http://www.abs.gov.au/AUSSTATS/abs@.nsf/DetailsPage/6310.0Aug

19. **Organized Labor as a Proportion of Employees by Age: U.S., 1995 and 2010**

    SOURCES: For 1995, *Employment and Earnings,* January 1997, p. 211; for 2010, http://www.stats.bls.gov/news.release/union2.t01.htm

20. **Organized Labor: Selected Membership Features, Australia, U.K., and U.S., 1995 and 2010**

    SOURCES:

    Australia: http://www.abs.gov.au/AUSSTATS/abs@.nsf/DetailsPage/6310.0Aug%202010?OpenDocument

    U.K.: http://www.bis.gov.uk/policies/employment-matters/research/trade-union-stats

    U.S.: http://www.stats.bls.gov/news.release/union2.t01.htm

Appendix E
Glossary of Terms

Like any other movement, organized labor has its own specialized terms, which can appear in the primary sources or in the secondary literature. What follows is a sample of terms intended to provide a starting point for a reader; further information about some of them can be found in the specialized works listed in the bibliography. Cross-references to other terms in the glossary are in bold.

Agency shop   U.S. term referring to a collective agreement that excludes free-riders by forcing them to pay the equivalent of the union membership fee in order to retain employment at that workplace.

Angestellte   German term for private sector white-collar employee, in contrast to *Beamte*.

Antiunion discrimination   Any practice that disadvantages a worker or a group of workers on grounds of their past, current, or prospective trade union membership, their legitimate trade union activities, or their use of trade union services. Can constitute dismissal, transfer, demotion, harassment, and the like.

Arbeiter   German term for manual or blue-collar workers, in contrast to *Angestellte* and *Beamte*.

Arbitration   A means of resolving **industrial disputes** outside the courts through the involvement of a neutral third party, which can either be a single arbitrator or an arbitration board. Arbitration can be nonbinding or compulsory.

Beamte   German term for publicsector employees, including civil servants and employees in state-run enterprises such as postal services, railroads, and schools, in contrast to *Angestellte*.

Betriebsräte German term for works' councils. They began in the late 19th century, were enacted in legislation in 1920, and were incorporated into co-determination (*Mitbestimmung*).

Black list A list of workers compiled by and circulated among employers identifying union members and activists who are to be boycotted or otherwise penalized.

Boycott A collective refusal to buy or use the goods or services of an employer to express disapproval with its practices.

Brownfield site A workplace where there are established unions and a long-standing system of industrial relations characterized by customs and practices recognized by employers and unions, in contrast to a **greenfield** site.

Ca'canny Originally a Scottish term meaning "to go carefully," it was first recorded in 1896 to refer to employees deliberately reducing the pace of their work or the quantity of their output. By 1918, "ca'canny" had entered standard English usage in Britain.

Candy men Term used in 19th-century England to describe the men employed by coal owners to evict miners from company-owned housing during labor disputes. The term originated in the English coal miners' strike of 1844, when some sellers of "dandy candy" in Newcastle-upon-Tyne were employed as bailiffs to evict miners from company-owned houses.

Casualization The practice of increasing the flexibility of the workforce by replacing permanent, full-time workers with workers on temporary, irregular contracts.

Checkoff A formal arrangement between an employer and a union whereby the employer deducts union fees and dues from their employees' pay and remits them to the union.

Closed (or union) shop A workplace where union membership is a condition of employment; *closed shop* is British usage and *union shop* is American usage. There are two main forms of the closed shop: workplaces where an individual must be a member of a particular union before being employed and those where the individual must join a particular union after being employed at the workplace. The opposite term is **open shop**.

Collective bargaining The process of negotiating mutually acceptable terms and conditions of employment as well as regulating **industrial relations**. Negotiations take place between one or more workers' representatives, unions of trade union centers on the one hand and employers or employers' representatives on the other hand.

Collective bargaining agreement An agreement, generally in writing, that incorporates the results of negotiations between an employer and labor unions. The agreement stipulates the working conditions, work regulations, and conflict settlement. The contract is legally binding and valid for a certain period of time.

Company union A company union is one formed by the management of a company among its employees and run for the benefit of the employer. Such unions are also variously called *house unions,* **yellow unions**, and even *employee representation plans.* Although a company union was formed in France in 1899, company unions were largely a feature of American labor relations. They flourished in the 1920s and early 1930s, but were effectively killed off by the National Labor Relations Act in 1935. Some observers regard the relatively docile unions of large Japanese companies as a form of company union.

Conseils de prud'hommes French labor tribunals that date from 1806.

Contracting-out The practice whereby an employer transfers an aspect of its business operation to an external provider. Also called **outsourcing**.

Corporatism The organization of large interest groups in society into corporate bodies as originally promoted by the Roman Catholic Church at the end of the 19th century. The term specifically refers to industry groups, unions, and governments. The creation of such umbrella organizations was a feature of the fascist governments of Italy and Germany. Hence, the term *neocorporatism* has been coined to describe the close cooperation between government, business, and unions in Western European countries since the 1960s to develop and implement economic policies such as over wages or managing technological change.

Demarcation. *See* **Jurisdiction.**

Density. *See* **Union density.**

Downsizing   Reduction of a company's workforce generally in an attempt to cut costs and improve efficiency.

Employers' organization   A body of employers associated for the collective protection and promotion of their interests. Can engage in **collective bargaining**.

Enterprise union   A union whose membership is limited to workers in one particular enterprise. Sometimes confusingly called a *company union.*

Export processing zone (EZP)   A special industrial area in a country where imported materials are processed before being reexported. Designed to attract mostly foreign investors by offering incentives such as exemptions from certain trade barriers, taxes, business regulations, or labor laws.

Free-riders   Employees who are not union members but who nevertheless benefit from the collective bargaining arrangements on pay and conditions achieved by organized labor at their place of work.

Freedom of association   The right to form and join the trade union of one's choosing as well as the right of unions to operate freely and carry out their activities without undue interference.

Freeloaders. *See* **Free-riders.**

Gherao (plural **gheraos**)   Indian term for a labor dispute in which employees harass employers and prevent them from leaving the workplace until the employees' claims are granted.

Greenfield site   A new workplace where there are no established unions or system of industrial relations. Often such sites are objects of competition between unions to recruit members and to gain exclusive recognition from management, in contrast to a **brownfield** site.

Industrial action   Any form of action taken by a group of workers, a union, or an employer during an industrial dispute. See **Strike, Lockout, Work-to-rule**.

Industrial dispute   A conflict between workers and employers concerning conditions of work or terms of employment. May result in **industrial action**.

Industrial relations   A general term for the interaction between management and its employees; it implies that both sides are organized. Industrial relations can also include governments and their representatives. As a term, *industrial relations* dates from the 1920s. Since 1945, the term *labor–management relations*—or just *labor relations*—has also come into use.

Industry   A general description of the type of goods or services produced or provided by the various sectors of the economy. Industries can be classified in a number of ways. One approach is to divide the economy into three parts: primary (agriculture and mining), secondary (manufacturing), and tertiary (other industries, also called service industries). For statistical purposes, most countries use a variant of the United Nations' International Standard Industrial Classification. Generally, unions recruit their members by occupations rather than industries.

Inflation/deflation   These terms refer to movements in the level of prices of goods and services in an economy. *Inflation* refers to rising prices and *deflation* refers to falling prices. If **nominal wages** do not match the changes of prices in an inflationary period, organized labor is more likely to engage in disputes for higher wages.

Internal labor market   The labor market that operates in a large enterprise such as the railroads. In the past, it has often been characterized by clearly defined points of entry, vertical organization, bureaucratic rules, and promotion of employees within the organization.

Journeymen   Term first recorded in 14th-century England to describe an artisan or mechanic who had completed an apprenticeship and then worked as an employee. Journeymen were the main groups in the formation of early labor unions in 18th-century England and the United States.

Jurisdiction   *Jurisdiction* refers to the work boundaries recognized by unions for recruiting members for a particular union. Unions can, and do, disagree over which union has the right to recruit members carrying out certain kinds of work, and this can lead to disputes. Work boundaries can also be altered by technological change. In British usage, jurisdiction is **demarcation**.

Kragenlinie   German noun literally meaning "collar line" but really referring to the social distinction between blue- and white-collar employees.

Labor aristocracy   The term *labor aristocracy* was used by Marx and Engels to describe the emergence of labor unions by skilled, relatively well-paid employees in Britain after 1850. Such employees included stone-masons, engineers, railroad engine drivers, carpenters, and printers. Because of their better-off condition, such unions were less likely to support radical social change and more likely to identify with middle-class ideas and values. The labor aristocracy made up about 15 percent of working-class employees in late 19th-century Britain.

Labor dispute. *See* **Industrial dispute.**

Labor economics The branch of economics that studies the supply and demand for human beings. Theoretical advances and the availability of computerized data sets have enabled labor economics to advance greatly since the 1960s through the use of quantitative analysis or econometrics. One topic that has received attention from labor economists has been the economic effects of organized labor.

Labor force The economically active part of the population. It includes those who are employed (the employed labor force) and the unemployed.

Lockout A labor dispute initiated by an employer or group of employers in contrast to a strike (that is, a labor dispute initiated by employees). The word was first recorded in 1860 to describe a labor dispute in which the employees were literally locked out of their workplace. In practice, lockouts are difficult to measure because provocation by an employer can mean that the dispute takes the form of a strike. An example of a national lockout occurred in the United States in October 2002 when a lockout of the longshoremen resulted in the closure of 19 ports on the West Coast.

Luddism *Luddism* was the name given to a systematic if sporadic campaign of **machine breaking** by employees in the English textile industry between 1812 and 1818. Luddism drew its name from an imaginary leader, Ned Ludd, who was also referred to as Captain Ludd and General Ludd.

Machine breaking Machine breaking, that is, the wrecking of new machinery by employees, was a form of industrial protest dating from at least the late 17th century and a feature of industrial relations before the recognition of labor unions.

New economy A catchall term for a host of economic and labor market trends evident since about 1980. The new economy has been described as being based on information manipulation, transformation, and transfer and using computers. New economy or postindustrial economy trends are particularly evident in finance and banking. Optimistic predictions about the future development of the economy based on the new computer technology were shaken by the end of the dot-com bubble in 2000.

Nominal wages   The amount of wages received without taking account of inflation, in contrast to **real wages**.

Normative   In economic and sociological literature, *normative* refers to what ought to be, that is, the outcome predicted by a theory in contrast to "positive" or what actually happens in reality.

Occupation   The specific job an individual is paid to carry out. There are two main kinds of occupation: manual, or blue-collar, occupations and nonmanual, or white-collar, occupations. Unions generally base their recruitment of members on groups of occupations. Historically, unions drawn from manual occupations tend to be more militant than those drawn from white-collar occupations.

Occupational status   Refers to the division of the employed **labor force** into employers, self-employed, employees, and unpaid helpers.

Open shop   In contrast to a **closed shop**, an open shop is a place of employment where employees may not be union members, either by choice or by coercion by the employer.

Order 1305   A British wartime regulatory measure issued in June 1940 to enforce compulsory arbitration as a final resort in labor disputes, but they continued. Order 1305 was withdrawn in August 1951, although the tribunal it established survived until 1958.

Osbourne Judgement   The Osbourne Judgement was a landmark decision by the British House of Lords in December 1909, which declared that it was illegal for labor unions to contribute funds to the British Labour Party. Organized labor was only able to get redress from the Osbourne Judgement after the Liberal Party, led by Lloyd George, was elected to government in 1911.

Outsourcing. *See* **contracting-out.**

Outworker   Literally, someone who works "out"—that is, outside a factory and from home. Outworkers are common in the textile industry. Outworkers typically work under poor conditions for very low pay. The word has been used in this sense since 1856.

Piece worker   An employee paid on the basis of defined tangible results (literally the production of "pieces") as opposed to attendance time at work. The term *piece worker* was used by 1884, but piece work dates from much earlier.

Primary labor market   A labor market characterized by high or difficult entry qualifications, high pay, good working conditions, and good promotion prospects, in contrast to the **secondary labor market**.

Pull economy   Refers to the tendency in Western economies since the 1970s for supply to exceed demand, thereby forcing businesses to compete harder for customers. Lower business profits and more difficult trading conditions have made it harder for labor unions to gain pay increases. The rise of the pull economy is a reflection of greater economic maturity and the growth of more demanding and knowledgeable consumers.

Push economy   Refers to the tendency in Western economies from the end of World War II to the 1970s for demand to exceed supply. In these favorable economic conditions, business profits were good and labor unions were able to demand and receive pay increases relatively easily.

Real wages   Real wages are **nominal wages** taking account of inflation or deflation. Changes in levels of real wages, particularly falls, have been a potent cause of labor unrest. An older term for real wages was *effective wages.*

Recognition   The designation by a government agency of a union as the workers' representative or acceptance by an employer that its employees can be collectively represented by a union.

Rights and interest   A distinction sometimes made between types of labor disputes: *Rights* refers to the interpretation of the rights of unions and management in a contract or employment agreement, whereas *interest* refers to the making of those terms. For example, an interest dispute could be over the recognition of a union by management; rights disputes are usually about alleged violations of agreed conditions of employment by one of the parties to the agreement.

Round Robin   A petition to employers from employees with the signatures made around the sides to disguise the identity of its initiators. Round robins originated in the British navy and the term was first recorded in 1731. Organized labor in the 19th century found them to be a useful device for dealing with repressive managements who refused to engage in collective bargaining.

Saint Monday   A custom observed from about the mid-17th century by shoemakers, tailors, and other **journeymen** of taking Monday as a holiday and sometimes even Tuesday. The custom also seems to have been observed by French textile employees. By 1764, it was observed by bricklayers, painters, and handloom employees. Work not performed on Monday was made up later in the week at night. The purpose of the custom was to create a period of leisure and to exert more control over when work was done. Its opponents claimed that "Saint Monday" was observed mainly in ale-houses and taverns. The custom was gradually eliminated by the factory system and replaced by a regulated system of hours.

Salting   A U.S. term that refers to the placing of paid union organizers as employees in the workplace with the object of recruiting new union members. The term probably comes from the mining industry and the addition of outside ore to a mine to make it seem richer than it really is.

Scab   *Scab* is a pejorative term used by organized labor in the United States and elsewhere to describe persons brought in by employers to replace employees on strike. In the United States, its use was first recorded in 1806 to describe employees who would not join a union of their occupation. Used as a term for *strikebreaker,* its usage was recorded in the United Kingdom by 1890.

Secondary labor market   A labor market usually characterized by low entry qualifications, low pay, poor working conditions, and limited opportunities for promotion, in contrast to the **primary labor market**.

Segmented labor market   A labor market that is dominated by one sex, race, or other group. Sex is a common characteristic of a segmented labor market; for example, most librarians are female and most engineers are male.

Shop stewards   Also known as *delegates,* shop stewards are the representatives of a union at the workplace but are not officials of the union. Shop stewards have been very important in British labor unions since 1918.

Sick-out   A form of **industrial action** in which groups of workers absent themselves from work, claiming they are sick.

Sit-down strike   A form of **industrial action** whereby employees occupy their workplace but do not carry out any work.

Sliding scale   A system of payment that linked wages directly to the price obtained for the good being produced by an **industry**. In 1795, agricultural laborers in Norfolk, England, suggested a sliding scale that would have tied their wage rate to the price of wheat. Sliding scales that linked wages to the price of coal were prevalent in the coal mining industry in the 1870s and 1880s in Britain and the United States. Although the system could yield higher wages when coal prices were high, it could have disastrous effects on miners' earnings if the coal price fell sharply.

Social dialogue   A term that came into vogue in the 1980s to describe formal discussions between representatives of labor unions and employers or governments on ways to achieve shared outcomes, such as economic growth and the reduction of unemployment. Social dialogue between the **social partners** has been successful in Western Europe, but not elsewhere, generally speaking.

Social dumping   A term coined in Western Europe in the late 1980s to refer to the adverse effects on affluent countries of economic competition from poorer countries. These effects can take the form of unemployment caused by the displacement of relatively highly paid employees because of the import of goods produced by poorly paid employees, the relocation of centers of employment from countries of high pay to ones with low pay, and attempts to lower the pay and conditions of employment in affluent societies by pitting them against workers in developing countries. The term has also been applied to the migration of workers from low-wage countries to high-wage countries.

Social partners   Unions and employers or their representative organizations.

Structural adjustment   A term that came into vogue in the 1980s to describe the economic changes that debtor Third World nations had to implement to receive economic assistance from organizations such as the International Monetary Fund and the World Bank. These changes typically include privatization and reductions in government expenditure.

Tolpuddle Martyrs   The Tolpuddle Martyrs were a group of six English agricultural laborers who were convicted of unlawful oaths and conspiracy at the village of Tolpuddle in Dorset. Led by George Loveless (1797–1874), who was also a lay Methodist preacher, the six men seemed to have used an initiation ceremony in the process of setting up a union to seek higher wages. Their union may have been part of the expansion of the Grand National Consolidated Trades Union. After a summary trial in March 1834, the six were convicted under conspiracy and mutiny laws of 1797 and 1819 and transported to New South Wales, Australia. They were not pardoned until 1838.

Tripartite Bodies made up of representatives of employers, unions, and government. Tripartite bodies of this kind are usually designed to address a problem of labor relations such as a dispute, training, or occupational health and safety. They may also be engaged in **social dialogue**. The International Labor Organisation has a tripartite structure.

Truck A term first recorded in England in 1665 to describe the payment of employees' wages in kind rather than money. The abuse arose from the goods often having a lesser value than the wages owed. Truck was first outlawed in 1701 but remained an abuse throughout the 19th century despite laws passed in 1831, 1887, and 1896. Truck was also an abuse in Germany and the United States. By the late 19th century, the term was extended to refer to an employer's fines or unauthorized deductions from an employee's wages.

Unemployment rate The number of unemployed as a percentage of the total labor force or of the total number of employees. The level of unemployment is important for labor unions as a factor in determining their strength in negotiations with employers.

Union busting Attempts by an employer to prevent the establishment of a trade union or remove an existing union, for example, by firing union members, challenging unions in court, or by forming a **yellow union**.

Union density Union members as a percentage of potential union members, usually defined as the percentage of employees in the **labor force** or a particular occupation or industry who are members of a labor union.

Union shop. *See* **Closed shop.**

Warnstreik German term for "warning strike." A labor dispute of short duration in support of union claims for higher pay or better working conditions. The purpose of the strike is to indicate that the claims are serious and that longer strikes may occur.

Work-to-rule   A form of **industrial action** whereby the workers strictly adhere to all laws, rules, and principles that apply to their work, effecting a slowdown.

Yellow dog contracts   One of the means by which English employers defeated the Grand United Council of Trade Unions in 1834 was by requiring employees to sign "The Document" by which they would give an undertaking to leave a union and not join another one. In the United States, this tactic was known as a *yellow dog contract,* from *yellow dog,* meaning a contemptible person. In the 1890s, yellow dog contracts that forbade union membership became more common and were not outlawed until 1932 by the Anti-Injunction (Norris-LaGuardia) Act.

Yellow union. *See* **Company union.**

Bibliography

CONTENTS

INTRODUCTION

Labor unions have always attracted interest from different disciplines, each offering its own insights. Labor unions are regularly studied not only by historians, but by economists, political scientists, sociologists, and lawyers. As the literature on this subject is vast, the bibliography is restricted mainly to scholarly books with their own bibliographies. Preference has been given to works published since 1980; earlier works are listed where they have become sources in their own right or where they have attained the status of classics in the field or simply because there was no obvious later work.

Because the study of organized labor is often controversial, the inclusion of a work in the bibliography does not necessarily imply recommendation; it is simply to note its importance and possible interest to the reader. It should be noted, too, that this bibliography makes no claim to be complete, particularly for the topics not expressly about organized labor, but rather to indicate what works are available and might be consulted with profit.

The bibliography contains a comprehensive listing of international comparative studies of industrial relations because these works, both old and new, are convenient starting points for investigating countries as well as being useful sources of information on organized labor. Although they typically stress contemporary developments, they usually contain a summary of past historical developments.

Given that this dictionary is part of a series about religions, philosophies, and movements, it is also important not to overlook the more general guides to reference material. Of special importance is Alan Day and Joan M. Harvey (eds.), *Walford's Guide to Reference Material Volume 2: Social and Historical Sciences, Philosophy and Religion* (7th ed. London: The Library Association, 1998).

Scarecrow Press publishes a series of historical dictionaries on most countries, some of which have special relevance for the history of organized labor. Robert F. Gorman and Edward S. Mihalkanin, *Historical Dictionary of Human Rights and Humanitarian Organizations* (2007), provides a general context for organized labor. For individual countries, volumes of special note are James C. Docherty, *Historical Dictionary of Australia* (2007); Paula S. Fichtner, *Historical Dictionary of Austria* (2009); Mark F. Gilbert and K. Robert Nilsson, *Historical Dictionary of Modern Italy* (2007); Joop W. Koopmans and Arend H. Huussen, *Historical Dictionary of the Netherlands* (2007); George Maude, *Historical Dictionary of Finland* (1995); Kenneth J. Panton and Keith A. Cowlard, *Historical Dictionary of the United Kingdom* (2 vols., 1997, 1998); Irene Scobbie, *Historical Dictionary of Sweden* (2006); Angel Smith, *Historical Dictionary of Spain* (2008); Robert Stallaerts, *Historical Dictionary of Belgium* (2006); Alastair H. Thomas, *Historical Dictionary of Denmark* (2008); Wayne C. Thompson, Susan S. Thompson, and Juliet S. Thompson, *Historical Dictionary of Germany* (1994); and Derek Lewis and Ulrike Zitzlsperger, *Historical Dictionary of Contemporary Germany* (2007).

Current information and references can be found in the journals listed in section A.7 of the bibliography and in works such as National Labor Relations Board, *New Books and Current Labor Articles* (Washington, D.C.). In addition, since the late 1980s, the U.S. Department of Labor has published a series on all the major countries in the world called *Foreign Labor Trends.* John Harper Publishing, *Trade Unions of the World* (London: John Harper, 2005) is the best current guide to global organized labor, with detailed entries for every country. In recent years, the Internet has become an indispensable source of information and many of the books mentioned in this bibliography can be downloaded, especially the older publications. A growing number of books are published in modern electronic formats such as .epub. Details of relevant websites are given at the end of this section.

THE STUDY OF ORGANIZED LABOR

For anyone just beginning to study organized labor, the best place to start is by gaining a general appreciation of economic history, specifically the Industrial Revolution and the economic, social, and intellectual ferment it created. Useful starting points are *The Fontana Economic History of Europe*, edited by Carlo M. Cipolla (6 vols. Glasgow: Collins/Fontana Books, 1972–1976); Fernand Braudel, *Civilization and Capitalism: 15th–18th Centuries* (3 vols. London: Fontana Press, 1981–1984); Sidney Pollard, *Peaceful Conquest: The Industrialization of Europe, 1760–1970* (Oxford: Oxford University Press, 1981); M. Teich and R. Porter (eds.), *The Industrial Revolution in National Context: Europe and the U.S.A.* (Cambridge: Cambridge University Press, 1996); and Derek H. Aldcroft and Steven Morewood, *The European Economy, 1914–2000* (4th ed., London: Routledge, 2001). For the United States, see Robert Heilbroner and Aaron Singer, *The Economic Transformation of America: 1600 to the Present* (Fort Worth, Tex.: 3rd ed., Harcourt Brace, 1994). Charles P. Kindleberger, *World Economic Primacy, 1500–1990* (New York: Oxford University Press, 1996), provides an up-to-date account of global economic history in a single volume. There is a wealth of ideas, as well as scholarship, in David Hackett Fischer, *The Great Wave: Price Revolutions and the Rhythm of History* (New York: Oxford University Press, 1996).

For economic history in the 20th century, the five-volume *Pelican History of the World Economy in the Twentieth Century* under the general editorship of Wolfram Fischer, published between 1977 and 1987, is still also recommended. The last work in this series, Herman Van der Wee, *Prosperity and Upheaval: The World Economy, 1945–1980* (1987), is most relevant as a backdrop to modern organized labor.

On the crowded developments in world economic history and economic thought since 1980, easily the best single work is Daniel Yergin and Joseph Stanislaw, *The Commanding Heights: The Battle for the World Economy* (New York: Simon and Schuster, 2002). It provides not only a readable account of difficult issues but also a good bibliography. For anyone who wants to gain a good understanding of the economic problems that have beset organized labor in Western economies since 1980, it is indispensable. Developments since 1980 as regard labor unions are described in Gary Daniels and John McIlroy, *Trade Unions in a Neoliberal World* (London: Routledge, 2009). Also interesting is Paul Kubicek's *Organized Labor in Postcommunist States: From Solidarity to Infirmity* (Pittsburgh: University of Pittsburgh Press, 2004).

For the social and economic ferment of 19th-century Europe, two good introductions from different points of view are given in the opening chapters of Philip Taylor, *The Distant Magnet: European Emigration to the U.S.A.* (New York: Harper Torchbooks, 1971) and in Dick Geary, *European Labour Protest, 1848–1939* (London: Methuen, 1984). Although not about organized labor as such, John Carey, *The Intellectuals and the Masses, 1800–1939: Pride and Prejudice among the Literary Intelligentsia* (London: Faber, 1992) gives a valuable, if chilling, alternative perspective on one level of response to population growth and the rise of the modern working class. On social class, Arthur Marwick, *Class: Image and Reality in Britain, France, and the USA since 1930* (Glasgow: Fontana/Collins, 1980) provides stimulating reading. Works like these are important for helping to place the study of organized labor in a wider historical perspective, a perspective that can all too easily become lost in the forest of specialist studies.

For economic thought, Robert L. Heilbroner, *The Worldly Philosophers* (6th ed., New York: Touchstone, 1986), provides a masterly introduction to the world of economic ideas written with a wit and humor seldom found in such works. More recent is Alessandro Roncaglia, *The Wealth of Ideas: A History of Economic Thought* (Cambridge University Press, 2005), which traces the history of economic thought from the Bible and classical antiquity to the present day. For economic issues generally, the major reference work is John Eastwell, Murray Milgate, and Peter Newman (eds.), *The New Palgrave: A Dictionary of Economics* (4 vols. London: Macmillan, 1987), which has bibliographies after each entry; the entries on arbitration, collective bargaining, strikes, and trade unions are of particular interest. Also worth noting as a background reference work is Carl Heyel (ed.), *The Encyclopedia of Management* (3rd ed., New York: Van Nostrand Reinhold, 1982).

Although organized labor has never lacked students since Adam Smith's famous reference to it in the *Wealth of Nations* (1776) as "combinations," it mainly attracted attention from economists and lawyers or from political theorists such as Karl Marx. By 1920, pioneers like Sidney and Beatrice Webb in Britain and John R. Commons and Selig Perlman in the United States established organized labor as an academically respectable field of study. Under their influence, organized labor tended to be studied from the viewpoint of its institutions; this was a "top down" approach with a strong emphasis on leaders.

Modern labor history dates from about 1960 with the works of American scholars like Irving Bernstein and David Brody and Eric Hobsbawm and E. P. Thompson in Britain. The publication of E. P. Thompson, *The Making of the English Working Class* (London: Victor Gollancz, 1963 and Penguin Books, 1968) was an inspirational milestone in labor history and a foundation work of modern social history.

What united the British and American works was their concern with the social and political setting of employees and to show the diversity of the experiences of particular groups. Over the past 50 years the output of social histories has been huge, although their quality has often been variable.

At this point, a word of warning is needed for the beginner. The study of organized labor is intimately bound up with the study of the Industrial Revolution, the effects of which have been hotly disputed by generations of participants and scholars. The older optimistic view of the Industrial Revolution, which E. P. Thompson rightly attacked, was that it represented general material progress. He was able to show that for many groups in the labor force conditions deteriorated.

Like any revolution, the Industrial Revolution had its good and bad sides, but all too often only the bad is presented. Many of the sources are fiercely polemical, and the secondary works have been similarly influenced. Studies often focus on the negative aspects of industrialization, on what went wrong rather than on what succeeded. It has often been more appealing to write about dramatic, noble failures, or the distressed condition of particular groups of workers than the slow, if duller process of general material improvement. Consider, for instance, the general absence of modern scholarly works about the cooperative movement compared with the abundance of books on the left wing of labor.

The debate about the Industrial Revolution continues to the present, though in different forms. This is particularly evident in the attitudes of the various disciplines. The works of many of the economic writers, for example, tend to take a far more positive view of the Industrial Revolution than those of social historians. For these reasons, it is vital to keep an open mind about the subject and to be mindful of the political ideologies that often still color much of the writing about organized labor.

Despite the maturing of labor history, there is a relative lack of studies of its historiography. An important exception is the U.S. study by Melvyn Dubofsky, *Hard Work: The Making of Labor History* (Urbana: University of Illinois Press, 2000). In this work, Dubofsky argued that labor history is no longer the cutting edge in historical research because it has been largely successful in entering the historical mainstream. This may be true for the United States and the United Kingdom, but this should not be taken to mean that labor history generally is a problem "solved" and that there are no more worlds for the researcher to conquer. Especially freeing labor history from the Eurocentric approach has been a challenge over the past decades. Good introductions to the study of a global labor history are Marcel Van der Linden, *Transnational Labour History: Explorations* (Aldershot, Hampshire: Ashgate, 2003), an invaluable resource for all students of European labor history, and Marcel Van der Linden, *Workers of the World: Essays toward a Global Labor History* (Leiden, Netherlands: Koninklijke Brill, 2008).

FINDING OUT ABOUT ORGANIZED LABOR

After gaining a broad appreciation of the Industrial Revolution, the following works provide a sound introduction to the study of labor unions. W. E. J. McCarthy (ed.), *Trade Unions: Selected Readings* (2nd ed., Harmondsworth: Penguin, 1985) contains a valuable selection of important readings, some of which are hard to locate in their original form. The political side of labor is approached in an interesting way by Walter Korpi in his *The Democratic Class Struggle* (London: Routledge Kegan Paul, 1983). There is an excellent view of the topic by Jelle Visser, "Trade Unions from a Comparative Perspective," in Joris Van Ruysseveldt et al. (eds.), *Comparative Industrial and Employment Relations* (London: Sage, 1995), pp. 37–67.

For critical labor union functions and collective bargaining, see Allan Flanders (ed.), *Collective Bargaining: Selected Readings* (Harmondsworth: Penguin, 1969), and H. Katz and T. Kochan, *An Introduction to Collective Bargaining and Industrial Relations* (New York: McGraw-Hill, 1992). For labor economics, a useful introductory text is Lloyd G. Reynolds et al., *Labor Economics and Labor Relations* (9th ed., Englewood Cliffs, N.J: Prentice-Hall, 1986).

There are numerous ways of approaching the many topics within the study of organized labor. For American studies, there are excellent bibliographical essays in Foster R. Dulles and Melvyn Dubofsky, *Labor in America: A History* (4th ed., Arlington Heights, Ill.: Harlan Davidson, 1984), Bruce Laurie, *Artisans into Workers: Labor in Nineteenth-Century America* (New York: Hill and Wang, 1989), and Robert H. Zieger, *American Workers, American Unions, 1920–1985* (2nd ed., Baltimore, Md.:

Johns Hopkins University Press, 1994). For British works, there are bibliographic guides in Henry Pelling, *A History of British Trade Unionism* (5th ed., London: Macmillan, 1992) and Dick Geary, *European Labour Protest, 1848–1939* (London: Methuen, 1984).

Students of American and British labor are blessed with comprehensive and high-quality bibliographies that were published in the early 1980s, particularly those by Maurice F. Neufeld for the United States and Arthur Marsh for Britain. These can be readily supplemented by recourse to book reviews and book notices in journals like *Labor History, Monthly Labor Review,* and *British Journal of Industrial Relations. Labor History,* for instance, has published an annual bibliography of labor journal articles and other scholarly work since 1965. There is also important bibliographical information in the *International Review of Social History.*

The *Journal of Economic Literature* (Pittsburgh) contains a useful annotated listing of new books. For sheer convenience as well as breadth, there is an outstanding bibliography organized by country in Marcel van der Linden and Jürgen Rojahn (eds.), *The Formation of Labour Movements, 1870–1914: An International Perspective* (Leiden, Netherlands: E.J. Brill, 1990), Vol. II, pp. 701–781.

Another important bibliographical source is the International Labour Organization, *International Labour Documentation,* which has been issued monthly since 1965. This source covers all topics pertaining to labor and is international in coverage. The 200,000 records it contains can be accessed at www.ilo.org/labordoc.

SPECIFIC TOPICS

Because the study of organized labor is often about the details of work, it is essential to gain some familiarity with industrial archaeology, which is concerned with the study of the physical remains and processes of the Industrial Revolution. As well as being important for its own sake, industrial archaeology gives many insights into the organization and conditions of work and living in past times. There is a useful encyclopedia devoted to this subject, Barrie Trinder (ed.), *The Blackwell Encyclopedia of Industrial Archaeology* (Oxford: Basil Blackwell, 1992), which is international in scope and contains an excellent bibliography. In addition, Shire, a British publisher, specialized in this field, and their Shire Album series of over 100 booklets written by experts covers topics from chain making to woodworking tools. Several of these are listed in the bibliography. Also highly recommended is the informative as well as entertaining British Channel 4 television series *The Worst Jobs in History.*

Since the late 1970s, students of organized labor have some excellent labor-saving reference works at their disposal. There are historical directories of labor unions for Britain and the United States. The British series compiled by Arthur Marsh and Victoria Ryan consists of four volumes, *Historical Directory of Trade Unions* (Westmead: Gower Press, 1980–1994). This remarkable series covers about 6,000 unions.

American unions are well covered by Gary M. Fink (ed.), *Labor Unions* (Westport, Conn.: Greenwood Press, 1977), which has entries on over 200 U.S. unions, each entry with its own bibliography. The work also contains national union affiliation details, a chronology, union genealogies, union executive lists, membership statistics, and a glossary.

No comparable work is currently available for Australia, but in 1982, Michael Quinlan and Margaret Gardner at the School of Industrial Relations, Griffith University, Queensland, began to prepare a computer database covering Australian unions and labor disputes between 1825 and 1925. This database contains reasonably full entries on 1,506 unions that operated between 1825 and 1900.

One of the most welcome developments of the past 30 years has been the appearance of biographical dictionaries of labor leaders. The labor movement is often ignored in many national biographical dictionaries, and it is often hard to find even the most elementary background information about its leaders, let alone its rank-and-file. For Britain, the leading work is the nine volumes edited by Joyce Bellamy and John Saville, *Dictionary of Labour Biography* (London: Macmillan, 1972–1993). For the United States, there is a one-volume work edited by Gary M. Fink, *Biographical Dictionary of American Labor* (rev. ed., Westport, Conn.: Greenwood Press, 1985) that has entries on about 750 individuals.

A biographical register of Australian labor since 1788 is being prepared by Andrew Moore and John Shields at the University of Western Sydney. The finished work may not be published in printed form, but might be made available on the Internet.

With the exception of Britain, all these efforts seem small compared with what is available for French labor. Jean Maitron (ed.), *Dictionnaire Biographique du Mouvement Ouvrier Français* (Paris: Les Editions Ouvriers, 1964–1997) consists of 44 volumes and covers the period from 1789 to 1939. It includes leaders as well as rank-and-file members of the labor movement. A new series has begun to cover the period from 1940 to 1968. Jean Maitron was also general editor of another series, *Dictionnaire Biographique du Mouvement Ouvrier International,* which consists of dictionaries for Austria, China, and Japan (two volumes) and Germany. Section A.3 lists labor biographical dictionaries.

Most studies of organized labor are of Britain, the United States, and Western Europe. Henry Pelling, *A History of British Trade Unionism* (5th ed., London: Macmillan, 1992) remains the best known survey work. It can be supplemented by Chris Wrigley, *British Trade Unions since 1933* (Cambridge: Cambridge University Press, 2002). Keith Laybourn, *A History of British Trade Unionism, c. 1770–1990* (Wolfeboro Falls, N.H.: Allan Sutton, 1992), is a good guide to the academic debates of recent years. Hugh A. Clegg, *A History of British Trade Unions since 1889* (3 vols. Oxford: Oxford University Press, 1964–1994) is the standard scholarly work; the first volume was written with Alan Fox and A. F. Thompson. Although often heavy going, it covers the period up to 1951. It is invaluable as a reference work.

For the United States, good, comprehensive single-volume surveys are available in Foster Rhea Dulles and Melvy Dubofsky, *Labor in America* (4th ed., Arlington Heights, Ill.: Harlan Davidson, 1984) and Ronald L. Filippelli, *Labor in the USA: A History* (New York: Knopf, 1984). For Germany, John A. Moses, *Trade Unionism in Germany from Bismarck to Hitler, 1869 to 1933* (2 vols. London: George Prior Publishers, 1982) provides a valuable survey with translations of some key documents. Moses's history can be profitably supplemented with the more recent work by Michael Schneider, *A Brief History of the German Trade Unions* (trans. Barrie Selman, Bonn: J. H. W. Dietz Nachf., 1991), which covers the whole period up to the present and is good for biographical details and statistics.

C. R. Dobson, *Masters and Journeymen: A Prehistory of Industrial Relations, 1717–1800* (London: Croom Helm, 1980) is a short but valuable work largely devoted to labor disputes in the 18th century. It is a reminder that labor unions and labor disputes were evident *before* the Industrial Revolution and, therefore, may presumably still be in existence in the often predicted postindustrial world.

For the ideas that have influenced organized labor and its general development, see James C. Docherty, *Historical Dictionary of Socialism* (Lanham, Md.: Scarecrow Press, 1997), which provides a general global survey and was updated in 2006 by Peter Lamb and James Docherty. Michael Poole, *Theories of Trade Unionism* (rev. ed., London: Routledge and Kegan Paul, 1984), offers a sociological approach to labor unions.

Because of the variable coverage they give to organized labor, the bibliography does not include a separate section on histories of particular industries, although this is not to say they are unimportant; on the contrary, they must be investigated by serious students. That said, an exception needs to be made for John Hatcher and others, *The History of the British Coal Industry* (5 vols. Oxford: Clarendon Press, 1984–1993), which deals with an industry that played a central role in British organized labor up to the 1950s.

A. RESEARCH GUIDES, SOURCES, AND JOURNALS

A.1 Bibliographies and Finding Aids

ABC-Clio Information Services. *Labor in America: A Historical Bibliography.* Santa Barbara, Calif.: ABC-Clio, 1985.

Addison, John T., and Claus Schnabel (eds.). *International Handbook of Trade Unions.* Northampton, Mass.: Edward Elgar, 2003.

Allen, V. L. (ed.). *International Bibliography of Trade Unionism.* London: Merlin Maspero, 1968.

Allison, Peter B. *Labor, Worklife and Industrial Relations: Sources of Information.* New York: Haworth Press, 1984.

Amorim, Anita, Una Murray, and Pallavi Rai. *A Selected Annotated Bibliography on Girl Child Labour: A Gender Perspective.* International Labour Office. Geneva: ILO, 2004.

Bain, George S., and John Bennett (eds.). *Bibliography of British Industrial Relations, 1971–1979.* Cambridge: Cambridge University Press, 1985.

Bain, George S., and Gillian B. Woolven (eds.). *Bibliography of British Industrial Relations.* Cambridge: Cambridge University Press, 1979. (Covers the period from 1880 to 1970.)

Bennett, John, and Julian Fawcett (eds.). *Industrial Relations: An International and Comparative Bibliography.* London: Mansell, 1985.

Bishoff, Ros, Richard Mitchell, and Andrea Steer (eds.). *Australian Labour Law: A Selected Bibliography.* Melbourne: Labour Studies Programme, University of Melbourne, 1985.

Burnett, John, David Vincent, and David Mayall (eds.). *The Autobiography of the Working Class: A Critical and Annotated Bibliography.* 3 vols. Brighton, Sussex, U.K.: The Harvester Press/New York: New York University Press, 1984, 1987, 1989.

Campbell, Anne, et al. (eds.). *Industrial Relations: A Select Annotated Bibliography.* London: Commonwealth Secretariat, 1980.

Carrington, Arthur V. (ed.). *Human Rights: A Bibliography.* Huntington, N.Y.: Nova Science Books, 2000.

Chan, Ming K. (ed.). *Historiography of the Chinese Labor Movement, 1895–1949: A Critical Survey and Bibliography of Selected Chinese Source Materials at the Hoover Institution.* Stanford, Calif.: Hoover Institution Press, 1981.

Chester, A. E. *Aspects of Australian Industrial Relations: A Select Bibliography.* Adelaide: South Australian Institute of Technology, 1980.

Dowe, Dieter (ed.). *Führer zu den Archiven, Bibliotheken und Forschungseinrichtungen zur Geschichte der europäischen Arbeiterbewegung.* Bonn: Verlag Neue Gesellschaft, 1984.

Feldman, Shelley, and Eveline Ferretti (eds.). *Informal Work and Social Change: A Bibliographic Survey.* Ithaca, N.Y.: ILR Press, 1998.

Fowler, Simon (ed.). *Sources for Labour History.* London: Public Record Office, 1995.

Fox, M. J., and P. C. Howard. *Labor Relations and Collective Bargaining: A Bibliographical Guide to Doctoral Research.* Metuchen, N.J: Scarecrow Press, 1983.

Gibbney, H. J. (comp.). *Labor in Print: A Guide to the People Who Created a Labor Press in Australia between 1850 and 1939.* Canberra: History Department, Research School of Social Sciences, Australian National University, 1975.

Harrison, Royden, Gillian Woolven, and Robert Duncan (eds.). *The Warwick Guide to British Labour Periodicals, 1790–1970: A Check List.* Atlantic Highlands, N.J.: Harvester Press, 1977.

Harzig, Christiane, and Dirk Hoerder (eds.). *The Immigrant Labor Press in North America, 1840s–1970s: An Annotated Bibliography.* New York: Greenwood Press, 1987.

Hessisches Hauptstaatsarchiv, Volker Eicherler (ed.). *Inventar zur Geschichte der deutschen Arbeitwegung in den staatlichen Archiven der Bundesrepublik Deutschland.* Berlin: Colloquium Verlag, 1996.

Hill, John. *Strikes in Australia: A Select Bibliography.* Canberra: Canberra College of Advanced Education Library, 1983.

Houkes, John M. *Industrial Relations Theses and Dissertations, 1949–1969: A Cumulative Bibliography.* Ann Arbor, Mich.: Xerox University Microfilms, 1973.

Huls, Mary E. (ed.). *United States Government Documents on Women, 1800–1900: A Comprehensive Bibliography. Vol. II: Labor.* Westport, Conn.: Greenwood, 1993.

International Labour Office. *Annotated Bibliography on Child Labour.* Geneva: International Labour Office, 1986. (See also the online updates.)

——. *International Labour Documentation.* Geneva: International Labour Office, 1965 to date.

——. *Women Workers: An Annotated Bibliography, 1983–94.* Geneva: International Labour Office, 1995.

Jadeja, Raj. *Parties to the Award: A Guide to the Pedigrees and Archival Resources of Federally Registered Trade Unions, Employers' Associations and Their Peak Councils in Australia.* Canberra: Noel Butlin Archives Centre, Research School of Social Sciences, Australian National University, 1994.

Jones, Gregory P. *A Guide to Sources of Information on Australian Industrial Relations.* Sydney: Pergamon Press, 1988.

Lily, Terry Ann, et al. (eds.). *Work-Family Research: An Annotated Bibliography.* Westport, Conn.: Greenwood Press, 1997.

Magnaghi, Russell M. (ed.). *Indian Slavery, Labor, Evangelization, and Captivity in the Americas: An Annotated Bibliography.* Lanham, Md.: Scarecrow Press, 1998.

Maley, Barry, et al. (eds.). *Industrial Democracy and Worker Participation.* Sydney: Department of Organizational Behaviour, University of New South Wales, 1979. (Covers Australia and other countries during 1960–1976.)

Marsh, Arthur (ed.). *Employees Relations Bibliography and Abstracts.* Oxford: Employees Relations Bibliography and Abstracts, 1985.

——. (ed.). *Employee Relations Bibliography & Abstract Journal.* Oxford: Employee Relations Bibliography and Abstracts, 1989 to date. (Issued four times a year, this work supplements the same editor's 1985 *Employees Relations Bibliography and Abstracts.*)

Martens, G. R. (ed.). *African Trade Unionism: A Bibliography with a Guide to Trade Union Organizations and Publications.* Boston, Mass.: G. K. Hall, 1977.

McBrearty, James (ed.). *American Labor History and Comparative Labor Movements: A Selected Bibliography.* Tucson: University of Arizona Press, 1973.

Neufeld, Maurice F., Daniel J. Leab, and Dorothy Swanson (eds.). *American Working Class History: A Representative Bibliography.* New York: R. R. Bowker, 1983.

Pettman, Barrie O. (ed.). *Industrial Democracy: A Selected Bibliography.* Bradford, West Yorkshire: MCB, 1978.

——. (ed.). *Strikes: A Selected Bibliography.* Bradford, U.K.: MCB Books, 1976. (Covers 32 countries.)

Robertson, David. *A Dictionary of Human Rights.* London; New York: Europa, 2004.

Roth, Herbert O. (ed.). *New Zealand Trade Unions: A Bibliography.* 2nd ed. Wellington: Oxford University Press, 1977.

Russell, Thyra K. (ed.). *Job Sharing: An Annotated Bibliography.* Lanham, Md.: Scarecrow Press, 1994. (Covers the United States, United Kingdom, Canada, and Australia.)

Shimakoa, H. R. *Selected Bibliographies on Labor and Industrial Relations in Australia, India, Japan, New Zealand and the Philippines.* Honolulu: University of Hawaii Industrial Relations Center, 1961.

Smart, John (ed.). *Records of the Department of Labour.* Ottawa: National Archives of Canada, 1988.

Smethurst, John B. (ed.). *A Bibliography of Co-operative Societies' Histories.* Manchester: Co-operative Union, n.d.

Smith, Harold (ed.). *The British Labour Movement to 1970: A Bibliography.* London: Mansell, 1981.

Sri Lanka. Ministry of Labour. *Bibliography of Labour Relations.* 2 vols. Colombo, Sri Lanka: Ministry of Labour, 1981.

Staatsarchiv Bremen, Werner Garbas, and Margo Müller (eds.). *Inventar zur Geschichte der deutschen Arbeitbewegung in den staatlichen Archiven der Bundesrepublik Deutschland.* Berlin: Colloquium Verlag, 1991.

Staatsarchiv Hamburg, Klaus Weinhauer, et al. (eds.). *Inventar zur Geschichte der deutschen Arbeitbewegung in den staatlichen Archiven der Bundesrepublik Deutschland.* Berlin: Colloquium Verlag, 1992.

Stern, Robert, and Daniel B. Cornfield (eds.). *The U.S. Labor Movement: References and Resources.* New York: G. K. Hall, 1996.

Switzer, Teri R. (ed.). *Telecommuters: The Workforce of the 21st Century.* Lanham, Md.: Scarecrow Press, 1996.

Tuskan, Erhan (ed.). *Inventory of the Archives of the International Confederation of Free Trade Unions (ICFTU), 1949–1993.* Amsterdam: Stichting beheer IISG, 1997.

University of the Philippines, Asian Labor Education Center, Research Section. *An Annotated Bibliography on Philippine Labor.* Quezon City: National Book Store, 1979.

Vaisey, G. Douglas (ed.). *The Labour Companion: A Bibliography of Canadian Labour History Based on Materials Printed from 1950 to 1975.* Halifax, Nova Scotia: Committee on Canadian Labour History, 1980.

Vocino, Michael C., and Lucille W. Cameron (eds.). *Labor and Industrial Relations Journals and Serials: An Analytical Guide.* New York: Greenwood Press, 1989.

Whitaker, Marian, and Ian Miles (eds.). *Bibliography of Information Technology: An Annotated Critical Bibliography of English Language Sources since 1980.* London: Edward Elgar (Gower), 1989.

Wilson, Joseph (comp. and ed.). *Black Labor in America, 1865–1983: A Selected Annotated Bibliography.* Westport, Conn.: Greenwood Press, 1986.

Zaniello, Tom. *Working Stiffs, Union Maids, Reds, and Riffraff: An Organized Guide to Films about Organized Labor.* Ithaca, N.Y.: Cornell University Press, 1996.

Zappala, Jon. *Workplace Industrial Relations in Australia: An Annotated and Selected Bibliography.* Sydney: Centre for Industrial Relations Research, University of Sydney and Business Council of Australia, 1988.

A.2 Directories and Reference Works

Arrowsmith, J. D. *Canada's Trade Unions: An Information Manual.* Kingston, Ontario: Queen's University Industrial Relations Centre Press, 1992.

Blanpain, Roger (ed.). *International Encyclopaedia for Labour Law and Industrial Relations.* 10 vols. Deventer, Netherlands: Kluwer, 1977 to date. (This work is in loose-leaf form and updated monthly.)

Bottomore, Tom (ed.). *A Dictionary of Marxist Thought.* 2nd ed. Oxford: Blackwell, 1991.

Buhle, Mari Jo, Paul Buhle, and Dan Georgakas (eds.). *Encyclopedia of the American Left.* New York: Garland, 1990.

Campbell, Joan (ed.). *European Labor Unions.* Westport, Conn.: Greenwood Press, 1993.

Coldrick, A. P., and Philip Jones. *The International Directory of the Trade Union Movement.* London: Macmillan, 1979.

Craft, Donna, and Terrance W. Peck (eds.). *Profiles of American Labor Unions.* 2nd ed. Farmington Hills, Mich.: Gale, 1998.

European Communities. *Glossary of Labour and the Trade Union Movement.* Luxembourg: European Communities, 1984. (English, French, Spanish, German, Italian, Dutch, Greek, Danish, Swedish, and Norwegian.)

Filippelli, Ronald L. (ed.). *Labor Conflict in the United States: An Encyclopedia.* New York: Garland, 1990.

Fink, Gary M. (ed.). *Labor Unions.* Westport, Conn.: Greenwood Press, 1977.

Gabaglio, E., and R. Hoffman (eds.). *European Trade Union Yearbook.* Brussels: European Trade Union Institute, 1996 to 2004.

Garlock, Jonathan. *Guide to the Local Assemblies of the Knights of Labor.* Westport, Conn.: Greenwood Press, 1982.

Gifford, Courtney D. (ed.). *Directory of U.S. Labor Organizations, 1988–89 Edition.* 4th ed. Washington, D.C.: Bureau of National Affairs, 1988. (Published annually since.)

Greenfield, Gerald M., and Maram Sheldon. (eds.). *Latin American Labor Organizations.* Westport, Conn.: Greenwood Press, 1987.

Harbridge, Raymond, and Kevin Hince. *A Sourcebook of New Zealand Trade Unions and Employee Organisations.* Wellington: Industrial Relations Centre, Victoria University of Wellington, 1994.

Huntley, Pat. *Australia's Super Unions.* Northbridge, New South Wales: Huntley, 1993. (A loose-leaf subscription work that supersedes the author's *Australian Trade Union Monitor.*)

Industrial Relations Center, University of Hawaii. *Robert's Dictionary of Industrial Relations.* 4th ed. Washington, D.C.: Bureau of National Affairs/University of Hawaii Industrial Relations Center, 1994.

Information Australia. *Industrial Relations Index: A Guide to Unions, Employer Groups and the Industrial Relations Industry.* Melbourne: Information Australia, 1985 to date.

John Harper Publishing. *Trade Unions of the World.* London: John Harper, 2005. (An updated version of a work first published in 1987.)

Jones, J., and M. Morris (eds.). *A-Z of Trade Unionism and Industrial Relations.* London: Heinemann, 1982.

Kittner, Michael (ed.). *Gewerkschafts Jahrbuch 1991.* Cologne: Bund-Verlag, 1991.

Lawson, Edward (comp.). *Encyclopedia of Human Rights.* 2nd ed. Washington, D.C.: Taylor and Francis, 1996.

Lecher, W. (ed.). *Trade Unions in the European Union: A Handbook.* London: Lawrence and Wishart, 1994.

Marsh, Arthur. *Concise Encyclopedia of Industrial Relations.* Westmead: Gower Press, 1979.

———. (ed.). *Trade Union Handbook.* 5th ed. Aldershot, U.K.: Gower, 1991.

Marsh, Arthur, and Victoria Ryan (eds.). *Historical Directory of Trade Unions.* 4 vols. Westmead, U.K.: Gower Press, 1980, 1984, 1987, and 1994 (with John B. Smethurst, Scolar Press, Aldershot).

Murray, R. Emmett. *The Lexicon of Labor: More than 500 Key Terms, Biographical Sketches, and Historical Insights Concerning Labor in America.* New York: New Press, 1998.

O'Connor, David. *Encyclopedia of the Global Economy: A Guide for Students and Researchers.* 2 vols. Westport, Conn.: Greenwood Press, 2005.

Paradis, Adrian A. *The Labor Reference Book.* Philadelphia: Chilton, 1972.

Peters, Lawrence H., et al. (eds.). *The Blackwell Encyclopedic Dictionary of Human Resource Management.* Oxford: Blackwell, 1998.

Rifkin, Bernard, and Susan Rifkin (eds.). *American Labor Sourcebook.* New York: McGraw-Hill, 1979.

Russell, Spomer C., and J. M. Nixon. *American Directory of Organized Labor: Unions, Locals, Agreements, and Employers.* Detroit, Mich.: Gale Research , 1992.

Schlager, Neil (ed.). *St. James Encyclopedia of Labor History Worldwide: Major Events in Labor History and Their Impact.* 2 vols. Detroit: St. James Press/Gale Group/Thomson Learning, 2004.

Schneider, Dorothy, and Carl J. Schneider (eds.). *The ABC-CLIO Companion to Women in the Workplace.* Santa Barbara, Calif.: ABC-Clio, 1993.

Stearns, Peter N., and John H. Hinshaw (eds.). *The ABC-CLIO World History Companion to the Industrial Revolution.* Santa Barbara, Calif.: ABC-Clio, 1996.

Sutcliffe, Paul, and Ron Callus (eds.). *Glossary of Australian Industrial Relations Terms.* Sydney: Australian Centre for Industrial Relations Research and Teaching, University of Sydney, and Australian Centre in Strategic Management, Queensland University of Technology, 1994.

Trinder, Barrie (ed.). *The Blackwell Encyclopedia of Industrial Archaeology.* Oxford: Basil Blackwell, 1992.

Weir, Robert, and James P. Hanlan (eds.). *Historical Encyclopedia of American Labor.* 2 vols. Westport, Conn.: Greenwood Press, 2004.

Yerbury, Di, and Maria Karlsson (eds.). *The CCH Macquarie Dictionary of Employment and Industrial Relations.* Sydney: CCH Australia and Macquarie Library, 1992.

A.3 Biographical Dictionaries

Andreucci, Franco, and Detti Tommasco (eds.). *Il Movimento Operaio Italiano: Dizionario Biografico, 1853–1943.* 5 vols. Rome: Riuniti, 1975–1978. (On the Italian labor movement.)

Bellamy, Joyce, and John Saville (eds.). *Dictionary of Labour Biography.* 10 vols. London: Macmillan, 1972–2000.

Bianco, L., and V. Chevrier (eds.). *Dictionnaire Biographique du Mouvement Ouvrier International: La Chine.* Paris: Editions Ouvrières, 1985. (On the Chinese labor movement.)

Bourdet, Y., et al. (eds.). *Dictionnaire Biographique du Mouvement Ouvrier International: Autriche.* Paris: Editions Ouvrières, 1982.

Droz, Jacques (ed.). *Dictionnaire Biographique du Mouvement Ouvrier International: L'Allemagne.* Paris: Editions Ouvrières, 1990. (Covers the German labor movement up to the 1930s.)

Fink, Gary M. (ed.). *Biographical Dictionary of American Labor.* rev. ed. Westport, Conn.: Greenwood Press, 1985.

Gupte, V., et al. (eds.). *Profiles: Short Biographies of 101 Trade Union Leaders in India Based on Their Memoirs.* Bombay: Mumbai, 1996.

Knox, William (ed.). *Scottish Labour Leaders, 1918–39: A Biographical Dictionary.* Edinburgh: Mainstream, 1984.

Lane, A. Thomas (ed.). *Biographical Dictionary of European Labor Leaders.* 2 vols. Westport: Conn.: Greenwood Press, 1995.

Maitron, Jean (ed.). *Dictionnaire Biographique du Mouvement Ouvrier Français.* 44 vols. Paris: Editions Ouvrières, 1964–1997.

Meertens, van P. J., et al. (eds.). *Biografisch Woordenboek van het Socialisme en de Arbeidersbeweging in Nederland.* 9 vols. Amsterdam: Stichting beheer IISG, 1986–2003. (A biographical dictionary about socialists and labor leaders from 1840 to 1940. A follow-up is published online.)

Nyathi, Pathisa (ed.). *Masotsha Ndlovu.* Edinburgh: Longman, 1998. (Biographies of trade union officials and employees in Zimbabwe.)

Shiota, S. (ed.). *Dictionnaire Biographique du Mouvement Ouvrier International: Japon.* 2 vols. Paris: Editions Ouvrières, 1982.

Zimmermann, Rüdiger (ed.). *100 Jahre ÖTV: Biographien. Die Geschichte einer Gewerkschaft und ihrer Vorläuferorganisationen.* Frankfurt: Union-Druckerei und Verlagsanstalt, 1996. (The second volume of the official history of the German *Gewerkschaft Öffentliche Dienste, Transport and Verkehr* (ÖTV).)

A.4 Statistics

Australian Bureau of Statistics. *A Guide to Labour Statistics.* Canberra: Australian Bureau of Statistics, 1986. (ABS Catalogue No. 6102.0.)

———. *Employee Earnings, Benefits and Trade Union Membership.* Canberra: Australian Bureau of Statistics, Catalogue No. 6310.0. Issued from August 1995 to date (title varies).

Bain, G. S., and R. Price. *Profiles of Union Growth: A Comparative Statistical Portrait of Eight Countries.* Oxford: Basil Blackwell, 1980. (The countries were Great Britain, United States, Australia, Canada, Germany, Sweden, Denmark, and Norway.)

Bairoch, Paul, et al. *The Working Population and Its Structure.* Brussels: Free University of Brussels, 1968.

Bean, R. (ed.). *International Labour Statistics: A Handbook, Guide, and Recent Trends.* London: Routledge, 1989. (Includes data on labor union membership as well as labor disputes.)

Bureau of Labor Statistics, U.S. Department of Labor. *National Compensation Survey: Employee Benefits in Private Industry in the United States.* Washington, D. C.: Bureau of Labor Statistics, 2002–03 to date.

Conk, Margo. *The United States Census and Labor Force Change: A History of Occupational Statistics, 1870–1940.* Ann Arbor, Mich.: UMI Research Press, 1980.

Ebbinghaus, Bernard, and Jelle Visser. *Trade Unions in Western Europe since 1945.* London: Macmillan Reference, 2000. (For a follow-up visit www.uva.aias.net.)

Flora, Peter, Franz Kraus, and Winfried Pfenning (eds.). *State, Economy, and Society in Western Europe, 1815–1975: A Data Handbook.* 2 vols. Chicago: St. James Press, 1983, 1987. (Contains annual time series on the labor force and labor disputes.)

Hirsh, Barry T., and David A. Macpherson (eds.). *Union Membership and Earnings Data Book: Compilations from the Current Population Survey.* Washington, D.C.: Bureau of National Affairs, 1994 to date.

India, Labour Bureau. *Indian Labour Year Book.* Simla: Labour Bureau, 1947 to date.

International Labour Office. *Sources and Methods: Labour Statistics, Volume 7, Strikes and Lockouts.* Geneva: International Labour Office, 1993.

———. *Year Book of Labour Statistics.* Geneva: International Labour Office, 1935–1936 to date. (The principal international source of labor force data, but not labor unions.)

———. *Year Book of Labour Statistics: Retrospective Edition on Population Censuses, 1945–1989.* Geneva: International Labour Office, 1990.

Jacobs, Eva E. (ed.). *Handbook of U. S. Labor Statistics: Employment, Earnings, Prices, Productivity, and Other Labor Data.* 9th ed. Lanham, Md.: Bernan Press, 2006. (No labor union membership statistics.)

Lacey, Michael, and Mary Fumer (eds.). *The State and Social Investigation in Britain and the United States.* Cambridge: Cambridge University Press, 1993.

Organisation for Economic Co-operation and Development. *Historical Statistics 1960–1997.* Paris: OECD, 2000.

Philippines, Department of Labor. *Yearbook of Labor Statistics.* Manila: Department of Labor, 1981 to date.

Plowman, D. H. *Australian Trade Union Statistics.* 2nd ed. Sydney: Industrial Relations Research Centre, University of New South Wales, 1981.

Prywes, Ruth W. *The United States Labor Force: A Descriptive Analysis.* Westport, Conn.: Quorum Books, 2000.

Rawson, D. W., and Sue Wrightson. *Australian Unions 1984.* Sydney: Croom Helm Australia, 1985. (First published in 1970.)

Ross, John M. *Employment/Unemployment and Earnings Statistics: A Guide to Locating Data in U.S. Documents.* Lanham, Md.: Scarecrow Press, 1996.

Routh, Guy. *Occupation and Pay in Great Britain, 1906–79.* 2nd ed. London: Macmillan, 1980. (First published in 1965.)

United States Department of Labor, Bureau of Labor Statistics. *Directory of National Unions and Employee Associations.* Washington, D.C.: Bureau of Labor Statistics, 1930–1980. (In recent years as *Directory of U.S. Labor Organizations.*)

———. *Employment and Earnings.* Washington, D.C.: Department of Labor, Bureau of Labor Statistics, 1969 to date.

Visser, Jelle. *European Trade Unionism in Figures, 1913–1985.* Deventer, Netherlands, and Boston, Mass.: Kluwer, 1989.

———. *In Search of Inclusive Unionism.* Special Issue, *Bulletin of Comparative Industrial Relations*, No. 18. Deventer, Netherlands: Kluwer Law and Taxation Publishers, 1990.

Walsh, Kenneth. *Industrial Disputes: Methods and Measurement in the European Community.* Luxembourg, Office for the Official Publications of the European Communities: Eurostat, 1982.

———. *Trade Union Membership: Methods and Measurement in the European Community.* Brussels: Eurostat, 1985.

A.5 Sources

Auerbach, Jerold S. (ed.). *American Labor: The Twentieth Century.* Indianapolis: Bobbs-Merrill, 1969.

Baxandall, Rosalyn, et al. (eds.). *America's Working Women: A Documentary History—1600 to the Present.* New York: Random House, 1976.

Bernhardt, Debra E., and Rachel Bernstein (eds.). *Ordinary People, Extraordinary Lives: A Pictorial History of Working People in New York City.* New York: New York University Press, 2000.

Blewett, Mary H. (ed.). *We Will Rise in Our Might: Working Women's Voices from Nineteenth-Century New England.* Ithaca, N.Y.: Cornell University Press, 1991.

Cole, G. D. H., and A .W. Filson (eds.). *British Working Class Movements: Select Documents, 1789–1875.* London: Macmillan, 1951. (Reprinted in 1965 and again in 1967.)

Commons, John R., et al. (eds.). *A Documentary History of American Industrial Society.* 10 vols. New York: Russell and Russell, 1910–1911.

Dubofsky, Melvyn, and Joseph A. McCartin (eds.). *American Labor: A Documentary Collection.* New York: Palgrave Macmillan, 2004.

Foner, Philip S., and Herbert Shapiro (eds.). *Northern Labor and Antislavery: A Documentary History.* Westport, Conn.: Greenwood Press, 1994.

Gorman, John. *To Build Jerusalem: A Photographic Remembrance of British Working Class Life, 1875–1950.* London: Scorpion, 1980.

Hagan, Jim (ed.). *Australian Trade Unionism in Documents.* Melbourne: Longman Cheshire, 1986.

Hurley, F. Jack. *Industry and the Photographic Image: 153 Great Prints from 1850 to the Present.* New York: Dover in Association with George Eastman House, 1980.

International Labour Office. *Legislative Series.* Geneva: International Labor Office, 1919–1989; continued as *Labour Law Documents,* 1990 to date.

———. *World Labour Report 2*. Geneva: International Labor Office, 1985. (Includes a report on organized labor.)

International Trade Union Conference. *Annual Survey of Violations of Trade Union Rights*. Brussels: International Trade Union Conference, 1985 to date.

Lack, John, et al. (eds.). *"The Workers' Paradise?" Robert Schachner's Letters from Australia, 1906–07*. Melbourne: University of Melbourne, 1990.

McKinlay, Brian (ed.). *Australian Labor History in Documents*. 3 vols. Burwood, Victoria: Collins Dove, 1990. (A revised version of a work originally published in 1979.)

Morton, Desmond. *Working People: An Illustrated History of the Canadian Labour Movement*. 4th ed. Montreal, Ontario: McGill-Queen's University Press, 1998.

O'Farrell, Brigid, and Joyce L. Cornbluh (eds.). *Rocking the Boat: Women's Voices, 1915–1975*. New Brunswick, N.J.: Rutgers University Press, 1996.

Rock, Howard B. (ed.). *The New York Artisan, 1789–1825: A Documentary History*. Albany: State University of New York Press, 1989.

Traugott, Mark (ed.). *The French Worker: Autobiographies from the Early Industrial Era*. Berkeley: University of California Press, 1993.

Troy, Leo, and Neil Sheflin. *Union Sourcebook—Membership, Structure, Finance, Directory*. West Orange, N.J: Industrial Relations Data and Information Services, 1985.

Walker, Charles R. *Steel: The Diary of a Furnace Worker*. Annotated and edited by Kenneth J. Kobus. Warrendale, Pa.: Iron and Steel Society, 1999.

Ward, J. T., and W. Hamish Fraser (eds.). *Workers and Employers: Documents on Trade Unions and Industrial Relations in Britain since the Eighteenth Century*. London: Macmillan, 1980.

Wrigley, Chris (eds.). *British Trade Unions, 1945–1995*. Manchester: Manchester University Press, 1997.

A.6 Selected Classic Labor Studies

Bell, Lady Florence. *At the Works: A Study of a Manufacturing Town*. London: Virago Press, 1985. (Reproduction of the first edition published by Edward Arnold, London, in 1907; it was a study of Middlesborough, Yorkshire.)

Chile, Vere G. *How Labour Governs: A Study of Workers' Representation in Australia*. Melbourne: Melbourne University Press, 1964. (First published in 1923.)

Coghlan, Timothy A. *Labour and Industry in Australia from the First Settlement in 1788 to the Establishment of the Commonwealth in 1901*. 4 vols. Oxford: Oxford University Press, 1918. (Reissued by Macmillan, Melbourne, in 1968.)

Commons, John R., et al. *History of Labor in the United States*. 4 vols. New York: Macmillan, 1918–1935.

Coombes, B. L. *These Poor Hands: The Autobiography of a Miner Working in South Wales*. London: Victor Gollancz, 1939.

Drake, Barbara. *Women in Trade Unions*. London: Virago Press, 1984. (First published in 1920.)

Engels, Frederick. *The Condition of the Working Class in England.* Cambridge Library Collections, 2010 (First published in 1887 in German.)

Fynes, Richard. *The Miners of Northumberland and Durham: A History of Their Social and Political Progress.* Sunderland, U.K.: Thos. Summerbell, 1963. (First published in 1873.)

Mayhew, Henry. *London Labour and the London Poor.* 4 vols. New York: Dover, 1968. (Reproduction of the edition of 1861–1862.)

Orwell, George. *The Road to Wigan Pier.* Harmondsworth, U.K.: Penguin Books, 1962, reprinted many times thereafter. (First published in 1937.)

Paris, Le Comte de. *The Trade Unions of England.* Trans. Nassau J. Senior. London: Smith Elder, 1869.

Roberts, Peter. *Anthracite Coal Communities: A Study of the Demography, the Social, Educational and Moral Life of the Anthracite Regions.* New York: Macmillan, 1904.

Sutcliffe, James T. *A History of Trade Unionism in Australia.* Melbourne: Macmillan, 1967. (First published in 1921.)

Thompson, E. P., and Eileen Yeo (eds.). *The Unknown Mayhew: Selections from the Morning Chronicle, 1849–50.* London: Merlin Press, 1971.

Tressell, Robert (pen-name of Robert Noonan). *The Ragged Trousered Philanthropists.* London: Panther Books, 1965. (A full version was not published until 1955.)

Walker, Charles R. *Steel: The Diary of a Furnace Worker.* Annotated and edited by Kenneth J. Kobus. Warrendale, Pa.: Iron and Steel Society, 1999. (First published in 1922.)

Webb, Sidney, and Beatrice Webb. *History of Trade Unionism,* rev. ed. 2 vols. London: Longmans, Green, 1907. (First published in 1894.)

——. *Trade Union Democracy.* London: Longmans, Green, 1898.

Wilkinson, Ellen. *The Town That Was Murdered: The Life-Story of Jarrow.* London: Victor Gollancz, 1939.

Wilson, John. *A History of the Durham Miners' Association, 1870-1904.* Durham, U.K.: J. H. Veitch & Sons, 1907.

Zola, Émile. *Germinal.* Harmondsworth, London: Penguin Books, 2004. (First published in 1885.)

A.7 Journals

Asian Labour Update (Kowloon), 1980 to date.

British Journal of Industrial Relations (London School of Economics), 1963 to date.

Bulletin of Comparative Labour Relations (Deventer), 1970 to date.

Conditions of Work Digest (International Labour Office, Geneva), 1986 to date.

Economic and Industrial Democracy (Industrial Relations Services, London), 1980 to date.

Economic & Labour Market Review. (Department of Employment, London), 2007 to 2011. (successor of *Labour Gazette* (Department of Labour, London), 1893–1995, and *Labour Market Trends* (Department of Employment, London), 1996–2006).

Employee Relations (Bradford), 1978 to date.

European Industrial Relations Review (London), 1974 to date.

European Journal of Industrial Relations (London), 1995 to date.

Free Labour World (International Confederation of Free Trade Unions, Brussels), 1950–1997. (Replaced by *Trade Union World*.)

Gender, Work, and Organization (Oxford), 1994 to date.

Government Employee Relations Report (Bureau of National Affairs, Washington, D.C), 1952 to date. (Weekly report on federal, state, and local government industrial relations in the United States.)

Historical Abstracts (New York), 1955 to date.

Historical Studies in Industrial Relations (Keele), 1996 to date.

IDS Pay Report (Income Data Services, London), 1966 to date.

Indian Journal of Industrial Relations (New Delhi), 1965 to date.

Indian Journal of Labour Economics (New Delhi), 1957 to date.

Industrial and Labor Relations Review (Ithaca, N.Y.), 1947 to date.

Industrial Law Journal (London/Oxford), 1971 to date.

Industrial Relations (Berkeley, Calif.), 1967 to date.

Industrial Relations Journal (Oxford), 1966 to date.

Industrial Relations Review and Report (Industrial Relations Services, London), 1971 to date.

International Journal of Comparative Labour Law and Industrial Relations (Deventer), 1977 to date.

International Journal of Human Resource Management (London), 1990 to date.

International Journal of Labour Research. Trade Union Strategies towards Global Production Systems (Geneva), 2009 to date.

International Labor and Working Class History (Los Angeles), 1976 to date.

International Labour Review (International Labour Office, Geneva), 1921 to date.

International Review of Social History (Cambridge), 1956 to date.

International Union Rights (London), 1993 to date.

Japan Labor Bulletin (Tokyo), 1961 to date.

Journal of Communist Studies (London), 1985 to 1994.

Journal of Communist Studies and Transition Politics, 1994 to date.

Journal of Economic Literature (Pittsburgh), 1969 to date. (Includes annotated lists of new books that cover labor and economic history topics.)

Journal of Industrial Relations (Sydney), 1959 to date.

Journal of Labor Economics (Chicago), 1983 to date.

Journal of Labour Research (Fairfax, Va.), 1980 to date.

Journal of Management Studies (Oxford), 1964 to date.

Journal of Social History (Fairfax, Va.), 1967 to date.

Labor Developments Abroad (U.S. Department of Labor, Bureau of Labor Statistics), 1956–1972. (A useful compendium of international labor events and developments for this period.)

Labor History (New York), 1960 to date.

Labor Law Journal (Riverwoods, Ill.), 1949 to date.

Labor Studies Journal (Rutgers University, N.J), 1975 to date.

Labour: Review of Economics and Industrial Relations (Oxford), 1987 to date.

Labour & Industry (Brisbane/Geelong), 1987 to date.

Labour and Society (Geneva), 1977 to date.

Labour, Capital and Society (Montreal), 1979 to date.

Labour History (Canberra/Sydney), 1962 to date.

Labour Research (London), 1980 to date.

Labour: Review of Labour Economics and Industrial Relations (Oxford), 1987 to date.

Labour/Le Travail (Halifax), 1976 to date.

Monthly Labor Review (U.S. Bureau of Labor Statistics, Washington, D.C.), 1915 to date.

New Zealand Journal of Industrial Relations (Dunedin), 1976 to 2003. (Replaced with New Zealand Journal of Employment Relations (Auckland), 2003 to date.)

Policy Studies (London), 1979 to date.

Regional Labor Review (New York), 1998 to date.

Socialist Register (London), 1964 to date.

South African Journal of Labour Relations (Pretoria), 1976 to date.

South-East Europe Review for Labour and Social Affairs (Brussels), 1998 to date.

Trade Union World (International Confederation of Free Trade Unions, Brussels), 1997 to July–August 2002. (A continuation of *Free Labour World* in a magazine format.)

Transport International (London: International Transport Workers' Federation), 2000 to date.

Work, Employment and Society (Durham, U.K.), 1987 to date.

B. INTERNATIONAL STUDIES

B.1 International Unionism

Barnouin, Barbara. *The European Labor Movement and European Integration.* London: Frances Pinter, 1986.

Bartolomei de la Cruz, Héctor, et al. *The International Labor Organization: The International Standards System and Basic Human Rights.* Boulder, Colo. and Oxford: Westview Press and HarperCollins, 1996.

Bendiner, Barton. *International Labour Affairs: The World Trade Unions and the Multinational Companies.* Oxford: Oxford University Press, 1987.

Busch, Gary K. *Political Currents in the International Trade Movement.* 2 vols. London: The Economist Intelligence Unit, 1980.

———. *The Political Role of International Trade Unions.* London: Macmillan, 1983.

Carew, Andrew, et al. (ed.). *The International Confederation of Free Trade Unions.* Bern, Switzerland: P. Lang, 2000.

Ghebali, Victor-Yves. *The International Labour Organisation: A Case Study on the Evolution of U.N. Specialised Agencies.* Dordrecht, Netherlands: Kluwer Academic Publishers, 1989.

Goethem, Geert van. *The Amsterdam International: The World of the International Federation of Trade Unions (IFTU), 1913–1945.* Amsterdam: Amsab-Instituut voor Sociale Geschiedenis, 2005.

Gordon, Michael E., and Lowell Turner (eds.). *Transnational Cooperation among Labor Unions*. Ithaca, N.Y.: ILR Press, 2000.

Holthoon, F. van, and Marcel van der Linden (eds.). *Internationalism in the Labour Movement, 1830–1940*. Leiden, Netherlands: E.J. Brill, 1990.

Horne, John N. *Labour at War: France and Britain, 1914–1918*. Oxford: Clarendon Press, 1991.

International Confederation of Free Trade Unions. *The Challenge of Change: Report to the 14th ICFTU World Congress on the Tasks Ahead for the International Free Trade Union Movement*. Brussels: International Confederation of Free Trade Unions, 1988.

International Labour Organization. *Industrial Relations, Democracy, and Social Stability*. Geneva: International Labour Organization, 1997. (An examination of international organized labor in the mid-1990s.)

———. *World Labour Report*. Geneva: International Labour Office, 1984 to date. (*Reports* 2 and 6 contain chapters on the state of labor unions in the world.)

World Labour Report. Geneva: International Labour Office, 1984 to date. (*Reports* 2 and 6 contain chapters on the state of labor unions in the world.)

International Metalworkers' Federation. *World of the IMF—IMF and the World: An Introduction to the International Metalworkers' Federation*. Geneva: International Metalworkers' Federation, 1996.

International Transport Workers' Federation. *Solidarity: The First 100 Years of the International Transport Workers' Federation*. London: Pluto Press, 1996.

Johansson, Knut, and Jan-Erik Norling. *Building the Future*. Geneva: International Federation of Building and Wood Workers, 1997.

Linden, Marcel van der, and Jürgen Rojahn (eds.). *The Formation of Labour Movements: An International Perspective, 1870–1914*. 2 vols. Leiden, Netherlands: E. J. Brill, 1990.

Lis, Katharina, Jan Lucassen, and Hugo Soly (eds.). *Before the Unions: Wage Earners and Collective Action in Europe, 1300–1850*. Cambridge: Cambridge University Press, 1995.

MacShane, Denis. *International Labour and the Origins of the Cold War*. Oxford: Clarendon Press, 1992.

Milner, Susan. *The Dilemmas of Internationalism: French Syndicalism and the International Labor Movement, 1900–1914*. New York: Berg, 1990.

Newton, Douglas J. *British Labour, European Socialism and the Struggle for Peace, 1889–1914*. Oxford: Clarendon Press, 1985.

Pasture, Patrick, and Johan Verberckmoes (eds.). *Working-Class Internationalism and the Appeal of National Identity: Historical Debates and Current Perspectives*. Oxford: Berg, 1998.

Prochaska, Alice. *History of the General Federation of Trade Unions*. London: Allen & Unwin, 1982.

Reinalda, Bob (ed.). *The International Transport Workers' Federation, 1914–1945: The Edo Fimmen Era*. Amsterdam: Stichting beheer IISG, 1997.

Rodriguez Garcia, Magaly. *Liberal Workers of the World, Unite?: the ICFTU and the Defence of Labour Liberalism in Europe and Latin America (1949–1969)*. New York: Peter Lang, 2010.

Schevenels, Walther. *Forty-Five Years: International Federation of Trade Unions.* Brussels: Board of Trustees of the International Federation of Trade Unions, 1956.

Southall, Roger. *Imperialism or Solidarity: International Labour and South African Trade Unions.* Rondebosch, South Africa: UCT Press, 1995. (A study based on events since about 1970.)

Teague, Paul, and John Gahl. *Industrial Relations and European Integration.* London: Lawrence & Wishart, 1992.

Thorpe, W. *The Workers Themselves: Revolutionary Syndicalism and International Labour.* Dordrecht, Netherlands: Kluwer, 1990.

Van Daele, Jasmien, et al. (eds.). *ILO Histories. Essays on the International Labour Organization and Its Impact on the World During the Twentieth Century.* Bern, Switzerland, 2010.

Wallerstein, I. (ed.). *Labor in the World Social Structure.* London: Sage, 1983.

Western, Bruce. *Between Class and Market: Postwar Unionization in the Capitalist Democracies.* Princeton, N.J.: Princeton University Press, 1999.

Windmuller, J. P. *The International Trade Union Movement.* Deventer: Kluwer, 1980.

World Federation of Trade Unions. *The World Federation of Trade Unions, 1945–1985.* Prague: World Federation of Trade Unions, 1985.

Yates, Michael D. *Why Unions Matter.* New York: Monthly review press, 1998.

B.2 International Comparative Studies

Adams, R. A. (ed.). *Comparative Industrial Relations: Contemporary Research and Theory.* London: HarperCollins, 1991.

———. (ed.). *Industrial Relations under Liberal Democracy: North America in Comparative Perspective.* Columbia: University of South Carolina Press, 1995.

Ananaba, Wogu. *The Trade Union Movement in Africa: Promise and Performance.* London: Hurst, 1979.

Baglioni, Guido, and Colin Crouch (eds.). *European Industrial Relations: The Challenge of Flexibility.* London: Sage, 1990.

Ballot, M., et al. *Labor-Management Relations in a Changing Environment.* 2nd ed. New York: John Wiley, 1996.

Bamber, Greg J., et al. (eds.). *Employment Relations in Asia-Pacific: Changing Approaches.* Sydney: Allen and Unwin, 2000. (Contains contributions on Australia, China, Indonesia, Japan, South Korea, New Zealand and Taiwan.)

Bamber, Greg J., and Russell D. Lansbury (eds.). *International and Comparative Industrial Relations: A Study of Industrialised Market Economies.* Sydney: Allen & Unwin, 1993.

Barbash, Jack, and Kate Barbash (eds.). *Theories and Concepts in Comparative Industrial Relations.* Columbia: University of South Carolina Press, 1989.

Bean, R. *Comparative Industrial Relations: An Introduction to Cross-National Perspectives.* London: Croom Helm, 1985. (reprint in 1991.)

Berger, Stefan, and David Broughton (eds.). *The Force of Labour: The Western European Labour Movement and the Working Class in the Twentieth Century.* Oxford: Berg Publishers, 1995.

Bergquist, Charles. *Labor in Latin America: Comparative Essays on Chile, Argentina, Venezuela, and Colombia.* Stanford, Calif.: Stanford University Press, 1986.

Beyme, Klaus von. *Challenge to Power: Trade Unions and Industrial Relations in Capitalist Countries.* London: Sage, 1980.

Blanchflower, David G. *A Cross-Country Study of Union Membership.* Institute for the Study of Labor, 2006. (Available as an electronic publication.)

Boyd, Rosalind E., Robert Cohen, and Peter C. Gutkind (eds.). *International Labour and the Third World: The Making of a New Working Class.* Aldershot, U.K.: Avebury, 1987.

Brandell, I. (ed.). *Workers in Third World Industrialization Struggles and Strategies.* London: Macmillan, 1991.

Buchanan, Paul G., and Kate Nicholls. *Labour Politics in Small Open Democracies: Australia, Chile, Ireland, New Zealand, and Uruguay.* New York: Palgrave Macmillan, 2003.

Córdova, Efren (ed.). *Industrial Relations in Latin America.* New York: Praeger, 1984.

Crouch, Colin. *Industrial Relations and the European State Traditions.* Oxford: Clarendon Press, 1992.

Ferner, Anthony, and Richard Hyman (eds.). *Changing Industrial Relations in Europe.* Oxford: Blackwell, 1998. (A revised version of a work first published in 1992.)

———. *New Frontiers in European Industrial Relations.* Cambridge, Mass.: Blackwell, 1994.

Frenkel, Stephen J. (ed.). *Organized Labor in the Asia-Pacific Region: A Comparative Study of Trade Unionism in Nine Countries.* Ithaca, N.Y.: ILR Press, 1993. (Studies Australia, China, Malaysia, New Zealand, Hong Kong, Singapore, South Korea, and Taiwan.)

Frenkel, Stephen J., and Jeffrey Harrod (eds.). *Industrialization and Labor Relations: Contemporary Research in Seven Countries.* Ithaca, N.Y.: ILR Press, 1995. (A study of South Korea, Malaysia, Hong Kong, Singapore, South Africa, Thailand, and Taiwan.)

Frenkel, Stephen J., et al. *Organization of Work in the Information Economy.* Ithaca, N.Y.: ILR Press, 1999.

Galenson, Walter. *Labor and Economic Growth in Five Asian Countries: South Korea, Malaysia, Taiwan and the Philippines.* New York: Praeger, 1992.

Geary, Dick (ed.). *Labour and Socialist Movements in Europe before 1914.* Oxford: Berg, 1989. (Deals with the United Kingdom, France, Germany, Russia, Italy, and Spain.)

Hanson, Charles, Sheila Jackson, and Douglas Miller. *The Closed Shop: A Comparative Study in Public Policy and Trade Union Security in Britain, the USA and West Germany.* New York: St. Martin's Press, 1982.

Kaufman, Bruce E. *The Global Evolution of Industrial Relations: Events, Ideas and the IIRA.* Geneva, International Labour Office, 2004.

Kirk, Neville. *Comrades and Cousins: Globalization, Workers and Labour Movements in Britain, the USA and Australia from the 1880s to 1914.* London: Merlin Press, 2003.

Lipset, Seymour Martin, and Noah M. Meltz. *The Paradox of American Unionism: Why Americans Like Unions More Than Canadians Do, but Join Much Less.* Ithaca, N.Y.: ILR Press, 2004.

Martin, Ross M. *Trade Unionism: Purposes and Forms.* Oxford: Clarendon Press, 1989.

Maurice, M., F. Sellier, and J. Silvestre. *The Social Foundations of Industrial Power: A Comparison of France and Germany.* Cambridge, Mass.: MIT Press, 1986.

Mommsen, Wolfgang, J., and Hans-Gerhard Husung (eds.). *The Development of Trade Unionism in Great Britain and Germany, 1880–1914.* London: George Allen and Unwin, 1986.

Peetz, David, Alison Preston, and Jim Docherty (eds.). *Workplace Bargaining in the International Context: First Report of the Workplace Bargaining Research Project.* Canberra: Department of Industrial Relations, 1993. (Studies Australia, Germany, Sweden, Britain, Japan, Canada, United States, and New Zealand.)

Phelan, Craig. *Trade Union Revitalisation: Trends and Prospects in 34 Countries.* Bern: Peter Lang, 2007.

———. *Trade Unionism since 1945: Towards a Global History.* Bern: Peter Lang, 2009.

Phelan, Craig (ed.). *The Future of Organized Labour: Global Perspectives.* Bern: Peter Lang, 2006.

Poole, Michael. *Industrial Relations: Origins and Patterns of National Diversity.* London: Routledge & Kegan Paul, 1986.

Pravada, A., and B. A. Ruble (eds.). *Trade Unions in Communist States.* London: Allen & Unwin, 1987.

Regini, Marino (ed.). *The Future of Labour Movements.* London: Sage, 1992.

Rigby, Mike, Roger Smith, and Teresa Lawlor (eds.). *European Trade Unions: Change and Response.* London: Routledge, 1999.

Rothman, M., et al. (eds.). *Industrial Relations around the World: Labor Relations for Multinational Companies.* Berlin: De Gruyter, 1992.

Ruysseveldt, J. van, and Jelle Visser. *Industrial Relations in Europe: Tradition and Transformations.* London: Sage, 1996.

Sisson, K. *The Management of Collective Bargaining: An International Comparison.* Oxford: Basil Blackwell, 1987.

Smith, E. Owen (ed.). *Trade Unions in the Developed Economies.* London: Croom Helm, 1981.

Southall, Roger (ed.). *Trade Unions and the New Industrialisation of the Third World.* London: University of Ottawa Press, 1988.

Sraïeb, Noureddine, A. Ben Hamida, and J. Bessis (eds.). *Le Mouvement Ouvrier Magrébin.* Paris: Editions du Centre National de la Recherche Scientifique, 1985. (Organized Labor in the Magreb.)

Sturmthal, Adolf F. *Left of Center: European Labor since World War II.* Urbana: University of Illinois Press, 1983.

Thirkell, John, et al. (eds.). *Labour Relations and Political Change in Eastern Europe: A Comparative Perspective.* London: UCL Press, 1995.

Valenzuela, J. Samuel, and Jeffrey Goodwin. *Labor Movements under Authoritarian Regimes.* Cambridge, Mass.: Center for European Studies, Harvard University, 1983.

Waddington, Jeremy, and Reiner Hoffman (eds.). *Trade Unions in Europe: Facing Challenges and Searching for Solutions.* Brussels: European Trade Union Institute, 2001.

Wilkinson, Barry. *Labour and Industry in the Asia-Pacific: Lessons for the Newly Industrialized Countries.* New York: Walter de Gruyter, 1994.

Wood, Geoffrey, and Chris Brewster (eds.). *Industrial Relations in Africa.* Hampshire, U.K.: MacMillan, 2007.

C. NATIONAL STUDIES

C.1 Histories of Peak National Organizations of Unions

Agyeman, Opoku. *The Failure of Grassroots Pan-Africanism: The Case of the All-African Trade Union Federation.* Lanham, Md.: Lexington, 2003.

Andrews, Gregg. *Shoulder to Shoulder? The American Federation of Labor, the United States and the Mexican Revolution, 1910–1924.* Berkeley: University of California Press, 1991.

Baskin, Jeremy. *Striking Back: A History of COSATU.* Johannesburg: Raven Press, 1991.

Boudali, Nouri. *L'Union Génerale Tunisienne du Travail: Souvenirs et Récits.* Tunis: N. Boudali, 1998. (A history of the Tunisian General Union of Labor.)

Clark, Jon, H. Hartmann, C. Lau, and D. Winchester. *Trade Unions, National Politics and Economic Management: A Comparative Study of the TUC and the DGB.* London: Anglo-German Foundation for the Study of Industrial Society, 1980.

Dorfman, Gerald A. *British Trade Unionism against the Trades Union Congress.* Stanford, Calif.: Hoover Institution Press, 1983.

Draper, Alan. *A Rope of Sand: The AFL-CIO Committee on Political Education.* New York: Praeger, 1988.

Hagan, Jim. *The History of the A.C.T.U.* Melbourne: Longman Cheshire, 1981.

Hearn, Mark, and Harry Knowles. *One Big Union: A History of the Australian Workers Union.* Melbourne: Cambridge University Press, 1996.

Kersten, Andrew E. *Labor's Home Front: The American Federation of Labor during World War II.* New York: New York University Press, 2006.

Levenstein, Nelson. *Communism, Anti-Communism and the CIO.* Westport, Conn.: Greenwood Press, 1981.

Lichtenstein, Nelson N. *Labor's War at Home: The CIO in World War II.* Philadelphia: Temple University Press, 2003. (First published in 1982.)

Martin, Ross M. *TUC: The Growth of a Pressure Group, 1868–1976.* Oxford: Oxford University Press, 1980.

Mort, Jo-Ann (ed.). *Not Your Father's Union Movement: Inside the AFL-CIO.* New York: Verso, 1998.

Nicholson, Marjorie. *The TUC Overseas: The Roots of Policy*. London: Allen & Unwin, 1986.

Peirats, José. *The CNT in the Spanish Revolution*. Hastings, U.K.: Meltzer Press, 2001.

Prochaska, Alice. *History of the General Federation of Trade Unions*. London: Allen & Unwin, 1982.

Scipes, Kim. *AFL-CIO's Secret War against Developing Country Workers: Solidarity or Sabotage?* Lanham, Md.: Lexington Books, 2010.

Stillman, Donald Dennis. *Stronger Together: The Story of SEIU*. Washington, D.C.: SEIU, 2010.

Taylor, Robert. *The TUC: From the General Strike to New Unionism*. New York: St. Martin's Press, 2000.

Tine, Warren Van, et al. *In the Workers' Interest: A History of the Ohio AFL-CIO, 1958–1998*. Columbus: Ohio State University Center for Labor Research, 1998.

Tuckett, Angela. *The Scottish Trade Union Congress: The First 80 Years, 1897–1977*. Edinburgh: Mainstream, 1986.

Wehrle, Edmund F. *Between a River and a Mountain: The AFL-CIO and the Vietnam War*. Ann Arbor, Mich.: The University of Michigan Press, 2005.

C.2 Histories of Organized Labor in Individual Countries

C.2.1 Africa

Andr, Gunilla. *Union Power in the Nigerian Textile Industry: Labour Regime and Adjustment*. New Brunswick, N.J.: Transaction Publishers, 1999.

Asante, S. *The Democratization Process and the Trade Unions in Africa*. Brussels: Worldsolidarity, 1993.

Awad, Ibrahim. *Employment and Decent Work in North Africa*. Cairo: ILO, 2004.

Bauer, Gretchen. *Labor and Democracy in Namibia, 1971–1996*. Athens: Ohio University Press, 1998.

Bekko, Gregg J., and George M. Muchai. *Protecting Workers in Micro and Small Enterprises: Can Trade Unions Make a Difference? A Case Study of the Bakery and Confectionery Sub-Sector in Kenya*. Geneva: International Labour Organization, 2002.

Du Toit, M. A. *South African Trade Unions*. Johannesburg: McGraw-Hill, 1976.

Hashim, Yahaya. *The State and Trade Unions in Africa: A Study in Macro-Corporatism*. The Hague, Netherlands: Institute of Social Studies, 2003.

Hirson, B. *Yours for the Union: Class and Community Struggles in South Africa, 1930–1947*. London: Zed Books, 1989.

Holdt, Karl von. *Transition from Below: Forging Trade Unionism and Workplace Change in South Africa*. Pietermaritzburg: University of Natal Press, 2003.

Kanyenze, Godfrey. *Giving Voice to the Unprotected Workers in the Informal Economy in Africa: the Case of Zimbabwe*. Geneva: International Labour Organization, 2004.

Kester, Gérard, and Akua O. Britwum. *Trade Unions and Workplace Democracy in Africa*. Aldershot, Hampshire, U.K.: Ashgate, 2007.

Kraus, Jon. *Trade Unions and the Coming of Democracy in Africa*. Palgrave Macmillan, 2007.

Lewis, Jon. *Industrialisation and Trade Union Organization in South Africa 1924–1955: The Rise and Fall of the South African Trades and Labour Council*. Cambridge: Cambridge University Press, 1984. (Paperback edition available since 2011.)

Luckhardt, Ken, and B. Wall. *Organise or Starve! A History of the South African Congress of Trade Unions*. London: Lawrence and Wishart, 1980.

Mogalakwe, Monageng. *The State and Organised Labour in Botswana: "Liberal Democracy" in Emergent Capitalism*. Aldershot, U.K.: Ashgate, 1997.

Mwamadzingo, Mohammed, and Ditiro Saleshando. *Trade Unions and Poverty Alleviation in Africa*. Geneva: International Labour Organization, 2003.

Odigie, S. A. *State Intervention in Industrial Relations in Nigeria, 1861–1989*. Benin City: privately printed, 1993.

Otobo, D. *Trade Union Movement in Nigeria: Yesterday, Today, and Tomorrow*. Lagos: Malthouse Press, 1995.

Panford, Kwamina. *IMF-World Bank and Labor's Burdens in Africa: Ghana's Experience*. Westport, Conn.: Praeger, 2001.

Sikainga, Ahmad A. *Organized Labor and Social Change in Contemporary Sudan*. Durham, U.K.: University of Durham, Institute for Middle Eastern and Islamic Studies, 2003.

C.2.2 British Isles

Boyle, John W. *The Irish Labor Movement in the Nineteenth Century*. Washington, D.C.: Catholic University of America Press, 1988.

Brown, Henry Phelps. *The Origins of Trade Union Power*. Oxford: Oxford University Press, 1986. (Although mainly about Great Britain, this work contains chapters on the United States, Canada, and Australia.)

Bryson, Alex. *The Size of the Union Membership Wage Premium in Britain's Private Sector*. London: Policy Studies Institute, 2003.

Charlton, John. *The Chartists: The First National Workers' Movement*. London: Pluto Press, 1997.

Chase, Malcolm. *Early Trade Unionism: Fraternity, Skill, and the Politics of Labour*. Aldershot, U.K.: Ashgate, 2000.

Clegg, Hugh A. *A History of British Trade Unions since 1889: Volume II, 1911–1933*. Oxford: Oxford University Press, 1985.

———. *A History of British Trade Unions since 1889: Volume III, 1934–1951*. Oxford: Oxford University Press, 1994.

Clegg, Hugh A., Alan Fox, and A. F. Thompson. *A History of British Trade Unions since 1889: Volume I, 1889–1910*. Oxford: Oxford University Press, 1964.

Coates, Ken, and Tony Topham. *Trade Unions in Britain*. Nottingham, U.K.: Spokesman, 1980.

Daniels, Gary, and John McIlroy (eds.). *Trade Unions in a Neoliberal World: British Trade Unions under New Labour*. London: Routledge, 2008.

Dijkstra, A. Geske, and Gregor Gall. *Union Organizing: Campaigning for Trade Union Recognition.* London: Routledge, 2003.

Dobson, C. R. *Masters and Journeymen: A Prehistory of Industrial Relations, 1717–1800.* London: Croom Helm, 1980.

Fraser, W. Hamish. *A History of British Trade Unionism, 1700–1998.* Basingstoke, U.K.: Macmillan, 1999.

Kenefick, W., and A. McIvor. *Roots of Red Clydeside, 1910–1914: Labour Unrest and Industrial Relations in West Scotland.* Edinburgh: John Donald, 1996.

Laybourn, Keith. *History of British Trade Unionism, c. 1770–1990.* Wolfeboro Falls, N.H.: Allan Sutton, 1992.

Leeson, R. A. *Travelling Brothers: The Six Centuries' Road from Craft Fellowship to Trade Unionism.* London: George Allen & Unwin, 1979.

McCarthy, C. *Trade Unions in Ireland, 1894–1960.* Dublin: Institute of Public Administration, 1977.

Pelling, Henry. *A History of British Trade Unionism.* 5th ed. Basingstoke, U.K.: Macmillan, 1992. (First published in 1963.)

Price, Richard. *Labour in British History: An Interpretative History.* London: Routledge, 1990. (First published by Croom Helm in 1986.)

Sewell, Rob. *In the Cause of Labour. History of British Trade Unionism.* London: Wellred Publications, 2003.

Wrigley, Chris. *British Trade Unions since 1933.* Cambridge: Cambridge University Press, 2002.

C.2.3 Middle East and Asia

Balasubramanian, A. *Trade Union Movement.* Pune, India: Everest Publishing House, 2002. (On the trade union movement in India.)

Benson, John, and Ying Zhu. *Trade Unions in Asia: An Economic and Sociological Analysis.* London: Routledge, 2008.

Chalmers, Norma. *Industrial Relations in Japan: The Peripheral Workforce.* London: Routledge, 1989.

Chen, P. K. *The Labour Movement in China.* Hong Kong: Swindon Books, 1985.

China, Anita (ed.). *China's Workers Under Assault: The Exploitation of Labor in a Globalizing Economy.* Armonk, N.Y.: M. E. Sharpe, 2001.

Choi, Jang Jip. *Labor and the Authoritarian State: Labor Unions in South Korean Manufacturing Industries, 1961–1980.* Seoul: Korea University Press, 1989.

Dejillas, Leopoldo J. *Trade Union Behavior in the Philippines, 1946–1990.* Manilla: Anteneo De Manilla University Press, 1994.

Elmhirst, Rebecca, and Ratna Saptari. *Labour in Southeast Asia: Local Processes in a Globalised World.* London: Routledge: 2004.

Geffken, Rolf, et al. *Labor and Trade Unions in China.* Brussels: ETUI-REHS, 2006.

Gibbs, Michael H. *Struggle and Purpose in Postwar Japanese Unionism.* Berkeley, Calif.: Institute of East Asian Studies, 2000.

Heller, Patrick. *The Labor of Development: Workers and the Transformation of Capitalism in Kerala, India.* Ithaca, N.Y.: Cornell University Press, 1999.

Hensman, Rohini. *Workers, Unions, and Global Capitalism: Lessons from India.* New York: Columbia University Press, 2011.

Hong, Yu. *Labor, Class Formation, and China's Informationized Policy of Economic Development.* Lanham, Md.: Lexington Books, 2011.

Hutchinson, Jane, and Andrew Brown (eds.). *Organising Labour in Globalising Asia.* London: Routledge: 2001.

Ingleson, John. *In Search of Justice: Workers and Unions in Colonial Java, 1908–1926.* Singapore: Oxford University Press, 1986.

Khan, B. A. *Trade Unionism and Industrial Relations in Pakistan.* Karachi: Royal, 1980.

Kim, S. J. *Trade Unionism in Korea.* Seoul: Federation of Korean Trade Unions, 1996.

King-Chi Chan, Chris, and Pun Ngai. "The Making of a New Working Class: A Study of Collective Actions of Migrant Workers in South China." In *China Quarterly* 198(1): 287–303.

Kume, Ikuo. *Disparaged Success: Labor Politics in Postwar Japan.* Ithaca, N.Y.: Cornell University Press, 1998.

Ladjevardi, Habib. *Labor Unions and Autocracy in Iran.* New York: Syracuse University Press, 1985.

Lambert, R. *Authoritarian State Unionism in New Order Indonesia.* Perth, Western Australia: Murdoch University, 1993.

Lee, Chang Hee. *Industrial Relations and Collective Bargaining in China.* Geneva: International Labour Organization, 2009.

Lee, Ching Kwan. *Against the Law: Labor Protests in China's Rustbelt and Sunbelt.* Berkeley, University of California Press, 2007.

———. *Gender and the South China Miracle: Two Worlds of Factory Women.* Berkeley, University of California Press, 1998.

Lee, Ching Kwan (ed.). *Working in China: Ethnographies of Labor and Workplace Transformation.* London: Routledge, 2006.

Lee, Lai To. *Trade Unions in China, 1949 to the Present: The Organization and Leadership of the All-China Federation of Trade Unions.* Singapore: Singapore University Press, 1986.

Matsuzaki, H. *Japanese Business Unionism: The Historical Development of a Unique Labour Movement.* Sydney: University of New South Wales, 1992.

Mehta, B. L. *The Trade Union Movement in India.* New Delhi: Kanishka, 1991.

Narayana Chetty, Y. *Dynamics of Trade Unionism in India.* New Delhi: Anmol Publications, 2004.

Ng, Hong Sek, and Malcolm Warner. *China's Trade Unions and Management.* New York: St. Martin's Press, 1998.

Oakley, Sheila. *Labor Relations in China's Socialist Market Economy.* Quorum Books, 2002.

Philion, Stephen E. *Workers' Democracy in China's Transition from State Socialism.* New York: Taylor & Francis, 2008.

Pringle, Tim. *Trade Unions in China: the Challenge of Labour Unrest.* Abingdon, U.K.: New York: Routledge, 2011.

Pun, Ngai. *Made in China: Women Factory Workers in a Global Workplace*. Durham, U.K.: Duke University Press, 2005.

Qiu, Jack Linchuan. *Working-Class Network Society: Communication Technology and the Information Have-Less in Urban China*. Cambridge: MIT Press, 2009.

Ramachandran, Selvakumaran, and Kris Arjunan. *Trade Unionism in the Malaysian Plantation Industry*. Sydney: University of New South Wales Studies in Human Resource Management and Industrial Relations in Asia, No. 2, 1993.

Ramasamy, P. *Plantation Labour, Unions, Capital, and the State in Peninsular Malaysia*. Kuala Lumpur: Oxford University Press, 1994.

Sen, Ratna. *Industrial Relations in India: Shifting Paradigms*. New Delhi: Macmillan India, 2003.

Shaheed, Zafar. *The Labor Movement in Pakistan: Organization and Leadership in Karachi in the 1970s*. Karachi: Oxford University Press, 2007.

Shalev, Michael. *Labour and the Political Economy in Israel*. New York: Oxford University Press, 1992.

Sheehan, Jackie. *Chinese Workers: A New History*. London: Routledge, 1998.

Solinger, Dorothy. *Contesting Citizenship in Urban China: Peasant Migrants, the State, and the Logic of the Market*. Berkeley: University of California Press, 1999.

Song, Ho Keun. *Labour Unions in the Republic of Korea*. Geneva: International Institute for Labour Studies, 1999.

Verma, Pramod, and S. Mookherjee. *Trade Unions in India*. New Delhi: Oxford and IBA, 1982.

Warner, Malcolm (ed.). *Changing Workplace Relations in the Chinese Economy*. London: Macmillan, 2000.

Woodiwiss, Anthony. *Law, Labour and Society in Japan: From Repression to Reluctant Recognition*. London: Routledge, 1991.

Yan, Hairong. *New Masters, New Servants: Migration, Development, and Women Workers in China*. Durham, U.K.: Duke University Press, 2008.

C.2.4 Europe

Agóes, Sándor. *The Troubled Origins of the Italian Catholic Labor Movement, 1878–1914*. Detroit, Mich.: Wayne State University Press, 1988.

Andersen, Søren Kaj, and Mikkel Mailand. *The Role of Employers and Trade Unions in Multipartite Social Partnerships: 20 Case Studies from Five EU Member States*. Copenhagen: Employment Relations Research Centre, 2002. (Covers Spain, Denmark, Netherlands, Germany and the United Kingdom.)

Ashwin, Sarah. *Russian Workers: The Anatomy of Patience*. Manchester: Manchester University Press, 1999.

———. *Russian Trade Unions and Industrial Relations in Transition*. Houndmills, Basingstoke, Hampshire: Palgrave Macmillan, 2003.

Barkan, J. *Visions of Emancipation: The Italian Workers' Movement since 1945*. New York: Praeger, 1984.

Berghahn, V. R., and D. Karsten. *Industrial Relations in West Germany*. Oxford: Berg, 1987.

Borisov, V., et al. *The Workers' Movement in Russia.* Aldershot, U.K.: Edward Elgar, 1995.

Bridgford, Jeff. *The Politics of French Trade Unionism.* Leicester: Leicester University Press, 1991.

Carley, Mark. *Trade Union Membership 2003–2008.* (Available in electronic format only. The European Union and Norway.)

Chapman, Herrick, Mark Kesselman, and Martin Schain (eds.). *A Century of Organized Labor in France: A Union Movement for the Twenty-First Century?* New York: St. Martin's Press, 1998.

Christiansen, Paul T. *Russian Workers in Transition: Labor, Management, and the State under Gorbachev and Yeltsin.* De Kalb: North Illinois University Press, 1999.

Davis, Sue. *Trade Unions in Russia and the Ukraine, 1985–95.* Basingstoke, U.K.: Palgrave, 2001.

Dawen, Wolfgang Uellenberg-van. *Gewerkschaften in Deutschland von 1848 bis heute: Ein Überblick.* Munich: Olzog, 1997. (A general survey about German labor unions.)

Degryse, Christophe, and Philippe Pochet. *Social Developments in the European Union 2003: Fifth Annual Report.* Brussels: European Trade Union Institute, 2004.

Dickens, Richard, Paul Gregg, and Jonathan Wadsworth. *The Labour Market under New Labour: the State of Working Britain.* Houndmills, Basingstoke, Hampshire; New York: Palgrave Macmillan, 2003.

Dimitrova, Dimitrina, and Jacques Vilrokx. *Trade Union Strategies in Central and Eastern Europe: Towards Decent Work.* Budapest: International Labour Organization, 2005.

European Commission. *The Evolution of Labor Law in the EU-12 (1995–2005)*: volume 3. Luxembourg: Office for Official Publications of the European Communities, 2009. (This report completes Volume 1 entitled The evolution of labor law (1992–2003) General report and Volume 2 entitled The evolution of labor law (1992–2003) National reports.)

Galenson, Walter. *The World's Strongest Trade Unions: The Scandinavian Labor Movement.* Westport, Conn.: Quorum, 1998.

Golden, Miriam. *Labor Divided: Austerity and Working-Class Politics in Contemporary Italy.* Ithaca, N.Y.: Cornell University Press, 1988.

Gospel, Howard F., and Stephen Wood. *Representing Workers: Trade Union Recognition and Membership in Britain.* London: Routledge, 2003.

Hein, Eckhard. *Macroeconomic Policy Coordination in Europe and the Role of the Trade Unions.* Brussels: European Trade Union Institute, 2005.

Katzenstein, Peter J. *Corporatism and Change: Austria, Switzerland and the Politics of Industry.* Ithaca, N.Y.: Cornell University Press, 1984.

———. (ed.). *Industry and Politics in West Germany.* Ithaca, N.Y.: Cornell University Press, 1989.

Kauppinen, T., et al. *Labour Relations in Finland.* Helsinki: Ministry of Labour, 1990.

Kesselman, M. (ed.). *The French Workers' Movement: Economic Crisis and Political Change.* London: Allen & Unwin, 1984.

Lange, P., G. Ross, and M. Vannicelli (eds.). *Unions, Change and Crisis: French and Italian Union Strategy and the Political Economy, 1945–1980.* London: Allen & Unwin, 1982.

Lewis, Jill. *Fascism and the Working Class in Austria, 1918–1934: The Failure of Labour in the First Republic.* New York: Berg, 1991.

Macgraw, Roger. *A History of the French Working Class.* 2 vols. Oxford: Blackwell Publishers, 1992.

Markovits, Andrei S. *The Politics of the West German Trade Unions: Strategies of Class and Interest Representation in Growth and Crisis.* Cambridge: Cambridge University Press, 1986.

Moses, John A. *Trade Unionism in Germany from Bismarck to Hitler, 1869 to 1933.* 2 vols. London: George Prior, 1982.

Murray, Andrew. *A New Labour Nightmare: the Return of the Awkward Squad.* London; New York: Verso, 2003. (Discusses the future of trade unionism in the United Kingdom.)

Sassoon, Donald. *Contemporary Italy: Politics, Economy and Society since 1945.* London: Longman, 1986.

Schneider, Michael. *A Brief History of the German Trade Unions.* Trans. Barrie Selman. Bonn: J. H. W. Dietz Nachf., 1991. (First published in German in 1989.)

Shkliarevsky, Gennady. *Labor in the Russian Revolution: Factory Committees and Trade Unions, 1917–1918.* New York: St. Martin's Press, 1993.

Simoni, Marco. *The Renegotiated Alliance between the Left and Organised Labour in Western Europe.* London: University of London, 2007. (Electronic resource.)

Stefancic, D. R. *Robotnik: A Short History of the Struggle for Worker Self-Management and Free Trade Unions in Poland, 1944–1981.* New York: Columbia University Press, 1992.

Thelen, Kathleen A. *Union of Parts: Labor Politics in Postwar Germany.* Ithaca, N.Y.: Cornell University Press, 1992.

Torigian, Michael. *Every Factory a Fortress: The French Labor Movement in the Age of Ford and Hitler.* Athens: Ohio University Press, 1999.

Wrigley, Chris (ed.). *Challenges of Labour: Central and Western Europe, 1917–1920.* New York: Routledge, 1993.

C.2.5 Latin America and the Caribbean

Alexander, Robert J. *History of Organized Labor in Argentina.* New York: Praeger, 2003.

———. *History of Organized Labor in Bolivia.* New York: Praeger, 2005.

———. *A History of Organized Labor in Brazil.* Westport, Conn.: Praeger, 2003.

———. *A History of Organized Labor in Cuba.* Westport, Conn.: Praeger, 2002.

———. *History of Organized Labor in the English-Speaking West Indies.* New York: Praeger, 2004.

———. *A History of Organized Labor in Panama and Central America.* New York: Praeger, 2008.

——. *A History of Organized Labor in Peru and Ecuador.* New York: Praeger, 2006.

——. *History of Organized Labor in Uruguay and Paraguay.* New York: Praeger, 2005.

Alexander, Robert J. (With the collaboration of Eldon M. Parker). *International Labor Organizations and Organized Labor in Latin America and the Caribbean. A History.* New York: Praeger, 2009.

Barros, Maurício Rands. *Labour Relations and the New Unionism in Contemporary Brazil.* London: Macmillan, 1999.

Decker, David R. *The Political, Economic, and Labor Climate of Argentina.* Philadelphia: University of Pennsylvania Press, 1983.

Drake, Paul W. *Labor Movements and Dictatorships in the Southern Cone in Comparative Perspective.* Baltimore, Md.: Johns Hopkins University Press, 1996.

Epstein, Edward C. *Labor Autonomy and the State in Latin America.* Boston, Mass.: Unwin Hyman, 1989.

French, John D. *The Brazilian Workers' ABC: Class Conflict and Alliances in Modern São Paulo.* Chapel Hill: University of North Carolina Press, 1992.

Greenfield, Gerald M., and Sheldon L. Maram. *Latin American Labor Organizations.* New York: Greenwood Press, 1987.

Look Lai, Walton. *Indentured Labour, Caribbean Sugar: Chinese and Indian Migrants to the British West Indies, 1838–1918.* Baltimore, Md.: Johns Hopkins University Press, 1993.

Middlebrook, K. J. *Paradox of Revolution: Labor, the State, and Authoritarianism in Mexico.* Baltimore, Md.: Johns Hopkins University Press, 1995.

——. *Unions, Workers, and the State in Mexico.* San Diego: University of California Press, 1991.

Murillo, Maria V. *Labor Unions, Partisan Coalitions, and Market Reforms in Latin America.* Cambridge: Cambridge University Press, 2001.

Nurse, Lawrence A. *Trade Unionism and Industrial Relations in the Commonwealth Caribbean: History, Contemporary Practice and Prospect.* Westport, Conn.: Greenwood Press, 1992.

Ramdin, Ron. *From Chattel Slave to Wage Earner: A History of Trade Unionism in Trinidad and Tobago.* London: Martin Brian & O'Keefe, 1982.

Roberts, Kenneth M. *Deepening Democracy: The Modern Left and Social Movements in Chile and Peru.* Stanford, Calif.: Stanford University Press, 1998.

Rodney, Walter. *A History of Guyanese Working People, 1881–1905.* Baltimore, Md.: Johns Hopkins University Press, 1981.

Vaillancourt-Laflamme, Catherine. *Trade Unions and Informal Workers' Associations in the Urban Informal Economy of Ecuador.* Geneva: International Labour Organization, 2005.

C.2.6 North America

Bacon, David. *The Children of NAFTA: Labor Wars on the U.S./Mexico Border.* Berkeley, Calif.: University of California Press, 2004.

Baldwin, Robert E. *The Decline of U.S. Labor Unions and the Role of Trade.* Washington, D.C.: Institute for International, 2003.

Beik, Millie Allen. *Labor Relations.* Westport: Greenwood Press, 2005. (Over 100 annotated primary documents.)

Block, Richard N., Karen Roberts and R. Oliver Clarke. *Labor Standards in the United States and Canada.* Kalamazoo, Mich.: W. E. Upjohn Institute for Employment Research, 2003.

Brody, David. *Workers in Industrial America: Essays on the Twentieth Century Struggle.* New York: Oxford University Press, 1980.

Camfield, David. *Canadian Labour in Crisis: Reinventing the Workers' Movement.* Halifax, N.S.: Fernwood, 2011.

Danver, Steven L. (ed.). *Revolts, Protests, Demonstrations, and Rebellions in American History. An Encyclopedia.* 3 vols. ABC-CLIO/Greenwood, 2010.

Derber, Milton, et al. *Labor in Illinois: The Affluent Years, 1945–80.* Urbana: University of Illinois Press, 1989.

Dubofksy, Melvyn. *Industrialism and the American Worker, 1865–1920.* 3rd ed. Wheeling, Ill.: Harlan Davidson, 1996.

Dubofksy, Melvyn, and Foster Rhea Dulles. *Labor in America: A History.* 6th ed. Wheeling, Ill.: Harlan Davidson, 1999.

Dulles, Foster R., and Melvyn Dubofsky. *Labor in America: A History.* 4th ed. Arlington Heights, Ill.: Harlan Davidson, 1984.

Ferrie, Joseph P. *The End of American Exceptionalism? Mobility in the U.S. Since 1850.* Cambridge, Mass.: National Bureau of Economic Research, Inc., 2005. (Working Paper 11324.)

Feurer, Rosemary. *Radical Unionism in the Midwest, 1900–1950.* Chicago: University of Illinois Press, 2006.

Forsey, Eugene. *Trade Unions in Canada, 1812–1902.* Toronto: University of Toronto Press, 1982.

Galenson, Walter. *The American Labor Movement, 1955–1995.* Westport, Conn.: Greenwood Press, 1996.

Godard, John. The Exceptional Decline of the American Labor Movement. *Industrial and Labor Relations Review* 63(1), 2009.

Gross, James A. *Workers' Rights as Human Rights.* Ithaca, N.Y.: Cornell University Press, 2003.

Hillstrom, Kevin. *Workers Unite! the American Labor Movement.* Detroit, Mich.: Omnigraphics, 2010.

Jacobs, James B. *Mobsters, Unions, and Feds: The Mafia and the American Labor Movement.* New York: New York University Press; London: Eurospan, 2006.

Jacoby, Daniel. *Laboring for Freedom: A New Look at the History of Labor in America.* Armonk, N.Y.: M. E. Sharpe, 1998.

Kochan, T., H. Katz, and R. McKerzie. *The Transformation of American Industrial Relations.* New York: Basic Books, 1986.

Le Blanc, Paul. *Work and Struggle: Voices from U.S. Labor Radicalism.* New York: Routledge, 2011.

Lee, R. Alton. *Farmers vs. Wage Earners: Organized Labor in Kansas, 1860–1960.* Lincoln, Neb.: University of Nebraska Press, 2005.

McCartin, Joseph. *Labor's Great War: The Struggle for Industrial Democracy and the Origins of Modern American Labor Relations.* Chapel Hill: University of North Carolina Press, 1997.

Mendel, Ronald. *"A Broad and Ennobling Spirit": Workers and Their Unions in Late Gilded Age New York and Brooklyn, 1886–1898.* Westport, Conn.: Praeger, 2003.

Mishel, Lawrence, Jared Bernstein, and Sylvia Allegretto. *The State of Working America, 2006/2007.* Ithaca, N.Y.: ILR Press, 2006.

Montgomery, David. *The Fall of the House of Labor: The Workplace, the State and American Labor Activism, 1860–1987.* Cambridge: Cambridge University Press, 1987.

Peirce, Jon. *Canadian Industrial Relations.* Scarborough, Ontario: Prentice Hall Canada, 2000.

Phillips-Fein, Kim. *Invisible Hands. The Making of the Conservative Movement from the New Deal to Reagan.* New York: Norton, 2009.

Roof, Tracy. *Congress, and the Welfare State, 1935–2010.* Baltimore: Johns Hopkins University Press, 2011.

Schiavone, Michael. *Unions in Crisis? The Future of Organized Labor in America.* Westport, Conn.: Praeger Publishers, 2007.

Shogan, Robert. *The Battle of Blair Mountain: The Story of America's Largest Labor Uprising.* Boulder, Colo.: Westview, 2004.

Sinyai, Clayton. *Schools of Democracy: A Political History of the American Labor Movement.* Ithaca, N.Y., Cornell University Press, 2006.

Troy, Leo. *The Twilight of the Old Unionism.* Armonk, N.Y., M. E. Sharpe Publishers, Inc., 2004. (The third book in a trilogy on labor relations in the United States. The first, *The New Unionism in the New Society* (1994), analyzed the rise of public sector unionism. The second, *Beyond Unions and Collective Bargaining* (1999), analyzed nonunion labor relations.)

Weir, Robert E. (ed.). *Class in America. An Encyclopedia.* 3 vols. Santa Barbara, Calif.: ABC-CLIO/Greenwood 2007.

Weir, Robert E., and James P. Hanlan (eds.). *Historical Encyclopedia of American Labor.* Westport, Conn.: Greenwood Press, 2004.

White, Samuel W. *Fragile Alliances. Labor and Politics in Evansville, Indiana, 1919–1955.* Westport, Conn.: Greenwood Publishing Group, 2005.

Zieger, Robert H. *American Workers, American Unions, 1920–1994.* 2nd ed. Baltimore, Md.: Johns Hopkins University Press, 1994.

C.2.7 Oceania

Ford, Bill, and David Plowman (eds.). *Australian Unions: An Industrial Relations Perspective.* Melbourne: Macmillan, 1983.

Hess, Michael. *Unions under Economic Development: Private Sector Unions in Papua New Guinea.* Melbourne: Oxford University Press, 1992.

Mallory, Greg. *Uncharted Waters: Social Responsibility in Australian Trade Unions.* Brisbane: Bollarong, 2005.

Markey, Ray. *In Case of Oppression: The Life and Times of the Labor Council of New South Wales.* Sydney: Pluto Press, 1994.

Martin, Ross M. *Trade Unions in Australia.* 2nd ed. Harmondsworth, U.K.: Penguin, 1980.

Roth, H. *Trade Unions in New Zealand: Past and Present.* Wellington: A. H. and A. W. Reed, 1973.

Thickett, Glen, and Raymond Harbridge. *A Sourcebook of New Zealand Trade Unions and Employee Organisations.* Wellington: Industrial Relations Centre, Victoria University of Wellington, 2002.

C.3 Industrial Relations in Specific Countries

Adams, Roy J., and Noah M. Meltz (eds.). *Industrial Relations Theory: Its Nature, Scope, and Pedagogy.* Management and Labor Relations Series No. 4. Lanham, Md.: Scarecrow Press, 1993.

Alexander, R., and J. Lewer. *Understanding Australian Industrial Relations.* 4th ed. Sydney: Harcourt Brace, 1996.

Anderson, J., M. Gunderson, and A. Ponak (eds.). *Union-Management Relations in Canada.* 2nd ed. Don Mills, Ontario: Addison-Wesley, 1989.

Appelbaum, Eileen, Annette D. Bernhardt, and Richard J. Murnane. *Low-Wage America: How Employers are Reshaping Opportunity in the Workplace.* New York: Russell Sage, 2003.

Ashwin, Sarah, and Simon Clarke. *Russian Trade Unions and Industrial Relations in Transition.* Houndmills, Basingstoke, Hampshire: Palgrave Macmillan, 2003.

Brown, William (ed.). *The Changing Contours of British Industrial Relations.* Oxford: Blackwell, 1981.

Chaykowski, R., and A. Verma (eds.). *Industrial Relations in Canadian Industry.* Toronto: Dryden, 1992.

Chelius, James, and James Dworkin (eds.). *Reflections on the Transformation of Industrial Relations.* Management and Labor Relations Series No. 1. Lanham, Md.: Scarecrow Press, 1990.

Deeks, John, Jane Parker, and Rose Ryan. *Labour and Employment Relations in New Zealand.* Auckland: Longman Paul, 1994. (Second edition of a text first published as *Labour Relations in New Zealand* in 1989.)

Deery, Stephen, and David Plowman. *Australian Industrial Relations.* 3rd ed. Sydney: McGraw-Hill, 1991.

Edwards, Paul K. (ed.). *Industrial Relations: Theory and Practice.* Oxford: Blackwell, 2003. (Previously called *Industrial Relations: Theory and Practice in Britain.*)

Kessler, Sid, and Fred Bayliss. *Contemporary British Industrial Relations.* Basingstoke, U.K.: Macmillan, 1992.

Lipsky, D., and C. Donn (eds.). *Collective Bargaining in American Industry.* Lexington, Mass.: Lexington Books, 1987.

McQuarrie, Fiona Anne Elizabeth. *Industrial Relations in Canada*. Etobicoke, Ont.: J. Wiley, 2003.

Murphy, T., B. Hillery, and A. Kelly (eds.). *Industrial Relations in Ireland: Contemporary Issues and Developments*. Dublin: University College, Dublin, 1989.

Quinn, Patrick. *Freedom of Association and Collective Bargaining: A Study of Indonesian Experience 1998–2003*. Geneva: International Labour Organization, 2003.

Roomkin, Myron J. *Profit Sharing and Gain Sharing*. Management and Labor Relations Series No. 2. Lanham, Md.: Scarecrow Press, 1990.

Slomp, Hans. *Labor Relations in Europe: A History of Issues and Developments*. Westport, Conn.: Greenwood Press, 1990.

Taylor, Bill, Kai Chang, and Qi Li. *Industrial Relations in China*. Cheltenham: Edward Elgar, 2003.

Thirkell, J. E. M., K. Petkov, and S. A. Vickerstaff. *The Transformation of Labour Relations: Restructuring and Privatization in Eastern Europe and Russia*. New York: Oxford University Press, 1998.

Wooden, Mark, et al. *The Transformation of Australian Industrial Relations*. Leichhardt, New South Wales: Federation Press, 2000.

Wrigley, Chris (ed.). *A History of British Industrial Relations*. 2 vols. Brighton, Sussex: Harvester Press, 1982, 1987. (Covers the period from 1875 to 1939.)

D. FEATURES OF LABOR UNIONS

D.1 Histories of Specific Unions

Bagwell, P. S. *The Railwaymen: The History of the National Union of Railwaymen*. 2 vols. London: Allen & Unwin, 1963, 1982.

Beasley, Margo. *The Missos: A History of the Federated Miscellaneous Workers' Union*. Sydney: Allen and Unwin, 1996.

———. *Wharfies: A History of the Waterside Workers' Federation of Australia*. Sydney: Halstead Press in Association with the Australian National Maritime Museum, 1996.

Bowden, Badley. *Driving Force: The History of the Transport Workers' Union of Australia, 1883–1992*. Sydney: Allen and Unwin, 1993.

Bray, Mark, and Malcolm Rimmer. *Delivering the Goods: A History of the Transport Workers' Union in New South Wales 1886–1986*. Sydney: Allen & Unwin, 1987.

Carpenter, Mick. *They Still Go Marching On: A Celebration of the COHSE's First 75 Years*. Banstead, U.K.: Confederation of Health Service Employees, 1985.

Clinton, Allen. *Post Office Workers: A Trade Union and Social History*. London: Allen & Unwin, 1984.

Coates, Ken, and Tony Topham. *The History of the Transport and General Workers' Union*. Oxford: Basil Blackwell, 1991.

Croucher, Richard. *Engineers at War*. London: Merlin Press, 1982. (A study of the British engineering unions during World War II.)

Freeman, Joshua B. *In Transit: The Transport Workers' Union in New York City, 1933–1966*. New York: Oxford University Press, 1989.

Galenson, Walter. *The United Brotherhood of Carpenters.* Cambridge, Mass.: Harvard University Press, 1983.

Gennard, John. *A History of the National Graphical Association.* London: Unwin Hyman, 1990.

Halpern, Martin. *UAW Politics in the Cold War Era.* Albany: State University of New York Press, 1988. (Deals with the United Auto Workers.)

Laslett, John H. M. (ed.). *The United Mine Workers of America: A Model of Industrial Solidarity?* University Park: State University of Pennsylvania, 1996.

Maguire, Martin. *Servants to the Public: A History of the Local Government and Public Services Union, 1901–1990.* Dublin: Institute of Public Administration, 1998.

Marsh, Arthur, and Victoria Ryan. *The Clerks: A History of Apex, 1890–1989.* Oxford: Malthouse, 1997.

Mitchell, Glenn. *On Strong Foundations: The BWIU and Industrial Relations in the Australian Construction Industry, 1942–1992.* Sydney: Harcourt Brace, 1996.

Murray, Robert, and Kate White. *The Ironworkers: A History of the Federated Ironworkers' Association of Australia.* Sydney: Hale and Iremonger, 1982.

Nachmann, Walter. *100 Jahre ÖTV: Geschichte: Die Geschichte einer Gewerkschaft und ihrer Vorläuforganisationen.* Frankfurt: Union-Druckerei und Verlagsanstalt, 1996. (This is the official history of the German Public Service, Transportation, and Traffic Labor Union. The book was issued as two volumes of which this is the first; the second is a biographical dictionary whose details are listed under Rüdiger Zimmerman in the earlier section [A.3] for biographical dictionaries.)

Schatz, Ronald. *The Electrical Workers: A History of Labor at General Electric and Westinghouse, 1923–1960.* Urbana: University of Illinois Press, 1983.

Spaull, Andrew. *Australian Education Union: From Federal Registration to National Reconciliation.* Sydney: ACER Press, 2000.

Strachan, Glenda. *Labour of Love: The History of the Nurses' Association in Queensland.* Sydney: Allen and Unwin, 1996.

Tyler, Gus. *Look for the Union Label: A History of the International Ladies' Garment Workers Union.* Armonk, N.Y.: M. E. Sharp., 1995.

Wellman, David. *The Union Makes Us Strong: Radical Unionism on the San Francisco Waterfront.* Cambridge: Cambridge University Press, 1995.

Yates, C. A. B. *From Plant to Politics: The Autoworkers' Union in Postwar Canada.* Philadelphia, Pa.: Temple University Press, 1993.

Zieger, Robert H. *Rebuilding the Pulp and Paper Workers' Union, 1933–1941.* Knoxville: University of Tennessee Press, 1984.

D.2 Unions in Specific Industries or Occupations

Aaron, B., J. Najita, and J. Stern. *Public-Sector Bargaining.* 2nd ed. Washington, D.C.: Bureau of National Affairs, 1988.

Andræ, Gunilla, and Björn Beckman. *Union Power in the Nigerian Textile Industry: Labour Regime and Adjustment.* New Brunswick, N.J.: Transaction, 1999.

Arnold, Gordon B. *The Politics of Faculty Unionization: The Experience of Three New England Universities.* Westport, Conn.: Bergin and Garvey, 2000.

Bach, Stephen, et al. (eds.). *Public Service Employment Relations in Europe: Transformation, Modernisation, or Inertia?* London: Routledge, 1999.

Bahl, V. *The Making of the Indian Working Class: A Case Study of the Tata Iron and Steel Company, 1880–1946.* New Delhi: Sage, 1995.

Baxter, Vern K. *Labor and Politics in the U. S. Postal Service.* New York: Plenum, 1994.

Benin, Leigh D. *The New Labor Radicalism and New York City's Garment Industry: Progressive Labor Insurgents in the 1960s.* New York: Garland, 2000.

Berger, Stefan, Andy Croll, and Norman LaPorte (eds.). *Towards a Comparative History of Coalfield Societies.* Burlington, Vt.: Ashgate, 2005.

Burgmann, Meredith, and Verity Burgmann. *Green Bans, Red Union: Environmental Activism and the New South Wales Builders' Federation.* Sydney: University of New South Wales Press, 1998.

Cobble, Dorothy Sue. *Dishing It Out: Waitresses and Their Unions in the Twentieth Century.* Chicago: University of Illinois Press, 1991.

Cooper, Bruce S. (ed.). *Labor Relations in Education: An International Perspective.* Westport, Conn.: Greenwood Press, 1992.

Cooper, Patricia A. *Once a Cigar Maker: Men, Women, and Work Culture in American Cigar Factories, 1900–1919.* Urbana: University of Illinois Press, 1987.

Creese, Gillian L. *Contracting Masculinity: Gender, Class, and Race in a White-Collar Union, 1944–1994.* Toronto: Oxford University Press, 1999.

Cullum, Linda K. *Narratives at Work: Women, Men, and Unionization, and the Fashioning of Identities.* St. John's, Newfoundland: ISER, 2003. (A study of the fishery processing industries of Newfoundland and Labrador.)

Daniel, Cletus E. *Bitter Harvest: A History of California Farmworkers, 1870–1941.* Ithaca, N.Y.: Cornell University Press, 1981.

Davies, Sam, et al. (eds.). *Dock Workers: International Explorations in Comparative Labour History, 1790–1970.* 2 vols. Aldershot, U.K.: Ashgate, 2000.

Docherty, C. *Steel and Steelworkers: The Sons of Vulcan.* London: Heinemann Educational Books, 1983. (A British study.)

Edwards, C., and E. Heery. *Management Control and Union Power: A Study of Labour Relations in Coal-Mining.* Oxford: Clarendon Press, 1989.

Ellem, Bradon. *In Women's Hands: A History of Clothing Trades Unionism in Australia.* Sydney: University of New South Wales Press, 1989.

Feldman, G. D., and K. Tenfelde (eds.). *Workers, Owners and Politics in Coal Mining: An International Comparison of Industrial Relations.* New York: Berg, 1990.

Freeman, Richard B., and Casey Ichniowksi. *When Public Sector Workers Unionize.* Chicago: University of Chicago Press, 1988.

Gavroglou, Stavros. *Labor's Power and Industrial Performance: Automotive Production Regimes in the U.S., Germany, and Japan.* New York: Garland Press, 1998.

Green, W. C., and E. J. Yanarella. *North American Auto Unions in Crisis: Lean Production as Contested Terrain.* Albany: State University of New York Press, 1996.

Griffin, Gerard. *White-Collar Militancy: The Australian Banking and Insurance Unions.* Sydney: Croom Helm, 1985.

Harris, Howell J. *Bloodless Victories: The Rise and Fall of the Open Shop in the Philadelphia Metal Trades, 1890–1940.* Cambridge: Cambridge University Press, 2000.

Hatcher, John, et al. *The History of the British Coal Industry.* 5 vols. Oxford: Clarendon Press, 1984–1993.

Ironside, Mike. *Facing up to Thatcherism: The History of NALGO, 1979–1993.* Oxford: Oxford University Press, 2000.

Jaffe, James A. *The Struggle for Market Power: Industrial Relations in the British Coal Industry, 1800–1840.* Cambridge: Cambridge University Press, 2002.

Jowitt, J. A., and A. J. McIvor (eds.). *Employers and Labour in the English Textile Industries, 1850–1939.* New York: Routledge, Chapman & Hall, 1988.

Katz, H. C. (ed.). *Telecommunications: Restructuring Work and Employment Relations Worldwide.* Ithaca, N.Y.: ILR Press, 1997.

Kazin, Michael. *Barons of Labor: The San Francisco Building Trades and Union Power in the Progressive Era.* Urbana: University of Illinois Press, 1987.

Kimeldorf, Howard. *Reds or Rackets? The Making of Radical and Conservative Unions on the Waterfront.* Berkeley: University of California Press, 1988.

Langemann, Ellen C. (ed.). *Nursing History: New Perspectives, New Possibilities.* New York: Teachers College Press, 1983.

Lawn, Martin (ed.). *The Politics of Teacher Unionism: International Perspectives.* London: Croom Helm, 1985.

Levitan, Sar A., and Alexandra B. Noden. *Working for the Sovereign: Employee Relations in the Federal Government.* Baltimore, Md.: Johns Hopkins University Press, 1983.

Licht, Walter. *Working for the Railroad: The Organization of Work in the Nineteenth Century.* Princeton, N.J.: Princeton University Press, 1983.

Mangum, Garth L., and John Walsh. *Union Resilience in Troubled Times, AFL-CIO, 1960–1993.* Armonk, N.Y.: M. E. Sharpe, 1994.

Markholt, Ottilie. *Maritime Solidarity, Pacific Coast Unionism: 1929–1938.* Tacoma, Wash: Pacific Coast Maritime History Committee, 1999.

McKelvey, Jean T. (ed.). *Cleared for Takeoff: Airline Labor Relations Since Deregulation.* New York: ILR Press, 1988.

Murphy, Marjorie. *Blackboard Unions: The AFT and the NEA, 1900–1980.* Ithaca, N.Y.: Cornell University Press, 1990.

Palmer, David. *Organizing the Shipyards: Union Strategy in Three Northeast Ports, 1933–1945.* Ithaca, N.Y.: ILR Press, 1998.

Peterson, Joyce S. *American Automobile Workers, 1900–1933.* Albany: State University of New York Press, 1987.

Schact, John N. *The Making of Telephone Unionism, 1920–1947.* New Brunswick, N.J: Rutgers University Press, 1985.

Sheridan, Tom. *Australia's Own Cold War: The Waterfront under Menzies.* Melbourne: Melbourne University Press, 2006.

Simms, Marian. *Militant Public Servants: Politicisation, Feminisation, and Selected Public Service Unions.* Melbourne: Macmillan, 1987. (An Australian study.)

Smith, David F. *White-Collar Unionism in New Zealand.* Wellington: New Zealand Institute of Industrial Relations Research, 1987.

Stein, Margot B. *The Social Origins of a Labor Elite: French Engine Drivers, 1837–1914.* New York: Garland, 1987. (Includes a comparison with U.S. engine drivers.)

Street, Richard S. *Beasts of the Field: A Narrative History of California Farmworkers, 1769–1913.* Stanford, Calif.: Stanford University Press, 2004.

Stromquist, Shelton. *A Generation of Boomers: The Pattern of Railroad Labor Conflict in Nineteenth Century America.* Champaign: University of Illinois Press, 1987.

Synott, John P. *Teacher Unions, Social Movements, and the Politics of Education in Asia.* Aldershot, U.K.: Ashgate, 2002.

Tuman, John P. *Reshaping the North American Automobile Industry: Restructuring, Corporatism, and Union Democracy in Mexico.* London: Continuum, 2003.

Turnbull, P., and V. Wass. *Reform and Structural Adjustment in the World's Ports: The Future for Labour and the Unions.* London: International Transport Workers' Federation, 1994.

Tyler, Gus. *Look for the Union Label: A History of the International Ladies' Garment Workers' Union.* Armonk, N.Y.: M. E. Sharpe, 1995.

Upham, Martin. *Tempered—Not Quenched: The History of the ISTC, 1851–1997.* London: Lawrence and Wishart, 1997. (A history of the Iron and Steel Industry Confederation.)

Vicary, Adrian. *In the Interests of Education: A History of Education Unionism in South Australia.* Sydney: Allen and Unwin, 1997.

Weir, Robert E. *Beyond Labor's Veil: The Culture of the Knights of Labor.* University Park: Pennsylvania State University Press, 1996.

Welch, Cliff. *The Seed Was Planted: The São Paulo Roots of Brazil's Rural Labor Movement, 1924–1964.* University Park: Pennsylvania State University Press, 1999.

Wellman, David. *The Union Makes Us Strong: Radical Unionism on the San Francisco Waterfront.* Cambridge: Cambridge University Press, 1995.

D.3 Unions and the Workplace or in Specific Regions

Ackers, Peter, et al. (eds.). *The New Workplace and Trade Unionism: Critical Perspectives on Work and Organization.* London: Routledge, 1995.

Appelbaum, Eileen, and Rosemary Batt. *The New American Workplace: Transforming Work Systems in the United States.* Ithaca, N.Y.: Cornell University Press, 1994.

Blewett, Mary H. *Men, Women, and Work: Class, Gender, and Protest in the New England Shoe Industry, 1780–1910.* Chicago: University of Illinois Press, 1988.

Callus, Ron, et al. *Industrial Relations at Work: The Australian Workplace Industrial Relations Survey.* Canberra: Australian Government Publishing Service, 1991. (A second survey was held in 1995.)

Cully, Mark, et al. *Britain at Work: As Depicted by the 1998 Workplace Employee Relations Survey.* London: Routledge, 1999. (Previous studies were conducted in 1980, 1984, and 1990.)

Cully, Mark, and Richard Fraser. *The Australian Workplace Industrial Relations Survey (AWIRS): The State Dimension.* Canberra: Department of Industrial Relations, 1993.

Daniel, W. W., and Neil Millward. *Workplace Industrial Relations in Britain.* London: Heinemann, 1983.

Ewing, K. D., and Anne Hock. *Trade Union Recognition in Small Enterprises.* Kingston upon Thames: Popularis Ltd., 2003.

Heerma van Voss, Lex, Els Hiemstra-Kuperus, and Elise Van Nederveen Meerkerk. *The Ashgate Companion to the History of Textile Workers, 1650–2000.* Farnham, U.K.: Ashgate, 2010.

Hershatter, Gail. *The Workers of Tianjin, 1900–1949.* Stanford, Calif.: Stanford University Press, 1986. (A case study of a Chinese city.)

Johnson, Claudia D. *Labor and Workplace Issues in Literature.* Westport, Conn.: Greenwood Press, 2006.

Kahmann, Marcus. *Trade Unions and Migrant Workers Examples from the United States, South Africa and Spain.* Brussels: European Trade Union Institute, 2002. (Available in electronic format only.)

Kaufman, Robert L. *Race, Gender, and the Labor Market: Inequalities at Work.* Boulder, Colo.: Lynne Rienner Publishers, 2010.

Kulczycki, John. *The Polish Coal Miners' Union and the German Labor Movement in the Ruhr, 1902–1934: National and Social Solidarity.* Oxford: Berg, 1997.

Kumar, Pradeep. *Unions and Workplace Change in Canada.* Kingston, Ontario: IRC Press, 1995.

Lynd, Staughton (ed.). *"We Are All Leaders": The Alternative Unionism of the 1930s.* Urbana: University of Illinois Press, 1996.

Markowitz, Linda. *Worker Activism after Successful Union Organizing.* Armonk, N.Y.: M. E. Sharpe, 2000.

Martin, Ron, Peter Sunley, and Jane Willis. *Union Retreat and the Regions: The Shrinking Landscape of Organized Labour.* London: J. Kingsley Publishers, 1996.

Millward, Neil, Alex Bryson, and John Forth. *All Change? British Employment Relations, 1980–1998, as Portrayed by the Workplace Industrial Relations Survey.* London: Routledge, 2000.

Millward, Neil, and Mark Stevens. *British Workplace Industrial Relations.* Aldershot, U.K.: Gower, 1986.

Morehead, Alison, et al. *Changes at Work: The 1995 Australian Workplace Industrial Relations Survey.* Melbourne: Longman, 1997.

Nissen, Bruce (ed.). *Unions and Workplace Reorganization.* Detroit, Mich.: Wayne State University Press, 1997.

Potterfield, Thomas A. *The Business of Employee Empowerment: Democracy and Ideology in the Workplace.* Westport, Conn.: Quorum Books, 1999.

Ross, Andrew. *No-Collar: The Humane Workplace and Its Hidden Costs.* Philadelphia, Pa.: Temple University Press, 2004.

Tillman, Ray M., and Michael S. Cummings (eds.). *The Transformation of U.S. Unions: Voices, Visions, and Strategies from the Grassroots.* Boulder, Colo.: Lynne Rienner, 1998.

D.4 Ideas, Movements, and Religion

Barrow, Logie. *Democratic Ideas and the British Labour Movement.* Cambridge: Cambridge University Press, 1996.

Buhle, Paul. *Marxism in the United States: Remapping the History of the American Left.* London: Verso, 1987.

Cannistraro, Philip, and Gerald Meyer. *The Lost World of Italian American Radicalism.* New York: Praeger, 2003.

Docherty, James C. *Historical Dictionary of Socialism.* Lanham, Md.: Scarecrow Press, 1997.

Dubofsky, Melvyn. *We Shall Be All: A History of the Industrial Workers of the World.* 2nd ed. Urbana: University of Illinois Press, 1988.

Fulcher, James. *Capitalism: A Very Short Introduction.* Cary, N.C.: Oxford University Press, 2004.

Heineman, Kenneth J. *A Catholic New Deal: Religion and Reform in Depression Pittsburgh.* University Park: Pennsylvania State University Press, 1999.

Holton, Bob. *British Syndicalism, 1910–14: Myths and Realities.* London: Pluto Press, 1976.

Kimeldorf, Howard. *Battling for American Labor: Wobblies, Craft Workers, and the Making of the Union Movement.* Berkeley: University of California Press, 1999.

Lieberman, Sima. *Labor Movements and Labor Thought: Spain, France, Germany and the United States.* New York: Praeger, 1986.

Linden, Marcel van der, and Wayne Thorpe (eds.). *Revolutionary Syndicalism: An International Perspective.* Aldershot, U.K.: Scolar Press, 1990.

Marshall, Peter. *Demanding the Impossible: A History of Anarchism.* London: HarperCollins, 1992.

Olssen, Erik. *The Red Feds: Revolutionary Industrial Unionism and the New Zealand Federation of Labour, 1908–14.* Auckland: Oxford University Press, 1988.

Roberts, David D. *The Syndicalist Tradition and Italian Fascism.* Chapel Hill: University of North Carolina Press, 1979.

Seaton, Douglas P. *Catholics and Radicals: The Association of Catholic Trade Unionists and the Labor Movement, from Depression to Cold War.* Lewisburg, Pa.: Bucknell University Press, 1981.

Strath, Bo. *The Organisation of Labour Markets: Modernity, Culture, and Governance in Germany, Britain, and Japan.* London: Routledge, 1996.

Stepan-Norris, Judith, and Maurice Zeitlin. *Left Out: Reds and America's Industrial Unions.* Cambridge: Cambridge University Press, 2002.

D.5 Autobiographies and Biographies of Labor Leaders

Bobumil, Walter. *A Biography of Florida Union Organizer—Frank E'Dalgo.* Lewiston, N.Y.: Edward Mellen Press, 2000.

Bull, Tas. *Life on the Waterfront: An Autobiography.* Melbourne: HarperCollins, 1998.

Bussel, Robert. *From Harvard to the Ranks of Labor: Powers Hapgood and the American Working Class*. University Park: Pennsylvania State University Press, 1999.

Carlson, Peter. *Roughneck: The Life and Times of Big Bill Haywood*. New York: Norton, 1983.

Clark, Paul, et al. *Forging a Union of Steel: Philip Murray, SWOC, & the United Steelworkers*. Ithaca, N.Y.: Cornell ILR Press, 1987.

Cook, Alice H. *A Lifetime of Labor: The Autobiography of Alice H. Cook*. New York: Feminist Press at the City University of New York, 1998.

Day, David. *Ben Chifley*. London: HarperCollins, 2001.

Dickmyer, Elizabeth R. *Reuther: A Daughter Strikes*. Southfield, Mich.: Spelman Publishers Division, 1989.

Dubofsky, Melvyn, and Warren Van Tine (eds.). *Labor Leaders in America*. Urbana: University of Illinois Press, 1986.

Estreiche, Samuel, Harry C. Katz, and Bruce E. Kaufman. *The Internal Governance and Organisational of Labor Unions: Essays in Honor of George Brooks*. New York: Kluwer Law International, 2001.

Fraser, Steven. *Labor Will Rule: Sidney Hillman and the Rise of American Labor*. New York: The Free Press, 1991.

Guy, Bill. *A Life on the Left: A Biography of Clyde Cameron*. Adelaide: Wakefield Press, 1999.

Jones, Jack. *Union Man: An Autobiography*. London: Collins, 1986.

Kirby, Diane. *Alice Henry—The Power of Pen and Voice: The Life of an Australian-American Labor Reformer*. New York: Cambridge University Press, 1991.

Lichtenstein, Nelson. *The Most Dangerous Man in Detroit: Walter Reuther and the Fate of American Labor*. New York: Basic Books, 1995.

Morgan, Kenneth O. *Labour People: Hardie to Kinnock*. 2nd ed. Oxford: Oxford University Press, 1992.

Mortimer, Jim W. *A Life on the Left*. Lewes, East Sussex, U.K.: The Book Guild, 1998.

Norington, Brad. *Jennie George*. Sydney: Allen and Unwin, 1998.

Phelan, Craig. *Divided Loyalties: The Public and Private Life of Labor Leader John Mitchell*. Albany: State University of New York Press, 1995.

———. *Grand Master Workman: Terence Powderly and the Knights of Labor*. Westport, Conn.: Greenwood Press, 2000.

Rickard, John. *H.B. Higgins: The Rebel as Judge*. Sydney: Allen & Unwin, 1985.

Robinson, Archie. *George Meany and His Times: A Biography*. New York: Simon & Schuster, 1981.

Salvatore, Nick. *Eugene V. Debs: Citizen and Socialist*. Urbana: University of Illinois Press, 1982.

Sloane, Arthur A. *Hoffa*. Cambridge, Mass.: MIT Press, 1991.

Tsuzuki, Chushichi. *Tom Mann, 1856–1941: The Challenge of Labour*. Oxford: Clarendon Press, 1991.

Ziegler, Robert H. *John L. Lewis, Labor Leader*. Boston, Mass.: Twayne, 1988.

D.6 Women's Labor and Labor Unions

Anker, Richard. *Gender and Jobs: Sex Segregation of Occupations in the World.* Washington, D.C.: International Labour Organization, 1998.

Baron, Ava (ed.). *Work Engendered: Toward a New History of American Labor.* Ithaca, N.Y.: Cornell University Press, 1991.

Belcher, P., et al. *Women Seafarers: Global Employment Policies and Practices.* Geneva: International Labour Organization, 2003.

Blewett, Mary H. *Men, Women, and Work: Class, Gender and Protest in the New England Shoe Industry, 1780–1910.* Urbana: University of Illinois Press, 1988.

Briskin, Linda, and Patricia McDermott (eds.). *Women Challenging Unions: Feminism, Democracy and Militancy.* Toronto: University of Toronto Press, 1994.

Chalmers, Lee V. *Marketing Masculinities. Gender and Management Politics in Marketing Work (Contributions in Labor Studies).* Westport, Conn.: Greenwood Press, 2001.

Chateauvert, Melinda. *Marching Together: Women of the Brotherhood of Sleeping Car Porters.* Champaign: University of Illinois Press, 1998.

Chaykowski, Richard P., and Lisa M. Powell (eds.). *Women and Work.* Montreal, Quebec: McGill-Queen's University Press, 1999. (Canadian study.)

Clark, Anna. *The Struggle for the Breeches: Gender and the Making of the British Working Class.* Berkeley: University of California Press, 1995.

Cobble, Dorothy S. (ed.). *Women and Unions: Forging a Partnership.* Ithaca, N.Y.: ILR Press, 1993.

Cobble, Dorothy Sue. *The Other Women's Movement: Workplace Justice and Social Rights in Modern America.* Princeton, N.J.: Princeton University Press, 2004.

Cook, Alice, et al. (eds.). *Women and Trade Unions in Eleven Industrialized Countries.* Philadelphia, Pa.: Temple University Press, 1984.

Cunnison, S., and J. Stageman. *Feminizing the Unions: Challenging the Culture of Masculinity.* Aldershot, U.K.: Avebury, 1995.

D'Aprano, Zelda, and Kath Williams. *The Unions and the Fight for Equal Pay.* North Melbourne: Spinifex Press, 2001.

Downs, Laura L. *Manufacturing Inequality: Gender Division in the French and British Metalworking Industries, 1914–1939.* Ithaca, N.Y.: Cornell University Press, 1995.

Dublin, Thomas. *Women at Work: The Transformation of Work and Community in Lowell, Mass., 1826–1860.* New York: Columbia University Press, 1979.

Dye, Nancy S. *As Equals and as Sisters: Feminism, Unionism, and the Women's Trade Union League of New York.* Columbia: University of Missouri Press, 1980.

Foner, Philip S. *Women and the American Labor Movement.* 2 vols. New York: Free Press, 1979, 1980.

Franzway, Suzanne. *Sexual Politics and Greedy Institutions: Union Women, Commitments, and Conflicts in Public and Private.* Sydney: Pluto Press, 2001. (An Australian study.)

Gabin, Nancy F. *Feminism in the Labor Movement: Women and the United Auto Workers, 1935–1975.* Ithaca, N.Y.: Cornell University Press, 1990.

Gordon, Eleanor. *Women and the Labour Movement in Scotland, 1850–1914*. Oxford: Clarendon Press, 1991.

Greenwald, Maurine W. *Women, War, and Work: The Impact of World War I on Women Workers in the United States*. Ithaca, N.Y.: Cornell University Press, 1990.

Gronman, Carol, and Mary B. Norton (eds.). *"To Toil the Livelong Day": America's Women at Work, 1780–1980*. Ithaca, N.Y.: Cornell University Press, 1987.

Groote, Gertjan de, and Marlou Schrover (eds.). *Women Workers and Technological Change in the Nineteenth and Twentieth Centuries*. London: Taylor and Francis, 1995.

International Confederation of Free Trade Unions, Asian and Pacific Regional Organisation. *Women and Trade Unions in the New Millennium*. Singapore: ICFTU-APRO, 2000.

Kessler-Harris, Alice. *Out to Work: A History of Wage-Earning Women in the United States*. New York: Oxford University Press, 1982.

Kraus, Vered. *Secondary Breadwinners: Israeli Women in the Labor Force*. Westport, Conn.: Greenwood Press, 2002.

Kurian, Rachel. *Women Workers in a Global Economy: Trends and Issues*. The Hague, Netherlands: Institute of Social Studies, 2003.

Lawrence, Elizabeth. *Gender and Trade Unions*. Bristol, Pa.: Taylor and Francis, 1994.

Levine, Susan. *Labor's True Women: Carpet Weavers, Industrialization, and Labor Reform in the Gilded Age*. Philadelphia: Temple University Press, 1984.

Lindsay, Lisa. *Working with Gender*. Portsmouth, N.H.: Heinemann, 2003.

Lindsey, Charles, and Lorna Duffin (eds.). *Women and Work in Pre-industrial England*. London: Croom Helm, 1985.

Louie, Miriam C.Y. *Sweatshop Warriors: Immigrant Women Workers Take on the Global Factory*. Cambridge, Mass.: South End Press, 2001. (A study of the U.S. garment industry.)

Milkman, Ruth (ed.). *Women, Work, and Protest*. Boston, Mass.: Routledge, 1985.

———. *Gender at Work: The Dynamics of Job Segregation by Sex during World War II*. Chicago: University of Illinois Press, 1987.

Nash, June, and Maria P. Fernández-Kelly (eds.). *Women, Men, and the International Division of Labor*. Albany: State University of New York Press, 1983.

Norwood, Stephen H. *Labor's Flaming Youth: Telephone Operators and Workers' Militancy, 1878–1923*. Urbana: University of Illinois Press, 1990.

Pathy, Suguna. *Sexual Division of Labour: The Engendered Labour Dynamics*. New Delhi: Serials Publications, 2011.

Pocock, Barbara (ed.). *Strife: Sex and Politics in Labour Unions*. Sydney: Allen and Unwin, 1997. (The countries covered are Australia, Canada, the United States, and the United Kingdom.)

Riccucci, Norma M. *Women, Minorities, and Unions in the Public Sector*. Westport, Conn.: Greenwood Press, 1990.

Roberts, Ron E. *Mother Jones and Her Sisters: A Century of Women Activists in the American Coal Fields*. Dubuque, Iowa: Kendall/Hunt, 1998.

Rose, Sonya. *Limited Livelihoods: Gender and Class in Nineteenth-Century England.* Berkeley: University of California Press, 1992.

Roth, Silke. *Building Movement Bridges: The Coalition of Labor Union Women.* New York: Praeger, 2003.

Ruiz, Vicki L. *Cannery Women/Cannery Lives: Mexican Women, Unionization and the Californian Food Processing Industry, 1930–1950.* Albuquerque: University of New Mexico Press, 1987.

Soldon, Norbert C. (ed.). *The World of Women's Trade Unionism: Comparative Historical Essays.* Westport, Conn.: Greenwood Press, 1985.

Steedman, Mercedes. *Angels of the Workplace: Women and the Construction of Gender Relations in the Canadian Clothing Industry, 1890–1949.* Don Mills, Ontario: Oxford University Press, 1997.

Summerfield, Penny. *Women Workers in the Second World War: Production and Patriarchy in Conflict.* London: Croom Helm, 1984.

Turbin, Carol. *Working Women of Collar City.* Chicago: University of Illinois Press, 1992.

Ward, Kathryn (ed.). *Women Workers and Global Restructuring.* Ithaca, N.Y.: ILR Press, Cornell University, 1990.

White, Jenny B. *Money Makes Us Relatives: Women's Labor in Urban Turkey.* Florence, Ky.: Routledge, 2004.

D.7 Democracy in Labor Unions and Rank-and-File Studies

Blanpain, Roger (ed.). Trade Union Democracy and Industrial Relations. Special Issue, *Bulletin of Comparative Industrial Relations,* No. 17. Deventer, Netherlands: Kluwer Law and Taxation Publishers, 1988.

Botz, Dan. *Rank and File Rebellion: Teamsters for a Democratic Union.* London: Verso, 1990.

Clark, Paul F. *The Miners' Fight for Democracy: Arnold Miller and the Reform of the United Mine Workers.* Ithaca: New York State School of Industrial and Labor Relations, Cornell University, 1981.

Clinton, Allen. *The Trade Union Rank and File: Trades Councils in Britain, 1900–1940.* Manchester: Manchester University Press, 1977.

Davis, Edward M. *Democracy in Australian Trade Unions: A Comparative Study of Six Unions.* Sydney: Allen & Unwin, 1987.

Dickenson, Mary. *Democracy in Trade Unions: Studies in Membership Participation and Control.* St. Lucia: University of Queensland Press, 1982.

Elias, Patrick, and Keith Wing. *Trade Union Democracy, Members' Rights and the Law.* London: Mansell, 1987.

Estreicher, Samuel, et al. (eds.). *The Internal Governance and Organizational Effectiveness of Labor Unions: Essays in Honor of George Brooks.* New York: Kluwer Law International, 2001.

Fosh, Patricia, and Edmund Heery. *Trade Unions and Their Members: Studies in Union Democracy and Organisation.* London: Macmillan, 1990.

Green, Max. *Epitaph for American Labor: How Union Leaders Lost Touch with America.* Washington, D.C.: AEI Press, 1996.

Kelber, Harry. *A New Game Plan for Union Organizing: How Union Members Can Become Involved to Protect Their Livelihood and Future,* 2003. (Only available electronically.)

Kelly, John. *Working for the Union: British Trade Union Officers.* Cambridge: Cambridge University Press, 1994.

Lynd, Staughton, and Alice Lynd (eds.). *The New Rank and File.* Ithaca, N.Y.: Cornell University Press, 2000.

Nyden, Philip W. *Steelworkers' Rank-and-File: The Political Economy of a Union Reform Movement.* New York: Praeger, 1984.

Sisya, Frank D. *The Political Life of a Public Employee Labor Union: Regional Union Democracy.* Lewiston, N.Y.: Edwin Mellen, 2000.

Undy, R., and R. Martin. *Ballots and Trade Union Democracy.* Oxford: Basil Blackwell, 1984.

D.8 Industrial Democracy

Dickman, Howard. *Industrial Democracy in America.* La Salle, Ill.: Open Court, 1987.

European Trade Union Institute. *Workers' Representation and Rights in the Workplace in Western Europe.* Brussels: European Trade Union Institute, 1990.

Industrial Democracy in Europe, International Research Group. *Industrial Democracy in Europe Revisited.* Oxford: Oxford University Press, 1993.

Knudsen, H. *Employee Participation in Europe.* London: Sage, 1995. (A study covering the 1950s to 1993.)

Lammers, Cornelius J., and György Széll (eds.). *International Handbook of Participation in Organizations: Vol. I—Organizational Democracy: Taking Stock.* Oxford: Oxford University Press, 1988.

Lichtenstein, Nelson, and John H. Howell (eds.). *Industrial Democracy in America: The Ambiguous Promise.* New York: Woodrow Wilson Center Press and Cambridge University Press, 1993.

Pencavel, John. *Worker Participation: Lessons from the Worker Co-ops of the Pacific Northwest.* New York: Russell Sage Foundation, 2001.

Rogers, Joel, and Wolfgang Streeck (eds.). *Works Councils: Consultation, Representation and Cooperation in Industrial Relations.* Chicago: University of Chicago Press, 1995.

Russell, R., and V. Rus (eds.). *International Handbook of Participation in Organizations for the Study of Organizational Democracy, Co-operation and Self-Management: Vol. II—Ownership and Participation.* Oxford: Oxford University Press, 1991.

D.9 Interunion Relations

Chaison, G. N. *Union Mergers in Hard Times: The View from Five Countries.* Ithaca, N.Y.: ILR Press, 1996.

Elgar, J., and R. Simpson. *The TUC's Bridlington Principles and Inter-Union Competition.* London: London School of Economics, Centre for Economic Performance, Discussion Paper No. 160, 1993.

Waddington, Jeremy. *The Politics of Bargaining: The Merger Process and British Trade Union Structural Development, 1892–1987.* London: Mansell, 1995.

D.10 Labor Disputes

Aris, Rosemary. *Trade Unions and the Management of Industrial Conflict.* Basingstoke, U.K.: Macmillan, 1998.

Brecher, Jeremy. *Strike.* rev. ed. Boston, Mass.: South End Press, 1997. (A U.S. rank-and-file study.)

Brenner, Aaron, Benjamin Day, and Immanuel Ness. *The Encyclopedia of Strikes in American History.* Armonk, N.Y.: M. E. Sharpe, 2009.

Brisbin, Richard, Jr. *A Strike Like No Other Strike: Law & Resistance during the Pittston Coal Strike of 1989–1990.* Baltimore, Md.: The Johns Hopkins University Press, 2002.

Burns, Joe. *Reviving the Strike: How Working People Can Regain Power and Transform America.* New York: Ig, 2011.

Charlesworth, Andrew, et al. *An Atlas of Industrial Protest in Britain, 1750–1990.* Basingstoke, U.K.: Macmillan, 1996.

Cohn, Samuel. *When Strikes Make Sense—and Why: Lessons from the Third Republic of French Coal Miners.* New York: Plenum Books, 1993.

Connor, Walter D. *Tattered Banners: Labor, Conflict, and Corporatism in Postcommunist Russia.* Boulder, Colo.: Westview Press, 1996.

Dobson, C. R. *Masters and Journeymen: A Prehistory of Industrial Relations, 1717–1800.* London: Croom Helm, 1980. (Much of this work deals with labor disputes.)

Dubrovskii, Oleg. *Fighting Back in Ukraine: A Worker Who Took on the Bureaucrats and Bosses.* London: Index Books, 1997.

Edwards, P. K. *Strikes in the United States, 1881–1974.* Oxford: Basil Blackwell, 1981.

Filippelli, Ronald L. (ed.). *Labor Conflict in the United States: An Encyclopedia.* New York: Garland, 1990.

Fleming, P., and Spicer, A. *Contesting the Corporation: Struggle, Power and Resistance in Organizations.* Cambridge: Cambridge University Press, 2007.

Franzosi, Roberto. *The Puzzle of Strikes: Class and State Strategies in Postwar Italy.* Cambridge: Cambridge University Press, 1995.

Godard, John. What Has Happened to Strikes? *British Journal of Industrial Relations* 49(2): 282–305, 2011.

Haimson, L. H., and C. Tilley (eds.). *Strikes, Wars, and Revolutions in an International Perspective.* Cambridge: Cambridge University Press, 1989.

Hanami, Tadashi, and Roger Blanpain (eds.). *Industrial Conflict Resolution in Market Economies: A Study of Australia, the Federal Republic of Germany, Italy, Japan and the USA.* Deventer, Netherlands: Kluwer Law and Taxation Publishers, 1984.

Hyman, Richard. *Strikes.* 3rd ed. Aylesbury: Fontana, 1984.

Jackson, Michael P. *Strikes.* New York: St. Martin's Press, 1987. (A study of Britain, the United States, and Australia.)

Jennings, Kenneth M. *Labor Relations at the New York Daily News: Peripheral Bargaining and the 1990 Strike.* Westport, Conn.: Praeger, 1993.

Juravich, Tom, and Kate Bronfenbrener. *Ravenswood: The Steelworkers' Victory and the Revival of American Labor.* Ithaca, N.Y.: Cornell University Press, 1999.

Kapsa, Michael. *Labor Strife and the Economy in the 1970s: A Decade of Discord.* New York: Garland, 1998.

Kawanishi, Hirosuke (ed.). *The Human Face of Industrial Conflict in Post-War Japan.* London: Kegan Paul International, 1999.

Loewenberg, J. J., et al. *Compulsory Arbitration: An International Comparison.* Lexington, Mass.: D. C. Heath, 1976.

Metcalf, David, and Simon Milner (eds.). *New Perspectives on Industrial Disputes.* London: LSE/Routledge, 1993.

Morris, Margaret. *The General Strike.* Harmondsworth, U.K.: Penguin, 1976. (Deals with the British General Strike in 1926.)

Ness, Immanuel. *Trade Unions and the Betrayal of the Unemployed: Labor Conflicts during the 1990s.* New York: Garland Press, 1998.

Nordlund, Willis J. *Silent Skies: The Air Traffic Controllers' Strike.* Westport, Conn.: Praeger, 1998.

Rachleff, Peter. *Hard-Pressed in the Heartland: The Hormel Strike and the Future of the American Labor Movement.* Boston: South End Press, 1993.

Reddy, Y. R. K. *Trends, Patterns and Impact of Strikes: The Indian Case.* New Delhi, India: Society for Policy Analysis and Development, 1990.

Reiss, Matthias, and Matt Perry (eds.). *Unemployment and Protest: New Perspectives on Two Centuries of Contention.* Oxford: Oxford University Press, 2011.

Rondinone, Troy. *The Great Industrial War: Framing Class Conflict in the Media, 1865–1950.* New Brunswick, N.J.: Rutgers University Press, 2010.

Silver, Beverly. *Forces of Labor: Workers' Movements and Globalization since 1870.* Cambridge: Cambridge University Press, 2003.

Svensen, Stuart. *The Sinews of War: Hard Cash and the 1890 Maritime Strike.* Sydney: University of New South Wales Press, 1995.

Van der Velden, Sjaak, et al. (eds.). *Strikes around the World, 1968–2005. Casestudies of 15 Countries.* Amsterdam: Aksant, 2007. (Covers Australia, the United Kingdom, the United States, Korea, New Zealand, Sweden, Germany, Belgium, Netherlands, South Africa, Canada, Mexico, Argentine, France, and Denmark.)

Walsh, Kenneth. *Strikes in Europe and the United States: Management and Incidence.* London: Frances Pinter, 1983.

Waters, Malcolm. *Strikes in Australia: A Sociological Analysis of Industrial Conflict.* Sydney: George Allen & Unwin, 1982.

Winterton, Jonathan, and R. Winterton. *Coal, Crisis and Conflict: The 1984–5 Miners' Strike in Yorkshire.* Manchester: Manchester University Press, 1989.

Zetka, James R., Jr. *Militancy, Market Dynamics and Workplace Authority: The Struggle over Labor Process Outcomes in the U.S. Automobile Industry, 1946 to 1973.* Albany: State University of New York Press, 1995.

E. LABOR AND SOCIETY

E.1 The Experience and Study of Work

Applebaum, Herbert A. *The American Work Ethic and the Changing Work Force: An Historical Perspective.* Westport, Conn.: Greenwood Press, 1998.

Arnold, John, et al. *Work Psychology: Understanding Human Behaviour in the Workplace.* 4th ed. Old Tappan, N.J.: Financial Times/Prentice Hall, 2004.

Bakke, Dennis W. *Joy at Work: A Revolutionary Approach to Fun on the Job.* Seattle, Wash.: Pvg, 2005.

Barringer, Tim. *Men and Work: Art and Labour in Victorian Britain.* New Haven, Conn.: Yale University Press, 2005.

Basu, Kaushik. *International Labor Standards: History, Theory, and Policy Options.* Malden, Mass.: Blackwell Publishers, 2003.

Bermeo, Nancy (ed.). *Unemployment in the New Europe.* Cambridge: Cambridge University Press, 2001.

Biernacki, Richard. *The Fabrication of Labor: Germany and England, 1640–1914.* Berkeley: University of California Press, 1995.

Bina, Cyrus, Laurie Clements, and Chuck Davis (eds.). *Beyond Survival: Wage Labor in the Late Twentieth Century.* Armonk, N.Y.: M. E. Sharpe, 1996.

Blackwell, Trevor, and Jeremy Seabrook (eds.). *Talking Work: An Oral History.* London: Faber and Faber, 1996.

Blau, Joel. *Illusions of Prosperity: America's Working Families in an Age of Economic Insecurity.* New York: Oxford University Press, 1999.

Boris, Eileen. *Home to Work: Motherhood and the Politics of Industrial Housework in the United States.* New York: Cambridge University Press, 1994.

Braverman, Harry. *Labor and Monopoly Capital: The Degradation of Work in the Twentieth Century.* New York, Monthly Review Press, 1998.

Brody, David. *In Labor's Cause: Main Themes on the History of the American Worker.* New York: Oxford University Press, 1993.

Bunting, Madeline. *Willing Slaves: How the Overwork Culture Is Ruling Our Lives.* London: HarperCollins, 2004.

Burnett, John (ed.). *Useful Toil: Autobiographies of Working People from the 1820s to the 1920s.* London: Allen Lane, 1974.

Chappell, Duncan, and Vittorio Di Martino. *Violence at Work.* 3rd ed. Geneva: International Labour Office, 2006.

Chinoy, E. *Automobile Workers and the American Dream.* 2nd ed. Urbana: University of Illinois Press, 1992.

Cross, Gary. *A Quest for Time: The Reduction of Work in Britain and France, 1840–1940.* Berkeley: University of California Press, 1989.

Derickson, Alan. *Workers' Health, Workers' Democracy: The Western Miners' Struggle, 1891–1925.* Ithaca, N.Y.: Cornell University Press, 1989.

Dinerstein, Ana C., and Mike Neary. *The Labour Debate: An Investigation into the Theory and Reality of Capitalist Work.* Aldershot, U.K.: Ashgate, 2002.

Dooley, David, and Joann Prause. *The Social Costs of Underemployment: Inadequate Employment as Disguised Unemployment.* New York: Cambridge University Press, 2004.

Edgar, Don. *The War over Work: The Future of Work and Family.* Carleton, Victoria: Melbourne University Press, 2005. (An Australian study.)

Edwards, R. *Contested Terrain: The Transformation of the Workplace in the Twentieth Century.* London: Heinemann, 1979.

Fraser, Ronald (ed.). *Work: Twenty Personal Accounts.* 2 vols. Harmondsworth: Penguin, 1968, 1969.

Freeman, Richard B., and Joel Rogers. *What Workers Want.* Ithaca, N.Y.: Cornell University Press, 1999.

Frenkel, Stephen J., et al. *On the Front Line: Organization of Work in the Information Economy.* Ithaca, N.Y.: Cornell University Press, 1999.

Gordon, D. M., R. Edwards, and M. Reich. *Segmented Work, Divided Workers: The Historical Transformation of Labor in the United States.* Cambridge: Cambridge University Press, 1982.

Gorz, André. *Reclaiming Work: Beyond the Wage-Based Society.* Cambridge: Polity Press, 1999.

Grint, Keith. *The Sociology of Work: An Introduction.* Oxford and Cambridge: Basil Blackwell and Polity Press, 1991.

Harrison, Royden, and Jonathan Zeitlin (eds.). *Divisions of Labour: Skilled Workers and Technological Change in 19th Century Britain.* Urbana: University of Illinois Press, 1985.

Head, Simon. *The New Ruthless Economy: Work and Power in the Digital Age.* New York: Oxford University Press, 2005.

Honoré, Carl. *In Praise of Slow: How a Worldwide Movement Is Challenging the Cult of Speed.* Toronto, Ontario: A. A. Knopf, 2004.

Howard, Ann (ed.). *The Changing Nature of Work.* San Francisco, Calif.: Jossey-Bass, 1995.

International Labour Organization, Social Security Department. *World Social Security Report 2010–2011. Providing Coverage in Times of Crisis and Beyond.* Geneva: International Labour Organization, 2010.

Jacoby, Daniel. *Laboring for Freedom: A New Look at the History of Labor in America.* Armonk, N.Y.: M. E. Sharpe, 1998.

Jacoby, S. M. *Employing Bureaucracy: Managers, Unions and the Transformation of Work in American Industry, 1900–1945.* New York: Columbia University Press, 1985.

Jaffe, James A. *Striking a Bargain: Work and Industrial Relations in England, 1815–1865.* Manchester: Manchester University Press, 2000.

Jones, Jacqueline. *American Work Four Centuries of Black and White Labour.* New York: W. W. Norton, 1998.

Joyce, Patrick (ed.). *The Historical Meanings of Work.* Cambridge: Cambridge University Press, 1987.

Kamata, Satoshi. *Japan in the Passing Lane: An Insider's Account of Life in a Japanese Auto Factory.* New York: Pantheon, 1982.

Karoly, Lynn A., and Constantijn W. A. Panis. *The 21st Century at Work: Forces Shaping the Future Workforce and Workplace in the United States.* Santa Monica, Calif.: RAND, 2004.

Koester, Almut. *The Language of Work.* Florence, Ky.: Routledge, 2004.

Lane, Joan. *Apprenticeship in England, 1600–1914.* London: UCL Press, 1996.

Lincoln, J. R., and A. L. Kalleberg. *Culture, Control and Commitment: A Study of Work Organization and Work Attitudes in the United States and Japan.* Cambridge: Cambridge University Press, 1990.

Lowenstein, Wendy. *Weevils at Work: What's Happening to Work in Australia—An Oral Record.* Sydney: Catalyst Press, 1997.

McCreery, David. *The Sweat of Their Brow: A History of Work in Latin America.* Armonk, N.Y.: M. E. Sharp, 2000.

McIvor, Arthur. *A History of Work in Britain, 1880–1950.* Basingstoke, U.K.: Palgave, 2001.

Meldrum, Timothy. *Domestic Service and Gender, 1660–1750.* New York: Pearson Education, 2000.

Nobel, A. *Forces of Production: A Social History of Industrial Automation.* New York: Alfred A. Knopf, 1984.

Osterman, Paul, Thomas A. Kochan, Richard M. Locke, and Michael Piore. *Working in America: A Blueprint for the New Labor Market.* Cambridge, Mass.: MIT Press, 2001.

Pahl, R. E. (ed.). *On Work: Historical, Comparative and Theoretical Perspectives.* Oxford: Basil Blackwell, 1988.

Pollert, Anna. *Transformation of Work in the New Market Economies of Central Eastern Europe.* London: Sage, 1999.

Ransome, Paul. *The Work Paradigm: A Theoretical Investigation of Concepts of Work.* Aldershot, U.K.: Avebury, 1996.

Roediger, David R., and Philip S. Foner. *Our Own Time: A History of American Labor and the Working Day.* New York: Verso Paper, 1989.

Rule, J. *The Experience of Labour in Eighteenth Century England.* London: Croom Helm, 1981.

Sennett, Richard. *The Corrosion of Character: The Personal Consequences of Work in the New Capitalism.* New York: Norton, 1998.

Shaiken, Harley. *Work Transformed.* New York: Holt, Rinehart and Winston, 1984.

Shields, John (ed.). *All Our Labours: Oral Histories of Working Life in Twentieth Century Sydney.* Sydney: University of New South Wales, 1992.

Silverman, Dan P. *Hitler's Economy: Nazi Work Creation Programs, 1933–1936.* Cambridge, Mass.: Harvard University Press, 1998.

Spector, Paul E. *Industrial and Organizational Psychology: Research and Practice.* New York: John Wiley & Sons, 2005.

Starbuck, William, and Cary Cooper. *Work and Workers.* New York, Russell Sage Foundation, 2005.

Strom, Sharon H. *Beyond the Typewriter: Gender, Class and the Origins of Modern American Office Work, 1900–1930.* Urbana: University of Illinois Press, 1992.

Terkel, Studs. *Working.* New York: Pantheon Books, 1972. (Also available in paperback by Avon.)

Thomas, Keith (ed.). *The Oxford Book of Work.* Oxford: Oxford University Press, 1999.

Tilly, Chris, and Charles Tilly. *Work under Capitalism.* Boulder, Colo.: Westview Press, 1998.

Whipp, Richard. *Patterns of Labour: Work and Social Change in the Pottery Industry.* London: Routledge, Chapman and Hall, 1990.

E.2 Forced or Involuntary Labor

Andrees, Beate, and Patrick Belser. *Forced Labor: Coercion and Exploitation in the Private Economy.* Boulder, Colo.: Lynne Rienner, 2009.

Bales, Kevin. *New Slavery. A Reference Handbook.* ABC-CLIO, 2005.

Brass, Tom, and Marcel van der Linden (eds.). *Free and Unfree Labour: The Debate Continues.* Bern, Switzerland: Peter Lang, 1997.

Gillespie, Michele. *Free Labor in an Unfree World: White Artisans in Slaveholding Georgia, 1789–1860.* Athens: University of Georgia Press, 2000.

Lichtenstein, Alex. *Twice the Work of Free Labor: The Political Economy of Convict Labor in the New South.* London: Verso, 1996.

Nicholas, Stephen (ed.). *Convict Workers: Interpreting Australia's Past.* Sydney: Cambridge University Press, 1988.

Patel, Klaus, and Christof Mauch. *Soldiers of Labor: Labor Service in Nazi Germany and New Deal America, 1933–1945.* Cambridge: Cambridge University Press, 2005.

Postma, Johannes. *Slave Revolts.* ABC-CLIO/Greenwood, 2008.

Rodriguez, Junius P. (ed.). *The Historical Encyclopedia of Slavery.* 2 vols. Santa Barbara, Calif.: ABC-CLIO, 1997.

———. *Slavery in the Modern World. A History of Political, Social, and Economic Oppression.* ABC-CLIO/Greenwood, 2011.

Shapiro, Karin. A. *A New South Rebellion: The Battle against Convict Labor in the Tennessee Coalfields, 1871–1896.* Chapel Hill: University of North Carolina Press, 1998.

E.3 Occupational Health and Safety

Aldrich, Mark. *Safety First: Technology, Labour, and Business in the Building of American Work Safety, 1870–1939.* Baltimore, Md.: Johns Hopkins University Press, 1997.

Bohle, Phil, and Michael Quinlan. *Managing Occupational Health and Safety: A Multidisciplinary Approach.* 2nd ed. Melbourne: Macmillan Education Australia, 2000.

Derickson, Alan. *Workers' Health, Workers' Democracy: The Western Miners' Struggle, 1891–1925.* Ithaca, N.Y.: Cornell University Press, 1988.

International Labour Organization. *Encyclopaedia of Occupational Health and Safety*. 3rd ed. Geneva: International Labour Office, 1983. (First published in 1930.)

International Metalworkers' Federation. *Stress and Burnout a Growing Problem for Non-manual Workers*. Geneva: International Metalworkers' Federation, 2003. (Available in electronic format only.)

Kodz, J. *Working Long Hours: A Review of the Evidence*. London: Dept. of Trade and Industry, 2003.

Treble, John, and Tim Barmby. *Worker Absenteeism and Sick Pay*. New York: Cambridge University Press, 2011.

E.4 Industrial Archaeology and Iconography

Cohen, Ronald D. *Work and Sing: a History of Occupational and Labor Union Songs in the United States*. Crockett, Calif.: Carquinez Press, 2009.

Dennis, James M. *Robert Koehler's The Strike: The Improbable Story of an Iconic 1886 Painting of Labor Protest*. Madison, Wisc.: The University of Wisconsin Press, 2011.

Fogg, Charles. *Chains and Chainmaking*. Aylesbury, Buckinghamshire: Shire, 1981.

Gale, W. K. V. *Ironworking*. Aylesbury, Buckinghamshire: Shire, 1981.

Gorman, John. *Banner Bright: An Illustrated History of the British Trade Union Movement*. London: Allen Lane, 1974.

———. *Images of Labour: Selected Memorabilia from the National Museum of Labour History*. London: Scorpion, 1985.

Griffin, A. R. *The Collier*. Aylesbury, Buckinghamshire: Shire, 1982.

Mace, Rodney. *British Trade Union Posters: an Illustrated History*. Sutton: Sutton Publishing, 1999.

Martin, Paul. *The Trade Union Badge: Material Culture in Action*. Aldershot, U.K.: Ashgate, 2002.

Trinder, Barrie (ed.). *The Blackwell Encyclopedia of Industrial Archaeology*. Oxford: Basil Blackwell, 1992.

E.5 Unions and Politics (*see also* D.4)

Arnesen, Eric, et al. *Labor Histories: Class, Politics, and the Working Class Experience*. Urbana: University of Illinois Press, 1998.

Asher, H., E. Ripley, and R. B. Snyde. *American Labor Unions in the Electoral Arena: People, Passions, and Power*. Lanham, Md.: Rowman & Littlefield, 2000.

Brennan, James P. *The Labor Wars in Córdoba, 1955–1976: Ideology, Work, and Labor Politics in an Argentine Industrial City*. Cambridge, Mass.: Harvard University Press, 1994.

Burwood, Stephen. *American Labor, France, and the Politics of Intervention, 1945–1952: Workers and the Cold War*. Lewiston, N.Y.: Mellen Press, 1998.

Campbell, Alan, et al. *British Trade Unions and Industrial Politics: The Post-War Compromise, 1945–64*. Aldershot, U.K.: Ashgate, 1999.

Carsten, F. L. *The German Workers and the Nazis*. Aldershot, U.K.: Scolar Press, 1995.

Chatterji, Rakhahari. *Unions, Politics and the State: A Study of Indian Labour Politics*. New Delhi: South Asian Publishers, 1980.

Cherny, Robert W., William Issel, and Kieran Walsh Taylor (eds.). *American Labor and the Cold War: Grassroots Politics and Postwar Political Culture*. New Brunswick, N.J.: Rutgers University Press, 2004.

Conner, Valerie J. *The National War Labor Board: Stability, Social Justice and the Voluntary State in World War I*. Chapel Hill: University of North Carolina Press, 1983.

Dark, Taylor E. *The Unions and the Democrats: An Enduring Alliance*. Ithaca, N.Y.: ILR Press, 1999.

Davidson, Roger. *Whitehall and the Labour Problem in Late-Victorian and Edwardian Britain*. London: Croom Helm, 1985.

Davis, Mike. *Prisoners of the American Dream: Politics and Economy in the History of the U.S. Working Class*. London: Verso, 1986.

Dorey, Peter. *The Conservative Party and the Trade Unions*. London: Routledge, 1995.

Draper, Alan. *A Rope of Sand: The AFL-CIO Committee on Political Education, 1955–1967*. New York: Praeger, 1989.

Filippelli, Ronald L. *American Labor and Postwar Italy, 1943–1953: A Study of Cold War Politics*. Stanford, Calif.: Stanford University Press, 1989.

Fink, Leon. *Workingmen's Democracy: The Knights of Labor and American Politics*. Urbana: University of Illinois Press, 1983.

Form, William. *Segmented Labor, Fractured Politics: Labor Politics in American Life*. New York: Plenum Press, 1995.

Francia, Peter L. *The Future of Organized Labor in American Politics*. New York: Columbia University Press, 2006.

Friedman, Gerald. *State Making and Labor Movements: France and the United States, 1876–1914*. Ithaca, N.Y.: Cornell University Press, 1998.

Fulcher, James. *Labour Movements, Employers and the State: Conflict and Cooperation in Britain and Sweden*. Oxford: Clarendon Press, 1991.

Gall, Gilbert. *The Politics of Right to Work: The Labor Federations as Special Interests, 1943–1979*. Westport, Conn.: Greenwood Press, 1988.

Gordon, Colin. *New Deals: Business, Labor, and Politics in America, 1920–1935*. New York: Cambridge University Press, 1994.

Greene, Julie. *Pure and Simple Politics: The American Federation of Labor and Political Activism, 1881–1917*. Cambridge: Cambridge University Press, 1998.

Gupta, Partha S. *Imperialism and the British Labour Movement, 1914–1964*. London: Macmillan, 1975.

Haydu, Jeffrey. *Between Craft and Class: Skilled Workers and Factory Politics in the US and Britain, 1890–1922*. Berkeley: University of California Press, 1988.

Katzenstein, Peter J. *Corporatist and Change: Austria, Switzerland and the Politics of Industry.* Ithaca, N.Y.: Cornell University Press, 1984.

Korpi, Walter. *The Democratic Class Struggle.* London: Routledge and Kegan Paul, 1983.

Kosciel, Frank. *Divided Loyalties: American Unions and the Vietnam War.* New York: Garland, 1999.

Kume, Ikuo. *Disparaged Success: Labor Politics in Postwar Japan.* Ithaca, N.Y.: Cornell University Press, 1998.

Large, Stephen S. *Organized Workers and Socialist Politics in Interwar Japan.* New York: Cambridge University Press, 1981.

Marks, Gary. *Unions in Politics: Britain, Germany, and the United States in the Nineteenth and Early Twentieth Centuries.* Princeton, N.J.: Princeton University Press, 1989.

McMullin, Ross. *The Light on the Hill: The Australian Labor Party, 1891–1991.* Melbourne: Oxford University Press, 1991.

Mink, Gwendolyn. *Old Labor and New Labor in American Political Development: Union, Party and State, 1875–1920.* Ithaca, N.Y.: Cornell University Press, 1986.

Minkun, Lewis. *The Contentious Alliance: Trade Unions and the Labour Party.* New York: Columbia University Press, 1993. (A study of the British Labour Party and organized labor.)

Montgomery, David. *The Fall of the House of Labor: The Workplace, the State, and American Radicalism, 1865–1925.* New York: Cambridge University Press, 1987.

Obach, Brian K. *Labor and the Environmental Movement: The Quest for Common Ground.* Cambridge, Mass.: MIT Press, 2004.

Perusek, Glenn, and Kent Worcester (eds.). *Trade Union Politics: American Unions and Economic Change, 1960s–1990s.* Atlantic Highlands, N.J.: Humanities Press, 1995.

Pimlott, Ben, and Chris Cook (eds.). *Trade Unions in British Politics: The First 250 Years.* 2nd ed. New York: Longman, 1991.

Robertson, David B. *Capital, Labor, and State: The Battle for American Labor Markets from the Civil War to the New Deal.* Lanham, Md.: Rowman & Littlefield, 2000.

Roxborough, Ian. *Unions and Politics in Mexico: The Case of the Automobile Industry.* Cambridge: Cambridge University Press, 1984.

Simeon, Dilip. *The Politics of Labour under Late Colonialism: Workers, Unions, and the State in Chota Nagpur.* New Delhi: Manohar, 1995.

Singleton, Gwynnoth. *The Accord and the Australian Labour Movement.* Melbourne: Melbourne University Press, 1990.

Taylor, R. *The Trade Union Question in British Politics: Government and Unions since 1945.* Oxford: Blackwell, 1994.

Tolliday, S., and J. Zeitlin (eds.). *Shopfloor Bargaining and the State.* Cambridge: Cambridge University Press, 1985.

Turner, Lowell. *Fighting for Partnership: Labor and Politics in Unified Germany.* Ithaca, N.Y.: Cornell University Press, 1998.

Wilentz, Sean. *Chants Democratic: New York City and the Rise of the Working Class, 1788–1850.* New York: Oxford University Press, 1984.

E.6 Employers

Amerasinghe, E. F. G. *Employers' Federation of Ceylon, 1929–1994.* Colombo: Employers' Federation of Ceylon, 1994.

Chubb, B. *FIE: Federation of Irish Employers, 1942–1992.* Dublin: Gill and Macmillan, 1992.

Cohen, Isaac. *American Management and British Labor: A Comparative Study of the Cotton Spinning Industry.* Westport, Conn.: Greenwood Press, 1990.

Gillespie, Richard. *Manufacturing Knowledge: A History of the Hawthorne Experiments.* New York: Cambridge University Press, 1991.

Gospel, H. F., and C. R. Littler (eds.). *Managerial Strategies and Industrial Relations.* London: Heinemann, 1983.

Harris, Howell J. *The Right to Manage: Industrial Relations Politics of American Business in the 1940s.* Madison: University of Wisconsin Press, 1982.

Hattam, Victoria C. *Labor Visions and State Power: The Origins of Business Unionism in the United States.* Princeton, N.J.: Princeton University Press, 1993.

Jacoby, S. (ed.). *Masters to Managers: Historical and Comparative Perspectives on American Employers.* New York: Columbia University Press, 1991.

Jacques, Roy. *Manufacturing the Employee: Management Knowledge from the Nineteenth to Twenty-First Centuries.* London: Sage, 1996.

Jowitt, J. A., and A. J. McIvor (eds.). *Employers and Labour in the English Textile Industries, 1850–1939.* London: Routledge, Chapman & Hall, 1988.

Kaufman, Bruce, and Daphne Taras (eds.). *Nonunion Employee Representation: History, Contemporary Practice, and Policy.* Armonk, N.Y.: M. E. Sharpe, Inc., 2000.

McIvor, Arthur J. *Organised Capital: Employers' Associations and Industrial Relations in Northern England, 1880–1939.* Cambridge: Cambridge University Press, 1996.

Myer, Stephen. *The Five Dollar Day: Labor Management and Social Control in the Ford Motor Company, 1908–1921.* Albany: State University of New York Press, 1981.

Sheldon, Peter, and Louise Thornthwaite (eds.). *Employer Associations and Industrial Relations Changes: Catalysts or Captives.* Sydney: Allen and Unwin, 1999.

Tolliday, S., and J. Zeitlin (eds.). *The Power to Manage? Employers and Industrial Relations in Comparative-Historical Perspective.* London: Routledge, 1991.

Windmuller, J. P., and A. Gladstone (eds.). *Employer Associations and Industrial Relations: A Comparative Study.* New York: Oxford University Press, 1984.

Wood, John C., and Michael C. Wood. *George Elton Mayo: Critical Evaluations in Business and Management.* Florence, Ky.: Routledge, 2004.

Wright, Christopher. *The Management of Labour: A History of Australian Employers.* Melbourne: Oxford University Press, 1995.

E.7 Social Histories and Immigration

Atkinson, Frank. *North-East England: People at Work, 1860–1960.* Ashbourne, Derbyshire, U.K.: Moorland, 1980. (Contains a comprehensive collection of photographs.)

Babson, Steve. *Working Detroit: The Making of a Union Town.* Detroit, Mich.: Wayne State University Press, 1984.

———. *Building the Union: Skilled Workers and Anglo-Gaelic Immigrants in the Rise of the UAW.* New Brunswick, N.J.: Rutgers University, 1991

Bahl, Vinay. *The Making of the Indian Working Class.* New Delhi: Sage, 1995.

Berlanstein, Lenard R. *Rethinking Labor History: Essays on Discourse and Class Analysis.* Champaign: University of Illinois Press, 1993.

Bodnar, John. *Workers' World: Kinship, Community, and Protest in an Industrial Society, 1900–1940.* Baltimore, Md.: Johns Hopkins University Press, 1982.

Briggs, Vernon M. *Immigration and American Unionism.* Ithaca, N.Y.: Cornell University Press, 2001.

Brody, David. *Workers in Industrial America: Essays on the Twentieth Century Struggle.* New York: Oxford University Press, 1980.

Cantor, Milton (ed.). *American Working-Class Culture: Explorations in American Labor and Social History.* Westport, Conn.: Greenwood Press, 1979.

Cherwinski, W., and G. Kealey (eds.). *Lectures in Canadian Labour and Working-Class History.* St. Johns, Newfoundland: Committee on Canadian Labour History, St. Johns, 1985.

Cornford, Daniel (ed.). *Working People of California.* Berkeley: University of California Press, 1995.

Crew, David. *Town in the Ruhr: A Social History of Bochum, 1860–1914.* New York: Columbia University Press, 1979.

Docherty, James C. *Newcastle: The Making of an Australian City.* Sydney: Hale & Iremonger, 1983.

Drummond, Diane K. *Crewe: Railway Town, Company and People, 1840–1914.* Aldershot, U.K.: Scolar Press, 1995.

Ellis, P. Berresford. *A History of the Irish Working Class.* rev. ed. London: Pluto Press, 1996.

Emberson-Bain, 'Atu. *Labour and Gold in Fiji.* Melbourne: Cambridge University Press, 1994.

Fagge, Roger. *Power, Culture, and Conflict in the Coalfields: West Virginia and South Wales, 1900–1922.* Manchester: Manchester University Press, 1996.

Faue, Elizabeth. *Community of Suffering & Struggle: Women, Men and the Labor Movement in Minneapolis, 1915–1945.* Chapel Hill: University of North Carolina Press, 1991.

Frisch, Michael, and Daniel J. Walkowitz (eds.). *Working-Class America: Essays on Labor, Community and American Society.* Urbana: University of Illinois Press, 1983.

Fry, Eric (ed.). *Common Cause: Essays in Australian and New Zealand Labour History.* Wellington and Sydney: Allen & Unwin/Port Nicholson Press, 1986.

Gardner, James B., and George R. Adams (eds.). *Ordinary People and Everyday Life: Perspectives on the New Social History.* Nashville, Tenn.: American Association for State and Local History, 1983.

Gerstle, Gary. *Working-Class Americanism: The Politics of Labor in a Textile City, 1914–60.* New York: Cambridge University Press, 1989.

Guerin-Gonzales, Camile, and Carl Strikwerda (eds.). *The Politics of Immigrant Workers: Labor Activism and Migration in the World Economy since 1830.* New York: Holmes and Meier, 1993.

Heerma van Voss, Lex, and Marcel van der Linden (eds.), *Class and Other Identities: Gender, Religion, and Ethnicity in the Writing of European Labour History.* Oxford and New York: Berghahn, 2002.

Hoerder, Dirk (ed.). *"Struggle a Hard Battle": Essays on Working-Class Immigrants.* De Kalb: North Illinois University Press, 1986.

Isaacman, Allen, and Richart Roberts (eds.). *Cotton, Colonialism, and Social History in Sub-Saharan Africa.* Portsmouth, N.H.: Reed Elsevier, 1995.

Kealey, G., and G. Patmore (eds.). *Canadian and Australian Labour History: Towards a Comparative Perspective.* Brisbane: Australian Society for the Study of Labour History, 1990.

Kleinberg, S. J. *The Shadow of the Mills: Working-Class Families in Pittsburgh, 1870–1907.* Pittsburgh: University of Pittsburgh Press, 1989.

Kornblum, William. *Blue-Collar Community.* Chicago: University of Chicago Press, 1974. (Deals with U.S steelworkers.)

Krause, Paul. *The Battle for Homestead, 1880–1892: Politics, Culture, and Steel.* Pittsburgh: Pittsburgh University Press, 1992.

Laslett, John H. M. *Nature's Noblemen: The Fortunes of the Independent Collier in Scotland and the American Midwest, 1855–1889.* Los Angeles: UCLA Institute of Industrial Relations Monograph and Research Series No. 34, 1983.

Lever-Tracy, Constance. *A Divided Working Class: Ethnic Segregation and Industrial Conflict in Australia.* London: Routledge & Kegan Paul, 1988.

Lichtenstein, Nelson, and Stephen Myer (eds.). *On the Line: Essays in the History of Auto Work.* Champaign: University of Illinois Press, 1989.

Littlefield, Alice, and Martha C. Knack (eds.). *Native Americans and Wage Labor: Ethnohistorical Perspectives.* Norman: University of Oklahoma Press, 1996.

Look Lai, Walton. *Indentured Labor, Caribbean Sugar: Chinese and Indian Migrants to the British West Indies, 1838–1918.* Baltimore, Md.: Johns Hopkins University Press, 1993.

Lummis, Trevor. *The Labour Aristocracy, 1850–1914.* Aldershot, U.K.: Scolar Press, 1994.

Lynch, John. *A Tale of Three Cities: Comparative Studies in Working Class Life.* Basingstoke, U.K.: Macmillan, 1998.

MacRaild, Donald M. *Labour in British Society, 1830–1914.* New York: St. Martin's Press, 2000.

Mohl, Raymond A., and Neil Betten. *Steel City: Urban and Ethnic Patterns in Gary, Indiana, 1906–1950.* New York: Holmes and Meier, 1986.

Moody, J. Carroll, and Alice Kessler-Harris (eds.). *Perspectives on American Labor History: The Problems of Synthesis.* De Kalb: Northern Illinois University Press, 1989.

Norris, P., A. R. Townsend, and J. C. Dewdney. *Demographic and Social Change in the Durham Coalfield.* Working Papers 23, 24, 25. Durham, U.K.: University of Durham, Department of Geography, Census Research Unit, 1983 and 1984.

O'Donnell, L. A. *Irish Voice and Organized Labor in America: A Biographical Study.* Westport, Conn.: Greenwood Press, 1997.

Oestreicher, Robert L. *Solidarity and Fragmentation: Working People and Class Consciousness in Detroit, 1875–1900.* Urbana: University of Illinois Press, 1986.

Penninx, Rinus, and Judith Roosblad (eds.). *Trade Unions, Immigration, and Immigrants in Europe, 1960–1993.* New York: Berghahn Book, 2000.

Prude, Jonathan. *The Coming of Industrial Order: Town and Factory Life in Rural Massachusetts, 1800–1860.* New York: Cambridge University Press, 1983.

Rorabaugh, W. J. *The Craft Apprentice: From Franklin to the Machine Age in America.* New York: Oxford University Press, 1986.

Saunders, Kay (ed.). *Indentured Labour in the British Empire, 1834–1920.* London: Croom Helm, 1984.

Schultz, Ronald. *The Republic of Labor: Philadelphia Artisans and the Politics of Class, 1720–1830.* New York: Oxford University Press, 1993.

Shergold, Peter R. *Working-Class Life: The "American Standard" in Comparative Perspective, 1899–1913.* Pittsburgh: Pittsburgh University Press, 1982. (Standards in Pittsburgh, Pensylvania, and Birmingham, U.K.)

Zippay, Allison. *From Middle Income to Poor: Downward Mobility among Displaced Steelworkers.* New York: Praeger, 1991.

E.8 Labor and Race

Alexander, Peter. *Workers, War and the Origins of Apartheid: Labour and Politics in South Africa, 1939–48.* Oxford: James Currey, 2000.

Boswell, Terry, Cliff Brown, John Brueggemann, and T. Ralph Peters, Jr. *Racial Competition and Class Solidarity.* Albany, State University of New York Press, 2006.

Brown, Cliff. *Racial Conflict and Violence in the Labor Market: Roots in the 1919 Steel Strike.* New York: Garland Press, 1998.

Draper, Alan. *Conflict of Interests: Organized Labor and the Civil Rights Movement in the South, 1954–1968.* Ithaca, N.Y.: ILR Press, 1994.

Gould, William. *Black Workers in White Unions: Job Discrimination in the United States.* Ithaca, N.Y.: Cornell University Press, 1977.

Harris, William H. *The Harder We Run: Black Workers since the Civil War.* New York: Oxford University Press, 1982.

Honey, Michael K. *Southern Labor and Black Civil Rights: Organizing Memphis Workers.* Urbana: University of Illinois Press, 1993.

———. *Going Down Jericho Road. The Memphis Strike, Martin Luther King's Last Campaign.* New York: Norton 2007.

Huntley, Horace, and David Montgomery (eds.). *Black Workers' Struggle for Equality in Birmingham*. Champaign, Ill.: University of Illinois Press, 2004.

Iton, Richard. *Solidarity Blues: Race, Culture, and the American Left*. Chapel Hill: University of North Carolina Press, 2000.

Kent, Ronald C., et al. (eds.). *Culture, Gender, Race, and U.S. Labor Relations*. Westport, Conn.: Greenwood Press, 1993.

Letwin, Daniel. *The Challenge of Interracial Unionism: Alabama Coal Miners, 1878–1921*. Chapel Hill: University of North Carolina Press, 1998.

Minchin, Timothy J. *Hiring the Black Worker: The Racial Integration of the Southern Textile Industry, 1960–1980*. Chapel Hill: University of North Carolina Press, 1999.

Moreno, Paul D. *Black Americans and Organized Labor: A New History*. Baton Rouge, La.: Louisiana State University Press, 2006.

Nelson, Bruce. *Divided We Stand: American Workers and the Struggle for Black Equality*. Princeton, N.J.: Princeton University Press, 2001.

Rachleff, Peter S. *Black Labor in the South: Richmond, Virginia, 1865–1890*. Philadelphia, Pa.: Temple University Press, 1984.

Ramdin, Ron. *The Making of the Black Working Class in Britain*. Aldershot, U.K.: Gower, 1987.

Roediger, David R. *The Wages of Whiteness: Race and the Making of the American Working Class*. London: Verso, 1991.

E.9 Child Labor

Dachi, H. A., and R. M. Garrett. *Child Labour and Its Impact on Children's Access to and Participation in Primary Education: A Case Study from Tanzania*. London: Dept. for International Development, 2003.

Grier, Beverly Carolease. *Invisible Hands. Child Labor and the State in Colonial Zimbabwe*. Portsmouth, N.H.: Heinemann, 2005.

Hindman, Hugh D. *Child Labor: An American History*. Armonk, N.Y.: M. E. Sharpe, 2002.

Hobbs, Sandy, Jim McKechnie, and Michael Lavalette. *Child Labor. A World History Companion*. Calif.: ABC-CLIO, 1999.

Kent, George. *Children in the International Political Economy*. Basingstoke, U.K.: Macmillan, 1995.

Lavalette, Michael (ed.). *A Thing of the Past? Child Labour in Britain, 1800 to the Present*. Liverpool: Liverpool University Press, 1999.

Levine, Marvin J. *Children for Hire*. New York: Praeger, 2003.

McIntosh, Robert. *Boys in the Pits: Child Labour in Coal Mines*. Montreal, Quebec: McGill-Queen's University Press, 2000.

Robinson, J. Dennis. *Striking Back: The Fight to End Child Labor Exploitation*. Mankato, Minn.: Compass Point Books, 2010.

Schmidt, James D. *Industrial Violence and the Legal Origins of Child Labor*. New York: Cambridge University Press, 2010.

Schmitz, Cathryne L., et al. (eds.). *Child Labor: A Global View.* Westport, Conn.: Greenwood Press, 2004.

E.10 Labor Sociology

Bruno, Robert. *Steelworker Alley: How Class Works in Youngstown.* Ithaca, N.Y.: Cornell University Press, 1999.

Charles, Maria, and David B. Grusky. *Occupational Ghettos: The Worldwide Segregation of Women and Men.* Palo Alto, Calif.: Stanford University Press, 2005.

Due, Jesper, et al. *The Survival of the Danish Model: A Historical Sociological Analysis of the Danish System of Collective Bargaining.* Copenhagen: DJØF, 1994.

Ehrenberg, Ronald G., and Robert S. Smith. *Modern Labor Economics: Theory and Public Policy.* Boston: Pearson/Addison Wesley, 2006.

Freeman, Richard B., and Joel Rogers. *What Workers Want.* Ithaca, N.Y.: Cornell University Press, 2006.

Halle, David. *America's Working Man: Work, Home, and Politics among Blue-Collar Property Owners.* Chicago: University of Chicago Press, 1984.

Heyes, Jason. *Labor Administration in the United Kingdom.* Geneva: International Labour Organization, 2001.

International Labour Organization. *Decent Work for Domestic Workers.* Geneva: International Labour Organization, 2009.

Jepsen, Maria, David Foden, and Martin Hutsebaut. *Lifelong Strategy for Active Ageing.* Brussels: European Trade Union Institute, 2003.

Kim, Hyunhee. *Working Class Stratification and the Demand for Unions in the United States.* New York: Garland, 1997.

Lubrano, Alfred. *Limbo: Blue-Collar Roots, White-Collar Dreams.* New York: John Wiley and Sons, 2003. (A U.S. account of the differences between blue-collar and white-collar cultures.)

Marwick, Arthur. *Class: Image and Reality in Britain, France and the USA since 1930.* Glasgow: Fontana/Collins, 1980.

Munger, Frank (ed.). *Laboring Below the Line: A New Ethnography of Poverty, Low-Wage Work, and Survival in the Global Economy.* New York, Russell Sage Foundation, 2001.

Poole, Michael. *Theories of Trade Unionism.* rev. ed. London: Routledge & Kegan Paul, 1984.

Robertson, James E. *Japanese Working Lives.* London: Routledge, 1998.

Theriault, Reg. *The Unmaking of the American Working Class.* New York: New Press, 2003.

Torlina, Jeff. *Working Class: Challenging Myths about Blue-collar Labor.* Boulder, Colo.: Lynne Rienner Publishers, 2011.

E.11 Labor and the Law

Atleson, J. *Values and Assumptions in American Labor Law.* Amherst: University of Massachusetts Press, 1983.

Bennett, Laura. *Making Labour Law in Australia: Industrial Relations, Politics and Law.* Sydney: Law Book, 1994.

Betten, Lammy. *International Labor Law: Selected Issues.* Deventer, Netherlands, and Boston: Kluwer, 1993.

Blanpain, Roger. *Labour Law and Industrial Relations of the European Union: Maastricht and Beyond, from a Community to a Union.* Deventer, Netherlands: Kluwer Law and Taxation, 1992.

———. *The Global Workplace: International and Comparative Employment Law: Cases and Materials.* Cambridge; New York: Cambridge University Press, 2007. (Covers nine countries, the United States, Canada, Mexico, the United Kingdom, Germany, France, China, Japan, and India.)

Blanpain, Roger, and C. Engels (eds.). *Comparative Labour Law and Industrial Relations in Industrialized Market Economies.* 5th ed. Deventer, Netherlands: Kluwer Law and Taxation Publishers, 1993.

Blanpain, R., and J. Baker. *Comparative Labour Law and Industrial Relations in Industrialized Market Economies.* The Hague: London: Kluwer Law International, 2007.

Bronstein, Arturo. *International and Comparative Labour Law: Current Challenges.* International Labour Office. Houndmills, Basingstoke: Palgrave Macmillan; Geneva: International Labour Organization, 2009.

CCH Canada. *Canadian Master Labour Guide: A Guide to Canadian Labour Law.* 8th ed., Don Mills, Ontario: CCH Canada, 1993.

Creighton, Breen, and Andrew Stewart. *Labour Law: An Introduction.* 2nd ed. Sydney: Federation Press, 1994.

Deery, Stephen J., and J. Mitchell (eds.). *Labour Law and Industrial Relations in Asia: Eight Country Studies.* Melbourne: Longman Cheshire, 1993. (The countries covered are Hong Kong, Malaysia, Singapore, South Korea, Japan, Philippines, Thailand, and Taiwan.)

England, J., and J. Rear. *Industrial Relations and Law in Hong Kong.* Hong Kong: Oxford University Press, 1981.

Ewing, K. D. *Trade Unions, the Labour Party and the Law: A Study of the Trade Union Act, 1913.* Edinburgh: Edinburgh University Press, 1982.

———. *The Right to Strike: from the Trade Disputes Act 1906 to a Trade Union Freedom Bill 2006.* Liverpool: Institute of Employment Rights, 2006.

Forbath, W. E. *Law and the Shaping of the American Labor Movement.* Cambridge, Mass.: Harvard University Press, 1991.

Gould IV, William B. *Labored Relations—Law, Politics, and the NLRB: A Memoir.* Cambridge, Mass.: The MIT Press, 2000.

Hanson, Charles. *The Closed Shop: A Comparative Study of Public Policy and Trade Union Security in Britain, the USA and West Germany.* London: Gower, 1982.

Hepple, Bob (ed.). *The Making of Labour Law in Europe: A Comparative Study of Nine Countries up to 1945.* London: Mansell, 1986. (Covers Belgium, Britain and Ireland, Denmark, France, Germany, Italy, the Netherlands, and Luxembourg.)

Hogler, Raymond. *Employment Relations in the United States: Law, Policy, and Practice.* Thousand Oaks, Calif.: Sage Publications, 2004.

International Labour Organization. *Freedom of Association: Digest of Decisions and Principles of the Freedom of Association Committee of the Governing Body of the ILO.* 3rd ed. Geneva: International Labour Office, 1985.

———. *Freedom of Association and Collective Bargaining.* Geneva: International Labour Office, 1994.

———. *Celebration of the 60th Anniversary of Convention No. 98: The Right to Organize and Collective Bargaining in the 21st Century.* Geneva: International Labour Organization, 2009.

Kahn-Freund, Otto, et al. *Labour Law and Politics in the Weimar Republic.* Oxford: Basil Blackwell, 1981.

Koniaris, T. B. *Labour Law and Industrial Relations in Greece.* Deventer, Netherlands: Kluwer and Taxation Publishers, 1990.

Kucera, David, and Ritash Sarna. *Trade Union Rights, Democracy, and Exports: A Gravity Model Approach.* Oxford, U.K.: Blackwell Publishing Ltd, 2006. (Based on data from 162 countries.)

Linnick, Stuart, et al. *The Developing Labor Law.* 2nd ed., 3rd supplement. Washington, D.C.: Bureau of National Affairs, 1988.

Nigeria Employers' Consultative Association. *Compendium of Nigerian Social and Labour Laws.* Lagos: NECA, 2004.

Peetz, David. *Brave New Workplace.* Sydney: Allen & Unwin, 2006. (An Australian study of radical changes to federal labor law in 2006.)

Prondzynski, Ferdinand von. *Freedom of Association and Industrial Relations.* London: Mansell, 1987.

Ray, Douglas E., Calvin William Sharpe, and Robert N. Strassfeld. *Understanding Labor Law.* 3rd ed. New Providence, N.J.: LexisNexis, 2011.

Schmitt, M. N., et al. *Turkish Labor Law.* Irvington-on-Hudson, N.Y.: Transaction Publishers, 1996.

Sugeno, Kazuo. *Japanese Labor Law.* Seattle: University of Washington Press, 1992.

Tomlins, Christopher L. *The State and the Unions: Labor Relations, Law, and the Organized Labor Movement in America, 1880–1960.* New York: Cambridge University Press, 1985.

———. *Law, Labor and Ideology in the Early American Republic.* New York: Cambridge University Press, 1993. (Covers the period from 1790 to 1850.)

Undy, R., P. Fosh, H. Morris, and P. Smith. *Managing the Unions: The Impact of Legislation on Trade Unions' Behaviour.* Oxford: Clarendon Press, 1996. (Concerned with British legislation since 1980.)

E.12 Labor, Films, Theater, and the Media

Booker, Keith. *Film and the American Left: A Research Guide.* Westport, Conn.: Greenwood Press, 1999.

Duffy, Susan (ed.). *The Political Left in the American Theatre of the 1930's: A Bibliographical Sourcebook.* Metuchen, N.J.: Scarecrow Press, 1992.

Filewod, Alan, and David Watt. *Workers' Playtime: Theatre and the Labour Movement since 1970.* Sydney: Currency Press, 2001.

Godfried, Nathan. *WCFL: Chicago's Voice of Labor, 1926–1978.* Champaign: University of Illinois Press, 1997.

Jones, Stephen G. *The British Labour Movement and Film, 1918–1939.* London: Routledge & Kegan Paul, 1988.

Manning, Paul. *Spinning for Labour: Trade Unions and the New Media Environment.* Aldershot, U.K.: Ashgate, 1998.

Milner, Lisa. *Fighting Films: A History of the Waterside Workers' Federation Film Unit.* North Melbourne: Pluto, 2003.

Puette, W. J. *Through Jaundiced Eyes: How the Media View Organized Labor.* Ithaca, N.Y.: ILR Press, 1992. (Covers the period from 1930 to 1991.)

F. LABOR AND THE ECONOMY

F.1 General Works

Aldcroft, Derek H., and Michael Oliver. *Trade Unions and the Economy, 1870–2000.* Aldershot, U.K.: Ashgate: 2000.

Aldcroft, Derek H., and Steven Morewood. *The European Economy, 1914–2000.* 4th ed. London: Routledge, 2001.

Auerbach, James A., and Richard S. Belous (eds.). *The Inequality Paradox: Growth of Income Disparity.* Washington: National Policy Association, 1998.

Backhouse, Roger E. *The Ordinary Business of Life: A History of Economics from the Ancient World to the Twenty-First Century.* Princeton, N.J.: Princeton University Press, 2002.

Bishel, Lawrence, Jared Bernstein, and John Schmitt. *The State of Working America, 1996–97.* Armonk, N.Y.: M. E. Sharpe, 1997.

Bluestone, B., and B. Harrison. *The Great U-Turn: Corporate Restructuring and the Polarizing of America.* New York: Basic Books, 1985.

Booth, Alison L. (ed.). *The Economics of Trade Unions.* Cheltenham, U.K.: Edward Elgar, 2002.

Brunetta, R., and C. Dell'Aringa (eds.). *Labour Relations and Economic Performance.* London: Macmillan, 1990.

Bruno, Michael, and Jeffrey D. Sachs. *The Economics of Worldwide Stagflation.* Cambridge, Mass.: Harvard University Press, 1985.

Burtless, G. (ed.). *A Future of Lousy Jobs? The Changing Structure of U.S. Wages.* Washington, D.C.: The Brookings Institution, 1990.

Cahuc, Pierre, and Andre Zylberberg. *The Natural Survival of Work: Job Creation and Job Destruction in a Growing Economy.* Cambridge, Mass.: The MIT Press, 2006.

Clarke, Thomas (ed.). *International Privatisation: Strategies and Practices.* Berlin: Walter de Gruyter, 1994.

Dabir-Alai, Parvis, and Mehmet Odekon (eds.). *Economic Liberalization and Labor Markets.* Westport, Conn.: Greenwood Press, 1999.

Dobbin, Frank (ed.). *The Sociology of the Economy.* New York: Russell Sage Foundation, 2004.

Ehrenberg, R. G., and R. S. Smith. *Modern Labour Economics: Theory and Public Policy.* 3rd ed. Glenview, Ill.: Scott Foresman, 1988.

Ellwood, David T., et al. *A Working Nation: Workers, Work, and Government in the New Economy.* New York: Russell Sage Foundation, 2000.

Fallick, J., and R. Elliott (eds.). *Incomes Policies, Inflation and Relative Pay.* London: Allen & Unwin, 1981.

Federico, Giovanni. *Feeding the World: An Economic History of Agriculture, 1800–2000.* Princeton, N.J.: Princeton University Press, 2005.

Flanagan, R. J., D. W. Soskice, and L. Ulman. *Unionism, Economic Stabilisation and Incomes Policies: European Experience.* Washington, D.C.: The Brookings Institution, 1983.

Frieden, Jeffry A. *Global Capitalism: Its Fall and Rise in the Twentieth Century.* New York: W. W. Norton, 2006.

Handy, L. J. *Wages Policy in the British Coalmining Industry: A Study of National Wage Bargaining.* Cambridge: Cambridge University Press, 1981.

Hart, Robert A. *The Economics of Overtime Working.* New York: Cambridge University Press, 2004.

Hart, Vivien. *Bound by Our Constitution: Women, Workers, and the Minimum Wage.* Princeton, N.J: Princeton University Press, 1994. (A comparison between the United States and Great Britain.)

Hirsch, Barry T. *Labor Unions and the Economic Performance of Firms.* Kalamazoo, Mich.: W. E. Upjohn Institute, 1991.

Hyman, R., and W. Streeck. *New Technology and Industrial Relations.* Oxford: Basil Blackwell, 1988.

Iversen, Torben et al. *Unions, Employers, and Central Banks: Macroeconomic Coordination and Institutional Change in Social Market Economies.* Cambridge: Cambridge University Press, 2000. (A study of northern European countries.)

Kaufman, Bruce E. *The Economics of Labor Markets and Labor Relations.* 2nd ed. Chicago: Dryden Press, 1989.

Kleinknecht, A., E. Mandel, and I. Wallerstein (eds.). *New Findings in Long Wave Research.* London: Macmillan, 1992.

Lane, Christel. *Management and Labour in Europe.* Aldershot, U.K.: Edward Elgar, 1989.

Levine, David I. *Working in the Twenty-First Century: Policies for Economic Growth through Training, Opportunity, and Education.* Armonk, N.Y.: M. E. Sharpe, Inc., 1998.

Lewis, H. G. *Union Relative Wage Effects: A Survey.* Chicago: University of Chicago Press, 1986.

Lindberg, Leon N., and Charles S. Maier (eds.). *The Politics of Inflation and Economic Stagnation.* Washington, D.C.: The Brookings Institution, 1985.

Locke, Richard, et al. (eds.). *Employment Relations in a Changing World Economy.* Cambridge, Mass.: MIT Press, 1995.

Luce, Stephanie. *Fighting for a Living Wage.* Ithaca, N.Y.: Cornell University Press, 2004.

Magnusson, Lars, Lilja Mosesdottir, and Amparo Serrano Pascual. *Equal Pay and Gender Mainstreaming in the European Employment Strategy.* Brussels: European Trade Union Institute, 2003.

Marshall, Ray. *Unheard Voices: Labor and Economic Policy in a Competitive World.* New York: Basic Books, 1987.

Mishels, Lawrence, and Paula Voos (eds.). *Unions and Economic Competitiveness.* Armonk, N.Y.: M. E. Sharpe, 1992.

Neumark, David, and Olena Nizalova. *Minimum Wage Effects in the Longer Run.* Cambridge, Mass.: National Bureau of Economic Research, Inc., (Working Paper 10656), 2004.

Osterman, Paul. *Securing Prosperity: The American Labor Market: How It Has Changed and What to Do about It.* Princeton, N.J.: Princeton University Press, 1999.

Palokangas, Tapio. *Labour Unions, Public Policy and Economic Growth.* Cambridge: Cambridge University Press, 2000.

Piore, Michael J., and Charles F. Sabel. *The Second Industrial Divide.* New York: Basic Books, 1984.

Pomeranz, Kenneth, and Steven Topik. *The World That Trade Created: Society, Culture, and the World Economy.* Armonk, N.Y.: M. E. Sharpe, 2006.

Posusney, Marshall P. *Labor and the State in Egypt: Workers, Unions, and Economic Restructuring.* New York: Columbia University Press, 1997.

Ratnam, Venkata. *Industrial Relations.* New Dehli: Oxford University Press, 2006.

Reynolds, Lloyd G., et al. *Labor Economics and Labor Relations.* 9th ed., Englewood Cliffs, N.J: Prentice-Hall, 1986. (A useful introductory text.)

Roncaglia, Alessandro. *The Wealth of Ideas: A History of Economic Thought.* Cambridge: Cambridge University Press, 2005.

Ryscavage, Paul. *Income Inequality in America: An Analysis of Trends.* Armonk, N.Y.: M. E. Sharpe, 1998.

Scholliers, Peter, and Vera Zamagni (eds.). *Labour's Reward: Real Wages and Economic Change in Nineteenth and Twentieth-Century Europe.* Aldershot, U.K.: Elgar, 1995.

Sengenberger, Werner, and Duncan Campbell (eds.). *International Labour Standards and Economic Interdependence.* Geneva: International Institute for Labour Studies, 1994.

Slomp, H. *Labor Relations in Europe: A History of Issues and Developments.* Westport, Conn.: Greenwood Press, 1990.

Villa, Paola. *The Structuring of Labour Markets: An Analysis of the Italian Construction and Steel Industries.* Oxford: Oxford University Press, 1987.

Western, Bruce. *Between Class and Market: Postwar Unionisation in Capitalist Democracies.* Princeton, N.J.: Princeton University Press, 1997. (A study of 18 Organisation for Economic Co-operation and Development countries from 1950 to 1990.)

Wilson, Kenneth G. *The Impact of Unions on United States Economy-Wide Productivity.* New York: Garland, 1995.

F.2 Globalization and Work Practices since 1980

Aidt, Toke. *Unions and Collective Bargaining: Economic Effects in a Global Environment.* Washington, D.C.: World Bank, 2002.

Anner, Mark Sebastian. *Solidarity Transformed: Labor Responses to Globalization and Crisis in Latin America.* New York: Ithaca, 2011.

Beaumont, P. B. *The Decline of Trade Union Organisation.* London: Croom Helm, 1987.

Bhagwati, Jagdish. *In Defense of Globalization.* New York: Oxford University Press, 2005.

Bishop, Beverley. *Globalization and Women in the Japanese Workforce.* London, New York: Routledge, 2005.

Brierley, William (ed.). *Trade Unions and the Economic Crisis of the 1980s.* London: Gower, 1987.

Brown, Clair, Barry Eichengreen, and Michael Reich. *Labor in the Era of Globalization.* New York, N.Y.: Cambridge University Press, 2010.

Clark, G. L. *Unions and Communities Under Siege: American Communities and the Crisis of Organized Labor.* Cambridge: Cambridge University Press, 1989.

Coates, D. *The Crisis of Labour: Industrial Relations and the State in Contemporary Britain.* Oxford: Philip Allan, 1989.

Craver, C. B. *Can Unions Survive? The Rejuvenation of the American Labor Movement.* New York: New York University Press, 1993.

De la Dehesa, Guillermo. *Winners and Losers in Globalization.* Malden, Mass.: Blackwell Publishing, 2006.

Dobbs, Lou. *Exporting America: Why Corporate Greed Is Shipping American Jobs Overseas.* Business Plus, 2004.

Elliott, Kimberly Ann, and Richard B. Freeman. *Can Labor Standards Improve under Globalization?* Washington, D.C.: Institute for International Economics, 2003.

Galenson, Walter. *Trade Union Growth and Decline: An International Study.* Westport, Conn.: Praeger, 1994.

Gereluk, Winston. *Sustainable Development of the Global Economy: A Trade Union Perspective.* Geneva: International Labour Organisation, 2002.

Ghose, Ajit K. *Jobs and Incomes in a Globalizing World.* Geneva: International Labour Organization, 2003.

Goldfield, Michael. *The Decline of Organized Labor in the United States.* Chicago: University of Chicago Press, 1985.

Gourevitch, P., et al. *Unions and Economic Crisis: Britain, West Germany and Sweden.* London: George Allen & Unwin, 1984.

Grant, John. *Blood Brothers: The Division and Decline of British Trade Unions.* London: Weidenfeld & Nicholson, 1992.

Hammer, Michael. *Beyond Reengineering: How the Process-Centered Organization Is Changing Our Work and Lives.* New York: HarperBusiness, 1996.

Hartman, Laura, Denis Arnold, and Richard Wokutch. *Rising above Sweatshops: Innovative Management Approaches to Global Labor Challenges.* New York: Praeger, 2003.

Heckscher, Charles C. *The New Unionism*. Ithaca, N.Y.: ILR Press, 1996. (A U.S. study.)

Hoerr, John P. *And the Wolf Finally Came: The Decline of the American Steel Industry*. Pittsburgh: University of Pittsburgh Press, 1988.

Hyman, Richard. *Understanding European Trade Unionism: Between Market, Class, and Society*. London: Sage, 2001.

International Confederation of Free Trade Unions. *A Trade Union Guide to Globalisation*. Brussels: International Confederation of Free Trade Unions, 2002.

Jacobs, David C. *Collective Bargaining as an Instrument of Social Change*. Westport, Conn.: Quorum Books, 1994.

Juris, H., et al. (eds.). *Industrial Relations in a Decade of Change*. Madison, Wisc.: Industrial Relations Research Association Series, 1985.

Kelly, Dominic, and Wyn Grant (eds.). *Politics of International Trade in the 21st Century. Actors, Issues and Regional Dynamics*. Palgrave Macmillan, 2005.

Kochan, T. (ed.). *Challenges and Choices Facing American Unions*. Cambridge, Mass.: MIT Press, 1985.

Kubicek, Paul. *Organized Labor in Postcommunist States: From Solidarity to Infirmity*. Pittsburgh, Penn.: University of Pittsburgh Press, 2004.

Lash, Scott, and J. Urry. *The End of Organized Capitalism*. Madison: Wisconsin University Press, 1987.

Leisink, Peter, et al. (eds.). *The Challenge to Trade Unions in Europe: Innovation and Adaptation*. Aldershot, U.K.: Edward Elgar, 1996.

Littek, W., and T. Charles (eds.). *The New Division of Labour*. Berlin: De Gruyter, 1994.

Martin, Andrew, et al. *The Brave New World of European Labor: European Trade Unions at the Millennium*. New York: Berghahn Books, 1999.

Masters, Marick F. *Unions at the Crossroads: Strategic Membership, Financial and Political Perspectives*. Westport, Conn.: Quorum Books, 1997.

Meiksins, Ellen, et al. (eds.). *Rising from the Ashes? Labor in the Age of "Global Capitalism."* New York: Monthly Review Press, 1998. (Covers East Asia, Eastern Europe, Germany, Sweden, Mexico, the United States, and the United Kingdom.)

Messina, Julián, Claudio Michelacci, Jarkko Turunen, and Gylfi Zoega (eds.). *Labor Market Adjustments in Europe*. Northampton, Mass.: Edward Elgar Publishing, Inc., 2006.

Moody, Kim. *An Injury to All: The Decline of American Unionism*. London: Verso, 1988.

Olney, Shauna. *Unions in a Changing World*. Washington, D.C.: International Labour Organization, 1996. (A study of Australia, Germany, Italy, Japan, the Netherlands, Sweden, the United Kingdom, and the United States.)

Perelman, Michael. *The Invisible Handcuffs of Capitalism: How Market Tyranny Stifles the Economy by Stunting Workers*. New York: Monthly Review Press, 2011.

Perrucci, C., et al. (eds.). *Plant Closings: International Context and Social Costs*. New York: Walter de Gruyter, 1988.

Rama, Martin. *Globalization and Workers in Developing Countries*. World Bank. Development Research Group. Public Services, 2003.

Rieger, Elmar, and Stephan Leibfried. *Limits to Globalization: Welfare States and the World Economy*. Cambridge: Polity Press, 2003.

Roozendaal, Gerda van. *Trade Unions and Global Governance: The Debate on a Social Clause*. London: Continuum, 2002.

Ross, Andrew. *Low Pay, High Profile: The Global Push for Fair Labor*. New York: New Press, 2004.

Schwartz, Herman M. *States Versus Markets: The Emergence of a Global Economy*. 3rd ed. Houndmills, Basingstoke, Hampshire; New York: Palgrave Macmillan, 2010.

Sennett, Richard. *The Corrosion of Character: The Personal Consequences of Work in the New Capitalism*. New York: W. W. Norton, 1999.

Smith, Chris, et al. (eds.). *The New Workplace and Trade Unionism*. New York: Routledge, 1995. (A British study.)

Stearns, Peter N. *Globalization in World History*. New York: Taylor and Francis, 2009.

Strauss, George, et al. (eds.). *The State of the Unions*. Madison, Wisc.: Industrial Relations Research Association Series, 1991.

Thomas, H. *Globalization and the Third World Trade Unions: The Challenge of Rapid Economic Change*. London: Zed Books, 1995.

Trinca, Helen, and Catherine Fox. *Better Than Sex: How a Whole Generation Got Hooked on Work*. Sydney: Random House Australia, 2004.

Uchitelle, Louis. *The Disposable American: Layoffs and Their Consequences*. New York: Knopf, 2006.

Waddington, Jeremy (ed.). *Globalization and the Patterns of Union Resistance*. New York: Mansell, 1999.

Willman, Paul, et al. *Union Business: Trade Union Organisation and Financial Reform in the Thatcher Years*. Cambridge: Cambridge University Press, 1993.

G. ORGANIZED LABOR AND THE FUTURE

Bennett, James T., and Bruce E. Kaufman. *What Do Unions Do?: A Twenty-Year Perspective*. New Brunswick, N.J.: Transaction Publishers, 2007.

Boeri, Tito, et al. (eds.). *The Role of Trade Unions in the Twenty-First Century: A Report for the Fondazione Rodolfo Debenedetti*. Oxford: Oxford University Press, 2001.

Bramble, Thomas, and Rick Kuhn. *Labor's Conflict: Big Business, Workers and the Politics of Class*. Port Melbourne, Vic.: Cambridge University Press, 2011.

Bronfenbrenner, Kate (ed.). *Global Unions. Challenging Transnational Capital through Cross-Border Campaigns*. New York: Cornell University Press, 2007.

Bryson, Alex. *Working with Dinosaurs? Union Effectiveness in Delivering for Employees*. London: Policy Studies Institute, 2003.

Cohen, Sheila. *Ramparts of Resistance: Why Workers Lost their Power and How to Get It Back*. London: Pluto, 2006. (Experiences of British and U.S. workers during the period 1968–2005.)

Crouch, C., and F. Traxler. *Organized Industrial Relations in Europe: What Future?* Aldershot, U.K.: Avebury, 1995.

Danford, Andy, Mike Richardson, and Martin Upchurch. *New Unions, New Workplace: A Study of Union Resilience in the Restructured Workplace.* London: Routledge, 2003.

Dunn, Bill. *Global Restructuring and the Power of Labour.* Basingstoke: Palgrave Macmillan, 2004.

Evatt Foundation. *Unions 2001: A Blueprint for Trade Union Activism.* Sydney: Evatt Foundation, 1995.

Fairbrother, Peter. *Trade Unions at the Crossroads.* London, New York: Mansell, 2000. (Covers the West Midlands.)

Fernie, Sue, and David Metcalf. *Trade Unions: Resurgence or Demise?* London, New York: Routledge, 2005.

Fletcher, Bill, Jr., and Fernando Gapasin. *Solidarity Divided: The Crisis in Organized Labor and a New Path toward Social Justice.* Berkeley, London: University of California Press, 2008.

Freeman, Richard B., Joni Hersch, and Lawrence R. Mishel. *Emerging Labor Market Institutions for the Twenty-first Century.* Chicago: University of Chicago Press, 2005.

Fulcher, James. *Capitalism: A Very Short Introduction.* Cary, N.C.: Oxford University Press, 2004.

Gollan, Paul J. *Employee Representation in Non-Union Firms.* London: Sage Publications, 2006.

Hannigan, Thomas A. *Managing Tomorrow's High-Performance Unions.* Westport, Conn.: Quorum Books, 1998.

Harrod, Jeffrey, and Robert O'Brien. *Global Unions: Theories and Strategies of Organized Labor in the Global Political Economy.* New York: Routledge, 2002.

Heery, Ed, and John Kelly. *Union Revitalization in the United Kingdom.* Geneva: International Institute for Labour Studies, 2002.

International Confederation of Free Trade Unions. World Congress. *Globalising Social Justice: Trade Unionism in the 21st Century.* Brussels: ICFTU, 2000.

Jayaraman, Sarumathi, and Immanuel Ness (eds.). *The New Urban Immigrant Workforce: Innovative Models for Labor Organizing.* Armonk, N.Y.: M. E. Sharpe, 2005.

Mantsios, Gregory (ed.). *A New Labor Movement for the New Century.* New York: Monthly Review Press, 1998.

Milkman, Ruth, and Kim Voss (eds.). *Rebuilding Labor: Organizing and Organizers in the New Union Movement.* Ithaca, N.Y.; London: Cornell University Press, 2004.

Nissen, Bruce (ed.). *Which Direction for Organized Labor? Essays on Organizing, Outreach, and Internal Transformation.* Detroit, Mich.: Wayne State University Press, 1999.

———. *Unions in a Globalized Environment.* Armonk, N.Y., M. E. Sharpe, Inc., 2002.

Peetz, David. *Unions in a Contrary World: The Future of the Australian Trade Union Movement.* Cambridge: Cambridge University Press, 1998.

Prosten, David (ed.). *The Union Steward's Complete Guide. A Survival Manual*. 2nd ed. Maryland: Union Communication Services, 2006 (1997).

Schnabel, Claus, and Joachim Wagner. *Who Are the Workers Who Never Joined a Union? Empirical Evidence from Germany*. Bonn: Institute for the Study of Labor, 2005. (Available in electronic format only.)

Shostak, Arthur B. *The Cyberunion Handbook: Transforming Labor through Technology*. Armonk, N.Y.: M. E. Sharpe, 2002.

Sverke, Magnus (ed.). *The Future of Trade Unionism: International Perspectives on Emerging Union Structures*. Aldershot, U.K.: Ashgate, 1997.

Tait, Vanessa. *Poor Workers' Unions: Rebuilding Labor from Below*. Cambridge, Mass.: South End Press, 2005. (Emphasizes the importance of building workplace power through grassroots organization and rank-and-file control.)

Tattersall, Amanda. *Power in Coalition: Strategies for Strong Unions and Social Change*. Ithaca: ILR Press/Cornell University Press, 2010.

Turner, Lowell, and Daniel B. Cornfield (eds.). *Labor in the New Urban Battlegrounds: Local Solidarity in a Global Economy*, with a foreword by Peter Evans. Ithaca, N.Y.: ILR; Bristol: University Presses Marketing, 2007.

Turner, Lowell, et al. (eds.). *Rekindling the Movement: Labor's Quest for Relevance in the Twenty-First Century*. Ithaca, N.Y.: ILR Press, 2001.

Verma, Anil, and A. Thomas. *Unions in the 21st Century: An International Perspective*. Houndmills, Basingstoke, Hampshire; New York: Palgrave Macmillan, 2004.

Weil, David. *Turning the Tide: Strategic Planning for Labor Unions*. New York: Lexington Books, 1994.

Wheeler, Hoyt N., and Lynn S. Williams. *The Future of the American Labor Movement*. Cambridge: Cambridge University Press, 2002.

Wheeler, Hoyt N., Brian S. Klaas, and Douglas M. Mahony. *Workplace Justice without Unions*. Kalamazoo, Mich.: W.E. Upjohn Institute for Employment Research, 2004.

Wunnava, Phanindra V. *The Changing Role of Unions: New Forms of Representation*. Armonk, N.Y.: M. E. Sharpe, 2004.

INTERNET SITES: A SELECTED GUIDE

Whether for sending messages or accessing websites, the Internet has become an indispensable tool for researchers, making it possible for them to obtain directly the latest information about a subject or an organization. Unlike a book, websites are ephemeral and there is no guarantee that they will be available for consultation at some future time. Labor unions began displaying their own websites on the Internet in about 1995 and by 1999 there were about 2,000 of these websites. This figure is still growing because unions and union activists are learning how to use the Internet not only as a source of information but also as a tool in the day-to-day union activities. This short guide is designed to complement and expand the works listed in the bibliography and in the appendixes. It provides a brief, selected guide to the main websites relating to organized labor in 2011. It does not claim to be comprehensive, but it does provide starting points for research. It should be noted that these websites are extensively linked to other websites. For further information on specific organizations, see John Harper Publishing, *Trade Unions of the World* (London: John Harper Publishing, 2005), which contains websites and contact addresses. Good guides to the use of the Internet by labor are Eric Lee, *The Labour Movement and the Internet: The New Internationalism* (London: Pluto Press, 1997) and Peter Waterman, Alternative International Labour Communication by Computer After Two decades, in *Interface: A Journal For and About Social Movements Labour Communications* 2(2): 241–269, 2010, from which we have bluntly picked many sites.

The guide lists websites relating to:

A. International Guides
B. International Labor Organizations and Guides
C. National Councils of Labor Unions
D. Labor Unions with More Than One Million Members in 2010
E. Government Departments Concerned with Labor Issues
F. Academic Websites
G. Regional Websites
H. Other Websites

A. International Guides

www.ilo.org/labordoc
Provides access to the main library catalog of the International Labour Organisation.

www.labourstart.org
Has links to organized labor websites. LabourStart is an online news service maintained by a global network of volunteers that aims to serve the international trade union movement by collecting and disseminating information, and by assisting unions in campaigning and other ways.

www.unions.org
Online union directory listing all labor unions in the United States.

B. International Labor Organizations and Guides

www.bwint.org
Building and Wood Workers International

www.etuc.org
European Trade Union Confederation

www.eurofound.europa.eu/eiro/
The European Industrial Relations Observatory (EIRO) is a monitoring instrument offering news and analysis on European industrial relations. A project of the *European Foundation for the Improvement of Living and Working Conditions,* EIRO began its operations in 1997. Its aim is to "collect, analyze, and disseminate high-quality and up-to-date information on key developments in industrial relations in Europe." An important EIRO report by Mark Carley was published in 2004. It examines trade union membership trends in 23 EU Member States.

www.global-unions.org
The website for the international trade union bodies based on particular industries.

www.idcdockworkers.org
International Dockworkers Council. "An association formed by organizations of dockworkers from all over the world. It is defined by its basic principles as being a unitary, independent, democratic, assembly-based, working-class organisation."

www.ifj.org
International Federation of Journalists

www.ioe-emp.org
International Organisation of Employers

www.itfglobal.org
International Transport Workers' Federation (ITF)

www.ituc-csi.org
International Trade Union Confederation

rmc.library.cornell.edu/EAD/htmldocs/KCL05028.html
Guide to the archives of the International Confederation of Free Trade Unions, 1949–1993.

www.tuac.org
The Trade Union Advisory Committee (TUAC) is an advisory group within the Organisation for Economic Co-operation and Development to give advice on its policies and programs.

www.wftucentral.org
World Federation of Trade Unions

C. National Councils of Labor Unions

www.actu.asn.au
Australian Council of Trade Unions

www.aflcio.org
American Federation of Labor–Congress of Industrial Organizations

www.cgb.info
Christlicher Gewerkschaftsbund Deutschlands

www.clc-ctc.ca
Canadian Labour Congress

www.cosatu.org.za
Congress of South African Trade Unions

www.dbb.de/
Deutscher Beamtenbund und Tarfiunion

www.dgb.de
Deutscher Gewerkschaftsbund (German Confederation of Labor Unions)

www.fnv.nl
Federatie Nederlandse Vakbeweging (Dutch Confederation of Labor Unions)

www.ictu.ie
Irish Congress of Trade Unions

http://kctu.org/
Korean Confederation of Trade Unions

www.lo.se
Landsorganisationen I Sverige (Swedish Labor Union Confederation)

www.nlc.edu/archives/using.html
George Meany Memorial Archives, which hold the records of the AFL-CIO.

www.nlcng.org
Nigeria Labour Congress

www.tuc.org.uk
Trades Union Congress (United Kingdom)

www.tucnigeria.org
Trade Union Congress of Nigeria

http://union.org.nz
New Zealand Council of Trade Unions

D. Labor Unions with More Than One Million Members in 2010

www.afscme.org
American Federation of State, County, and Municipal Employees. A model website, skillfully organized with high-quality past as well as current material.

www.igmetall.de
IG Metall (Metal Workers' Union, Germany)

www.nea.org
National Education Association (U.S.)

www.seiu.org
Service Employees International Union (U.S.)

www.teamster.org
Teamsters (U.S.)

www.ufcw.org
United Food and Commercial Workers' International Union (U.S.)

www.unison.org.uk
Unison (U.K.)

www.unitetheunion.org
Unite the Union (U.K.)

www.verdi.de
Ver.di (United Services Labor Union, Germany).

E. Government Departments Concerned with Labor Issues

www.bis.gov.uk/
Department for Business Innovation and Skills. Contains a vital source on labor union statistics: Trade union membership.

www.nlrb.gov
The National Labor Relations Board is the U.S. federal agency that administers the National Labor Relations Act.

www.state.gov
Country Reports on Human Rights Practices. U.S. State Department, Bureau of Democracy, Human Rights and Labor.

stats.bls.gov
U.S. Department of Labor, Bureau of Labor Statistics. (Search for "labor union.")

F. Academic Websites

www.archives.anu.edu.au/nbac/html/index.php
Noel Butlin Archives Centre–Australian National University Library

www.iisg.nl
International Institute of Social History, Amsterdam, Netherlands. A major website with important links to other websites relevant to labor studies, including a global virtual library for labor history organized by country, as well as links to women's history and economic history. It incorporates an online biographical register of 575 Dutch labor leaders, a database of almost 17,000 labor conflicts that occurred in the Netherlands since 1372, and a repository of international data of labour conflicts.

www.lib.berkeley.edu/IIRL/iirlnet.html
University of California, Berkeley—Labor Links. A labor research portal compiled by the library to labor unions, history archives, international organizations, and government agencies.

www.statistics.gov.uk/
The major source of British labor statistics.

www.uva-aias.net
Access to an international database with union characteristics from 34 countries from 1960 to date.

G. Regional Websites

www.aawl.org.au.
Australia Asia worker links; "Workers Change the World."

www.amrc.org.hk.
"To support and contribute toward the building of a strong, democratic, and independent labor movement in Asia."

www.clb.org.hk/en/
China Labour Bulletin. "A proactive outreach organisation that seeks to defend and promote the rights of workers in China."

www.labournet.de/
LabourNet Deutschland/Germany. "Trade union meeting place, linking the disobedient with and without a job." Part of the global LabourNet initiatives, which, however, are not actually connected.

http://worldlabour.org/eng/
China Labour Net. Their "understanding of the labour movement and workers' rights extends beyond union rights and economic rights, it includes the emancipation of labour."

H. Other Websites

www.channel4.com/history/microsites/W/worstjobs/index.html
Important source for work in history.

www.domesticworkerrights.org/
Respect and Rights for Domestic Workers. An initiative of domestic workers' unions together with support organizations.

http://en.maquilasolidarity.org/
Maquila Solidarity Network. "A labor and women's rights organization that supports the efforts of workers in global supply chains to win improved wages and working conditions and a better quality of life."

flag.blackened.net/revolt/ws99/ws56_union.html
Anarchists and the Trade Unions

www.globallaborstrategies.org/
Global Labour Strategies. "To contribute to building global labor solidarity through research, analysis, strategic thinking, and network building around labor and employment issues."

http://icsf.net
International Committee in Support of Fishworkers. "An international nongovernmental organisation that works toward the establishment of equitable, gender-just, self-reliant, and sustainable fisheries, particularly in the small-scale, artisanal sector."

www.ictur.org
International Centre for Union Rights. "An organising and campaigning body defending and improving the rights of trade unions and trade unionists worldwide."

iira.free.fr
International Industrial Relations Association. Operates under the auspices of the International Labour Organization and maintains an international directory of labour and industrial relations institutes and centers.

www.labornet.org
LaborNet. "Community of labor unions, activists, and organizations offers a network for the discussion of economic justice and rights issues."

http://labortech.net/
LaborTech. "Brings together labor video, computer, and media activists in the United States and from around the world to build and develop labor communication technology and media."

www.newunionism.net/
New Unionism Network. "New Unionism is about unions setting agendas, rather than just reacting to them."

www.nosweat.org.uk/
No Sweat. "No Sweat exists to fight against sweatshop exploitation. We organise solidarity for sweatshop workers from the UK to the four corners of the world. We stand for workers' self-organisation, international solidarity and for the right to organise in every workplace."

www.nswp.org/
Global Network of Sex Work Projects (NSWP). An informal alliance of sex worker rights activists working within sex work projects around the world.

http://reinventinglabour.wordpress.com/
"ReinventingLabour is for people who organize, struggle, analyze, critique and strategize within and around the international labour movement."

www.sigtur.com/
Southern Initiative on Globalisation and Trade Union Rights. "An active and living voice of workers in the Global South representing a diverse and broad spectrum of trade unions."

www.streetnet.org.za/
StreetNetInternational. "To promote the exchange of information and ideas on critical issues facing street vendors and market vendors and hawkers (mobile vendors) and on practical organising and advocacy strategies."

www.tie-germany.org/
Transnationals Information Exchange—Germany (but also active in other countries such as Russia and the Netherlands). A global network of both union and nonunion activists in the formal and informal sectors.

utopia.knoware.nl/users/modijk
Trade Unions and Homosexuality. Report of a global conference of 1998 to discuss the role of trade unions in fighting for the rights of lesbians and gay men.

http://viacampesina.org
Via Campesina. "La Via Campesina is the international movement which brings together millions of peasants, small and medium-size farmers, landless people, women farmers, indigenous people, migrants and agricultural workers from around the world."

www.wiego.org/
Women in Informal Employment: Globalising and Organising. "A global action-research-policy network that seeks to improve the status of the working poor, especially women, in the informal economy."

www.women-ww.org
WomenWorkingWorldwide. An international network of women workers. Their central aim is that women themselves call for change in their working conditions and networks such as WWW can make sure that their voices are heard and not ignored.

www.worldmarchofwomen.org
World March of Women. "An international feminist action movement connecting grass-roots groups and organizations working to eliminate the causes at the root of poverty and violence against women."

About the Authors

SJAAK VAN DER VELDEN was born in Rotterdam, the Netherlands, in 1954. He studied history at Leiden University. During his career as a carpenter (1980–2000), he wrote a thesis on strikes in the Netherlands. He graduated from Leiden University in 2000 and worked with the Historical Sample of the Netherlands from 2000 to 2007. Since then he worked with the Socialist Party until 2012 when he started his own historical investigation office. In 2007, he took on a part-time job at the International Institute of Social History (IISH) to build an international HUB on labor conflicts. Since the beginning of 2010, he is an affiliated fellow with the IISH and masters the repository on labor conflicts hosted there. In March 2011, he co-organized the International Conference Strikes and Social Conflicts in Lisbon.

His publications include 10 books in Dutch, *Strikes around the World: Case Studies of 15 Countries 1968–2005* (co-editor, 2007), and numerous articles in Dutch and English.

JAMES C. DOCHERTY was born in Gosford, New South Wales, in 1949. He is a second-generation Australian; both of his parents were born in Scotland. He graduated from the University of Newcastle, New South Wales, with the University Medal in History in 1972 and went on to gain a master's and a doctorate in history from the Australian National University. Between 1978 and 2004 he was an Australian federal government employee in various departments and a union member. He was an Honorary Research Associate with the National Centre for Australian Studies at Monash University from 1990 to 1996.

His publications include *Selected Social Statistics of New South Wales, 1861–1976* (1982); *Newcastle: The Making of an Australian City* (1983); and, "English Settlement in Newcastle and the Hunter Valley" in James Jupp (ed.), *The Australian People: An Encyclopedia of the Nation, Its People and Their Origins* (1988). He was an editorial consultant and contributor to *Australians: Historical Statistics* (1987), contributed the entries on Australian history, politics, industrial relations, and institutions in David Crystal (ed.), *The Cambridge Encyclopedia* (1990), and was an editor and contributor to *Workplace Bargaining in the International Context* (1993). He is the author of three historical dictionaries: *Historical Dictionary of Australia* (1992, 1999, 2007), *Historical Dictionary of Socialism* (1997), and *Historical Dictionary of Organized Labor* (1996, 2004). Since 2005, his research interests have changed to Scottish population history and migration. He also has some carpentry skills.

CPSIA information can be obtained at www.ICGtesting.com
Printed in the USA
BVOW010524070612

291795BV00001B/3/P